Communications
in Computer and Information Science 7

David C. Wyld   Michal Wozniak
Nabendu Chaki   Natarajan Meghanathan
Dhinaharan Nagamalai (Eds.)

Trends in Networks and Communications

International Conferences
NeCoM, WeST, WiMoN 2011
Chennai, India, July 15-17, 2011
Proceedings

 Springer

Volume Editors

David C. Wyld
Southeastern Louisiana University, Hammond, LA 70402, USA
E-mail: david.wyld@selu.edu

Michal Wozniak
Wroclaw University of Technology, 50-370 Wroclaw, Poland
E-mail: michal.wozniak@pwr.wroc.pl

Nabendu Chaki
University of Calcutta, Calcutta, India
E-mail: nchaki@gmail.com

Natarajan Meghanathan
Jackson State University Jackson, MS 39217-0280, USA
E-mail: nmeghanathan@jsums.edu

Dhinaharan Nagamalai
Wireilla Net Solutions PTY Ltd, Melbourne, VIC, Australia
E-mail: dhinthia@yahoo.com

ISSN 1865-0929   e-ISSN 1865-0937
ISBN 978-3-642-22542-0   e-ISBN 978-3-642-22543-7
DOI 10.1007/978-3-642-22543-7
Springer Heidelberg Dordrecht London New York

Library of Congress Control Number: 2011931557

CR Subject Classification (1998): C.2, H.4, I.2, H.3, D.2, J.1

Typesetting: Camera-ready by author, data conversion by Scientific Publishing Services, Chennai, India

Printed on acid-free paper

Springer is part of Springer Science+Business Media (www.springer.com)

Preface

The 4th International Conference on Network Security & Applications (CNSA 2011) was held in Chennai, India, during July 15–17, 2011. The conference focuses on all technical and practical aspects of security and its applications for wired and wireless networks. The goal of this conference is to bring together researchers and practitioners from both academia and industry to focus on understanding the present-day security threats and to propose and discuss counter-measures to defend against such attacks. In the past few years, the enthusiastic participation of a large number of delegates in different AIRCC–organized conferences, like the International Conference on Network Security and Applications (CNSA), International Conference on Networks and Communications (NECOM), International Conference on Web and Semantic Technology (WEST), International Conference on Wireless and Mobile Networks (WIMON), the First International Conference on Advances in Computing and Information Technology (ACITY), reflect the fact that the parent body of the Academy and Industry Research Collaboration Center (AIRCC) is successful in providing a platform toward promoting academic collaboration. We believe that this spirit of co-working was further strengthened during CNSA 2011.

The CNSA 2011, NECOM 2011, WEST 2011, WIMoN 2011 and AICTY 2011 committees invited original submissions from researchers, scientists, engineers, and students that illustrate research results, projects, survey works, and industrial experiences describing significant advances in the areas related to the relevant themes and tracks of the conferences.

Thanks to the authors whose effort as reflected in the form of a large number of submissions for CNSA 2011 on different aspects of network security including Web security, cryptography, performance evaluations of protocols and security application, etc. All the submissions underwent a scrupulous peer-review process by a panel of expert reviewers. Besides the members of the Technical Committee, external reviewers were invited on the basis of their specialization and expertise. The papers were reviewed based on their technical content, originality, and clarity. The entire process, which includes the submission, review, and acceptance processes, was done electronically. This hard work resulted in the selection of high-quality papers that expand the knowledge in the latest developments in networks security and applications.

There were a total of 1,285 submissions to the conference, and the Technical Program Committee selected 195 papers for presentation at the conference and subsequent publication in the proceedings. The book is organized as a collection of papers from the 4th International Conference on Network Security and Applications (CNSA 2011), the Third International Conference on Networks and Communications (NeCoM 2011), the Third International Conference on Web and Semantic Technology (WeST 2011), the Third International Conference on

Wireless and Mobile Networks (WiMoN 2011), and the First International Conference on Advances in Computing and Information Technology (ACITY 2011). This small introduction incomplete would be without expressing our gratitude, and thanks to the General and Program Chairs, members of the Technical Program Committees, and external reviewers for their excellent and diligent work. Thanks to Springer for the strong support. Finally, we thank all the authors who contributed to the success of the conference. We also sincerely wish that all attendees benefited academically from the conference and wish them every success in their research.

David C. Wyld

Michal Wozniak
Nabendu Chaki
Natarajan Meghanathan
Dhinaharan Nagamalai

Organization

General Chairs

David C. Wyld	Southeastern Louisiana University, USA
S. K. Ghosh	Indian Institute of Technology, Kharagpur, India
Michal Wozniak	Wroclaw University of Technology, Poland

Steering Committee

Krzysztof Walkowiak	Wroclaw University of Technology, Poland
Dhinaharan Nagamalai	Wireilla Net Solutions PTY LTD, Australia
Natarajan Meghanathan	Jackson State University, USA
Nabendu Chaki	University of Calcutta, India
Chih-Lin Hu	National Central University, Taiwan
Selma Boumerdassi	CNAM/CEDRIC, France
John Karamitsos	University of the Aegean, Samos, Greece
Abdul Kadhir Ozcan	The American University, Cyprus
Brajesh Kumar Kaushik	Indian Institute of Technology - Roorkee, India

Program Committee Members

A.P. Sathish Kumar	PSG Institute of Advanced Studies, India
Abdul Aziz	University of Central Punjab, Pakistan
Abdul Kadir Ozcan	The American University, Cyprus
Ahmed M. Khedr	Sharjah University, UAE
Alejandro Garces	Jaume I University,Spain
Andy Seddon	Asia Pacific Institute of Information Technology, Malaysia
Ashutosh Dubey	NRI Institute of Science and Technology, Bhopal, India
Ashutosh Gupta	MJP Rohilkhand University, Bareilly, India
Atilla Elci	Toros University, Turkey
Atilla Elci	Eastern Mediterranean University, Cyprus
B. Srinivasan	Monash University, Australia
Babak Khosravifar	Concordia University, Canada
Balaji Sriramulu	drsbalaji@gmail.com
Balakannan S.P.	Chonbuk National University, Jeonju, Korea
Balasubramanian Karuppiah	MGR University, India
Bhupendra Suman	IIT Roorkee, India
Bong-Han Kim	Cheongju University, South Korea

Boo-Hyung Lee   KongJu National University, South Korea
Carlos E. Otero   The University of Virginia's College at Wise,
                                  USA
Chandra Mohan   Bapatla Engineering College, India
Charalampos Z. Patrikakis   National Technical University of Athens,
                                  Greece
Chih-Lin Hu   National Central University, Taiwan
Chin-Chih Chang   Chung Hua University,Taiwan
Cho Han Jin   Far East University, South Korea
Cynthia Dhinakaran   Hannam University, South Korea
Danda B. Rawat   Old Dominion University, USA
David W. Deeds   Shingu College, South Korea
Debasis Giri   Haldia Institute of Technology, India
Dimitris Kotzinos   Technical Educational Institution of Serres,
                                  Greece
Dong Seong Kim   Duke University, USA
Durga Toshniwal   Indian Institute of Techniology, India
Emmanuel Bouix   iKlax Media, France
Farhat Anwar   International Islamic University, Malaysia
Firkhan Ali Bin Hamid Ali   Universiti Tun Hussein Onn Malaysia, Malaysia
Ford Lumban   Gaol University of Indonesia
Genge Bela   Joint Research Centre, European Commission,
                                  Italy
Girija Chetty   University of Canberra, Australia
Govardhan A.   JNTUH College of Engineering, India
H.V. Ramakrishnan   MGR University, India
Haller Piroska   Petru Maior University, Tirgu Mures, Romania
Henrique Joao Lopes Domingos   University of Lisbon, Portugal
Ho Dac Tu   Waseda University, Japan
Hoang Huu Hanh   Hue University, Vietnam
Hwangjun Song   Pohang University of Science and Technology,
                                  South Korea
Jacques Demerjian   Communication & Systems, Homeland
                                  Security, France
Jae Kwang Lee   Hannam University, South Korea
Jan Zizka   SoNet/DI, FBE, Mendel University in Brno,
                                  Czech Republic
Jayeeta Chanda   jayeeta.chanda@gmail.com
Jeong-Hyun   Park Electronics Telecommunication Research
                                  Institute, South Korea
Jeong-Hyun   Park Electronics Telecommunication Research
                                  Institute, South Korea
Jeyanthy N.   VIT University, India
Jivesh Govil   Cisco Systems Inc., USA
Johann Groschdl   University of Bristol, UK

Rajendra Akerkar   Technomathematics Research Foundation,
                                    India
Rajesh Kumar Krishnan   Bannari Amman Institute of Technology, India
Rajesh Kumar P.   The Best International, Australia
Rajeswari Balasubramaniam   Dr. MGR University, India
Rajkumar Kannan   Bishop Heber College, India
Rakhesh Singh Kshetrimayum   Indian Institute of Technology, Guwahati, India
Ramayah Thurasamy   Universiti Sains Malaysia, Malaysia
Ramin Karimi   Universiti Teknologi Malaysia
Razvan Deaconescu   University Politehnica of Bucharest, Romania
Reena Dadhich   Govt. Engineering College Ajmer, India
Rituparna Chaki   rituchaki@gmail.com
Roberts Masillamani   Hindustan University, India
S. Bhaskaran   SASTRA University, India
Sagarmay Deb   Central Queensland University, Australia
Sajid Hussain   Acadia University, Canada
Salah M. Saleh Al-Majeed   Esses University, UK
Saleena Ameen   B.S. Abdur Rahman University, India
Salman Abdul Moiz   Centre for Development of Advanced
                                    Computing, India

Sami Ouali   ENSI, Campus of Manouba, Manouba, Tunisia
Samodar Reddy   India School of Mines, India
Sanguthevar Rajasekaran   University of Connecticut, USA
Sanjay Singh   Manipal Institute of Technology, India
Sara Najafzadeh   Universiti Teknologi Malaysia
Sarada Prasad Dakua   IIT-Bombay, India
Sarmistha Neogy   Jadavpur University, India
Sattar B. Sadkhan   University of Babylon, Iraq
Seetha Maddala   CBIT, Hyderabad, India
Serban   Ovidius University of Constantza, Romania
Sergio Ilarri   University of Zaragoza, Spain
Serguei A. Mokhov   Concordia University, Canada
Seungmin Rho   Carnegie Mellon University, USA
Sevki Erdogan   University of Hawaii, USA
Shivan Haran   Arizona state University, USA
Shriram Vasudevan   VIT University, India
Shubhalaxmi Kher   Arkansas State University, USA
Solange Rito Lima   University of Minho, Portugal
Sriman Narayana Iyengar   VIT University, India
Subir Sarkar   Jadavpur University, India
Sudip Misra   Indian Institute of Technology, Kharagpur,
                                    India
Suhaidi B. Hassan   Office of the Assistant Vice Chancellor,
                                    Economics Building
Sundarapandian Vaidyanathan   Vel Tech Dr. RR & Dr. SR Technical University,
                                    India

SunYoung Han	Konkuk University, South Korea
Susana Sargento	University of Aveiro, Portugal
Swarup Mitra	Jadavpur University, Kolkata, India
Tsung Teng Chen	National Taipei University, Taiwan
Virgil Dobrota	Technical University of Cluj-Napoca, Romania
Vishal Sharma	Metanoia Inc., USA
Wei Jie	University of Manchester, UK
William R. Simpson	Institute for Defense Analyses, USA
Wojciech Mazurczyk	Warsaw University of Technology, Poland
Yannick Le Moullec	Aalborg University, Denmark
Yedehalli Kumara Swamy	Dayanand Sagar College of Engineering, India
Yeong Deok Kim Woosong	University, South Korea
Yuh-Shyan Chen	National Taipei University, Taiwan
Yung-Fa Huang	Chaoyang University of Technology, Taiwan

External Reviewers

Abhishek Samanta	Jadavpur University, Kolkata, India
Amit Choudhary	Maharaja Surajmal Institute, India
Anjan K.	MSRIT, India
Ankit	BITS, PILANI, India
Aravind P.A.	Amrita School of Engineering, India
Cauvery Giri	RVCE, India
Debdatta Kandar	Sikkim Manipal University, India
Doreswamyh Hosahalli	Mangalore University, India
Gopalakrishnan Kaliaperumal	Anna University, Chennai, India
Hameem Shanavas	Vivekananda Institute of Technology, India
Hari Chavan	National Institute of Technology, Jamshedpur, India
Kaushik Chakraborty	Jadavpur University, India
Lavanya	Blekinge Institute of Technology, Sweden
Mydhili Nair	M. S. Ramaiah Institute of Technology, India
Naga Prasad Bandaru	PVP Siddartha Institute of Technology, India
Nana Patil	NIT Surat, Gujrat
Osman B. Ghazali	Universiti Utara Malaysia, Malaysia
P. Sheik Abdul Khader	B.S.Abdur Rahman University, India
Padmalochan Bera	Indian Institute of Technology, Kharagpur, India
Pappa Rajan	Anna University, India
Pradeepini Gera	Jawaharlal Nehru Technological University, India
Rajashree Biradar	Ballari Institute of Technology and Management, India
Ramin Karimi	University Technology, Malaysia
Reshmi Maulik	University of Calcutta, India
Rituparna Chaki	West Bengal University of Technology, India

S.C. Sharma	IIT - Roorkee, India
Salini P.	Pondichery Engineering College, India
Selvakumar Ramachandran	Blekinge Institute of Technology, Sweden
Soumyabrata Saha	Guru Tegh Bahadur Institute of Technology, India
Srinivasulu Pamidi	V.R. Siddhartha Engineering College Vijayawada, India
Subhabrata Mukherjee	Jadavpur University, India
Sunil Singh	Bharati Vidyapeeth's College of Engineering, India
Suparna DasGupta	suparnadasguptait@gmail.com
Valli Kumari Vatsavayi	AU College of Engineering, India

Technically Sponsored by

Software Engineering & Security Community (SESC)
Networks & Communications Community (NCC)
Internet Computing Community (ICC)
Computer Science & Information Technology Community (CSITC)

Organized By

ACADEMY & INDUSTRY RESEARCH COLLABORATION CENTER (AIRCC)
www.airccse.org

Table of Contents

Networks and Communications

Wireless and Mobile Networks

Web and Semantic Technology

Adaptation of MAC Layer for QoS in WSN

Sukumar Nandi and Aditya Yadav

IIT Guwahati

Abstract. In this paper, we propose QoS aware MAC protocol for Wireless Sensor Networks. In WSNs, there can be two types of traffic one is event driven traffic which requires immediate attention and another is periodic reporting. Event driven traffic is classified as Class I(delay sensitive) traffic and periodic reporting is classified as Class II(Best Effort) Traffic. MAC layer adaptation can take place in terms of (i) Dynamic contention window adjustment per class, (ii) Reducing the delay suffered by difference in Sleep schedules(DSS) of communicating nodes by dynamically adjusting Duty Cycle based on Utilization and DSS delay of class I traffic, (iii) Different DIFS (DCF Inter Frame Spacing) per class, (iv) Adjusting all the three schemes proposed above simultaneously.

Keywords: Wireless Sensor Networks, QoS.

1   Introduction

WSNs are deployed for critical monitoring applications, some of these applications are delay-sensitive and have stringent requirement on end-to-end latencies. Apart from this delay-sensitive traffic, they also support periodic reporting of environment to their base stations. WSNs deployment for forest fire monitoring is one of the type of applications that we are emphasizing on. This calls for QoS specific mechanisms to be in place for supporting the application requirements. There has been a lot of research and development carried out in architecture, protocol design, energy saving and location in WSNs, but only a few studies have been done regarding network efficiency (i.e. Quality of Service QoS) in WSNs.

We consider SMAC[1], as one of the widely accepted MAC layer implementations in WSNs and use it as our base MAC protocol for implementing the QoS features at MAC level. SMAC pays no attention to latency and end to end delay, and nodes form virtual clusters in terms of their common sleep-wakeup schedule to reduce control overhead. For supporting delay-sensitive traffic and periodic reporting for above mentioned application requirements, our prototype defines two classes of traffic classI(immediate attention) and classII(periodic reporting) respectively. In our prototype, we propose to adjust MAC level parameters Contention Window[7], DIFS[7], Sleep schedules of nodes[1],[2] to provide QoS for the classes of traffic specified. In [9] MAC level parameters are adjusted for QoS guarantees, In [2], duty cycle is being adapted, but efficient QoS classes specific way of adapting duty cycle in case of SMAC[1], and adapting MAC level parameters Contention Window and DCF- IFS in case of Sensor Networks is our contribution, that this paper proposes.

D.C. Wyld et al. (Eds.): NeCoM/WeST/WiMoN 2011, CCIS 197, pp. 1–10, 2011.

MAC layer is responsible for scheduling and allocation of the shared wireless channel, which eventually determines the link level QoS parameters namely MAC delay. To maintain the per class service guarantees in dynamic environment, MAC layer is made adaptive to current network conditions. The proposed dynamic adaptation of the behavior of MAC layer is done by, (i) dynamically varying the contention window based on the class of traffic, (ii)Reducing the delay suffered by Difference in Sleep Schedules(DSS) of communicating nodes by dynamically adjusting Duty Cycle based on Utilization and DSS delay of class I traffic, (iii) By differentiating the DCF Inter Frame Spacing for different class of Traffic, (iv) Combining all the three proposed schemes for MAC Layer Adaptation.

The rest of the paper is organized as follows. In section 2 we briefly discuss about the related work. Section 3 describes our proposed scheme. Section 4 presents the simulated results to show the the efficiency of our proposed scheme. Section 5 concludes the paper.

2   Related Work

Some of the works in improving end-to-end latency by duty cycle adaptation are DSMAC[2] and UMAC[6].

In DSMAC[2], when duty cycle of a node is changed, for maintaining same sleep schedule of this node with its neighbors, duty cycle is always doubled or halved, so that neighbors can follow the same schedule and still communicate with duty cycle changed node. The only difference in the new duty cycle node now either wakes up more or less frequently than its neighbors. In DSMAC [2], they take into account the delay faced by the sending nodes to a receiving node for changing the duty cycle, but change of twice or half, increases the energy consumption in Sensor networks. Moreover, it doesn't consider the adaptation for different types of traffic in WSNs.

In another scheme, UMAC [6] duty cycle is changed dynamically and its not always doubled or halved, but its changed according to Utilization of the node, it pays no attention to delay suffered by one hop neighbors of a node in sending data. It also neglects the different service requirements for different class of traffic.

There has been some works done on providing QoS in WSNs at different layers, mainly on Network and MAC layer. One of such work is, Energy aware QoS Routing. In [3], the authors propose a QoS-aware protocol for realtime traffic generated by WSNs, consisting of image sensors. This protocol implements a priority system that divides the traffic flows in two classes: best effort and realtime. All nodes use two queues, one for each traffic class. This way, different kinds of services can be provided to these types of traffic.

Another MAC level contribution for QoS in WSNs is B-MAC [4]. It stands out for its design and implementation simplicity, which has an immediate effect in memory size occupation and power saving. B-MAC does not implement any specific QoS mechanism; however, this fact is compensated by its good design. Some parts of this design are addressed to improve the efficiency for avoiding collisions, efficiency in the channel occupation at low and high data rates, the tolerance to changeable environments, or the good scalability properties.

In [5], author proposes a traffic-aware MAC protocol which dynamically adjusts the duty cycle adapting to the traffic load. Adaptive scheme operates on a tree topology, and nodes wake up only for the time measured for successful transmissions. By adjusting the duty cycle, it can prevent packet drops and save energy.

3 Dynamic MAC Layer Adaptation for QoS in WSNs

In our framework, MAC layer is designed to adapt their behavior based on the dynamic network conditions(which can be obtained through continuous monitoring) and service quality requirements of the admitted traffic.

3.1 Estimation of MAC Delay

The measurement technique for MAC delay is very simple. A node computes the MAC delay(d) by subtracting the time (t_r), that a packet is passed to the MAC layer from the time (t_s), an the packet is actually sent onto the link. Here d^i and d_{avg}^{i-1} are measured MAC delay and previously stored average MAC delay for a service class. η is a positive constant, which determines how much effect the previously stored average MAC delay have on the current average MAC delay.The contention window rules for our two service classes are given below.

$$d_{avg}^i = (1 - \eta) * d^i + \eta * d_{avg}^{i-1} \tag{1}$$

3.2 Contention Window Adaptation

One of the schemes that we propose for adapting MAC Layer for providing QoS in WSNs is Dynamic Contention Window adaptation for different class of traffic. The contention window parameters namely CWmin and CWmax provides intra node service differentiation among different class of traffic. The different service classes are assigned a non overlapping ranges of contention window in default setting. These default contention window ranges are adjusted by the CW Adaptation based on dynamic network conditions and required service level of a QoS class. To provide service differentiation across different classes of traffic, the non overlapping contention window ranges are maintained while performing contention window adaptation.

Class I (Delay sensitive service). This class of traffic corresponds to event driven traffic(immediate attention) in WSNs. We have assumed that each node ensure a maximum MAC Delay of D_I for traffic of class I, and try to maintain it by periodically monitoring the observed delay in that class and adjusting the CW range accordingly. In this case, based on the per hop delay requirements of the class I, given as D_I, and the current MAC delay, D, measured in the node for Class I traffic, $CWmax$ is adjusted as shown in Algorithm 1. In the algorithm, $CWmax^{prev}$ represents the value of CWmax for class I before applying CW adaptation, and $CWmax$ is the new value of CWmax obtained by applying the dynamic adaptation of contention window, due to the difference between expected maximum delay, D_I, and the current measured delay, D, for class I. To avoid the possibility of unnecessary fluctuation in setting of CWmax, a threshold value namely Contention Window Threshold , $CWthresh_I$ is used in the algorithm. Here α_I is a small positive constant, that should be selected appropriately to enable faster adaptation of $CWmax$ to prevailing network condition.

Algorithm 1. Procedure for Contention Window Adjustment of Class I

{$CWmax$ is calculated based on Mac delay}
$CWmax := CWmax^{prev} * (1 - \alpha_I * (D - D_I) \div D)$
if $(abs(CWmax - CWmax^{prev}) < CWthresh_I)$ **then**
  $CWmax := CWmax^{prev}$
  return
end if
if $(CWmax < CWmax^{prev})$ **then**
  $CWmax := max(CWmax, CWmax^{def})$
else
  if $(CWmax > CWmax^{prev})$ **then**
    $CWmax := min(CWmax, CWmax^{max})$
  end if
end if

Class II (Best Effort Service). This class of traffic corresponds to periodic reporting in WSNs. Traffic in this class has no delay guarantee requirements. Contention window adaptation for this class of service is required to properly utilize the available resources in the network, without degrading the service quality of other high quality service class. Because the contention window of Class II traffic, should not degrade the performance of ongoing higher priority traffic, a checking is performed such that the CWmin value of Best Effort traffic will not be smaller than CWmax of the other high priority traffic.

For class I, CWmin(default) value is 7, CWmax(default) is 15 and CWmax(max) is 31. For class II, CWmin(default) value is 32, CWmax(default) is 63 and CWmax(max) is 63.

3.3 Duty Cycle Adaptation

Second scheme, that we propose for adapting MAC Layer for providing QoS in WSNs is Dynamic Duty Cycle change based on Utilization of a node and one hop delay to the receiving node for classI traffic. In our proposed scheme of duty cycle adaptation, we change duty cycle taking into account both the criteria of Utilization and delay suffered by one hop neighbors. We change the duty cycle by appropriate percentage, by taking into account two factors mentioned above, as specified in Algorithm 2.

In Wireless Sensor Networks, the MAC layer protocol SMAC[1], we noticed that main reason behind delays in WSNs is the different sleep schedules followed by the nodes. In SMAC[1], Nodes form virtual clusters based on common sleep schedules to reduce control overhead and enable traffic-adaptive wake-up. So when data is sent from source to sink, at many nodes it has to go from one virtual clusters to another virtual cluster, and the bordering node follows both the sleep schedules. This difference in sleep schedule is incorporated in total end-to-end delay.

For the Class I(delay sensitive) traffic, this delay is undesirable. One of the solutions to this problem that we propose, is to dynamically vary the duty cycle of the nodes which are receiving more of Class I traffic. Suppose some Node 1 tries to transmit some class I traffic to Node 2, due to difference in sleep schedule, it will incur a delay, If many nodes wants to transmit to Node 2, almost all will be incurring this delay, which will increase the overall end to end delay of class I traffic. So we propose to increase the duty cycle of Node 2 based on utilization of the node and delay information received in the data frames by the sending nodes.

Estimation of Difference in Sleep Schedules (DSS) Delay. The measurement technique for Difference in Sleep Schedules Delay is very simple. A transmitting node computes this delay(s), by subtracting the time (ts_s) that a packet is passed to the MAC layer from the time (ts_c) it starts carrier sensing for sending the packet. Then it includes this delay ($ts_s - ts_c$) in the MAC frame header and sends the frame. Receiving node then extracts this delay as s^i, and calculates the average delay s^i_{avg}. Here s^i and s^{i-1}_{avg} are measured DSS delay, and previously stored average DSS delay for a service class. ζ is a positive constant, which determines how much effect the previously stored average DSS delay have on the current average DSS delay.

$$s^i_{avg} = (1 - \zeta) * s^i + \zeta * s^{i-1}_{avg} \tag{2}$$

We vary the duty cycle at the time of synchronization, when in SMAC it broadcasts the SYNC packets for the neighbor discovery, and each node also periodically broadcasts the SYNC packets so that its synchronized with its neighboring nodes. So, when a node changes its duty cycle, it broadcasts in its SYNC packets its new updated time before it goes to sleep, and in this way changing the duty cycle doesn't desynchronize the nodes. Moreover by this, we reduce the difference in sleeping schedules of all other nodes with this node, which has just updated its duty Cycle.

For changing the duty cycle by appropriate amount as calculated in Algorithm 2, duty cycle of a node should be updated at the time of sending SYNC packets, so that its not desynchronized with other nodes as we are not changing Duty Cycle by double or half. A node may be in many different sleep synchronized virtual clusters, it is following many common sleep schedules. So when duty cycle is changed it should be changed in all the schedules and all the nodes following those schedules which are at one hop distance to current node, should be informed by SYNC packets.

SYNC packets are sent after some periods defined in SMAC[1] as SYNCPE-RIOD. We implement this scheme by choosing the primary or first schedule followed by node, as the schedule to change the duty cycle. Algorithm 2 , is performed when SYNC has to be broadcasted in this schedule. Suppose duty cycle needs to be changed, then we broadcast the SYNC in this schedule to indicate the change in duty cycle, and for other schedules which till now also has some non-zero periods left before they transmit SYNC packets, we make number of periods left to zero, so that neighboring nodes following those schedules can perceive the change in duty Cycle of the SYNC packet sending node, and by this way nodes are not desynchronized even after varying duty cycle dynamically.

Duty Cycle Adaptation for Class I(Delay sensitive service): We have assumed that each node ensure a maximum DSS Delay of S_I for traffic of class I, and try to maintain it by periodically monitoring the observed delay in that class, and adjusting the Duty Cycle accordingly based on Utilization. In this case, based on the per hop delay requirements of the class I, given as S_I, and the current DSS delay, S, measured in the node for Class I traffic, Duty Cycle(DC) is adjusted as shown in Algorithm 2. In the algorithm, DC^{prev} represents the value of DC for class I before applying Duty Cycle adaptation, and DC is the new value of Duty Cycle obtained by applying the dynamic adaptation of Duty Cycle, due to the difference between expected maximum delay, S_I, and the current measured delay, S, for class I. To avoid the possibility of unnecessary fluctuation in setting of DC, a threshold value namely Duty Cycle Threshold, $DCthresh$ is used in the algorithm. Here, U_{min} is min Utilization to change DC, DC_U is permissible DC calculated from Utilization, ρ is ratio of classI and class II packets.

For classI DC_{min} is 30, and DC_{max} is 60, and $DC_{default}$ for classI and classII is 30. $DCthresh$ can be chosen as 5% DC^{prev}. We don't want to fluctuate on very small changes. U_{min} is dependent on the traffic rate, according to our traffic rate we took U_{min} as 10%. ρ_{min} is application dependent, depending on how delay sensitive is application. We took ρ_{min} to be 30%. U_{min} and ρ_{min} these are traffic and application dependent parameters, that depends on functionality performed by WSNs. U_{prev} is the previous value of Utilization, we increase the DC in proportion to increase in Utilization(U).

3.4   DCF Inter Frame Spacing (DIFS) Adaptation

Third scheme that we propose for adapting MAC Layer for providing QoS in WSNs is DIFS Adaptation per class. DIFS, is the time interval since the last sending of frame, after which any node can try to acquire the channel to send a new frame. In proposed framework, we provide intra node service differentiation based on DIFS, for different class of traffic. So, for class I we define parameter denoted by difsI and for class II we define difsII. Values of DIFS for different classes of traffic are, for class I, difsI is 8 and for class II, difsII is 15. Class I has to wait less after sending of last frame to send a new Class I traffic frame, than the Class II frame. In this differentiated service is provided based on MAC layer parameter DIFS. In this case, the DIFS of the SYNC packets has to be adjusted to the DIFS value of Class I, for maintaining the synchronization in the nodes.

Algorithm 2. Procedure for Duty Cycle Adjustment of Class I

$U := (T_{rx} + T_{tx}) \div (T_{rx} + T_{tx} + T_{idle})$
$\{T_{rx}$ is the receiving time, T_{tx} is transmitting time, T_{idle} is the idle time, in last SYNC period $\}$
if $(U < U_{min})$ **then**
  $DC := DC_{def}$
  return
end if
$\{DC_U$ is calculated duty cycle of node according to its utilization $\}$
if $(U > U_{min})$ **then**
  $DC_U = min(DC(1 + (U - Uprev)/Uprev), DC_{max})$
  $DC_U = max(DC_U, DC_{min})$
  $\{DC$ is calculated based on DSS delay $\}$
  if $\rho > \rho_{min}$ **then**
    $DC := DC^{prev} * (1 + (S - S_I) \div S_I)$
    if $(abs((DC - DC^{prev})/DC^{prev}) < DCthresh)$ **then**
      $DC := DC^{prev}$
      return
    end if
    $\{$if DC based on DSS delay is less than DC^{prev}, then DC is based on utilization$\}$

    if $(DC < DC^{prev})$ **then**
      $DC := max(DC_U, DC_{min})$
    else
      $\{$if DC based on DSS delay is greater than DC^{prev}, then DC is minimum of DC_U and DC based on DSS delay, so to minimize energy consumption$\}$
      if $(DC > DC^{prev})$ **then**
        $DC := min(DC, DC_U)$
      end if
    end if
  end if
end if
end if

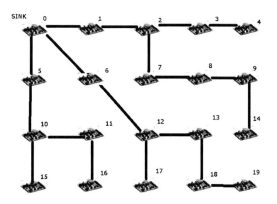

Fig. 1. Network Topology

3.5   Combining All the Schemes

Fourth scheme that we propose for adapting MAC Layer for providing QoS in WSNs is implementing all the previous three approaches together, CW Adaptation, Duty Cycle Adaptation, DIFS Adaptation. In this, contention window adaptation is done as specified in Algorithm 1. MAC Delay is measured as specified in Equation 1 and CW is adapted according to the class of traffic to be transmitted. Duty Cycle adaptation also occurs simultaneously, each node sends the information of DSS delay of class I packet to the receiving node, and receiving node keeps on updating the average DSS delay of classI packets in that round, until its time to broadcast the SYNC packets. At this instant it runs the Algorithm 2, to determine the change and inform the nodes. DIFS Adaptation is done before the nodes starts communicating, different DIFS intervals are set for class I traffic and class II traffic for intra node service differentiation. SYNC packets follow DIFS interval of classI packets, as they are important messages for synchronization. In this way all the three proposed schemes works together in a node to improve the end-to-end delay for classI(delay sensitive) traffic in presence of classII(periodic reporting) traffic.

4   Simulation and Results

The simulation of proposed scheme is implemented in ns2.29 simulator[10]. The topology that we used for our simulations is shown in Figure 1. In Figure 1, the Node numbered 0 is sink and all other sensors transmit to this node. Equal number of Class I and Class II packets are generated by each node. In this topology, distance between two nodes horizontally and vertically is 140 meters, and diagonally its around 196 meters. Communication range of each node is around 200 meters. Lines shown in the Figure 1, are routes. For simplicity, we have used static routing with only one next hop from each node, but our approach is not constrained by the topology.

Figure 2, shows the Contention Window Adaptation, Figure 4, Duty Cycle Adaptation, Figure 3, shows the DIFS Adaptation and Figure 5, shows the combination of all three proposals together. In every graph, the X axis is the Number of packets of each class received at the sink, and the Y axis is the cumulative end to end delay of packets of each class received at the sink. Since the number of packets received at sink in SMAC and Proposed scheme are same, average latency of two schemes are reported for all traffic.

Contention Window Adaptation, leads to 30% benefit in average end-to-end delay of Class I Packets compared to SMAC. DIFS Adaptation, leads to 25% benefit in average end-to-end delay of Class I Packets compared to SMAC. Duty Cycle Adaptation, leads to 37% benefit in average end-to-end delay of Class I Packets compared to SMAC. Duty Cycle, CW, DIFS Adaptation combined leads to 60% benefit in average end-to-end delay of Class I Packets compared to SMAC.

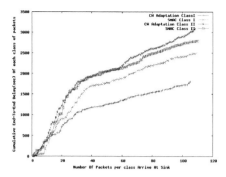

Fig. 2. Cumulative end-to-end delay of packets at sink with, CW adaptation

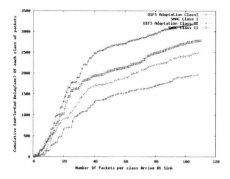

Fig. 3. Cumulative end-to-end delay of packets at sink, with DIFS Adaptation

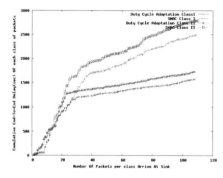

Fig. 4. Cumulative end-to-end delay of packets at sink, with Duty Cycle Adaptation

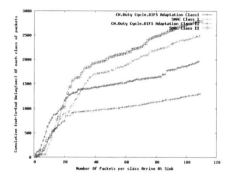

Fig. 5. Cumulative end-to-end delay of packets at sink, with all three adaptations (CW,Duty Cycle,DIFS)

5   Conclusion

The paper, proposed schemes to deal with delay sensitive(event driven) traffic in presence of periodic reporting traffic. This is achieved by adapting (i) CW, different contention window for different class of traffic (ii) Duty Cycle, adapted appropriately according to Utilization and DSS delay,unlike the previous works in literature (iii) DIFS parameters at MAC layer (iv) Combination of all three schemes proposed above. In dynamic duty cycle adaptation, our scheme adapts duty cycle by appropriate amount instead of doubling or halving it as done in previous approaches[2], so our scheme reduces energy consumption for duty cycle adaptation, but at cost of extra control messages overhead. The simulation results establish superiority of all the proposed schemes over SMAC. All the four proposed schemes shows the improvement in end-to-end delay of class I traffic in presence of class II traffic.

References

1. Ye, W., Heidemann, J., Estrin, D.: Medium Access Control With Coordinated Adaptive Sleeping for Wireless Sensor Networks. IEEE/ACM Transactions on Networking 12(3) (June 2004)
2. Lin, P., Qiao, C., Wang, X.: Medium Access Control With A Dynamic Duty Cycle For Sensor Networks. In: WCNC 2004 (2004)
3. Akkaya, K., Younis, M.: An energy-aware QoS routing protocol for wireless sensor network. In: Proceedings of the Workshops in the 23rd International Conference on Distributed Computing Systems, pp. 710–715 (May 2003)
4. Polastre, J., Hill, J., Culler, D.: Versatile low power media access for wireless sensor networks. In: SenSys 2004: Proceedings of the 2nd International Conference on Embedded Networked Sensor Systems, pp. 95–107. ACM Press, New York (2004)
5. Bac, S., Kwak, D., Kim, C.: Traffic-Aware MAC Protocol using Adaptive Duty Cycle for Wireless Sensor Networks. In: Vazão, T., Freire, M.M., Chong, I. (eds.) ICOIN 2007. LNCS, vol. 5200, pp. 142–150. Springer, Heidelberg (2008)
6. Yang, S.-H., Tseng, H.-W., Wu, E.H.-K., Chen, G.-H.: Utilization Based Duty Cycle Tuning MAC Protocol for Wireless Sensor Networks. In: Global Telecommunications Conference, GLOBECOM 2005. IEEE, Los Alamitos (2005)
7. Wireless LAN Medium Access Control (MAC) and Physical Layer (PHY) Specification IEEE Std. 802.11-1999 edition
8. Dam, T.V., Langendoen, K.: An Adaptive Energy-Efficient MAC Protocol for Wireless Sensor Networks. In: The First ACM Conference on Embedded Networked Sensor Systems (Sensys 2003), Los Angeles, CA, USA (November 2003)
9. Xiao, Y.: IEEE 802.11e: A QoS provisioning at the MAC layer. IEEE Wireless Commun. 11(3), 72–79 (2004)
10. McCanne, S., Floyd, S.: ns Network Simulator, http://www.isi.edu/nsnam/ns/

Audio Steganography Using Modified LSB and PVD

R. Darsana and Asha Vijayan

Center For Cyber Security
Amrita Vishwa Vidyapeetham
Coimbatore, India
{darsanaraj1,asha03vijayan}@gmail.com

Abstract. In Audio Steganography we find a way so that an audio file can be used as a host media to hide textual message without affecting the file structure and content of the audio file. In this system a novel high bit rate LSB audio data hiding and another method known as Pixel value differencing is proposed. This scheme reduces embedding distortion of the host audio. The hidden bits are embedded into the higher LSB layers resulting in increased robustness against noise addition. To avoid major differences from the cover audio and the embedded audio this algorithm helps in modifying the rest of the bits. To enlarge the capacity of the hidden secret information and to provide an imperceptible stego-audio for human perception, a pixel-value differencing (PVD) is used for embedding. The difference value of audio samples is replaced by a new value to embed the value of a sub-stream of the secret message. The method is designed in such a way that the modification is never out of the range interval. This method provides an easy way to produce a more imperceptible result than those yielded by simple least-significant-bit replacement methods. The SNR value is good for LSB scheme and the capacity is high for PVD scheme.

Keywords: Audio Steganography, LSB, PVD, substitution Techniques, SNR.

1 Introduction

In Audio Steganography we find a way so that an audio file can be used as a host media to hide textual message without affecting the file structure and content of the audio file. Because of degradation in the perceptual quality of the cover object may leads to a noticeable change in the cover object, may leads to the failure of objective of steganography. The two primary criteria for embedding the covert message are that the stego signal resulting from embedding is indistinguishable from the host audio signal and the message should be correctly received at the receiver side. Audio data hiding method provides the most effective way to protect privacy.

In the past few years, several algorithms for the embedding and extraction of message in audio sequences have been presented.[3] All of the developed algorithms take advantage of the perceptual properties of the human auditory system (HAS) in order to add a message into a host signal in a perceptually transparent manner. Embedding additional information into audio sequences is a more tedious task than that of images, due to dynamic supremacy of the HAS over human visual system. On the other hand, many attacks that are malicious against image steganography

D.C. Wyld et al. (Eds.): NeCoM/WeST/WiMoN 2011, CCIS 197, pp. 11–20, 2011.
© Springer-Verlag Berlin Heidelberg 2011

algorithms cannot be implemented against audio steganography schemes. Audio Steganography should guarantee Undetectability, Capacity, Robustness, Perceptual transparency, Security and Accurate Extraction[1].

The rest of this paper is organized as follows. Section 2 reviews previous works related to Audio steganographic methods. Section 3 summarizes the proposed scheme and has 2 effective methods to embed message in audio. Section 4 presents performance analysis. Section 5 concludes this paper with a summary of the main contributions of this work and future works.

2   Related Work

In audio steganography, secret message is embedded into digitized audio signal which result slight altering of binary sequence of the corresponding audio file. There are several methods are available for audio steganography.

LSB Coding:-Least significant bit (LSB) coding is the simplest way to embed secret message in a digital audio file. This is done by replacing the LSB of each sample with a binary message. This coding helps in embedding large amount of data to be encoded.

Parity Coding:-The parity coding method breaks a signal down into separate regions of samples and encodes each bit from the secret message in a sample region's parity bit. If the parity bit of a selected region does not match the secret bit to be encoded, the process flips the LSB of one of the samples in the region.

Phase Coding:- Phase components of sound are not clearly perceptible to the human ear. Rather than introducing disturbances, the technique encodes the message bits as phase shifts in the phase spectrum of a digital signal, achieving an inaudible encoding in terms of signal-to-perceived noise ratio.

Echo Hiding:-In this information is embedded in a sound file by giving an echo into the discrete signal. It allows for a high data transmission rate and provides superior robustness. To hide the data three parameters of the echo are varied: Amplitude, decay rate, and offset (delay time) from the original signal[11].

Spread Spectrum:-In the context of audio steganography, the basic spread spectrum (SS) method attempts to spread secret information across the audio signal's frequency spectrum as much as possible. This method spreads the secret message over the sound file's frequency spectrum, using a code that is independent of the actual signal. So the final signal occupies a bandwidth in excess of what is actually required for transmission.

3   Proposed Scheme

In this paper we introduce 2 methods for effective embedding in audio files. Here substituting the least significant bit of each sampling point with a binary representation of message. First method uses substitution in appropriate bit positions then reducing the amount of distortion using a modified LSB algorithm. Second method uses another algorithm where the secret message that can be embed is more that also with less distortion. The embedded secret message can be extracted from the resulting stego-audio without referencing the original cover audio.

3.1   Reduced Distortion Bit Embedding (Modified LSB Scheme)

In this method it is able to shift the limit for transparent data hiding in audio from the lower LSB layer to the higher LSB layers such as fourth to sixth layer, using a two-step approach. In the first step, a message bit is embedded into the ith LSB layer of the host audio using a novel LSB coding method. In the second step, the impulse noise caused by embedding is shaped in order to change its white noise properties. The standard LSB coding method simply replaces the original host audio bit in the ith layer (i=1,…,16) with the bit from the message bit stream. In the case when the original and watermark bit are different and ith LSB layer is used for embedding the error caused by embedding is 2^{i-1} (amplitude range is [-32768, 32767]). The embedding error is positive if the original bit is 0 and message bit is 1 and vice versa.

A key idea of the proposed LSB algorithm is message bit embedding that causes minimal embedding distortion of the host audio. It is clear that, if only one of 16 bits in a sample is fixed and equal to the message bit, the other bits can be flipped in order to minimize the embedding error. For example, if the original sample value was $0…01000_2=8_{10}$, and the watermark bit was zero is to be embedded into 4th LSB layer, instead of value $0…00000_2=0_{10}$ that the standard algorithm would produce, the proposed algorithm produces a sample that has value $0…00111_2=7_{10}$, which is far closer to the original one[3]. However, the extraction algorithm remains the same; it simply retrieves the message bit by reading the bit value from the predefined LSB layer in the embedded audio sample.

In the embedding algorithm, the $(i+1)^{th}$ LSB layer (bit a_i) is first modified by insertion of the present message bit. Then the algorithm given below is run. In a case where the bit a_i need not be modified at all due to already being at correct value, no action is taken with the signal sample. The proposed embedding algorithm is implemented 4.1.1.In addition to decreasing objective measure as signal to noise ratio (SNR) value, in the second step of embedding the proposed method introduces noise shaping in order to increase perceptually transparency of the overall method. LSB watermark embedding in a silent or non-dynamic part of the audio sequence causes perceptible hissing noise as significant audio values are introduced where they did not exist in the host audio signal. In order to decrease these perceptual artifacts, the second part of the algorithm is executed. In our algorithm, embedding error is spread to the four consecutive samples, as samples that are predecessors of the current sample cannot be altered because information bits have already been embedded into their LSBs. Let e(n) denote the embedding error of the sample a(n), For the case of embedding into the 4th LSB layer, the next four consecutive samples of the host audio are modified according to these expressions:

$$a(n+1)=a(n+1)+ \lfloor e(n) \rfloor$$
$$a(n+2)=a(n+2)+ \lfloor e(n)/2 \rfloor$$
$$a(n+3)=a(n+3)+ \lfloor e(n)/3 \rfloor$$
$$a(n+4)=a(n+4)+ \lfloor e(n)/4 \rfloor$$

where $\lfloor A \rfloor$ denotes floor operation that rounds A to the nearest integer less than or equal to A. Error diffusion method shapes input impulse noise, introduced by LSB embedding, by smearing it. The effect is most emphasized during silent periods of the audio signal and in fragments with low dynamics e.g. broad minimums or maximums. In these cases, there are several hundreds of samples with the same value (e.g. all sixteen bits in a sample are zeros) and error diffusion method shifts the sample levels towards the mean value of expected additive noise. Therefore, the perceptual distortion is not as high as it would be without this step [3]. Both the steps jointly increase the subjective quality of stego object as noise made by LSB embedding has perceptually better-tuned distribution. The proposed LSB scheme thus tries to avoid large modification in the cover and robustness of embedding increases with the increase of the LSB depth used for hiding.

3.1.1 Algorithm
If bit 0 is to be embedded

        if $a_{i-1}=0$ then $a_{i-1}a_{i-2}\ldots a_0=11\ldots 1$

        if $a_{i-1}=1$ then $a_{i-1}a_{i-2}\ldots a_0=00\ldots 0$ and

            if $a_{i+1}=0$ then $a_{i+1}=1$

            else if $a_{i+2}=0$ then $a_{i+2}=1$

            $\ldots$

            else if $a15=0$ then $a15=1$

    else if bit 1 is to be embedded

        if $a_{i-1}=1$ then $a_{i-1}a_{i-2}\ldots a_0=00\ldots 0$

        if $a_{i-1}=0$ then $a_{i-1}a_{i-2}\ldots a_0=11\ldots 1$ and

     if $a_{i+1}=1$ then $a_{i+1}=0$

        else if $a_{i+2}=1$ then $a_{i+2}=0$

        $\ldots$

        else if $a_{15}=1$ then $a_{15}=0$

3.2 Embedding Using Pixel Value Differencing Algorithm

Hiding data in the LSBs of the samples of an audio is a common information hiding method that utilizes the characteristic of the human Auditory System to small changes in the audio. This simple LSB embedding approach is easy for computation, and a large amount of data can be embedded without great quality loss. The more LSBs are used for embedding, the more distorted result will be produced. Not all samples in an audio can tolerate equal amounts of changes without causing notice to a listener. In the PVD embedding method, the cover audio is simply divided into a number of samples. A flowchart of the proposed embedding method is sketched in Fig. 1.

3.2.1 Quantization of Sample Differences
A difference value d is computed from every two consecutive samples, say s_i and s_{i1}, of a given cover audio. Assume that the values of si and s_{i1} are vi and v_{i1} respectively, and then d is computed as $v_i - v_{i+1}$ which may be in the range from 0 to 255 if 8 bit quantization is used. A block with d close to 0 is considered to be an extremely smooth block, whereas a block with d close to -255 or 255 is considered as a sharply edged block. By symmetry, we only consider the possible absolute values of d (0 through 255) and classify them into a number of contiguous ranges, say R_i where i =1,2,...n. These ranges are assigned indices 1 though n. The lower and upper bound values are l_i and R_i respectively, where l_i is 0 and u_i is 255. The width of R_i is the selected range intervals are based on the human visual capability mentioned previously.

The widths of the ranges which represent the difference values of smooth samples are chosen to be smaller while those which represent the difference values of highly varying samples are chosen to be larger. That is, we create ranges with smaller widths when d is close to 0 and ones with larger widths when d is far away from 0 for the purpose of yielding better undistorted results. A difference value which falls in a range with index k is said to have index k. All the values in a certain range (i.e., all the values with an identical index) are considered as close enough. That is, if a difference value in a range is replaced by another in the same range, the change presumably cannot be easily noticed by human ears. Here some bits of the secret message is embedded into a audio samples by replacing the difference value of the block with one with an identical index, i.e., we change a difference value in one range into any of the difference values in the same range. In other words, in the proposed data embedding process, we adjust the sample values in each two sample pair by two new ones whose difference value causes changes unnoticeable to a listener of the stego-audio.

3.3   Data Embedding and Extraction

We consider the secret message as a long bit stream. We want to embed every bit in the bit stream into the sample pair of the cover audio. The number of bits which can be embedded in each block varies and is decided by the width of the range to which the difference value of the two samples belongs[2]. Given a sample pair B with index k and value difference d, the number of bits, say n, which can be embedded in this block, is calculated by Since the width of each range is selected to be a power of 2,the value of $n=\log_2(u_k - l_k + 1)$ is an integer.

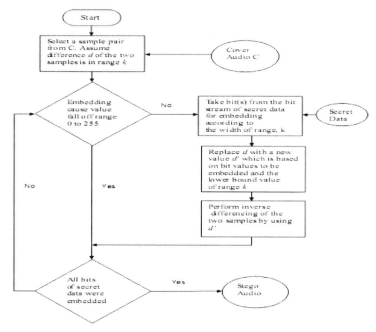

Fig. 1. The data embedding process in PVD

3.3.1 Procedure

1) Calculate the difference value di between two consecutive samples pi and P_{i+1} for each block in the cover audio. The value is given by $d_i = v_{i+1} - v_i$

2) Using d_i to locate a suitable R_k in the designed range table, to compute $j = \min(u_k - |d_i|)$ where $u_k >= d_i$ for all $1 <= k <= n$ is the located range.

3) Compute the amount of secret data bits t that can be embedded in each pair of two consecutive samples by R_i. The value t can be estimated from the width w of R_j this can be defined by $t = \log 2w_j$

4) Read t bits from the binary secret data and transform the bit sequence into a decimal value b. For instance, if bit sequence $= 110$, then the converted value $b = 6$.

5) Calculate the new difference value d to replace the original difference

$$di' = \begin{cases} lj + b & if\ di \geq 0 \\ -(lj + b) & if\ di < 0 \end{cases}$$

6) Modify the values of p_i and p_{i+1}l by the following formula

$$(v_i', v'_{i+1}) = (v_i - ceil(m), v_{i+1} + floor(m))\ \text{if } d \text{ is odd}$$

$$(v_i', v'_{i+1}) = (v_i - floor(m), v + ceil(m))\ \text{if d is even where } m = (d'-d)/2_{i+1}$$

Repeat Step 1-6 until all secret data are embedded into the cover audio, then the stego-audio is obtained. During the phase of secret extraction, the original designed range table is required. In the beginning, the same method in the embedding phase is used to partition the stego-audio into sample pairs. Then the difference value d for each pair of two consecutive samples pi*and P^* the stego-audio is calculated. Next, d_i^* is used to locate the suitable R_{i+1} in Step 2 during the embedding phase. Therefore, b^* is obtained by subtracting l_j from d_i^*. If the stego-audio is not altered, b^* is equal to b. Finally, b^* is transformed from a decimal value into a binary sequence with t bits, where $t = \log 2w_j$.

The above equations satisfy the requirement that the difference between v'$_i$ and v'$_{i+1}$ is d'. It is noted that a distortion reduction policy has been employed in designing for producing v'$_i$ andv'$_{i+1}$ from v$_i$ and v$_{i+1}$, so that the distortion caused by changing v$_i$ and v$_{i+1}$ is nearly equally distributed over the two samples. The effect is that the resulting change is less perceptible. An illustration of the data embedding process is shown in Figure 2. In the inverse calculation, a smaller value of d' produces a smaller range interval between v'$_i$ and v'$_{i+1}$ while a larger d' produces a larger interval. Some of the calculation may cause the resulting (v'$_i$, v'$_{i+1}$) to fall off the boundaries of the range [0,255] Although we may re-adjust the two new values into the valid range of [0, 255] by forcing a falling off boundary value to be one of the boundary values of 0 and 255, and adjusting the other to a proper value to satisfy the difference d', yet this might produce some distortions. To solve this problem, a checking process is employed to detect such falling off boundary cases, and abandon the samples which yield such cases for data embedding[2]. The sample values of the abandoned blocks are left intact in the stego-audio. This strategy helps us to distinguish easily samples with embedded data from abandoned blocks in the process of recovering data from a stego audio. The proposed falling-off-boundary checking proceeds by producing a pair (v^*_i and v^*_{i+1}) by replacing m as $m=(uk-d)/2$. Since u_k is the maximum value in the range l_k to u_k the resulting pair of v^*_i, v^*_{i+1}) produced by the use of u_k will yield the maximum difference That is, this maximum range interval (v^*_i - v^*_{i+1})covers all over the ranges yielded by the other (v^*_i, v^*_{i+1}). So the falling off boundary checking for the block can proceed by only examining the values of (v^*_i, v^*_{i+1}) which are produced by the case of using u_k If either v^*_i or v^*_{i+1} falls off the boundary of 0 or 255, we regard the block to have the possibility of falling-o ff, and abandon the block for embedding data. In addition, the inverse calculation in is designed in such a way that the inverse calculation can proceed directly or progressively. This property is useful for judging the existence of embedded data in each block in the data recovering process. Assume that blocks in stego audio has the values (v_i, v_{i+1}) and that the difference d' of the two values is with index k. we apply the falling off boundary the two values is with index k.

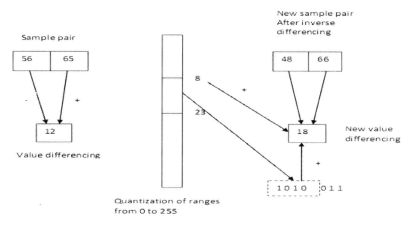

Fig. 2. Illustration of the data embedding process

We apply the falling-off-boundary checking process to (v'_i , v'_{i+1}) by using $m = (u_k - d')/2$ and (v''_i , v''_{i+1}) is the resulting values We now want to prove that the resulting (v''_i , v''_{i+1}) are identical to the values (v^*_i, v^*_{i+1})which were computed by $m = (u_k - d')/2$ in the embedding process The proof is as follows

$$(v'_i, v'_{i+1}) = f((v'_i, v'_{i+1}), u_k - d) = f((v_i, v_{i+1}), d'-d + u_k - d')$$

Also, the inverse calculation is designed in such a way that it satisfies the following property: $f((v_i, v_{i+1)}, m) = f(f((v_i, v_{i+1})m')m'')$ for $m=m'+m''$

The above result can be transformed further to be

$$f(v_i, v_{i+1}), d'-d + u_k - d') = f(f(v_i, v_{i+1}), d'-d)u_k - d')$$
$$= f((v_i, v_{i+1}), u_k - d') = (v''_i, v''_{i+1})$$

This completes the proof. The above property shows that the results of both of the falling-off-boundary checking processes, one in data embedding and the other in data recovery, are identical. Note that in the recovery of the secret message from the stego-audio using the previously described extraction process, there is no need of referencing the cover audio.

4 Performance Analysis

The goal of research is to develop quantitative measures that can automatically improve audio quality. The simplest and most widely used full-reference quality metric is the Signal to Noise ratio (SNR). Steganography capacity is the maximum message size that can be embedded subject to certain constraints. Tables 1 & 2 shows SNR values of different audios. We have randomly taken audios after embedding in those audios the SNR values are still around 40 db. Figures 3 to 6 shows the histogram analysis of original and embedded audios using two methods. Results show that quality is preserved in both methods. In audios 20 % embedding has done. Compared to LSB method PVD method can hold more secret data but LSB method shows high SNR value.

Table 1. SNR value of different audios using PVD method

Audio	SNR	BER
a.wav	39.2836	0
b.wav	40.3233	0
c.wav	39.4464	0

Table 2. SNR value of different audios using LSB method

Audio	SNR	BER
d.wav	47.7574	0
e.wav	42.2260	0
f.wav	48.2812	0

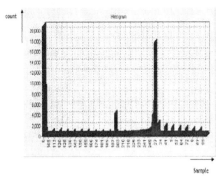

Fig. 3. Histogram of original audio using PVD

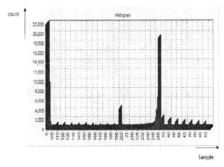

Fig. 4. Histogram of embedded audio using PVD

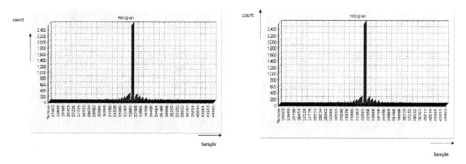

Fig. 5. Original audio using Modified LSB   **Fig. 6.** Embedded audio using Modified LSB

5 Conclusion and Future Work

A new approach is proposed to resolve two problems of substitution technique of audio steganography. First problem is having low robustness against attacks which try to reveal the hidden message and second one is having low robustness against distortions with high average power. Substitution algorithm will try to embed the message bits in the deeper layers of samples and other bits are altered to decrease the error and if alteration is not possible for any samples it will ignore them. Using the proposed scheme, message bits could be embedded into vague and deeper layers to achieve higher robustness. We tested the proposed algorithms with 5 music clips. The clips are sampled at 44.1 KHz with the length of about 1 minute and quantized by 8 bits. The performance of the proposed scheme in terms of SNR (Signal to NoiseRatio)and histogram is analyzed and listed in Table 1 & 2 and Figures 3 to 6. In modified LSB method the distortion are reduced when compared with standard method and in PVD method the capacity of secret data that can be embedded is more. In the future, more effective methods should be taken into account to further increase the embedding capacity and embedding should be done in live audio.

References

1. Zamani, M., Manaf, A.B.A., Ahmad, R.B., Jaryani, F., Hamed, Taherdoost, Zeki, A.M.: A Secure Audio Steganography Approach. IEEE Xplore (2009)
2. Wu, D.C., Tsai, W.H.: A Steganographic Method for Images By Pixel Value Differencing. Pattern Recognition Letters 24, 1613–1626 (2003)
3. Cvejic, N., Seppanen, T.: Increasing Robustness of LSB Audio Steganography Using a Novel Embedding method. In: Proceedings of the International Conference on Information Technology: Coding and Computing, ITCC 2004 (2004)
4. Basu, P.N., Bhowmik, T.: On Embedding of Text in Audio – A case of Steganography. In: 2010 International Conference on Recent Trends in Information, Telecommunication and Computing (2010)
5. Zamani, M., Manaf, A.B.A., et al.: An Approach to Improve the Robustness of Substitution Techniques of Audio Steganography. IEEE Xplore (2009)

6. Gopalan, K.: Audio Steganography Using Bit Modification. In: Proceedings of the 2003 IEEE Intematianal Conference (2003)
7. Katzenbeisser, S., Petitcolas, F.A.P.: Information Hiding Techniques for Steganography and Digital Watermarking. Artech House, Norwood (2000)
8. Cvejic, N.: Algorithms for audio watermarking and steganography. In: Information Processing Laboratory. University of Oulu, Oulu (2004)
9. Wang, H., Wang, S.: Cyber warfare: Steganography vs. Steganalysis. Communications of the ACM 47(10) (October 2004)
10. Artz, D.: Digital Steganography: Hiding Data within Data. IEEE Internet Computing (May-June 2001)
11. Geetha, K., Vanitha Muthu, P.: Implementation of ETAS (Embedding Text in Audio Signal) Model to Ensure Secrecy. (IJCSE) International Journal on Computer Science and Engineering 02(04), 1308–1313 (2010)

An Adaptive Cross Layer Design to Enhance Throughput for Multimedia Streaming over Mobile Adhoc Networks

N. Gomathi[1], P. Seethalakshmi[2], and A. Govardhan[3]

[1] Research Scholar,
JNTU, Hyderabad
gomathi1974@gmail.com
[2] Director, CAE,
Anna University
Triuchirappalli
seetha@tau.edu.in
[3] Principal,
JNTUH College of Engg.,
Hyderabad
govardhan_cse@yahoo.co.in

Abstract. The main objective of this paper is to propose a novel method for enhancing the Quality of Service (QoS) of multimedia applications in wireless adhoc networks. The enhancement is achieved by implementing a cross layer mapping algorithm, between application layer and Medium Access Layer where Connectionless Light Weight Protocol (UDPLite) is used in transport layer that supports multimedia applications. The Proposed method achieves 16% improvement in reduction of delay and 12.5% improvement in PSNR as compared to the conventional UDP Protocol under heavy traffic conditions.

Keywords: Enhanced Distributed Channel Access, MANETs, PSNR, UDPLite, Video Streaming.

1 Introduction

Recent advancements in computing techniques have become an integral part of wireless communication networks. Mobile Ad hoc networks (MANETs) have emerged amid the unprecedented growth of Internet and are increasingly attracting attention because of its ability to connect across nodes without relying on pre-existing network infrastructure. The widespread emergence of real-time voice, audio and video applications, stimulates the successful development of viable technologies to provide these multimedia applications over mobile adhoc networks. The performance of MANET is affected by various factors such as mobility of node, battery life and routing protocols, topology change etc. Hence providing Quality of service for multimedia applications in adhoc networks is difficult.

Quality of Service requirements of multimedia applications in adhoc networks have been supported by IEEE 802.11e standard. 802.11e defines four Access

D.C. Wyld et al. (Eds.): NeCoM/WeST/WiMoN 2011, CCIS 197, pp. 21–32, 2011.
© Springer-Verlag Berlin Heidelberg 2011

Categories (ACs) with different transmissions priorities. The transmission priority is the probability of successfully earning the chance to transmit when individual ACs are competing to access the wireless channel. Higher the transmission priority, better is the opportunity to transmit. But in a wireless channel the unavoidable burst loss, due to excessive delays and limited bandwidth there are challenges for good transmission over wireless network.

In this paper we argue that for 802.11e based adhoc networks, a partial checksum approach at the transport layer along with an adaptive cross layer mapping scheme between application layer and Medium Access Layer, can improve the performance of video transmission. In this paper an attempt has been made to get benefits of UdpLite along with cross layer approach. The rest of the paper is organized as follows. In this section 2 we discuss the aspects of an adaptive cross layer mapping algorithm and UdpLite. In this section 3 we discuss about proposed system. Section 4 establishes system simulation model and Section 5 gives results to illustrate the performance while conclusion are drawn in section 6.

2   UDPLite and Cross Layer Approach

The quality of video can be increased by enabling the application layer to specify about the importance of packets and those packets can be preserved by the UDPLite protocol [1] in the transport layer along with Cross Layer Mapping approach. The notion of application-layer over transport-layer protection is not new and hence traditional real- time multimedia services have been realized as Realtime Transport Protocol (RTP) over User Datagram Protocol (UDP). User Datagram Protocol (UDP) is an unreliable protocol that is suitable for delay sensitive applications such as   real-time media applications that are sensitive to network delays. UDPLite is an extension to UDP that even needs damaged data to be delivered rather than discarded by networks, so it allows partial checksums on multimedia data by enabling the applications to specify, the sensitive and insensitive parts of the multimedia stream on a per-packet basis. Errors in the sensitive part cause a packet to be discarded whereas an error in the insensitive part allows it to be delivered. The check sum is carried out on the sensitive part of the packet. UDP has a strict checksum where corrupted packets will be discarded if they contain any transmission errors. The UDPLite protocol allows the application to receive the corrupted packets instead of dropping them altogether. This is achieved by a partial checksum which only covers a fixed amount of sensitive data. Integrating UDPLite into existing UDP framework is simple. The length field in the UDP header is replaced by the coverage field, which signifies the number of bytes of the packet that are to be checksummed. With a checksum coverage value replacing the packet length, UDPLite packets are treated as classic UDP packets with the checksum enabled. To address security concerns and handle the multiplexing of other transport level flows, the packet header should always be checksummed. If corruption occurs in the Sensitive region or in the header, the packet is dropped at the receiver otherwise the packet is passed up to the application through the interface.

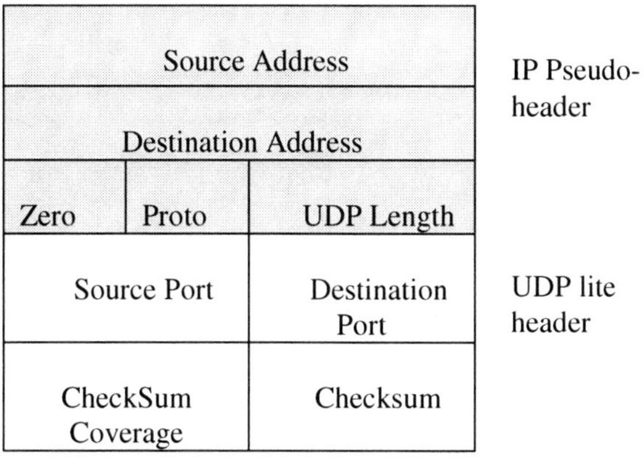

Source Address			IP Pseudo-header
Destination Address			
Zero	Proto	UDP Length	
Source Port		Destination Port	UDP lite header
CheckSum Coverage		Checksum	

Fig. 1. The UDPLite Header

The UDPLite protocol headers are shown in Figure 2. Shaded fields are the fields of the pseudo header provided by the IP layer, and white fields belong to the UDPLite header. The UDPLite checksum covers the conceptual IP pseudo-header in order to protect against misrouted packets.

The Checksum Coverage field in the UDP Lite header denotes the number of octets (counting from the first octet of the header) that are covered by the checksum. The value of Checksum Coverage is zero indicating that the entire UDP-Lite packet is covered by the checksum. This explains that the value of the Checksum Coverage field MUST be either 0 or at least 8. The UDP Lite header and the IP pseudo-header are always verified by the checksum, which means that the least acceptable value of the coverage field is eight (the number of bytes in the UDP Lite header). A UDP-Lite packet with a Checksum Coverage value of 1 to 7 MUST be discarded by the receiver.

Cross Layer Mapping Scheme

From the Application Layer the video significance information is generated and transmitted to Enhanced Distributed channel access used in Medium Access Layer. In EDCA, packets arriving from Application layer and Transport layer (UDPLite layer) packets are tagged with four different user priorities and each priority is mapped to one of four Access Categories (ACs). The four different Access Categories (ACs) are Voice traffic, Video traffic, Best Effort traffic and Back Ground traffic that are represented as AC0, AC1, AC2 and AC3 respectively. Each AC maintains a local queue and an independent back off instance with a specific set of contention parameters. All ACs contend independently for access to the channel and internal collisions may occur, but are solved by allowing the AC with the highest priority to gain access to the channel.

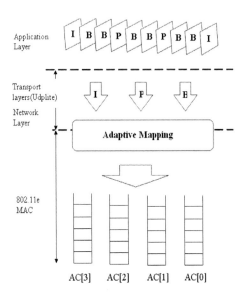

Fig. 2. Architecture of adaptive mapping

To achieve differentiation between Access Categories (ACs), Contention Window (CW) parameters such as CW_{min} and CW_{max} and Arbitrary Interframe Space (AIFS) are used. to Instead of waiting for the normal Differentiated Inter Frame Space (DIFS) time, each AC waits a specific AIFS time. Higher priorities have lower values of the Contention Window (CW) parameters and AIFS. This leads to a higher fraction of the capacity and lower delays since the channel access frequency is increased. An additional parameter is the Transmission Opportunity (TXOP) that specifies the length of time the channel is occupied by a station. Depending on this limit, one or several packets may be transmitted when an AC has acquired the channel. Priority differentiation used by EDCA ensures better service to high priority class while offering a minimum service for low priority classes.

The AC with the smallest AIFS has the highest priority, and a station needs to defer for its corresponding AIFS interval. From Table 1 it is inferred that the smaller the parameter values (such as AIFS, CWmin and CWmax) the greater the probability

Table 1. Default EDCA parameter set values

Priority	Access Category	Designation	AIFSN	CWmin	CWmax	TXOPlimit
3	AC_VO	Voice	2	(CWmin+1)/4-1	(CWmin+1)/2-1	0.003008
2	AC_VI	Video	2	(CWmin+1)/2-1	CWmin	0.006016
1	AC_BE	Best Effort	3	CWmin	CWmax	0
0	AC_BK	Background	7	CWmin	CWmax	0

to access the medium. Each Access Category within a station behaves like an individual virtual station, it contends for access to the medium and independently starts its backoff procedure after detecting the channel being idle for at least an AIFS period. When a collision occurs among different access categories within the same station, the higher priority access category is granted the opportunity to transmit, while the lower priority access category suffers from a virtual collision, similar to a real collision outside the station.

In the cross-layer approach, the frames of the MPEG-4 video packets are dynamically mapped to the appropriate Access Category based on both the significance of the video frame and the network traffic load. Based on this Access Category the MPEG4 video packets are mapped dynamically to the appropriate Access Category (AC). Typically a MPEG video contains B-Frames, I-Frames and P-Frames. Loss of Important frames in MPEG4 video stream would degrade the delivered video quality, whereas loss of B-Frame doesn't affect all the frames of Group of Pictures (GOP) but itself. Loss of I-Frame would cause all frames in Group of Pictures (GOP) to be undecodable. Based on the significance of the video frame, the channel access priorities are used to prioritize the transmission opportunity at the MAC layer are set with the I frame as the highest; the P frame below I but above B's priority, and the B frame set at the lowest priority. Mapping probability defined as Prob_TYPE is assigned according to its coding significance of video data. This way the important video data is alloted to high priority AC queue in 802.11e MAC layer which has been discussed in [2]. If allocating a frame into a lower priority queue is inevitable, the transmission allocating probability of lower significant frames is higher than that of important video frames. When larger Prob_TYPE is assigned to less important video frames the MPEG4 downward mapping probability relationship of the video frame types become Prob_B> Prob_ and Prob_I, values lying between 0 and 1. Moreover, to support dynamic adaptation to changes in network traffic loads, MAC queue length has been used as an indication of the current network traffic load. According to the IEEE 802.11e specification, when transmitted over an IEEE 802.11e wireless network, MPEG-4 video packets are placed in AC2 category which has better opportunity to access the channel than lower priority Access Categories (ACs). The tradeoff is, when the video stream increases, this queue rapidly jams and drops occur. So an adaptive, cross-layer mapping algorithm approach has been implemented and it is already discussed in [3]. This mapping algorithm re-arranges most recently received video packets into other available lower priority queues, while the AC2 queue is getting filled. Two parameters, **threshold_low** and **threshold_high** which was denoted in *[2]* has been used predicatively to avoid the upcoming congestion by performing queue management in advance. The integrated function to introduce these two parameters in the cross layer mapping approach is in the following expression:

$$Prob\_New = Prob\_Type * \frac{qlen\,(AC[2]) - threshold\_low}{threshold\_high - threshold\_low}$$

In this function, the original predefined downward mapping probability of each type of video frame, **Prob_TYPE**, will be adjusted according to the current queue length and threshold values, and about the result is a new downward mapping probability, **Prob_New**. The higher **Prob_New**, the greater the opportunity for the packet to be mapped into a lower priority queue.

In the cross layer mapping approach when a video packet arrives, first the queue length of AC2 is checked and it is compared with values of threshold_high and threshold_low. If queue length is lower than the threshold_low (light load), the video data is mapped to AC[2] irrespective of the type of video data being transferred. But if the queue length is greater than the threshold_high (heavy video traffic load) the video data is directly mapped to lower priority queues, AC[1] or AC[0]. However if queue length of AC[2] is between threshold_high and threshold_low, the mapping decision considers both the mapping probability (Prob_TYPE) and the current buffering size condition of the queue. Hence, the video data packet will be mapped to different AC's according to the calculated downward mapping probability. With such a priority scheme in mac layer along with UDPLite in Transport layer the transmissions are prioritized and the drop rate of video is minimized.

3 Related Work

EDCA has been improved by adjusting the parameter adaptively to channel state or congestion level in [4]. adaptive EDCA had been implemented, where the access point adopted the contention window based on the network congestions was discussed in [5]. a two level protection had been applied for voice and video traffic by distributed admission control. The Budget calculation had been done in EDCA to protect existing video streams and the issue of bandwidth allocation for video streams had been investigated in [6]. The cross layer architecture was used which is based on the data partitioning and they have been associated to each partition within the access layer categories of EDCA was discussed in [7]. The macro and micro rate control schemes had been used at the application layer and network layer which uses bandwidth estimation and adaptive   mapping of packets using video classifications was discussed in [8]. A wireless video system had been built using the error resilient low bit rate video coder by implementing UDPlite and PPP lite in transport and link layer protocols for cellular video was discussed in [9]. The H.264 had been transmitted for video over an adhoc scenario using Udplite which has reduced retransmission using unequal error protection was discussed in [10]. A multimedia network asic design had been implemented which includes the characteristics of H.264 with Udplite to reduce packet loss was discussed in [11]. A distributed algorithm had been implemented for channel time allocation among multiple video streams, and they had investigated several heuristic packet pruning schemes for rate adaption of high definition video streams were discussed in [12]. A distributed rate allocation scheme had been implemented with a goal of minimizing the total video distortion of all peers without excessive network utilization was discussed in [13]. This scheme relied on cross-layer information exchange between MAC and application layers. A work had been done on 802.11e, where the parameters of MAC layer had been adjusted to provide very good quality by adding UDPlite in transport layer was discussed in [14].

4   Proposed System

The figure 3 depicts the main components of the system architecture for wireless media streaming. The media source which can be a real time encoder or pre compressed media file, generated media packets that are initially sent to the application layer buffer. Subsequently the UDPLite header is added by the transport layer, IP header is added by the network layer. The IP packet is sent to the 802.11e MAC layer and creates an MAC protocol data unit for wireless transmission. All packets are stored in link layer buffer. Similarly the above process is been reversed at the receiver end.

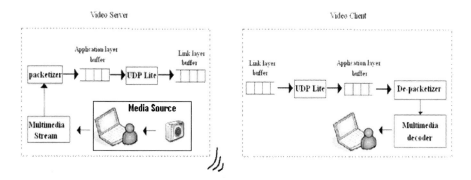

Fig. 3. Multimedia Streaming System

5   Simulation Results and Discussions

A. Implementation and simulation setup of Cross Layer Mapping along with UDPLite.

The simulation of Cross Layer Mapping approach along with UDPLite using NS2 simulator has been done, and the performance of the received video at the receiver has been examined. We simulate a Cross Layer Mapping approach along with UDPLite over a ad-hoc network using the NS2 simulator. By exploiting the cross layer mapping approach, prioritization is done in the transmission of essential video data that improves the queue space utilization and also support dynamic adaptation for changes in network traffic loads. MAC queue is used as the indication of the current network traffic load. When video is transmitted over an IEEE 802.11e WLAN, MPEG4 video packets are placed in AC2 which increase efficiency of accessing channels when the video stream increases in the AC2 queue rapidly filled and problems such as jams and drops occur. Inorder to overcome these problems, the proposed approach arranges most recently received video packets into other available lower priority queues. since UDPlite is used in the transport layer the packets, which are prone to errors due to radio channel variations are also delivered to the receiver by the UDPlite protocol in the transport layer, if the error has occurred in the payload. the corrupted packet will be discarded, if the error has occurred in the header.

5.1 Simulation Topology

The simulation is performed with 3 types of video sources like YUV QCIF (176 x 144) Foreman, Claire, Akiyo. Each video frame was fragmented into packets before transmission and the maximum packet size over the simulator network is 1000 bytes. Figure 4 presents the simulation topology in the experiment. There are eight ad hoc wireless nodes where one is video server and another is video receiver. The data rate of wireless link is 1Mbps.

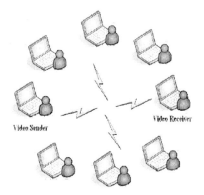

Fig. 4. Network topology used in simulation

5.2 Experiments and Results

In all simulation experiments the performance of 4 cases -MPEG4 UDP, MPEG4 UDPLite, cross layer mapping with UDP and cross layer mapping with UDPLite has been compared, for the video sequences.

Delay

Figure 5 represents the delay produced by cross layer mapping with UDP and cross layer mapping with UDPlite, Figure 6 represents the delay produced by MPEG4 UDP and MPEG4 UDPLITE while transmitting Foreman of 400 frames as video source. The delay produced by cross layer mapping with UDP is 0.72 sec because no priority is given for the video packet.

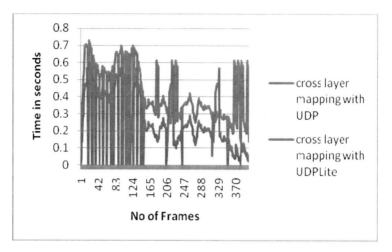

Fig. 5. Delay produced by cross layer mapping with UDP and cross layer mapping with UDPLite (Foreman)

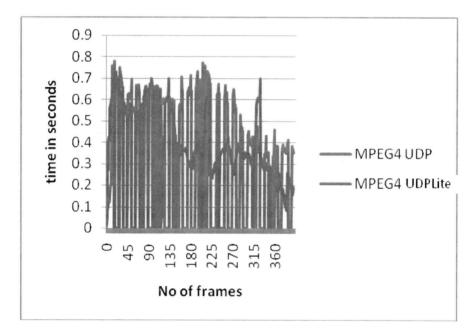

Fig. 6. Delay produced by MPEG4 UDP and MPEG4 UDPLITE (Foreman)

Peak Signal Noise Ratio

Similarly PSNR produced by cross layer mapping with UDP and cross layer mapping with UDPLite. Figure 7 represents the PSNR produced by cross layer mapping with

UDP and cross layer mapping with UDPLite while the video source transmitted is Foreman, Figure 8 represents the PSNR produced by MPEG4 UDP and MPEG4 UDPLITE while the video source transmitted is Foreman.

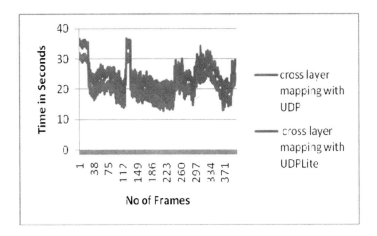

Fig. 7. PSNR produced by cross layer mapping with UDP and cross layer mapping with UDPLite (Foreman)

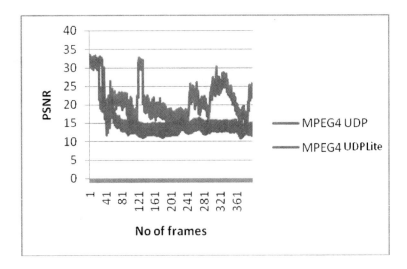

Fig. 8. PSNR produced by MPEG4 UDP and MPEG4 UDPLITE (Foreman)

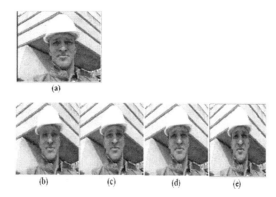

Fig. 9. (a). Original video frame (Foreman), (b). PSNR of MPEG4 with UDP, (c). PSNR of MPEG4 with UDPLITE, (d). PSNR of cross layer mapping with UDP, (e). PSNR of cross layer mapping with UDPLite.

6 Conclusion

Although, IEEE 802.11e EDCA has some features for QoS support it is not effective in providing priority to real time traffic such as delay sensitive video. By using dynamic mapping technique, video packets are mapped to the appropriate access category based on the significance of video data and network traffic load. Our proposed approach combines the benefits of UDPLite along with cross layer mapping thereby increasing the PSNR and decreasing the delay to a great extent.

References

[1] Larzon, L.-A., Degermark, M., Pink, S.: UDP lite for Real Time Multimedia Applications. In: IEEE International Conference of Communications, ICC (1999)
[2] http://140.116.72.80/~jhlin5/ns2/crosslayer/NS-2_crosslayer.htm
[3] Lin, C.-H., Ke, C.-H., Shieh, C.-K., Chilamkurti, N.K., Zeadally, S.: A Novel Cross-Layer Architecture for MPEG-4 Video Stream over IEEE 802.11e Wireless Network. Special Issue of International Journal of Telecommunications System (2008)
[4] Ge, Y., Hou, J.C., Choi, S.: An Analytic Study of Tuning Systems Parameters in IEEE 802.11e Enhanced Distributed Channel Access. Computer Networks 51(8), 1955–1980 (2007)
[5] Hu, C., Hou, J.C.: A Novel Approach to Contention Control in IEEE 802.11e-Operated WLANs. In: Proc. IEEE Infocom 2007 (May 2007)
[6] Xiao, Y., Li, H., Choi, S.: Protection and Guarantee for Voice and Video Traffic in IEEE 802.11e Wireless LANs. In: Proc. IEEE Infocom 2004, Hongkong, pp. 2153–2163 (March 2004)
[7] Ksentini, A., Naimi, M., Gueroui, A.: Toward an improvement of H.264 video transmission over IEEE 802.11e through a cross-layer architecture. IEEE Communications Magazine, 107–114 (January 2006)

[8] Foh, C.H., Zhang, Y., Ni, Z., Cai, J.: Scalable Video Transmission over the IEEE 802.11e Networks using Cross-Layer Rate Control. In: Proc. IEEE ICC 2007, Glasgow, UK (June 2007)

[9] Sing, A., Konrad, A., Joseph, A.D.: Performance Evaluation of UDP Lite for Cellular Video. In: Proceedings of the 11th International Workshop on Network and Operating Systems Support for Digital Audio and Video, NOSSDAV 2001 (2001)

[10] Masala, M.B., De Martin, J.C.: MAC–Level Partial Checksumfor H.264 Video Transmission over 802.11 Ad Hoc Wireless Networks. In: Vehicular Technology Conference, VTC 2005, June 1, vol. 5, pp. 2864–2868 (Spring 2005)

[11] Hsiao, Y.-M., Chang, F.-P., Chen, J.-S., Su, Y.-L., Yang, Z.-W., Chen, W.-S., Chu, Y.-S.: High Speed ASIC Design of Multimedia. In: 2010 the 5th IEEE Conference Network Industrial Electronics and Applications (ICIEA), June 15-17, pp. 155–159 (2010)

[12] Zhu, X., Girad, B., Van Beek, P.: Distributed channel time allocation and rate adaption for multiuser video streaming over wireless home networks. In: IEEE International Conference on Image Processing (ICIP 2007), San Antonio, TX, USA (September 2007)

[13] Zhu, X., Girad, B., Schiert, T., Wiegand, T.: Video multicast over Wireless Mesh Networks with Scalable Video Coding (SVC) in Visual communication and Image processing. In: Proc. of SPIE, vol. 6822, pp. 682205-682205-8 (2008)

[14] Gomathi, N., Seethalakshmi, P., Govardhan, A.: Cross Layer Design To Enhance Throughput For Multimedia Streaming Over Mobile Adhoc Networks. International Journal on Computer Science and Engineering 3(1), 114–126 (2011)

Implementation of Fault Secure Encoder and Decoder for Memory Application

K. RajaSekhar[1,*], B.K.V. Prasad[1], T. Madhu[2], P. SatishKumar[3],
and B. Stephen Charles[4]

[1] ASRCOE, Tanuku, Andhra Pradesh, India
rajasekharkassey@yahoo.com, baditakali@gmail.com
[2] SIET, Narsapur, Andhra Pradesh, India
tennetimadhu@yahoo.com
[3] CVRCOE, Hyderabad, Andhra Pradesh, India
satishkumar_1968@rediffmail.com
[4] SJCET, Kurnool, Andhra Pradesh, India
bstephen_charles@rediffmail.com

Abstract. Memory cells have been protected from soft errors for more than a decade; due to the increase in soft error rate in logic circuits, the encoder and decoder circuitry around the memory blocks have become susceptible to soft errors as well and must also be protected. An attempt is made to implement the FPGA based fault-tolerant memory architecture which tolerates transient faults both in the storage unit and in the supporting logic (i.e., encoder, corrector, and detector circuitries) by using the Euclidean Geometry Low-Density Parity-Check (EG-LDPC) code. This architecture is authorized in Verilog, behavior simulation using the ISE simulator and synthesis by using the synthesis Xilinx ISE 9.1. This is a new approach to design fault-secure encoder and decoder circuitry for memory designs and to identify and define a new class of error correcting codes whose redundancy makes the design of fault-secure detectors (FSD) particularly simple.

Keywords: Encoder, Fault Tolerance, Memory, Decoder, Fault –Diagnosis.

1 Introduction

Electronic space provided by silicon (semiconductor memory) chips or magnetic/ optical media can be used as temporary or permanent storage for data and/or instructions to control a computer or execute one or more programs. The major drawback of these chips is the errors that occur i.e. both hard and soft errors. Hard errors are caused due to fabrication defects in the memory chip and cannot be corrected once they start appearing. On the other hand, Soft errors are caused predominantly by electrical disturbances. Error detection and correction techniques enable reliable delivery of digital data over unreliable channels by detecting and

---

* Corresponding author.

D.C. Wyld et al. (Eds.): NeCoM/WeST/WiMoN 2011, CCIS 197, pp. 33–43, 2011.
© Springer-Verlag Berlin Heidelberg 2011

correcting the errors introduced by the channel and thereby recovering the original transmitted information. The "Error Correction Code" (ECC) [1] or forward error correction (FEC) code[2] is one such method used to detect and correct for the errors introduced during storage or transmission of data. In this technique, redundant or parity *data* is added to a message such that the original information can be recovered by a receiver even when a number of errors (up to the capability of the code being used) were introduced. The code is embedded into the RAM and such RAM chips are called as ECC Memory. These ECC memory chips are predominantly used in servers rather than in client computers for protection and reliability. The servers contain several Gigabytes of RAM that operate 24 hours a day and the likelihood of errors cropping up in their memory chips is comparatively high. If the Memory errors are not corrected immediately, then the computer/server may eventually crash. When a client crashes, it normally does not affect other computers even when it is connected in a network, but when a server crashes it brings the entire network down with it. Hence ECC memory is mandatory for servers but optional for clients when they are used for mission critical applications. Further, the code saves a lot of time as the receiver need not ask the sender for retransmission of data and hence a back-channel is not required. Error-correcting codes are frequently used in simplex communication such as broadcasting, as well as for reliable storage in media such as CDs, DVDs, RAM and ROM. FEC codes such as low-density parity-check codes (LDPC) achieve

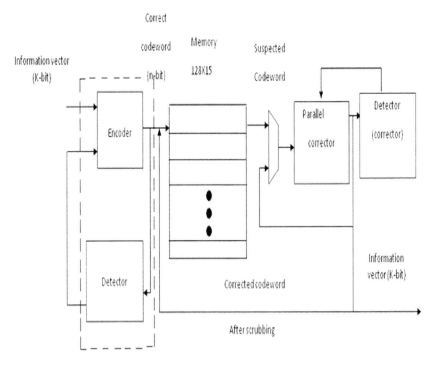

Fig. 1. Fault-tolerant memory architecture, with parallel corrector

a remarkable performance with iterative decoding that is very close to the Shannon limit[3]. Consequently, these codes have become strong competitors to turbo codes for error control in many communication and digital storage systems where high reliability is required. LDPC codes can be constructed using random or deterministic approaches. In this paper focus is made on Euclidean Geometric (EG) LDPC codes, which are constructed deterministically using the points and lines of a Euclidean geometry [1], [4]. The EG LDPC codes are cyclic and consequently their encoding can be efficiently implemented with linear shift registers. Minimum distances for EG codes are also reasonably good and can be derived analytically. Iteratively decoded EG LDPC codes does not have the serious error- floors that plague randomly-constructed LDPC codes[5] as they do not have pseudo-code words of weight smaller than their minimum distance. For these reasons, EG LDPC codes are good candidates for use in applications like optical communications that require very fast encoders and decoders and very low bit error-rates. Hence, a fault tolerant memory architecture is implemented using the EG LDPC codes as depicted in Fig. 1.

2   Fault –Tolerant Memory System

The proposed memory system design (Fig. 1) can tolerate errors in any part of the system, including the storage unit and encoder and corrector circuits using the fault-secure detector. For a particular ECC used for memory protection, let E be the maximum number of error bits that the code can correct and D be the maximum number of error bits that it can detect, and in one error combination that strikes the system, let e_e, e_m, and e_c be the number of errors in encoder, a memory word, and corrector, and let e_{de} and e_{dc} be the number of errors in the two separate detectors monitoring the encoder and corrector units. In conventional designs, the system would guarantee error correction as long as $e_m \leq E$ and $e_e = e_c = 0$. In contrast the system can correct any error combination as long as $e_m \leq E$, $e_c + e_{dc} \leq D$ and $e_m + e_c + e_{dc} \leq D$. This design is feasible when the following two fundamental properties are satisfied:

- Any single error in the encoder or corrector circuitry can at most corrupt a single codeword bit (i.e., no single error can propagate to multiple codeword bits).

- There is a fault secure detector that can detect any combination of errors in the received codeword along with errors in the detector circuit. This fault-secure detector can verify the correctness of the encoder and corrector operation.

The information bits are fed into the encoder to encode the information vector, and the fault secure detector of the encoder verifies the validity of the encoded vector. If the detector detects any error, the encoding operation must be redone to generate the correct codeword. The codeword is then stored in the memory. During memory access operation, the stored code words will be accessed from the memory unit. Code words are susceptible to transient faults while they are stored in the memory; therefore a parallel corrector unit is designed to correct potential errors in the retrieved code words. In our design all the memory words pass through the corrector and any potential error in the memory words will be corrected. Similar to the encoder unit, a fault-secure detector monitors the operation of the corrector unit. The entire circuitry is implemented using the flowchart given in Fig. 2.

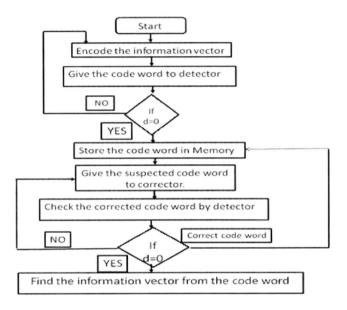

Fig. 2. Flow chart for fault-tolerant memory system

3   Circuit Implementation

Let I = (1_0, i_1, i_2----i_{k-1}) be the k-bit information vector that will be encoded into an n-bit codeword, c= (c_0, c_1----c_{n-1}). For linear codes, the encoding operation essentially performs the following vector-matrix multiplication: c=i. G, Where G is a k*n generator matrix. The validity of a received encoded vector can be checked with the Parity-Check matrix, which is a (n-k)*n binary matrix named H. The checking or detecting operation is basically summarized as s=c.H^T. The (n-k) -bit vector s is called the syndrome vector. A syndrome vector is zero if c is a valid codeword, and nonzero if c is an erroneous codeword. Each code is uniquely specified by its generator matrix or parity-check matrix. A code is a systematic code if every codeword consists of the original k-bit information vector followed by n-k parity bits. With this definition, the generator matrix of a systematic code must have the following structure: G= [I:X] Where I is a k*k identity matrix and X is a k*(n-k) matrix that generates the parity-bits. The advantage of using systematic codes is that there is no need for a decoder circuit to extract the information bits. The information bits are simply available in the first k bits of any encoded vector. A code is said to be a cyclic code if for any codeword c, all the cyclic shifts of the codeword are still valid. A code is cyclic if the rows of its parity-check matrix and generator matrix are the cyclic shifts of their first rows. The minimum distance of an ECC, d, is the minimum number of code bits that are different between any two code words. The maximum number of errors that an ECC can detect is d-1, and the maximum corrections d/2. Any ECC is represented with a triple (n, k, d), representing code length, information bit length and minimum distance respectively.

3.1 Encoder

The cyclic ECC codes are converted into systematic codes using the procedure mentioned in [1, 6]. The Fig. 3 shows the systematic generator matrix to generate (15, 7, 5) EG-LDPC code. The reason for selecting (15, 7, 5) among other LDPC codes is that the difference between number of errors detected and corrected should be minimum (1 bit).The encoded vector consists of information bits followed by parity bits, where each parity bit is simply an inner product of information vector and a column of X, from G=[I:X], for generating the matrix, we select a generator polynomial such that density in each row should be 5 according to LDPC code which is represented in binary form. The next step is to apply circular right shift to that row and continue until k times to get non systematic matrix. Now convert non systematic generator matrix to systematic generator matrix ie G= [I:P] by xor one row with any other row to see that only 5 ones are present.

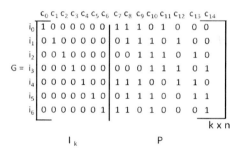

Fig. 3. Generator matrix for the (15, 7, 5) EG-LDPC in systematic format

Fig.4 shows the encoder circuit to compute the parity bits of the (15, 7, 5) EG-LDPC code. The i= $\{i_0,i_1,i_2----i_6\}$ is the 7-bit information vector and will be copied to (c_0----c_6) bits of the encoded vector, and the rest of encoded vector, the parity bits, are linear sums (XOR) of the information bits. If the building block is a two-input gate, then the encoder circuitry will take 22 two-input XOR gates. Each of the XOR gates generates one parity bit of the encoded vector. The codeword consists of seven information bits followed by eight parity bits.

i_0 i_1 i_2 i_3 i_4 i_5 i_6 $i_0 i_4 i_6$ $i_0 i_1 i_4 i_5 i_6$ $i_0 i_1 i_2 i_4 i_5$ $i_0 i_1 i_2 i_4 i_5$ i_0 $i_2 i_3$ $i_1 i_3 i_4$ $i_2 i_4 i_5$ $i_3 i_5 i_6$

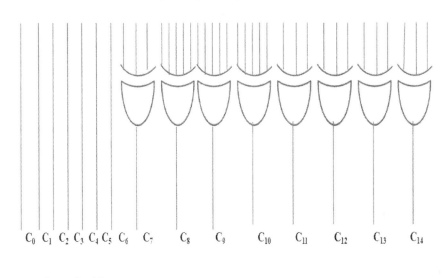

C_0 C_1 C_2 C_3 C_4 C_5 C_6 C_7 C_8 C_9 C_{10} C_{11} C_{12} C_{13} C_{14}

Information bits

Parity Bits

Fig. 4. Structure of encoder circuit for the (15, 7, 5) EG-LDPC code

3.2 Detector

The core of the detector operation is to generate the syndrome vector, $S = c.H^T$, which is basically implementing the following vector-matrix multiplication on the received encoded vector c and parity-check matrix H. Therefore each bit of the syndrome vector is the product of c with one row of the parity-check matrix. This product is a linear binary sum over digits of c where the corresponding digit in the matrix row is 1. This binary sum is implemented with an XOR gate. Fig. 5 shows the detector circuit for the (15, 7, 5) EG-LDPC code. Since the row weight of the parity-check matrix is ρ, to generate one digit of the syndrome vector we need a ρ-input XOR gate, or $(\rho - 1)$ 2-input XOR gates. For the whole detector, it takes n $(\rho - 1)$ 2-input XOR gates. Note that implementing each syndrome bit with a separate XOR gate satisfies the assumption of Theorem I of no logic sharing in detector circuit implementation. An error is detected if any of the syndrome bits has a nonzero value. The final error detection signal is implemented by an OR function of all the syndrome bits. The output of this -input OR gate is the error detector signal.

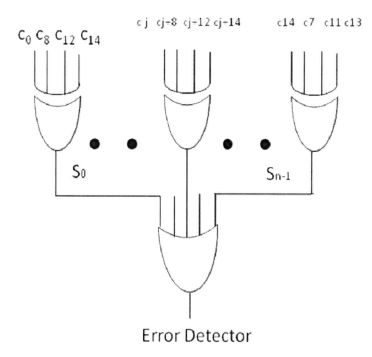

Fig. 5. Fault-secure detector for (15, 7, 5) EG-LDPC code

3.3 Corrector

For high error rates, the corrector is used more frequently and its latency can impact the system performance. Therefore we can implement a parallel one-step majority corrector which is essentially n copies of the single one-step majority-logic corrector. All the memory words are pipelined through the parallel corrector. This way the corrected memory words are generated every cycle. The detector in the parallel case monitors the operation of the corrector, if the output of the corrector is erroneous; the detector signals the corrector to repeat the operation. Faults detected in a nominally corrected memory word arise solely from faults in the detector and corrector circuitry and not from faults in the memory word. Since detector and corrector circuitry are relatively small compared to the memory system, the failure rate of these units is relatively low. Assuming our building blocks are two-input gates, γ number of ρ -input parity-check sums will require $(\gamma*\rho-1)$ two-input XOR gates. The size of the majority gate is defined by the sorting network implementation. The parallel implementation consists of exactly n copies of the serial one-step majority- logic corrector.

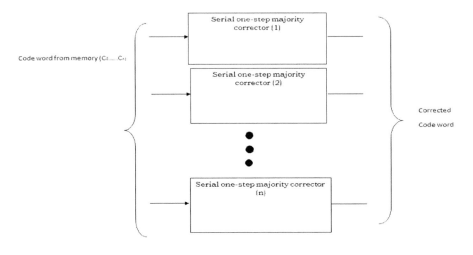

Fig. 6. Parallel corrector

3.4   One-Step Majority-Logic Correction

It is the fast and relatively compact error-correcting technique [1]. There is a limited class of ECCs that are one-step-majority correctable which include type-I two-dimensional EG-LDPC. The procedure identifies the correct value of each bit in the codeword directly from the received codeword; this is in contrast to the general message-passing error correction strategy (e.g., [5]) which may demand multiple iterations of error diagnosis and trial correction. Avoiding iteration makes the correction latency small and deterministic. This technique can be implemented serially to provide a compact implementation or in parallel to minimize correction latency.

This method consists of (1) Generating a specific set of linear sums of the received vector bits and (2) Finding the majority value of the computed linear sums. A linear sum of the received encoded vector bits can be formed by computing the inner product of the received vector and a row of a parity-check matrix. This sum is called Parity-Check sum. The core of the one-step majority-logic corrector is generating γ parity-check sums from the appropriate rows of the parity-check matrix. The one-step majority logic error correction is summarized in the following procedure. These steps correct a potential error in one code bit let's say, e.g. c_{n-1}.

- Generate γ parity-check sums by computing the inner product of the received vector and the appropriate rows of parity-check matrix.

- The γ check sums are fed into a majority gate. The output of the majority gate corrects the bit c_{n-1} by inverting the value of if the output of majority gate is "1".

The circuit implementing a serial one-step majority logic corrector for (15, 7, 5) EG-LDPC code is shown in Fig.7. This circuit generates γ parity-check sums with γ XOR gates and then computes the majority value of the parity-check sums. Since each parity-check sum is computed using a row of the parity check matrix and the row density of EG-LDPC codes are ρ, each XOR gate that computes the linear sum has ρ inputs.

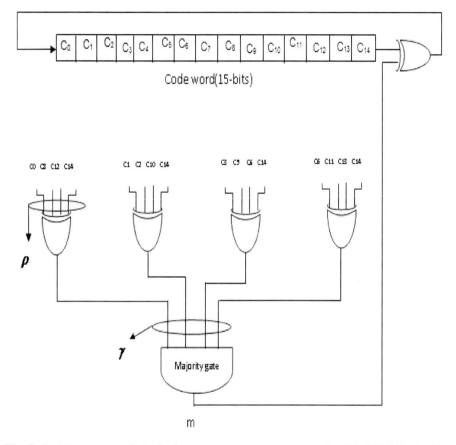

Fig. 7. Serial one-step majority logic corrector structure to correct last bit (bit14th) of 15-bit (15, 7, 5) EG-LDPC code

The single XOR gate on the right of Fig. 7 corrects the code bit c_{n-1} using the output of the majority gate. Once the code bit c_{n-1} is corrected, the codeword is cyclic shifted and code bit c_{n-2} is placed at c_{n-1} position and will be corrected. The whole codeword can be corrected in n rounds. If the fault rate is low, the corrector block is used infrequently; since the common case is error-free code words, the latency of the corrector will not have a severe impact on the average memory read latency. The serial corrector must be placed off the normal memory read path. The memory words retrieved from the memory unit are checked by detector unit. If the detector detects an error, the memory word is sent to the corrector unit to be corrected, which has the latency of the detector plus the round latency of the corrector.

4   Results Analysis

The behavioral simulation waveform for the fault secure encoder is shown in Fig.8. In Fig.8, the input is information i(k-bit) vector and output is the c(n-bit)encoded codeword.

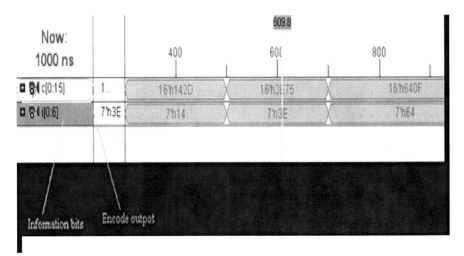

Fig. 8. Behavioral simulation waveform for the fault secure encoder

The behavioral simulation waveform for the fault secure memory system is shown in Fig.9. In Fig.9 inputs are I(k-bit) (information vector), clk, wen(write enable), ren(read enable), and e (error vector) is to introduce an error. In this detector output d which detects the errors in the encoded code word. First information vector is given to encoder it gives encoded vector as an output which is n-bit length. This encoded vector is given as input to the detector. If any error is present in the encoded code word the detector output is '1' else '0' encoded codeword is correct. The correct encoded codeword is given to the memory when 'wen' is '1'(high) data is write into memory in a perticular address location, here address line is the information vector. when 'ren' is high data is read and given as an output of memory. The memory output is combination of coded vector and error vector. This memory output is given as an input to the corrector which corrects the suspected coded word. This corrected coded word is given to the detector to check whether coded word is correct or not.At the corrector side detector sinal is 'md'. The above action is observed by signal 'ed' where 'ed' is the output of the detector before corrector.

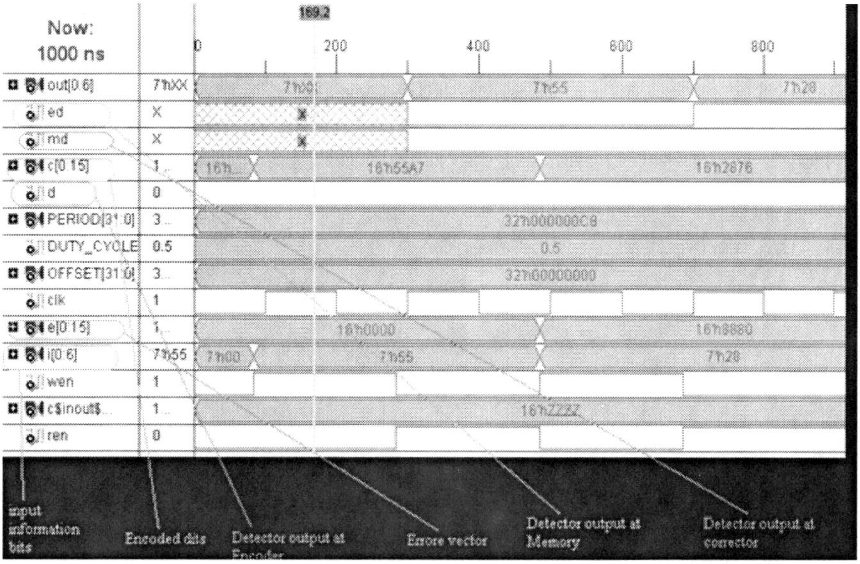

Fig. 9. Behavioral simulation waveform for the fault-tolerant memory system

The above results prove that the procedure adopted for recognizing and correcting the faults is being done with much accuracy and speed. The method can be extended to achieve much higher speeds and redundancy in nano memory cells.

5   Conclusion and Future Scope

The FPGA implementation of fault tolerant memory architecture will tolerate the transient faults both in the storage unit and in the supporting logic (i.e., encoder, corrector and detector circuitries). The potential transient errors in the encoder or corrector output can be corrected by the detect-and-repeat technique. This new technique also takes less area and time compared to other ECC/FEC techniques as there is no need of decoder. Efforts can be made to use nano memory which provides smaller, faster, and lower energy devices which allow more powerful and compact circuitry in the near future.

References

1. Lin, S., Costello, D.J.: Error Control Coding, 2nd edn. Prentice Hall, Englewood Cliffs (2004)
2. Edwards, L.: Low cost alternative to Hamming codes corrects memory errors. Cornput. Des., 132–148 (July 1981)
3. MacKay, D.J.C., Neal, R.M.: Near Shannon limit performance of low density parity check codes. Electronics Letters 32(18), 1645–1646 (1997)
4. Kou, Y., Lin, S., Fossorier, M.: Low density parity check codes based on_nite geometries: a rediscovery and more. IEEE Trans. Inform. Theory 47, 2711–2736 (2001)
5. Knuth, D.E.: The Art of Computer Programming, 2nd edn. Addison Wesley, Reading (2000)
6. McEliece, R.J.: The Theory of Information and Coding. Cambridge University Press, Cambridge (2002)

Performance Analysis of Energy Efficient Routing Protocol for Homogeneous Wireless Sensor Network

S. Taruna, Jain Kusum Lata, and G.N. Purohit

Computer Science Department, Banasthali University, India
staruna71@yahoo.com
kusum_2000@rediffmail.com
gn_purohitjaipur@yahoo.co.in

Abstract. Wireless Sensor Networks, are made of low-cost, low-power, small in size, and multifunctional sensor nodes. The efficient energy utilization is one of the important performance factors for wireless sensor networks survivability be-cause nodes operate with limited battery power. In this paper we propose and analyze a new approach of zone based clustering head selection algorithm for wireless sensor network of homogeneous nodes. Nodes in the network are uniformly distributed. In this clustering algorithm, network performance is improved by selecting cluster heads on the basis of the residual energy of existing cluster heads, and nearest hop distance of the node. In this paper we evaluate various performance metrics like energy consumption, network life time, number of channel heads metrics in each round and compare these with respect to random algorithm i.e. LEACH. We conclude that proposed protocol effectively extends the network lifetime without degrading the other critical overheads and performance metrics.

Keywords: Wireless Sensor network, Zone, Clustering Algorithm, Residual Energy.

1 Introduction

A sensor network consists of a large number of very small nodes that are deployed in some geographical area. The purpose of the network is to sense the environment and report what is happening in the area in which it is deployed. These tiny sensor nodes, which consist of sensing, data processing, and communicating components, leverage the idea of wireless sensor networks [1]. Due to recent technological advances, the manufacturing of small and low cost sensors became technically and economically feasible. The sensing electronics measure ambient conditions related to the environment surrounding the sensor and transform them into an electric signal. Processing such a signal reveals some properties about objects located and/or events happening in the vicinity of the sensor [2]. Sensors have the ability to communicate either among each other or directly to an external base-station. A greater number of sensors allows for sensing over larger geographical regions with greater accuracy. Each sensor node

D.C. Wyld et al. (Eds.): NeCoM/WeST/WiMoN 2011, CCIS 197, pp. 44–54, 2011.

comprises sensing, processing, transmission, mobilization, position finding system, and power units. Despite the innumerable applications of WSNs, these networks have several restrictions, e.g., limited energy supply, limited computing power, and limited bandwidth of the wireless links connecting sensor nodes.

The main constraint in designing a routing protocol in WSNs is limited power of sensor nodes that mandates the design of energy-efficient communication protocol. There are many protocols proposed for other wireless networks like mobile or ad-hoc. However, these protocols cannot be used directly due to resource constraints of sensor nodes like limited battery power, computational speed, and human interface of node device and density of nodes in network. Much research has been done in recent years, but even after many efforts, there are still many design options open for improvement. Thus, there is a need of a new protocol scheme, which enables more efficient use of energy at individual sensor nodes to enhance the network survivability. In this paper, we analyze energy efficient homogeneous clustering head selection algorithm for WSN. We first describe the protocol and then we provide simulation results in MATLAB [9] and determine performance analysis of given protocol compared with benchmark clustering algorithm LEACH.

The paper is organized as follows. Section 2 summarizes the related previous works Section 3 discusses the basic radio energy model. Section 4 describes the proposed homogeneous clustering algorithm. Simulation results are presented in section 5 Comparisons with random LEACH algorithm in section 6. Conclusions and suggestions for future work are given in section 6.

2 Related Work

Routing is a process of determining a path between source and destination upon request of data transmission. A variety of protocols have been proposed to enhance the life of WSN and for routing the correct data to the base station. Battery power of individual sensor nodes is a precious resource in the WSN [3]. For example, the power consumed by a Berkeley mote to transmit 1-bit of data is equivalent to the computation of 800m instructions. When the battery power at a sensor node expires, the node is called as a dead node and the sensor node discontinues its operations in the network.

In general, routing in WSN can be divided into **flat-based routing, hierarchical-based routing, and location-based[10]** routing depending on the network structure. In flat-based routing, all nodes are typically assigned equal roles or functionality. In hierarchical-based routing, however, nodes will play different roles in the network. In location-based routing, sensor nodes positions are exploited to route data in the network.

Hierarchical routing performs energy-efficient routing in WSN, and contributes to overall system scalability and lifetime. In a hierarchical architecture, sensors organize themselves into clusters and each cluster has a cluster head, i.e. sensor nodes form clusters where the low energy nodes are used to perform the sensing in the proximity of the phenomenon. For the cluster based wireless sensor network, the cluster information and Cluster Head (CH) selection are the basic issues. The cluster head coordinates the communication among the cluster members and manages their data [11].

According to the manner the data are collected, cluster based WSNs are classified into three broad categories namely (i) homogeneous sensor networks, (ii) heterogeneous sensor network, (iii) hybrid sensor network.

(i) In the homogeneous sensor networks, all the sensor nodes and base stations are identical in terms of hardware capability and initial battery power. In this method, the static clustering elects cluster heads (CH) only once for the entire lifetime of the network. This results in overload on cluster heads. As proposed in LEACH [4], the role of cluster heads is randomly and periodically rotated over all the nodes to ensure the same rate of dissipation of battery power for all the sensor nodes.

(ii) Heterogeneous sensor networks, has two or more different types of sensor nodes with different hardware capabilities and battery power are used. The sensor nodes with higher hardware capabilities and more battery power compared to other sensor nodes act as cluster heads and perform as a normal sensor node.

(iii) In hybrid sensor networks several mobile base stations work cooperatively to provide fast data gathering in a real-time manner.

Low-energy adaptive clustering hierarchy (LEACH) is a popular energy-efficient adaptive clustering algorithm that forms node clusters based on the received signal strength and uses these local cluster heads as routers to the base station [7]. LEACH is an application-specific data dissemination protocol that uses clusters to prolong the life of the wireless sensor network. LEACH utilizes randomized rotation of local cluster heads to evenly distribute the energy load among the sensors in the network [4]. LEACH uses three techniques namely (i) randomized rotation of the cluster heads and corresponding clusters, (ii) localized coordination and control for cluster set-up and operation, and (iii) local compression to reduce global communication. LEACH clustering terminates in a finite number of iteration, but does not guarantee good cluster head distribution and assumes uniform energy consumption for cluster heads.

The author in [8] has proposed a theoretical model for energy efficient routing in homogeneous sensor network but did not implement and evaluate the performance of the protocol in any simulator. In this study we consider the impact of the model and its behavior with respect to benchmark LEACH protocol. Our paper has highlighted the practical implementation of protocol in MATLAB and determines various performance metrics like energy consumption, network lifetime, number of cluster heads in each round.

3 Network and Energy Consumption Model

We assume that the energy consumption of the sensor is due to data transmission and reception. Cluster head consume energy for the data aggregation before it sends the data to BS. We use the same radio model as stated in [4] and shown in Figure 1, using this model the energy consumed in transmitting one message of size k bits over a transmission distance d, is given by

$$E_{Tx}(k,d) = k(E_{elec} + \varepsilon_{AMP}d^{\lambda}) = E_{elec}\,k + k\varepsilon_{AMP}d^{\lambda},$$

where   k=length of the message,
          d=transmission distance between transmitter and
          receiver, E_{elec}= electronic energy,

ε_{AMP}=transmitter
amplifier, λ= Path Loss
(2<=λ<=4),

Also, the energy consumed in the message reception is given by

$$E_{rx} = E_{elec}\ k,$$

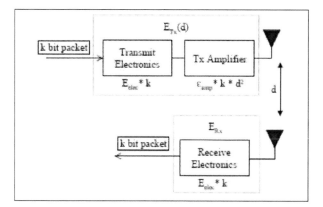

Fig. 1. Energy Model for algorithm

4   The Proposed Homogeneous Clustering Algorithm [8]

4.1   Basic Assumptions for the Clustering Algorithm

- Number of nodes in network are 100.
- The base station (BS) is located outside the deployed area and fixed.
- All nodes can send data to BS.
- The BS has the information about the location of each node.
- Data compression is done by the Cluster Head.
- Data Compression energy is different from the reception and transmission.
- In the first round, each node has a probability p of becoming the cluster head.
- A node, which has become cluster head, shall be eligible to become cluster head after 1-$1/p$ rounds.
- All nodes are of same specification.
- All nodes in the network are having the same energy at starting point and having maximum energy.
- All nodes consume same energy for transmission and reception.

- Energy of transmission depends on the distance (source to destination) and data size.
- Nodes are uniformly distributed in network.

4.2 Proposed Algorithm

The proposed algorithm works in round. Each round has the setup and transmission phase.

Setup phase:
1. Network is virtually divided in grid of 6 rectangles

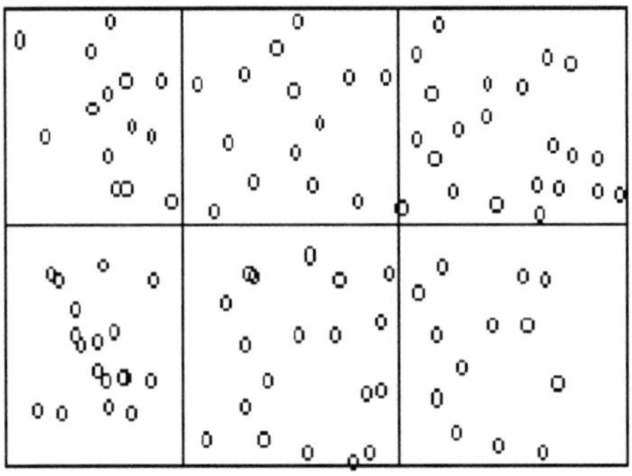

Fig. 2. Homogeneous Network with 100 nodes

1. All nodes send data to BS about their location.
2. Nodes belonging to a rectangle create a group called pre-cluster.

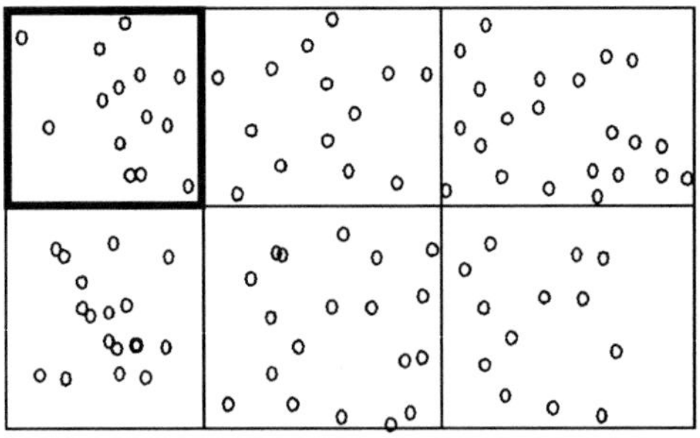

Fig. 3. Precluster

3.   A random node from the pre-cluster is selected as cluster head.

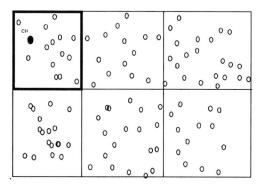

Fig. 4. Cluster head

4. Selected cluster head sends advertisement of their cluster as joining request to all other nodes in the network.

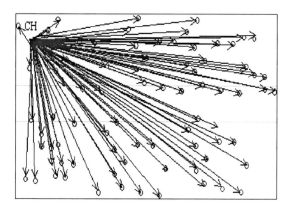

Fig. 5. Selected cluster head send JOIN request to all other node in network

5. On the basis of the distance the nodes select one cluster head, which is most near to it.
6. The nodes send confirmation by **ACK** to cluster head. And final cluster formation is done.

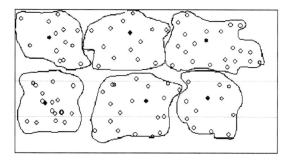

Fig. 6. Final Cluster formation

7.   The node of a pre-cluster may lie in another final cluster.

Transmission Phase
Nodes send the sensed data to the Cluster Head and CH performs aggregation and compression on data and sends it to Base Station.

New Cluster Head (CH) Formation
New CH is selected by checking the residual energy of cluster head. If the energy of the current CH is less then threshold level, new CH is selected. New CH is to be selected depending on the following criteria:

- A node has not become a CH for the past $(1-1/p)$ round.
- The node is having the maximum residual energy in the cluster.
- The node, which is nearest to existing cluster head in cluster.

5   Performance Evaluations

The performance analysis of above routing protocol is evaluated with the MATLAB. Then the protocol is compared to the LEACH algorithm (in which cluster selection is done by random selection) in terms of the network lifetime.

5.1   Simulation Parameter

Table 1. Simulation Parameters

Parameter	Values
Simulation Round	2000
Topology Size	200 X 200
Number of nodes	100
CH probability	0.5
Initial node power	0.5 Joule
Nodes Distribution	Nodes are uniformly distributed
BS position	Located at (100,250)
Energy for Transmission (ETX)	50*0.000000001 Joule
Energy for Reception (ERX)	50*0.000000001 Joule
Energy for Data Aggregation	5*0.000000001 Joule

5.2   Simulation Result

1.   **Energy Consumption:** -We simulated the proposed and random algorithm (LEACH) for 10 times and determined the cluster with the maximum number of nodes. We calculated the energy for the control packet size (ctrPack-etLength) of 100 bytes.

Power consumption in random selection method for cluster head is

$$E_{consume} = \text{Energy for the reception of data for all nodes in cluster}$$
+ Send the CH information to Base station.
=(ERX*ctrPacketLength *N)
+ EDA
+ (ETX * ctrPacketLength + Emp* ctrPacketLength)

(* λ Is path loss and we consider the same path loss for all the nodes. Path Loss can be in the range 2 to 4) (In the simulation we assumed path loss as 3.)

2. **Network Life Time:** -Number of rounds when first node is dead. In the random selection method cluster head selection in each round is done on the basis of 1/p, but not on the basis of residual energy.

Table 2. Simulation result

Simu-lation No.	Max. No. of nodes in Proposed Selection	Max. No.of nodes in Random Selection	Energy Consumed in Random Selection in J/mS	Energy Consumed in Proposed Selection J/mS
1	25	50	25.50050001	13.00050001
2	27	46	23.50050001	14.00050001
3	24	38	19.50050001	12.50050001
4	23	29	15.00050001	12.00050001
5	21	37	19.00050001	11.00050001
6	22	30	15.50050001	11.50050001
7	27	32	16.50050001	14.00050001
8	24	39	20.00050001	12.50050001
9	26	35	18.00050001	13.50050001
10	24	42	21.50050001	12.50050001

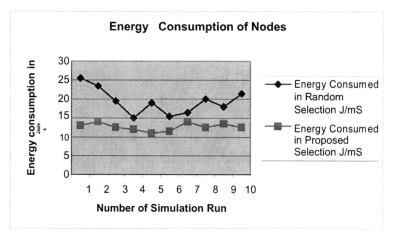

Fig. 7. Energy consumption of nodes for cluster selection

The cluster head is determined by the following function: -

$$
T(n) = \begin{cases} \dfrac{P_t}{1-P_t \cdot (r.\bmod\ i/P_t)^2} & \textit{if } n \in G \\[4mm] 0, & \textit{Otherwise} \end{cases}
$$

Where Pt is the desired percentage of cluster heads, r is the current round number; G is the set of nodes that have not been cluster-heads in the last 1/Pt rounds.

When a node is dead in the network it will not be the part of the network. It shows that if a dead node occurs in early rounds of the algorithm, this may affect lifespan of the network or drag towards the early dead of all nodes.

Table 3. Network Life Time

No. of Simulation	No.of Round in which first dead node occur in random selection	No. of Round in which first dead node occur in proposed selection
1	516	745
2	552	792
3	541	683
4	494	782
5	511	743
6	520	740
7	535	692
8	549	699
9	562	763
10	501	635

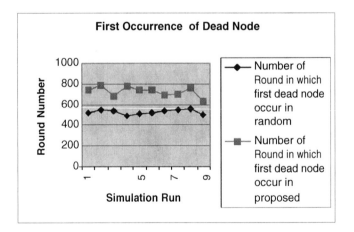

Fig. 8. Network Life Time

3.   **Energy Consumption with varying message size:-** We simulated with the maximum number of node that is 46 in random selection and 27 in the proposed method with different message size; energy consumption is shown in following table.

Table 4. Energy Consumption for cluster head selection for different message size

Message size in Byte	Energy Consumed in Random Selection J/mS	Energy Consumed in Proposed Selection J/mS
1000	235.0005001	*140.0005001*
2000	470.0005003	*280.0005003*
3000	705.0005004	*420.0005004*
4000	940.0005005	*560.0005005*
5000	1175.000501	*700.0005007*
6000	1410.000501	*840.0005008*
7000	1645.000501	*980.0005009*
8000	1880.000501	*1120.000501*
9000	2115.000501	*1260.000501*
10000	2350.000501	*1400.000501*

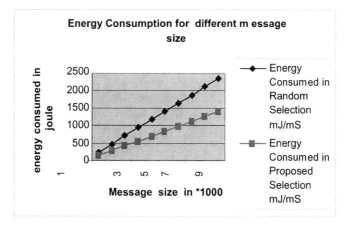

Fig. 9. Energy Consumption for different message size

6   Conclusion and Future Work

Energy consumption is the main design issue in routing of wireless Sensor Network. We concluded that energy consumed for the cluster head selection is less in the proposed algorithm, which directly shows the increased network survivability. Further the network lifetime of the proposed algorithm has greater span than the LEACH protocol. We have also determined the impact of message length in the energy consumption. Since energy assumption increases with the message size, so if the message length can be decreased the residual energy of node is more and it increases the lifetime of the node and that directly increase the life of network. The proposed algorithm is for the homogeneous network and we propose to extend this work for the heterogeneous network.

References

1. Akyildiz, I.F., Su, W., Sankarasubramaniam, Y., Cayirci, E.: A Survey on Sensor Network. IEEE Communication Magazine 40(8), 102–114 (2004)
2. Martin, G.: An Avaluation of Ad-hoc Routing Protoco ls for Wireless Sensor Networks. Master's thesis, School of Computing Science, Newcastle University upon Tyne, U.K. (May 2004)
3. Heinzelman, W.R., Chandrakasan, A., Balakrishnan, H.: Energy-Efficient Communication Protocol for Wireless Microsensor Networks. In: Proceedings of the Thirty Third Hawaii International Conference on System Sciences (HICSS 2000). IEEE Computer Society, Washington, DC (2000)
4. Heinzelman, W.R., Chandrakasan, A., Balakrishnan, H.: An Application-Specific Protocol Architecture for Wireless Microsensor Networks. IEEE Transactions on Wireless Communications 1(4), 660–670 (2002)
5. Pottle, G.J., Kaiser, W.J.: Embedding the Internet: Wireless Integrated Network Sensors. Communications of the ACM 43(5), 51–58 (2000)
6. Baker, D.J., Ephremides, A.: The Architectural Organization of a Mobile Radio Network via a Distributed Algorithm. IEEE Transactions on Communications 29(11), 1694–1701 (1981)
7. Heinzelman, W.R., Chandrakasan, A., Balakrishnan, H.: An Application-specific Protocol Architecture for Wireless Microsensor Networks. IEEE Transactions on Wireless Communications 1(4) (October 2002)
8. Singh, S.K., Singh, M.P., Singh, D.K.: Energy Efficient Homogenous Clustering Algorithm for Wireless Sensor Networks. International Journal of Wireless & Mobile Networks (IJWMN) 2(3) (August 2010)
9. http://www.Mathworks.com
10. Al-Karaki, J., Kamal, A.: Routing Techniques in Wireless Sensor Networks: A Survey. IEEE Communications Magazine 11(6), 6–28 (2004)
11. Lin, C.R., Gerla, M.: Adaptive Clustering for Mobile Wireless Networks. IEEE Journal on Selected Areas in Communication 15(7), 11265–11275 (1997)

Mobile Communication
Implementation Techniques to Improve Last Mile High Speed FSO Communication

R. Srinivasan[1] and A. Vijayaraj[2]

[1] Research Scholar, Dept. of Computer Science and Engineering,
Sathyabama University, Chennai, India
rsbdrd@gmail.com
[2] Faculty of Computer Science and Engineering, Saveetha Engineering College
Chennai, India
satturvijay@yahoo.com

Abstract. As an affordable alternative solution for the current generation last mile wireless communication network access, the FSO – Free Space Optical Communication has vast development in supporting of FSO communication. The primary advantages of FSO system are the license free optical nodes, higher data rates, easy to install with less expensive setup. However, obtaining the reliable communication link and higher bandwidth rate still having some difficulties due to environmental interferences. These difficulties plays important role in designing of a strong and high efficient FSO network. In this paper, we propose new approaches based on mixed Integer Programming formulations to design optimized FSO network structure to improve the link availability and high data rate, and also considered the allocation of limited bandwidth. In our analyses result provide right directions to design high efficient reconfigurable FSO network design.

Keywords: FSO network structure, Bandwidth, FSO routing, FSO network design.

1 Introduction

The global telecommunications network has seen massive expansion over the last few years. First came the tremendous growth of the optical fiber long-haul, wide-area network (WAN), followed by a more recent emphasis on metropolitan area networks (MANs). Meanwhile, local area networks (LANs) and gigabit ethernet ports are being deployed with a comparable growth rate. In order for this tremendous network capacity to be exploited, and for the users to be able to utilize the broad array of new services becoming available, network designers must provide a flexible and cost-effective means for the users to access the telecommunications network. Presently, however, most local loop network connections are limited to 1.5 Mbps (a T1 line). As a consequence, there is a strong need for a high-bandwidth bridge (the "last mile" or "first mile") between the LANs and the MANs or WANs. A recent New York Times article reported that more than 100 million miles of optical fiber was laid around the

D.C. Wyld et al. (Eds.): NeCoM/WeST/WiMoN 2011, CCIS 197, pp. 55–63, 2011.

world in the last two years, as carriers reacted to the Internet phenomenon and end users' insatiable demand for bandwidth. Despite the huge investment in trenching and optical cable, most of the fiber remains unlit, 80 to 90% of office, commercial and industrial buildings are not connected to fiber, and transport prices are dropping dramatically. Free Space Optics (FSO) systems represent one of the most promising approaches for addressing the emerging broadband access market and its "last mile" bottleneck. Free Space Optics (FSO) systems offer many features, principal among them being low start-up and operational costs, rapid deployment, and high fiber-like bandwidths due to the optical nature of the technology [19].

The optical link can reach 1 Gbps or more to support wide bandwidth range over a long distance communication; Due to above characteristics the optical network will offer wide range of directions for new era communication. Let us have a situation, i.e., it's too difficult to setup optical fibres and also we have to go for huge budget, time to setup, even though RF wireless structure its not supporting higher bandwidth, and also less secured. An FSO structured network using Biphase shift keying method can interconnect multiple wireless LANs using IEEE 802.11 without modulating and demodulating radio signals [1], [5]. A basic FSO system is illustrated in Figure 1.

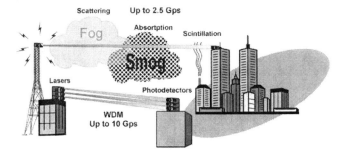

Fig. 1.

Even though the FSO structure supporting high bandwidth, long distance cost efficient communication the environmental factors such as weather related factors like fog, rain, clouds and high density obstacle like high density clouds and buildings remain great challenges to reduce and may limit the data rate and availability of link through LOS(Line of Sight)[8]. For example, the primary challenge to FSO-based communications is dense fog. Rain and snow have little effect on FSO technology, but fog is different. Fog is vapor composed of water droplets, which are only a few hundred microns in diameter but can modify light characteristics or completely hinder the passage of light through a combination of absorption, scattering, and reflection. The primary answer to counter fog when deploying FSO-based optical wireless products is through a network design that shortens FSO link distances and adds network redundancies. FSO installations in extremely foggy cities such as San Francisco have successfully achieved carrier-class reliability [1]

Recent surveys and research schemes having lot of directions to overcome LOS line of sight problems with low bit-error-rate (BER) performance in FSO communication system under severe interference conditions [9]. But the increasing of laser power can solve this problem upto some extent. When the optical transmitter reaching maximum power limit, we have to decrease the bandwidth or transmission distance of the physical links which are under severe weather conditions such as heavy fog which will lead to do some modifications in logical and physical structures of FSO networks, due to above reason the efficiency and performance of Free Space Optical network will be affected. So, our idea of improving optimum structure of FSO network in the topological level. That we discussed in this paper.

The rest of the paper, in part II, we reviewed the problems related with FSO network structure management while implementing our ideas. Part III and IV we represented the integer programming models to design optimized FSO network structure. In Part V, we discussed about the all other issues like reconfiguration, reliability and other challenges in design of FSO network structure. Finally we concluded the paper in final section.

2 Optical Wireless Network Structure – Design and Management

The wired network structure well studied for this purpose including multiplexing techniques especially WDM (wavelength division multiplexing) [10], [12]. Since the physically connected optical communication networks establishes direct transmission path through the fibre optic cables which combines both physical and logical network structure. However, in case of FSO design, the weather conditions, transmission length etc., plays important role in deciding the quality of service through the link availability, and high data rates. With this, the wireless network radio frequency transmissions (ref: IEEE802.11), a transmitted signal in FSO system can able to reach one specified receiver (LOS), and no issues about hidden terminal problem[13]. Based on this, we have to analyze both physical and logical architecture design, and wireless related algorithms cannot be directly used to design FSO network.

While the majority of research in optical wireless literature has focused on the physical components, modulation and coding schemes (for example, [1], [5], [14]), network structure design is generating increased attention recently [15]–[18]. The study in [15] presented network structure control heuristics to jointly minimize congestion and cost by defining a weighting formulation for specifying preferences in the physical or network layer in 2-degree Free Space Optical (FSO) ring networks. Given the nature of heuristic algorithms, this work does not guarantee any optimal topologies and is limited to ring network structure without consideration of multi-hop routing in mesh topologies with diverse node degrees (e.g., ≥ 2). The authors of [16], [17] considered network structure control and routing in a model with limited number of transceivers at each node. In [18], the authors developed cross layer heuristics to design FSO network structure control (without routing) in bi-connected networks by using the Bit Error Rate as the weight of each link. However, none of previous work considered the availability of the physical FSO link when designing the network structure. In addition, previous work assumes one request either is 100% satisfied or blocked without considering how to split or partially satisfy a traffic request (constrained by a lower bound) by effectively designing both the physical and logical FSO network topologies, which does not take full advantage of the benefits of FSO system. In this paper we for the first time, conduct a comprehensive study on optimizing physical and logical network structure design in FSO network while taking into the link availability, splittable flow and partial bandwidth allocation into consideration. As to be described in next sections, we develop mixed Integer Programming formulations to model the network structure design problems.

3 Design in Physical Level Structure

For example, In designing of FSO network structure in a city with number of connection originating or terminating building for the traffic and also other buildings which is not part of any connectivity also should be considered to ensure Line of Sight (LOS), In other words, though some buildings may not join the FSO network, they could stand in-between of the buildings joined the network and hence hampering the creation of some potential FSO links[1]. Hence, when using FSO, each building is eligible for connecting to only a subset of the buildings that have line of sight and locate within a specified maximum transmission range. In fact, the limited number of transceivers due to cost concerns at each FSO node and requiring line-of-sight between the senders and the receivers prevent the setup of a direct physical FSO link between all node pairs. The scalability problems can also arise when connecting N FSO nodes with $N-1$ transceivers at each node, and O ($N2$) FSO links in the whole network. Furthermore, the available bandwidth on each physical FSO link depends on the distance between the nodes. Hence, the selection of FSO links to be established is very critical as that affects the robustness and performance of the FSO system. This problem is referred as *physical network structure design*. The *physical design* problems can be formulated as follows: assume that the FSO network having N nodes and the location, signal interference/weather condition, distance between each node pair, and the number of transceivers at node i, ∇i, are given 2; then the problem is how to design a physical network structure that achieves optimum performance in terms of network capacity or accommodating more traffic demands. At the same time any

For instance, given buildings A and C are in the FSO network and B is not, we cannot create a direct FSO link from A to C if B blocks the line of sight between A and C. Building A has to rely on other buildings in the network to reach Building C. node that may generate or receive traffic cannot be isolated from the FSO network. To comprehensively model the problem of physical network structure design, for each node pair (i, j), we define $\Lambda i,j$ as the potential effective link bandwidth if one FSO link is established between node i and j, which can be determined as Equation (1).

$$\Lambda_{i,j} = \begin{cases} 0 \text{ if no line-of-sight between node } i \text{ and } j; \\ 0 \text{ if node } I \text{ is too far away from node } j; \\ \rho_{i,j}B_{i,j} + (1 - \rho_{i,j}) F_{i,j} \text{ otherwise} \end{cases} \quad (1)$$

where $\rho_{i,j}$ is the probability that the FSO link between node i and j operates at normal condition with link bandwidth of $B_{i,j}$. The bandwidth of the FSO link can degrade to $F_{i,j}$ under interferences such as fog, which occurs with probability $1 - \rho_{i,j}$. With the definition of effective link bandwidth, we can model the problem of physical network structure design by using following formulations.

A. Notations

N: the number of nodes in the FSO network;

∇i: the number of transceivers at node i;

$\Lambda_{i,j}$:   the potential effective link bandwidth between node i and j;

$L_{i,j}$:   1, if there is a physical FSO link in the FSO network, and 0 otherwise;

$\gamma_{i,j}$:   the actual link bandwidth between node i and j in the FSO network..

B. Integer programming formulations(IPF)

The main objective is to improve the available bandwidth of the whole FSO network as shown in Equation (2) and the secondary objective is to maximize the minimum available bandwidth of individual FSO link as in Equation (3).

$$\text{Maximize} \sum_{i,j} \Upsilon_{i,j} \tag{2}$$

$$\text{Maximize} \ \min_{i,j} \ \Upsilon_{i,j} \tag{3}$$

The following constrains are also required. Equations (4) and (5) are the transceivers constraint at each FSO node; Equations (6) and (7) ensure that each node has at least one physical link connected to the FSO network; The actual link bandwidth between node i and j is specified in Equation (8).

$$\sum_i L_{i,j} \leq \nabla_j \forall_j \tag{4}$$

$$\sum_j L_{i,j} \leq \nabla_i \forall_i \tag{5}$$

Transceivers constraint of each FSO node

$$\sum_i L_{i,j} > 0 \forall_j \tag{6}$$

$$\sum_j L_{i,j} > 0 \forall_i \tag{7}$$

Ensuring that each node has atleast one physical connection

$$\Upsilon_{i,j} = \Lambda_{i,j} x L_{i,j} \forall_{i,j} \tag{8}$$

Actual bandwidth in-between node i and j

4 Design in Logical Level Structure

In the case of *Logical network structure design*, the physical network structure including the set of nodes and links as well as the actual link bandwidth (i.e., Yi,j) is fixed. Given a set of traffic demands that can be projected by monitoring the traffic pattern in the network or can be inferred from the Service Level Agreements (SLAs) [16], the basic problem is how to satisfy *as many* traffic demands as possible or maximize the network throughput by establishing logical connections among the node pairs. While each logical connection may travel through multiple intermediate FSO links, a certain amount of bandwidth is reserved on each corresponding physical link. We refer to such logical connection as FSO flow.

The following additional parameters and variables are defined for describing the mathematic model to optimally establish the FSO flows in the network.

$\Gamma^{s,d}$ the projected traffic demand of the node pair (s, d);
$M^{s,d}$ the minimum bandwidth request for the node pair (s, d);
$V^{s,d}_{i,j}$ 1, if the FSO flow from s to d utilizes physical link between node i and node j, and 0 otherwise;
$\Omega^{s,d}$ the reserved bandwidth on physical link between node i and node j, for the FSO flow from s to d;
$\Pi^{s,d}$ the assigned/satisfied bandwidth for the FSO flow from s to d.

Equation (9) shows the objective function which is to satisfy as many traffic demands as possible.

$$\text{maximize } \sum_{s,d} \Pi^{s,d} \tag{9}$$

Note that two parameters are used to specify the traffic demand for each node pair (s, d), wherein $M_{s,d}$ is the lower bound and $\Gamma_{s, d}$ is the projected demand or upper bound of the assigned bandwidth for the FSO flow from s to d as shown in Equations (10)-(11).

$$\Pi^{s,d} \geq M^{s,d} \forall_{s,d} \tag{10}$$

$$\Pi^{s,d} \leq \Gamma^{s,d} \forall_{s,d} \tag{11}$$

$$\Omega_{i,j}^{s,d} \leq V_{s,j}^{s,d} \times \Upsilon_{s,j} \ \forall_{s,d,j} \tag{12}$$

$$\Omega_{i,j}^{s,d} \leq V_{i,d}^{s,d} \times \Upsilon_{i,d} \ \forall_{s,d,i} \tag{13}$$

$$\sum_i V_{i,s}^{s,d} = 0 \forall_{s,d} \tag{14}$$

$$\sum_j V_{d,j}^{s,d} = 0 \forall_{s,d} \tag{15}$$

$$\Pi^{s,d} = \sum \Omega_{s,j}^{s,d} \forall_{s,d} \tag{16}$$

$$\Pi^{s,d} = \sum_i \Omega_{i,d}^{s,d} \forall_{s,d} \tag{17}$$

$$\sum_i \Omega_{i,n}^{s,d} - \sum_i \Omega_{n,j}^{s,d} = 0 \forall_{s,d,n \neq s,d} \tag{18}$$

$$\sum_{s,d} \Omega_{i,j}^{s,d} \leq \Upsilon_{i,j} \ \forall_{i,j} \tag{19}$$

Equations (12) - (17) are the traffic flow constraints which ensure each FSO flow only starts from the source node and ends at the destination node while Equations (18) and (19) specify the traffic continuity and FSO link capacity constraints, respectively.

Given a set of traffic demands and N nodes, one can adopt a *two-stage* scheme or *joint* scheme to optimize the network structure. With the *two-stage* scheme, after using the model in Section 3 to establish the physical network structure in the first stage, the model in Section 4 is applied to satisfy as many traffic as possible in the second stage. With the *joint* scheme, the mathematical models in Section 3 and 4 are combined to design an FSO network from scratch by excluding the objective equations (2) - (3), wherein the optimized physical network structure and FSO flows can be set up by jointly considering the physical network structure and logical network structure design while taking into the link availability, partial and minimum bandwidth allocation into consideration.

5 Performance Analysis

In our simulation and experiments, we focus on the performance analysis and results to compare the proposed *two-stage* scheme and *joint* scheme. A random 5-node FSO system is considered and each node has two transceivers available for establishing bidirectional links as shown in Figure 2(a).

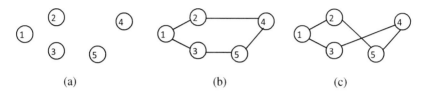

(a)   (b)   (c)

Fig. 2. Wireless Optical network structure with five nodes

The link availability and bandwidth parameters are randomly generated and calculated according to Equation (1). The total projected traffic demands (i.e., $\Sigma_{s,d}\Gamma_{s,d}$ are 1.92*Gbps* and the minimum bandwidth request for a node pair is 11*Mbps*. Figure 2(b) and Figure 2(c) show the network structure after running the *two stage* scheme and *joint* scheme, respectively. In the experiment, the *joint* scheme accommodates about 87% of the total traffic demand while the *two-stage* scheme only satisfy about 80% of the total traffic demand. Our other simulation results also show that the *joint* scheme outperforms the *two-stage* scheme by a noticeable margin.

This can be explained as follows: in the *two-stage* scheme, the objective function (i.e., Equation (2)) of the first stage is aggressive in achieving maximal bandwidth of the whole FSO network, which may actual create some bottleneck FSO links. And those bottleneck links may in turn hurt the performance of *two-stage* scheme when accommodating traffic demand in the second stage.

Note that, even though the proposed schemes are based on the case with static (projected) traffic, the schemes can be used (with minor modifications) to minimize the blocking probability or maximize the throughput for dynamic traffic demands. Nevertheless, there are several related research issues such as how to enhance the current network structure with new (updated) links/nodes to accommodate additional traffic among the same set of source and destination nodes or include new source or destination nodes, which deserve further investigation.

6 Conclusion and Future Directions

Free Space Optical communication (FSO) technology is evolving fast as a cost-effective and high-capacity alternative solution to broadband access. The FSO system owns prominent features such as very high bit rates, quick and inexpensive setup without digging up roads, and no licensing requirements or tariffs for their utilization. In an FSO system, at least one part of the optical channel passes through the Earth's atmosphere. As a result, the available FSO link bandwidth is vulnerable to interferences such as attenuation, scintillation and weather, which may significantly affect the system performance if the system is not considered and optimized properly.

In this study, we proposed and investigated Mix Integer Programming formulations for optimum design of FSO network structure while considering the link and bandwidth availability, and partial bandwidth allocation. Our goal in setting out the formulations is not to provide a computational tool, but rather to provide a corresponding problem definition/model and draw further research attention in optimizing and modeling FSO network.

Acknowledgment

I would like to thank the entire researcher those who are participating, participated in the field of network structure enhancement, with their references we prepared some reviews on FSO network structure design.

References

[1] Kedar, D., Arnon, S.: Urban optical wireless communication networks: the main challenges and possible solutions. IEEE Communications Magazine 42, S2–S7 (2004)

[2] Langer, K., Grubor, J.: Recent developments in optical wireless communications using infrared and visible light. In: Proceedings of International Conference on Transparent Optical Networks, vol. 3, pp. 146–151 (2007)

[3] Katz, G., Arnon, S., Goldgeier, P., Hauptman, Y., Atias, N.: Cellular over optical wireless networks. IEE Proceedings of Optoelectronics 153, 195–198 (2006)

[4] Last, M., Leibowitz, B., Cagdaser, B., Jog, A., Zhou, L., Boser, B., Pister, K.: Toward a wireless optical communication link between two small unmanned aerial vehicles. In: Proceedings of IEEE International Symposium on Circuits and Systems, vol. 3, pp. 930–933 (2003)

[5] Liu, Q., Qiao, C., Mitchell, G., Stanton, S.: Optical wireless communication networks for first- and last-mile broadband access. Journal of Optical Networking 4, 807–828 (2005) (invited)

[6] Mahdy, A., Deogun, J.: Wireless optical communications: a survey. In: Proceedings of IEEE Wireless Communications and Networking Conference, vol. 4, pp. 2399–2404 (2004)

[7] Ari, F., Ozek, F., Ozturk, O., Geren, O.: Techniques for link security in outdoor mobile laser optical wireless. In: Proceedings of International Conference on Transparent Optical Networks, vol. 3, pp. 160–163 (2006)

[8] Leitgeb, E., Muhammad, S., Flecker, B., Chlestil, C., Gebhart, M., Javornik, T.: The influence of dense fog on optical wireless systems, analyzed by measurements in graz for improving the link-reliability. In: Proceedings of International Conference on Transparent Optical Networks, vol. 3, pp. 154–159 (2006)

[9] Arnon, S., Kopeika, N.S.: Adaptive optical transmitter and receiver for space communication through thin clouds. Applied Optics 36(9), 199–1987 (1997)

[10] Leonardi, E., Mellia, M., Marsan, M.A.: Algorithms for the logical topology design in WDM all-optical networks. Optical Network Magazine 1(1), 35–46 (2000)

[11] Ramaswami, R., Sivarajan, K.: Design of logical topologies for wavelength-routed optical networks. IEEE Journal on Selected Areas in Communications 14, 840–851 (1996)

[12] Xin, C., Wang, B.: Logical topology design for dynamic traffic grooming in mesh WDM optical networks. In: Proceedings of IEEE ICC, vol. 3, pp. 1792–1796 (2005)

[13] IEEE, IEEE std 802.11- Wireless LAN media access control (MAC) and physical layer (PHY) specifications (1997)

[14] Chang, G., Jia, Z., Yu, J., Ellinas, G.: Super broadband optical wireless over optical fiber network architecture. IEEE Lasers & Electro-Optics Society, 344–345 (2006)

[15] Zhuang, J., Casey, Milner, S., Gabriel, S., Baecher, G.: Multi-objective optimization techniques in topology control of free space optical networks. In: Proceedings of IEEE Military Communications Conference, vol. 1, pp. 430–435 (2004)

[16] Kashyap, A., Lee, K., Kalantari, M., Khuller, S., Shayman, M.: Integrated topology control and routing in wireless optical mesh networks. Computer Networks 51(15), 4237–4251 (2007)

[17] Gurumohan, P., Hui, J.: Topology design for free space optical networks. In: Proceedings of IEEE International Conference on Computer Communications and Networks, pp. 576–579 (2003)

[18] Llorca, J., Desai, A., Milner, S.: Obscuration minimization in dynamic free space optical networks through topology control. In: Proceedings of IEEE Military Communications Conference, vol. 3, pp. 1247–1253 (2004)

[19] http://www.fsona.com/technology.php?sec=fso_guide

Binary Tree Based Cluster Key Management Scheme for Heterogeneous Sensor Networks

Rajender Dharavath[1], K. Bhima[2],
K. Sri Vidya Shankari[3], and A. Jagan[4]

[1] Asst. Professor, CSE Dept. BVRIT, Narsapur, India
[2] Sr. Asst. Professor, IT Dept. BVRIT, Narsapur, India
[3] Asst. Professor, Dept. of CSE, Aditya Engineeering College, Kakinada, India
[4] Professor & HOD, CSE Dept. BVRIT, Narsapur, India
{raja.dharavath,bhima.mnnit,accessvidya}@gmail.com,
jagan.amgoth@bvrit.ac.in

Abstract. Many applications of wireless sensor networks are used to achieve energy efficiency and require secure data communications. To achieve security in wireless sensor networks, it is important to be able to encrypt the messages sent between sensor nodes. The key management task is challenging due to resource constrained nature of wireless sensor networks. We are introducing two key management methods for wireless sensor networks, which can handle events like node addition, node compromise and key refresh at regular intervals. The first one is *Binary Tree Based Method*, used to generate Cluster Key *CK*, for intra cluster communication and Common Cluster Key *CCK*, for inter cluster communication. The second one is *DH Key Exchange Method* performs key management with minimum communication and storage at each node which ensures the security from eavesdropping and internal attacks. Our Key management methods avoid the usage of public key in communications.

Keywords: Binary Trees, DH Key Exchange, Hierarchical wireless sensor networks, Cluster Head, Sensor node, Base Stations.

1 Introduction

Wireless Sensor Networks (WSN) are composed of small autonomous devices, or sensor nodes, that are networked together. Sensor networks can facilitate large scale, real-time data processing in complex environments. Their applications involve protecting and monitoring critical military, environmental, safety-critical or domestic infrastructures and resources. Wireless communication employed by the WSN facilitates eavesdropping and packet injection by an adversary. This factor demand security for sensor network to ensure operation safety, secrecy of sensitive data and privacy for people in sensor environment.

The *key management schemes* discussed in [1,2,3,6,7,9,11] consider homogeneous sensor networks, where all sensor nodes have identical capabilities in terms

D.C. Wyld et al. (Eds.): NeCoM/WeST/WiMoN 2011, CCIS 197, pp. 64–77, 2011.
© Springer-Verlag Berlin Heidelberg 2011

of communication, computation and storage. Large scale homogeneous networks suffer from high costs of communication, computation and storage requirements. Hence Hierarchical Sensor Networks (HSNs) (also called as Heterogeneous Sensor Networks) are preferred as they provide better performance and security solutions. In WSN's hierarchical clustering provides scalability, self organization and energy efficient data dissemination.

In *Hierarchical networks*, there is a hierarchy of nodes in terms of resources and functions. The most powerful node is the Base Station (*BS*), which is at top level. *BS* is a powerful data processing and storage unit which collects sensor readings, perform costly operations and manage the network. It interfaces the network to outside world. Transmission power of BS is usually enough to reach all nodes. The next level of sensors is called *group heads or Cluster Heads* (we call these nodes as CH-Sensors). These nodes have better resources compared to the sensor nodes which form the lowest level of this model. The special category of nodes are called virtual sensor node used for building Binary Tree and generating for Cluster Key and Common Cluster Key *CCK*.

Cluster heads are responsible for intermediate data processing, data aggregation e.g. collect and process the readings of other nodes in the cluster and send a single reading to base station. The *BS* in turn performs computation on readings from multiple cluster heads. The sensor nodes i.e., nodes with least resources and used for sensing a particular data form the majority of the network. They provide the readings for the parameters being sensed.

Hierarchical Sensor Networks (HSN) are considered in [8,4,10,5]. In the scheme [8] proposed by *Sajid et.a*l. Key management based on key pre distribution is discussed. Routing driven key management scheme is discussed in [4], the scheme is based on Elliptic Curve Cryptography. The scheme [10] focuses on achieving higher key connectivity and system performance using the combination of nodes with higher capability and nodes with lower capability in terms of computation, communication and storage. In [5] algorithms are discussed to improve the degree of sensing coverage using heterogeneous sensor networks.

In this paper we are proposing key management methods for Heterogeneous Sensor Networks. The first method is called as *Binary Tree Based Method* which is based on the scheme in [16][13]. The second method is based on *Diffie-Hellman Key Exchange Algorithm* which is proposed for wired network [14] which is called as *DH Key Exchange-Based Method* in this paper.

Here, hierarchical architecture of sensor networks is considered, where data is routed from sensor nodes to the base station through cluster head. Base station interfaces sensor network to the outside network. Sensor nodes are assumed to be immobile; these nodes organize themselves into clusters. The size of the cluster we are assuming here is a small group of sensor nodes. A cluster head is chosen from each cluster to handle the communication between the cluster nodes and the base station.

2   Related Work

Due to the resource constraints, the extremely large network size and the lack of the infrastructure support, traditional public-key based asymmetrical key distribution protocols and trusted infrastructure authentication security mechanisms are not suitable for WSNs. Pre-distributing secret keys into sensor nodes before they are deployed is a applicable solution for key management in wireless sensor environment [23].

Eschenauer et al. [23] proposed a *random key predistribution scheme* in 2002. In their scheme, a subset of keys from a large size key pool is randomly selected and pre-loaded into sensors. If two nodes can find a common key, they can setup a secure link by it. Otherwise, they need to establish a path-key between them. According to the random graph theory, if the probability that any two nodes have at least one common key satisfies a critical value, the network is connected with high probability. In our approach private Key K_{ij} selection is different.

In the *key management scheme* discussed in [8] node revocation is not considered in detail. This scheme discusses about the percentage of links that are compromised when a node is compromised, but how these compromised links are reconfigured and what is the effort involved to reconfigure the compromised links in not discussed. The proposed methods present how actually the keys are changed (rekey operation: is nothing but changing the keys that are known to compromised node and distributing them securely to existing nodes) in order to reconfigure the compromised links when a node is compromised.

In this paper, we adopt a *heterogeneous sensor network model* to overcome the poor scalability and performance bottleneck of homogeneous sensor networks. We propose a novel key management schemes for wireless sensor networks.

The proposed methods are analyzed in detail by considering various performance metrics like storage, communication and computation. The analysis shows that *Binary Tree based Method* achieves rekey operation by performing n communication with additional storage, whereas [8] achieves the same goal using $2n$ communication. The *DH Key Exchange Based Method* achieves rekeys operation by avoiding public key usage and no additional communication cost is incurred.

The paper is organized as follows: In Section 3 we explain notations, security goals and the threat model. Section 4 explains in detail the Binary Tree Based Method. In Section 5 we explain the *DH Key Exchange based Method.*In section 6 we explain the security analysis of the Key Management Scheme and Section 7 presents the performance analysis of the proposed methods and finally we conclude in Section 8.

3   System Model

In this section we discuss about assumptions and notations, security goals and threat model used in this paper to construct the key management methods

3.1   Notations

Following are some of the notations used in this paper.

BS	Base Station
CH_i	Cluster Head of ith cluster
S_{ij}	i^{th} cluster j^{th} sensor node
K_{ij}	Secret key of ith cluster j^{th} sensor node
V_{ij}	i^{th} cluster j^{th} virtual sensor node
V_0	Root node of both cluster(virtual sensor node)
CK_i	common Key for i^{th} cluster
CCK	Common Cluster Key
HCH	Head of the Cluster Heads

3.2   Security Goals

The main security goal considered in this paper is confidentiality: only the authorized nodes should be able to read the messages transmitted between the nodes. The confidentiality requirements that we are achieving in the *Tree based Method* and *DH Key Exchange based Methods* are:

Non-group confidentiality: Nodes that are not in the cluster should not be able to access any key that can be used to decrypt the message sent to the legitimate nodes.

Forward confidentiality: When a node is compromised, the scheme should ensure that the compromised node does not have access to any key used to encrypt the future messages.

Backward confidentiality: When a new node is added to the cluster, the scheme should ensure that the node does not have access to any key such that it can decrypt the previous messages.

3.3   Threat Model

The types of attacker we are considering in this paper are of two types. First type of attacker is an outside attacker who is able to eavesdrop on the communications. Second type of attacker is inside attacker a compromised node which is able to get all the secrets.

4   Description of the Binary Tree Based Method

Sensors within a cluster are organized as binary tree [16] which is balanced with two cluster sensor nodes at the leaf level as shown in Fig.1 Each cluster's binary tree is maintained by the cluster head CH, and two clusters binary tree is maintained by the head of the cluster head HCH i.e. Base Station.

In Fig.1 S_{11}, S_{12}, S_{13}, S_{14} represents sensor nodes within the cluster C_1, and V_{10}, V_{11}, and V_{12} are virtual sensor nodes, which are used to build binary tree for generation of cluster key CK_1. S_{21}, S_{22}, S_{23}, and S_{24} represent sensor nodes of cluster C_2 and V_{20}, V_{21}, V_{22} are virtual sensor nodes, which are used to form binary tree for generation of cluster key CK_2. Nodes within a cluster are of

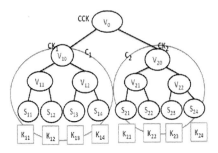

Fig. 1. Hierarchical Binary Tree for Clustered Wireless Sensor Networks

fixed size based on the m value. Every sensor node shares a key with the cluster head called its secret key used to communicate with the cluster head securely. K_{11}, K_{12}, K_{13}, K_{14} are secret keys correspond to sensor nodes of cluster C_1.The keys KV_{11}, KV_{12} are generated (explained in section 5) by CH_1 for generating CK_1. K_{21}, K_{22}, K_{23}, and K_{24} are secret keys of correspond to sensor nodes of cluster C_2. The keys KV_{21}, KV_{22} are generated(explained in section 5) by CH_2 for generating CK_2.

The key at the root of hierarchical binary tree is the Common Cluster Key (CCK) i.e., KV_0. The key CCK is computed by BS and shared by all CH-Sensor which is used for inter cluster communications. Nodes within a cluster can communicate securely using CK. In Fig.1 S_{11}-S_{14} are cluster C_1 sensor nodes, S_{21}-S_{24} are cluster C_2 sensor nodes, V_{10}-V_{12} are Cluster C_1 virtual sensor nodes, V_{20}-V_{22} are virtual sensor node of C_2 and V_0 is root node for C_1, C_2. CK_1, CK_2 are Cluster Keys for C_1 and C_2. CCK is Common Cluster Key.

5   Description of the DH Key Exchange Method

In this section we explain the basic Diffie-Hellman key exchange algorithm, followed by the detailed description of the protocol for key establishment using *DH Key exchange method*.

5.1   Diffie-Hellman Key Exchange Algorithm

Consider a sensor node S_a and S_b, let the global pubic elements p and α where p is prime number and $\alpha < p$ and α is a primitive root of p.

Let K_a is secret key or contribution of sensor node S_a then secret-public key (Blinded Key) pair becomes as follows.

$$\{K_a, BK_a = \alpha^{K_a} mod p\} \tag{1}$$

Let K_b is secret key or contribution of sensor node S_b then secret-public key (Blinded Key) pairs becomes as follows.

$$\{K_b, BK_b = \alpha^{K_b} mod p\} \tag{2}$$

The sensor node S_a calculates communication key as follows.

$$\{SK_a = (BK_b)^{K_a} mod p\} \tag{3}$$

The sensor node S_b calculates communication key as follows.

$$\{SK_b = (BK_a)^{K_b} mod p\} \tag{4}$$

SK_a or SK_b ($SK_a = SK_b = KV_0$) are communications key for S_a and S_b.

Key generation and Binary Tree Methods are adopted from [17][16]. In *TGDH* [17] every node on the key tree has a *Diffie-Hellman key* pair based on the prime p and generator α, used to generate the group key. Secret-public key pair for real member M_i is as follows.

$$\{KM_i, BKM_i = \alpha^{KM_i} mod p\} \tag{5}$$

And Secret-public key pair for virtual member V_i is as follows.

$$\{KV_i, BKV_i = \alpha^{KV_i} mod p\} \tag{6}$$

Consider a node Mv whose left child is Mlv and right child node is Mrv (to simplify the description, we do not distinguish real members from virtual members here). Secret key of M_i's can be computed in the usual *Diffie-Hellman key exchange* fashions as follows.

$$\{KMv \equiv (BKMlv)^{KMrv} \equiv (BKMrv)^{KMlv} mod p\} \tag{7}$$

5.2   Key Establishment Using DH Key Exchange Method

Following steps explain the key establishment process.

Initialization. Every sensor node and Cluster Head are loaded with private key K_{ij} that it shares with the base station as well as with the cluster head. These private keys are chosen from a key pool K of pairwise relatively prime numbers such that no two private keys are not same, it is possible by selecting randomly one private key after other without replacement, once selected private keys are not replaced again and it is removed from pool, and new keys are added into the key pool.

Initially each *CH* is loaded with the information of all sensors in the network (i,e, Node ID and its corresponding private key of all the nodes are stored). Each sensor will now construct a m-ary tree and assigns keys for each node in the tree as shown in fig1. Now, *CH* will distribute all the keys along the path from leaf to root of respective nodes by encrypting the keys using private keys of the sensors. Upon receiving the set of keys, sensors can communicate with cluster head as well as other sensors between the clusters using the cluster key *CCK*.

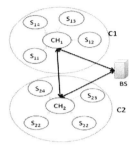

Fig. 2. Clustered Wireless Sensor Network

Cluster Formation. After deployment all *CH* broadcast Hello message to other sensors in the network. Each sensor selects the nearest CH-Sensor as its Cluster Head. After receiving reply from sensor nodes, each Cluster Head will delete the keys of the sensor nodes that are not there in its cluster. The cluster formation and initializations are shown in Fig.2.

Key Generations Scheme. In this step each CH_i calculates the Cluster Key (CK_i) for intra cluster communications from all sensor nodes S_{ij} using DH Key Exchange Method.

The steps for the generating Cluster Key CK_1 for cluster C_1 (from Fig.1 clustered network):

The cluster head CH_1 of cluster C_1 calculates its CK_1 (i.e. KV_{10}) based on the *DH Key exchange algorithm.*

The K_{11} is the secret key of sensor node S_{11} then secret-public key pair of sensor node S_{11} is calculated by CH_1 is as follows.

$$\{K_{11}, BK_{11} = \alpha^{K_{11}} modp\} \tag{8}$$

The K_{12} is secret key of sensor node S_{12} then secret-public key pair of sensor node S_{12} is calculated by CH_1 is as follows.

$$\{K_{12}, BK_{12} = \alpha^{K_{12}} modp\} \tag{9}$$

The secret- public key pair of virtual sensor node V_{11} is calculated as follows from sensor node S_{11} and S_{12} by CH_1.

$$\{KV_{11} \equiv (BK_{11})^{K_{12}} \equiv (BK_{12})^{K_{11}} modp\ BKV_{11} = \alpha^{KV_{11}} modp\} \tag{10}$$

The K_{13} is secret key of sensor node S_{13} then secret-public key pair of sensor node S_{13} is calculated by CH_1 is as follows.

$$\{K_{13}, BK_{13} = \alpha^{K_{13}} modp\} \tag{11}$$

The K_{14} is secret key of sensor node S_{14} then secret- public key pair of sensor node S_{14} is calculated by CH_1 is as follows.

$$\{K_{14}, BK_{14} = \alpha^{K_{14}} modp\} \tag{12}$$

The secret- public key pair of virtual sensor node V_{12} is calculated as follows from sensor node S_{13} and S_{14} by CH_1.

$$\{KV_{12} \equiv (BK_{13})^{K_{14}} \equiv (BK_{14})^{K_{13}} modp \; BKV_{12} = \alpha^{KV_{12}} modp\} \qquad (13)$$

Now the KV_{10}, which is treated as the Cluster Key CK_1 is calculated by CH_1 as follows (from virtual sensor node V_{11} and V_{12} i.e. from KV_{11}, BKV_{11} and KV_{12}, BKV_{12}).

$$\{KV_{10} \equiv (BK_{11})^{K_{12}} \equiv (BK_{12})^{K_{11}} modp \; BKV_{10} = \alpha^{KV_{10}} modp\} \qquad (14)$$

The cluster head CH_1 distributes the CK_1 to all sensor nodes within the cluster C_1. And CK_1 is used for intra cluster communication in C_1.

The steps for generating Cluster Key CK$_2$ for cluster C$_2$ (from Fig.1):

The cluster head CH_2 of C_2, calculates its Cluster Key CK_2 (i.e. KV_{20}) according DH key $exchange$ $method$.

The K_{21} is the secret key of sensor node S_{21} then secret-public key pair of sensor node S_{21} is calculated by CH_2 is as follows.

$$\{K_{21}, BK_{21} = \alpha^{K_{21}} modp\} \qquad (15)$$

The K_{22} is the secret key of sensor node S_{22} then secret-public key pair of sensor node S_{22} is calculated by CH_2 is as follows.

$$\{K_{22}, BK_{22} = \alpha^{K_{22}} modp\} \qquad (16)$$

The secret- public key pair of virtual sensor node V_{21} is calculated as follows from sensor node S_{21} and S_{22} by CH_1.

$$\{KV_{21} \equiv (BK_{21})^{K_{22}} \equiv (BK_{22})^{K_{21}} modp \; BKV_{21} = \alpha^{KV_{21}} modp\} \qquad (17)$$

The K_{23} is the secret key of sensor node S_{23} then secret-public key pair of sensor node S_{23} is calculated by CH_2 is as follows.

$$\{K_{23}, BK_{23} = \alpha^{K_{23}} modp\} \qquad (18)$$

The K_{24} is the secret key of sensor node S_{24} then secret-public key pair of sensor node S_{24} is calculated by CH_2 is as follows.

$$\{K_{24}, BK_{24} = \alpha^{K_{24}} modp\} \qquad (19)$$

The secret- public key pair of virtual sensor node V_{22} is calculated as follows from sensor node S_{23} and S_{24} by CH_2.

$$\{KV_{22} \equiv (BK_{23})^{K_{24}} \equiv (BK_{24})^{K_{23}} modp \; BKV_{22} = \alpha^{KV_{22}} modp\} \qquad (20)$$

Now the KV_{20}, which is treated as the Cluster Key CK_2 is calculated as follows (from virtual sensor node V_{21} and V_{22} i.e. from KV_{21}, BKV_{21} and KV_{22}, BKV_{22}).

$$\{KV_{20} \equiv (BK_{21})^{KV_{22}} \equiv (BK_{22})^{KV_{21}} modp \; BKV_{20} = \alpha^{KV_{20}} modp\} \qquad (21)$$

The cluster head CH_2 of cluster C_2 distributes the CK_2 to all sensor nodes within the cluster C_2. And CK_2 is used for intra cluster communication in C_2.

Steps for generating Common Cluster Key CCK:

The BS (or HCH) calculates CCK (or KV_0) from CK_1 and CK_2 (i.e. from KV_{10}, BKV_{10} and KV_{20}, BKV_{20}) according to the *DH Key Exchange Method as shown below.*

$$\{KV_0 \equiv (BKV_{10})^{KV_{20}} \equiv (BKV_{20})^{KV_{10}} mod p\} \tag{22}$$

HCH or BS distributes the CCK to the all CH's and to all cluster sensor nodes by using corresponding secret keys. CCK is used for inter cluster communication.

6   Security Analysis of Key Management Scheme

Security analysis of Key management scheme (includes the both methods *Binary Tree Based Method* and *DH Key Exchange Based Method*) is explained in this section by considering the following issues: Key establishment, rekey operation as a result of events like node addition, node compromise and key refresh at regular intervals.

6.1   Key Establishment

Each sensor is pre loaded with a secret key that it shares with its cluster head before deployment. Initially all CH-Sensors are pre loaded with all the keys that are assigned to sensor nodes. After deployment all CH-Sensors broadcast hello message to sensor nodes. Each sensor node selects the nearest CH-Sensor as its cluster head. After receiving reply from sensor nodes each CH-Sensor will delete the keys of sensor nodes that are not there in its cluster. Each CH-Sensor will now construct an m-ary binary tree and assigns keys for each node in the tree as explained in section 3. Now, initially CH-Sensor will distribute all the keys (CK_{ij}, and CCK) i.e. except all public keys and secret keys of virtual sensor nodes) along the path from leaf to root of respective nodes by encrypting the keys using secret keys of the sensors. Upon receiving the set of keys (CK_i, CCK) sensor nodes can communicate with cluster head as well as other sensors within the cluster using the Cluster Key CK_i and sensor node of one cluster can communicate with other cluster sensor node using Common Cluster Key CCK.

6.2   Node Revocation or Node Compromise

We assume that we have intrusion detection mechanism to detect node compromise. As soon as a node is compromised corresponding cluster head will change all the keys that are known to compromised node (i.e., keys along the path from compromised node's position to root of the tree). The changed CK_i and CCK are distributed securely to existing nodes.

Suppose if the compromised node is S_{24} with secret key K_{24} in cluster C_2 then the CH_2 construct a new binary tree as shown in Fig.3 and keys KV_{22}, BKV_{22},

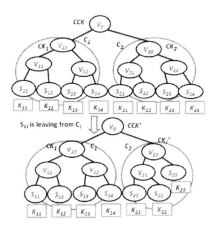

Fig. 3. Sensor Node S_{24} Revocation from Cluster C_2

CK_2 and CCK are changed to KV'_{22} $BKV'_{22}, CK2'$. The base station generates the CCK' from CK_1 and CK'_2.The generated new keys CK'_2 is distributed to the all sensor nodes of cluster C_2 and CCK' is distributed to the all cluster heads and sensor nodes of both clusters by encrypting with private keys of respective sensor nodes. If a single node is compromised then number of encryptions required to distribute CCK' key securely is mk (to distribute CK'_2, m encryptions required) where m is the cluster size and $k$is number of cluster.

Steps for generating CCK$'$ and CK$'_2$:

Now the KV_{20}which is treated as the Cluster Key CK'_2 is calculated as follows from virtual sensor node V_{21} and sensor node S_{23} i.e. from KV_{21}, BKV_{21} and K_{23}, BK_{23} (eq 18).

$$\{KV'_{20} \equiv (BKV_{21})^{K_{23}} \equiv (BK_{23})^{KV_{21}} modp \, BKV'_{20} = \alpha^{KV'_{20}} modp\} \qquad (23)$$

The *BS (or HCH)* calculates CCK' *(or KV'_0)* from CK_1 (eq.14) and CK'_2 (i.e. from KV_{10}, BKV_{10} and KV'_{20}, BKV'_{20}) as shown below according to the *DH Key Exchange Method.*

$$\{KV'_0 \equiv (BKV_{10})^{K'_{20}} \equiv (BKV'_{20})^{KV_{10}} modp\} \qquad (24)$$

Now *BS* distributes CCK' to the both clusters and CH_2 distributes CK'_2 to C_2.

6.3   Addition of New Node

A new node is pre loaded with a secret key that it shares with the cluster head. Base station encrypts the secret key of the new sensor node using the CCK that is maintained for cluster heads and for inter cluster communication the same is sent. Upon receiving the message from base station each CH-Sensor will have the information regarding the new node. Each CH-Sensor node will now broadcast Hello message to newly added sensor node. Now as in initial setup phase sensor

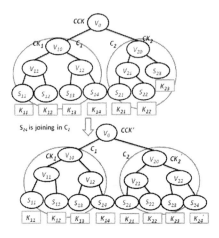

Fig. 4. Addition of new sensor node S_{24} in cluster C_2

node will choose nearest CH-Sensor as its cluster head. Now the cluster head will find an appropriate position for the new node in the binary tree and tree is updated (i.e., all the keys along the path including KV_{ij}, BKV_{ij}, CK_i and CCK are changed). Cluster head will now distribute new set of keys (CK_i' and CCK') to corresponding nodes as well as the new node will receive all the keys along the path. In order to distribute the changed keys securely cluster head uses secret key of the new node and for other nodes it uses previous CK_i.

If the new node added is say S_{24} with secret key K_{24} then the binary tree formed by the CH_2 is as shown in Fig.4. And new CK_2' is generated as explained in key generations scheme and distributes to all sensor nodes of cluster C_2.

Steps for generating CCK' and CK_2':

The K_{24}' is the secret key of new sensor node S_{24} then secret-public key pair of sensor node S_{24} is calculated by CH_2 is as follows.

$$\{K_{24}', BK_{24}' = \alpha^{K_{24}'} modp\} \tag{25}$$

The secret- public key pair of virtual sensor node V_{22} is calculated as follows from sensor node S_{23} and S_{24} by CH_2.

$$\{KV_{22}' \equiv (BK_{23})^{K_{24}'} \equiv (BK_{24})^{KV_{23}} modp \, BKV_{22}' = \alpha^{KV_{22}'} modp\} \tag{26}$$

The KV_{20}', which is treated as the Cluster Key CK_2' is calculated as follows (from virtual sensor node V_{21} and V_{22} i.e. from KV_{21}, BKV_{21} and KV_{22}, BKV_{22}).

$$\{KV_{20}' \equiv (BKV_{21})^{KV_{22}'} \equiv ((BKV_{22})')^{KV_{21}} modp \, BKV_{20}' = \alpha^{KV_{20}'} modp\} \tag{27}$$

The BS (or HCH) calculates CCK' (or KV_0') from CK_1 and CK_2' (i.e. from KV_{10}, BKV_{10} and KV_{20}', BKV_{20}') according to the DH Key $Exchange$ $Method$.

$$\{KV_0' \equiv (BKV_{10})^{KV_{20}'} \equiv (BKV_{20}')^{KV_{10}} modp\} \tag{28}$$

Now *BS* distributes CCK' to all CH-Sensor nodes and all nodes of both clusters. CH_2 distribute CK_2 to C_2.

6.4   Key Refresh

In order to achieve key freshness it is required to change the cluster key CK_i periodically. To change the key at regular interval the Cluster Head will generates a new CK_i' by changing the private keys of sensor nodes in clusters. *CH* broadcasts the new CK_i' to all cluster sensor nodes.

7   Performance Analysis

7.1   Storage

In the Binary Tree-Based Scheme each sensor node is required to store three (3) keys (i.e., self secret key K_{ij}, CK_i, and CCK). Each CH-Sensor is required to store $(2n+2)$keys where n is total nodes in binary tree (virtual sensor nodes and sensor nodes) or $(2 \sum K_{ij} + 2)$. And BS required to store $(kn+2m+1)$ keys where k is number of clusters, n is the number of sensor nodes and m is the number of CH-Sensors. In the *DH Key Exchange Based Method* no additional storage is required by sensor node, each sensor node will store only its secret key K_{ij}. CH- Sensor generates keys where n is number of sensor nodes in cluster and k is number of virtual sensor nodes in binary tree. For the scheme in [8] the storage is : for a key sharing probability of 0.8 sensor node stores 5 generation keys and CH-Sensor approximately 250 generation keys.

7.2   Computation

In *Binary Tree-Based Scheme*, computation costs are measured in terms of number of encryptions. Total numbers of encryptions performed by CH-Sensor in case of node addition is n, where n is the number of sensor nodes in cluster. Total numbers of encryptions performed by BS in case of node addition $(m+n)$ where m is number of CH-Sensors and n is total number of sensor nodes in all clusters.

7.3   Communication

Communication costs are studied in terms of number of messages that are exchanged in order to change the required keys. In *Binary Tree-Based Method* for events like node addition and node compromise, the number of messages constructed and communicated are two, which is the communication cost incurred at CH-sensor and at *BS*. Similarly each sensor node performs either two receive operations.

For key refresh each CH-sensor performs one transmits operations and sensor nodes performs two receive operation in order to update the *CK* and *CCK*. In *DH Key Exchange Method*, when a node is added or compromised the cluster head constructs Binary Tree in order to change the key. The communication cost incurred in the *DH Key Exchange Method* is: one transmits operation by CH-Sensors and two receive operation by sensor nodes.

The table below summarizes the communication costs incurred by the proposed schemes and the scheme in [8].

Table 1. Depicts Storage and Communication Requirement for the proposed Method and The Scheme by Sajid et.al.

–	Storage CH-Sensor	Storage Sensor node	Communication CH- Sensor	Communication Sensor node
BTBM	$(2n+2)$	3 keys	1 to n transmit+2 receive	1 transmit+1-2 receive
DH KE	$(n+2k)$keys	1 or 3 keys	1 to n transmit+ 2 receive	2 receive messages
SS	250(app) keys	5 (app)keys	n transmit + n receive	2 tranmit +(p+1) receive

BTBM - Binary Tree based Method, DH KE - DH KE Method, SS - Schemem by Sajid et.al. and app - approximate.

8 Conclusion

The paper presents new methods for key management for confidential communication between node and its cluster head in hierarchical sensor networks. The methods are analyzed in detail with respect to security and performance. Performance analysis shows that *Binary Tree- Based Method* exhibits better performance which achieves rekey operation by performing n communications with some additional storage. In *DH Key Exchange Method* key is established in an efficient way for node addition, node compromise and also key refresh at regular intervals.

References

1. Chan, H., Perrig, A., Song, D.: Random key pre distribution schemes for sensor networks. In: IEEE Symposium on Research in Security and Privacy, pp. 197–213 (2003)
2. Cheng, Y., Agrawal, D.P.: Efficient pairwise key establishment and management in static wireless sensor networks. In: Second IEEE International Conference on Mobile Ad Hoc and Sensor Systems (2005)
3. Du, W., Deng, J., Han, Y.S., Varshney, P.K.: A pairwise key pre distribution scheme for wireless sensor networks. In: Proc. of the 10th ACM Conference of Computers and Communication Security (CCS 2003), pp. 42–51 (2003)
4. Du, X., GUizani, M., Xiao, Y., Ci, S., Chen, H.H.: A Routing-Driven Elliptic Curve Cryptography based Key Mangement scheme for Heterogeneous Sensor Networks. IEEE Transactions on Wireless Communications
5. Du, X., Lin, F.: Maintaining Differential coverage in heterogeneous sensor network. EURASIP Journal of Wireless Communications and Networking (4), 565–572 (2005)
6. Eschenauer, L., Gligor, V.D.: A key management scheme for distributed sensor networks. In: Proceedings of the 9th ACM Conference Computer and Communications Security, pp. 41–47 (November 2002)

 7. Hwang, J., Kim, Y.: Revisiting random key pre distribution schemes for WSN. In: Proc. of the 2nd ACM Workshop on Security of Ad Hoc and Sensor Networks, pp. 43–52 (2004)
 8. Hussain, S., Kausar, F., Masood, A.: An Efficient Key Distribution Scheme for Heterogeneous Sensor Networks. In: IWCMC 2007 (2007)
 9. Liu, D., Ning, P.: Establishing pairwise keys in distributed sensor networks. In: Proceedings of the 10th ACM Conference on Computers and Communication Security (CCS 2003), pp. 52–61 (2003)
10. Lu, K., Qian, Y., Hu, J.: A framework for distributed key management schemes in heterogeneous wireless sensor networks. In: IEEE International Performance Computing and Communications Conference, pp. 513–519 (2006)
11. Pietro, R.D., Mancini, L.V., Mei, A.: Random Key assignment to secure wireless sensor networks. In: 1st ACM Workshop on Security of Ad Hoc and Sensor Networks (2003)
12. Samuel, S.: Cryptanalysis of Number Theoretic Ciphers. CRC Press, Boca Raton (2003)
13. Wong, C., Gouda, M., Lam, S.: Secure Group Communication Using key Graphs. In: Proceedings of the ACM SIGCOMM 1998 (October 1998)
14. Zheng, X., Huang, C.-T., Matthews, M.: Chinese Remainder Theorem Based Group Key Management. In: ACMSE (2007)
15. Zhu, S., Setia, S., Jajodia, S.: LEAP: Efficient Security Mechanisms for Large Scale Distributed Sensor Networks. In: Proc. of 10th ACM Conference on Computers and Communication Security, CCS 2003 (2003)
16. Zhou, L., Ravishankar, C.V.: Efficient, authenticated, and fault-tolerant key agreement for dynamic peer groups. Technical Report 88, Dept. of Computer Science and Engineering, University of California, Riverside (2003)
17. Kim, Y., Perrig, A., Tsudik, G.: Simple and fault-tolerant key agreement for dynamic collaborative groups. In: Proceedings of the CCS 2000 (2000)
18. Shen, L., Shi, X.: A Dynamic Cluster-based Key Management Protocol in Wireless Sensor Networks. International Journal of Intelligent Control and Systems 13(2), 146–151 (2008)
19. McGrew, D.A., Sherman, A.T.: Key Establishment in Large Dynamic Groups Using One Function Trees
20. Lee, P., Lui, J., Yau, D.: Distributed collaborative key agreement protocols for dynamic peer groups. Technical report, Dept. of Computer Science and Engineering, Chinese University of Hong Kong (2002)
21. Kim, Y., Perrig, A., Tsudik, G.: Simple and fault-tolerant key agreement for dynamic collaborative groups. In: Proceedings of the CCS 2000 (2000)
22. Steiner, M., Tsudik, G., Waidner, M.: Key agreement in dynamic peer groups. IEEE Transactions on Parallel and Distributed Systems 11 (2000)
23. Eschenauer, L., Gligor, V.D.: A key-management scheme for distributed sensor networks. In: Proceedings of the 9th ACM Conference on Computer and Communications Security (November 2002)

A Hierarchical Mobile Agent Monitoring Mechanism with XML-Based Mobile Agents

C. Valliyammai and S. Thamarai Selvi

Department of Computer Technology, Anna University, Chennai,
Chromepet, Chennai-600044, India
{cva,stselvi}@annauniv.edu

Abstract. Mobility management is a necessity in highly dynamic and large-scale Mobile Agent (MA) networks, especially in a multi-region environment, in order to control and communicate with agents after launching. In this paper, we have proposed a hierarchical mobile agent monitoring mechanism using Mobile Monitor Agents (MMA's). The mobile agent system is implemented in XML. This XML based system provides a system independent, standardized, effective and customized solution for application development. Distributing MMA dynamically solves the scalability issue of Centralized monitoring mechanism, and still has the advantages of Hierarchical monitoring mechanism to decrease the information processing bottleneck issue at centralized server. The MMA takes care of a certain number of agent servers and it reduces the traffic in the centralized server by bypassing queries from the agent servers under its control. XML helps to decrease the amount of data transferred and the processing part with the Java parsers is not transferred in network. There is less transfer of data because only data representation is migrated.

Keywords: Agent Server, Mobile Agents, Mobile Monitor Agent.

1 Introduction

The dynamic change and huge size of networks need for a dynamic adaptive and scalable agent monitoring system, preferably in a distributed trend. Monitoring of mobile agents is one of the important aspects of an agent system, everything from the location and the present status of the mobile agents must be kept track of. But many Agent systems including Grasshopper [9] and Mole do not offer this properly [2]. The IBM aglets is one system that offers mobile agent monitoring but it does it in a centralized fashion, leading to performance bottlenecks and also poses some problems when it comes to issues like scalability and network utilization [12]. Information processing is difficult to handle on a large scale in such a centralized agent system. In many agent systems, the implementation is not fully programming language independent.

The identification of key features like persistence, resource allocation, orphan detection, state capture, security, communication and co-ordination are important to make efficient use and successful deployment of mobile agents. To achieve inter-operability, a set of established XML-related standards such as XML web services is

D.C. Wyld et al. (Eds.): NeCoM/WeST/WiMoN 2011, CCIS 197, pp. 78–87, 2011.

added to support XML-based mobile agents. The mobile agents capture the data and logic in the form of XML and thus allow easy communication between different technology and language-based agent systems. Even if we use Java byte code transfer, the transfers create a huge overload in the network. In Java if a modification is done to an agent, the compiled Java byte codes need to be sent fully. The XML coded agents eliminate this problem. The XML codes are like handling of web services [8]. True language independence is achieved with XML. The intercommunication and migration of the agents are handled through web services [4]. Here the XML agents help in decreasing the total transfers. Dynamic code modification can be done in XML using X-Path facility. For these reasons, the agents are coded in XML [7].

2 Related Work

Mobile agents move the computation to another host high throughput and low latency[6]. The mobile agents can avoid transmitting a large amount of data across the network even when the network is slow and migrate with partial results from one server to another until it has accomplished its task, then return the result to the originating host. The framework proposed by [1] provides the development of agents and deployment further, an agent hierarchy can be maintained to facilitate an agent to accomplish its goal; sometimes facilitator itself becomes a communication bottleneck, or a critical point of failure. Mole provides a stable environment for the development and usage of mobile agents in the area of distributed applications [9]. Most of the mobile agent-based mechanisms use hierarchical monitoring structure to resolve the scalability issues, so the network is partitioned into a set of domains arranged hierarchically and a new monitoring agent is deployed in each domain [16]. The IBM aglets offers mobile agent monitoring in a centralized fashion. The proposed mobile agent location monitoring is based on footprints, broadcast, centralized, and hierarchical which limit the scalability [11]. An XML-based agent system is also proposed but not hierarchically in [8].

3 Agent Storage Location Mechanism

There are two commonly used storage mechanisms of agent location. When an agent migrates to new agent server, the old agent server can either retain the old record and store the new location or simply delete the record [11]. The agents list can be stored in two ways: Entire Agents list can be stored locally in every agent server or only agents in control can be stored in Agent Server. In the latter case, entire list is found only in centralized server.

> Let K be the Number of agent servers
>
> N is the Number of agents.

Let us analyze the storage mechanisms based on four parameters: Total Space required Network Traffic with Agent Server, Centralized Server space and the Centralized Server traffic.

3.1 Storage of All Records in Every Agent Server

Information about all the agents can be stored in every agent server. An agent query is asked directly to the agent server's MMA. Here an agent server which runs an MMA has to answer queries from agents under its control. The Total Space required is O(K*N). Traffic with Agent Servers O(N/K). Space consumed in Centralized Server space is O(N). There is no Traffic with the Centralized Server. Here the Centralized Server just acts as an MMA deployment initiator. Centralized server does not have to handle any queries.

3.2 Storage of All Records Only Centrally

Information about all agents need not be stored in all agent servers. Total list is stored only in the centralized server. Only the list of agents which are under control is stored in an agent server running an MMA. Only less space is consumed and the total Space required is O(N). There is no Traffic associated with the Agent Server. Space consumed in Centralized Server is O(N) and the traffic in Centralized Server is O(N). A new scheme is proposed to overcome the drawbacks of the above schemes. All records are stored in the Agent Server within the timestamp. A timestamp is added, a time limit to store the old records. Once the time for a record resides exceeds the max limit, the record is deleted and the agent has to contact the centralized server for location information. Due to the involvement of timestamps only frequently visiting agents' location are retained [5]. This works well since the storage is unnecessary only if never used. If the agent visits frequently, the storage cannot be said to be wasted. If it had been stored centrally then network traffic would have been very high with the central server. So this scheme gains complete superiority over both the commonly used schemes.

4 Implementation

The information is stored in the form of hashed two columned tables called hash map. The first column of the hash map is the primary key. The advantage of having a hash map is that all basic operations like adding an entry, modifying an entry and removing an entry are done in O(1). The list of key-value pairs used in the centralized data section is shown in Table 1.

The complexity involved in maintaining the hash map is the rehash functionality which is executed only when the hash map exceeds a particular limit or decreases below a threshold. Agents are implemented in XML. Agents migrate frequently in the system environment. So XML is used to support inter-operability and takes less size. The other main advantage is that the facility of dynamic modification of code is available. The XML file can be represented as a DOM tree and a piece of code is added to any node in the DOM tree conveniently. The code can be easily sent to be updated using the X-path facility that the web services offer in the presence of XML, where an agent has already migrated and needs to be updated. An XML agent is executed by a parser written in any convenient language, which needs to be interoperable, so the host environment can be programmed in any language. JAVA is used to implement the parser and have defined customized tags that are the prominent aspect of the XML agent [10]. These tags are understood by the parser, and are treated accordingly. The Depth First Traversal (DFS) is used to traverse the tags in the DOM tree. Since the DFS offers the scope for expanding the child through the last in first out (LIFO) mechanism. It was still needed to reverse the children node stack formed after every step, so that the first come child is expanded first. The operations are mapped to the specific tag then and there when the tags are tapped out from the stack that is formed after the reversal. MMA operations are implemented in the parser itself.

Table 1. Data Structures Used

Data Structure	Key	Value	Use
Agent Servers	Agents Server name	IP:port in which the agent server running	Used for communicating with the agent server
Hier	Child agent sever	Parent agent server	Describes the hierarchy in the agent server
Clients	Client Name	Agent server name where the client is connected to	Used for the client to communicate with the agent server
MMA	Agent Server name	A Boolean which is true if an MMA runs in the agent server, and false otherwise	Used for deployment
Ag0	Free Agent Name	Agent server where the Agent is running	Used for selecting operations and describes the status 0 agents
Ag1	Busy Agent Name	Agent server where the agent is executed or is transferred from	Describes the busy agents

4.1 Centralized Server

Centralized server has all the information regarding agents, agent server, MMAs and the clients stored efficiently. The Centralized server is the one where the deployment of the MMA begins. Initially the list of agents, the number of instances to be created is written in a file "init.mmaproj". Each line in the file represents an agent type. The format of each line is "<type> <XML file> <number of instances>". The required agents are created in a new directory "./agents/root". The server runs in the port 9001 and listens infinitely for connections. It answers various queries. The queries can be for the IP:port where the agent server is running, the agent server where the client is connected, the parent agent server of a particular agent server, if an MMA is running in an agent server or the agent server where the agent is located. When a new agent server connects to the centralized server, the centralized server runs the deployment algorithm to check if the threshold is met with. To check the total value, total value of the children is calculated recursively. For an agent server which runs an MMA this value is zero, as the region of control under this MMA has no influence for the calculated region. Also the region under that MMA is not expanded. The total value is the summation of the children's values plus 1. If this value exceeds the threshold, then a "makemma" message is sent to the child having the maximum value. Following this message the MMA file is transferred. If an agent server is removed, the apployment procedure is run. This is similar to the deployment mechanism but is triggered once a removal of agent server takes place. This procedure checks for an MMA which may be running without any use, as a result of the agent server's removal. i.e if an agent server is removed the value count to be considered for threshold decreases and if the value of another MMA is very low and lesser than the value of the removal that corresponding MMA can be removed. The load is reduced by using low threshold and MMAs that divert the query messages pertaining to the agents. The status messages say about the change of status or the location of an agent.

4.2 Agent Server

The agent server is the one that deals with agent operations. An MMA may or may not run in an agent server. Every agent server in this hierarchical system should be under some agent server which can be the centralized server too. For every agent server a name and the IP:Port is stored. For Centralized server name is "root" and Port is 9001. The Port value for MMA in Centralized server is 9002. To run an agent server in the system, a free port is found and assigns that port to listen the agent server. When an agent server starts listening a new folder is created in "./Agent" in its name. All agents are stored in that folder including the Mobile Monitoring Agent(MMA). When an agent server deploys MMA to another agent server it sends a copy of its static MMA file in current directory to the agent server. So there are two instances of MMA file such as static and executing. When the agent server is disconnected, the listening should end only after all the running threads finish their work. For this purpose, there is a thread counter in the agent server and for every connection accepted, the counter is incremented and decremented when the thread ends. Disconnection module waits for the counter to become 0. The deployment taking place here is similar to that in the Centralized server.There are some additional functionalities like parsing and communication with clients. If an agent operation is requested by a client, the agent server checks if an agent of that type is available with it. If yes, it uses that agent. If no, it asks its MMA for an agent. This message format is "agent <type> <Source Agent server> <Source Agent Server IP>". If MMA has an agent under its monitoring area of that type, it forwards the message to the centralized server. On receiving the message the agent server having the free agent sends the "takeagent" message to the source agent server. When the agent server has the agent it simply parses the corresponding agent with an Input provided by the client. Agent is then migrated to destination(s) if needed. Agent migration is implemented as a parsed XML file transfer. A message "recv <agent name>" is sent before sending the agent. The agent server parses the received agent file if the message is "recv". It does not parse if the message is "takeagent".

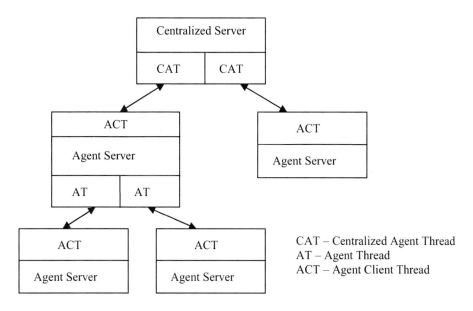

Fig. 1. Interaction between Agent Servers

Agent server interacts with its parent agent server through AgentClientThread. An agent server interacts with its children agent servers through AgentThreads. The interaction is shown in Figure 1. When an agent server is disconnecting it has to check issues like the agents that are in the agent server should be handed over to some other agent server, and the agent server is made to give the agents to its parents. When an agent server sends the disconnecting message, the centralized server chooses an alternative agent server for the clients that are under the agent server. The client messages in the agent server are handed over to the alternate agent server so that they are retained for the clients. An Agent Server running an MMA cannot disconnect.

Also an Agent Server cannot disconnect if there is no other agent server running. The Figure 2 shows the sequence of actions taking place when an MMA is deployed to an agent server.

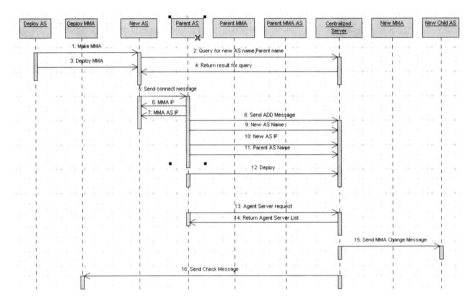

Fig. 2. Process of a new MMA deployment

5   Results

The two different agent systems such as centralized agent system are depicted in Figure 3 and the hierarchical agent system shown in Figure 4 can be compared with respect to the traffic in the centralized server.

Let N be the number of Agent servers.

Traffic of Centralized server in centralized agent system $- O(N)$ (1)

Let M be the number of MMAs in the hierarchical agent system.

T   be the Threshold value in hierarchical agent system

Nc be the number of agent servers monitored by centralized server.

Traffic of centralized server with hierarchical agent System $- O(N_c + M)$ (2)

Here $M = O(N/T)$ - Since MMA is deployed for every threshold value.

And $Nc = O(T)$ so,

$$Traffic = O(T+N/T)$$ (3)

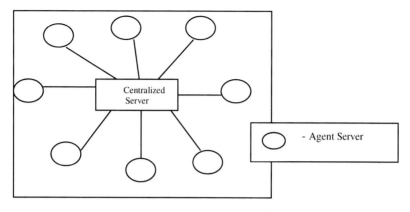

Fig. 3. Centralized Agent System

Both the systems are compared with 20 Agent servers. The hierarchy in the hierarchical agent system taken for comparison is shown in Figure 4.

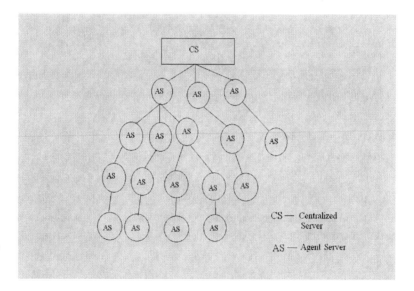

Fig. 4. A Hierarchical Agent System

The agent server1 is the Centralized server. The traffic with centralized server is calculated for each addition of an agent server. For Centralized system, traffic is N. For hierarchical system, traffic is Nc + M which is shown in Figure 5 proves the experimental. Three Systems are taken for comparison such as centralized scheme, hierarchical scheme with threshold-3 and hierarchical scheme with threshold-5.

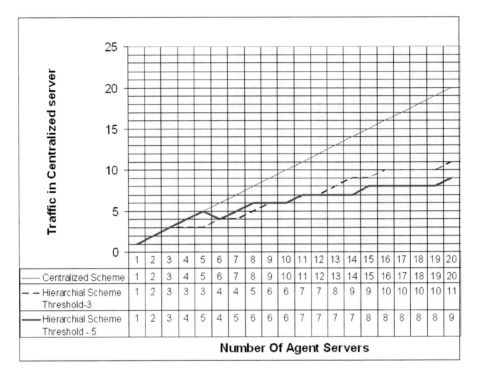

Fig. 5. Traffic in Centralized Scheme versus Hierarchical Scheme

6 Conclusion and Future Work

A Hierarchical mobile monitoring system is proposed and the role of the Mobile Monitoring Agent is bypassing selective tasks of centralized server. The MMAs do not know about the traffic to the centralized server at a given instant. There are two agent servers connected under centralized server which are very active and contribute more traffic to the centralized server and an MMA is running for four agent servers which are idle. So the traffic is taken into account and need to change MMA dynamically. All the agent servers and MMAs depend on the presence of the centralized server. If the centralized server crashes, system becomes inconsistent, but the system can be extended to distribute the role of centralized server dynamically.

References

[1] Brenner, A., Zarnekow, R., Wittig, H.: Intelligent Software Agents: Foundation and Applications. Springer, Heidelberg (1998)
[2] Baumann, J., Hohl, F., Rothermel, K., Strasser, M., Theilmann, W.: Mole: A mobile agent system. International Journal of Software: Practice and Experience 32(6), 575–603 (2002)

[3] Baumann, J., Hohl, F., Rothermel, K., Straber, M.: Mole,-Concepts of a Mobile Agent System. WWW Journal, Special Issue on Applications and Techniques of Web Agents 1(3) (1998)

[4] Fuggetta, A., Picco, G., Vigna, G.: Understanding Code Mobility. IEEE Transactions on Software Engineering 24(5), 342–362 (1998)

[5] Kendall, E.A., Krishna, V., Suresh, C.B., Pathak, C.V.: An Application framework for Intelligent and Mobile Agents. ACM Computing Surveys 32(1) (2000)

[6] Kotz, D., Gray, R., Rus, D.: Future Directions for Mobile Agent Research. IEEE Distributed Systems (2002),
http://dsonline.computer.org/0208/f/kot_print.htm

[7] Goyal, R., Chandra, P., Singh, Y.: XML based Safe and Scalable Multi-Agent Development Framework. Proceedings of World Academy of Science, Engineering and Technology 11 (2006)

[8] Steele, R., Dillon, T., Pandya, P., Ventsov, Y.: XML –based Mobile Agents. In: Proceedings of the International Conference on Information Technology: Coding and Computing, ITCC 2005 (2005)

[9] Magedanz, T.: IKV++ GmbH Germany, Grasshopper-Agent platform: A Universal Agent Platform Based on OMG MASIF and FIPA Standards (1999),
http://cordis.europa.eu/infowin/acts/analysys/products/thematic/agents/ch4/ch4.htm

[10] Wong, D., Paciorek, N., Moore, D.: Java-based mobile agents. Communications of the ACM 42(3), 92–102 (1999)

[11] Ye, D.-Y., Wang, T.I., Taiwan, C.K.: University Department of Engineering Science The Mechanism of Tracking Mobile Agent. Master paper (2000)

[12] Wang, Y.-H., Keh, H.-C., Hu, T.-C., Liao, C.-H.: A hierarchical dynamic monitoring mechanism for mobile agent location. In: 19th International Conference on Advanced Information Networking and Applications (2005)

[13] The MIT encyclopedia for Artificial Intelligence,
http://www.aaai.org/AITopics/html/agents.htm

[14] Consortium, W. W. W. XML Schema Part 0: Primer,
http://www.w3.org/TR/xmlschema-0/

[15] IBM Aglet, http://www.trl.ibm.co.jp/aglets

[16] Ahn, J.: Fault-tolerant Mobile Agent-based Monitoring Mechanism for Highly Dynamic Distributed Networks. IJCSI International Journal of Computer Science Issues 7(3) (May 2010) ISSN (Online): 1694-0784

Mutual Authentication for Mobile Communication Using Symmetric and Asymmetric Key Cryptography

Tumpa Roy and Kamlesh Dutta

National Institute of Technology, Hamirpur
Himachal Pradesh, India
{tumpa.nit,kdnith}@gmail.com

Abstract. The Global System for mobile communication (GSM) is widely used for mobile communication where the mobile users can make and receive call when they are moving independent of time, location, and network access. The wireless mobile systems are more vulnerable to deceitful access and eaves dropping. Though the authentication process on GSM is giving a reasonable security level but have some drawbacks such as: 1. overloading the network traffic and increasing the call set up time 2. Not support the mutual authentication 3. Storage overhead of visitor location registers (VLR) 4. Overload on home location registers (HLR) with authentication of mobile station. There are many protocol already proposed to overcome the above drawback but they can not overcome all the point. In this paper we are going to propose a authentication to overcome the drawback of GSM security process by using the combination the symmetric and asymmetric key cryptographic method.

Keywords: Global system for mobile communication, Symmetric key Cryptography, Asymmetric key Cryptography, Authentication, Mobile communication, Security.

1 Introduction

The global system for mobile communication is the most popular standard for mobile telephony system in the world. It has become the worldwide wireless communication standard and is used by over 4.3 billion people across more than 213 countries, since it has been offering higher digital voice quality at a lower cost[1]. The subscriber can use their phone enabled by the international ramming agreement between the network operators. For its popularity the security is on of the most vital issue as far as the wireless communication is concerned. The confidentiality of radio transmission, i.e., the privacy, and the subscriber identity authentication of the user are two major issues in the protocols [1-3] of the mobile communications. Privacy is the most obvious need for a cryptosystem. It ensures the private messages will not be disclosed to illegal users. Authentication is a mechanism to ensure only legal users can access the network. When a mobile user tries to setup a communication session with another user, he/she must verify the identity of the other. It verifies the claimed identity of a participant in mobile communications. In the original design, mobile users are authenticated by using a shared-secret crypto graphical system. GSM only authenticates the mobile user to the network. GSM network divided into

D.C. Wyld et al. (Eds.): NeCoM/WeST/WiMoN 2011, CCIS 197, pp. 88–99, 2011.

three broad pert: Mobile station that carried by the subscriber, the Base Station Subsystem control the radio link with the mobile station, and the Network and Switching Subsystem (NSS) it manages the switching functions through the Mobile Switching Centre (MSC) and provides an external access to several customer databases authentication.

The mobile station (MS) consists of the physical equipment, such as the radio transceiver, display and digital signal processors, and a smart card called the Subscriber Identity Module (SIM). The mobile equipment is uniquely identified by the International Mobile Equipment Identity (IMEI). The SIM card contains the International Mobile Subscriber Identity (IMSI), identifying the subscriber, a secret key for authentication, and other user information. The SIM card may be protected against unauthorized use by a password or personal identity number. Base Station subsystem is responsible to manage the radio network, and it is controlled by an MSC. Typically one MSC contain several BSSs. A BSS itself may cover a considerably large graphical area consisting of many cells.

In the NSS, we find four basic customers databases: The Home Location Register (HLR): contains the permanent subscriber parameters and features for a group of subscribers within a given network.

The Visited Location Register (VLR): a dynamic data base, whose entries move with subscribers, containing information for all users within one or more location area (group of cells).

The Authentication Centre (AuC): a strongly protected database which contains all the authentication and encryption information, needed by the HLR and VLR, for every mobile user. The Equipment Identity Register (EIR): used to prevent the use of stolen or fraudulent MS equipments.

The rest of this paper we organize as follows: in section 2 we discuss the general GSN security architecture and point out different drawback of that architecture, then in section 3 we review the GSM security related paper, in the section 4 we proposed a new authentication protocol to improve the GSM authentication protocol and then we compare and analyze our proposal with other protocol in the section 5 and lastly we conclude in the section 6.

2   GSM Security Architecture

The security of GSM is based on algorithms A3, A5, and A8. The authentic --cation protocol of GSM is shown in fig 1. The notation used throughout the paper is given in

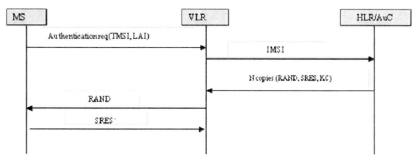

Fig. 1. The authentication protocol of GSM

Table 1. It contains two aspects, privacy and authentication. It contains two aspects, privacy and authentication. To achieve privacy, the KC (Cipher Key) is output as a session key between the mobile station and the home subsystem to encrypt/decrypt the communication messages on the safety basis of algorithm A5 against interception by an eavesdropper.

As for authentication, the SRES (Signed RESponse) is output as a certi -ficate to authenticate mobile stations. The SRES and KC are computed, respect -tively, by using Ki and RAND as inputs through algorithms A3 and A8, where Ki is the mobile station's secret key shared between the mobile station and the HLR and saved in the SIM card and HLR's database, and RAND is a random number generated by the home subsystem.

The authentication architecture of GSM is shown in the fig. 2.

1. The MS sends an authentication request to the VLR. This request contains the Temporary Mobile Subscriber Identity (TMSI) and Location Area Identity (LAI).

2. After receiving the TMSI, the new VLR can use the TMSI to get the IMSI from the old VLR. Then the new VLR sends the IMSI to HLR.

3. For the IMSI of the MS, the HLR/AuC generates several triplets, (RAND, SRES, KC), say n copies, at a time. Then HLR/AuC sends these copies to the visited VLR and for subsequent use.

4. The VLR then selects a pair, (RAND, SRES, KC) and sends the RAND to the MS. The VLR then asks the MS to compute the SRES and send it back.

5. When the MS receives the RAND, he/she computes SRES and KC with his/her secret key Ki and the RAND using Algorithms A3 and A8. The MS keeps the KC to communicate secretly and sends the SRES back to the VLR.

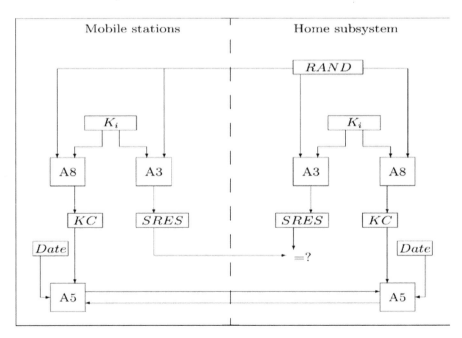

Fig. 2. The security architecture of GSM

Notation	Description
MS	Mobile Subscriber
SIM	Subscriber Identity Module
BTS	Base Transceiver Station
BSC	Base Station Controller
MSC	Mobile switching center
VLR	Visitor Location Register
HLR	Home Location Register
AuC	Authentication Center
EIR	Equipment Identity Register
IMSI	International Mobile Subscriber Identity
IMEI	International Mobile Equipment Identity
RAND	Random number generated by HLR
K_i	Secret key shared between the MS and HLR
SRES	Signed result generated by VLR
SRES´	Signed result generated by MS
KC	Cipher key
NSS	Network and Switching Subsystem
SRT	Signed result generated by VLR for mutual authentication
SRT´	Signed result generated by MS for mutual authentication
K	Secret key for mutual authentication
RANDj	Random number generated by LR. j= 1…… n
RANDy	Random number generated by foreign VLR. y= 1…… n
na, nb	Secret key o MS and HLR/VLR respectively for mutual authentication.
PMS, PV-H	Public key of MS and VLR/HLR
CERT	Certificate of VLR

6. Once the VLR receives the SRES from the MS, the SRES is compared with the stored select-SRES. If the two SRESs are equal, the MS passes the authentication process and is permitted to access the system; otherwise, the VLR rejects the MS.

As long as the MS stays in the area covered by this VLR, the VLR can use the n copies of the triplet authentication parameters to authenticate the MS for each call until the VLR uses up the set of parameters. Once the VLR uses up the set, she/he just makes a request for another set of parameters from HLR.

Drawback of GSM Security Protocol:

(i) It is not a mutual authentication mechanism between mobile stations and base stations (VLR). GSM only provides unilateral authentication for the mobile stations. Using the challenge/response mechanism, the identity of a mobile station is verified. However, the identity of VLR cannot be authenticated. It is therefore possible for an intruder to pretend to be a legal network entity and thus to get the mobile stations.

(ii) The VLR must turn back t the HLR to make a request for another set of authentication parameters when the MS stays in the VLR for a long time and exhausts its set of authentication parameters for authentication. There is bandwidth consumption between the VLR and HLR.

(iii) Every mobile station in the particular VLR has n copies of the authentication parameters. The parameters are stored in the particular VLR database, and then space overhead occurs.

(iv) The authentication of an MS is done in the VLR and thus must be helped by the HLR of the MS for each communication.

3   Literature Review

To fix the above drawbacks, some revised GSM authentication protocols have been proposed [6-8] but those protocol change the basic security architecture of the GSM. Some of this protocol are not suitable for the ramming users and none of the protocols can fix all of the above drawbacks at a time. Furthermore, some protocols require that some additional hardware be added to the system, and others are changed to public-key cryptography, which means more computational costs. In 2004, Hwang et al. proposed an anonymous channel protocol where the mobile station could request services privately under the visit network [5]. The protocol uses tickets, secret key cryptosystem, and public key cryptosystem techniques. The architecture of the protocol is different from the GSM. Since the protocol uses a public key cryptosystem, the computational cost is very high. However, they cannot properly address the roaming users, furthermore their protocols are not suitable for roaming users. To a mobile user frequently roaming to another VLR, communication overheads occur. In 2004, Hahn et al. proposed an improved GSM authentication protocol for roaming users [9] They improved the GSM authentication protocol to reduce the signaling load for a roaming user. The protocol exploits the enhanced user profile containing a few VLR IDs a mobile user is most likely to visit. However, the protocol cannot solve all of the above problems and is not flexible. In 2006, Kumar et al. proposed an efficient identity based mutual authentication scheme for GSM[10]. It support the mutual authentication and reduce the storage overhead of VLR. But it change the basic security architecture of the GSM and is not suitable for the roaming users. In 2006, Ammayappan et al. proposed an improvement to the GSM authentication protocol, based on Elliptic Curve Cryptography (ECC)[11] change the architecture and the computational cost is high for public key cryptography.

4   Proposed Protocol

In this algorithm we use the asymmetric key cryptography for mutual authentication purpose over the symmetric key cryptography and symmetric key cryptography for data communication purpose for reduce the computational power. In this protocol there are two phase:

      1. Initial Registration Phase
      2. Mutual authentication phase.
      3. For ramming Users.

4.1 Initial Registration Phase

In this algorithm we assume that the HLR and valid VLR have the same public key and the same private key for simplicity. Other wise we also can use the different public key and private key.

The MS register in its home network for first time then the prime number G which is known by SIM and the HLR. At the time of initial registration with HLR, MS and HLR compute the secret key using diffe-Hallman algorithm. This
Phase consist of the following steps :

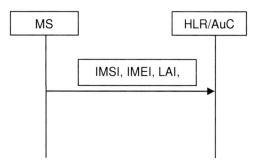

Fig. 3. Initial registration architecture

1. The MS sends the IMSI, the serial no. of the mobile phone, the current location with the public key of mobile station through the secure channel. Public key $P_{MS} = n_a * G$, where n_a is the private key of the mobile station.

2. After receiving the registration message the HLR check the IMSI no. If the no. is valid then the HLR generate the secret key $(K) = n_b * P_{MS}$ where n_b is the private key and sends the public key $P_{H-V} = n_b * G$ to the MS.

3. After receiving the public key the MS also calculate the secret key $(K) = n_a * P_{H-V}$.

4.2 Mutual Authentication in Home Network

After the registration phase first time when the mobile station communicate then the following steps occurs for the mutual authentication and the diagram shown in the fig 4.

1. The MS sends the IMSI number time stamp T1which is encrypted by the public key of VLR/HLR.

2. VLR decrypt the message by using its private key, and save the IMSI, T1 and send this data with its own authenticated Id i.e V_{Id}. And encrypted this data by using its own public key, send to the HLR.

3. HLR decrypt the message and check the V_{Id} ,IMSI no. and T1 . if they are valid then it generate the certificate for VLR and send its encrypted form to the VLR and another copy of certificate for the MS which is encrypted by the public key of the MS. CERT = $K_i * T1$.

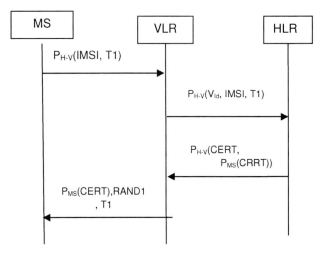

Fig. 4. Architecture for mutual authentication

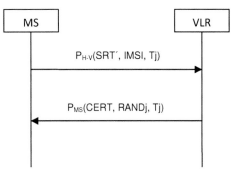

Fig. 5. J^{th} registration phase

4. VLR send the encrypted CERT with the T1 and RAND1. RAND1 is generated by the random no. generator which is stored in the VLR and use to generate the session key between MS and VLR. KC_1= RAND1* K. And save the CERT for further use.

5. MS check the T1 , if it is valid then it calculate the CERT´ = K_i * T1. If CERT= CERT´ then it calculate the session key which is used for the data encryption. And save CERT´ to its database for further use.

If the MS stay for longer time in the same network, then the following steps occur from the second time. For j^{th} time:

1. MS calculate SRT´ = A3(K * Tj). And send the SRT´ IMSI and Tj which are encrypted by the punlic key of VLR.

2. After getting this message the VLR Calculate the SRT= A3(K * Tj) and check whether it is or not with SRT´. If it is equal then it Generate RANDj and send the CERT to the MS . it calculate the cipher key KC_j = RANDj* k

3.MS compare it with the saved CERT´. if they are equal then it calculate the cipher key KC_j= RANDj* k.

4.3 Authentication Protocol for Roaming Users

When the Mobile Station visit from its home network to the foreign network then it need to authentication to the foreign network. Let the Mobile Station move from the VLR1 to VLR2 then the authentication takes the following steps:

1. The MS send an authentication request to the foreign VLR. The request contain the TMSI1, signed result (SRT´ = A3(K* Ty)), and the time stamp Ty.

2. the VLR2 send the TMSI1 to the VLR1 .

3. the VLR1 then send the IMSI, CERT, and the secret key K encrypted by the public key of the VLR2.

4. The VLR2 decrypted the message which is coming from the VLR1 and calculate the SRT = A3(K*Ty) and compare with SRT´ , if both are same the it send the CERT, the random number which is generated by the VLR2 (RANDy), and the time stamp(Ty).

5. after getting the message from the VLR2, the MS first check the Ty, then it compare the CERT which are initially saved to the MS database to the CERT which is coming from the VLR2. If they are equal then the VLR2 is authenticate. Then the MS calculate the cipher key KC_y = A8(K* RANDy).

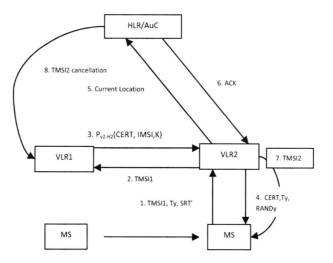

Fig. 6. Roaming protocol architecture

After the authentication the VLR2 send the location update message to the HLR, then the HRL send the ACK to the VLR2. After get the ACK reply the VLR2 send the TMSI2 to the MS and the HLR send the cancellation message to the previous VLR.

5 Analysis of Proposed Protocol

The GSM authenticate protocol must not only be secure but also efficient. In this section we compare the performance of our proposed protocol to the original GSM authentication and other GSM security protocol.

5.1 Comparison Goal Analysis

Here we compare our protocol with other existing protocol base on the drawback point of the GSM authentication protocol in the table 2.

Roaming (RO): If a MS roams frequently, then the previous VLR only forward one copy of IMSI, CERT, K instead of n copy of authentication parameter. So it reduce the communication parameter and suitable for the roaming users.

Reduction of Bandwidth consumption (RBC):   As the HLR gives the secret key to the VLR and MS for authentication so as long MS stay in the coverage area of the same VLR or roams between VLRs. That is to say, the VLR does not turn back to the HLR to require another set of authentication parameter and thus bandwidth consumption between the HLR and the VLR is reduced.

Reduction of storage overhead in the VLR database (ROV): The VLR store only one copy of secret key, and CERT instead of saving n no of triplet and thus the storage space of VLR is reduce.

Reduction of overload of HLR (ROH): Our protocol reduces the overload of the HLR because the VLR communicate to the HLR for only one time and the output parameter just a single copy instead of n copy.

Mutual authentication: Here we assume that the HLR is a dependable authority with the capability of identifying the VLR using the Vid . Once the VLR can be verified the HLR can assign the certificate (CERT) and send the CERT to the VLR with one copy of CERT encrypted by the public key of MS which is used the authenticate the VLR to the MS . The SRJ is use to authenticate the MS to the VLR.

Table 2. Compression among GSM protocols

Ref. no	RO	RBC	RSO	ROH	MA	AC
Original	N	N	N	N	N	_
Our	Y	Y	Y	Y	Y	N
[12]	N	Y	Y	Y	Y	N
[14]	N	Y	N	N	N	Y
[13]	N	Y	Y	Y	Y	N
[15]	N	Y	N	N	N	Y
[9]	Y	N	N	N	N	N
[7]	N	Y	Y	Y	Y	Y

The AC means it change the actual architecture of the GSM security, Y denotes yes, N denotes no.

5.2 Delay Comparison

The authentication delay in the GSM network consists of the time from when the subscriber begins the authentication process until the network decides to either accept or reject the subscriber. In fact, the exchange of authentication messages between the subscriber and the BTS results in a transmission delay. Let us assume that the time delay due to the network database (DB) message exchange is TDB and it is the same between all of them. And the time between MS and BTS is TRF. The Authentication delay of the original GSM security protocol [14] is TAd = 4TDB + 3TRF. The authentication delay of our protocol is TAd = 2 TFR from the fig. 7.

5.3 Comparison with the Signaling Messages

The term signaling refers to the set of actions required to set up a connection between hosts across the network under software control. Actions here are messages sent from different GSM entities. Using the same model and analysis used in analyzing GSM protocol, we find that the number of messages is clearly less than the conventional GSM protocol. In Table 3, we find the number of signaling message per authentication request for each database register (AuC, VLR and HLR) using the rate of authentication requests per second for each type of activity (registration, call termination and origination).

Table 3. Signaling message per authentication request

Activity	Original GSM HLR VLR		Ref. 14 HLR VLR		Ref. 8 HLR VLR		Ref. 1 HLR VLR		Proposed HLR VLR	
Registrati on	4	5	2	2	4	4	2	2	1	2
Call origination	4	5	2	2	0	1	0	1	0	1
Calltermination	4	5	2	2	0	1	0	1	0	1

5.4 Security Analysis

In this section, we discuss the security of the proposed scheme. The proposed mutual key agreement protocol will be considered to be a secure authenticated   key establishment protocol, if it satisfies the following properties:

know-key Security: Suppose that adversary E has derived session keys of past communication sessions, But that is useless for E to obtain the new session or counterfeit any participants since in our proposed protocol, the server generate new RANDj every new session, and in addition the shared key is generated with every new session also. Another important aspect of our protocol is that the shared secret key is calculated independently on both sides and protected by the secure hash function. thus our proposed protocol is secure against any adversary known key attacks.

Dictionary attack: The dictionary attack could be performed in offline or online mode. An on-line password guessing attack cannot succeed since service provider can choose appropriate trail intervals. On the other hand, in an off- line password guessing attack, it is impossible to get the real password since a one way hash function is applied to the password. During the protocol process, the shared Key   used to generate the session key in every new session; and by assuming the intractability of elliptic curve discrete logarithm problem. Therefore the proposed protocol resists the offline and online dictionary attack.

Perfect forward secrecy: We assume that adversary E had known the card reader's or service provider's private key (even both) , it is also difficult for E to obtain the old session key consulted between card reader or service provider. the session key Kc = RANDj*k,RANDj is a random numbers generated form service provider. Thus, our protocol satisfies the property of perfect forward secrecy.

Passive attack: A passive attack can be possible if adversary E, the attacker, make a guess at the session key using only information obtainable over network. If the attacker E perform a passive attack, then the session will terminate with both parties accepting. That is, service provider and card reader successfully identify themselves to each other, and they both compute the session key. So, E the adversary, cannot compute any information about the   common   shared   session   key   due   to   the intractability of elliptic curve discrete logarithm problem. Therefore the proposed protocol resists against the passive attack.

Man in middle attack: It can be considered as an active attack. In this protocol no useful information about the secret key   is revealed during a successful run. this protocol resists the man in middle attack.

6 Conclusion

Presently 3G and 4G mobile systems are becoming more and more dominant in the market. But for the low cost and simplicity the old standard of Pan-European digital cellular system (GSM) still very popular. Many telecommunication companies still use the GSM technology or it integrated with their 3G or 4G system. Many authentication protocols have been developed to improve the original authentication protocol of GSM, but they have not taken the roaming users into account and mostly cannot solve the problems without modifying the architecture of GSM. But in our proposed protocol the GSM security drawbacks solved without changing the actual GSM security architecture.

References

1. Lee, C.-C., Liaol-En, Hwang, M.-S.: An efficient authentication protocol for mobile communications. Telecommun. Syst. (2010), doi:10.1007/s11235-009-9276-4.2010
2. Dominguez, A.P.: Cryptanalysis of Parka's authentication protocol in wireless mobile communication systems. International Journal of Network Security 3(3), 279–282 (2006)
3. Hwang, M.-S.: Dynamic participation in a secure conference scheme for mobile communications. IEEE Transactions on Vehicular Technology 48(5), 1469–1474 (1999)
4. http://www.roggeweck.net/uploads/media/StudentGSM_Architecture.pdf

5. Hwang, M.-S., Lee, C.-C., Lee, J.-Z.: A new anonymous channel protocol in wirelesscommunications. International Journal on Electronics and Communications 58(3), 218–222 (2004)
6. Kumar, K.P., Shailaja, G., Kavitha, A., Saxena, A.: Mutual authentication and key agreement for GSM. In: International Conference on Mobile Business, pp. 25–28 (June 2006)
7. Ammayappan, K., Saxena, A., Negi, A.: Mutual authentication and key agreement based on elliptic curve cryptography for GSM. In: International Conference on Advanced Computing and Communications, pp. 183–186 (December 2006)
8. Fanian, A., Berenjkoub, M., Gulliver, T.A.: A new mutual authentication protocol for GSM networks. In: Canadian Conference on Electrical and Computer Engineering, pp. 798–803 (May 2009)
9. Hahn, G., Kwon, T., Kim, S., Song, J.: Design and analysis of improved GSM authentication protocol for roaming users. In: Jin, H., Gao, G.R., Xu, Z., Chen, H. (eds.) NPC 2004. LNCS, vol. 3222, pp. 451–458. Springer, Heidelberg (2004)
10. Kumar, K.P., Shailaja, G., Kavitha, A., Saxena, A.: Mutual authentication and key agreement for GSM. In: International Conference on Mobile Business, pp. 25–28 (June 2006)
11. Ammayappan, K., Saxena, A., Negi, A.: Mutual authentication and key agreement based on elliptic curve cryptography for GSM. In: International Conference on Advanced Computing and Communications, pp. 183–186 (2006)
12. Smith, T.F., Waterman, M.S.: Identification of Common Molecular Subsequences. J. Mol. Biol. 147, 195–197 (1981)
13. May, P., Ehrlich, H.C., Steinke, T.: ZIB Structure Prediction Pipeline: Composing a Complex Biological Workflow through Web Services. In: Nagel, W.E., Walter, W.V., Lehner, W. (eds.) Euro-Par 2006. LNCS, vol. 4128, pp. 1148–1158. Springer, Heidelberg (2006)
14. Foster, I., Kesselman, C.: The Grid: Blueprint for a New Computing Infrastructure. Morgan Kaufmann, San Francisco (1999)
15. Czajkowski, K., Fitzgerald, S., Foster, I., Kesselman, C.: Grid Information Services for Distributed Resource Sharing. In: 10th IEEE International Symposium on High Performance Distributed Computing, pp. 181–184. IEEE Press, New York (2001)
16. Foster, I., Kesselman, C., Nick, J., Tuecke, S.: The Physiology of the Grid: an Open Grid Services Architecture for Distributed Systems Integration. Technical report, Global Grid Forum, National Center for Biotechnology Information (2002), http://www.ncbi.nlm.nih.gov

Optimization of Prefetching in Peer-to-Peer Video on Demand Systems

Parag Bafna and B. Annappa

Department of Computer Science and Engineering
National Institute of Technology Karnataka, Surathkal, India - 575025
bafnaparag@gmail.com, annappa@ieee.org

Abstract. In Peer-to-Peer Video on Demand System like Video Cassette Recording (VCR) various operations (i.e. forward, backward, resume) are found to be used very frequently. The uncertainty of frequent VCR operations makes it difficult to provide services like play as download. To address this problem, there exist algorithms like random prefetching, distributed prefetching, etc. But each such algorithm has its own advantage and disadvantages. So to overcome the problem of prefetching we propose optimize prefetching for Peer-to-Peer(P2P) Video on Demand systems.The simulation result proves that the proposed prefetching algorithm significantly reduces the seeking delay as compared with the random prefetching scheme.

Keywords: Peer-to-Peer, Video on Demand, Distributed Prefetching, Random Prefetching, Seeking delay.

1 Introduction

Multimedia communication has been in continuous state of evolution over the past few decades. After the application level multicast, video streaming is boosted by Peer-to-Peer(P2P) networks. Multimedia streaming can be categorized into live streaming and on-demand streaming. In live streaming systems, the source servers broadcast videos, and all the clients are synchronous.Successful examples include CoolStreaming[1], and PPLive[2]. On the other hand, On-demand streaming or Video on Demand is an interactive multimedia service, which delivers video content to the users on his/her demand. Differing live streaming, for on-demand streaming, clients mostly demands different videos or different parts of the same video[10].

It is found that Video on Demand (VoD) is increasingly popular with Internet users. VoD is compelling because it provides users with video stream control, such as pause and random seek which results in increase seeking delay and stress on streaming server.The uncertainty of frequent VCR operations makes it difficult to provide high quality real-time streaming services. To address this problem, prefetching is proposed. In a data prefetching, peers prefetch and store various portions of the streaming media ahead of their playing position, which grants peers the ability to overcome the departure of source peer and to smooth

D.C. Wyld et al. (Eds.): NeCoM/WeST/WiMoN 2011, CCIS 197, pp. 100–106, 2011.

video playing experience. The prefetched portion of content can also serve to other peers on the network which requires some additional bandwidth and storage.Considering the increasing stress on bandwidth, storage capability on local peers nowadays, it certainly offers a more desirable tradeoff between quality and cost. In this paper we proposed an optimized prefetching strategy and compared our strategy with strategies like random prefetching strategy.

The rest of this paper is organized in different sections as follows. In section 2, we discuss the related work. In section 3, we discuss our proposed optimize prefetching strategy. Section 4 illustrates the performance evaluation and comparison of our strategy with random prefetching strategy. Section 5 presents final conclusion.

2   Related Work

In random prefetching[6] it has been observed that it randomly start to select the media chuck which is actually not required for proper functioning of on demand video streaming .The behavior of user while accessing the video chunk is unpredictable so random prefetching does not provides effective solution to such problem. Where as, in case of distributed prefetching[5], user viewing behavior logs are maintained by a tracker server which improves hit ratio by considering users access patterns, however extracting a user viewing pattern from user viewing behavior logs require large computation to be performed by tracker server.

3   Optimization of Prefetching

In order to overcome drawbacks of various prefetching techniques discussed in earlier section, we proposed a new prefetching technique called optimize prefetching strategy. In this technique, every peer node maintains the record of playback media chunks (video divided into media chunks) by other peers in the same session-interval. This information is obtained through mutual sharing basis. After collecting state information from all peers (in same session-interval), a table of available media chunks is constructed by each peer in that particular session-interval. Table 1 shows peers obtained state information.

Table 1. Information received by peer I

Peer ID	Records
I	1 2 5 8 11 20
J	5 6 7 8 9 11
K	1 2 8 15 16 17
L	6 8 9 11 12 17
M	9 10 11 12 13
N	4 5 6 7 8 9 20
O	2 3 4 6 7 8
P	3 4 5 6 7 8 9

Table 2. List created by peer I

media chunk number	media chunk count
1	2
2	3
3	2
4	4
5	4
6	5
7	4
8	7
9	5
10	0
11	4
12	2
13	1
14	0
15	1
16	1
17	2
18	0
19	0
20	2

Each peer performs the necessary computation to create a list shown below (Table 2). First column of the list contain media chunk number and second column contain number of occurrence of that media chunk in record. The peer then requests for a media chunk near to its play head position, which does not exist in that session-interval (count=0). In case of Table 2 missing media chunks like 10, 14, 18, and 19 would be requested from peers in other session-interval depending on current play head position. If there is no such media chunk exists than peer request for a media chunk which has highest count in list (count is present in second column of list). Dead response from shortcut neighbors results in the desired media chunk request from server as a last resort. Each peer also prefetch the media chunks near to its play head position as an urgent downloading target. If bandwidth allows, the peer also tries to fetch *anchors*. Anchors are media chunks each consisting of 10 continuous seconds and are distributed throughout the media file with fixed interval (e.g. 300 seconds). The algorithm for optimize prefetching strategy is as shown below.

3.1 Proposed Prefetching Algorithm

```
Media chunk select ()
/* find the next segment to prefetch*/
{
    Find the media chunk MCi that didn't exist in buffermap // count =0
    Return MC ; // MC is the desired media chunk
}
```

```
Media chunk select1 ()
{
    Find the media chunk MCi that did exist in buffermap with highest count
    Return MC; // MC is the desired media chunk
}
Void Prefetch () // the function to do prefetching
{
    While (true or prefetching set is not empty)
    {
        Media chunk MC = select ();
        If (MC != NULL)
        Goto : Download
        Else
        Media chunk MC = select1 ();
        If (MC != NULL)
        Goto : Download
        Else if (bandwidth_is_available)
        {
            Downlaod anchor;
            Exit ;
        }
        Else
        Exit ;
        Download :
        Broadcast(MC);
        /* broadcast the prefetching of media chunk*/
        If (Media chunk MC is cached by a peer in same session-interval)
        /*situation where same Media chunk is also requested by some other
        peer */
        {
            Download media chunk MC;
            Remove the media chunk MC from prefetching list;
        }
        Else if (Media chunk MC is located on a remote peer P)
        {
            Connect with the peer P;
            Download media chunk MC;
            Remove media chunk MC from the prefetching set;
        }
        Else // when timeout expires
        {
            Send the media chunk request to server;
            Connect with server;
            Download media chunk MC;
            Remove media chunk MC from prefetching set;
        }
    }
}
```

4   Performance Evaluation

We implemented an event-driven simulator coded in C++ to conduct a series of simulations. For end-to-end latency setup we employed real world node-to-node latency matrix (2500*2500) measured on internet[8]. One should note that we do not consider the queuing management in the routers. The default streaming rate is set to 500kbps. The upload and download bandwidth of peers is set to 500kbps.

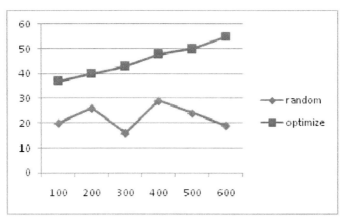

X-axis=Number of peers, Y-axis= VCR request satisfied by segments prefetched(%)

Fig. 1. Comparison of percentage of VCR request satisfied by segments prefetched

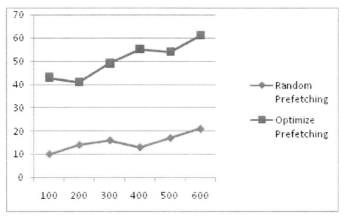

X-axis=Number of peers, Y-axis= ratio of the amount of played data to the amount of download data(%)

Fig. 2. Comparison of ratio of the amount of played data to the amount of download data

Figure 1 shows the comparison of percentage of VCR request satisfied by media chunks prefetched for optimize and random prefetching[6]. Optimize prefetching focus on downloading media chunk which is near to its play head position and rarest in the session-interval or have highest count where as in random prefetching media chunk is prefetched without following any rule.Figure 1 shows our scheme has satisfied higher percentage of VCR request of media chunk prefetching as compared with random prefetching.

Figure 2 shows comparison of the ratio of the amount of played data to the amount of download data of random prefetching and optimize prefetching. Figure 2 shows that optimize prefetching have higher ratio of the amount of played data to the amount of download data than random prefetching since random prefetching arbitrarily fetches media chunks.

5 Conclusion

Simulation and experimental study shows that there is need to provide Peer-to-Peer(P2P) based video on Demand service to users. But as most prefetching algorithms has their own limitations which makes them insufficient while providing Peer-to-Peer Video on Demand service.Therefore we proposed a novel method of Peer-to-Peer video prefetching technique which has minimal overhead of calculations, greater access to frequently accessed video/media chunks and reduced network traffic and efficient use of peers in network. The result obtained also helps us to track the frequently used media chunks by user and helps them to make available as per users request. The comparison of proposed technique with random prefetching shows the advantage of our proposed system over it. In future we are trying to develop the system that will help to utilize the available bandwidth efficiently by using our technique.

References

1. cool Streaming (March 11, 2011), http://www.coolstreaming.us
2. PPTV (March 11, 2011), http://www.pptv.com
3. He, Y., Liu, Y.: VOVO: VCR-Oriented Video-on-Demand in Large-Scale P2P Networks. In: Proc. of IEEE Trans. Parallel and Distributed Systems, vol. 20 (April 2008)
4. Yu, H., Zheng, D., Zhao, B., Zheng, W.: Understanding User Behavior in Large-Scale Videoon-Demand Systems. In: Proc. of EuroSys 2006 (2006)
5. Zheng, C., Shen, G., Li, S.: Distributed Prefetching Scheme for Random Seek Support in P2P Streaming Applications. In: Proc. of ACM Workshop on Advances in P2P Multimedia Streaming 2005 (2005)
6. Cheng, B., Jin, H., Liao, X.: Supporting VCR functions in P2P VoD services using ring assisted overlays. In: Proc. of ICC 2007 (2007)
7. Huang, C., Li, J., Ross, K.W.: Can Internet Video-on-Demand be Profitable. In: Proc. of ACM SigComm 2007 (2007)

8. Meridian node to node latency matrix (2500*2500) (2005), meridian project, http://www.cs.cornell.edu/People/egs/meridian/data.php
9. Cheng, B., Liu, X., Zhang, Z., Jin, H.: A Measurement Study of a Peer-to-Peer Video-on-Demand System. In: Proc. of IPTPS 2007, Belleue, USA (April 2007)
10. Cheng, B.: Huazhong University of Science and Technology; Stein, L.: Microsoft Research Asia; Jin, H., Liao, X., Huazhong University of Science and Technology; Zhang, Z.: Microsoft Research Asia. GridCast: Improving Peer Sharing for P2P VoD

Testing Resilience of Router against Denial of Service Attacks

Vishal Maruti Karande[1], Sandeep Nair Narayanan[1],
Alwyn Roshan Pais[1], and N. Balakrishnan[2]

[1] Information Security Lab, Dept. of Computer Science and Engineering,
National Institute of Technology Karnataka, Surathkal, India - 575025
{vishalmkarande,sandeepnairnarayanan,alwyn.pais}@gmail.com
[2] Dept. of SERC, Indian Institute of Science, Bangalore, India - 560012
balki@serc.iisc.ernet.in

Abstract. Provisioning data security and integrity in an IP network requires a detailed understanding of both the architecture and the performance of devices that are used within the network. A router interconnects two or more computer networks, and it becomes most common target for attackers to carry out Denial of Service Attacks. Thus it is necessary to study the effect of resource exhaustion attack on router with respect to its performance and security. In this paper, the proposed framework provides an effective method to evaluate router performance and its resilience against denial of service attacks. The feasibility of the framework has been demonstrated by carrying out different resource exhaustion attacks on device under test (DUT) i.e. router, and the resilience against the attacks is measured using a defined set of performance metrics.

Keywords: Denial of service attacks, Performance Testing, Resilience, Router Performance.

1 Introduction

Today most organizations are dependent on the performance and security of their network infrastructures. Building and securing network infrastructure in both normal and attack scenarios require a detailed understanding of the performance of devices that constitute the network infrastructure [12]. Enterprise networks are commonly based on a three tier model. The first layer includes Access Routers located in small offices which do not require hierarchical routing of their own. The second layer includes Distribution Routers which aggregate data from multiple Access Routers. These routers provide functionalities like QoS, VPN etc. The third layer includes the Core Routers which form the backbone network interconnecting different Distribution Routers. As router interconnects two or more computer networks by providing packet routing service, it becomes the most common target for attackers to carry out denial of service attacks.

Today different varieties of routers are provided by router vendors like Cisco, Juniper, Linksys etc. each having its own resilience against security attacks.

D.C. Wyld et al. (Eds.): NeCoM/WeST/WiMoN 2011, CCIS 197, pp. 107–116, 2011.
© Springer-Verlag Berlin Heidelberg 2011

Resilience is the ability of the router to cope with stress and adversity. Active routers offer the combined benefits of intrusion detection, firewall protection and work collaboratively to provide resilience against security threats. However combining all security measures in a single device for defense against security threats can result in a significant performance loss. Thus router vendors have to find balance point between performance and security while providing functionalities like QoS, VPN etc. Efficient router testing for finding its resilience level helps in building performance and security balance point.

This paper focuses on the generic router resilience testing framework independent of router architecture and underlying protocols, analyzing the potential threats and entry points. We have performed various denial of service attacks on device under test (DUT) i.e. router and performance of the router is measured with respect to performance metrics such as throughput (connections per second, packets per second), scalability, request/response delay, transaction duration, allocation of resources etc.

2   Background

2.1   Traffic Types

The different types of traffic handled by the routers include Transit IP packets, Receive IP packets and Exception IP/Non-IP Packets as shown in Fig 1.

- *Transit IP Packets.* These are the packets with the destination IP address which is not owned by any of the interfaces of the router, but an IP address which is accessible through the router. When a router sees a transit packet, the decision it makes is to forward the packet out to one of its interfaces.
- *Receive IP Packets.* IP packets that arrive at a router, and that are destined to an IP address owned by that router itself are called receive-adjacency packets. With receive-adjacency packets, the router cannot engage any specialized forwarding hardware; the router must process the packet itself using its own local CPU resources.

Fig. 1. Router Traffic

– *Exception IP and Non-IP Packets.* Exception IP packets (e.g. packet with TTL value 0) include transit or receive IP packets that have some exceptional characteristic about them and that cannot be handled by normal processing by the router. Non-IP packets (LCP, ARP etc) are the packets that are not part of the IP protocol.

2.2 Entry Points for Denial of Service Attacks

A Denial of Service attack on a router is an attempt to make a router resource unavailable to its intended users. These are also known as resource exhaustion attacks. The resources affected by such attacks are CPU, Packet Memory, Network Bandwidth, Route Memory, VTY Lines etc.[9] As CPU serves as a master controller of the router, packet flood attacks aim to saturate them with attack traffic, causing high CPU utilization. Packet memory is used to buffer the packets. Route memory is used to store route information and is used to provide IP reachability and traffic forwarding. When a router's buffers are exhausted, legitimate traffic is discarded, which may result in a DoS condition. A packet flood attack may be engineered to saturate a network link, affecting legitimate traffic forwarding across that link and resulting in a DoS condition.

3   Problem Statement

3.1   Conceptual Model

Conceptual models are used to help reduce the amount of complexity that must be comprehended at one time. The conceptual model of a router depicts how the packets are handled in a router, once it reaches the ingress interface of a router from any other network node. Here we have scoped our view above the data link layer. So the input to this model will be the Payload of a valid frame. Fig 2 describes how this input will be handled in any generic router.

Integrity check module does the initial check on IP packets like validation of header checksum, failing which the packet is dropped. Now the packet reaches the Header Processing and Route lookup module where the IP header will be

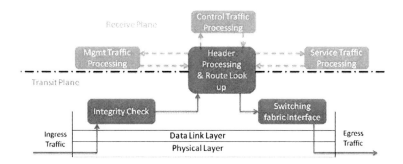

Fig. 2. Router Conceptual model

examined and reconstructed to decide on the action to be performed on the packet. The processing's done here include Packet Validation and Reconstruction, Inbound/Outbound Filtering, Packet Classification into different traffic types, Higher Layer Protocol Classification, Route Lookup etc. Now the receive IP packets will be sent to the different processing units for further processing. For the transit IP packets, the next hop interface will be found and are sent to the switching fabric interface. In case of any exceptions this unit will generate the exception IP packets. Once the next hop router is found the packets will be sent to the Switching Fabric Interface where it will be sent to the required interface. Some of the different switching mechanisms include shared medium switch, shared memory switch fabric, cross bar switch, space time division switch etc.

The management processing unit is the logical unit responsible for handling the management traffic, which are used for managing the various activities of the router. Some of the most common management protocols found in routers are FTP, TFTP, HTTP, HTTPS etc. The Control processing unit handles the control traffic related to the routing protocols. They make the router intelligent such that the packets are routed to the correct interface to reach its destination, through the shortest path. The different protocols which come under this category are BGP, OSPF, RIP etc. The logical handling of the traffic related to the extra services provided by a router, apart from its core functionality of routing is performed by the Service Processing unit. E.g. NAT, QoS etc.

3.2   Adversary Model

Fig.3 shows the classification of vulnerabilities based on the conceptual model presented in the above section. Each of the vulnerabilities defined here has, *Vulnerability Name* which is the position of the vulnerability in the model, *Vulnerability Action* which is the action which causes the vulnerability to be exploited. For e.g., flooding, malformed packets, protocol mismatch etc., and *Vulnerability Result* which is the result which will be produced, once the vulnerability is exploited. The major categories are,

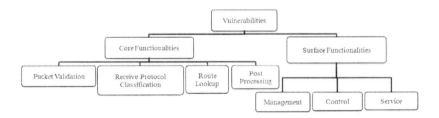

Fig. 3. Router Vulnerablities

Core Functionalities. The vulnerabilities related to the core functions of the router like Packet validation, Receive Protocol Classification, Route Lookup, and Post processing come under this section. They are enlisted in Table 1.

Table 1. Entry Points for Core Functionalities attacks

Type	Name	Action	Result
Packet Validation	TTL expiry Attack	Flooding	Denial of Service
Receive Protocol Classification	SYN Flood Attack	Flooding	Denial of Service
Receive Protocol Classification	UDP Flood Attack	Flooding	Denial of Service
Route Look Up	Invalid Route Attack	Flooding	Denial of Service
Post Processing	Options Filed Attack	Flooding	Denial of Service

Surface Functionalities. This subsection includes all the vulnerabilities possible for the functionalities other than the core functions of the router. The surface functionalities are broadly classified as Management Processing, Control Processing, and Service Processing. The vulnerabilities relating to each of these surface functionalities are enlisted in Table 2, Table 3, and Table 4 respectively. Each protocol can have design or implementation vulnerability[4].

Table 2. Entry Points for Management Processing Attacks

Protocol	Type	Name	Action	Result
Telnet, FTP	Design	Plain Password	Injection	Unauthorized Access
Telnet	Implementation	Authentication Bypass	Injection	Unauthorized Access
FTP	Implementation	Authentication Bypass	Injection	Information Disclosure
TFTP	Implementation	Long File Name	Injection	Denial of Service
TFTP	Design	No Authentication	Injection	Unauthorized Access
SSH	Implementation	Protocol Mismatch	Injection	Unauthorized Access

Table 3. Entry Points for Control Processing Attacks

Protocol	Type	Name	Action	Result
RIPv1	Design	No Authentication	Injection	DoS, Information Disclosure
RIPv2	Design	Clear Text Authentication	Injection	DoS, Information Disclosure
OSPF	Design	Clear Text Authentication	Injection	DoS, Information Disclosure

Table 4. Entry Points for Service Processing Attacks

Protocol	Type	Name	Action	Result
VPN	Implementation	Malformed Packet	Injection	Denial of Service
NAT	Implementation	NAT Skinny Call Control Protocol Vulnerability	Injection	Denial of Service
OSPF	Implementation	Virtual Private Dial-up Network Vulnerability	Injection	Denial of Service
MVPN	Implementation	MVPN Data Leak	Injection	Unauthorized Access

3.3   Performance Metrics

In our study we have used the following standard performance testing metrics for router testing[9][11].

- *Throughput*. It is measured in terms of Connections per second. Connections per second (c/s) refer to the rate at which a device can establish state parameters for new connections.
- *Packets per second*. It is the maximum number of packets per second processed by the router.
- *Scalability*. It is measured in terms of maximum concurrent connections per second. It refers to the total number of sessions (connections) about which a device can maintain its state simultaneously.
- *Request/Response Delay*. It measures the response time of the router for a particular type of processing request traffic sent to it.
- *Transaction Duration*. It is the time taken by the router to process particular type of traffic (Transit traffic/ Receive traffic).
- *Allocation of Resources*. It measures resources allocated while processing particular type of traffic. Resources are router CPU, VTY lines, route memory, temporary buffers etc.

4   Performance and Resilience Testing

4.1   Testing Framework

Fig.4 shows the framework used for testing router performance and resilience. Denial of Service attacks can be carried out using both normal and unusual traffic. As the router performance degrades with the introduction of more services, the testing is performed with router services enabled and services disabled[3].

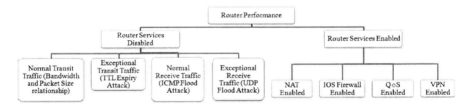

Fig. 4. Router Testing Framework

4.2   System under Test

To test the routers performance and resilience we have set up the test bed as shown in Fig.5. The entities involved in the test bed are DUT i.e. Cisco 2600 and Cisco 2821 router[10], User hosts (Linux/Windows machines), Switches, IXIA traffic generator running using IXExplore and IXLoad[13].

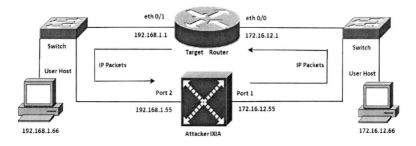

Fig. 5. Experimental Test Bed

4.3   Performance Measurement and Results

Normal Transit Traffic.
Traffic Type.

- Unidirectional traffic routed from port-1 to port-2 of IXIA.
- 3 streams of 30,000 packets per burst each looped 100 times.
- Line rate: 1000Mbps Max, which keeps changing, to observe the packet loss.
- Different packet sizes: 64,256, 512, 1024, 1500 (in bytes)[1].

Inference. For smaller packet size the packet drop occurs for lower line rate as compared to large sized packets. This proves the inverse relationship of the packet size with the line rate. Thus router performance is largely dependent on the packet size and line rate as shown in the Fig.6.

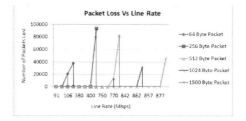

Fig. 6. Number of Packets Lost Vs Line Rate

```
[root@localhost ~]# telnet 172.16.12.1
Trying 172.16.12.1...
telnet: connect to address 172.16.12.1: No route to host
telnet: Unable to connect to remote host: No route to host
[root@localhost ~]# ▮
```

Fig. 7. Unsuccessful Telnet Attempt to the Router

Exceptional Transit Traffic (TTL expiry attack). Under normal conditions, routers are capable of processing exception packets. However, under attack conditions where the number of TTL expiry packets is large, high CPU utilization may result, leading to denial of service to slow path traffic[8]. Fig.7 shows unsuccessful telnet attempt to the router.

Normal Receive Traffic (ICMP flood attack)
Traffic Type.

- Unidirectional traffic routed from port-1 to port-2 of IXIA.
- 3 streams of 30,000 packets per burst each looped 100 times, Frame size: 1024 bytes.

Case 1:

- 2 Streams sending normal IP transit traffic from port-1 to port-2 of IXIA.
- 1 Stream sending ICMP packets destined to router on some random port.

Case 2:

- 1 Stream sending normal IP transit traffic from port-1 to port-2 of IXIA.
- 2 Streams sending ICMP packets destined to router on some random port.

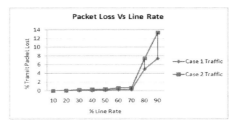

Fig. 8. Transit packet lost (%) Vs Line rate (%) in ICMP Flood Attack

For each case line rate is varied from 10% to 90%. (1000 Mbps max.) For both traffic cases as shown in Fig.8, when the line rate is increased beyond 70% the percentage of packets dropped by the router increases drastically. The drop rate increases with increase in attack traffic rate. (Percentage of drop in packets at the router is more in case-2 traffic). For attack traffic the ICMP error messages generated by the router are captured at host machine using Wireshark. Thus increase in line rate and attack traffic rate result in increased packet drop causing DoS attack by ICMP flooding.

Exceptional Receive Traffic (UDP flood attack).
Traffic Type.

- Unidirectional traffic routed from port-1 to port-2 of IXIA.
- 3 streams of 30,000 packets per burst each looped 100 times, Frame size: 1024 bytes.

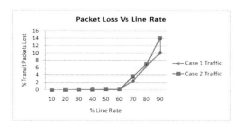

Fig. 9. Transit packet lost (%) Vs Line rate (%) in UDP Flood Attack

Case 1:

- 2 Streams sending normal IP transit traffic from port-1 to port-2 of IXIA.
- 1 Stream sending UDP packets destined to router on some random port.

Case 2:

- 1 Stream sending normal IP transit traffic from port-1 to port-2 of IXIA.
- 2 Streams sending UDP packets destined to router on some random port.

For each case line rate is varied from 10% to 90% (1000 Mbps max.). For both traffic cases as shown in Fig.9, when the line rate is increased beyond 60% the percentage of packets dropped by the router increases drastically. The drop rate increases with increase in attack traffic rate. (Percentage of drop in packets at the router is more in case-2 traffic). For attack traffic the ICMP error messages generated by the router are captured at host machine using Wireshark. Thus increase in line rate and attack traffic rate result in increased packet drop causing DoS attack by UDP flooding.

Tests Inference. Above results show that resilience of router varies with type of attacks performed. Thus based on position, in the organization's network infrastructure (Three Tier Architecture) proper choice of router can be made using proposed performance testing approach.

5   Conclusion and Future Work

In this paper we proposed a novel approach for testing the performance and resilience of the router against DoS attacks. We identified threats and their entry points for resource exhaustion attacks based on the conceptual model of DUT i.e. router. In order to test the compliance of router performance to the security requirements, we proposed a testing framework which is easily extensible by adding number of test case DoS attacks targeted on the router. Based on the testing framework we have successfully conducted a set of resource exhaustion attacks on DUT. Performance analysis clearly shows that routers have different resilience capability against different types of DoS attacks. This testing approach can be used to validate routers produced to build secure infrastructure.

Future work involves identifying new threats and their entry points in the router conceptual model. Proposed framework can be extended to test the router performance and resilience against number of denial of service attacks with number of router services enabled.

Acknowledgments. We would like to express our appreciation to Prof. N. Balakrishnan, Dept. of SERC, IISc Bangalore for valuable support of this research.

References

1. Antonios, I., Lipsky, L.: On the Relationship between Packet Size and Router Performance for Heavy-Tailed Traffic. In: Southern Connecticut State University, NCA 2004 Proceedings of the Network Computing and Applications. IEEE Press, Los Alamitos (2004)
2. Adami, D., Carlotti, N., Giordano, S., Pagano, M., Repeti, M.: Performance Analysis of the Control and Forwarding Plane in an MPLS Router. In: IFIP International Federation for Information Processing, pp. 254–262 (2005)
3. Zeng, H., Zhou, X., Song, B.: On testing of IP routers. In: Parallel and Distributed Computing, Applications and Technologies, p. 61 (2003)
4. Mirkovic, J., Reiher, P.: A taxonomy of DDoS attack and DDoS defense mechanisms. ACM SIGCOMM Comp. Comm. Review 34(2), 39–53 (2004)
5. Xu, Y., Gurin, R.: On the robustness of router-based denial-of-service (DoS) defense systems. ACM SIGCOMM Comp. Comm. Review 35(3) (2005)
6. Elmiligi, M., El-Kharash, G.: Performance Analysis of Networks-on-Chip Routers. In: 2nd Int'l Design and Test Workshop, IDT 2007, p. 232 (2007)
7. Hu, Y.-H., Choi, H., Choi, H.-A.: Packet Filtering for Congestion Control under DoS Attacks. IEEE Press, Charlotte (2004)
8. Vladimirov, A.A., Vizulis, J.N., Mikhailovsky, A.A.: Hacking Exposed Cisco Networks: Cisco Security Secrets and Solutions (2006)
9. Schudel, G., Smith, D.J.: Router Security Strategies - Securing IP Network Traffic Planes. Cisco Press (2008)
10. Portable product sheet- Router Performance, http://www.cisco.com/
11. Bandwidth, Packets per Second, and Other Network Performance Metrics, http://www.cisco.com/
12. Weidong, W.U.: Packet Forwarding Technologies (2008)
13. IxExplore, IxLoad, http://www.ixiacom.com/
14. Active Network Security Tool-hping, http://www.hping.org/

NetALM: Network Based Application Layer Multicast for Multiparty Video Conference in OverLay Networks

T. Ruso and C. Chellappan

Department of Computer Science & Engineering,
Anna University, Chennai
racingruso@gmail.com, drcc@annauniv.edu

Abstract. The purpose of this work is to maintain efficient backup routes for reconstructing overlay trees quickly. In most conventional methods, after a nodes leaves the trees, its children start searching for a new parent. In real time applications, this kind of reactive approach is not suited because this approach takes a lot of time to find a new parent. We propose a NetALM: Network based Application Layer Multicast protocol, which is used to form a multicast tree in a hierarchical order. In this proactive approach allows a node to finds its new parent immediately and switch to the backup smoothly. In our proposal, the structure of the overlay tree is resource aware. The higher capability resource nodes will be in the higher level of the tree. This tree structure is used to do smooth data distribution for our multiparty video conference application. In this application, we are dividing the users into two categories are Participants and Spectators. Participants can send both audio and video packets to other ends. However, Spectators can not send any audio and video packets; they can only receive the audio and video packets. Using these two methods we can utilize the internet bandwidth.

Keywords: Application Layer Multicast, Overlay tree, Participants, Spectator, peer to peer.

1 Introduction

Multicasting services are increasing in popularity as service providers take advantage of multicasting solutions to efficiently distribute content to a large number of users. For example, multicasting can be used to provide streaming content such as news or video to many subscribers. ALM (Application Layer Multicast) implements the multicast functionally at end-hosts[1]. Different from IP multicasting, which unrealistically needs global deployment of routers with IP multicasting capability, ALM needs only installation of application software and requires no change in the current network infrastructure. In addition, it provides flexibility in routing such as multipath packet transfer and load balancing. The most active research area in ALM is design of routing protocols [2]-[6]. There are several measures to evaluate the effectiveness of the routing protocols as the following: (a) quality of the data delivery path, that is measured by stress, stretch and node degree parameters of overlay multicast tree, (b) robustness of the overlay, that is measured by the recovery time to

D.C. Wyld et al. (Eds.): NeCoM/WeST/WiMoN 2011, CCIS 197, pp. 117–126, 2011.
© Springer-Verlag Berlin Heidelberg 2011

reconstruct a packet delivery tree after sudden end host failures, and (c) control overhead, that represents protocol scalability for a large number of receivers.

In the ALM session, each end host is a member of the delivery tree, and it leaves freely and may fail sometimes. This is not a problem in IP multicast, because the non-leaf nodes in the delivery tree are routers and do not leave the multicast tree without notification. In ALM, one of the problems which we have to consider is to reconstruct the overlay multicast tree after a node departure [3]. The time to receive the data flow again after a node departure is important for multicast applications such as live media streaming, because all the children nodes are disconnected. It is therefore quite important to maintain the media quality by quickly reconstructing the overlay trees, but little attention has been given to this problem. Most researchers use a reactive approach, in which nodes start searching for their new parent after departure of their old parent node. It usually takes several seconds to restore the overlay tree. It is therefore important to find an effective mechanism to reconstruct the overlay trees.

On the other hand, a proactive approach takes into account the node departure before it happens. The basic idea is that each nonleaf node in the overlay multicast tree pre-computes a backup route. In Probabilistic Resilient Multicast (PRM) [11], each host chooses a constant number of other hosts at random and forwards data to each of them with a low probability. It enables each host to have a backup route. However, PRM generates extra data overhead. Another proactive approach was proposed by Yang et al [12], which we call Yang's approach in this paper. It calculates the *degree* each host has, and ensures backup route proactively whenever a node leaves or joins. *Degree* represents a outbound link. It is inevitable to consider the degree bound in overlay multicast, which can be easily observed in streaming applications. Each host limits the number of children on the tree it is willing to support.

We therefore propose a new proactive approach in order to avoid the degree limitation and generating heavy overheads [4] [9]. By placing higher capability node in terms of available memory, processor speed etc., in the higher level of the tree. This method will produce the hierarchical structure tree. Using this tree, we can replace if any node failure in any level of the tree. Most of the video conference users are coming from the Local Area Network (LAN). The bandwidth of LAN is always same. So we are not considering this parameter to form the multicast tree. Furthermore, we implemented our proposal in software, and experimented with live video streaming over the actual network. The results of our implementation verify the effectiveness of our approach and convince us that our proposal achieved better streaming quality.

The rest of this paper is organized as follows. In section 2, we detail our related work. In section 3, we introduce the routing algorithms on different network topologies and under various traffic conditions. In section 4, we detail our video conference application. In section 5, we discuss some of the Experimental output we conclude in Section 6.

2   Application Layer Multicast Introduction

2.1   ALM Fundamentals

The basic idea of application-layer multicast is shown in Figure 1. Unlike native multicast where data packets are replicated at routers inside the network, in application layer multicast data packets are replicated at end hosts.

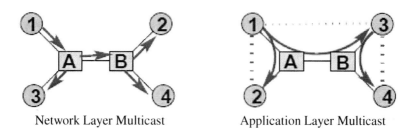

Network Layer Multicast   Application Layer Multicast

Fig. 1. Network-layer and application layer multicast. Square nodes are routers, and circular nodes are end circular nodes are end-hosts. The dotted lines represent peers on the overlay.

Logically, the end-hosts form an overlay network, and the goal of application-layer multicast is to construct and maintain an efficient overlay for data transmission. Since application-layer multicast protocols must send the identical packets over the same link, they are less efficient than native multicast. Two intuitive measures of "goodness" for application layer multicast overlays, namely *stress* and *stretch*, were defined in [9]). The stress metric is defined per-link and counts the number of identical packets sent by a protocol over each underlying link in the network. The stretch metric is defined per-member and is the ratio of path-length from the source to the member along the overlay to the length of the direct unicast path. Consider an application-layer multicast protocol in which the data source unicasts the data to each receiver.

It is obvious that ALM is less efficient than IP multicast. While routers in IP multicast try to avoid multiple copies of the same packet over the same link, by constructing optimal multicast trees, in ALM packets may traverse the same link several times. Furthermore, end hosts do not have detailed information about routing or network topology, so, they usually work with limited topology information, based on end-to-end measurements, like round-trip time (RTT) or end-to-end bandwidth, to construct the overlay tree.

2.2   Related Work

There are lot of ALM protocols have been addressed so for, from those protocols, there are three popular protocols such as NICE, ZIGZAG and OMNI [2]. NICE protocol talked about two important factors such as stress, and stretch. Stress is the number of redundant packets that are send in one link. Stretch deals with per member the ratio of path length to the total path length. Layer formation in nice protocol, at first all the nodes are at layer 0. With some basic Behavior they form the cluster in layer 0, this time layer 0 has no of clusters. A centre node is selected as leader in each cluster and all the leader is moved to the layer 1. In this layer they form the cluster. From this cluster another leader is chosen and that leader goes to layer2. This is how it repeats until it form single node at top NetALM Protocol. The conditions are a node at some layer Lj must be present in the all the lower layer and a node which is not in Lj should not be present in the Li where i>j. In a NICE hierarchy structure, members at that top have to maintain the state of the members which are at the lowest level and the members in the same group can only have some limited information about the other members in that group. While developing nice hierarchy the members which are closer to distance are considered to be same hierarchy. Nice hierarchy is created by assigning members to different layers [2].

If a node wants to join the tree, first it will query to the top layer one then the top node will give the information to the joining node about lower layer node. Then joining select one based on the rtt then sends to that node request. This is how they join the network when it comes to the lower layer that is layer0. There are two types of leaving one is Graceful: The leaving node informs other node of its departure and other one is Ungraceful: The leaving node "dies" suddenly without announcement. When nodes disappears from the tree, then we close all connections to the node and the method will inform to all other peers. Tree refinement is based on the following three methods: Cluster split, Cluster merge and Cluster leader transfer These refinements are done when the boundaries are violated. If it exceeds based on that merge or split or transfer can takes place.

ZIGZAG protocol is similar to nice protocol while forming tree hierarchy but there are differences. First one is node on the same layer receives packet only from the higher node and a node on the same cluster receives from the same higher node. Second one is there is no connection or link between two nodes which are in the same cluster. Third one is the cluster nodes receives packet from the foreign node not from the parent node. This helps even if the parent node fails able to reconstruct easily. This is one of the advantage in ZIGZAG protocol. Here no scalability related things are considered. The node which wants to join to hierarchy should go from the parent node as similar to the nice[2].

In OMNI protocol there is no leader and layered like structure as like in the previous two protocols. In this case service providers deploy multicast service nodes(MSN) that act as a application layer forwarding entities for set of client. OMNI helps in reducing the latencies to the entire client set. MSN are also assigned priority based on the number of client that are attached to it. The main advantage is it minimizes the maximum latency[2].

3 NetALM Protocol

Here we took six metrics to form the Multicast tree. The six metrics are type of Network, Hop Distance, Available Memory, Processing power, delay and bandwidth. Using this metrics we can reduce the height of the tree. Data distributions are two types one is Back bone distribution and another one is Tree Bone distribution. Back bone distribution is used to distribute the packets to the public network and tree bone distribution is used to distribute the packets to the private networks.

3.1   Tree Bone Formation and Refinement

At the time of login, each user will send the parameters such as IP-Address, port number, type of network, bandwidth and system configuration (Processor Speed, available memory, bandwidth, etc..,) to the server. Server will form the multicast tree based on the parameters. A Basic tree is constructed based on the parameters bandwidth, Processing power and the available memory with nodes identified by their ip address. This tree is constructed using priority queue with the following constraints.

- RAM SPEED (It includes available physical memory, Front Bus speed, SWAP space).
- Processing Power. (This comprises of CPU frequency, No. of processors, type of processor).
- Bandwidth (Network Bandwidth).

3.2   Member Join Process

When a new host joins the multicast group, it must be mapped to some cluster in layer. We illustrate the join procedure in Figure 2. Assume that host wants to join multicast group. First, it contacts the Tree Head (TH) with its join query. The TH responds with the hosts that are present in the highest layer of the hierarchy. The joining host then contacts all members in the highest layer to identify the member closest to itself. In the example, the highest layer has just one member, which by default is the closest member to amongst layer members. Host informs of the three other members in its cluster then contacts each of these members with the join query to identify the closest member among them, and iteratively uses this procedure to find its cluster.

   It is important to note that any host, which belongs to any layer, is the center of its cluster, and recursively, is an approximation of the center among all members in all clusters that are below this part of the layered hierarchy. Hence, querying each layer in succession from the top of the hierarchy to layer results in a progressive refinement by the joining host to find the most appropriate layer cluster to join that is close to the joining member.

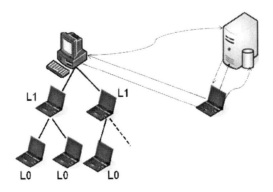

Fig. 2. New member join

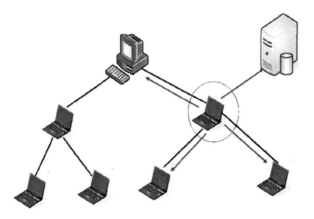

Fig. 3. Member Departure

3.3 Member Failure and Host Departure

When a host leaves the multicast group, it sends a *Remove* message to all clusters to which it is joined. This is a graceful-leave.

However, if it fails without being able to send out this message to all cluster peers, the algorithm will detects this departure through non-receipt of the periodic *HeartBeat* message from. A leader of a cluster, this triggers a new leader selection in the cluster. Each remaining member, of the cluster independently selects a new leader of the cluster, depending on who estimates to be the center among these members. Multiple leaders are re-conciled into a single leader of the cluster through exchange of *LeaderTransfer* message between the two candidate leaders, when the multiplicity is detected. It is possible for members to have an inconsistent view of the cluster membership, and for transient cycles to develop on the data path. These cycles are eliminated once the protocol restores the hierarchy invariants and reconciles the cluster view for all members.

4 Video Conferencing Process

Every user has to first register with the server by giving their user name and password. Once the user gives the username and password it is authenticated by the server. After successful authentication the server sends the list of on-going conference to the corresponding user, the user and chooses the conference of his preference then the server allows him to participate in that conference. After that the corresponding user's audio and video packets will be sending to all the participants in the conference. The user is allowed to create their own conference. Conference Management is discussed in the following sessions.

4.1 Conference Management System

NetALM conference management protocol is a real time conference control protocol that is ready to use for everyday communications. It supports all types of Internet

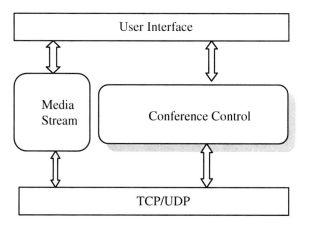

Fig. 4. Video Conference System Module

connections, including LAN, broadband, and even dial-up. It can be integrated with all kinds of instant messaging services, and a version for MSN messenger has been developed. The full mesh conferencing structure is first introduced in [12], where Lennox et al. also point out that the full mesh conferencing architecture is not suitable for bandwidth-limited end systems, such as wireless devices and users with 56 kbps modems. To break this limitation, in our system, we entirely separate the transmission module from the media stream engine and define a whole set of APIs that are open for both Unicast and application-level multicast (ALM). When there are multiple data receivers, multicast allows data replication to be performed outside of the data source. Application-level multicast is different from traditional IP multicast in that data replication is conducted at end systems instead of multicast-enabled routers. With a proper ALM algorithm, we are able to alleviate the scalability problem of full mesh conferencing architecture.

Our protocol is designed based on the full mesh architecture, where conference members are united by a fully connected communication mesh. And all the members are equivalent in terms of position in topology or rights in the conference. Different from [12], our protocol is so concise that it uses only four communication messages:

♦ JOIN_CONFERENCE as a Participant

A peer can join a conference as a Participant only if it is in the list of allowed participants specified by the conference Host. A peer intending to join a conference as a Participant generates a (private key, public key) pair and sends a JOIN_CONFERENCE message containing the conference name and its public key to the Server. The Server checks the list of allowed participants for that conference and if the peer is allowed then it sends the public key of the peer to other Participants and Spectators and also sends the public key of other Participants to the peer. Now the peer can subscribe to multicast AV data (encrypted) of other Participants and decrypt it before rendering using corresponding public keys. Also other Participants and Spectators can subscribe to the multicast AV data (encrypted) of the new Participant and decrypt it before rendering using the public key of the new Participant.

♦ JOIN_CONFERENCE as a Spectator

A peer can join a conference as a Spectator only if it is in the list of allowed spectators specified by the conference Host. A peer intending to join a conference as a Spectator sends a JOIN_CONFERENCE message containing just the conference name to the Server. The Server checks the list of allowed spectators for that conference and if the peer is allowed then it sends the public key of all Participants to the Spectator. Now the new Spectator can subscribe to the entire Participants' multicast AV data (encrypted) and decrypt it before rendering using the corresponding public key.

♦ LEAVE_CONFERENCE as a Participant

The Participant sends a bye message LEAVE_CONFERENCE containing the conference name to the server. The Server sends messages to all the Spectators and other Participants saying this particular Participant has left the conference . The Spectators and other Participants unsubscribe to the ex-Participant's multicast data.

♦ LEAVE_CONFERENCE as a Spectator

The Spectator can silently leave the conference unless the server wants to maintain a log of conference activities, in which case the Spectator sends a bye message LEAVE_CONFERENCE containing the conference name to the Server and the Server appropriately logs the incident.

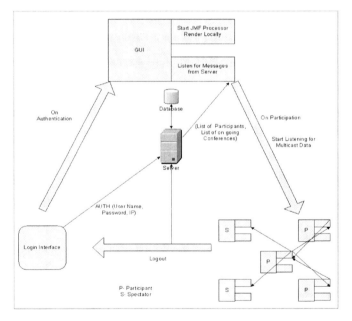

Fig. 5. Peer Life Cycle

4.2 Peer Life Cycle

- Every peer has to get authenticated by the Authentication Server using its username and password. The server stores the IP of the peer's machine which can be used by other peers.
- On successful login, the system starts audio/video capture and renders only video locally.
- It continuously listens over a port for UDP update messages from the server. For e.g. list of online peers, list of on-going conferences.
- The peer can interact with other peers or join a conference [7].
  On logout, peer should send a "BYE" message to the server and exit gracefully.

5 Experimental Output

JAVA language is used to develop this application. And other two important API's are JMF2.0 and JXTA. JMF2.0 is to capturing the data source from the input devices such as Web Camera and head phone. JXTA is used to setting up the P2P environment. The video standard is H323 and the video format is H236, It can capture 30 frames per seconds. The audio format is GSM. The minimum requirements of this software are Pentium IV processor, 1.8GHz processor speed and 512MB memory. The following output is showing you the four persons are talking to each other using this application.

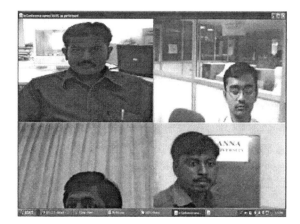

6 Conclusion

Using this protocol we can give good quality of service to the Low bandwidth users. The two types of Data distribution will be one efficient distribution compare than other protocols like NICE, ZIGZAG and OMNI. The well structured tree will avoid the DDOS attacks. Heterogeneous users can participate the conference. Application itself We have reduced internet bandwidth using Participant and Spectator concept and avoided server overload and latency between the peers using peer to peer communication. This application also allows Text Chat and Online Presentation.

Acknowledgement

This work is supported by the NTRO, Government of India. NTRO provides the fund for collaborative project "Smart and Secure Environment" and this paper model for this project. Authors would like to thanks the project coordinators and the NTRO members.

References

1. Besharati, R., Dezfouli, M.A.: A Topology-aware Application Layer Multicast Protocol. In: Proceedings IEEE CCNC 2010, 978-1-4244-5176-0/10/$26.00 © 2010 IEEE
2. Hosseini, M., Ahmed, D.T., Shirmohammadi, S., Georganas, N.D.: A Survey of Application-Layer Multicast Protocols. IEEE Communications Surveys 9(3), 3rd Quarter (2007)
3. Kobayashi, M., Nakayama, H., Ansari, N., Kato, N.: Reliable Application Layer Multicast Over Combined Wired and Wireless Networks. IEEE Transactions on Multimedia 11(8), 1520-9210/$26.00 © 2009 IEEE
4. Wu, X., Dhara, K., Krishnaswamy, V.: Enhancing Application-Layer Multicast for P2P Conferencing. In: Proc. of IEEE Consumer Communications and Networking Conference, pp. 986–990 (2007)
5. Moreno-Vozmediano, R.: Application Layer Multicast for Efficient Grid File Transfer. International Journal of Computer Science and Application@2009 Techno Mathematics Research Foundation 6(1), 70–84 (2009)
6. Ping, L.B.: Bandwidth Fair Application Layer Multicast for Multi-party Video Conference Application, 978-1-4244-2309-5/09/$25.00@2009 IEEE
7. Wu, X., Dhara, K., Krishnaswamy, V.: Enhancing Application-Layer Multicast for P2P Conferencing. In: Proc. of IEEE Consumer Communications and Networking Conference, pp. 986–990 (2007)
8. Kim, M.S., Lam, S.S., Lee, D.Y.: Optimal Distribution Tree for Network Streaming Media. In: Proc. of IEEE International Conference on Distributed Computing Systems (2003)
9. Strufe, T., Schafer, G., Chang, A.: BCBS: An efficient load balancing Strategy for cooperative overlay live-streaming. In: Proc. of IEEE International Conference on Communications, pp. 304–309 (2006)
10. Pendarakis, D., Verma, D., Shi, S., Waldvogel, M.: ALMI: an application Level multicast infrastructure. In: Proc. of USENIX Symposium on Network Technologies and Systems (2001)
11. Chu, Y., Rao, S.G., Zhang, H.: A case of end system multicast. In: SIGMetrics. ACM, New York (2000)
12. Chen, L., Luo, C., Li, J., Li, S.: Digiparty – a decentralized multi-party Video conferencing system. In: Proc. of IEEE International Conference On Multimedia and Expo (2004)
13. Ronasi, K., Firooz, M.H., Pakravan, M.R., Avanaki, A.N.: A Fast Algorithm for Construction of Minimum Delay Multicast Trees in P2P networks. In: International Symposium on Communications and Information Technologies, ISCIT 2006 (2006); IEEE NO: 04141529

Transmit Diversity Technique for Wireless Communication over Rayleigh Channels Using 16 QAM Modulation Schemes

N.S. Murthy[1], S. Sri Gowri[2], and J.N.V. Saileela[3]

[1] Associate Professor, ECE Dept., VR Siddhartha Engg. College, Vijayawada-7, India
nsmmit@gmail.com
[2] Professor& HOD, ECE Dept., SRK Institute of Technology, Vijayawada, India
sajjasrigowri@yahoo.com
[3] Student, ECE Dept., VR Siddhartha Engg. College, Vijayawada-7, India

Abstract. The increasing demand for higher data rates and higher quality in wireless communications has motivated the use of multiple antenna elements at the transmitter and single antenna at the receiver in a wireless link. Space-time block coding over Rayleigh fading channels using multiple transmit antennas was introduced. In this work Data is encoded using a space-time block code and the encoded data is split into n streams which are simultaneously transmitted using n transmit antennas. The received signal at each receive antenna is a linear superposition of the n transmitted signals perturbed by noise. Maximum likelihood decoding is carried out by dividing the signals transmitted from different antennas. This uses the orthogonal structure of the space-time block code and gives a maximum-likelihood decoding algorithm, which is based only on linear processing at the receiver. Space-time block codes are designed to achieve the maximum diversity order for a given number of transmit and receive antennas subject to the constrain of having a simple decoding algorithm. This paper presents a simple two-branch transmit diversity scheme. Using two transmit antennas and one receive antenna using QAM modulation technique the performance of OSTBC with Alamouti is compared with no STBC scheme at lower as well as higher SNRs. This paper evaluates the performance of the system by increasing data lengths in terms of blocks.

Index Terms: Codes, diversity, multi-path channels, multiple antennas, diversity, multi-path channels, multiple antennas, Rayleigh fading channel, space-time coding.

1 Introduction

Wireless communication is the transfer of information over a distance without the use of cables. It has made a tremendous impact on the lifestyle of a human being. It is very difficult to survive without wireless in some form or the other. As compared to fixed wireless systems, today's wireless networks provide high-speed mobility (mobile users in fast vehicles) for voice as well as data traffic. The time-varying

D.C. Wyld et al. (Eds.): NeCoM/WeST/WiMoN 2011, CCIS 197, pp. 127–137, 2011.
© Springer-Verlag Berlin Heidelberg 2011

nature of wireless channels, such as fading, multi-path makes it difficult for wireless system designers to satisfy the ever-increasing expectations of mobile users in terms of data rate.

In most situations, the wireless channel suffers attenuation due to destructive addition of multi-paths in the propagation media and to interference from other users. The channel statistic is significantly often Raleigh, which makes it difficult for the receiver to reliably determine the transmitted signal unless some less attenuated replica of the signal is provided to the receiver. This technique is called diversity, which can be provided using temporal, frequency, polarization, and spatial resources. In many situations, however, the wireless channel is neither significantly time variant nor highly frequency selective. This forces the system engineers to consider the possibility of deploying multiple antennas at both the transmitter and receiver to achieve spatial diversity.

Communications technologies have become very important part of human life. People can be reached at any time and at anyplace. Over 700million people around the world subscribe to existing second & third generation cellular system supporting data rates of 9.6Kbps to 2Mbps. More recently, IEEE 802.11 wireless LAN networks enable communication at the rate of around 54Mbps and have attracted more than 1.6 billion's equipment sales. Over next ten years, the capabilities of these technologies are expected to move towards the 100Mbps-1Gbps ranges and to subscriber members over two billion. At the present time, the wireless communication research community and industry discuss standardization for the fourth mobile generation. In other words, the next generation systems are supposed to have better quality and coverage, be more power and bandwidth efficient, and be deployed in diverse environments. Because of the enormous capacity increase MIMO systems offer, such systems gained a lot of interest in mobile communication research [9],[10]

Receiver diversity is used in present cellular mobile systems such as GSM, IS-136, etc. But receiver diversity is very complex to design Recently Transmit diversity has been studied extensively as a method of combating impairments in wireless fading channels [2]–[4]. It is particularly appealing because of its relative simplicity of implementation and the feasibility of multiple antennas at the base station.

2 Space Time Coding

Space-Time Codes (STCs) have been implemented in cellular communications as well as in wireless local area networks. Space time coding is performed in both spatial and temporal domain introducing redundancy between signals transmitted from various antennas at various time periods[8]. It can achieve transmit diversity and antenna gain over spatially encoded systems without sacrificing bandwidth. The researches on STC focuses on improving the system performance by employing extra transmit antennas. In general, the designs of STC amounts to finding transmit matrices that satisfy certain optimality criteria. Constructing STC, researchers have to trade-off between three goals: decoding, minimizing the error probability, and maximizing the information rate. The space time encoding and decoding as shown in fig 1.

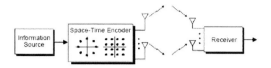

Fig. 1. System Block Diagram

A. Space Time Coded Systems

Consider a space-time coded communication system with n_t transmit antennas and n_r receive antennas. A space-time encoder encodes the transmitted data[8]. At each time slot, a block of $m \cdot n_t$ binary information symbols

$$c_t = \left[c_t^1, c_t^2, ..., c_t^{m \cdot n_t} \right]^T \tag{1}$$

is fed into the space-time encoder. The encoder maps the block of m binary data into n_t modulation symbols from a signal set of constellation $M = 2^m$ points. After serial-to-parallel (SP) conversion, the n_t symbols

$$s_t = \left[s_t^1, s_t^2, ...s_t^{n_t} \right]^T, 1 \le t \le N \tag{2}$$

Are transmitted simultaneously during the slot t from n_t transmit antennas, Symbol $s_t^i, 1 \le i \le n_t$, is transmitted from antenna and all transmitted symbols have the same duration T sec. The vector in (2) is called a space-time symbol and by arranging the transmitted sequence in an array, a $n_t \times N$ space-time codeword matrix [8]

$$S = \left[s_1, s_2, ..., s_N \right] = \begin{bmatrix} s_1^1 & s_2^1 & \cdots & s_N^1 \\ s_1^2 & s_2^2 & \cdots & s_N^2 \\ \vdots & \vdots & \ddots & \cdots \\ s_1^{n_t} & s_2^{n_t} & \cdots & s_N^{n_t} \end{bmatrix} \tag{3}$$

can be defined. The i-th row $s^i = \left[s_1^i, s_2^i, ..., s_N^i \right]$ is the data sequence transmitted from the i-th transmit antenna and the $j - th$ column $s_j = \left[s_j^1, s_j^2, ...s_j^{n_t} \right]$ is the space-time symbol transmitted at time $j, 1 \le j \le N$.

The received signal vector can be calculated as

$$\mathbf{Y=HS + N} \tag{4}$$

The MIMO channel matrix H corresponding to n_t transmit antennas and n_r receive antennas can be represented by a $n_r \times n_t$ matrix:

$$H = \begin{bmatrix} h_{1,1}^t & h_{1,2}^t & \cdots & h_{1,n_t}^t \\ h_{2,1}^t & h_{2,2}^t & \cdots & h_{2,n_t}^t \\ \vdots & \vdots & \ddots & \cdots \\ h_{n_r,1}^t & h_{n_r,2}^t & \cdots & h_{n_r,n_t}^t \end{bmatrix} \tag{5}$$

Where the ji-th element, denoted by $h_{j,i}^t$, is the fading gain coefficient for the path from transmit antenna i to receive antenna j. Perfect channel knowledge is assumed at the receiver side and the transmitter has no information about the channel available at the transmitter side. At the receiver, the decision metric is computed based on the squared Euclidian distance between all hypothesized receive sequences and the actual received sequence:

$$d_H^2 = \sum_t \sum_{j=1}^{n_r} \left| y_t^j - \sum_{j=1}^{n_t} h_{j,i}^t s_t^i \right|^2 \tag{6}$$

Given the receive matrix **Y** the ML-detector decides for the transmit matrix **S** with smallest Euclidian distance d_H^2.

B. Space-Time Codes

A space–time code (STC) is a method employed to improve the reliability of data transmission in wireless communication systems using multiple transmit antennas. STCs rely on transmitting multiple, redundant copies of a data stream to the receiver in the hope that at least some of them may survive the physical path between transmission and reception in a good enough state to allow reliable decoding. Two different space-time coding methods, namely space-time trellis codes (STTCs) and space-time block codes (STBCs) have been proposed. STTC has been introduced as a coding technique that promises full diversity and substantial coding again at the price of a quite high decoding complexity. To avoid this disadvantage, STBCs have been proposed by the pioneering work of Alamouti. The Alamouti [1] code promises full diversity and full data rate (on data symbol per channel use) in case of two transmit antennas. The key feature of this scheme is the orthogonality between the signals vectors transmitted over the two transmits antennas. This scheme was generalized to an arbitrary number of transmit antennas by applying the theories of orthogonal design. The generalized schemes are referred to as space-time block codes. However, for more than two transmit antennas no complex valued STBCs with full diversity and full data rate exist. Thus, many different code design methods have been proposed providing either full diversity or full data rate.

C. Space Time Block Codes

A Space-Time Block Code is generally represented by a matrix. Each row represents a time slot and each column represents one antenna's transmission over time.[8]

$$\begin{bmatrix} s_{11} & s_{12} & \cdots & s_{1n_t} \\ s_{21} & s_{22} & \cdots & s_{2n_t} \\ \vdots & \vdots & \ddots & \vdots \\ s_{T1} & s_{T2} & \cdots & s_{Tn_t} \end{bmatrix}$$

Here, s_{ij} is the modulated symbol to be transmitted in time slot i from antenna j.

There are T time slots and n_t transmit antennas as well as n_r receive antennas. This block is usually considered to be of 'length' T

The code rate of an STBC measures how many symbols per time slot it transmits on average over the course of one block. If a block encodes k symbols, the code-rate is

$$r = \frac{k}{T} \tag{7}$$

3 Orthogonal Designs

A. *Real Orthogonal Designs*

Definition: A real orthogonal design[6] of order n and type $(s_1, s_2, \cdots\cdots, s_k), s_1 > 0$ in real commuting variables $x_1, x_2, \cdots\cdots, x_k$ is a $n \times n$ matrix A with entries from the set $\{0, \pm x_1, \pm x_2, \cdots\cdots \pm x_k\}$ satisfying

$$AA^T = A^T A = \sum_{l=1}^{k} s_l x_l^2 I_n \tag{8}$$

Where $I_n = n \times n$ is an identity matrix

$$\text{Eg. } A_2 = \begin{bmatrix} x_1 & x_2 \\ -x_2 & x_1 \end{bmatrix}$$

B. *Complex Orthogonal Designs*

Definition: A complex orthogonal design of order n and type $(s_1, s_2, \cdots\cdots, s_k), s_1 > 0$ in real commuting variables $x_1, x_2, \cdots\cdots, x_k$ is a $n \times n$ matrix C with entries in the set $\{0, \pm x_1, \pm x_2, \cdots\cdots \pm x_k, \pm ix_1, \pm ix_2, \cdots\cdots \pm ix_k\}$ satisfying

$$C^H C = \sum_{l=1}^{k} s_l x_l^2 I_n \qquad (9)$$

An alternative definition for complex orthogonal design C has entries from the set

$\left\{0, \pm z_1, \pm z_2, \cdots \cdots \pm z_k, \pm z_1^*, \pm z_2^*, \cdots \cdots \pm z_k^*\right\}$, where the z_l are complex

commuting variable and z_l^* denotes the complex conjugate of z_l, such that

$$C^H C = \sum_{l=1}^{k} s_l |z_l|^2 I_n \qquad (10)$$

C. Generalized Complex Orthogonal Designs

Definition: A generalized complex orthogonal design of order n is a $r \times n$ matrix
G with entries from $\left\{0, \pm z_1, \pm z_2, \cdots \cdots \pm z_k, \pm z_1^*, \pm z_2^*, \cdots \cdots \pm z_k^*\right\}$, or products
of these complex indeterminate with the imaginary unit i such that,

$$G^H G = \sum_{l=1}^{k} |z_l|^2 I_n \qquad (11)$$

If the entries of G are allowed to be complex linear combinations of the complex
variables and their conjugates, then the design G is called a Generalized Complex
Linear processing orthogonal designs.

D. Encoding Using Alamouti Code:

The Alamouti code is the first STBC that provides at full data rate for two transmit
antenna as shown in fig2.[1]. The information bits are first modulated using an M-ary
modulation scheme. The encoder takes the block of two modulated symbols s_1 and
s_2 in each encoding operation and hands it to the transmit antennas according to the
code matrix

$$S = \begin{bmatrix} s_1 & s_2 \\ -s_2^* & s_1^* \end{bmatrix} \qquad (12)$$

The first row represents the first transmission period and the second row the
second transmission period. During the first transmission, the symbols s_1 and s_2 are
transmitted simultaneously from antenna one and antenna two respectively. In the
second transmission period, the symbol $-s_2^*$ and s_1^* are transmitted simultaneously
from antenna one and antenna two respectively.

It is clear that the encoding is performed in both time (two transmission intervals) and space domain (across two transmit antennas). The two rows and columns of S are orthogonal to each other and the code matrix is orthogonal:

$$SS^H = \begin{bmatrix} s_1 & s_2 \\ -s_2^* & s_1^* \end{bmatrix} \begin{bmatrix} s_1^* & -s_2 \\ s_2^* & s_1 \end{bmatrix}$$

$$= \begin{bmatrix} |s_1|^2 + |s_2|^2 & 0 \\ 0 & |s_1|^2 + |s_2|^2 \end{bmatrix}$$

$$= \left(|s_1|^2 + |s_2|^2 \right) I_2 \qquad (13)$$

Where I_2 is a (2×2) identity matrix. This property enables the receiver to detect s_1 and s_2 by a simple linear signal processing operation.

At the receiver side only one receive antenna is assumed to be available. The channel at time t may be modeled by a complex multiplicative distortion $h_1(t)$ for transmit antenna one and $h_2(t)$ for transmit antenna two. Assuming that the fading is constant across two consecutive transmit periods of duration T,

$$h_1(t) = h_1(t+T) = h_1 = |h_1| e^{j\theta_1}$$
$$h_2(t) = h_2(t+T) = h_2 = |h_2| e^{j\theta_1} \qquad (14)$$

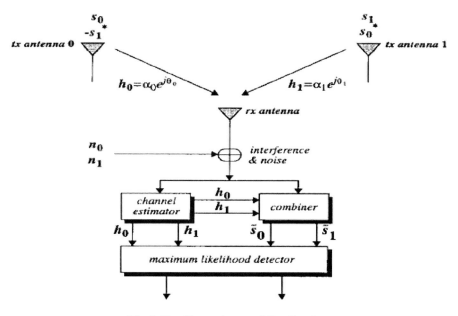

Fig. 2. Two Transmitters and One Receiver

Where $|h_i|$ and $\theta_i . i = 1, 2$ are the amplitude gain and phase shift for the path from transmit antenna i to the receive antenna. The received signals at the time t and $t + T$ can then be expressed as

$$r_1 = s_1 h_1 + s_2 h_2 + n_1$$
$$r_2 = -s_2^* h_1 + s_1^* h_2 + n_2$$

(15)

Where r_1 and r_2 are the received signals at time t and $t + T$, n_1 and n_2 are complex random variables representing receiver noise and interference. This can be written in matrix form as[7]:

$$r = Sh + n$$

(16)

Where $h = [h_1, h_2]^T$ the complex channel vector and n is is the noise vector at the receiver.

E. Decoding

One particularly attractive feature of orthogonal STBCs is that maximum likelihood decoding can be achieved at the receiver with only linear processing. In order to consider a decoding method, a model of the wireless communications system is needed.[5]

At time t, the signal r_j^t received at antenna j is:

$$r_j^t = \sum_{i=1}^{n_t} \alpha_{ij} s_t^i + n_t^i$$

(17)

Where α_{ij} is the path gain from transmit antenna i to receive antenna j, s_t^i is the signal transmitted by transmit antenna i and n_t^i is a sample of additive white Gaussian noise (AWGN).

Let $e_1, e_2, \cdots\cdots, e_n$ denote the permutations corresponding to the rows and let $\delta_k(i)$ denote the sign of x_i in the kth row. Then $e_k(p) = q$ means that x_p is up to a sign change the $(k, q)th$ element[11]

$$R_i = \sum_{t=1}^{n_t} \sum_{j=1}^{n_r} r_j^t \alpha_{e_t(i),j}^* \delta_t(i)$$

(18)

For $i = 1, 2, \cdots\cdots, n$ and decide in favor of s_i among all the constellation symbols s if:

$$s_i = \arg \min_{s \in A} |R_i - s|^2 + \left(-1 + \sum_{k,l} |\alpha_{k,t}|^2 \right) |s_i|^2$$

(19)

This is a very simple decoding strategy that provides diversity.

4   Result

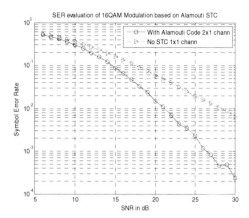

Fig. 3. Number of blocks=25000

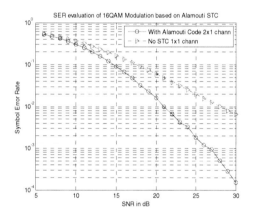

Fig. 4. Number of blocks=50000

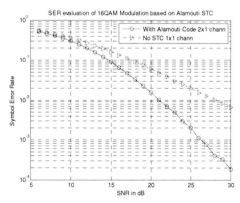

Fig. 5. Number of blocks=100000

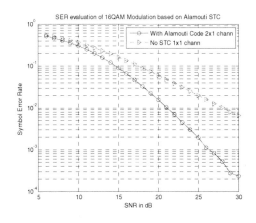

Fig. 6. Number of blocks=500000

5 Conclusion

The theory of space–time block coding, a simple and elegant method for transmission using multiple transmit antennas in a wireless Rayleigh environment is evaluated. These codes have a very simple maximum-likelihood decoding algorithm, which is only based on linear processing. Moreover, they exploit the full diversity given by transmit and receive antennas. The encoding and decoding algorithms are described. The encoding and decoding of these codes have very little complexity. Simulation results were provided to demonstrate that increasing number of transmit chains with very little decoding complexity. In this work QAM modulation technique is used to evaluate the performance of the system from the results obtained. It is concluded that implementing orthogonal STBC with Alamouti code using two transmitting and single receiving antenna decreases the symbol error rate. If we increase the data length shown in fig3-6 to be transmitted over the system, at higher SNR s the symbol error rate decreases even it is almost at lower SNRs

References

[1] Alamouti, S.M.: A simple transmitter diversity scheme for wireless communications. IEEE J. Select. Areas Commun. 16, 1451–1458 (1998)
[2] Balaban, N., Salz, J.: Dual diversity combining and equalization in digital cellular mobile radio. IEEE Trans. Veh. Technol. 40, 342–354 (1991)
[3] Foschini Jr., G.J.: Layered space-time architecture for wireless communication in a fading environment when using multi-element antennas. Bell Labs Tech. J., 41–59 (Autumn 1996)
[4] Foschini Jr., G.J., Gans, M.J.: On limits of wireless communication in a fading environment when using multiple antennas. Wireless Personal Commun. (March 1998)
[5] Guey, J.-C., Fitz, M.P., Bell, M.R., Kuo, W.-Y.: Signal design for transmitter diversity wireless communication systems over Rayleigh fading channels. In: Proc. IEEE VTC 1996, pp. 136–140 (1996)

[6] Adams, S.S.: Journey of discovery. Orthogonal matrices & Wireless communications

[7] Jafarkhani, H.: Space Time theory & practice, Text book. University Press, Cambridge

[8] Zwecke, z.: Thesis on Space-Time Block Coding For Multiple Antenna Systems

[9] Telatar, I.E.: Capacity of Multi-Antenna Gaussian Channels. AT&T Bell Labs (1995),
     http://mars.belllabs.com/cm/ms/what/mars/papers/proof

[10] Foschini, J., Gans, M.J.: On Limits of Wireless Communications in Fading Environments
     when Using Multiple Antennas. Wireless Personal Communications 6, 311–335 (1998)

[11] Tarokh, V., Jafarkhani, H., Calderbank, A.R.: Space-time block codes from orthogonal
     designs. IEEE Trans. Inform. Theory 45, 1456–1467 (1999)

T-RAP: (TCP Reply Acknowledgement Packet) a Resilient Filtering Model for DDoS Attack with Spoofed IP Address

L. Kavisankar and C. Chellappan

Department of Computer Science & Engineering,
Anna University
kavisankaar@gmail.com, drcc@annauniv.edu

Abstract. A Distributed Denial-of-Service (DDoS) attack is a strenuous attack to defend, mainly due to a server's inability to control the amount and the origin of requests. It is easily performed by utilizing the weakness of the network protocol. DDoS attack is considered to be a major threat among security problems in today's Internet. TCP/IP protocol suite is the most widely used protocol suite for data communication. While SYN flooding exploits the TCP three-way handshake process by sending many connection requests using spoofed source IP addresses to a victim server. The IP protocol specifies no method for validating the authenticity of the packet's source. This implies that an attacker can forge the source address to their desire. These kinds of attack are potentially severe. They bring down business of company drastically. DDoS attack can easily exhaust the computing and communication resources of its victim within a short period of time. This paper deals on attacks that consume all the bandwidth available to the victim machine. The TCP SYN flood works by exhausting the TCP connection queue of the host and thus denying legitimate connection requests. There are various methods used to detect and prevent this attack, one of which is to block the packet based on SYN flag count from the same IP address. This kind of prevention methods becomes unsuitable when the attackers use the Spoofed IP address. For the prevention of this kind of attacks, the TCP specific probing is used in the proposed scheme where the client is requested to change the windows size/ cause packet retransmission while sending the ACK in the three way hand shake. We also use the DHCP to statically assign the IP address based on the MAC address in a private environment. This is very useful to find the Spoofed IP Packets/TCP SYN flood and preventing them.

Keywords: TCP SYN flooding, DDoS, IP Spoofing, T-RAP, Static DHCP.

1 Introduction

IP Spoofing protection solutions can essentially be divided into three categories they are End-Host-Based Solutions, Router-Based Solutions, Solutions Requiring the Use of Both Routers and End-Hosts. Here we are concentrating on End-host-based solutions. The TCP/IP protocol suite, the most widely used protocol suite for data

D.C. Wyld et al. (Eds.): NeCoM/WeST/WiMoN 2011, CCIS 197, pp. 138–148, 2011.

communication assumes that all the hosts participating in the communication have no malicious intent. It is to be noted that internet was designed with functionality but not security in mind. There is no security built into the internet infrastructure to protect hosts from other hosts. Attackers can forge the source address of IP packets to maintain their concealment and also to redirect the blame for attacks. When attackers inject packets with spoofed source addresses into the Internet, routers forward those packets to their destination just like any other packet without checking the validity of the packets source addresses. These spoofing packets consume network bandwidth and are often part of some malicious activity, such as a DDoS attack. This attack prevents legitimate users from access the regular Internet services by exhausting the victim's resources .The main drawback in the present network is that authentication of the source address is not provided but the network is concerned with only the destination to be reached by the packet which are send for communication with that advantage the attacker try to impersonate the source address as a source which is genuine / accessible of the target.

The mitigation of IP spoofing by monitor packets using network-monitoring software here learning and recording of the packet is done. T-RAP (TCP Replay Acknowledgement Packet) a prevention model for DDoS attack with Spoofing IP address is designed and developed for the prevention of the DDoS attack using the spoofed IP packets. It is easy to detect the DDoS attack by monitoring the packets with SYN flag and using a threshold limit, packets from that IP address is not accepted if it exceeds the threshold limit. But an attacker can launch a DDoS attack on the target victim server using the Spoofed IP address. Using TCP-specific probes intelligently craft/append TCP acknowledgment messages to give another layer of protection. Since the sender of spoofing packets is often unable to see any replies, a recipient host can send acknowledgments that should change the TCP window size or cause packet retransmission, and then observe whether or not the supposed source responds correctly. If the supposed source does not change the window size or does not retransmit the packet, the recipient host considers the packet's source to be spoofed.

Ensuring that an IP packet carries a correct source address is highly difficult. There is no control over the request given by the client. So the filtering of the packet should be done before a malicious client gives the request to the server. Using Static DHCP, the DHCP server recognizes the MAC address of your device's NIC and assigns the static IP address to it in a private network. With help of this mapping between the IP address and MAC we can find out IP spoofing to some extent. While rest is taken care by the TCP probing method.

The rest of this paper is organized as follows. In section 2, we introduce IP Spoofing and the recent trends in IP Spoofing and little discussion about Botnets. In section 3, we detail our related work. In section 4, we detail about Static DHCP. In section 5, we detail about T-RAP .In section 6, we discuss about the result and we conclude in Section 7.

2   IP Spoofing Introduction

2.1   The IP Spoofing Techniques

The SYN flood attack exploits a vulnerability of the TCP three-way handshake, namely, that a server needs to allocate a large data structure for any incoming SYN packet regardless of its authenticity. During SYN flood attacks, the attacker sends SYN packets with source IP addresses that do not exist or are not in use. During the three-way handshake, when the server puts the request information into the memory stack, it will wait for the confirmation from the client that sends the request. While the request is waiting to be confirmed, it will remain in the memory stack. Since the source IP addresses used in SYN flood attacks can be nonexistent, the server will not receive confirmation packets for requests created by the SYN flood attack. Each half-open connection will remain on the memory stack until it times out, it will retransmit the SYN+ACK 5 times, doubling the time-out value after each retransmission. The initial time-out value is 3 seconds, so retries are attempted at 3, 6, 12, 24, and 48 seconds. More and more requests will accumulate and fill up the memory stack. Therefore, no new request, including legitimate requests, can be processed and the services of the system are disabled. Generally, the space for the memory stack allocated by the operating system is small, and even a small scale SYN flood attack can be disruptive. On the other hand, SYN floods can be also launched from compromised machines using spoofed IP address / genuine source IP addresses given these compromised machines are configured to ignore the SYN/ACK packets from the target.

3   Related Works

The methods used for preventing TCP SYN flood is done by the following way using the server as the detector of the attack and the local router of the attacker is used to prevent the attack. To establish the TCP connection with the server, every client should send the SYN signal and have to respond the SYN/ACK signal with the ACK signal. To identify the attack, the SYN request sent by the client is stored in the server data table (database) until the acknowledgement from the client received by the server for the SYN ACK signal. The client information stored in the table is the IP address and the SYN count. If the count (number of SYN request sent by the attacker without the ACK signal to establish the connection) in the table exceeds the threshold limit, the victim intimate the details of the attack to its local router and it will be sent to the local router of the attacker to drop all the packets from the respective node. If suppose the local router compromise with the attacking node, that router is also prevented from throwing the packet.

OS Fingerprinting [13] can detect spoofing packets if the spoofed source can be actively fingerprinted. The resulting active fingerprint is different from the passively deployed fingerprint then it is considered to be the spoofing packet. Even then, results can be complicated by a firewall between the target and the spoofed source, if the firewall filters the fingerprinting probes, or alters the responses. Fingerprinting is not reliable enough to depend on.

Hop-Count Filtering (HCF) [6] observes the hop-count of packets arriving at a given host/server. During normal times measurement is made where, HCF creates a mapping of IP addresses to hop counts. Then, if an attacker sends a spoofing packet to the host; it is likely the hop-count of the packet will not match the expected hop-count for packets from the spoofed source address. Because legitimate hop-counts may change due to routing changes, strictly filtering all packets that do not match would lead to false positives. In order to minimize false positives, HCF only begins filtering traffic if some threshold amount of packets does not match their expected hop counts.

The method used to prevent the opening of connections to spoofed source addresses is SYN cookies [15]. When a server uses SYN cookies it does not allocate resources to a connection until the 3-way TCP handshake completes. First the server sends a SYN + ACK packet with a specially encoded initial sequence number, or cookie, that includes a hash of the TCP headers from the client's initial SYN packet, a timestamp, and the client's Maximum Segment Size (MSS). Then when it receives the client's response, the server can check the sequence number and create the necessary state only if the client's sequence number is the cookie value plus one. Because the cookie uses a hash involving the server's secret key, attackers should not be able to guess the correct cookie values. However, because of performance concerns and some incompatibilities with TCP extensions, such as large windows, operating systems generally do not activate the SYN cookie mechanism until the host's SYN queue fills up. An attacker sending spoofing traffic at a low rate may avoid triggering the SYN cookie mechanism. Administrators may be able to forcibly enable SYN cookies for all connections, but should be aware of the side effects.

Another mechanism used for IP Spoofing prevention is using IP puzzles [5]. It provides active defense against spoofing. Here the server sends an IP puzzle to a client, and then the client needs to "solve" the puzzle by performing some computational task. Only after the server receives the puzzle solution from the client will the server allow the client to connect. It is prohibitively expensive for malicious hosts to send large numbers of packets as a side effect it is preventing attackers from successfully sending spoofing packets. Since the IP puzzle would be sent to the listed source and not the attacker, an attacker could not send a puzzle solution, thus preventing the attacker from spoofing.

4   Static DHCP Assignment of IP Address in a Private Environment

Static DHCP (DHCP reservation) is a useful feature which makes the DHCP server on your router always assigns the same IP address to a specific computer on your LAN. To be more specific, the DHCP server assigns this static IP to a unique MAC address assigned to each NIC on your LAN. Your computer boots and requests its IP from the router's DHCP server. The DHCP server recognizes the MAC address of your device's NIC and assigns the static IP address to it. For Example 4 MAC addresses are there and those are the only machines which should receive DHCP, you could probably create a pool of 4 addresses with all of them reserved (mapped).

This is used to determine whether the IP address has been changed. If IP address has been changed then the packets are filtered without reaching the victim system.

IP address	Hardware address	Lease expiration
10.0.0.1	0090.bff6.081e	Infinite
10.0.0.2	00b7.0813.88f1.66	Infinite
10.0.0.2	0090.bff6.081d	Infinite
10.0.0.2	0090.0813.081f	Infinite

5 T-RAP (TCP Reply Acknowledgement Packet)

T-RAP (TCP Reply Acknowledgement Packet) is the methods used for the mitigation of TCP SYN flood with IP spoofing. Here the simple TCP handshake may not be enough to prevent attackers from spoofing TCP packet, since attackers may be able to predict TCP sequence numbers. The sender of spoofing packets mostly unable to see any replies with this in mind, we use T-RAP (TCP Reply Acknowledgement Packet) which intelligently craft/append TCP acknowledgment messages to give another layer of protection. Here recipient host/server sends acknowledgment that should change the TCP window size or cause packet retransmission. It should be observed whether source responds correctly. If the supposed source does not change the window size /does not retransmit the packet, the recipient host/server considers the packet's source to be spoofed.

The recording of the TCP handshake is the key aspect in this method. The TCP acknowledgment message sends along with the SYN+ACK packet send from the victim server which undergoes the IP Spoofing for the TCP SYN flooding. If the packet retransmission is with change in TCP Window size the packet is not spoofed.

Fig.1. Shows T-RAP (TCP Reply Acknowledgement Packet) method used to determine TCP packet received is spoofed or not. Based on the detection the packet is dropped or accepted .Initially the server receives the   TCP packet with SYN flag in the packet so the protocol analyzer detect it as TCP protocol and send the client with the TCP Acknowledgement if the packet does not come from the spoofed IP address then the client reply with change in TCP Window size based on this reply the Packet Capture Engine record this and send it to the Decider. Based on the reply from the client using T-RAP the packet is dropped or accepted.

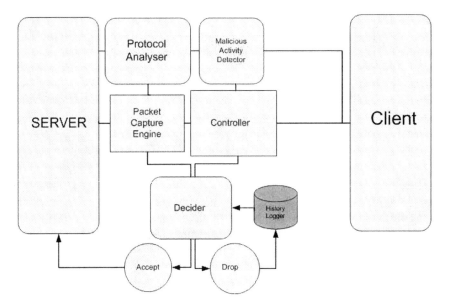

Fig. 1. TCP SYN flood detection model using T-RAP

This is a host-based architecture and it is developed using TCP Probing .Here the TCP probe is used to send the specification to the client trying to establish a new connection with the server. The decision is taken based on the reply from the client. Initially when the client tried to change the IP address mapped to the MAC address and connect to the server the malicious activity detector detects it and filter the packet without reaching the victim server. The Controller is used to send the specification to the client trying to establish a new connection with the server. The Specification contains the TCP probe which is TCP Reply Acknowledgement Packet (T-RAP) that should change the TCP window size or cause packet retransmission. The Protocol analyzer analyses the packet whether it follows the TCP protocol. The Packet Capture engine is used to record the packet used in the TCP handshake and it is useful in verifying the specification given by the TCP Probe. The Decider decides based on the information available (i.e.) it follows the Specification while replying back to the server, based on this accepts or rejects the packets. The dropped packet information is logged on to the History logger.

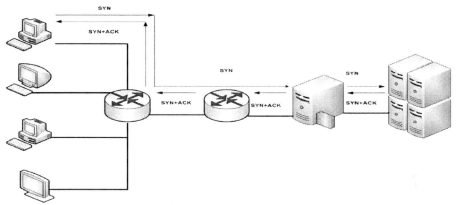

Fig. 2. TCP Three way handshake in normal scenario

The above figure gives the representation of the three way hand shake where SYN packets are send from the client to establish connection where it is responded with the SYN+ACK packet.

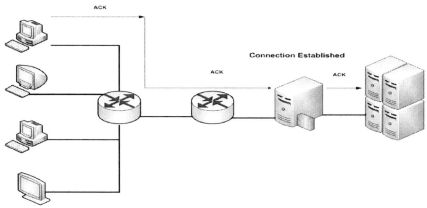

Fig. 3. TCP Three way handshake connection established

Fig.3 gives the representation of the three way hand shake where ACK packets are send from the client to finish the three way hand shake and to establish connection with the server.

Fig.4 gives the representation of the three way hand shake where SYN packets is send from the client to initiate the three way hand shake and to establish connection with the server. Here the static DHCP is assigned to each MAC address /Hardware address (i.e.) Each NIC card mapped with static IP address using Static DHCP.

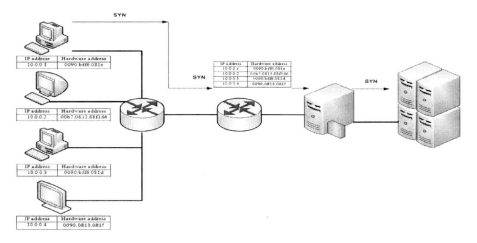

Fig. 4. TCP Three way handshake passes through filter

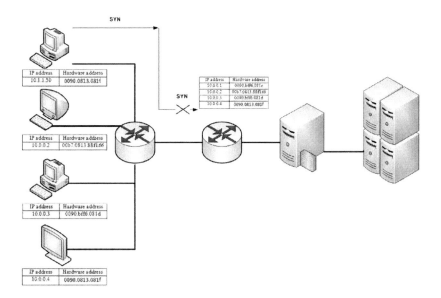

Fig. 5. Filtering of the malicious activity in the TCP three way handshakes

Fig.5 gives the representation of the three way hand shake where SYN packets is send from the client to initiate the three way hand shake and to establish connection with the server. Here the static DHCP is assigned to each MAC address /Hardware address when this is violated by the client and it also tries to establish the connection with the server. The Client which violates this static DHCP is prevented from communicating further with the server using the filter.

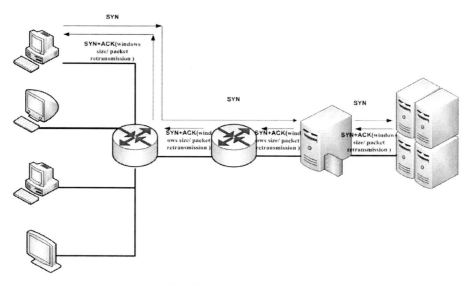

Fig. 6. TCP Three way handshake using T-RAP

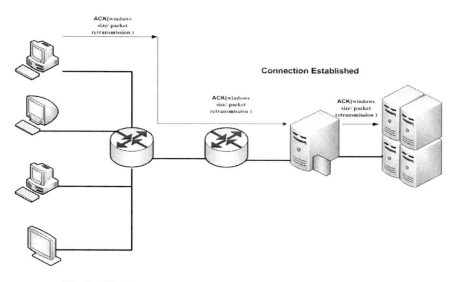

Fig. 7. TCP Three way handshake connection established using T-RAP

In this method using the T-RAP the extra specification is appended with the acknowledgment that is to change the TCP window size or cause packet retransmission. Based on this specification the packet send with ACK from client is changed as per the specification and send back to the server to establish the connection. The packet replied back should be with the correct specification send by the server. This is analysed using the protocol analyser .The decider accepts or rejects the packet based on the result from the Packet Capture engine.

Based on the results from the Packet Capture engine the check is made whether it satisfies the specification given by the server using TCP probing to change the TCP window size or cause packet retransmission. The decider decides to accept or drop based on specification reply of TCP probing.

6   Experimental Output

The T-RAP (TCP Reply Acknowledgement Packet) TCP probing method finds the spoofed Packet and drop the packet based on the specification given in the

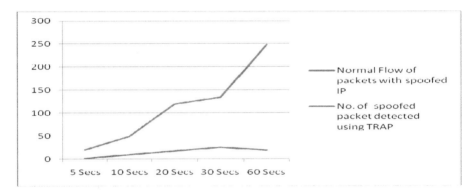

Fig. 8. TCP Three way handshake connection established using T-RAP

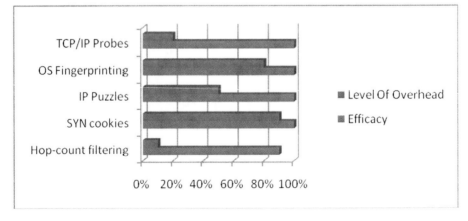

Fig. 9. TCP Three way handshake connection established using T-RAP

acknowledgement. Here the comparison is made between the normal flow of packet with spoofed IP and the No. of spoofed packet detected using the T-RAP (TCP Reply Acknowledgement Packet) TCP probing method. The implementation is done on the blades severs where T-RAP finds and detects the spoofed IP address and also drops the spoofed packets.

From fig. 9.the TCP/IP Probe seems to have better efficacy with less overhead as compared to other methods of IP Spoofing prevention for the purpose of DDoS attack protection.

7   Conclusion

The problem of ensuring that an IP packet carries a correct source address is a major concern. More over there is no control over the request given by the client. So the filtering of the packet should be done before a malicious client gives the request to the server. Using Static DHCP, the DHCP server recognizes the MAC address of your device's NIC and assigns the static IP address to it in a private network. With help of this mapping between the IP address and MAC we can find out IP spoofing to some extent. While rest is taken care by the TCP probing method. The T-RAP is very much useful in detecting the IP Spoofing done for TCP SYN flooding. The UDP flooding cannot be counter by this method. A common method should be developed to detect and traceback the spoofed IP packets in any form. TCP probing has good robustness against the TCP SYN flooding. Also, this method can effectively detect the IP Spoofing while reducing the TCP SYN flooding.

In future, we hope to analyze and provide IP Spoofing prevention system from the point of view of universal IP Spoofing security solution (i.e.) to provide prevention of IP Spoofing which occurs in any form.

Acknowledgement. This Work is supported by the NTRO, Government of India. NTRO provides the fund for collaborative project "Collaborative Directed Basic Research on Smart and Secure Environment" and this paper is modeled for this project. Authors would like to thank the project coordinators and the NTRO officials.

References

1. Krishna Kumar, B., Krishna Kumar, P.: Hop Count Based Packet Processing Approach to Counter DDoS Attacks. In: International Conference on Recent Trends in Information, Telecommunication and Computing (2010)
2. Cisco, Cisco 3600 Series Multiservice Platforms (2010),
   http://www.cisco.com/en/US/products/hw/routers/ps274/
   products_configuration_example09186a0080819289.shtml
3. Wang, H., Jin, C., Shin, K.G.: Defense Against Spoofed IP Traffic Using Hop-Count Filtering. IEEE/ACM Transactions on Networking (2007)
4. Lim, J.-D., Kim, Y.-H., Jung, B.-H., Kim, K.-Y., Kim, J.-N., Lee, C.-H.: Implementation of Multi-Thread Intrusion Prevention System for IPv6. In: International Conference on Control, Automation and Systems (2007)

5. Ma, M.: Mitigating denial of service attacks with password puzzles. In: Information Technology: Coding and Computing, ITCC 2005 (2005)
6. Liu, P.-E., Sheng, Z.-H.: Defending Against TCP SYN Flooding with a new kind of SYN-Agent. In: Proceedings of the Seventh International Conference on Machine Learning and Cybernetics, Kunming, pp. 1218–12221 (2008)
7. Kompella, R.R., Singh, S., Varghese, G.: On Scalable Attack Detection in the Network. International Journal on IEEE/ACM Transaction on Networking 15(1), 14–25 (2007)
8. Haggerty, J., Berry, T., Shi, Q., Merabti, M.: DiDDeM: A System for Early Detection of TCP SYN Flood Attacks. In: Proceedings of Globecom 2004, pp. 2037–2042 (2004)
9. Mirkovic, J.: D-WARD: Source-End Defense Against Distributed Denial-of-Service Attacks, PhD Thesis, University of California, los angels (2004)
10. Lemon: Resisting syn flooding dos attacks with a syn cache. In: Proc. USENIX BSDCon 2002, pp. 89–98 (2002)
11. Ferguson, P., Senie, D.: Network Ingress Filtering: Defeating Denial of Service Attacks which employ IP Source Address Spoofing. RFC 2267 (May 2000)
12. Internet System, RealSecure User's Guide and Reference Manual (1996)
13. Stopforth, R.: Techniques and countermeasures of TCP/IP OS fingerprinting on Linux Systems, Thesis, University of KwaZulu-Natal, Durban (2007)
14. Cisco Systems, Configuring TCP Intercept (Prevent Denial- of-Service Attacks), Cisco IOS Documentation (December 1997)
15. Schuba, C.L., Krsul, I.V., Kuhn, M.G., Spafford, E.H., Sundaram, A., Zamboni, D.: Analysis of a denial of service attack on TCP. In: Proc. IEEE Symp. Security and Privacy, pp. 208–223 (1997)
16. Bernstein, D.J.: SYN Cookies (1997), http://cr.yp.to/syncookies.html
17. Bradley, K.A., Cheung, S., Puketza, N., Mukherjee, B., Olsson, R.A.: Detecting Disruptive Routers: A Distributed Network Monitoring Approach. In: IEEE Symposium on Security and Privacy (1998)
18. Spatscheck, O., Petersen, L.L.: Defending Against Denial of Service Attacks in Scout. In: Proceedings of the 3rd Symposium on Operating Systems Design and Implementation (February 1999)
19. Sailan, M.K., Hassan, R., Patel, A.: A Comparative Review of IPv4 and IPv6 for Research Test Bed. In: 2009 International Conference on Electrical Engineering and Informatics Selangor, Malaysia (2009)
20. Yang, X., Ma, T., Shi, Y.: Typical DoS/DDoS threats under IPv6. In: Proceedings of the International Multi-Conference on Computing in the Global Information Technology (ICCGI 2007), pp. 50–55 (2007)
21. Zhang, X., Wu, S.F., Fu, Z., Wu, T.: Malicious Packet Dropping: How it might impact the TCP performance and How we can detect it. In: Proceedings of IEEE ICNP 2000 (2000)
22. Wang, X.F., Reiter, M.K.: Using Web-Referral Architectures to Mitigate Denial-of-Service Threats. IEEE Transactions on Dependable and Secure Computing 7(2) (April-June 2010)
23. Ma, Y.: An Effective Method for Defense against IP Spoofing Attack. In: Wireless Communications Networking and Mobile Computing, WiCom (2010)
24. Duan, Z., Yuan, X., Chandrashekar, J.: Controlling IP Spoofing through Interdomain Packet Filters. IEEE Transactions on Dependable and Secure Computing 5(1), 22–36 (2008)

Transmit Precoding for Time Varying Channel by Considering Channel Prediction Error

V. Kejalakshmi[1] and S. Arivazhagan[2]

[1] Department of Electronics and Communication Engineering,
K.L.N. College of Engineering,
Pottapalayam, 630611, Tamilnadu, India
[2] Department of Electronics and Communication Engineering, Mepco Schlenk Engineering
College, Sivakasi, 626005, Tamilnadu, India
Tel.:+91-04562-232652

Abstract. Transmit precoding techniques used at the base station(B.S) greatly reduces inter symbol interference(ISI) and inter channel interference(ICI), and allows the receiver to be complete simplified. These techniques needs full channel state information(CSI) at the B.S. But the CSI at the B.S is often outdated because of time varying nature of the channel. Hence, to adapt the transmit precoding technique, it is necessary to update the CSI at the transmitter. For reliable adaptive transmission, it is required to have the prediction of future CSI. In this paper we consider the kalman filter to predict the future channel, then the prediction error is corrected by the proposed technique. Then the prediction error corrected channel is used to construct the linear precoding matrix. Our simulation results show that the Bit error rate(BER) perfomance is improved if the prediction error is corrected to construct linear precoding matrix.

Keywords: Channel State information (CSI), Time Division Duplex (TDD), Kalman Prediction, Precoding, Doppler rate, Bit Error Rate (BER), MMSE.

1 Introduction

The performance of a wireless communication sytem can be improved by the well known Multiple Input Multiple Output (MIMO) antenna system [1], [2]. The degradation factors for the transmission of digital data over the MIMO high speed communication systems are Inter Symbol Interference (ISI) and Inter Channel Interference (ICI). The receiver based channel equalization has been used to mitigate such effects. Recently, research has been done in the area of precoding techniques to shift the signal processing burden from the receiver to the transmitter. The precoder design is expected to allow the receiver to be considerably simplified, which in turn reduces computational complexity and power consumption.

In the case of Time Division Duplex (TDD) systems, since the same frequency band is used for both transmission and reception. Hence, due to the channel reciprocity, the uplink channel estimates are used as the downlink channel estimates. In the case of Frequency Division Duplexing (FDD), CSI has to be obtained at the transmitter using a feedback channel. The feedback delay, channel estimation and

D.C. Wyld et al. (Eds.): NeCoM/WeST/WiMoN 2011, CCIS 197, pp. 149–158, 2011.
© Springer-Verlag Berlin Heidelberg 2011

quantization errors and processing delay degrade the performance of adaptive transmission, especially in rapidly time varying fading. Even in open loop channels (ie) TDD systems, the reciprocity will be valid only if the duplexing time is much shorter than the coherence time. Hence, current CSI is not sufficient and future channel conditions need to be known to adapt transmission parameters. The accuracy of the transmit channel estimation depends on the channel characteristics. In wireless communication systems, mobility can make the available channel information out of date. The Doppler spread induced by the motion of the subscribers and scatterers has a strong influence on time processing algorithm. The Doppler spread is large in macro cells which serve high mobility subscribers and it increases with high operating frequencies. Hence, for the case of a larger Doppler spread, the reciprocity cannot be applied i.e. the uplink channel estimates cannot be used for the downlink. A timely update of the CSI is an obvious solution to improve the system performance in a time varying channel. Hence it is necessary to estimate the downlink channel in accordance with the Doppler rate. Larger Doppler rate implies faster channel variation.

Since the CSI is known in the transmitter of TDD systems, it is possible for the transmitter to precode the signals according to the CSI. Esmailzadeh *et al.* also showed that the performance of pre-RAKE system is equivalent to the conventional RAKE receiver.In [3], Barreto *et al.* proposed pre/post RAKE to have remarkable performance improvement. While the pre-RAKE weights are determined in the same way as the pre-RAKE in [1] and [2], the post-RAKE weights are determined by Maximal ratio combining (MRC), to further improve the performance gain. The pre/post RAKE proposed by [3] & [4] is called as an Eigen precoder. The combining weights of the pre and post RAKE are jointly determined by the Eigen analysis to maximize the signal to noise ratio (SNR). A principal ratio combining (PRC) pre/post RAKE has been proposed in [5], which is a general expansion of Eigen precoder and it also utilizes the flexible number of pre-RAKE fingers.

When the CSI is available at the transmitter, multiple antenna systems are able to construct parallel sub channels without cross talk, by applying SVD to accomplish an optimal capacity [6], [7]. Han and Park in [8] proposed a pre/post RAKE structure called SVD pre/post RAKE, whose combining weights are determined by the SVD. Since the SVD establishes parallel sub channels in the multipath fading channel, the multiplexed transmission can be utilized.

Recently researchers have focused on preprocessing concepts based on channel prediction. . The benefits of using the channel prediction on adaptive rate control and power control schemes have been studied in [7]. In [8], A.H.Sayed etal, proposed channel prediction for equalization in MIMO wireless communication systems by considering the decision delay. In [9], a Pre-RAKE transmitter with long range prediction is employed over rapidly varying multipath fading channel. In [10], channel prediction based on wiener filtering is used in adaptive beam forming MISO systems. In [11], Giannakis etal analyzed the effect of channel prediction error on the BER performance of adaptive modulation based on transmit beam forming. The pre-RAKE beamforming for predicted channel was discussed in [12]. In [13], Raviraj and Adve proposed N frames ahead predictor based on the Kalman filter.

Here, we use a Kalman filter to track the time variation of the channel taps. These channel taps are typically modeled as mutually uncorrelated circular Gaussian random process. These time varying channel taps are predicted by the Kalman filter. The channel prediction error (i.e) the difference between the actual channel taps and the predicted channel is unavoidable. In our work, we derive the downlink channel coefficients by considering the channel prediction error. Then we use these channel coefficients to design the precoding system. The main contribution of this work is

(i) From the kalman recursion, the prediction error covariance is obtained and using this prediction error, the correlation coefficient between the actual channel and the predicted channel is derived.

(ii) Then using the relationship between the actual channel, predicted channel and the correlation coefficient, the actual channel is obtained. precoder is designed and BER performance is analyzed for the predicted channel and prediction error corrected channel.

The remainder of the paper is organized as follows. Section 2 deals with system model and the channel model. Kalman based tracking and the channel prediction are discussed in section 4. Section 5 presents the simulation results of the proposed algorithm and section 6 concludes the paper.

2 System Model

In this paper, we consider the downlink of a multiuser flat fading MIMO channel with K users, each with a single receive antenna, and a base station with M transmit antennas. Assuming that the transmitted signal is linearly precoded at the base station, the vector of the received signals at the K receivers is given by

$$y = HGS + n. \tag{1}$$

where H is the $K \times M$ channel matrix , whose $(i,j)^{th}$ element is the complex gain from transmit antenna j to receive antenna i and whose elements are independent and identically distributed (i.i.d.) zero mean complex Gaussian elements with unit variance , and the rank of a matrix H is K.

$$H = \begin{matrix} h11 & ... & h1N \\ \vdots & \vdots & \vdots \\ hK1 & ... & hNK \end{matrix}$$

G is the $M \times K$ precoding matrix, S is the vector consisting of K independent streams of data with zero mean and normalized variance, and n is an additive white Gaussian noise vector $CN(\mathbf{0}, N_0 I)$, where I denotes the identity matrix.

Then the decision statistics of the output of the receiver at the mobile station can be written as

$$\hat{y} = RHGS + Rn \tag{2}$$

where R = aI represents the simplified receiver (where I is an N×N identity matrix). Given the estimated channel matrix H, we are interested in designing the precoding matrix **G** at the base station such that the mean square error (MSE) signal at the different users' receivers is minimized.

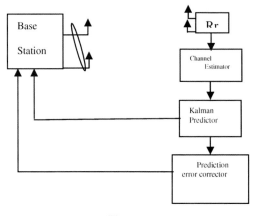

Fig. 1.

$$\text{Gopt} \quad = \quad \text{argmin} \quad E \left[\| \hat{y} - S \|_2^2\right]$$

$$E \left[\| G_{opt}S \|_2^2\right] = P_s \, E \left[\| s \|_2^2\right]$$

The power constraint states that the total average transmit energy per symbol after precoded by G is equal to P_s. By substituting $\hat{y} = RHGS + Rn$

$$\text{Gopt} \quad = \quad \text{argmin} \quad E \left[\| RHGS + Rn - S \|_2^2\right] \qquad (3)$$

$$E \left[\| G_{opt}S \|_2^2\right] = P_s \, E \left[\| s \|_2^2\right]$$

On substituting $R = aI$, and simplifying further as in [14],

$$\text{Gopt} = \sqrt{\frac{PsN}{trace(SS')}} \, \text{Topt} \qquad (4)$$

where $\text{Topt} = H^H \, (H \, H^H + \beta I)^{-1}$ and β is given as σ^2 / P_s.

3   Channel Model

The frequency selective channel is modeled as a chip-tapped multipath channel with L resolvable paths as

$$h(t) = \sum_{l=1}^{L} hl \, \delta \, (t - \tau l) \qquad (5)$$

where hl denotes the channel gain, $\tau l = (l - 1)T$ denotes propagation delay of the lth path, T is the bit duration and $\delta(t)$ is the Dirac delta function [8]. In the Rayleigh fading channel, hl has an independent zero mean complex Gaussian distribution and the channel vector h is defined as

$$h = [h_1 \dots h_L]^T \text{ such that } E \{\| h \|^2\} = 1.$$

In this section, we will model the channel time variations as a low order AR (Auto Regressive) process. Exact modeling of the time evolution of the vector process $\{h(t)\}$ with an ARMA (Auto Regressive and Moving Average) model is impossible, because the autocorrelation functions are non-rational. Even though the large order AR models for the fading channels are accurate, the first few correlation terms of small lag $|t_1 - t_2|$ are more important for the design of the receivers. Thus, even low order AR models, matching the Bessel auto correlation well for small lags, can capture most of the channel tap dynamics and lead to effective tracking algorithms i.e.

$$h(n) = \sum_{l=1}^{p} al\, h(n-l) + w(n) \qquad (6)$$

where $h(n) = [h(0)\, h(1) \ldots h(L-1)]^T$ and $w(n) = [w(0)\, w(1) \ldots w(L-1)]^T$. Generally w (n) is considered as zero mean *i.i.d.(Independent and identically distributed)* circular complex Gaussian vector process with correlation matrices $R_w(n) = \sigma_w^2 \delta(n)$. The discrete time fading channel sequence h(n) models a channel with maximum Doppler Frequency f_D and sampling period T_{fr}, which has a autocorrelation

$$R(k) = E\{h(t_1)\, h^*(t_2)\} = \zeta_0 (2\pi f_D k T_f) \qquad (7)$$

The AR coefficients Al are determined by solving the set of p×p Yule Walker equations, $A = R^{-1} W$, where

$$A = [a1\ a2 \ldots\ldots\ldots\ldots ap]^T,$$

$$R = \begin{matrix} R(0) & \cdots & R(-p+1) \\ \vdots & \ddots & \vdots \\ R(p-1) & \cdots & R(0) \end{matrix}$$

$$W = [R(1)\, R(2) \ldots\ldots\ldots R(p)]^T$$

The speed of the variation can be determined by the Doppler rate. In this paper, it is assumed that the random variations of the different channel taps are statistically independent among each other, and further, we assume that the Doppler rates are same for each tap. Larger Doppler rate imply faster channel variations and hence more diversity but a more difficult estimation task. In any case, the Doppler rate uniquely specifies a Bessel auto correlation as in (7). The modeling inaccuracy of the AR(p) approximation can be made arbitrarily small by increasing the order p [15].

4 Channel Prediction

In this section, we present an adaptive implementation of the precoding system. In TDD systems, the downlink channel vector can vary drastically from the uplink channel vector over a period of duplex time under fast Rayleigh fading. In Frequency Division Duplex (FDD) systems, not only does the channel vector vary rapidly, but also the uplink and downlink channels have independent fading. Therefore the prediction of future downlink channel is necessary at the base station for adaptive transmission over fast Rayleigh fading channels. In FDD systems, different frequency bands are allocated to uplink and downlink communication, so downlink CSI must be estimated at the receiver and provided to the transmitter using an uplink feedback mechanism. It has been recently demonstrated that this feedback mechanism may also be required in TDD systems [16]. The precoding matrix elements are updated in accordance with the Kalman predicted channel matrix.

Channel prediction: In this section, we are interested in deriving minimum variance estimators for the coefficients h (n) according to the model described by equation (6). The proposed method is based on an AR channel model and Kalman filtering ideas. In order to predict the channel, we first formulate the one step ahead Kalman predictor [15]. The system uses the following model to describe the evolution of the state $\mathbf{h}_n$ and the corresponding measurement $\mathbf{z}_n$. The time update (prediction) equations and the measurement (correction) equations are defined as follows.

$$\mathbf{h}_n = \mathbf{A}\,\mathbf{h}_{n-1} + \mathbf{w}_n$$
$$\mathbf{z}_n = \mathbf{C}\,\mathbf{h}_n + \mathbf{v}_n$$

with state transition matrix **A** and measurement matrix **C**

$$\mathbf{A} = \begin{matrix} a1 & a2 & \dots & ap\text{-}1 & ap \\ 1 & 0 & \dots & 0 & 0 \\ 0 & 1 & \dots & 0 & 0 \\ \vdots & \vdots & \ddots & 0 & 0 \\ 0 & 0 & \dots & 1 & 0 \end{matrix}$$

$$C = [1\ 0\ 0\ \dots\dots\dots 0]$$

where the predicted and corrected forms of the state vector **h** and the covariance matrix P are indicated by the subscripts [n/n-1] and [n/n] respectively.

Initialization

- Initial Error Covariance Matrix Prediction

$$P(n\text{-}1/n\text{-}1) = I \tag{8}$$

    where I is the L×L identity matrix, with L being the channel's length.
- Initial channel prediction

$$h(n\text{-}1/n\text{-}1) = [0\dots\dots 0]^{\mathrm{T}} \tag{9}$$

with h(n) being a column vector of length L.

Computation

- The best estimate of h(n) without the observation of output

$$h\,(n/n\text{-}1) = A(n\text{-}1)\,h(n\text{-}1/n\text{-}1) \tag{10}$$

- The error covariance matrix

$$P\,(n/n\text{-}1) = A\,(n\text{-}1)P(n\text{-}1/n\text{-}1)A^{\mathrm{H}}(n\text{-}1) + Q_{w(n)} \tag{11}$$

where $Q_{w(n)}$ is the covariance matrix for the noise process w(n)

Estimation
- The Kalman Gain

$$K(n)=P(n/n-1)C^H(n)*[C(n)P(n/n-1)C^H(n)+R(n)]^{-1} \tag{12}$$

where $C(n)$ represents the detected symbols stacked in a matrix of size $N \times L$, which we assume equal to true, $R(n) = N_0 I_{N*N}$ represents the measurement noise covariance matrix and $K(n)$ is the $L \times N$ gain matrix.
- Estimated Channel

$$h(n/n) = h(n/n-1)+K(n)[r(n)-C(n)h(n/n-1)] \tag{13}$$

where $r(n)$ is a $N \times 1$ vector containing the received signal at the channel output.
- Estimated Error Covariance Matrix

$$P(n/n) = [I-K(n)C(n)] P(n/n-1) \tag{14}$$

Prediction
- Predicted channel

$$h(n+1/n) = A h(n/n) \tag{15}$$

where A is the $L \times L$ of AR (1) model matrix.

- Predicted error covariance

$$P(n+1/n) = A P(n/n) A^H + Q_{w(n)} \tag{16}$$

$$= E[e(n+1/n) e(n+1)/n)^H]$$

where $e(n+1/n)$ is the prediction error i.e. the difference between the actual channel and the predicted channel,

$$e(n+1/n) = h_{act}(n+1/n) - h_{pred}(n+1/n) \tag{17}$$

The trace of the prediction error covariance matrix gives the Mean Square Error (MSE) of the channel prediction. Now, we can relate the normalized MSE of the channel prediction with the correlation coefficient ρ by $\epsilon = 2(1-\rho)$, where ρ is the correlation between the actual channel and the predicted channel

$$\rho = (E[h_{act} h_{pred}^H]) / (\sqrt{(E[|h_{act}|^2])} E[|h_{pred}|^2])$$

ρ lies between 0&1, $\rho = 1$ means that the predicted channel is equal to the actual 1 channel while $\rho = 0$ means that the predicted channel is independent of the actual channel. Using the fact that the channel gains form a Gaussian process, we can model the relationship between the actual channel and the predicted channel as in [14],

$$h_{act} = h_{pred} + \sqrt[2]{1 - \rho 2}\ v \tag{18}$$

where v is the zero mean unit variance Gaussian random variable independent of the channel. From this model, it is evident that given the predicted channel value h_{pred}, the actual channel can be modeled to be Gaussian with mean h_{pred} and variance $(1- \rho^2)$ i.e., $h_{act} = N (h_{pred} ; (1- \rho^2)$.The actual channel, h_{act}, now obtained can be used to design precoding matrix elements.

5 Simulation Results

In this section, we present simulation results to illustrate the Bit Error Rate (BER) performance of the Transmit precoding system for time varying channels. Here we consider the channel model as presented in section II, where we assume that the channel is flat fading with Rayleigh distribution, whose elements are i.i.d. zero mean complex random variables with unit variance. The channel parameters are selected to represent the typical values for a WiMAX system based on the IEEE 802.16e standard i.e., carrier frequency (fc) = 2.3 GHz, channel sampling rate (fs) = 200Hz, frame Duration (Tfr) = 5ms, Feedback delay = 3 frames. In our simulation, a system with four transmit antennas at the base station and 4 users and each with single receive antenna is considered. The BER performance for various Doppler rates is simulated.

Figure 2 shows the comparison of BER performance of the transmit precoding between the perfect channel, predicted channel and the predicted channel with error for various Doppler rates.

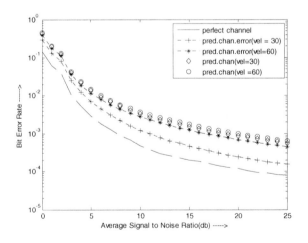

Fig. 2. BER performance under linear precoding

From this figure we can observe that, when the Doppler rate is reduced, (i.e.) the vehicular velocity is decreased, the gap between the perfect channel and the predicted channel is decreased.

Further, this figure clearly shows that the BER performance of the predicted channel with error is better than the predicted channel. It is also evident from the figure that, as Doppler frequency increases, the performance of the system degrades.

The gap between the perfect channel and the predicted channel increases as the speed of the vehicle increases. This is because the time correlation is stronger for the slow mobile speed and tracking task is easier.

It is also observed that the difference between the predicted channel and the channel considered with prediction error becomes larger as the Doppler frequency increases. As the Doppler rate increases the difference between the predicted channel and the predicted channel with error increases, due to the correlation coefficient between the actual channel and the predicted channel.

Figure 3.compares the prediction MSE with the prediction error corrected MSE. It is evident that the prediction corrected MSE is less than the kalman predicted MSE for all the mobile velocity. All the above simulations are done for AR model of order 2 and the measurement error in the kalman equations is assumed to have zero variance. The extension of this work can be for various measurement error variances and for the correlated MIMO channel.

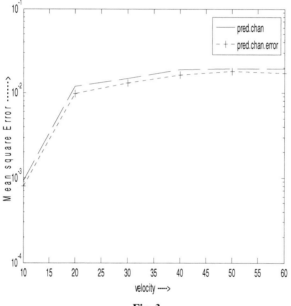

Fig. 3.

6 Conclusion

This paper proposed the transmit precoding system to track the time varying channel and the precoder matrix elements are calculated for the predicted channel and the prediction error corrected channel. The channel prediction is done using the Kalman filter, employing second order AR model to best fit the true statistics of the channel variation. Results show that the vehicular speed has strong influence on the BER performance. Hence it is concluded that the proposed system can tolerate the higher mobile speed than the system that uses the Kalman predicted channel.

References

1. Spencer, Q.H., Peel, C.B., Swindlehurst, A.L., Haardt, M.: An introduction to the Multiuser MIMO Downlink. IEEE Communication Magazine 42(10), 60–67 (2004)
2. Vishwanath, S., Jindal, N., Goldsmith, A.J.: On the capacity of MIMO Broadcast channels. In: Proc of IEEE International Conf. on Commun. (ICC), Newyork (April 2002)
3. Esmailzadeh, R., Sourour, E., Nakagawa, M.: Pre-RAKE diversity combining in time division duplex Diversity combining for direct sequence spread spectrum mobile communication systems. IEEE Trans. Veh. Technol. 47, 795–801 (1999)
4. Vojcic, B.R., Jang, W.M.: Transmitter precoding in Synchronous Multiuser Communications. IEEE Trans. Commun. 46(10), 1346–1355 (1998)
5. Stojnic, M., Vikalo, H., Hassibi, B.: Rate Maximisation in Multi Antenna Broadcast Channels with Linear Processing. In: Proc of IEEE Global Telecomm. Conf. (GLOBECOM 2004), vol. 6, pp. 3957–3961 (2004)
6. Irmer, R., Barreto, A.N., Fettwies, G.P.: Transmitter precoding for spread spectrum signals in frequency selective fading channels. In: Proc. IEEE 3G Wireless, pp. 939–944 (May 2001)
7. Marathe, D.V., Bhashyam, S.: Power control for Multi antenna Gaussian Channels with delayed feedback. In: Proc. of International Conf. on Signals, Systems and Computers, pp. 1598–1602 (November 2005)
8. Komninakis, C., Fragouli, C., Sayed, A.H.: Multi-Input Multi- Output fading channel tracking and equalization using Kalman estimation. IEEE Trans. Sig. Proc. 50(5), 1065–1075 (2002)
9. Guncavdi, S., Duel-Hallen, A.: A space time pre-RAKE transmitter diversity method for W-CDMA using long range prediction. In: Proc CISS, pp. 32–37 (March 2001)
10. Ramya, T.R., Bhashyam, S.: On Using Channel Prediction In Adaptive Beamforming Systems. In: Proceedings of IEEE COMSWARE 2007, Workshop on Wireless Systems: Advanced Research and Development (WISARD 2007), Bangalore, India (January 2007)
11. Zhou, S., Giannakis, G.B.: How Accurate Channel Prediction Needs to be for Transmit Beamforming With Adaptive Modulation Over Rayleigh MIMO Channels? IEEE Transactions on Wireless Commun. 3(4) (July 2004)
12. Dong, L., Xu, G., Ling, H.: Predictive Downlink Beamforming for Wideband CDMA Over Rayleigh Fading Channels. IEEE Trans. on Wireless Commun. TW02-134, 1–11
13. Tanenbaum, A.J., Adve, R.S.: Channel prediction and feedback in multiuser broadcast channels. In: Proc. CWIT 2009 (2009)
14. U-Choi, R.L., Murch, R.D.: New Transmit Schemes and Simplified Receivers for MIMO Wireless Communication Systems. IEEE Trans.on Wireless Commun. 2(6) (November 2003)
15. Haykin, S.: Adaptive Filter Theory, 3rd edn. Prentice Hall, Englewood Cliffs (1996)
16. Haartsen, J.C.: Impact of non-reciprocal channel conditions in broad band TDD-systems. In: Proc IEEE PIMRC 2008, Cannes, France (September 2008)

Design and Implementation CAM Architecture Memory Cell Using DMLSA Technique

I. Sreenivasa Rao, B.S.N.S.P. Kumar, S. Raghavendra, and V. Malleswara Rao

Department of ECE, GIT, GITAM University, Visakhapatnam, A.P., India
Isnaidu2003@gmail.com, bsnsp.kumar@gmail.com,
sirigiriraghu@gmail.com

Abstract. A low-power content-addressable memory (CAM) using a differential match line (DMLSA) sense amplifier is proposed in this work. The proposed self-disabled sensing technique can choke the charge current fed into the ML right after the matching comparison is generated. Instead of using typical NOR/NAND-type CAM cells with the single-ended ML, the proposed novel NAND CAM cell with the differential ML design can boost the speed of comparison without sacrificing power consumption. In addition, the 9-T CAM cell provides the complete write, read, and comparison functions to refresh the data and verify its correctness before searching. The CAM with the proposed technique is implemented on silicon to justify the performance by using a standard 90-nm complementary metal–oxide–semiconductor process.

Keywords: CAM, threshold voltage, 9-T, Low power.

1 Introduction

Content-addressable memory (CAM) is a special type of computer memory used in certain very high speed searching applications. It is also known as associative memory, associative storage, or associative array, although the last term is more often used for a programming data structure. Several custom computers, were built to implement CAM, and were referred to as associative computers. Unlike standard computer memory (random access memory or RAM) in which the user supplies a memory address and the RAM returns the data word stored at that address, a CAM is designed such that the user supplies a data word and the CAM searches its entire memory to see if that data word is stored anywhere in it. If the data word is found, the CAM returns a list of one or more storage addresses where the word was found. Thus, a CAM is the hardware embodiment of what in software would be called an associative array. In this paper we are performing the operation for single bit CAM for storing the data and searching the data using low power differential sense amplifier technique (DMLSA) in 90nm technology.

The paper is organized such that the CAM cell structure is explained in section 2. The CAM operation of the proposed SRAM is in section 3. The DMLSA technique is explained in section 4. The observations are explained in section 5. And the results are explained in section 6 and finally concluded in section 7.

D.C. Wyld et al. (Eds.): NeCoM/WeST/WiMoN 2011, CCIS 197, pp. 159–166, 2011.
© Springer-Verlag Berlin Heidelberg 2011

2   CAM Cell Structure

A conventional CAM storage cell is shown in Fig. 1. Its structure is similar to that of the normal RAM. Here in the CAM the memory element used to store the data is SRAM cell and for comparing operation we use another three more transistors for comparing the bit that is stored is matched or not.

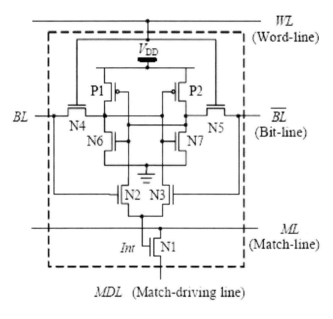

Fig. 1. CAM Cell block diagram

The sense amplifiers and latches provide an interface to give out the result of the search. The signal Pre is used to control pre-charging the match-lines. The address decoder is used for writing original data to CAM cells.

3   CAM Operation

A CAM cell has four different states it can be in: standby where the circuit is idle, reading when the data has been requested and writing when updating the contents and comparing the data that is stored. The four different states work as follows:

3.1   Stand By

If the word line is not asserted, the access transistors N4 and N7 disconnect the cell from the bit lines. The two cross coupled inverters formed by P1, N2 – P2, N3 will continue to reinforce each other as long as they are disconnected from the outside world. The CAM cell using tanner tools is shown in the below fig.2

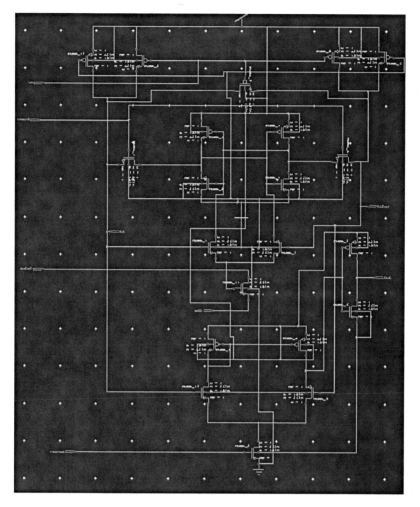

Fig. 2. CAM cell schematic diagram

3.2 Reading

Assume that the content of the memory is a 1, stored at Q. The read cycle is started by precharging both the bit lines to a logical 1, then asserting the word line WL, enabling both the access transistors. The second step occurs when the values stored in Q and Q are transferred to the bit lines by leaving BL at its precharged value and discharging BL through N4 and P1 to a logical 0. On the BL side, the transistors P2 and N3 pull the bit line toward VDD, a logical 1. If the content of the memory was a 0, the opposite would happen and BL would be pulled toward 1 and BL toward 0.

3.3 Writing

The start of a write cycle begins by applying the value to be written to the bit lines. If we wish to write a 0, we would apply a 0 to the bit lines, i.e. setting BL to 1 and BL to

0. This is similar to applying a reset pulse to a SR-latch, which causes the flip flop to change state. A 1 is written by inverting the values of the bit lines. WL is then asserted and the value that is to be stored is latched in. Note that the reason this works is that the bit line input-drivers are designed to be much stronger than the relatively weak transistors in the cell itself, so that they can easily override the previous state of the cross-coupled 3 inverters. Careful sizing of the transistors in a SRAM cell is needed to ensure proper operation.

3.4 Comparing

The search mode begins with pre-charging the match line to VDD, and then the complementary search data are loaded to the bit-lines, which are compared with the content of the storage cell. The CAM cell compares its stored bit with the bit on its corresponding search line. If the bit mismatches, the word's match-line will be pulled down, only when bit match, the match-line's state will be kept as pre-charged. Binary CAM is the simplest type of CAM which uses data search words consisting entirely of 1s and 0s. Ternary CAM (TCAM) allows a third matching state of "X" or "Don't Care" for one or more bits in the stored dataword, thus adding flexibility to the search. For example, a ternary CAM might have a stored word of "10XX0" which will match any of the four search words "10000", "10010", "10100", or "10110". The added search flexibility comes at an additional cost over binary CAM as the internal memory cell must now encode three possible states instead of the two of binary CAM.

4 DMLSA

The detailed schematic of the proposed DMLSA for our differential NAND-type CAM is shown in Fig. 3. The DMLSA senses the voltage on the ML_i_ and SML_i_ to tell if the word is "match" or "mismatch," and then automatically disables the charge path to save the power. Notably, a reset signal SEARCH_EN will set the DMLSA into an

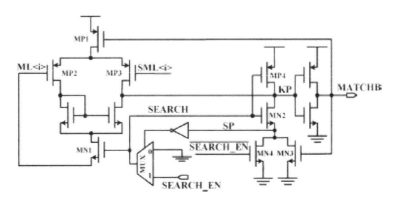

Fig. 3. CAM with DMLSA Block diagram

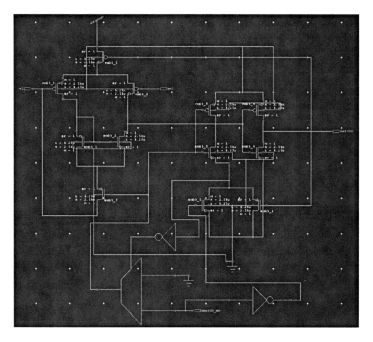

Fig. 4. DMLSA schematic diagram

initial state, where $ML\_i\_ = SML\_i\_ = 0$ and $SP = 0$ before the searching process. The detailed operation of DMLSA in the searching process is described here.

1) *"Mismatch"*: Before the searching process $SP = 0$, SEARCH = SEARCH_EN is pulled to high at the beginning of the searching process. Then, MN1 is turned on to charge the $ML\_i\_$ such that KP will be discharged but not totally pulled down to 0. If there is any "mismatch" By two feedback paths, MATCHB turns MN3 on and MP1 off, respectively, such that the current path of MP1 is shut off to choke the charge current of $ML\_i\_$ and SP is discharged via MN3 to turn off MN1. The former constitutes a positive loop from MATCHB to KP through MN3 and MN2, which more quickly pulls down KP. Therefore, the power consumption is reduced after the searching process. The design of DMLSA in Tanner tools is shown in fig.4.

2) *"Match"*: If all of the CAM cells are "match," $ML\_i\_$ and $SML\_i\_$ are isolated without any current path. The voltage difference between $ML\_i\_$ and $SML\_i\_$ creates an output current of the differential pair (MP2 and MP3) to charge the KP and SP. As soon as KP is charged to high, MATCHB becomes logic 0, indicating that the comparison is a "match." After the SP is raised to high, SEARCH will equal to logic 0 and turn off MN1 to choke the charge current to ML_i.

5 Practical Observations

Table 1. Power Dissipation calculated at 90nm technology for various temperatures

S.No	Temperature(T)	Power Dissipation
1	10	2.214141e-007 W
2	30	2.022490e-007 W
3	90	1.898992e-007 W

6 Results

It is observed that the value that is stored in the CAM cell is '1' and that is compared with the value '1' by driving on to the MDL. If both stored bit and MDL are matched the output will be '0', if it is mis-matched the output is'1'. Here it is observed that ML=0 as shown in fig.5.

The CAM cell output with DMLSA techniques shown in fig.6. When the stored bit and SML bit matches then the output of 'matchb' is '0'. If it is mis-matches the output is '1'. Here the below waveform shows for matched condition.

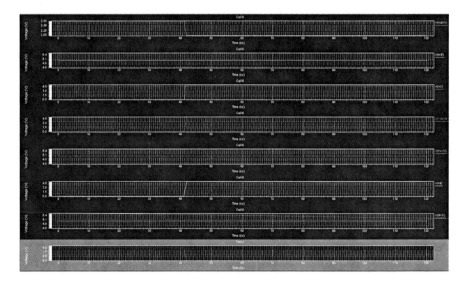

Fig. 5. CAM Cell output waveform using DMLSA

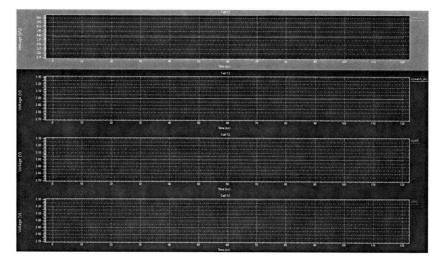

Fig. 6. DMLSA Output

7   Conclusion

The proposed self-disabled sensing technique can choke the charge current fed into the ML right after the matching comparison is generated. Instead of using typical NOR/NAND-type CAM cells with the single-ended ML, the proposed novel NAND CAM cell with the differential ML design can boost the speed of comparison without sacrificing power consumption. In addition, the 9-T CAM cell provides the complete write, read, and comparison functions to refresh the data and verify its correctness before searching. Power dissipation and output waveforms of the single bit CAM cell is calculated in 90nm BSIM3 technology at various temperatures and the DMLSA technique is proposed in this paper for CAM.

References

1. Chang, Y.-J., Liao, Y.-H.: Hybrid-Type CAM Design for Both Power and Performance Efficiency. IEEE Trans. Very Large Scale Integration (VLSI) Systems 16, 965–974 (2008)
2. Haigh, J., Clark, L.: Fast Translation Lookaside Buffers for Low power Embedded Microprocessors. Integration: The VLSI Journal 41(4), 509–523 (2008)
3. Pagiamtzis, K., Sheikholeslami, A.: A low-power contentaddressable memory (CAM) using pipelined hierarchical search scheme. IEEE J. of Solid-State Circuits 39(9), 1512–1519 (2004)
4. Wu, Y., Hu, J.: Low-power content addressable memory using 2N-2N2P Circuits. In: Proc. IEEE ICCCAS 2006, Guilin, China, pp. 2657–2661 (June 2006)
5. Arsovski, I., Sheikholeslami, A.: A mismatch-dependent power allocation technique for match-line sensing in content-addressable memories. IEEE J. of Solid-State Circuits 38(11), 1958–(1966)

6. Kramer, A., Denker, J.S., Flower, B., et al.: 2nd order adiabatic computation with 2N-2P and 2N-2N2P logic circuits. In: Proc. The International Symposium on Low Power Electronics and Design, Dana Point, pp. 191–196 (1995)
7. Hu, J., Xu, T., Li, H.: A lower-power register file based on complementary pass-transistor adiabatic logic. IEICE Trans. on Inf. & Sys. E88-D(7), 1479–1485 (2005)
8. Natarajan, A., Jasinski, D., Burleson, W., et al.: A hybrid adiabatic content addressable memory for ultra low-power applications. In: Proc. Great Lakes Symposium on VLSI, Washington, D.C., USA, April 28-29, pp. 72–75 (2003)
9. Wu, Y., Hu, J.: Low-power content addressable memory using 2N-2N2P Circuits. In: Proc. IEEE ICCCAS 2006, Guilin, China, pp. 2657–2661 (June 2006)
10. Maksimovic, D., Oklobdzija, V.G.: Integrated power clock generators for low energy logic. In: Proc. IEEE Power Electronics Specialists Conf., Atlanta, GA, June 18-22, pp. 61–67 (1995)
11. Moon, Y., Jeong, D.K.: A 32×32-bit adiabatic register file with supply clock generator. IEEE J. of Solid-State Circuits 33(5), 696–701 (1998)
12. Pagiamtzis, K., Sheikholeslami, A.: Content-addressable memory (CAM) circuits and architectures: A tutorial and survey. IEEE J. Solid-State Circuits 41, 712 (2006)
13. Juan, T., Lang, T., Navarro Reducing, J.: TLB power requirements. In: Proc. Int. Symp. Low Power Electronics and Design, p. 196 (1997)
14. Miyatake, H., Tanaka, M., Mori, Y.: A design for high-speed low-power CMOS fully parallel content-addressable memory macros. IEEE J. Solid-State Circuits 36, 956 (2001)
15. Arsovski, I., Sheikholeslami, A.: A mismatch-dependent power allocation technique for match-line sensing in content-addressable memories. IEEE J. Solid-State Circuits 38, 1958 (2003)
16. Zukowski, C.A., Wang, S.Y.: Use of selective precharge for low-power content-addressable memories. In: Proc. Int. Symp. Circuits and Syst., p. 1788 (1997)
17. Cheng, K.H., Wei, C.H., Jiang, S.Y.: Static divided word matching line for low-power content addressable memory design. In: Proc. Int. Symp. Circuits and Syst., p. 629 (2004)
18. Chang, Y.J., Lai, F., Yang, C.L.: Zero-aware asymmetric SRAM cell for reducing cache power in writing zero. IEEE Trans. Very Large Scale Integr. Syst. 12, 827 (2004)

Header Compression Scheme over Hybrid Satellite-WiMAX Network

Yung-Wey Chong, Imad J. Mohamad, and Tat-Chee Wan

National Advanced IPv6 Centre,
11800 Universiti Sains Malaysia, Penang, Malaysia
{chong,imad}@nav6.org, tcwan@cs.usm.my
http://www.nav6.usm.my

Abstract. Today the interest for global broadband access has led to the integration of hybrid networks that can provide wide area coverage and new services. Although satellite network plays a vital role in providing coverage over the surface of the earth, Line-Of-Sight (LOS) is still an obstacle in satellite communications. Thus a hybrid network between satellite and terrestrial wireless systems (IEEE802.16 WiMAX) will be the key to affordable services that can provide broadband connectivity to rural and remote areas. In this paper, a header compression scheme is proposed over hybrid satellite-WiMAX network. The proposed header compression scheme (Hybrid-ROHC or in short H-ROHC) will enable the saving of resources over the hybrid network where bandwidth is a premium.

Keywords: Satellite Communication, Header Compression, IEEE802.16 WiMAX, Hybrid Network, H-ROHC.

1 Introduction

The integration of satellite and terrestrial wireless system such as IEEE802.16 WiMAX [1] is an effective approach in providing anytime-anywhere connectivity to remote area and for disaster communication services. Although hybrid satellite-WiMAX system seems to be an ideal network, transporting IP based packet via satellite can be a challenge. Long propagation delay and significant packet losses often cause performance degradation in the satellite network. Moreover the high header overhead will seriously consume the bandwidth and lower the transmission efficiency. Thus it is vital to use the scarce radio resources for the hybrid network in an efficient way. By applying header compression to the IP traffic, incurred overhead in hybrid satellite-WiMAX network can be reduced.

There are a number of header compression mechanisms that can be used to compress the headers of IP traffic namely Robust Header Compression (ROHC) [2] and Payload Header Suppression (PHS). Although ROHC is more complex than PHS in terms of implementation, previous study [3] shows that ROHC has better efficiency over PHS. Since the compression scheme for hybrid network need to work not only over wireless network, it must be robust enough in error

D.C. Wyld et al. (Eds.): NeCoM/WeST/WiMoN 2011, CCIS 197, pp. 167–176, 2011.
© Springer-Verlag Berlin Heidelberg 2011

prone satellite link. Thus the proposed header compression scheme is based on ROHC algorithm due to its ability to tolerate losses and errors.

Section 2 describes hybrid satellite-WiMAX network overview and related work. Section 3 presents proposed header compression scheme over the hybrid network. Section 4 shows predicted performance of proposed approach. Section 5 concludes the proposal and ideas for future work.

2   Hybrid Satellite-WiMAX Network Overview and Related Work

In a hybrid satellite-WiMAX network, WiMAX Subscriber Station (SS) is integrated with WiMAX radio interface and access is made at MAC level through the setup of connections with the WiMAX Base Station (BS). SS will negotiate the QoS parameters with BS and if it grants the process, a MAC connection is established at WiMAX level. Dynamic bandwidth allocation is used in the satellite subnetwork for optimization. The WiMAX class of services is then mapped onto the DVB-RCS capacity requests.

Return Channel Satellite Terminal (RCST) is the gateway to/from the access network to the satellite gateway (satGW). It setup DVB-RCS channels and ensure the correct communication over satellite link. DVB-S2 is used on forward link whereas DVB-RCS is used on return link transmission. DVB-S2 is used because it supports Adaptive Coding and Modulation (ACM) and adapts per-time slot basis depending on the Signal-to-Noise-plus-Interference Ration (SNIR) at the destination terminal whereas on the return link, MF-TDMA and adaptive coding is used to enable bidimentional framing [4].

To transport IP data over DVB-S2/RCS system, ULE [5], a data link protocol defined in RFC 4326 to transport the IP packet directly over MPEG2 transport streams (TS) is used. The payload is first wrapped into a Sub-Network Data Unit (SNDU) structure with a 4-byte SNDU header. The SNDU header consists of destination address present field (D), length and payload type. If D is enabled, additional 6 bytes Destination Network Point of Attachment (NPA) Address will be allocated after the payload type. The receiver destination NPA Address is used to idenfity the receiver within MPEG2-TS transmission network.

Although, various systems for interworking of satellite and wireless terrestrial communication networks has been studied, to our best knowledge, there are no publicly released studies of header compression over hybrid satellite-WiMAX network. Centonza and McCann [6] presented a hybrid network solution which employs DVB-RCS domains as a backhaul for content delivery to WiMAX domains. Two different radio network choices were proposed for coorporation in the hybrid network environment. Mobility and QoS management solution for the hybrid network were tabled as well.

Fan et al. [7] presented an IP-based reference architecture which supports a range of transport requirements. It focused on the requirements and design constrains that were faced in the design of the network-layer of the reference system. Gur, Bayhan and Alagoz [8] discussed a heterogeneous system of satellite-WiMAX network for efficient delivery of multimedia services. Enhancements in

WiMAX Base Station (BS) and Multicast Broadcast Service Controller (MBSC) which allows interworking in multimedia delivery context were also proposed.

Despite the great interest in hybrid satellite-WiMAX technology, the large majority of studies focused on mobility, QoS or multicast capabilities. None has used header compression over the hybrid network. This paper fills this gap by proposing a header compression scheme over hybrid satellite-WiMAX network.

3 Proposed Header Compression Scheme (H-ROHC) over Hybrid Satellite-WiMAX Network

IEEE802.16 is a connection oriented access technology without bi-directional native multicast support. It has defined only downlink multicast support which may be a problem for some IPv6 protocols such as IPv6 Neighbour Discovery (ND) and ARP. Since commercial network models extend 802.16 MAC transport connection all the way to an access router (AR), there are multiple ways of deploying IP protocols that traditionally assume the availability of multicast at the link layer [9]. One way is to treat IEEE802.16 Message Authentication Code (MAC) transport connections between a SS and BS as point-to-point IP links so that IPv6 protocols can be run without any problem. Another method is to use bridging to support bidirectional multicast. The proposed header compression scheme (H-ROHC) is used to reduce the overhead for both model.

3.1 H-ROHC in Point-to-Point Link Model

In this model, WiMAX BS is anchored with an AR located at the RCST. In short, the satellite is not included in the WiMAX network. The WiMAX Subnet consists of a single BS/AR and multiple SS. Each link between a SS and AR is allocated a separate, unique prefix or a set of unique prefixes by the AR. In this case, a tunnel exist between the BS and AR as shown in Figure 1.

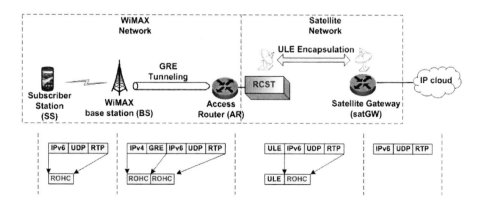

Fig. 1. Base Station connecting with Access Router through GRE tunneling

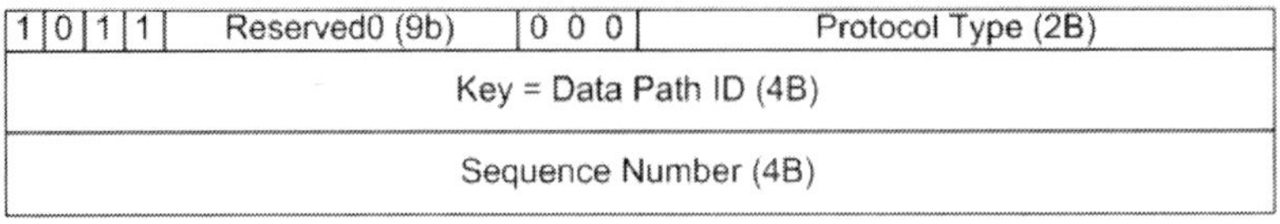

1	0	1	1	Reserved0 (9b)	0 0 0	Protocol Type (2B)
Key = Data Path ID (4B)							
Sequence Number (4B)							

Fig. 2. GRE header format

GRE encapsulation is used as the tunneling protocol for the data plane between BS and AR. The payload packet is encapsulated in a GRE packet and the resulting packet is then encapsulated again in IP protocol. The GRE protocol is used without Checksum and Routing option. Therefore Checksum Present and Routing Present bit are set to zero. The fields Reserved0 and Reserved1 are set to 0. Since it is not using PPTP, the 3 bits GRE protocol version is also cleared to 0. Figure 2 shows the GRE Header setting used in the hybrid network.

The BS maps the 802.16e Connection ID (CID) on the GRE Tunnels for both upstream and downstream traffic. There is a 1 to 1 correspondence between 802.16e connections and GRE keys. Sequence Number field is set for handover optimizations. Due to double headers (IP/IP), the GRE tunneling add overhead between the endpoints. For example, for each IPv4 packet transmitted, the extra overhead due to GRE tunnel is 20 bytes plus GRE Header which is 12 bytes. This leads to great wastage of resource. Thus there are two parts of compression that needs to be dealt with; inner header compression and outer header compression.

For the inner header compression, the original IP packet (IP/UDP/RTP) is compressed at the SS as if there is no encapsulation. The compression parameter of ROHC is negotiated during WiMAX Connection Admission Control. The IP packet is compressed with ROHC at the SS before GRE tunneling and ULE encapsulations are applied. At the satGW, on receiving the compressed packet, it is decompressed using corresponding ROHC profiles and finally the original packet is forwarded to the core network (CN).

A second compression happens at the outer IP header which is added at the BS (to the compressed packet). The compression scheme for the GRE header is similar to the scheme applied to the IP header. Since 8 out of 12 bytes of GRE headers are static (except for GRE sequence number) and do not change during the duration of the flow, ROHC over GRE is extremely simple to implement. Here, GRE header can be seen as part of extension header chains. By removing static fields from most of the messages, exploiting dependencies and the predictability of other fields, the total header size can be reduced significantly. The sequence number field in the GRE header contains a counter value for a GRE tunnel. The sequence number in the GRE header linearly increases with each new encapsulated IP datagram per GRE key, and when the compressor (BS) is confident that the decompressor (AR) has received the pattern, the sequence number will not be sent again. The decompressor will then applies linear extrapolation to reconstruct the sequence number in the GRE header.

The AR will decompresses the outer IP header and forwards the compressed packet (inner header compression) to the RCST where it encapsulates the IP packet in ULE SNDU. To differentiate between streams of uncompressed and compressed packets, the compressed packets carry payload type 0x00AC instead of using 0x8000 for IPv4 packet and 0x86DD for IPv6 packets. The resulting SNDU is further encapsulated in MPEG2-TS packet which has a fixed-length of 188 bytes consisting 4 byte header.

3.2   H-ROHC in Ethernet Link Model

In IEEE802.16 standard, packets going over the air between SS and BS are identified in the IEEE802.16 MAC header by the Connection Identifier (CID) of the particular connection and not unique 48-bit MAC addresses. To realize Ethernet over IEEE802.16 access network, the point-to-point connections between BS and AR is bridged. Figure 3 shows the Ethernet link model in the hybrid network.

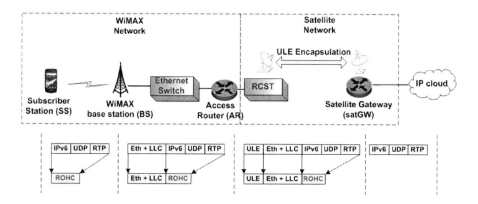

Fig. 3. Implementation of Ethernet link model in hybrid network

However due to its roots in CSMA/CD protocol, Ethernet needs to have a minimum frame size of 64 bytes in which 14 bytes are used for MAC header and 4 are used for Frame Check Sequence (FCS). This leaves a minimum payload of an Ethernet packet to 46 bytes in which may not be an advantage to use header compression since the frame will be padded to inflate the size to at least 46 bytes.

To implement H-ROHC in this model, LLC encapsulation is used over ROHC packet [10]. An SAP value (Logical Link Control Address which includes SSAP and DSAP) is allocated to ROHC packet. Thus when the LLC frame arrives at the decompressor, it will recognize the LLC encapsulation. The total per-packet overhead for this solution is 21 bytes, 18 bytes for the Ethernet MAC header and FCS plus three bytes for the LLC header carrying ROHC identification. The compressed packet will be sent via a bridge SNDU (Type 0x0001) at the satellite link as shown in Figure 4.

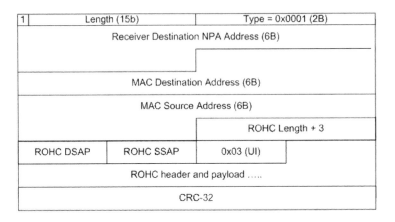

Fig. 4. SNDU format for a bridged payload

4   Performance Evaluation

This section estimates the performance of using H-ROHC over the hybrid satellite-WiMAX network. Although there are 3 compression state, namely Initialization and Refresh (IR), First Order (FO) and Second Order (SO), to simplify the analysis, only SO state is considered because compression operates at the highest efficiency in this state.

When compressor is operating at the highest efficiency at SS, it is capable of reducing the headers of IP packet down to 1 byte. However for IPv6 UDP datagrams, the UDP packet must be coupled with a 2 bytes UDP checksum thus the smallest compressed header for IPv6/UDP/RTP stream will be 3 bytes. Two cases are compared: (1) header compression is not used and (2) header compression is used. The header size is taken from the BS to the AR. The comparison is shown in three different profile, namely profile R1(IPv6/UDP/RTP), R2 (IPv6/UDP) and R4 (IPv6).

Figure 5 (a) shows the header size for IPv6/IPv6 in point-to-point link model. Without compression, the header size increased tremendously from the original IP packet due to IP-in-IP encapsulation. The double header can be reduced drastically by compressing the GRE tunneling overhead to 3 at the BS where 1 byte compressed header (for outer IP packet) is coupled with 2 bytes of GRE checksum.

Although IP packet are compressed in Ethernet link model, the Ethernet header and LLC header caused addditional overhead in order to support on-link multicast. As shown in Figure 5 (b), the BS will add 21 bytes of header to the compressed packet received from SS resulting greater header overhead as compared to point-to-point link model.

Figure 5 (c) shows the compression efficiency of header compression for different profiles in point-to-point link model and Ethernet model. The header compression solution (H-ROHC) in point-to-point link model is the most effective as it gives an average compression efficiency of 94% for IPv6 flows. In both

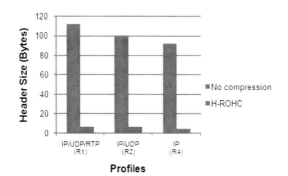

(a) Header compression for point-to-point link model

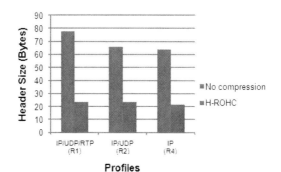

(b) Header compression for Ethernet link model

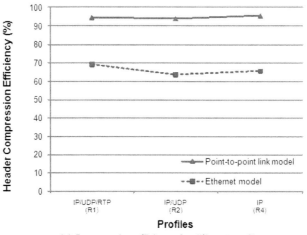

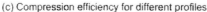

(c) Compression efficiency for different profiles

Fig. 5. Header compression for IPv6

model, profiles R1 gives the best results because the profile is defined to compress maximum headers.

A theoretical model of achievable data throughput for H-ROHC compressed IPv6/UDP/RTP stream and uncompressed IPv6/UDP/RTP over ULE/MPEG2-TS using packing mode can be calculated. The number of MPEG2-TS frames transmitted per second (TS) can be calculated using the following formula:

$$TS = \frac{Bandwidth}{188 \times 8} \tag{1}$$

where $Bandwidth$ represents the bandwidth of the link in bps

Each MPEG2-TS frame is 188 bytes and out of these 188 bytes, 184 bytes are used to carry its payload, the ULE SNDU. Assuming that the Payload Pointer (PP) of the MPEG2-TS frame is negligible, the number of bytes that can be used by an ULE SNDU (ULE) is

$$ULE = TS \times 184 \tag{2}$$

Each ULE packet adds 14 bytes of overhead with 4 bytes taken up by the ULE header, 6 bytes for the NPA address and 4 byes for 32-bit CRC. The number of uncompressed IPv6/UDP/RTP packets that can be sent in 1 second is denoted by $PPS_{uncompressed}$. Achievable data throughput in bps, denoted by $Throughput_{uncompressed}$ can be calculated as below:

$$PPS_{uncompressed} = \frac{ULE}{Payload + Header\_Size + ULE\_Packet\_Size} \tag{3}$$

$$Throughput_{uncompressed} = PPS_{uncompressed} \times Payload \times 8 \tag{4}$$

The number of compressed IPv6/UDP/RTP packets that can be sent in 1 second, denoted by $PPS_{compressed}$, and achievable data throughput in bps, $Throughput_{compressed}$ is derived using the following formula. Note that only the optimal mode (which is SO state) is considered in the calculation.

$$PPS_{compressed} = \frac{ULE}{Payload + HROHC\_Header\_Size + ULE\_Packet\_Size} \tag{5}$$

$$Throughput_{compressed} = PPS_{compressed} \times Payload \times 8 \tag{6}$$

where $HROHC\_Header\_Size$ for point-to-point link model is 3 bytes and $HROHC\_Header\_Size$ for Ethernet link model is 21 bytes. Figure 6 shows the maximum theoretical data throughput over ULE/MPEG2-TS packing mode for both point-to-point link model and Ethernet link model. It is noted that maximum theoretical data throughput for point-to-point link model is higher than Ethernet link model due to high overhead for H-ROHC in Ethernet model.

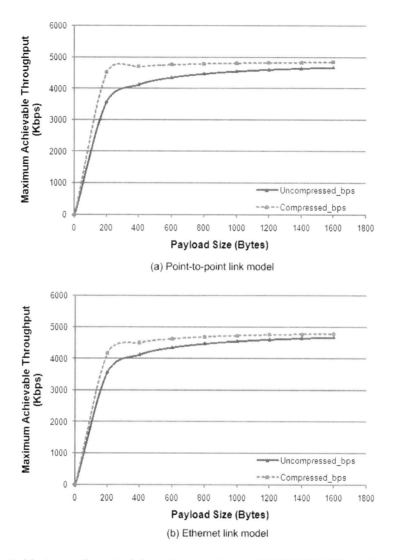

(a) Point-to-point link model

(b) Ethernet link model

Fig. 6. Maximum theoretical data throughput over ULE/MPEG2-TS packing mode

5   Conclusion

This paper proposed a header compression scheme based on ROHC over hybrid satellite-WiMAX network. The results showed that H-ROHC reduced overall header overhead drastically in both point-to-point and Ethernet link model. Although the complexity of H-ROHC is greater in point-to-point link model, header compression using GRE tunneling is more efficient and provides better utilization of the networks which have low bandwidth and scarce resources. Since bandwidth is costlier than the processing time which can be neglected in high processing router, the issue of complexity can be outweighted. H-ROHC Ethernet link model will be the prefer choice when deployment requires the use of Ethernet CS in WiMAX network since it is much simpler to be implemented. Future work may includes the implementation and testing of more profiles such as TCP over the hybrid satellite-WiMAX network.

References

1. IEEE 802.16e: IEEE Standard for local and metropolitan area networks, Air Interface for Fixed Broadband Wireless Access Systems. Amendment 2: Physical and Medium Access Control Layers for Combined Fixed and Mobile Operation in Licensed Bands and Corrigendum 1 (February 2006)
2. Bormann, C., et al.: Robust Header Conmpression (ROHC): Framework and four profiles: RTP, UDP, ESP and uncompressed. IETF RFC 3095 (July 2001)
3. Nuaymi, L., Bouida, N., Lahbil, N., Godlewski, P.: Header Overhead Estimation, Header Suppresion and Header Compression in WiMAX. In: Proc. Wireless and Mobile Computing, Networking and Communications, WiMOB (2007)
4. Castro, M.A.V., Fernandez, D.P., Kota, S.: VoIP Transmission Cross-Layer Design over Satellite-WiMAX Hybrid Network. Paper Presented at the Military Communications Conference, MILCOM (2007)
5. Fairhurst, G., Collini-Nocker, B.: Unidirectional lightweight encapsulation (ULE) for transmission of IP datagrams over an MPEG-2 transport stream (TS). IETF RFC 4326 (2005)
6. Centonza, A., McCann, S.: Architectural and Protocol Structure for Composite DVB-RCS/IEEE802.16 Platforms. Proc. Digital Video Broadcasting Over Satellite: Present and Future, 35–40 (2006)
7. Fan, L., Baudoin, C., Rodriguez, F., Ramos, A., Guerra, J., Cuesta, B., et al.: SATSIX: A Network Architecutre for Next-Generation DVB-RCS Systems. IP Networking over Next-Generation Satellite Systems, 103–125 (2007)
8. Gur, G., Hayhan, S., Alagoz, F.: Hybrid Satellite-IEEE 802.16 system for mobile multimedia delivery. International Journal of Satellite Communications and Networking (2010), 10.1002/sat.971
9. Madanapalli, S.: Analysis of IPv6 Link Models for 802.16 Based Networks. IETF RFC 4968 (2007)
10. Bormann, C.: Robust Header Compression (ROHC) over 802 networks. IETF work in progress (2009)

Comparing the Performance Parameters of Network on Chip with Regular and Irregular Topologies

S. Umamaheswari[1], J. Rajapaul Perinbam[2], K. Monisha[1], and J. Jahir Ali[1]

[1] Department Of Information Technology
Madras Institute Of Technology, Anna University
uma_sai@annauniv.edu,
{kmonisha90,zahir1010}@gmail.com
[2] Department of Electronics and Communication Engineering,
RMK Engineering College, Chennai
jrp.ece@rmkec.ac.in

Abstract. Scalability and reusability are the critical issues concerning any application. As far as Network on Chip is concerned the above said issues are addressed through generating application specific topologies. Application specific topologies are irregular in structure and take into account certain factors like communication weight, area and energy constraints while building up the topology. Regular topologies like 2D mesh, spidergon etc are more structured and are built not considering much about the system characteristics and other requirements. Consequently the throughput and power utilizations vary depending on the topology. Our aim is to provide a comparative analysis on the performance measures of irregular application specific networks against the regular topological structures.

Keywords: Network on Chip (NoC), Irregular topology, performance comparison, Topology generation, Throughput analysis.

1 Introduction

System-on-Chip (SoC) refers to integrating all components of a system like computer or other electronic system into a single chip. The components of a System on Chip are analog or digital in nature, like FPGAs, DSPs and other Intellectual Properties (IP). These IPs communicate with each other, in such a manner that they provide the functionality of the system. Earlier SoCs used normal bus based system for communication. But this causes problems like synchronization, energy consumption, area constraints, lack of modularity other clock skew problems. Scalability is very important for SoCs, because of the shrinking technology sizes and increasing scale of complexity.

Network on Chip (NoC) is the new emerging trend in the area of SoC. NoC replaces design-specific global on-chip wiring with a general-purpose on-chip interconnection network. As the system becomes general purpose, it supports scalability and reusability. Using a network in the place of wiring has several more

D.C. Wyld et al. (Eds.): NeCoM/WeST/WiMoN 2011, CCIS 197, pp. 177–186, 2011.
© Springer-Verlag Berlin Heidelberg 2011

advantages like structure, performance and interoperability. The major components in NoC are the IPs which act as the nodes of the network and the routers which hold the routing logic. NoCs reduce the length of wiring by splitting the wires between the nodes and the router and between the routers. The network concept provides modularity and high level optimization.

Though NoC provides scalability and reusability, it has certain challenges to face too. The growing components like the routers and the introduction of complex logic into the routers consume extra power. The system should be designed in such a way that, it works within the power constraints while providing the functionality.

There are two main phases involved in building up a system. They are network topology generation and floor-planning. Floor-plan determines the physical placing of cores and routers. This influences the overall area and the length of physical links. The network topology indicates the overall connection between cores and routers, and between routers. The network layout may be regular or irregular in structure. Regular topologies are 2D Mesh, Spidergon, Ring and Tree networks. These regular topologies have the advantages of topology reuse and low design complexity and are suitable for homogeneous cores, e.g., general purpose CPUs, FPGAs, etc. Application specific networks are developed by constructing irregular topologies. These networks are custom build and tailored to specific application.

The high level simulation of on chip network is still in progression. There are lots of trade off involved in choosing simulation tool and defining the physical constraints for it. Due to similarities between NoCs and networks, NS2 is emerging as the most suitable tool for evaluating NoC design.

In this paper we compare the performance of irregular topology networks against the regular ones. Focus is given on throughput and energy consumption. The paper is organized as follows; section 2 gives the background and related literature to our work. Section 3 discusses the regular topological structures. Section 4 describes the irregular topological structure with the algorithm for generation of the same.

2   Background and Related Work

In designing NoC systems, there are several issues to be concerned with, such as topologies, routing algorithms, performance, latency, complexity and so on. The design of system-on-chip (SoC) in [1],[4] provides integrated solutions to challenging design problems in the telecommunications, multimedia, and consumer electronics domains. Micro-network control [1] model provides good quality of service and manages the network resources by providing dynamic control. Focusing on using probabilistic metrics to quantify design objectives such as performance and power will lead to a major change in design methodologies.

The amount of energy utilized and hence the amount of power consumed varies in accordance with the number of cores in the chip [2]. The heterogeneous cores used in SoCs have varied functionalities to support highly sophisticated applications of SoCs. When these cores are structured with regular topologies, keeping in consideration of the sophisticated functionalities of the applications, they may degrade the performance of other components by overriding their needs [5],[6]. As a solution to this problem, irregular interconnection topologies understand the real need of the applications. The proposed low power irregular topology generation algorithm [8], builds application specific networks that have the interconnection architecture which suits the traffic characteristics of the application. This reduces the power consumption in the application by 49%.

Higher level protocols that are layered on top of simple network interface [3] provide a simple reliable datagram interface to each IP in the system.

The High Throughput Chip-Level Integration of Communicating Heterogeneous Elements (HT-CLICHÉ) [7], optimizes the system circuit and increases the number of virtual channels for communication from four to eight. This increase in the number of virtual channel increases the throughput while preserving the frequency.

The performance metrics of NoC are being studied under different topological structures. NoC mesh architecture is constructed and the behavior is observed under different traffic modes such as Exponential, Pareto and Constant Bit Rate(CBR) mode with the network simulator NS2 [9]. By this simulation, the authors analyzed the common network performance metrics such as packet delay, throughput, communication load and drop probability under different buffer sizes and different traffic injection rates.

For low power application specific NoCs, a two-phase flow-topology generation and floor planning algorithm is designed to reduce the number of routers, to guarantee deadlock free and minimize power [12].

The case study in [11] presents the multimedia application VOPD, which is the best suited application for obtaining more different topologies with more cores.

The website [10] provides guidelines for working in NS2 and programming in Tcl.

3   Regular Topologies

In this section we consider three network topologies under regular interconnection structure. They are,

1.   2D Mesh,
2.   WK Recursive and
3.   Spidergon.

3.1 2D Mesh Topology

Two-Dimensional mesh topology (Fig.1) consists of a grid structure with routers in the intersection of the lines in the grid. All routers placed in the topology are connected to routers on three sides. The boundary routers in 2D Mesh have connections with the neighboring routers on three sides and the core in the fourth side. The boundary routers in 2D Mesh have connections with the neighboring routers on three sides and the core in the fourth side. The edge routers, which are in the corners of the boundary, have connections with two routers in sides, in addition to the core. The inner routers have connections with routers in all four sides with the core being connected as the fifth.

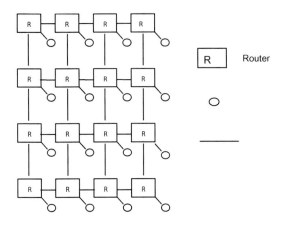

Fig. 1. A Mesh Network with 16 Nodes

3.2 WK Recursive Topology

WK[N_d, L] is a recursive network topology (fig.2). It is denoted as   WK(N_d, L), where,

    1. N_d represents the node degree. It means the amplitude that represents the number of virtual nodes that constitute the fully connected undirected graph.

    2.   L represents the expansion level. Each of the N_d virtual node represents a WK topology WK(N_d, L-1) for all L > 1.

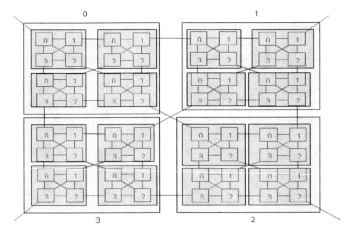

Fig. 2. A WK(4,3) Network

3.3 Spidegon Topology

The Spidergon NoC network is a combination star and ring topology. It is constructed based on elementary polygon network which is formed by arranging 4R+1 (R = 1, 2, etc.) routers in a fashion that combines the topological structures of ring and star. There is a single central router that connects to the 4R routers which giving star topology. The peripheral routers are connected to each other in the form of ring network. The valence (m) of the network is characterized by m=4R, which represents the number of peripheral nodes.

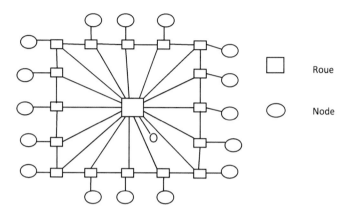

Fig. 3. Spidergon Topology

4   Irregular Topology

Irregular topologies are derived to make the system more application and specification oriented. This is achieved by taking several constraints into consideration while, forming the network layout. As a result, the optimization objectives such as power consumption, area of the chip, number of routers in the system can be optimized easily.

In [13] the authors proposed a two step topology generation algorithm, which we use in our paper to generate the irregular, interconnects. The first part of the algorithm, involves initial cluster formation based on the communication characteristics between the IPs. Each cluster is then assigned to a router. In the second part, the topology is constructed by connecting the clusters to each other one by one, based on the communication weights between the clusters. The pseudo code used in the generation of irregular topology is shown in the Figure 5.

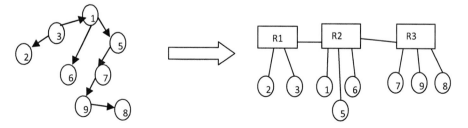

Fig. 4. Irregular Topology Generation

Pseudo code for irregular topology generation

```
#1 compute r: n <=  p*r-2*(r-1)
#2 call: create_cluster (leading_node)
#3 FOR each cluster formed in step2
       #3.1 find: total communication load
       #3.2 choose clusters based on total communication
            Load
END FOR
#4 optimize the number of clusters
#5 Assign routers to each cluster
#6 Form topology by connecting the routers
#7 Induce traffic in the topology
```

The number of routers to be used can be minimized by using the following equation.

$$n \leq pr-2(r-1) \tag{1}$$

where, n represents the number of nodes in the network, p represents the number of ports in each router, r represents the minimum number of routers that will be calculated with the Eq.(1).

5 Simulation

In this section we explain the parameters used for simulating the NoC model in NS2.

5.1 Traffic Models and Parameters

We use three different traffic models to make the comparative study of the NoC performance under different topologies. They are,

1. Constant Bit Rate(CBR) traffic model,
2. Exponential traffic model and
3. Pareto traffic model.

These three traffic models have different traffic generation patterns which provide ease in observing the behaviour of NoC under different traffic scenarios.

The number of flits generated under different traffic models under different traffic rates can be observed from the output trace files. The Table 1 shows the count of flits.

We observed the throughput achievements of all network layouts under the three traffic models and under the traffic rates 100,1400,200 Mbs.

Table 1. No. of Flits Generated in different Traffic Models

Traffic Model	Traffic Rate (Mbps)	No. of flits generated
	100	350000
CBR	140	525000
	200	650000
	100	300000
	140	475000
	200	575000
	100	300000
Pareto	140	475000
	200	575000

5.2 Simulation Parameters

In each traffic model we define set of traffic parameters to observe the perfect behaviour of the network under those models. We assign the flit size to be constant as 8 bytes. The ON and OFF times of Pareto and Exponential traffic models are taken to be the same as 0.1 s and 1 ms respectively. During the ON state, there will be a sudden burst of traffic all through the network.

With all the participating nodes as sources and all nodes sinks we analyse the performance of each network. The exponential and pareto traffic models are similar in the fact that they induce sudden burst of traffic during the ON time and no traffic in the OFF time. They differ only in the point that exponential traffic model follows normal distribution and Pareto model follows Pareto distribution

6 Results

The throughput achieved in different network models under CBR traffic model is analyzed. From the simulation results it becomes obvious that custom build application specific topology gives higher throughput compared to other network topologies. Among the regular topologies, WK outperforms Spidergon and mesh.

Here we present the graphs obtained while comparing the throughputs of regular and application specific networks under CBR and Pareto traffic models.

6.1 Throughput Comparison under CBR Traffic Model

CBR traffic model, as it name implies, induces a constant rate traffic in the network. We can fix the desired rate in NS2. In our simulation we considered three traffic rates 100, 140 and 200 Mps. The fig.5, gives the comparison of performance in terms of throughput for CBR model. The graph is plotted for throughput in Mbps against the time scale in microseconds (ms).

The CBR graph analyzes shows, application specific network achieves maximum throughput than any other regular topologies. This is due to the reason, when highly communicating nodes are placed under the same cluster the success rate of a packet being delivered to the target increases as direct communicating links connect the source and destination nodes.

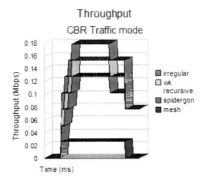

Fig. 5. Throughput achieved in different networks

WK recursive network also follows a cluster based topology like application specific network, with difference that the former is built without considering the parameters relating to communication weights and it is rigid in the choice of number of routers to be used and number of nodes in each cluster. These factors lead to the difference in throughput achievement.

The difference in throughput between Spidergon and Mesh topology is due to the fact that, though Mesh topology has higher number links between routers, the shortest path between any two communicating nodes includes minimum number of hops in the Spidergon network than in Mesh network.

6.2 Throughput Comparison under Pareto Traffic Model

The fig.6 gives the comparative analysis of throughput of different NoC topologies under pareto traffic model. This model generates traffic according to pareto distribution, which induces sudden burst of traffic with alternating periods of idleness characterized by zero traffic. The ON time and OFF time are set to 1ms and 0.1s respectively.

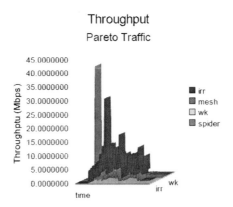

Fig. 6. Throughput achieved in different networks

The graph shows that, at the start of traffic burst, mesh topology seems to outweigh. But when ON and OFF periods alternates the performance of mesh declines. At the same time, application specific topologies maintains their packet delivery rate leading to higher throughput. The throughput of WK, Spidergon topologies varies between those of mesh and application specific topologies.

6.3 Energy Comparison

We use the energy model suggested in [6] to compare the energy consumed in the four topologies. The eqn. 2 is used in the calculation of energy.

$$E_{Av} = Nb_{flits}S_{flis} (h_{av} (0.39+0.12\times l_{avw}) + 09776 h_{av}-1)) \qquad (2)$$

The graph analyzes (Fig.8) shows that application specific topologies consume minimum energy while achieving higher throughput. Mesh and Spidergon topologies vary slightly in the total energy consumed and WK tops the analysis.

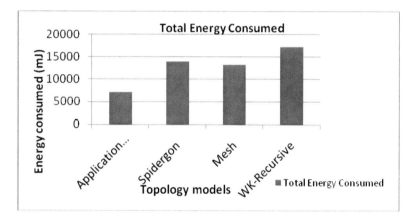

Fig. 7. Throughput achieved in different networks

7 Conclusion and Future Work

Thus the choice of topology depends upon the requirement of the application. The overall performance of application specific network is high compared to all other network topologies. At the same time, designing the topology generation algorithms for these networks is a challenge. There exists a tradeoff between the choice of network topology and the performance achieved.

In future work, we compare the various application specific topology generation algorithms. The objective is to suggest algorithm for well customized topology generation that suits most of the embedded system applications.

References

1. Benini, L., De Micheli, G.: Networks on Chips: A New SoC Paradigm. IEEE Computer 35(1), 70–78 (2002)
2. Chang, K.-C., Chen, T.-F.: Low-power algorithm for automatic topology generation for application-specific networks on chips. IET Comput. Digit. Tech. 2(3), 239–249 (2008)
3. Dally, W.J., Towles, B.: Route packets and not wires: on-chip interconnection networks. In: Proc. Design and Automation Conf., pp. 684–689 (2001)
4. Henkel, J., Wolf, W., Chakradhar, S.: On-chip networks: A scalable and communication-centric embedded system design paradigm. In: 17th International Conference on VLSI Design (2004)
5. Verdoscia, L., Roberto Vaccaro Istituto per la, Ricerca sui Sistemi Informatici, Paralleli CNR Via P. Castellino, 111 80131 Napoli-Italy: An Adaptive Routing Algorithm for WK-Recursive Topologies. Source Computing Journal 63 (1999)
6. Bakhouya, M.: Evaluating the energy consumption and the Silicon area of on-chip interconnect architectures. Journal of Systems Architecture (2009)
7. El-Moursy, M.A., El Ghany, M.A.A., Ismail, M.: High throughput architecture for CLICHÉ Network on Chip. In: IEEE International SOC Conference, SOCC 2009. Electron. Eng. Dept., German Univ. in Cairo, Cairo, Egypt (2009)
8. Suboh, S., Bakhouya, M.J., Gaber, El-Ghazawi, T.: An interconnection architecture for network-on-chip systems. Telecommunication Syst. and Springer Science+Businq2ess Media and LLC (2008)
9. Sun, Y.R., Kumar, S.R., Jantsch, A.: Simulation and evaluation of a network on chip architecture Using ns2. In: Proc. the IEEE NorChip Conference (2002)
10. The Network Simulator - ns-2, http://WWW.nsnam.org/
11. Van Der Tol, E.B., Jaspers, E.G.T.: Mapping of mepg-4 decoding on a flexible architecture platform. In: SPIE 2002, pp. 1–13 (2002)
12. Iris, W.-Y.L., Jiang, H.-R.: Topology Generation and Floorplanning for Low Power Application-Specific Network-on-Chips. IEEE Transactions (2008)
13. Ar, Y., Tosun, S., Kaplan, H.: TopGen: A New Algorithm for Automatic Topology Generation for Network on Chip Architectures to Reduce Power Consumption. In: 4th International Conference on Application of Information and Communication Technologies (2009)

A New Graph Model for Heterogeneous WSN

Jasmine Norman[1] and Paulraj Joseph[2]

[1] Vellor Institue of Technology, Vellore
[2] Manonmaniam Sudaranar University, Tirunelveli

Abstract. Random Geometric Graphs have been a very influential and well-studied model of large networks, such as sensor networks, where the network nodes are represented by the vertices of the RGG, and the direct connectivity between nodes is represented by the edges. In random geometric graph the n nodes locations are chosen uniformly and independently at random and two points are connected by an edge if they are within a distance less then a certain value r. This assumes homogeneous wireless nodes with uniform transmission ranges. The assumption of homogeneous nodes does not always hold in practice since even devices of the same type may have slightly different transmission power. Therefore, the standard RGG model is not suitable to represent real time heterogeneous WSN. In this paper, we propose a non uniform radii disk RGG model based on a new metric NSM for heterogeneous WSN.

Keywords: Sensor, Heterogeneous, Random Geometric Graph, Transmission Range.

1 Introduction

Unique characteristics of a WSN include limited power, ability to withstand harsh environmental conditions, ability to cope with node failures, mobility of nodes, dynamic network topology, communication failures, heterogeneity of nodes, large scale of deployment and unattended operation. The challenges of WSN were studied by Yao K in [15]. The key challenge in wireless sensor networks is maximizing network lifetime. Energy efficiency and network capacity are perhaps two of the most important issues in wireless ad hoc networks and sensor networks. Many to one communication paradigm are widely used in regard to sensor networks since sensor nodes send their data to a common sink for processing. This many-to-one paradigm also results in non-uniform energy drainage in the network. A typical network configuration consists of sensors working unattended and transmitting their observation values to some processing or control center, the so-called sink node, which serves as a user interface. Due to the limited transmission range, sensors that are far away from the sink deliver their data through multihop communications, i.e., using intermediate nodes as relays. The integration of different wireless access technologies combined with supported services in next-generation wireless systems creates a real heterogeneous network. In contrast to a traditional static wireless sensor network

D.C. Wyld et al. (Eds.): NeCoM/WeST/WiMoN 2011, CCIS 197, pp. 187–196, 2011.

which consists of a large number of small sensor nodes with low computational, storage and communication capabilities, such limitations no longer apply in a mobile sensor network.

Random graphs are typically used to represent sensor networks. The authors in [2,11] have studied the application of random geometric graph to wireless sensor networks. Also the topology and connectivity properties of random geometric graphs are well researched. In [7] we proposed optimization conditions based on RGG for efficient routing in heterogeneous WSN. All previous known structures are defined solely on the given point set or the unit disk graph. However, graphs representing communication links are rarely so completely specified as the unit disk graph. In wireless communications, different nodes may have different transmission radius. Consequently, two nodes can communicate directly only if they are within the transmission range of each other. Assume each wireless node u has a fixed transmission range r_u. Each sensor node can detect an event of interest within a distance of r, and this distance is termed as the sensing range. The disk centered at a sensor node and with a radius of r is termed as the coverage disk of this node. In this paper we propose a non uniform radii disk RGG model to represent heterogeneous WSN. We also have identified a routing metric for heterogeneous WSN based on our work in [6]. It is also proved through simulations, that the graph based on the new metric is better suitable to represent real time sensor networks.

The remainder of the paper is organized as follows. Section 2 provides a brief overview of the related work. Section 3 explains the system model. Section 4 gives the mathematical model of the system. Section 5 describes the implementation results. Section 6 provides the conclusion of the work and discusses future directions.

2   Related Work

Pervasive Computing promises a world where computational artifacts embedded in the environment will continuously sense our activities and provide services based on what is sensed [9]. Sensor networks enable to accomplish the goal of pervasive computing partially. Their new requirements need optimized solutions at all layers of the protocol stack in an attempt to optimize the use of their scarce resources. In particular, the routing problem, has received a great deal of interest from the research community with a great number of proposals being made. The authors in [3] have analyzed the performance of the popular protocols after classification. The common belief is that a multi-hop configuration with rather small per-hop distance is the only viable energy efficient option for wireless sensor networks.

There is very less research work done related to heterogeneous sensor networks. In [10,14] the authors proposed localized topology control algorithms for heterogeneous wireless multi-hop networks.Due to the limited transmission range, sensors that are far away from the sink deliver their data through multi-hop communications. Although there is active research on maximizing network lifetime or network capacity most of these work consider a sensor network under a given physical topology. Random graphs are often applied to model communication networks to highlight their randomness. Mathematically, a random graph is a graph that is generated by a stochastic process . The theory of random graphs began with Erdos and Renyi's pioneer work in the late 1950s and early 1960s, which considered a class of random graphs now called Erdos-Renyi graphs [5,11]. As the probability of an edge existing between each pair of nodes is equal in an Erdos-Renyi graph, this model is not well suited to WSNs, which are embedded in two (or three) dimensional space, and in which the probability of a link existing is very much higher between nodes which are geometrically close. Therefore, we need new methods to model networks with randomness. A natural candidate for random network modeling is the class of Random Geometric Graphs . With node set V , a geometric graph G = (V, r) is equivalent to a graph G1 = (V, E), in which the vertex set V is embedded in a metric space, and E = (u , v) , $\forall u, v \in V$, u-v $\leq r$.

Chen Avin in [2] had investigated the property of random geometric graphs that has implication for routing and topological control in sensor networks. The goal was to construct a special subgraph, the Restricted Delaunay Graph, that permits efficient routing, based only on local information. In [1,4,8] the authors studied the topology and connectivity properties of random geometric graphs. In this paper we propose a new routing metric called NSM for real time WSN and based on which a mathematical model for heterogeneous WSN is identified.

3   System Model

In real world, at a given time, there may be stationary, mobile and powerful base stations existing together in a region as shown in Fig 1. Assuming all the nodes know their destination ID, when an event occurs or when requested by the base station, they try to forward the data to their base station. The topology changes continuously due to the mobility of the nodes. It will be practically impossible most of the times to directly forward the data to the base station due to the nature of radio signals. Hence the problem is to find a neighbour (hop) towards the destination. This is done repeatedly till the destination is reached. In a heterogeneous setup there may be a few base stations in a region. So we

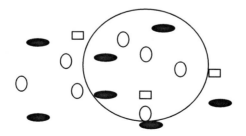

Fig. 1. Heterogeneous WSN

proposed in [6] that for a given node to forward the data, it is enough to find the nearest base station even if the node's base station is different. Also only high energy nodes get selected as relay nodes sparing the less energy stationary nodes thus prolonging the network life time.

The problem is to find a minimum cost path from a source to a destination. The optimum path in wireless sensor networks is the minimum energy conservation path. The algorithm works based on the type of node. Assuming high energy base stations and high bandwidth mobile nodes which could be recharged, the probabilities are set. The probability differs for each request. The static nodes with less energy level will not participate in routing in order to save energy. A* algorithm is applied to pick the best neighbour from the routing table of a node. The routing metric used in a function of R(i) and h(i).

R(i) = tr (i,j) , the transmission range between the source and the destination. h(i) = f(p(j) , T(j), L(j)) where p(j) is the probability of node j, T(j) is the time the reply packet is sent from j, L(j) is the location of j.

3.1   NSM Metric

Avoidance of congestion at nodes, high throughput, low levels of interference, isotonicity, efficient utilization of channel capacity, minimal transmission delay are some of the desired characteristics of a good routing metric for wireless sensor networks. We have proposed a new metric NSM which is defined as below. Nearest sink node metric (NSM) is defined as

$$NSM_{ij} = ETX_{ij} * T_j * NT_j * \frac{S}{\frac{Rc_i + Rc_j}{2 * \lambda_{ij}}} * R_{ij} \tag{1}$$

Where T_j represents the type of node.

$$T_j = \begin{cases} 2, & \text{if } i = \text{Sink node or Base station} \\ 1, & \text{if } i = \text{rechargeable mobile node} \\ 0, & \text{if } i = \text{Stationary node} \end{cases}$$

$$NT_j = max_{j=1}^{N} NSM_k$$

$$R_{ij} = \frac{10^{\frac{p_t + g_t + g_r - p_r}{20}}}{41.88 * f}$$

Where P_t is the Tx power in dBM for the wireless device that will be transmitting data
g_t is the Tx antenna gain in dBi
P_r is the Rx sensitivity in dBm
g_r is the Rx antenna gain in dBi
R_{ij} is the transmission distance in Km
f is the frequency in MHz
S is the packet size ,

Expected transmission time is ,

$$ETX_{ij} = \frac{1}{(1 - P_f) * (1 - p_r)}$$

where p_f is the probability of packet loss in the forward direction and p_r is the packet loss probability in the reverse direction. Remaining capacity is ,

$$Rc_i = B_i - \sum_{k=1}^{n} f_{ik} * \gamma_{ik}$$

where B_i is the transmission rate of node i,f_{ik} is the transmission rates of Ni current flows that traverse node i and γ_{ik} is the link quality factor.

4   Mathematical Model

Random Geometric Graphs (RGG) as shown in Fig 2 have been a very influential and well-studied model of large networks, such as sensor networks, where the network agents are represented by the vertices of the RGG, and the direct connectivity between agents is represented by the edges. Informally, given a radius r, a random geometric graph results from placing a set of n vertices uniformly and independently at random on the unit torus$[0, 1]^2$ and connecting two vertices if and only if their distance is at most r, where the distance depends on the chosen metric.

Connecting two vertices, u, v is possible if and only if the distance between them is at most a threshold r, ie.$d(i, j) \leq r$. Several probabilistic results are known about the number of components in the graph as a function of the threshold r and the number of vertices n. An edge appears iff d(i,j) is less than r and if the probability computed based on the distance between i and j , type of j , neighbours of j and energy level of j is greater than a threshold value(0.5).

Fig. 2. A typical RGG

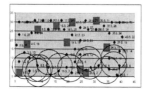

Fig. 3. Equal Radius RGG

We propose a dynamic random graph model (HRGG) for heterogeneous wireless sensor networks. Due to heterogeneity the nodes will have different transmission ranges. The graph has strong and weak links. Fig 3 shows the distribution of the sensors and equal radius RGG drawn at sample points.

4.1   Definitions

HRGG : A non uniform disk radii random geometric graph with strong and weak links.

Strong Links SL: Between two vertices v1 and v2 , the edge connecting v1 and v2 is said to be strong when $P(v1, v2) \geq 0.5$ where p(i,j) = f(d(i,j) , e(j), t(j),n(j)) [6]

Weak Links WL : Between two vertices v1 and v2 , the edge connecting v1 and v2 is said to be weak when $P(v1, v2) < 0.5$.

Path in HRGG : A set of (V, E) such that $E \in SL$ and are connected.

Fig. 4. HRGG - Non uniform radius

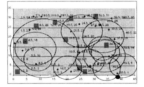

Fig. 5. Non uniform Range RGG

Guaranteed Delivery : If there exists a path in HRGG , the delivery is guaranteed.

Strong Node SN : A node is strong if it lies in a path in DRGG

Weak Node WN : A node that is within the transmission range of any other node X but is not in a path in DRGG.

Isolated Node : A node is isolated if there is no node within its transmission range.

4.2   Transmission Range vs. Radius

Friis transmission equation for free space loss is given by ,

$$\frac{P_r}{P_t} = \frac{G_r * G_t}{F_t}[\frac{\lambda}{4\pi R}]^2 \tag{2}$$

Where P_r is the Tx power for the wireless device that will be transmitting data G_r is the Tx antenna gain. P_t is the Rx sensitivity G_t is the Rx antenna gain R is the transmission distance in Km λ is the wavelength F_t is the loss factor

The same equation can be rewritten as,

$$R_{ij} = \frac{10^{\frac{p_t + g_t + g_r - p_r}{20}}}{41.88 * f}$$

There can be a big difference between the theoretical transmission distance and the actual results in the field. These calculations are based on an unobstructed line-of-sight signal with no electronic interference. However, the real world presents many variables that result in less-than-perfect wireless performance, such as mismatched impedance, electronic noise, building obstructions, reflected signals, etc.We reduce the distance based on the remaining energy level and the type of the node. So the modified equations are,

If $(E_r \approx E_{th} \& Tn = 0)$ then r = 0.
If $(E_r \approx E_{th} \& Tn = 1)$ then $r = r - \mu, \mu \propto E_r$.
Where E_r is the remaining energy level and E_{th} is the energy threshold value.

For the other cases we retain the actual transmission distance as computed by the formula. We will denote s(i) as the set of all nodes in $\varphi(i)$ whose distance to node N is smaller than radius r. Decisions at node i will be based on the following variables:

An estimation of the available energy at neighboring nodes, Eij, j $\in$ s(i). The distance to each of the neighbouring node , min d(i,j) < r The neighbours type and closeness to a base station , t(j) = 2 or 1 ,$\exists$ n(j) where t(n(j)) = 2.

4.3   Properties

The following operations are possible in the graph.

1. Adding an edge - When a node receives a reply packet with probability greater than 0.5, an edge will be added.
2. Deleting an edge - Since the nodes could be mobile, after a specific time period, the probability of an edge may go down. In this case the edge will be deleted.
3. From the definition of the graph it follows that, this graph is not symmetric. i.e, R(i,j) $\neq$ R(j,i) Proof: Assume i is not in the proximity of a base station and j is closer to a base station. So j's computed probability is high and the link exists between i and j. On the contrary, the probability computed by i will be low either because of its type or due to the proximity of the node. So j will not select i as the next Hop to reach its destination. So there is no edge between j and i.

Table 1. Reachability Matrix

0	2	1	32	34	36
1	2	24	0	35	-
2	26	30	33	45	7
3	30	22	-	-	-
4	5	-	-	-	-

4. There may be isolated vertices in this model as nodes with less energy level are less likely to participate in routing. So the graph is not a connected graph.
5. The graph is a monotonically increasing/ decreasing graph at time t.

Fig 5 represents a heterogeneous WSN with varying radius. A reachability matrix is formed as in Table 1 , representing each node and its neighbours arranged in the order of best neighbours. Thus if the node has a base station near it, it will occupy the first position. The matrix can be used for finding whether a path exists between the source and the destination at time 't'.

5   Performance Analysis

We simulate this protocol on GloMoSim, [12] a scalable discrete-event simulator developed by UCLA. This software provides a high fidelity simulation for wireless communication with detailed propagation, radio and MAC layers.

5.1   Simulation Model

The GloMoSim library [12] is used for protocol development in sensor networks. The library is a scalable simulation environment for wireless network systems using the parallel discrete event simulation language PARSEC.

Table 2 lists the assumed parameters. Intel Research Berkeley Sensor Network Data and WiFi CMU data from Select Lab [13] are used to get the positions for the nodes. The experiment is repeated for varying number of nodes. CBR traffic is assumed in the model. For mobility, trace file is used. The new protocol is written in Parsec and hooked to GloMoSim.

Table 2. Assumed Parameters

Transmission range	Computed
Simulation Time	5M
Topology Size	2000m x 2000m
Number of sensors	55
Number of sinks	16
Mobility	Trace File
Node Placement	Node File

5.2   Simulation Results

Fig 6 shows the transmission range of the nodes as computed. The fluctuations prove that the uniform radius RGG is not suitable to represent real time network.

Fig 7 shows NBS based node distribution. As per the routing metric NBS, optimized results can be obtained at time t if the nodes on 1 scale are selected to transmit. Those on the 0 scale do not have a base station within its transmission range.

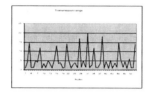

Fig. 6. Non uniform Range Graph

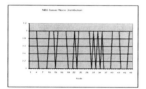

Fig. 7. NBS based Optimized Graph

6   Conclusion

Wireless sensor networks and radio frequency identification (RFID) devices are quickly becoming a vital part of our infrastructure. This leads to heterogeneous wireless networks in which devices have dramatically different capabilities. In this paper we proposed a new graph model HRGG based on energy efficient routing metric NSM for heterogeneous pervasive networks. We proved that the traditional random geometric graph is not suitable to represent heterogeneous WSN. Simulation results also support the model and show optimized results. Our next step is to study the formal aspects of the graph.

References

1. Gupta, B., Iyer, S.K.: Topological Properties Of The One Dimensional Exponential Random Geometric Graph. Random Structures and Algorithms 32(2), 181–204 (2008)
2. Avin, C.: Random Geometric Graphs: An Algorithmic Perspective. Ph.D dissertation, University of California, Los Angeles (2006)

3. Das, S., Castaneda, R., Yan, J.: Simulation-Based Performance Evaluation of Routing Protocols for Mobile Ad Hoc Networks. Mobile Networks and Applications 5(3), 179–189 (2000)

4. Díaz, J., Mitsche, D., Pérez-Giménez, X.: On the Connectivity of Dynamic Random Geometric Graphs, Symposium on Discrete Algorithms. In: Proceedings of the Nineteenth Annual ACM-SIAM Symposium on Discrete Algorithms, pp. 601–610 (2008)

5. Gupta, P., Kumar, P.R.: The Capacity of Wireless Networks. IEEE Transaction on Information Theory 46, 388–404 (2000)

6. Norman, J., Paulraj Joseph, J.: HLAODV - A Cross Layer Routing Protocol for Pervasive Heterogeneous Wireless Sensor Networks Based On Location. IJCSI (July 2010)

7. Norman, J., Paulraj Joseph, J.: Optimized Routing for Heterogeneous Wireless Sensor Networks. In: Proceedings of ICMCS 2011. Loyola College, Chennai (2011)

8. Li, J., Andrew, L.L.H., Foh, C.H., Zukerman, M., Chen, H.-H.: Connectivity, Coverage and Placement in Wireless Sensor Networks. Sensors 9, 7664–7693 (2009)

9. Lewis, F.L.: Wireless Sensor Networks - Smart Environments: Technologies, Protocols, and Applications. John Wiley, Chichester, Cook, D.J., Das, S.K. (eds.) (2004)

10. Li, N., Hou, J.C.: Topology Control in Heterogeneous Wireless Networks: Problems and Solutions. IEEE/ACM Transactions on Networking (TON) 13(6), 1313–1324 (2005)

11. Penrose, M.D.: Random Geometric Graphs. Oxford University Press, Oxford (2003)

12. Takai, M., Bajaj, L., Ahuja, R., Bagrodia, R., Gerla, M.: GloMoSim: A Scalable Network Simulation Environment, Technical report 990027, UCLA (1999)

13. Wireless Sensors Location Data,
http://www.select.cs.cmu.edu/data/index.html

14. Li, X.-Y., Song, W.-Z., Wang, Y.: Localized topology control for heterogeneous wireless sensor networks. ACM Transactions on Sensor Networks (TOSN) 2(1), 129–153 (2006)

15. Yao, K.: Sensor Networking: Concepts, Applications, and Challenges. ACTA Automatica Sinica 32(6) (2006)

Extending the Principles of Cloud Computing in Mobile Domain

Jitendra Maan

Tata Consultancy Services, TCS Towers, 249 D & E, Udyog Vihar Phase IV, Gurgaon,
Haryana, India – 122001
Jitendra.maan@tcs.com

Abstract. This paper outlines key considerations in extending cloud computing principles to mobile domain and platforms along with business challenges and obstacles faced in deploying over the mobile devices. This paper enlightens the benefits offered by Mobile Cloud Computing and also illustrate, how usinesses can utilizes Mobile Cloud services to get virtually infinite computing apabilities and resources on-demand.

This paper would also address the current challenges ith Mobile Cloud computing. And, it is intended for all business domains rrespective of application portfolios.

Keywords: Mobile computing, Mobile Cloud Computing, Mobile Internet, Mobile Cloud Service, Mobile web experience, Mobile Cloud applications.

1 Introduction

Today major business challenges in front of CIO and CEO are to "Get more with less" by reducing costs and improving productivity. Every investment need to be justified with pre-defined ROI as the time progresses. Enterprises are driven with lot of caution keeping future business demands and growth factors in mind.

In such a changing business environment, technology plays a crucial role in deciding on, how and where to access information, but organizations want to gain the operational and cost advantages by deploying rich interactive web applications over the Internet Cloud to achieve the scale and expand their market reach with the high penetration of mobile devices. On a broad industry perspective, IT is going through mobility evolution where focus is currently on deploying & accessing cloud applications on mobile channel.

Despite the known security challenges, Mobile Cloud Computing is gaining high traction among businesses of all sizes, due to the fact that Cloud allows both data storage and processing done entirely outside of the mobile devices/PCs environment. In the near term, a cloud-based mobile architecture will change the way the mobile applications are developed and consumed where Mobile Web technologies continue to evolve along with multiple dimensions of application offerings.

D.C. Wyld et al. (Eds.): NeCoM/WeST/WiMoN 2011, CCIS 197, pp. 197–203, 2011.
© Springer-Verlag Berlin Heidelberg 2011

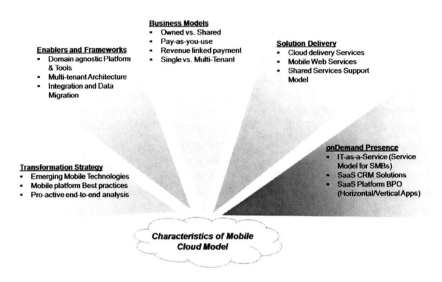

Fig. 1. Characteristics of Mobile Cloud Model

2   Mobile Internet and Cloud Applications

Mobile Cloud Computing Paradigm is different from the traditional client server based computing environment. Cloud Computing has a major impact on Mobile domain due to proliferation of smartphone and featured mobile devices. Mobile Web Applications, in general pose certain unique requirements and challenges, compared to their desktop versions, which primarily arise from small size of the device with low resolution, limited input and interaction capabilities, small memory footprint, lower processing power, slower rate of data transfers and need for tailored content depending on the dynamic context of use. Considering all such limitations, there is a need to borrow the compute and storage capabilities from cloud.

We see the trend, that cloud computing will bring unprecedented sophistication to mobile applications. Mobile cloud sync is emerging as a major new category of wireless services.

Cloud is a new capability and a delivery model that can help customers in defining their Mobility roadmap. A few characteristics of such model are illustrated in Fig.1 above.

There are several other factors contributing to adoption of running mobile applications in the cloud.

Easy Customization. Cloud services can make it easier for developers by minimizing the amount of code they have to customize for each of the mobile platforms. A new architecture for mobile applications based on the cloud will drastically change the way mobile apps are developed, acquired and used.

Support for Open APIs. Open APIs allow moving data from Mobile devices to Cloud-oriented environment and visa versa. Such simple, open APIs (based on Web Technologies) plays a transformational role in the way they are being exposed and consumed by mobile and cloud applications, with appropriate monitoring and management in place.

Over-The-Air deploy-ability. Mobility environment is highly heterogeneous, Over-The-Air provisioning/delivery of applications plays an important role as it enables easy deployment and upgrades to mobile applications using cloud services. Cloud based repository is emerging as a low-cost solution with compelling total cost of ownership (TCO) advantage over thick client applications.

3 Mobile Cloud Computing – Key Considerations

Cloud Computing is becoming a disruptive force in the mobility solution space. Cloud computing, in simple terms, is like a communication grid to share resources, information and software capabilities to different mobile devices/channels and computers where all computing devices work together like a single unified system.We see cloud computing as a promising technology which can offer many benefits for mobile devices. The primary motivations for the mainstream cloud computing are related to the elasticity of computing resources to usage. It offers virtually infinite resources that are available on demand and charged according. A shared problem between mobile and mainstream cloud computing is the data transfer bottleneck. For mainstream cloud computing the most important concern is the time and the cost of transferring massive amounts of data to the cloud while for mobile cloud computing the key issue is the energy consumption of such communication.

True Mobile Cloud Computing is about extending the principles of Cloud Computing – such as on-demand access, pay-as-you-go, everything-as-a-service and device-agnostic applications – to the mobile domain.

The form of Mobile Cloud Computing, which is gaining more traction among today's businesses where applications running in the Cloud are accessed from a thin client or a browser, providing huge amounts of storage, unlimited processing power, and the cross-device platform compatibility.

Mobile cloud computing alos differs from simple computation offloading in the sense that the cloud can offer services other than computing for mobile clients. Storage for backing up the mobile terminal data is one example. Another example could be a content sharing service, which by nature requires transferring locally produced data to the cloud.

Enterprise Collaboration solutions in particular, will be significant drivers for the growth of Mobile Cloud Computing. One reason for this is that there is a proven willingness amongst businesses, as well as other organization such as government departments, to pay for services that increase productivity and improve customer service.

4 Benefits of Mobile Cloud Computing

Cloud computing is mainly the internet-based computing, whereby shared resources, software, and information are provided to computers and other mobile devices on demand, same as with the electricity grid. Mobile-enabled applications keep their data in the cloud and keep it updated with all the changes made.

Mobile Cloud Computing delivers significant value across the entire mobile ecosystem. Mobile Cloud Computing offers the organizations, an easy way to access capabilities such as Direct2Mobile Billing, click-to-call/conference, and 2-way messaging, seamlessly across multiple network operators. There are several benefits of deploying cloud services over mobile channel -

- **Cloud becomes a new medium to share resources and applications through Mobile channel.** As users become more mobile, the applications they use will become mobile-enabled. By hosting data and applications in the cloud, mobile users do not need to worry about to actually carry and maintain the data but such cloud driven model allow them to access their data & applications in real-time, anywhere on their mobile devices.
- **Create New Stream of revenues.** Several analysts predict that enterprise-scale cloud services based model will propel the growth of traditional IT service market using Mobile Channel. Due to nature of cloud applications, Mobile Cloud computing has started creating a new stream of revenue for businesses and application vendors since business adoption of cloud based services and platforms is growing at phenomenal pace.
- **Foster effective collaboration among applications and people.** The power of cloud allows deploying different collaboration tools (e.g. email, web conferencing, instant messaging and team workspaces etc) at centralized, high speed distributed servers to foster effective collaboration among different stakeholders. Take, for example, email services which has been cloud-enabled, will allow user to update mails on one device, remove a few emails using another device, and update calendar on 3rd device and all of these devices are in complete sync using cloud services which offers a unique and connected user experience with up-to-date information in real-time. Solutions such as Microsoft's SharePoint, IBM's Lotus Live suite, and more recently Chatter from Salesforce.com, all aim to make it easier for employees to collaborate, whether they are producing a document, managing project tasks or simply wishing to communicate in real time as a group. Moreover, these solutions are increasingly being delivered as a cloud-based service and accessed via a desktop browser or mobile application.
- **Automatic backup of personal and enterprise data.** With cloud computing, you never lose your enterprise as well as personal data, because it always exists in the cloud. Since data would always be pulled from cloud stores, hence it becomes easy to replace one device with another, by simply registering a new device and get all your data from the cloud with no delay.
- **Easier and unique way to access computing resources.** Cloud makes it easy to login to various computing devices (e.g. desktop computer, notebook, tablet, cell phone, eBook reader) through single-sign on, a unified gateway to access all computing resources stored in the cloud environment.

- **More computing power on demand.** Cloud Computing offer the choice to select right services and deployment models in the interest of mobile users. Cloud computing opens up new innovative ways to use rich-media capabilities, such as integrating video into documents or presentations and computing power will become more and more disembodied and will be consumed as and when it is needed.

- **Offer bundled and unbundled services.** Cloud computing opens up ways to offer services bundled with video streaming and rich-media capabilities, such as integrating video into documents or presentations. And, the selection of such bundled or unbundled services over mobile domain, depends on various factors such as:

  1. Differentiated vs Commodity capabilities
  2. Core vs. non-core services
  3. Desire for flexibility and innovation vs. agility

We, at TCS believes in delivering on-demand business capability through "IT-as-a-Service" model, with an integrated suite of hardware, network, software and mobile solutions as a bundled service offering. More importantly, all the required technical, business and consulting services are provided in a "build-as-you-grow" or "pay-as-you-use" model through a combination of on-premise and shared services hosted platforms.

5   Challenges with Mobile Cloud Computing

5.1   Mobile Cloud Inter-Operability and Usability

Successful development and deployment of mobile Web applications demands for a better understanding of mobile user context and their challenges. With the screen resolutions, browser capabilities and speed (3G, 4G etc) are getting better now; mobile web experience is getting closer to desktop browsing. Generally, interoperability issues would stem from the platform fragmentation of mobile devices, mobile operating systems, and browsers.

From an engineering view of point, interoperability problems have to be addressed up-front for accessing cloud capabilities over mobile devices. Such problems would normally arise due to different form factors across mobile devices. Usability problems would be centered around the small physical size of the mobile phone form factors (limited resolution screens and user input/operating limitations.

Open Standards based interoperable services are necessary to preserve enterprise user data. The issue of mobile user freedom is surfacing with the emergence of more & more Mobile application stores available in the Cloud. Mobile Cloud success depends on interoperability among different computing devices like - mobile devices, desktop PCs and different app stores. For example – Syncing pictures with desktop PC and streaming videos from another Store; thereby giving unprecedented freedom to mobile users.

5.2 Network Dependent Factors Drive Mobile User Experience in the Cloud

Mobile cloud computing performance is dependent on various network factors like:-

- Network Latency
- Data transmission rate

It is customary to offload computer-intensive resources in the 'cloud,' and it requires special considerations in network design and application deployment.

5.3 Limited Battery Life of Mobile Device is Another Barrier

Another significant barrier in mobile cloud computing is the limited battery life of mobile devices. The more we execute in the cloud and more we save battery life, as the application execute burden is offloaded. Such execution offload is linked to device functions and cannot be completely transferred to the cloud.

5.4 Safeguard Critical Enterprise Data in the Cloud becomes an Issue

It is not an easy task to safeguard enterprise user data sitting in the public/private cloud. It is necessary to develop Cloud based framework for effective collaboration and information management, sharing and archiving by taking into account the mobile user needs.

6 Summary

It is quite obvious that with the emergence of Rich Mobile Internet applications and Cloud technologies, customer's immediate focus has shifted towards those tools, technologies or platforms that deliver rich user experience that is visibly different from what's delivered by traditional server-centric platforms.

Clearly, Cloud as a mobile delivery model is fast shedding its nascent image with many organizations examining the possibility of employing Mobile Cloud for operational agility. Adoption of a cost-effective Cloud model is on the rise across businesses. Using such model, it is extremely easy to create an entirely new breed of products and services on mobile channel that deliver previously unheard of value to customers and this capability has been one of the significant pointers to the relevance, effectiveness, and sustainability of Cloud services.

Though, there are challenges in deploying Applications and data on the cloud, but the benefits that businesses can accrue in long term, simply cannot be ignored. There are obvious reasons to complement the Mobile enablement.

I strongly believes that Cloud-based mobility solutions will come to be recognized as an increasingly viable option for enterprise IT. In the current market scenario, even though the benefits of early Cloud adoption are well understood, there still exist numerous reservations pertaining to Cloud's capacity to support business needs, applications and underlying infrastructure. Early adopters with the insight to address such reservations will reap Cloud benefits in the long term.

References

1. Gens, F.: IDC Predictions 2010: Recovery and Transformation. Filing Information, IDC #220987 1, 3–7 (2009)
2. Mun, K.: Corporate Technology Strategist, Alcatel-Lucent: Mobile Cloud Computing Challenges, TechZine, Technology and Research e-zone (September 2001),
   `http://www2.alcatel-lucent.com/blogs/techzine/2010/mobile-cloud-computing-challenges`

Hybrid Miniaturized Tri-band Planar Inverted-F Antenna (PIFA)

Mukta Jukaria and R.P.S. Gangwar

Deptt. of Electronics & Communication Engineering, College of Technology,
Gobind Ballabh Pant University of
Agriculture & Technology, Pantnagar (Uttrakhand), India
muktajukaria2010@gmail.com
profrpsgangwar@yahoo.co.in

Abstract. With the recent meteoric spread of wireless communication *PIFA antenna has been one of the major concept that is being implemented in various wireless communication systems.* the need for constant reduction in the size of wireless devices requires corresponding compactness in the antenna supporting the wireless devices. In this proposed work *PIFA antenna with slotted and meandered radiating patch is introduced. Paper research shows the effect of meandering in a dual band PIFA by performing double functions- tune the resonance frequency with increased band width (at a higher frequency) and to provide tri band controlled resonant frequency. Development of proposed antenna covers IEEE802.11, wireless local area network (WLAN), worldwide interoperability for microwave access (WiMax) applications for wireless communications. The antenna occupied a very compact size of (9.5mmX14.5mmX8mm). The main radiating Patch is injected with slots and meandering, to generate and control the three resonant frequencies covers 3.3, 3.7 and 5.7 GHz. The simulated result of antenna shows a gain of 1.58dBi, 1.5dBi, 4.12dBi respectively and radiation efficiency of 74%, 78.5% and 78% for three bands respectively. Proposed antenna possesses the properties of good performance, compact size (50% of typical antenna). 2D electromagnetic simulation IE3D version 12.22 is used in the design of simulation of proposed PIFA that includes the simulation and comparison within the parameters return loss, VSWR, efficiency and Radiation pattern to prove the advantage of meandered patch.*

Keywords: Hybrid, WLAN, WiMax, Tri band antenna.

1 Introduction

PIFA is a quarter wavelength ($\lambda/4$) low profile antenna with a rectangular planer element located above a ground plane constituting of feed-Probe, conical via and some shorting mechanism. PIFA antenna is a good candidate for the various mobile technologies in future with new bands, flexible structure, flexible impedance and fabrication and corporation. Inverted F antenna is a variant of the monopole where the top section has been folded down so as to be parallel with the ground plane .ground plane is useful for the excitation of current in the printed IFA and an electromagnetic field is formed by intersection of IFA and an image of itself below the ground plane that works as an energy reflector The requirement of latest communication system

D.C. Wyld et al. (Eds.): NeCoM/WeST/WiMoN 2011, CCIS 197, pp. 204–212, 2011.
© Springer-Verlag Berlin Heidelberg 2011

supports the optimization of PIFA by varying various parameters to get an efficient wide band with compact size multiple band with compact size multiband PIFA. In the proposed antenna the use of slots and meandering in radiating patch has been analysed as an alternative of antenna size reduction, shifting of band and triband operation [23, 4, 6,13]. The slot in ground plane is used to enhance the band width and to get direction operation. Slotting and meandering structure is synthesized in order to sustain three resonant mode. The propose PIFA consist of a Ground plane, a top patch, a feed, and shorting mechanism that short circuits the top patch to ground plane in antenna is fed By 50 Ω coaxial line. Shorting mechanism is obtained by using a conical via and a shorting pin leads to a quarter wave resonator or multiple resonant modes. Design of PIFA adopts contemporary techniques probe feeding. Inverted patch structure with air filled dielectric, slotted and meandered patch. This antenna takes the objective to facilitate laptop PCM CIA, Combo WLAN sys, WiMax and IEEE 80211/a/b/g [1, 2, 6, 14]. Simulation of conventional PIFA antenna provides limited bandwidth and resonant frequencies [2,6]. In this paper a novel slotted shape with meandering is investigated for enhancing the impedance bandwidth with a very compact radiating patch size (9.5mmX14.5mmX8mm) [2, 6, 10]. An additional substrate layer $\epsilon r = 4.882$ (woven fibreglass) tanδ=.002. Increases gain and band width of ant and also provide necessary mechanism protection for radiating element.

2 Antenna Design

The basic geometry of proposed antenna is simulated in three parts. In the first part the antenna with sided U shaped slot is simulated and patch is shown in Figure (1).Inverted U shaped slot in radiating patch produce a band of 760 MHz at resonant frequency 3.47GHz, peak gain 2.91 dBi with radiation frequency 80.5%. The antenna is printed on and FR4 PCB with Dielectric substrate $\epsilon r = 4.882$ and tan δ = 0.002. Implementation of slots in radiating patch can increase of decrease the frequency response of the antenna to Higher band or a lower band ,not only but also it can change bandwidth response due to the current on the patch has to travel then without slots. This is also responsible for the reduction of dimensions of the radiating patch.

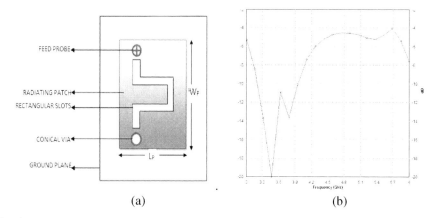

(a)   (b)

Fig. 1. (a) Basic14.5mm ×9.5mm PIFA above the ground plane with slotted radiating patch (b) Return loss of the single band PIFA

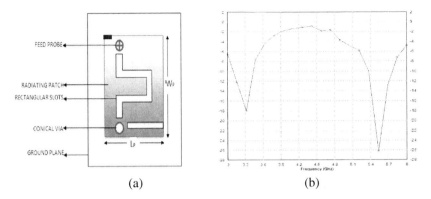

(a)   (b)

Fig. 2. (a) Dual band PIFA with single meandering (b) Return loss of the dual band PIFA

Second geometry introduced meandering in one side of slotted patch and simulated result at the same frequency shown in Figure. (2) .Meandering is useful in the reduction of dimension of antenna. Simulation shows shifting of frequency in higher frequency and provides dual band antenna with resonant frequency 3.36GHz and 5.6 GHz due to the coupling between the meandering and slot on the PIFA [2,3,6,15].

3   Compact Triband PIFA

Third geometry is aimed towards a novel miniaturized triband antenna for wireless systems. Dual meandering in a slotted patch supports the triband operation at resonant frequency 3.31, 3.68, 5.6 GHz. proposed antenna of compact size $(9.5 \times 14.5 \times 8)mm^3$ is located up to a compact size finite ground plane having dimension (35mmX70mm). This basic structure includes two substrate layer one air substrate of 7 mm from ground plane and woven fibre ($\epsilon r = 4.882$) of 1mm above the air substrate. Single feed Probe and conical via includes the inverted F structure in addition with a conducting pin of 1 mm as shown in Figure.(3).To get the triband operation and inverted U type slot and dual meandering is added to antenna structure.

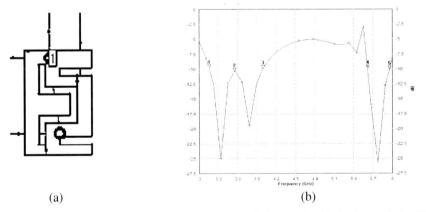

(a)   (b)

Fig. 3. (a) Proposed geometry of triband PIFA on the radiating patch with dual meandering (b) Return loss of the tri band PIFA

4 Proposed Antenna Structure

Lg=35mm, Wg=70mm, Lp=9.5mm, Wp=14.5mm, A6=4.5mm, r (width of slot and meandering)=1mm. for the figure probe feed cantered at (9.5mm,63.5mm), conical via(9.5.52.5) and top radiating patch is 8 mm above the ground and a shorting pin shorts the ground plane and radiating patch to achieve the proper impedance matching and sufficient band width. The substrate height from the ground plane 0 mm to 7mm is air and from 7mm to 8 mm is woven fibre ($\epsilon r = 4.882$).

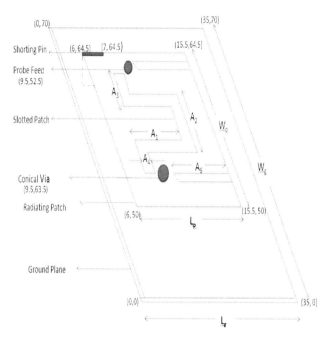

Fig. 4. (a) 2D geometry of miniaturized triband PIFA with a ground plane dimensions 35mm × 70mm

The narrow band width is typical problem for planar antennas and band width is inversely proportional to the quality factor Q is

$$Q = \text{energy stored/energy lost}$$

To decrease the quality factor Q we use a medium permittivity substrate because higher permittivity substrate radiate energy lesser than store it
   -Embedding the suitable slots into main patch in order to create dual band antenna.
   -Addition meandering provide gap coupled resonator to create a new band.
   -Width of shorting pin is responsible for the resonant frequency [9].

Equation for PIFA (if the width of the radiating patch is not equal to the width of the shorting pin) is given below [4,10]

$$f_r = L + W + h - w = \frac{\lambda_0}{3} \tag{1}$$

where L, W length and width of radiating patch w is width of shorting pin h is the height of patch from the ground plane. The resonant frequency of the antenna cab ne computed using the following equations,

$$L + h = \frac{\lambda_0}{4} \qquad (2)$$

Where λ_0 is the wave length hence resonance frequency

$$f_1 == \frac{c}{4(L+h)} \qquad (3)$$

Where c is the speed of light. The other case is for w = 0. A short-circuit plate with a width of zero cab ne physically represented by a thin short circuit pin. The effective length of the current is then L+W+h. For this case, the resonance condition is expressed by,

$$L + W + h = \frac{\lambda_0}{4} \qquad (4)$$

The other resonant frequency that is part of the linear combination is associated with the case 0<W<L and is expressed as:

$$f_2 = \frac{c}{4(L+W+h-w)} \qquad (5)$$

For the case when 0<W/L<1, the resonant frequency f, is the a linear combination of the resonant frequencies associated with the limiting cases. The resonant frequency f, is found using the experiment for f_1 and f_2 above in the following,

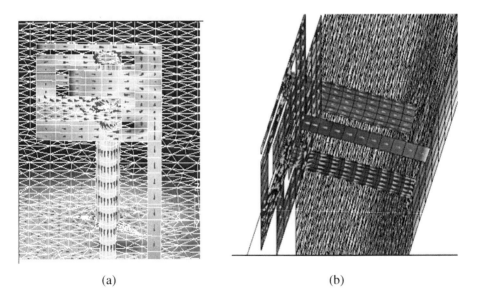

(a)   (b)

Fig. 5. (a) Simulated current distribution within the patch (b) Side view of current flow through shorting pin and probe feed in 3D geometry

$$f_r = rf_1 + (1 - r)f_2 \text{ for } \frac{L}{W} \leq 1 \tag{6}$$

$$f_r = r^k f_1 + (1 - r^k)f_2 \text{ for } \frac{L}{W} \geq 1 \tag{7}$$

Where, r= $\frac{W}{L}$ and $k = \frac{L}{W}$

Current distribution within the antenna, shorting pin and feed is shown in Figure (5):

5   Result and Discussion

Proposed structure is designed using transmission line model by taking dimensions as quarter wave length (λ /4). Proposed antenna is simulated by using Software

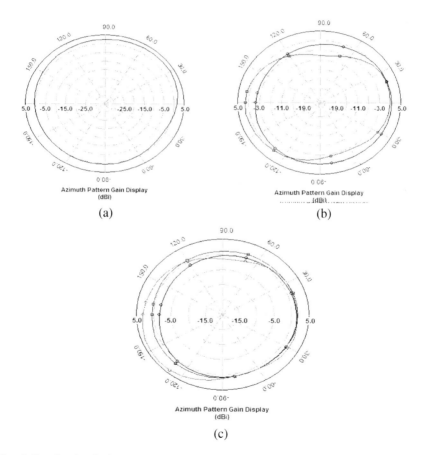

(a)   (b)

(c)

Fig. 6. Simulated radiation pattern for (a) single band antenna at 3.47GHz. (b) dual band PIFA at resonant frequencies 3.36GHz and 5.6 GHz. (c) tri band PIFA at resonant frequencies 3.3GHz, 3.7GHz and 5.69GH.

ZELAND IE3D version 12.22 software. A triband Compact size antenna is fabricated and simulated. Study of antenna shows how various structures and meandering in radiating patch effects the performance of antenna. The main attraction of proposed antenna is dimensions of antenna i.e. 50% reduced in comparison of reference paper[,2 4 ,6, 9 ,10,11,13,15,16] and the band width of proposed antenna is increased by more then 30% with respect to tri band reference antenna [5 ,6,9,11,15], As the width of shorting Pin decreases the resonant frequency is also decreases and also the finite ground plane plays an important role in PIFA. Here the antenna designing in three step shows a single band antenna of band width (3.20GHz-3.96GHz) when only slotting is done over the radiation patch. As we include meandering in either side of PIFA it provides dual resonant frequency at 3.36GHz and 5.6GHz and with the dual meandering a triple band structure at resonant frequency (3.3GHz ,3.7GHz, 5,69GHz) is obtained. Results are simulated and measured in form of return loss. Radiation pattern, gain, return loss of the proposed antenna is also studied. Figure (6) reveals radiation pattern is nearly omnidirectional in azumith plane and peak gain is case of single band band is equal to 2.91 dBi at $\theta = 45°$ and max 4.18 dBi in case of tri band antenna. Figure 7 shows max Antenna efficiency is 80.5% in case(1) ,85% in case(2) and 80% in case (3). Position of radiating patch and conical via in ground plane is also a big factor[2]. Change in position of radiating patch in finite ground plane change the characteristic of antenna .L shaped slot in ground plane increased the operational bandwidth because of the increased electrical length within the ground[8].

Simulated Results of Proposed antenna: Simulated results for three types of antenna are shown in Table (1).

Table 1.

Design	Resonant Frequency	Band width in MHz	Return Loss	Peak Gain	Radiation Efficiency
Antenna with slot on radiating patch	3.47 GHz	760	1.47	2.91	80.5%
Antenna with single meandering	3.36	312	1.19	1.47	76%
	5.6	400	1.2	2.31	85%
Antenna with dual meandering	3.3	322	1.1	1.58	75%
	3.7	306	1.2	1.70	80%
	5.69	384	1.001	4.18	79%

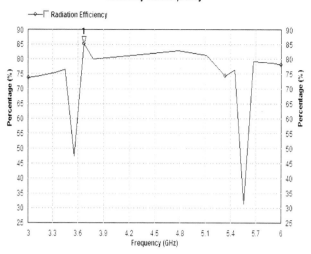

Fig. 7. Efficiency Vs Frequency for the proposed antenna

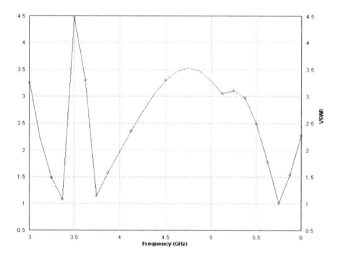

Fig. 8. VSWR Vs Frequency for the proposed antenna

6 Conclusion

A triple band slotted and meandered antenna design in a compact volume 9.5X14.5X8 mm^3 is achieved for wireless application..Bandwidth of triple band antenna is successfully designed and simulated at 3.3GHz (band width 288 MHz), 3.7GHZ (band width 306MHz) and 5.69GHz (band width 384 MHz). The gain of antenna is simulated 1.58dBi, 1.70 dBi and 4.18dBi at three bands respectively. The proposed antenna has radiation efficiency 75%, 80% and 79% respectively. Antenna has good return loss, good radiation pattern, good efficiency and good gain up to 4.18 dBi at θ = 45°. The proposed antenna can be used in wireless communication devices for WLAN, WiMax and radar application. L shaped cut in ground plane is used to increase the bandwidth of antenna and for Omni directional radiation. Finally simulation result shows that various structures into the radiating patch improve the antenna performance.

References

1. Bhattacharyya, A.K., Garg, R.: Generalised transmission line model for microstrip patches. IEE Proceedings 132, 93–98 (1985)
2. Arkko, A.T.: Effect of ground plane size on a free space performance of a mobile handset antenna (2002)
3. Chen, Wang, H.-T., Lu, K., Chiou, T.-W.: PIFA with a meandered and folded patch for a duel band mobile phone application. IEEE Transactions on Antennas and Propagations 51(9), September 9 (2003)
4. Ahmed, M.: Development of small wide band antenna (2005)
5. WP 2.3-1 Wide band Antenna Radiators. TRIBAND PIFA, University of Liverpool, Revision 1 (2005)
6. Sami, M.R., Majid Yaha, I.: A novel miniaturized triband PIFA for memo application microwave and optical technology letters. 49(3) (March 2007)
7. Ray, U.S., Chattoraj, N., Chattoraj, N.: Seain,: New dual frequency microstrip antennas for wireless application. Romanian Journal of Information Science and Technology 10(1) (2007)
8. Gandara, Tiago, Lucia, R.U., Peixeiro, Custodio: Planar inverted F antennas Integrated into small multi-standard handsets. ATKAFF 48(1-2), 45–52 (2007)
9. Pokorny, Pokorny, M., Horak, Jiri, Raida, Zbynek: Planar Tri-Band Antenna Design. Brno University of Technology, Pukynova 118, 612 00 Brno, Czech Republic (2008)
10. Raghavan, S., Jayanti, N.: Design of planer Inverted –F Antenna for wireless applications. WSEAS Transactions on communications NITT 8 (2009)
11. Tarboush, H.F., Abu, N.R., Raweshidy, H.S., Budimir, D.: Design of Planar Inverted F Antenna (PIFA) for multiband wireless application, wireless network and communication centre W.N.C.C., School of engineering and design, Brunel University, West London (2009)
12. Jeon, S., Choi, H., Kim, H.: Hybrid Planar-F Antenna with a T-Shaped Slot on the Ground Plane. ETRI Journal 31(5) (October 2009)
13. Alkanhal, M.A.S.: Composite compact triple-band microstrip antennas. Progress in Electromagnetics Research PIER 93, 221–236 (2009)
14. Anguera, Picher, C., Cabedo, J.A.: Multiband Handset Antenna using slots on the ground plane: Consideration to Facilitate the Integration of the Feeding Transmission Line. Progres. In: Electromagnetics Research, PIER 93, 221 (2009)
15. Cabedo, A., Anguera, J.: Multiband Handset Antenna combining a PIFA slots, and Ground Plane Modes. IEEE Transactions on Antennas and Propagation 57(9) (September 2009)
16. Tarboush, H.F., Abu, N.R., Raweshidy, H.S., Budimir, D.: Compact planar inverted antenna (PIFA) for WiMax application wireless network and communication centre W.N.C.C., School, London (2009)

A Novel Distributed Clustered Approach towards Building an Agent Based Routing Topology for MANET

Ditipriya Sinha[1], Uma Bhattacharya[2], and Rituparna Chaki[3]

[1] Department of Information Technology, CIEM, Kolkata, India
[2] Bengal Engineering & Science University, Howrah, India
[3] West Bengal University of Technology, Kolkata, India
ditipriya_sinha@yahoo.co.in, ub@cs.becs.ac.in, rchaki@ieee.org

Abstract. The problem of routing is a complex one in case of mobile ad hoc networks due to the dynamic topology. Clusterization is an efficient means of increasing the efficiency of a MANET. A study of several clustering algorithms has lead to the observation that stable, secure cluster head selection increases lifespan and security of the network. The current state of art also relies heavily on ant colony optimization technique for finding the optimum shortest route in case of MANET. This paper proposes an agent based routing protocol for routing packets in a cluster based MANET. The algorithm is proposed to work in a distributed manner, using the concept of dominating set of mobile nodes. The selection of cluster head is determined on the basis of parameters such as connectivity, stability and residual battery power.

Keywords: Dominating Node, Non dominating Node, Gateway Node, Cluster Head, Pheromone.

1 Introduction

A Mobile Ad Hoc Network (MANET) is a network built on ad hoc demand by some mobile wireless nodes geographically distributed over an area. These nodes can join or leave the network at any time. There is no fixed infrastructure and also no centralized administration. The network does not have a fixed station or access point. The inherent flexibility along with easy set-up and low maintenance cost causes MANETs to be increasingly useful in disaster management, battlefield surveillance, etc. The mobile nature of MANETs leads to frequently changing topology. Thus a route from a source to a destination does not remain valid after some time. Battery life, loss of packets due to mobility, network partition, changing topologies and transmission error are some of the inherent problems of MANETs. Most of the routing topology used in wired network fails to give good result in the case of MANETs. This is due to the dynamic nature of MANETs, which allows nodes to freely move within the network. As compared to traditional wired links, the wireless links have significantly lower capacities, which cause the assignment of routing paths more challenging. The ever-increasing level of congestion also creates difficulties to assign the route in MANET. Congestion control is a challenge of designing a good routing topology. It concerns controlling traffic entry into a telecommunication

D.C. Wyld et al. (Eds.): NeCoM/WeST/WiMoN 2011, CCIS 197, pp. 213–220, 2011.

network so as to avoid conjunctive collapse by attempting to avoid over subscription of any of the processing or link capabilities of the intermediate nodes and network as well as taking resource reducing steps, such as reducing the rate of sending packets. On the other hand the advantages of cluster based approaches are improving routing efficiency, scalability, supporting QOS and saving power consumption. Clustering mainly transforms a physical network into a virtual network of interconnected clusters or group of nodes. The main goal of cluster based network is to find the cluster head nodes and partition the network into clusters. These nodes take on a special role in managing routing information. Stable and reliable cluster head selection is another challenge in MANET. In this paper we propose a distributed based clustering algorithm for mobile ad-hoc networks. In this algorithm clustering set up phase is accomplished by dominating set. Among dominating sets most eligible node is selected as cluster head and some dominating nodes are selected as gateway nodes. This proposed algorithm chooses most reliable, stable, highly powerful node as cluster head. Agent based approaches use swarm intelligence techniques to generate routes between source and destination nodes. There are mainly two different types of agent based routing logic. One of them is multi-agent system in which multiple agents are interacting with each other. Another one is single-agent system]in which an individual agent solves the problem. Generally multi-agent system can be used to solve problems which are difficult or impossible for an individual agent to solve. One of the examples of swarm intelligence is ant colony optimization technique. This optimization technique has been used where concentration of pheromone deposition at different routes is used to construct a pheromone table. The ant based methods take care of the dynamic nature of MANETs. The present work is designed a multi-agent routing algorithm using ant colony optimization technique in cluster based network.

2   Review of Existing Works

In a cluster based mobile adhoc network, nodes are clustered in any form of hierarchical structure. The advantage of cluster based approaches are improving routing efficiency, scalability, supporting QOS and saving power consumption. The two main tasks involved in maintaining a cluster based network are (a) finding the cluster head nodes and (b) partitioning the network into clusters. The cluster head nodes have a special role in managing routing information. Some reviews of cluster based routing algorithms are given below.

2.1   CBRP

The idea of CBRP[6] is to divide the nodes in adhoc network into number of disjoint or overlapping clusters. A node in a cluster is selected as a cluster head. A cluster head elects a gateway node to communicate with other cluster heads. CBRP is based on source routing similar to DSR. A cluster head is elected for each cluster to maintain cluster membership information. Inter-cluster routes are discovered dynamically using the cluster membership information kept at each cluster head. By clustering nodes into groups, the protocol efficiently minimizes the flooding traffic during route discovery and speeds up this process as well. Furthermore, the protocol takes into consideration the existence of uni-directional links and uses these links for both intra-cluster and inter-cluster routing.

2.2 CBMPR

The main idea of this technique is to extend the hop-by-hop multi path into cluster by cluster multi path [3]. .Here each cluster works independently. There fore it reduces interference. The purpose of this scheme is to find less interfering path for wireless multi hop network.

2.3 SCAM

SCAM (Scenario-based Clustering Algorithm for Mobile ad hoc networks) [11] is a adaptive and distributed clustering algorithm. It is based on dominating sets (k, r). Non clustered nodes select the cluster head among k dominating nodes. The quality of cluster head is calculated based on different metrics such as connectivity, stability and residual battery power. It uses technique to maintain cluster.

Agent based approaches use swarm intelligence techniques to generate routes between source and destination nodes. There are mainly two different types of agent based routing logic. One of them is multi-agent system in which multiple agents are interacting with each other. Another one is single-agent system in which an individual agent solves the problem. The ant based methods help in talking the dynamic nature of MANETs. Some reviews of swarm intelligence based algorithms are given below.

2.4 SACO

The SACO[14] algorithm was created to solve the problem of finding shortest path between two nodes on a graph. In SACO algorithm, a number of ants are placed on the source node of the graph. In each iteration, each ant incrementally constructs a path to the destination node.

2.5 AntNet

Di Caro and *Dorigo* describe the application of ACO to dynamic routing in packet-switched networks, using an algorithm that they call AntNet. This is the first application where ACO is used for routing with a source routing mechanism, i.e. the entire route of the packet is listed in the header of the packet [13].

2.6 ARA

Gues et al presents an ACO-based routing scheme using distance vector routing. Route discovery in ARA[12] is done by broadcasting Forward Ants (FANT).

2.7 LCRACO

This algorithm[10] also concerns with load in the network. This algorithm uses two colony of ant, Red colony ant chooses the path where concentration of red pheromone is high and blue colony ant chooses the path where concentration of blue pheromone is high. This way it balances the load in the network.

3 The Proposed Algorithm

The proposed algorithm and the associated data dictionary have been described in this section.

3.1 Data Dictionary

Table 1. Variables list

Variable Name	Description
domnode[ ]	Id of dominating nodes.
nondomnode[ ]	Id of non dominating nodes
dg,[ ], t[ ], bp[ ], mob[ ]	Denote degree, trust value, battery power, mobility of all nodes in the network respectively
R	Denotes the radio range of the cluster
ACK[ ]	Node id of the neighbor nodes of sender in the cluster
Cluster[a, b]	Denotes the weight for nodes in a cluster
Ch[ ]	Cluster head array that stores address of cluster heads
Th	Denotes threshold value of weight
K	Denotes no of clusters in a network
D	Denotes no of dominating nodes.
R[x, y], b[x, y]	Denote red and blue pheromone array respectively.
rprob[ ][ ], bprob[ ][ ]	Probability of red and blue pheromone respectively.
rmax , bmax	Define maximum amount of red and blue pheromone respectively.
Lock[][]	Defines availability of the path
S, E	Denotes source and destination node respectively
M	Defines no of messages.
N	Denotes no of nodes in the network

3.2 The Algorithm

The review of the state of the art scenario leads to the conclusion that agent based approach for route selection has to be given extra care for achieving optimum throughput. In this paper, a new routing technique has been proposed. This algorithm takes care of congestion and load for routing in cluster based network.

Begin

Step 1: Weight of each node is calculated using equation 1.
$$w[i]=t[i]+dg[i]+1 / Mob[i]+bp[i] \qquad \dots 1$$

Step 2: Threshold value in the network is calculated. It is the average weight of all nodes in the network. To calculate threshold value, equation 2 is used.
$$Th= 1/n\sum_{i=(1..n)} (dg[i]+t[i]+bp[i]+1/Mob[i]). \qquad \dots 2$$

Step 3: A node is selected as non dominating node if **Weigh**t < Threshold and stored in nondomnode[ ] array, else it is selected as dominating node and stored in domnode [ ] array.

Step 4: Call **BuildCluster**(domnode,nondomnode,n) for formation of cluster using domnode as the dominating node.

End.

Procedure BuildCluster(domnode, nondomnode, n)

Step 1:
i. domnode[i] broadcasts FINDNEIGHBOUR message with in r hop distance to all nondomnode[ ] nodes.
ii. wait:=2r+(n-1)
iii. if(wait<=0) then
      i.   check for ACK from nodes.
      ii. store address of nodes in cluster[i][ ]
      iii. wait:=wait-1

Step 2: Highest weight node among all dominating nodes is selected as cluster head and stores in array ch[].

Step 3: Call procedure **Routing**(n,ch[],cluster[][],k,l) for finding the shortest route using cluster head ch with the help of ant colony optimization technique.

Procedure Routing(n,ch,cluster,k,l)

Step1: All nodes maintain two tables, one stores value of red pheromone and another stores value of blue pheromone.

Step2: Red pheromone and blue pheromone values are calculated
$$r[i][j]=t[i]+bp[i]+cost[i][j]; \hspace{2cm} ...3$$
$$b[i][j]=1/Mob[i]+dg[i]+cost[i][j]; \hspace{1.5cm} ...4$$

Step3: Calculate maximum value of red pheromone and blue pheromone among all paths in network and stores it in a variable rmax and bmax respectively.

Step4: Probability of red pheromone and blue pheromone are calculated :
$$phsum:=phsum+r[i][j]+b[i][j]; \hspace{2cm} ....5$$
$$rprob[i][j]=r[i][j]/phsum; \hspace{2.5cm} ...6$$
$$bprob[i][j]=b[i][j]/phsum; \hspace{2.5cm} ...7$$

Step5: For any path between node i, j
    if((r[i][j]+b[i][j])>=(rmax+bmax)) then
       set Lock[i][j] to zero to block the path;
    else
       set Lock[i][j]=1 to signify path availability.

Step6: Source node S sends m of packets to the destination via the cluster-head.

Step7: The clusterhead generates a sequence of 0 and 1 and stores in array V[].

Step8: The clusterhead chooses the next hop node, where lock[][]=1;
   if(lock[Ch][k]==0) then
      Ch checks value of V[ ];
      if V[i] is found to be zero then
         a red ant is generated, which chooses the node with maximum rprob as
         the next hop node;
      else
         a blue ant is generated and the node with maximum rprob is chosen as
         the next hop node.

Step9:
   If red ant chooses k as the next hop node then
      the amount of red pheromone deposited is calculated as
         Ch][k]=r[Ch][k]+(1/cost[Ch][k]);
   elseif blue ant chooses k as the next hop node then
      the amount of blue pheromone deposited is calculated as
         b[Ch][k]=b[Ch][k]+(1/cost[Ch][k]).

Step10: After sending 3 messages amount of red and blue pheromone decreased from the path and it is proportional to the cost on that path as follows:
      r[Ch][k]=r[Ch][k]-(.0005*cost[Ch][k]);
      b[Ch][k]=b[Ch][k]-(.0005*cost[Ch][k]);

Step11: Repeat steps 1 to 10 until the packet reaches destination node D.

4   Performance Analysis

The simulation experience conducted for the performance evaluations were implemented in NS2 simulation tool, widely used for wireless network. To determine the efficiency of proposed protocol, we monitored four parameters: no of dominating nodes, no of non dominating nodes, load in the network and the delivery time. Load is computed by total no packets transmitted during simulation period.

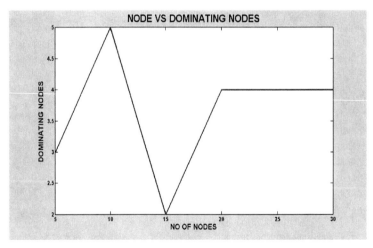

Fig. 1. Showing no of nodes vs. no of dominating nodes

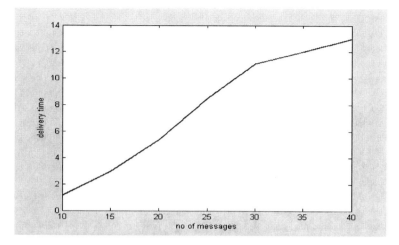

Fig. 2. Load vs. Delivery time

Figure 1 shows the no of dominating nodes as a function of number of nodes in the network. Figure 2 shows delivery time for the routing protocol as a function of load in the network.

Figure 1 shows, nodes vs dominating nodes graph. Here, it is found that if nodes increase, dominating nodes does not increase rapidly. From 5 to 10 nodes, dominating nodes increase with no of nodes in the network. After that, no of dominating nodes decrease with increase of nodes in the network. After from 20 th node, it's value again increase. Then after 22 nodes value of dominating nodes are same with increase of no of nodes in the network. Thus it is proved that value of dominating nodes' number does not keep on increasing with the increasing number of nodes in the network. After certain number of nodes it will be same. So, number of clusters also does not increase rapidly and overhead does not increase.

The Figure 2 shows load vs delivery time graph. From this figure, it is determined, if load in the network increases delivery time does not increase rapidly. From 30 to 40 load in the network, the delivery time stabilizes.

5 Conclusion

The proposed algorithm is an agent based routing protocol used for routing packets in a cluster based mobile adhoc network. A node is selected as cluster head using the concept of dominating and non dominating nodes. This proves to be beneficial for the stability of clusters in a dynamic network. Multiple agents are deployed using the concept of ant colony optimization for faster and more efficient packet routing throughout the network. Simulation results show that the proposed protocol ensures efficient packet delivery even in the face of congestion in the network. This algorithm is very useful where the bandwidth of the packets sent by a node exceeds the bandwidth of the channel.

References

1. Schwartz, M., Stern, T.E.: Routing Techniques used in Communication Networks. IEEE Trans. on Communications, 539–552 (April 1980)
2. Ramamoorthy, C.V., Bhide, A., Srivastava, J.: Reliable Clustering Techniques for Large, Mobile Packet Radio Networks. In: Proc. IEEE INFOCOM, pp. 218–226 (May 1987)
3. Zhang, J., Jeong, C.K., Lee, G.Y., Kim, H.J.: Cluster-based Multi-path Routing Algorithm for Multi-hop Wireless Network
4. Krishna, P., Vaidya, N.H., Chatterjee, M., Pradhan, D.K.: Cluster Based Routing Protocol. ACM SIGCOMM Computer Communication Review 27(2), 49–64 (1997)
5. Gerla, M., Tasai, J.: Multicluster,mobile,multimedia radio network. ACM-Baltzer Journal Wireless Networks 1(3), 255–256 (1997)
6. Jiang, M., Li, J., Tay, Y.C.: Cluster Based Routing Protocol (CBRP) Functional Specification Internet Draft, draft-ieft-manet-cbrp.txt (June 1999)
7. Zheng, Z.-w., Wu, Z.-h., Lin, H.-z., Zheng, K.-g.: CRAM: An Energy Efficient Routing Algorithm for Wireless Sensor Networks. Computer and Information Sciences, 341–350 (2004)
8. Dhurandher, S.K., Singh, G.V.: Power Aware Cluster Efficient Routing Wireless Ad Hoc Networks. In: Pal, A., Kshemkalyani, A.D., Kumar, R., Gupta, A. (eds.) IWDC 2005. LNCS, vol. 3741, pp. 281–286. Springer, Heidelberg (2005)
9. Wang, Y., Ling, T., Yang, X., Zhang, D.: Scalable and Effective Cluster Based Routing Algorithm Using Nodes' Location for Mobile Ad Hoc Networks. Information Technology Journal 7(7), 958–971 (2008)
10. Chaki, R., Sinha, D.: LCRACO - A new Load and Congestion Controlled Routing based on Ant Colony Optimization. In: Proc. of IEEE International Workshop on Internet and Distributed Computing Systems, Khulna Bangladesh, pp. 978–971 (Decembar 2008) ISBN:978-1-4244-2136-7
11. Anitha, V.S., Sebastian, M.P.: SCAM: scenario-based clustering algorithm for mobile ad hoc networks. In: Proceedings of the First International Conference on Communication Systems and Networks, Bangalore, India, vol. 7, pp. 375–382. IEEE Press, Piscataway (2009) ISBN:978-1-4244-2912-7
12. Gunes, M., Sorges, U., Bouazizi, I.: ARA- the ant colony based routing algorithm for MANET. In: ICPP Proc. of the 2002 Workshop on Adhoc Networks (2002)
13. Di Caro, G., Dorigo, M.: AntNet distributed stigmergetic control for communication networks. Journal on Artificial Intelligence Research (1998)
14. Dorrio, M., Di Caro, G.: Mobile Agents For Adaptive Routing. In: 31st International Conference Sys., Hawaii (January 1998)

New Paradigms in Checkpoint Processing and Recovery Techniques for Distributed Mobile Systems

Ruchi Tuli[1] and Parveen Kumar[2]

[1] Research Scholar, Singhania University, (Pacheri Bari) Rajasthan (India)
[2] Professor, Meerut Institute of Engineering & Technology, Meerut (India)

Abstract. A distributed application involving Mobile hosts consists of a set of cooperating processes in which some of them run on MHs. An MH is connected to the wired network through *mobile support stations* (MSS). Distributed systems are not fault-tolerant and the vast computing potential of these systems is often hampered by their susceptibility to failures. Many techniques have been developed to add reliability and high availability to distributed systems. These techniques have different tradeoffs and focus. The paper surveys a literature survey on the modern check pointing techniques in distributed and mobile environments. We have classified the various check pointing schemes and then discussed the related works in that category. The paper also presents a comparative study of the protocols/schemes with relative advantages and disadvantages and finally the features which make the checkpointing techniques to be suitable in a particular application scenario are also discussed.

Keywords: Mobile computing systems, co-ordinated checkpoint, rollback recovery, mobile host.

1 Introduction

Checkpointing / rollback-recovery strategy has been an attractive approach for providing fault-tolerance to distributed applications. A checkpoint is a snapshot of the local state of a process, saved on local nonvolatile storage to survive process failures. A global checkpoint of an n-process distributed system consists of n checkpoints (local) such that each of these n checkpoints corresponds uniquely to one of the n processes. A global checkpoint M is defined as a consistent global checkpoint if no message is sent after a checkpoint of M and received before another checkpoint of M. The checkpoints belonging to a consistent global checkpoint are called globally consistent checkpoints (GCCs). In distributed systems, rollback recovery is complicated because messages induce inter-process dependencies during failure-free operation. Upon a failure of one or more processes in a system, these dependencies may force some of the processes that did not fail to roll back, creating what is commonly called a rollback propagation. To see why rollback propagation occurs, consider the situation where the sender of a message m rolls back to a state that precedes the sending of m. The receiver of m must also roll back to a state that precedes m's receipt; otherwise, the states of the two processes would be inconsistent because they would show that message m was received without being sent, which is impossible in any correct

D.C. Wyld et al. (Eds.): NeCoM/WeST/WiMoN 2011, CCIS 197, pp. 221–231, 2011.
© Springer-Verlag Berlin Heidelberg 2011

failure-free execution. This phenomenon of cascaded rollback is called the *domino effect*. In some situations, rollback propagation may extend back to the initial state of the computation, losing all the work performed before the failure.

In a distributed system, if each participating process takes its checkpoints independently, then the system is susceptible to the domino effect. This approach is called *independent or uncoordinated checkpointing* [1], [2], [3]. It is obviously desirable to avoid the domino effect and therefore several techniques have been developed to prevent it. One such technique is *coordinated checkpointing* [4], [5], [6] where processes coordinate their checkpoints to form a system-wide consistent state. In case of a process failure, the system state can be restored to such a consistent set of checkpoints, preventing the rollback propagation. Alternatively, *communication-induced checkpointing* [7], [8], [9] forces each process to take checkpoints based on information piggybacked on the application messages it receives from other processes. Checkpoints are taken such that a system-wide consistent state always exists on stable storage, thereby avoiding the domino effect. *Log-based rollback recovery* [10], [11], [12], [13], [14], [15] combines checkpointing with logging of nondeterministic events. Log-based rollback recovery relies on the piecewise deterministic (PWD) assumption, which postulates that all non-deterministic events that a process executes can be identified and that the information necessary to replay each event during recovery can be logged in the event's determinant. By logging and replaying the non-deterministic events in their exact original order, a process can deterministically recreate its pre-failure state even if this state has not been checkpointed.. Table 1 below gives a comparison of rollback recovery protocols based on different parameters.

Table 1. Comparison of Rollback recovery protocols

Parameters	Uncoordinated Checkpointing	Coordinated Checkpointing	Communication Induced Check-pointing	Message logging protocols		
				Pessimistic logging	Optimstic logging	Casual logging
Domino Effect	Possible	No	No	No	No	No
Orphan Message	Possible	No	Possible	No	Possible	No
Recovery Line	Unbounded	Last global checkpoint	Possibly several checkpoints	Last check-point	Possibly several check points	Last check point
Output Commit	Not possible	Global Coordination required	Global Coordination required	Local decision	Global Coordination required	Local decision

2 System Model

The algorithms that are considered in this paper use the common system model in which a mobile computing system consists of a set of mobile hosts (MHs) and mobile support stations (MSSs). The static MSS provides various services to support the MHs and a region covered by a MSS is called a cell. A wireless communication link is established between a MH and a MSS; and a high speed wired communication link is assumed between any two MSSs. The wireless links support FIFO communication in both directions between a MSS and the MHs in the cell. A distributed computation is performed by a set of MHs or MSSs in the network.

3 Checkpointing Algorithms for Mobile Computing Systems

Checkpointing techniques are studied under Asynchronous or uncoordinated, Synchronous or coordinated and quasi-synchronous or communication-induced checkpointing schemes. In this section, we discuss the various algorithms that have been proposed in literature for each of these schemes. Figure 1 shows the classification of these schemes.

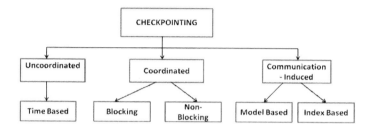

Fig. 1. Classification of checkpointing schemes

3.1 Asynchronous or Uncoordinated or Independent Checkpointing

In uncoordinated checkpointing, each process has autonomy in deciding when to take checkpoints. This eliminates the synchronization overhead as there is no need for coordination between processes and it allows processes to take checkpoints when it is most convenient or efficient.

Park, Woo and Ycom[16] proposed an algorithm based on independent checkpointing and asynchronous message logging. All the messages are delivered to mobile host (MH) through MSS, so message logs are saved by MSS for all MHs in its vicinity. The logs that are saved in MSS are used to recover state of process at MH after failure. Also, to reduce the message overhead, the mobile support stations take care of the dependency tracking.

Park, Woo and Ycom[17] proposed a scheme based on the message logging and independent checkpointing, and for the efficient management of the recovery information, such as checkpoints and message logs. They suggested a movement-based scheme which allows the movement of checkpoint and message logs to a nearby MSS when either distance between MH and MSS on which latest checkpoint is saved exceed a threshold value, or, when number of handoffs that number of MSS carrying message logs of a MH exceeds a threshold value. These schemes keep the recovery information of MH in certain range. The movement-based scheme considers both of the failure-free execution cost and the failure-recovery cost.

Zhang, Zuo, Zhi- Bowu and Yang [18] improved this scheme by migrating only partial recovery information of a MH when a MH moves out of the range. It means that recovery information of MH which is stored in some MSS due to mobility, is mapped to another set of MSSs. These MSSs are given by route function. The main advantage of this scheme is that one MSS is not burdened by transferring all the information to it.

Another movement-based algorithm was proposed by E. George, Chen and Jin [19] in which Independent checkpointing and optimistic message logging is used. MH takes checkpoint when its handoff_counter becomes greater than a predefined threshold.

3.2 Coordinated Checkpointing

In this we will discuss the algorithms for both blocking and non-blocking coordinated checkpointing schemes.

3.2.1 Blocking Coordinated Checkpointing

A straightforward approach to coordinated checkpointing is to block communications while the checkpointing protocol executes. After a process takes a local checkpoint, to prevent orphan messages, it remains blocked until the entire checkpointing activity is complete.

A two-level blocking checkpointing algorithm was proposed by Lotfi, Motamedi and Bandarabadi [20] in which local and global checkpoint are taken. Nodes take local checkpoint according to checkpoint interval calculated previously based on failure rate and save it in their local disk. These checkpoints when sent to stable storage become global checkpoint. Local checkpoints are used to recover from more probable failures where as global checkpoints are used to recover from less probable failures. After each checkpointing interval, system determines expected recovery time in case of permanent failure. System calculates amount of time taken (T1) to recover if system does not take global checkpoint and amount of time taken (T2) to recover if system takes global checkpoint. Then system compares these two times. If T2 < T1, system will take global checkpoint else system will only store checkpoint locally.

Awasthi and Kumar[21] proposed a synchronous checkpointing protocol for mobile distributed systems. They reduced the useless checkpoints and blocking of processes during checkpointing using a probabilistic approach. A process takes an induced checkpoint if the probability that it will get a checkpoint request in current initiation is high.

Another blocking coordinated scheme is proposed by Suparna Biswas and Sarmistha Neogy [22] in which each MSSp is required to maintain an array A[n] in which A[1] is 1 when MH1 is present in vicinity of cell of MSSp where number of MH (Mobile Host) are n starting from 0 to n-1. A MH initiates checkpointing procedure, calculates its dependency vector D and sends request to all the MH whose bit in dependency vector D is 1 via its MSS. If a MH is present in vicinity of current MSS, then checkpoint request is send directly to MH. Else current MSS will broadcast checkpoint request message to other MSS so that it can reach all those processes whose bit is 1 in dependency vector D calculated by checkpoint initiator. Thus all these processes take checkpoint and sends information to initiator via their local MSS.

Guohui Li and LihChyun Shu [23] designed an algorithm to reduce blocking time for checkpointing operation, in which each process Pi maintains a set of processes Si. A process Pj is included in this set if Pj has sent at least one message to Pi in current checkpoint interval. Checkpointing dependency information is transferred from sending process to destination process during normal message transmission. So when a process starts a checkpointing procedure, it knows in advance the processes on which it depends both transitively and directly.

Biswas & Neogy [24] proposed a checkpointing and failure recovery algorithm where mobile hosts save checkpoints based on mobility and movement patterns. Mobile hosts save checkpoints when number of hand-offs exceed a predefined handoff threshold value. They introduced the concept of migration checkpoint An MH upon saving migration checkpoint, sends it attached with migration message to its current MSS before disconnection.

S. Kumar, R.Garg [34] and P. Kumar [35] gave the concept of hybrid checkpointing algorithm, where in an all-process coordinated checkpoint is taken after the execution of minimum process coordinated checkpointing algorithm for a fixed number of times.

3.2.2 Non-blocking Coordinated Checkpointing Algorithm

In this approach the processes need not stop their execution while taking checkpoints. A fundamental problem in coordinated checkpointing is to prevent a process from receiving application messages that could make the checkpoint inconsistent.

Cao and Singhal [25] presented a non-blocking coordinated checkpointing algorithm with the concept of "Mutable Checkpoint" which is neither temporary nor permanent and can be converted to temporary checkpoint or discarded later and can be saved anywhere, e.g., the main memory or local disk of MHs. In this scheme MHs save a disconnection checkpoint before any type of disconnection .This checkpoint is converted to permanent checkpoint or discarded later. In this scheme only dependent processes are forced to take checkpoints. In this way, taking a mutable checkpoint avoids the overhead of transferring large amounts of data to the stable storage at MSSs over the wireless network.

Cao-Chen-Zhang-He [26] proposed an algorithm for Hybrid Systems. They presented an algorithm which was developed for integrating independent and coordinated checkpointing for application running on a hybrid distributed system containing multiple heterogeneous systems.

Bidyut – Rahimi- Liu [27] presented their work for mobile computing systems. In that work they presented a single phase non-blocking coordinated checkpointing suitable for mobile systems. This algorithm produces a consistent set of checkpoints without the overhead of temporary checkpoints.

Bidyut-Rahimi-Ziping Liu [28] proposed non-blocking checkpointing and recovery algorithms for bidirectional networks. The proposed algorithm allowed the process to take permanent checkpoints directly, without taking temporary checkpoint global snapshot algorithms for large scale distributed systems. Whenever a process is busy it takes a checkpoint after completing its current procedure. The algorithm was designed and simulate for Ring network.

Partha Sarathi Mandal and Krishnendu Mukhopadhyaya [29] proposed a non blocking algorithm that uses the concept of mobile agent to handle multiple initiations of checkpointing. Mobile Agent has id same as its initiator id and it migrates among processes, perform some work, take some actions and then moves to other node together with required information. Each process takes initial permanent checkpoint and sets version number of checkpoint to 0. Process sends application message m by piggybacking it with version number of its latest checkpoint. Receiver compares application message's version number with its own current checkpoint version number to decide whether to take checkpoint first or simply to process message only. There is a DFS which is maintained by each process which contains id of neighbors on which the process depends.

S. Kumar, R.K. Chauhan and P. Kumar [33] proposed a single-phase non-blocking coordinated checkpointing algorithm suitable for mobile computing environments in which processes take permanent checkpoints directly without taking temporary checkpoints and whenever a process is busy, the process takes a checkpoint after completing the current procedure.

3.3 Communication Induced or Quasi-Synchronous Checkpointing

It lies between synchronous and asynchronous (independent) checkpointing. Process takes communication induced checkpoints besides independent checkpoint to reduce number of useless checkpoints taken in independent checkpointing approach. Processes takes two kinds of checkpoints called local checkpoints and forced checkpoints. Local checkpoints are just like independent checkpoints taken in independent checkpointing approach. Forced checkpoints are taken to guarantee eventual progress of recovery line.

Qiangfeng Jiang and D. Manivannan [30] presented an optimistic checkpointing and selective message logging approach for consistent global checkpoint collection in distributed systems. In this work they presented a novel quasi-synchronous checkpointing algorithm that makes every checkpoint belong to a consistent global checkpoint. Under this algorithm every process takes tentative checkpoints and optimistically logs messages received after a tentative checkpoint is taken and before the tentative checkpoint is finalized. Since tentative checkpoint can be taken any time and sorted in local memory, tentative checkpoints taken can be flushed to stable storage anytime before that checkpoint is finalized.

Ajay D Kshemkalyani algorithm [31] presented a fast and message efficient algorithm and show that new algorithm is more efficient. He presented two new algorithms Simple Tree and Hypercube that use fewer message and have lower response time and parallel communication times. In addition the hypercube algorithm is symmetrical and has greater potential for balanced workload and congestion freedom. This algorithm have direct applicable in large scale distributed systems such as peer to peer and MIMD supercomputers

Jin Yang, Jiannong Cao, Weigang Wu [32] proposed a communication induced checkpointing scheme in which communication induced or forced checkpoints are taken by a process by analyzing piggybacked information that comes with received message. Each process has a logical clock or counter which is increased with every new checkpoint taken. When a process sends an application message, it piggybacks recent value of logical clock on message. Receiver compares its LC (logical clock) with received LC to decide whether to take a forced checkpoint before processing message or simply process the message. Algorithm uses a Mobile Agent (MA) system which has a globally unique id. Each MA executes on a node and takes an independent checkpoint before migration. It then determines next host to which it has to migrate, it reaches on that host and takes a checkpoint on it. This process will continue until all hosts have been visited. These checkpoints are called local checkpoints.

4   Comparison of Different Checkpoint Algorithms

Table 2 below highlights the features of different checkpoint algorithms proposed in literature and also discusses their relative advantages and disadvantages.

Table 2. Comparison of various checkpoint algorithms for distributed systems

S. No.	Algorithm	Advantages	Disadvantages	Approach
Uncoordinated Checkpointing				
1.	T.Park [16], 2002	1. Recovery of an MH is performed independently 2. Message logging & dependency tracking is performed by MSS to utilize volatile space at MSS	1. Distributed storage at MSS need to be managed so as to reduce the cost collection of message logs of MH after failure	Centralized
2.	T.Park [17], 2003	1. Movement based scheme used to handle distributed storage, controls transfer cost as well as recovery cost	1. All the recovery information of MH needs to be migrated to MSS when it moves out of the scope of current MSS 2. Only partial recovery information may be available if MH returns back to previous MSS	Centralized
3.	Zhang [18], 2008	1. Independent checkpointing algorithm 2. Failed nodes can recover independently 3. All the recovery information of a MH is not transferred to single MSS, so one MSS will not be bottleneck of failure and access	1. Storage overhead is high	Centralized
4.	E.George [19], 2006	1. When a MH crosses a distance threshold from the location of latest checkpoint, recovery information is collected and transferred to MH's local MSS 2. Storage management is done by removing the log entry from MSS when checkpoint is successfully taken.	-	Distributed
Blocking Coordinated Checkpointing				
5.	Lofti [20], 2009	1. Low overhead than one level scheme as local checkpoints are used for more probable failures and global checkpoints are used for less probable failures.	-	Distributed
6.	P. Kumar [21], 2007	1. low memory and computation overhead 2. Low communication overheads on wireless channels	1. A MH can remain disconnected for an arbitrary period of time without affecting checkpointing activity.	Distributed
7.	S. Negi [22], 2007	1. A solution how to handle mobility is given	1. If a MH is present in vicinity of current MSS, then checkpoint request is send directly to MH. Else current MSS will broadcast checkpoint request message to other MSS 2. Thus all these processes take checkpoint and sends information to initiator via their local MSS	Centralized
8.	Guohui [23], 2005	1. Blocking time is reduced	1. Storage overhead	Centralized
9.	Biswas [24], 2010	1. They introduced the concept of migration checkpoint 2. An MH upon saving migration checkpoint, sends it attached with migration message to its current MSS before disconnection	1. During checkpointing participating MHs are barred only from receiving execution	Distributed
10.	P. Kumar, R. Garg [34], 2011	1. Introduced the concept of soft checkpointing 2. Fewer control messages 3. Blocking time is reduced 4. Handles frequent aborts of checkpointing scheme.	1. Synchronization Message overhead is large. 2. It is a complex scheme-	Distributed
Non-Blocking Coordinated Checkpointing				

Table 2. (*continued*)

11.	Cao & Mukesh Singhal [25], 2001	1. Only dependent processes are forced to take checkpoints 2. Storage overhead is reduced	1. Useless Checkpoints 2. High Synchronization Message overhead 3. Checkpointing Tree is formed	Distributed
12.	Cao & Chen [26], 2004	1. Easy to implement 2. No change required for subsystems 3. No extra workload	-	Distributed
13.	Bidyut, Rahimi and Liu[27], 2006	1. Checkpoint overhead is reduced	1. Channel can loss messages	Distributed
14.	Bidyut-Rahimi-Ziping Liu [28], 2008	1. Eliminates the need of taking temporary checkpoint	-	Distributed
15.	Partha Sarathi Mandal and Krishnendu Mukhopadhyaya [29], 2007	1. Number of moves that an agent takes to complete checkpointing may be very large	1. Multiple concurrent checkpoints are possible	Distributive
16.	S. Kumar, R.K. Chauhan & P. Kumar [33], 2008	1. Free from avalanche effect 2. Fewer control messages are required	1. Possibility of useless checkpoints.	Distributive
17.	P.Kumar [35], 2007	1. No useless checkpoints 2. Minimizes blocking period 3. Controls loss of computation on recovery	1. Some blocking of processes takes place. 2. Checkpointing Overhead is larger than minimum process checkpointing.	Distributed
Communication Induced Checkpointing				
18.	Qiangfeng Jiang and D. Manivannan [30], 2007	1. Fast response time 2. Reduce overhead of checkpints	-	Distributed
19.	Ajay D Kshemkalyani algorithm [31], 2010	1. Useful in large distributive systems like supercomputers, MIMD, required less message and response time	-	Distributed
20.	Jin Yang, Jiannong Cao, Weigang Wu [32], 2006	1. Forced checkpoints maintain consistent recovery line	1. Deferred message processing scheme allow delaying the processing of received message (that can lead to forced checkpoint) until mobile agent takes a basic checkpoint. Thus, forced checkpoints are avoided but some messages cannot be processed immediately	Distributed

5 Application Scenarios

The checkpointing techniques discussed above have certain unique features which make them suitable to be used in a particular situation. Table 3 below discuses the application areas where each of these checkpointing techniques can be efficiently applied.

Table 3. Application scenarios of checkpointing techniques

Checkpointing technique	Features	Application Area
Un-coordinated checkpointing	The Independent Checkpoint pattern is ideal for the development of systems with demanding performance constraints during error-free executions, that do not experience errors often and when they do they can afford to go off service for repairing the failure.	Telecom operator network and ISP service network
Co-ordinated checkpointing	The Coordinated Checkpoint pattern is addressed more to the development of systems-that have bounded time constraints (yet not high performance once) on their execution, and they cannot afford long execution delays due to system recovery.	Automatic navigation control and embedded systems (e.g. mobile phones, PDAs)
Communication-induced checkpointing	The Communication-Induced Checkpoint pattern is meant for high-performance real time systems that can perform general purpose computations (as opposed to those system that can perform only special purpose computations such as signal processing).	Stock market software

6 Conclusion

We have reviewed and compared different approaches for failure free execution of a mobile host and to a greater extent failure free execution of mobile environment. We studied three checkpointing scheme- independent, coordinated and communication induced checkpointing and the various algorithms that have been developed under each of these scheme. We have also compared different approaches of checkpointing and compared the salient features of various snapshot recording algorithms in Table 2. Clearly, the higher the level of abstraction provided by a communication model, the simpler the snapshot algorithm. The requirement of global snapshots finds a large number of applications like: detection of stable properties, checkpointing, monitoring, debugging, analyses of distributed computation, discarding of obsolete information, etc. We have also shown what are the features that are needed to be considered while choosing a checkpointing technique for a particular system.

References

1. Bhargava, B., Lian, S.R.: Independent Checkpointing and Concurrent Rollback for Recovery in Distributed Systems – An Optimistic Approach. In: Proceedings of 17th IEEE Symposium on Reliable Distributed Systems, pp. 3–12 (1988)
2. Storm, R., Temini, S.: Optimistic Recovery in Distributed Systems. ACM Trans. Computer Systems, 204–226 (August 1985)
3. Ni, W., Vrbsky, S.V., Ray, S.: Low-cost Coordinated Checkpointing in Mobile Computing Systems". In: Proceeding of the Eighth IEEE International Symposium on Computers and Communications (2003)
4. Chandy, K.M., Lamport, L.: Distributed snapshots: Determining Global State of Distributed Systems. ACM Transaction on Computing Systems 3(1), 63–75 (1985)
5. Koo, R., Tueg, S.: Checkpointing and Rollback recovery for Distributed Systems. IEEE Trans. on Software Engineering 13(1), 23–31 (1987)

6. Elonzahy, E.N., Alvisi, L., Wang, Y.M., Johnson, D.B.: A survey of Rollback-Recovery protocols in Message-Passing Systems. ACM Computing Surveys 34(3), 375–408 (2002)

7. Baldoni, R., Hélary, J.-M., Mostefaoui, A., Raynal, M.: A Communication- Induced Checkpointing Protocol that Ensures Rollback-Dependency Trackability. In: Proceedings of the International Symposium on Fault-Tolerant-Computing Systems, pp. 68–77 (June 1997)

8. Hélary, J.M., Mostefaoui, A., Raynal, M.: Communication- Induced Determination of Consistent Snapshots. In: Proceedings of the 28th International Symposium on Fault-Tolerant Computing, pp. 208–217 (June 1998)

9. Manivannan, D., Singhal, M.: Quasi-Synchronous Checkpointing: Models, Characterization, and Classification. IEEE Trans. Parallel and Distributed Systems 10(7), 703–713 (1999)

10. Alvisi, L., Marzullo, K.: Message Logging: Pessimistic, Optimistic, Causal, and Optimal. IEEE Transactions on Software Engineering 24(2), 149–159 (1998)

11. Alvisi, L., Hoppe, B., Marzullo, K.: Nonblocking and Orphan-Free message Logging Protocol. In: Proc. of 23rd Fault Tolerant Computing Symp., pp. 145–154 (June 1993)

12. Alvisi, L.: Understanding the Message Logging Paradigm for Masking Process Crashes. Ph.D. Thesis, Cornell Univ., Dept. of Computer Science (January 1996); Available as Technical Report TR-96-1577

13. Elnozahy, Zwaenepoel, W.: On the Use and Implementation of Message Logging. In: 24th Int'l Symp. Fault Tolerant Computing, pp. 298–307. IEEE Computer Society, Los Alamitos (1994)

14. Johnson, D.: Distributed System Fault Tolerance Using Message Logging and Checkpointing. Ph.D. Thesis, Rice Univ. (December 1989)

15. Venketasan, S., Juang, T.Y.: Efficient Algorithms for Optimistic Crash recovery. Distributed Computing 8(2), 105–114 (1994)

16. Park, T., Woo, N., Ycom, H.Y.: An Efficient Optimistic Message Logging Scheme for Recoverable Mobile Computing Systems. IEEE Tran. On Mobile Computing (2002)

17. Park, T., Woo, N., Yeom, H.Y.: An Efficient Recovery Scheme for Fault Tolerant Mobile Computing Systems. FGCS-19 (2003)

18. Ci, Y.-W., Zhang, Z., Zuo, D.C., Bowu, Z., Yang, X.-Z.: Area Difference Based Recovery Information Placement for Mobile Computing System. In: 14th IEEE International Conference on Parallel and Distributed Systems (2008)

19. George, S.E., Chen, I.-R., Jin, Y.: Movement Based Checkpointing and Logging for Recovery in Mobile Computing Systems. ACM, New York (2006)

20. Lotfi, M., Motamedi, S.A., Bandarabadi, M.: Lightweight Blocking Coordinated Checkpointing for Cluster Computer Systems. In: Sym. on System Theory (2009)

21. Kumar, L., Kumar, P.: A synchronous ckeckpointing protocol for mobile distributed systems: probabilistic approach. Int. Journal of Information and Computer Security (2007)

22. Biswas, S., Neogy, S.: A Low Overhead Checkpointing Scheme for Mobile Computing Systems. In: Int. Conf. Advances Computing and Communications. IEEE, Los Alamitos (2007)

23. Li, G., Shu, L.: A Low-Latency Checkpointing Scheme for Mobile Computing Systems. In: Int. Conf. Computer Software and Applications. IEEE, Los Alamitos (2005)

24. Biswas, S., Neogy, S.: A Mobility-Based Checkpointing Protocol for Mobile Computing System. International Journal of Computer Science & Information Technology 2(1), 135–151 (2010)

25. Cao, G., Singhal, M.: Mutable Checkpoints: A New Checkpointing Approach for Mobile Computing Systems. IEEE Transactions on Parallel and Distributed System 12(2), 157–172 (2001) ISSN: 1045-9219
26. Cao, J., Chen, Y., Zhang, K., He, Y.: Checkpointing In Hybrid Distributed Systems. In: Proceedings of 7th International Symposium of Parallel Architetures. IEEE, Los Alamitos (2004)
27. Gupta, B., Rahimi, S., Liu, Z.: A new high performance checkpointing approach for mobile computing systems. International Journal of Computer Science and Network Security (2006)
28. Gupta, B., Rahimi, S., Liu, Z.: Design of high performance distributed snapshot/recovery algorithms for ring network. Journal of Computing and information Technology-CIT (2008)
29. Mandal, P.S., Mukhopadhyaya, K.: Mobile Agent based Checkpointing with Concurrent Initiations. International J. of Foundation of Computer Science (2007)
30. Jiang, Q., Manivannan, D.: An Optimistic Checkpointing and selective message logging approach for consistent global checkpoint collection in distributed systems. IEEE, Los Alamitos (2007)
31. Kshemkalyani, A.D.: A symmetric O(n log n) message distributed snapshot algorithm for large scale systems. IEEE, Los Alamitos (2010)
32. Yang, J., Cao, J., Wu, W.: CIC: An Integrated Approach to Checkpointing in Mobile Agent System. In: Proceedings of Second International Conference on Semantics, Knowledge and Grid (2006)
33. Kumar, S., Chauhan, R.K., Kumar, P.: Minimum process Error discovery algorithm for mobile Distributed system using Global Checkpoint. International Journal of Information Technology and Knowledge Management 1(1), 25–33 (2008)
34. Kumar, P., Garg, R.: Soft Checkpointing Based Hybrid Synchronous Checkpointing Protocol for Mobile Distributed Systems. International Journal of Distributed Systems and Technologies 2(1), 1–13 (2011)
35. Kumar, P.: A Low-Cost Hybrid Coordinated Checkpointing Protocol for Mobile Distributed Systems. An International Journal from Mobile Information Systems 4(1), 13–32 (2007); Listed in ACM Portal & Science Citation Index Expanded

A-Star Algorithm for Energy Efficient Routing in Wireless Sensor Network

Keyur Rana[1] and Mukesh Zaveri[2]

[1] Department of Computer Engineering,
Sarvajanik College of Engineering & Technology, Surat, India
Keyur.rana@scet.ac.in
[2] Department of Computer Engineering,
Sardar Vallabhbhai National Institute of Technology, Surat, India
mazaveri@coed.svnit.ac.in

Abstract. Various routing protocols have been designed and developed for Wireless Sensor Networks (WSN). They face various challenges. Sensor nodes are strongly energy and storage constrained and failure rate of sensor node is very high. While sending data to the Base station some routing mechanisms which consider all these parameters, are needed to extend life of the network.

There are several techniques for routing in WSN for data gathering with aggregation and for data gathering without aggregation. Using Minimum transmission energy model and Minimum hop routing model techniques it may happen that the same path is used for more times and nodes on this route gets drain from energy. This leads to network partition and routing algorithm failure. In this paper, we have presented routing algorithm based on informed search. We have used A-Star algorithm to search optimal route from source to the destination in such a way that overall life of network is extended. We have used a pre-defined minimum energy level (*Level1*) for sensor nodes so that sensor node don't participate in routing if its residual energy level is below this level and other better path is available. If there exist no such path, then this node can be part of routing.

Keywords: Wireless sensor network, Routing algorithm, A-Star algorithm, Energy aware routing in WSN.

1 Introduction

In Wireless Sensor Network, light-weight, low power and small size sensor nodes are used which are operated by a small battery. The energy they lose is proportionate to the distance of communication. There is no way to recharge these batteries in most of cases. Sensors nodes are used for monitoring physical phenomena like temperature, humidity, vibrations and so on [1]. The sensor network should have a lifetime long enough to fulfill the application requirements.

Deployment of sensor nodes is done either in random fashion or in pre-defined way. The sensor node performs needed measurements from its surroundings, process this data and transmit it to the Base Station (BS). The BS collects data from all these

D.C. Wyld et al. (Eds.): NeCoM/WeST/WiMoN 2011, CCIS 197, pp. 232–241, 2011.
© Springer-Verlag Berlin Heidelberg 2011

nodes and uses it as per the application. Nodes in sensor networks have limited computational power, limited energy resources and memory. These restrictions put a limit on routing algorithms to be used.

Generally in routing algorithm, the best path is chosen for transmission of data from source to destination. Over the period of time, if same path is chosen for all communications in order to achieve better performance in terms of quick transmission time, then those nodes which are on this path will get drained faster. The problem with many routing algorithms is that they minimize total energy consumption in the network with the expense of non uniform energy drainage in the network. Such approaches cause network partition because some nodes which are part of the efficient path are drained from their battery energy quicker. In many cases, the lifetime of a sensor network is over as soon as the battery power in critical nodes is depleted [2].

Some special nodes, called relay nodes can also be used within the network, for balanced data gathering to extend life of network. In case of hierarchical sensor network, cluster head is called as relay node.

A Genetic Algorithm (GA) based approach for energy efficient routing has been proposed by Ataul Bari et. al[3]. They have suggested this approach for two-tiered sensor network for data gathering with aggregation. In [4], GA based approach for data gathering without aggregation has been proposed. In this approach, a pre-defined threshold level (*Level1*) energy is considered as the threshold residual energy in the sensor node. If it is found, that one or more nodes having residual energy less than the *Level1* energy in the route between source to destination, then, another route with number of nodes below residual energy of *Level1* lesser than the previous route solution will be sought. In this approach, total energy consumed and total number of nodes below *Level1* has been used as criteria to choose best route.

In this paper, we have emphasized on heuristic search technique, called A-Star algorithm, for searching best path for routing in WSN. Criteria to search best path is not only to get path with minimum energy consumption but also to see that nodes selected in the path contain enough of residual energy. This will make sure, that overall lifetime of sensor network is extended. We have used concept of a pre-defined threshold level, *Level1*, of residual energy. We have simulated GA based approach of [4] and A-Star algorithm for routing in WSN for data gathering without aggregation for comparison.

To find best path, Warshall's algorithm [5, 6] can be used. Warshall's algorithm compares all possible paths through the graph between each pair of vertices. This is a non adaptive algorithm and it does not consider current level of energy of sensor nodes to decide route. We have also simulated Warshall's algorithm and compared with our approach.

2   Review

In this chapter, we will discuss informed and heuristic search, A-Star algorithm, Network model and two tired Wireless Sensor Network.

2.1 Overview of A-Star Algorithm

A-Star algorithm is used to find path and to traverse graph efficiently. A-Star algorithm performs better than Dijkstra's algorithm with respect to time. A-Star uses heuristics for decision making. The A-Star algorithm [7] is a best-first search algorithm that finds the optimal path from source to destination.

It uses a distance and a cost heuristic function (usually denoted $f(n)$) to determine the order in which the search visits nodes in the tree. The distance-plus-cost heuristic is a sum of two functions: (i) The path-cost function, which is the cost from the starting node to the current node (denoted by $g(n)$) and (ii) an admissible "heuristic estimate" of distance to the goal (denoted by $h(n)$).

Generally, the A-Star algorithm creates a tree of nodes and maintains two lists, an OPEN list and a CLOSED list. The OPEN list is a priority queue and keeps track of those nodes that need to be examined, while the CLOSED list keeps track of nodes that have already been examined. Each node n maintains $f(n)$ where $f(n) = g(n) + h(n)$; intuitively, this is the estimate of the best solution that goes through n.

The heuristic function must be admissible, i.e. it must not overestimate the distance to the goal or, in other words estimated cost must be less than the actual cost. This produces computationally optimal results. Thus, for an application like routing, $h(n)$ might represent the straight-line distance to the goal, since that is physically the smallest possible distance between any two nodes. The most essential part of the A-Star algorithm is a good heuristic estimate function. This can improve the efficiency and performance of the algorithm [8].

2.2 Network Model

Relay nodes can be used within the sensor network, for balanced data gathering to extend life of network. In case of hierarchical sensor network, relay nodes can be used as cluster head.

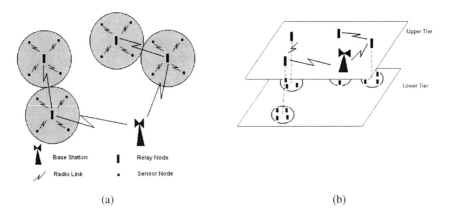

(a)   (b)

Fig. 1. (a) Two Tired Sensor Network (b) A Logical Topology of Two Tire

In this paper we will be refereeing mainly to the sensor network model shown in Fig. 1, which shows that sensor network is divided in cluster and each cluster contains one relay node and many sensor nodes. There is also one BS where information is forwarded by sensor nodes via relay nodes. Each relay node can communicate either with other relay nodes or to the BS. Clustering strategies for this model can be referred from [12].

For this model, a two-tiered WSN has been considered, with N relay nodes (acting as cluster heads). They are labeled as node numbers $1, 2, 3, \ldots, N$ and one BS, labeled as node number $N+1$. This labeling is done for representing the routing solution in form of an array. Let D be the set of all sensor nodes, and $D_i, 1 \leq i \leq N$, be the set of sensor nodes belonging to the ith cluster, which has relay node i as its cluster head. We assume that each sensor node belongs to exactly one cluster i.e., $D = D_1 \cup D_2 \cup \ldots \cup D_N$ and $D_i \cap D_j = \Phi$ for $i \neq j$.

A number of different metrics have been used in the literature to measure the lifetime of a sensor network. In [9], the lifetime of a sensor network has been defined as the minimum of (i) the time when the percentage of nodes that are alive drops below a specified threshold, (ii) the time when the size of the largest connected component of the network drops below a specified threshold, and (iii) the time when the volume covered drops below a specified threshold. The work of [10] has defined the lifetime of the network as the lifetime of the sensor node that dies first. In [11], a number of metrics are used to define the network lifetime. N-of-N lifetime (i.e., time till any relay/gateway node dies) metric has been used in this approach.

2.3   Routing in Sensor Network through Relay Nodes

The type of network shown in Fig. 1 consists of number of sensor clusters and a BS. Each cluster is deployed around a pre defined location. One of the important measures of WSN is the network life time. Since life time of each relay node depends on energy consumption, it is important to preserve residual energy of these relay node in such a way that overall network life time is extended. We have used non-flow splitting routing scheme using multi hop data transmission model [14].

In this paper, we consider two-tiered sensor networks and present an A-Star algorithm based approach to determine a suitable routing strategy for upper-tier relay node networks which is shown in Fig. 1(b).

3   A-Star Algorithm Based Routing

Given a collection of n relay nodes, numbered from 1 to n, and a BS, numbered as $n+1$ along with their locations, the objective of the A-Star algorithm is to find a schedule for data gathering in a sensor network, such that the lifetime of the network is maximized. Each sensor node transmits exactly one packet of data containing a fixed number of bits, in each round. Each period of data gathering is referred to as a round [13], and the lifetime is measured by the number of rounds until the first relay node runs out of power (N-of-N metric).

In our model, the routing schedule is computed by some center entity called as a Base Station. We have assumed that the number and location of relay nodes are predetermined, thus distances between various relay nodes are known. With the known distance, energy consumed for data communication can be calculated. BS can use these facts and can update energy level of each relay node after every round.

3.1 Routing Schedule

A-Star Algorithm is basically used to find efficient path between any sources to destination using $g(n)$ and $h(n)$ functions. In our model, BS will prepare routing schedule and will broadcast to all relay nodes. A-Star algorithm will be applied for each relay node. Relay node where this algorithm is applied will be the source node and the BS will be destination node. Such N different routes will be created and this information will be consolidated. This consolidated route information is put in an array. This is shown in Fig. 2(b). Fig. 2(a) shows two tiered WSN, as discussed earlier. Dotted lines are showing route for each relay nodes.

Array has N number of indices. Value at i^{th} index will represent node number as to where node i will be sending data, which in turn, will go to the BS in a same way. After the current routing schedule is broadcasted, all relay nodes will follow it.

3.2 Energy Consumed – Data Gathering without Aggregation

To avoid network partitioning and to balance the load in the network in terms of energy, a pre defined threshold level of residual energy is introduced. Say, a node having E_{init} initial energy has another mark of energy, *Level1* of energy (say 40% of residual energy), then alternate route is selected with node having more energy than *Level1*. This alternate route will give life extension to those nodes which were selected in the first attempt, thus the network life too, gets extended. Thus, healthy nodes will participate in routing and weak nodes will get rest, thus overall network lifetime can be extended.

To calculate life of a network, we are counting total number of rounds. This can also be counted, as follows:

$$R_{net} = \frac{E_{initial}}{E_{max}} \qquad (1)$$

where R_{net} is the network lifetime in terms of rounds and $E_{initial}$ is the initial energy of a relay node. We assume that the value of $E_{initial}$ is known beforehand and is the same for all relay nodes initially. E_{max} is the maximum energy dissipated by any relay node in the particular routing schedule.

The equation (1) can be useful when, we consider data gathering with aggregation. But for data gathering without aggregation, this approach of counting network life will not be useful. Aggregation can be performed when the data from different sensors are highly correlated but data aggregation is not applicable in all sensing environments. Imagine a scenario where the data being transmitted by the nodes are completely different (no redundancy) e.g. video images from distant regions of a battlefield. In such situations, it might not be feasible to fuse data packets from different sensors into a single data packet, in any meaningful way. This implies that the number and size of transmissions will increase, thereby draining the sensor energies much faster. The problem is finding an efficient schedule to collect and transmit the data to the BS, such that the system lifetime is maximized [15].

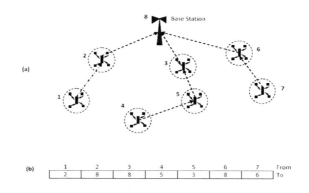

Fig. 2. (a) Two tired WSN with labeled relay nodes and base station (b) Routing schedule represented in form of an Array

To understand why we need special attention for those applications where data gathering is done without aggregation, let us understand from Fig. 2. For data aggregation case, node *3* will send data to BS only once hence energy will be consumed once. But in case of data gathering without aggregation, node *3* will send data to the BS, which has been sent by node *5*, node *4* and node *3* itself. This way, it will consume almost *3* times higher energy than the earlier case. While for node *4*, energy consumption will not differ in either of data gathering techniques.

4   Proposed A-Star Algorithm

A-Star algorithm creates tree structure in order to search optimal route from given source to the destination. A tree node will be explored based on its f(n) value, which A-Star algorithm uses for optimal path searching, where $f(n) = g(n) + h(n)$.

4.1   Threshold Energy Level, *Level1*

In our approach, in addition to $g(n)$ and $h(n)$, we have also taken another parameter to measure strength of a route. This parameter keeps track of the current energy level in the sensor node. As introduced earlier, a pre defined threshold energy level, *Level1* can be used as a threshold level for a sensor node. If sensor node's residual energy goes below this level, the algorithm should avoid this node while searching for a route, instead it should search for alternative path, where no node having residual energy below *Level1* is there. This new parameter, $l(n)$ is the path cost count of weak node having less energy. This will keep a counter of how many nodes in the current path are below *Level1* of energy level.

Thus, Estimated cost function f(n) carries two parameters shown in equation (2).

$$f(n) = (\ g(n) + h(n)\ ,\ l(n)\ ) \tag{2}$$

In this approach, routing decision is made based on value of $l(n)$. If value of $l(n)$ is same then only, value of $f(n)$ is checked for further comparison. For A-Star algorithm implementation, we have prepared and used following data structures with below mentioned members:

- A tree node: { A Sensor node element, M number of children pointers, A pointer to the parent node, value of $g(n)$, $h(n)$, $l(n)$ }
- A sensor node : { Identification of node, Residual energy, List of neighbours, Number of neighbours }

Pseudo Code for Proposed Efficient Routing Algorithm

```
Input    : Sensor Network
Output   :   Life of Sensor Network in terms of rounds
1.  BEGIN
2.  InitilizeNetwork()
3.  EstimateDistance() // finds distance to the BS
4.  WHILE NOT END_ASTAR() // N-of-N metric [11]
5.      InitializeSolArray() // initialize solution
                  //array to store routing schedule
6.      FOR each node i in the Network DO
7.        CreateTree (i)   //using A-Star algorithm
8.        PrepareSolArray() //prepare routing schedule
9.      END FOR
10.     BroadcastSolution()  // BS broadcasts routing
                          //schedule
11.     UpdateEnergy()   //Energy update for relay nodes
12.     CountRound = CountRound + 1  //count n/w life
13. END WHILE
14. PRINT CountRound  //print n/w lifetime in
15. END
```

In the pseudo code, meaning of each function is written in the same line as a comment. Estimation of distance from each node to the BS can be carried out from the methods mentioned in [16, 17]. This distance will be useful to calculate energy consumption between two nodes. This estimated distance is also useful to get our heuristic function, $h(n)$. BS will be able to update node's residual energy once routing schedule is prepared. CountRound variable will contain value of number of rounds which is a measure of network lifetime.

4.2   Calculation of Heuristic Values with Energy Level

Calculation of estimated cost function $f(n)$ in A-Star algorithm is as shown in equation (2). The parameter, path cost count of weak node $l(n)$, which is number of nodes below energy level, $Level1$ is calculated as follows.

For a node n whose parent node is p, is the intermediate node from source node to the destination node, $l(n)$ will keep count of total number of nodes which are on this route and are below pre-defined threshold level of energy $Level1$. Residual energy of the current node n will be checked, and if it is found less than $Level1$ energy, then $l(n)$

will be $l(p)$ + *Incremental_factor*, where $l(p)$ is the path cost count of parent node p and *Incremental_factor* is a value, which is added as per the strategy.

Assignment of value to the Incremental_factor in our approach is taken as proportionate value to the residual energy left in the sensor node. E.g. value of Incremental_factor will be more for residual energy left 0.1% of initial energy and will be less for residual energy left 30% of initial energy.

5   Experimental Results

For our experiments, we have used following first order radio model for communication energy dissipation [18].

$$E_{T_i}(b_{t_i}, d_{i,j}) = \alpha_2 b_{t_i} + \beta b_{t_i} d_{i,j}^m$$

Where $d_{i,j}$ is the Euclidian distance between node i and j, which varies from 25 to 40 meters. $\alpha 2$ is the transmit energy coefficient, β is the amplifier coefficient, b_{ti} is amount of data to transmit from node i to another node and m is the path loss exponent, $2 \leq m \leq 4$. E_{Ti} is total transmit energy dissipated.

Similarly, the receive energy, E_{Ri} is calculated as follows:

$$E_{R_i}(b_{r_i}) = \alpha_1 b_{r_i}$$

Where b_{ri} is the number of bits received by relay node i and $\alpha 1$ is the receive energy coefficient. Hence total energy dissipated by a node i for data to receive and then to transmit it further is E_i. Where $E_i = E_{Ti} + E_{Ri}$.

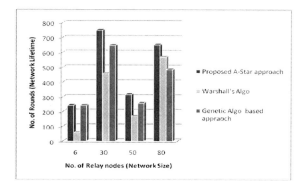

Fig. 3. Comparison of A-Star based, GA based approach and Warshall's algorithm

We consider both type of energy in computation of energy consumption. For simulation, the values for the constants are taken same as in [18] as (i) $\alpha 1 = \alpha 2 = 50$ nJ/bit, (ii) $\beta = 100$ pJ/bit/m^2 and (iii) the path loss exponent, m=4. The initial energy of each node, $E_{init} = 5$J.

Fig. 3 shows comparison of GA based approach with A-Star algorithm based approach and Warshall's algorithm. For data gathering without aggregation, GA based approach has been suggested in [4].

It can be seen from the Fig. 3 that, using A-Star algorithm, network lifetime is extended. In most of the cases it is extended around 15% than that of GA based approach and it is extended to more than 40% than that of Warshall's algorithm.

6 Conclusion

This paper focuses on A-Star algorithm based heuristic routing technique to extend lifetime of WSN. This approach is more useful for data gathering without aggregation. Data gathering without aggregation technique can be useful in applications where all nodes send data which are not redundant and are different all together such as, sending video images from distant regions of a battlefield, sending information while tracking objects etc. Apart from the traditional A-Star algorithm's parameters, we have introduced path cost count which depends on pre-defined level of minimum energy, *Level1*. This helps to protect a sensor node from draining out earlier and thus, enhance overall life of the WSN.

References

1. Akyildiz, I.F., Su, W., Sankarasubramaniam, Y., Cayirci, E.: Wireless sensor networks: a survey. Computer Networks 38(4) (2002)
2. Akkaya, K., Younis, M.: A survey on routing protocols for wireless sensor networks. IEEE Transactions on Mobile Computing 3(3), 325–349 (2005)
3. Bari, A., Wazed, S., Jaekel, A., Bandyopadhyay, S.: A genetic algorithm based approach for energy efficient routing in two-tiered sensor networks. Ad Hoc Networks 7(4), 665–676 (2009) ISSN:1570-8705
4. Rana, K.M., Zaveri, M.A.: Genetic Algorithm Based Routing Technique to Extend Lifetime of Wireless Sensor Network. International Journal of Advanced Research in Computer Science 1(2), 126–132 (2010)
5. An explanation on Network flows and Graphs,
   http://www.ieor.berkeley.edu/~ieor266/Lecture12.pdf
   (accessed : April 24, 2010)
6. A 'layman's' explanation on Floyd–Warshall algorithm,
   http://en.wikipedia.org/wiki/Floyd%E2%80%93Warshall_
   algorithm (accessed : April 24, 2010)
7. Hart, P.E., Nilsson, N.J., Raphael, B.: A formal basis for the heuristic determination of minimum cost paths. IEEE Transactions on Systems Science and Cybernetics SSC4(2), 100–107 (1968)
8. Williams, S.G.D.: Using the A-Star Path-Finding Algorithm for Solving General and Constrained Inverse Kinematics Problems (February 2008),
   http://www.oriontransfer.co.nz/research/InverseKinematicsA-
   star.pdf (accessed : October 29, 2010)
9. Blough, D.M., Santi, P.: Investigating upper bounds on network lifetime extension for cell-based energy conservation techniques in stationary ad hoc networks. In: Proceedings of the 8th ACM International Conference on Mobile Computing and Networking (ACM MobiCom 2002), pp. 183–192 (September 2002)

10. Madan, R., Cui, S., Lall, S., Goldsmith, A.: Cross-layer design for lifetime maximization in interference-limited wireless sensor networks. In: Proceedings of 24th IEEE Conference on Computer Communications (IEEE INFOCOM 2005), vol. 3, pp. 1964–1975 (2005)

11. Pan, J., Hou, Y.T., Cai, L., Shi, Y., Shen, S.X.: Topology control for wireless sensor networks. In: Proceedings of the Ninth Annual International Conference on Mobile Computing and Networking, pp. 286–299 (2003)

12. Bari, A., Jaekel, A., Bandyopadhyay, S.: Clustering strategies for improving the lifetime of two-tiered sensor networks. Computer Communications 31(14), 3451–3459 (2008)

13. Bari, A., Jaekel, A., Bandyopadhyay, S.: Maximizing the lifetime of two tiered sensor networks. In: The Proceeding of IEEE International Electro/Information Technology Conference (EIT 2006), MI, pp. 222–226 (May 2006)

14. Hou, Y.T., Shi, Y., Pan, J., Midkiff, S.F.: Lifetime-optimal data routing in wireless sensor networks without flow splitting. In: Workshop on Broadband Advanced Sensor Networks, San Jose, CA (2004)

15. Kalpakis, K., Dasgupta, K., Namjoshi, P.: Maximum lifetime data gathering and aggregation in wireless sensor networks. In: Proceedings of the IEEE International Conference on Networking (2002)

16. López Villafuerte, F., Schiller, J.: DIN: An Ad-Hoc Algorithm to Estimate Distances in Wireless Sensor Networks. In: Coudert, D., Simplot-Ryl, D., Stojmenovic, I. (eds.) ADHOC-NOW 2008. LNCS, vol. 5198, pp. 162–175. Springer, Heidelberg (2008)

17. Blumenthal, J., Reichenbach, F., Timmermann, D.: Position Estimation in Ad hoc Wireless Sensor Networks with Low Complexity. In: Proceedings of the 2nd Workshop on Positioning, Navigation and Communication (WPNC 2005) & 1st Ultra-Wideband Expert Talk 2005 (UET 2005), pp. 41–49 (2005)

18. Heinzelman, W., Chandrakasan, A., Balakrishnan, H.: Energy efficient communication protocol for wireless micro-sensor networks. In: Proceedings of the 33rd HICSS, Maui, Hawaii, pp. 3005–3014 (2000)

19. Tang, J., Hao, B., Sen, A.: Relay node placement in large scale wireless sensor networks. Computer Communications 29(4), 490–501 (2006)

Congestion Control Protocol for Traffic Control in Multimedia Applications Using WSN

Sushama Suryawanshi and S.R. Hiray

Computer Department, Sinhgad college of Engg., Pune University,
Pune, India
sushinpune@rediff.com, swapnajah@yahoo.com

Abstract. TCP/IP is reliable, connection oriented protocol for data transmission. It performs very well in wired network but in case of wireless sensor network it is not performing with good throughput. Congestion control is a major problem of TCP/IP performance. A sensor is congested if it receives more traffic than its maximum forwarding rate. The nature of sensor deployment leads to unpredictable patterns of connectivity and varied node density. This causes uneven bandwidth provisioning on the forwarding paths. The data sources are often clustered at sensitive areas under scrutiny. They may take similar paths to the base stations. When data converge toward a base station, congestion may occur at sensors that receive more data than they can forward. Similarly for multimedia applications UDP is unreliable. So Datagram Congestion Control Protocol is suggested for timely, reliable delivery in multimedia applications. It is a general purpose transport protocol for establishment, maintenance and teardown of an unreliable packet flow, and Congestion control of packet. For multimedia applications timely performance of TCP/IP is very important. So Extended Datagram Congestion Control Protocol is suggested for multiple flows. This protocol will reduce congestion in Wireless Sensor Network.

Keywords: WSN, Congestion control, Datagram, Packets, multimedia traffic, ELFN, Payload, CCID2, CCID3, TFRC.

1 Introduction

WSN typically consists of a large number of tiny wireless sensor nodes (often referred to as nodes or motes) that are densely deployed [1]. Nodes measure some ambient conditions in the environment surrounding them. These measurements are, then, transformed into signals that can be processed to reveal some characteristics about the phenomenon. The data collected is routed to special nodes, called sink nodes (or Base Station, BS), typically in a multi-hop basis. Then, the sink node sends data to the user. Sensor networks have a wide range of applications in habitat observation, health monitoring, object tracking, battlefield sensing, etc. They are different from traditional wireless networks in many aspects.

D.C. Wyld et al. (Eds.): NeCoM/WeST/WiMoN 2011, CCIS 197, pp. 242–251, 2011.
© Springer-Verlag Berlin Heidelberg 2011

Particularly, sensor nodes are limited in computation capability, memory space, communication bandwidth, and above all, energy supply. Nowadays, nodes are intended to be small and cheap.

Consequently, their resources are limited (typically, limited battery, reduced memory and processing capabilities). Because of the restrained transmission power, wireless sensor nodes can only communicate locally, with a certain number of local neighbors. So, nodes have to collaborate in order to accomplish their tasks: sensing, signal processing, computing, routing, localization, security, etc. Transmission Control Protocol (TCP) is a reliable, end-to-end transport protocol, which is widely used for data services and is very efficient for wired networks. However, experiments and research showed that TCP's congestion control algorithm performs very poorly over Wireless sensor networks with degraded throughputs [5]. Research therefore has focused on further improving TCP to address the special characteristics of Wireless sensor networks.

Two or more TCP/IP endpoints (user/server) communicate over WSN through gateways and intermediate nodes. The base WSN infrastructure, sensing operations, and data relaying are maintained simultaneously with TCP/IP communication. The path for TCP/IP communication is referred to as tcp route but WSN data are sent also along that route. In case of direct and proxy tcp, every WSN node may be a part or a communication endpoint of the tcp route, while in native tcp nodes only relay TCP/IP data between the gateways.

There are several conceptual differences between WSNs and TCP/IP networks in communication paradigm, flow control, and predictability. In contrast to data-centric WSNs, TCP communication is connection-oriented between specific endpoints.

The end-to-end connection maintenance and flow control generates considerable amount of control traffic between connection endpoints. In WSNs, the communication over wireless links is the dominant cause for energy consumption. Therefore, the flow control is performed over a single hop in order to avoid costly end-to-end retransmissions.

TCP flow control assumes that all communication errors are caused by congestion while the main reasons for errors in WSNs are random bit errors, topology changes, and temporarily unavailable nodes. Further, TCP assumes symmetric uplink and downlink in a connection, but in WSNs their delay and throughput may differ considerably .While direct tcp faces the general TCP/IP drawbacks in wireless environments, proxy tcp allows energy efficient WSN operation but leads to buffering and flow control adaptation challenges in gateway TCP/IP proxy. The generality of native tcp is limited but it is an energy efficient approach for random TCP/IP communication with moderate load.

1.1   TCP/IP Adaptation to WSNs

In direct tcp, WSN uses legacy TCP/IP for communication. Instead proxy tcp and native tcp require the adaptation of TCP flow control, IP addressing, and packet fragmentation. In proxy tcp, the TCP/IP proxy in gateway converts these to corresponding WSN counterparts. The TCP/IP adaptation layer in gateway handles the addressing and fragmentation in native tcp but relays the flow control over WSN. The transmission rate in TCP depends on the sizes of the peer receive window and sender congestion window (CWND). The congestion window is resized based on the networking conditions. The utilized window control algorithms depend on the TCP version. In general, the algorithms use received acknowledgements and timeouts for controlling their decisions.

The window-based congestion control algorithms of TCP may lead to the aggressive reduction of the transmission rate due to a single bit error or topology change. This is accounted in proxy tcp, which instead of legacy TCP algorithms uses WSN specific flow control algorithms.

2   Comparison of Existing Methods

Congestion causes many problems. When a packet is dropped, the energy spent by upstream sensors on the packet is wasted. The further the packet has traveled, the greater the waste. When a sensor X is severely congested, if the upstream neighbors attempt to send to X, their efforts (and energy) are deemed to be wasted and, worse yet, counter-productive because they compete for channel access with neighboring sensors. Finally, and above all, the data loss due to congestion may jeopardize the mission of the application. While fusion techniques can be used for data aggregation, applications may require some specifics (e.g., exact locations of the reporting sensors) to be kept, which place a limit on how much the fusion can do.

2.1   Explicit Link Failure Notification (ELFN)

Since all nodes acting as routers have the full TCP/IP protocols stack, they have access to the routing protocols of the IP layer. The routing protocol can detect the link failure when the next node in the connection goes out of range, and the packet cannot be delivered [5]. It sends the route error notification (RRER), which is flooded to all of the nodes including the source node.

This error notification however does not reach the transport protocol, and it is only used by routing protocol to update the routing table. The TCP/IP protocols stack can be altered to use the RRER packet as the link failure notification. After the modifications, when the RRER packet is received, TCP can distinguish this link failure from the congestion. It can enter the "standby" mode by freezing the regular transmission of the packets until the connection is reestablished and then resume the transmission.

The routing protocol can be modified to carry additional information in RRER packets, similar to the "host unreachable" ICMP message such as: sender address and port. This can identify at the sender of which connection this message is for. When sender receives the RRER packet and it detects that it is the source of the original message, it can notify the TCP layer about this link failure. TCP will probe the connection in a chosen probe intervals. When the acknowledgement packet is received TCP can leave the "standby" mode and restore the communication at the state as it was before the link failure. Explicit Link Failure Notification (ELFN) implemented using the Dynamic Source Routing (DSR) protocol. They compared the expected performance of TCP protocol with the actual results received from the node testing. Significant performance problems were caused by "the caching and propagation of stale routes" that can cause "the inability of the TCP sender's routing protocol to quickly recognize and purge stale routes from its cache resulted in repeated routing failures". It was suggested to turn off the replying from cache functionality however; in network with multiple data sources it still caused degradation of performance. The implementation of the ELFN however clearly improved the throughput. They tested the ELFN implementation for different node movement speeds and in general it showed performance improvement.

2.2 TCP-Feedback

TCP-F (TCP-Feedback) relies on the network layer at intermediate hosts to detect the route failures due to the mobility of downstream neighbors along the route. A sender can be in an active state or a snooze state. In the active state, transport is controlled by the normal TCP. A soon as an intermediate host detects a link failure, it explicitly sends a route failure notification (RFN) packet to the sender and records this event. After receiving the RFN, the sender goes into the snooze state by stopping sending further packets and freezing the values of state variables such as retransmission timer and congestion window size[4] The sender remains in the snooze state until it is notified of the restoration of the route through a route reestablishment notification (RRN) packet from an intermediate host. Then it enters the active state again. It is a similar feedback scheme in which the TCP sender utilizes the network layer feedback (Route Failure Notification or RFN) from intermediate nodes to distinguish route failure and network congestion.

On receiving a Route Reestablishment Notification (RRN), via the routing protocol, TCP knows the route is reestablished and leaves the frozen state and resumes transmission using the same variable states before the "snooze state". In addition, a route failure timer is used to prevent infinite wait for RRN messages. When a route failure timer expires, the TCP normal congestion control is invoked. TCP-Feedback performs significantly better than standard TCP when route re establishment delay grows. This is mainly due to the reduction of the number of unnecessary packet retransmission and timer back offs during the route failure interval. However, similar to the first approach, upon route re-establishment the TCP state reflects the conditions on the old route and not necessarily on the new route.

2.3 Fixed Retransmission Timeout Scheme (Fixed RTO)

The fixed RTO technique does not rely on the feedback from lower layers. In fact, a heuristic was employed to distinguish route failures and congestion. When timeouts occur consecutively, the sender assumes a route failure happened rather than network congestion. The unacknowledged packet is retransmitted again but the RTO is not doubled a second time. The RTO remains fixed until the route is reestablished and the retransmitted packet is acknowledged [10].This technique complements our out-of-order detection and response technique.

TCP Losses: Every route failure induces upto a TCP-window worth of packet loss.While the losses have a direct and absolute impact on the performance degradation, the TCP source will also react to the losses by performing congestion control.MAC Failure Detection Time: Since the MAC layer (802.11) has to go through the cycle of multiple retransmissions before concluding link failure, there is a distinct component associated with the time taken to actually detect link failure from when the failure occurs. Importantly, the detection time increases with increasing load in the network. A high MAC detection time will result in a higher likelihood of the TCP source pumping in more packets (upto a window's worth) into the broken path, and an eventual timeout.

2.4 Selective ACK

The Selective ACK scheme is particularly addressed toward lossy environments where the receiver buffer can have several holes, enabling the sender to retransmit only the holes and thus save on precious bandwidth. However, the current specification for TCP-SACK supports the advertisement of only three blocks of non-contiguous data. While the limit of three is suitable for the wire line Internet environment, it would be a severe limitation in an ad-hoc network environment. Since typical adhoc networks are expected to consist of a few hundred nodes at a maximum and considerable inter-layer interactions exist even in the current set-up of an ad-hoc network protocol stack, feedback from the intermediate routers in the network can significant help the transport layer's congestion control scheme. For instance, while it can be extremely difficult to distinguish between random wireless losses, congestion based losses, and mobility related losses based on purely end to end mechanisms, appropriate feedback from the routers can help in distinguishing between the loss types and reacting accordingly.

Prediction Accuracy: While in the first case, the performance will be as bad as a scheme without any prediction capabilities, the second case would lead to an additional overhead caused by the alternate route computation process.

There are two possible scenarios in which the proposed scheme can mispredict a route failure: (i) When two nodes A and B are relatively stationary, but the distance between them is marginally smaller than the transmission range (ii) When the received signal strength varies due to causes other than distance, say for example channel fading. However, recall that the proposed approach maintains a history of the received signal strengths and makes its link-failure prediction based on both the configured look-ahead time and the slope of the curve representing the progression of received signal strengths on that particular link. This simple mechanism of maintaining the history will prevent mispredictions from occurring due to both the above causes.

TCP with above discussed protocols shows quite promising results. However, none of these improvements will benefit UDP streams that are often used in streaming media content. Throughput is one of the QoS parameters of Transport layer. Throughput is number of user data transferred per second, measured over time interval. Throughput is measured separately over each direction. The study shows significant throughput increase with the use of ELFN. But it uses DSR as routing protocol choice and a single TCP flow. When multiple flows exist, this approach cannot achieve throughput improvements, and it even degrades the performance as the mobility rate increases. The connection establishment delay is another parameter for **QoS. It is the amount of time elapsing** between a transport connection being requested and the confirmation being received by the user of the transport service.

It includes the processing delay in the remote transport entity. If delay is shorter service will be better.

TCP-Feedback performs significantly better than TCP when route reestablishment delay grows. This is mainly due to the reduction of the number of unnecessary packet retransmission and timer backoffs during the route failure interval. However, similar to the first approach, upon route re-establishment the TCP state reflects the conditions on the old route and not necessarily on the new route. Significant improvement of throughput was achieved by the use of Fixed RTO. Study of TCP selective and delayed acknowledgments options, shows that they could only achieve marginal gains.

3 Proposed Protocol

One of the limitations of TCP is that there is no congestion control for the acknowledgements sent by the receiver to the sender. Ack congestion control can be useful any time there is congestion on the reverse path, but is particularly important for bandwidth asymmetric networks or packet radio subnetworks. It is useful for deployment as a standard feature in end hosts (PCs, VoIP codecs, and other internetenabled multimedia appliances).DCCP supports various QoS. DCCP gives minimal overhead. It gives general-purpose transport layer protocol providing only two core functions: The establishment, maintenance and teardown of an unreliable packet flow, and Congestion control of that packet flow. Again to add some more functions to transport layer Extended DCCP is suggested. In extended Protocol following functions are added to DCCP: Buffering of received packets at the receivers, retransmission of lost or corrupted packets by the senders, detection and deletion of duplicated packets at the receivers, and in-order delivery of received packets to the application program at the receivers.

These additional facilities will improve performance of DCCP for congestion control. DCCP, the Datagram Congestion Control Protocol [7], is a new transport protocol in the TCP/UDP family that provides a congestion-controlled flow of unreliable datagrams. Delay-sensitive applications, such as streaming media and telephony, prefer timeliness to reliability. These applications have historically used UDP and implemented their own congestion control mechanisms a difficult task or no congestion control at all. DCCP will make it easy to deploy these applications without risking congestion collapse. It aims to add to a UDP-like foundation the minimum mechanisms necessary to support congestion control, such as possibly-reliable transmission of acknowledgement information. This minimal design should make DCCP suitable as a building block for more advanced application semantics, such as selective reliability.

Application requirements

Any protocol designed to serve a specific group of applications should consider what those applications are likely to need (although this needs to be balanced carefully against a desire to be future-proof and general).

For the group of applications the most concerned requirements include:

☐ Choice of congestion control mechanism

While our applications are usually able to adjust their transmission rate based on congestion feedback, they do have constraints on how this adaptation can be performed to minimize the effect on quality. Thus, they tend to need some control over the short-term dynamics of the congestion control algorithm, while being fair to other traffic on medium timescales. This control includes influence over which congestion control algorithm is used for example, TFRC rather than strict TCP-like congestion control.

☐ Low per-packet overhead

Internet telephony and games in particular will tend to send small packets frequently, to achieve low delay and quick response time. Protocol overhead should not expand thepackets unduly.

☐ ECN support

Explicit Congestion Notification lets congested routers mark packets instead of dropping, them. ECN capability must be turned on only owns that react to congestion, but it is particularly desirable for applications with tight timing constraints, as there is often insufficient time to retransmit a dropped packet before its data is needed at the receiver.

☐ Middlebox traversal.

UDP's lack of explicit connection setup and teardown presents unpleasant difficulties to network address translators and rewalls, with the result that some middle boxes don't let UDP through at all. Any new protocol should improve on UDP's friendliness to middle boxes.

To support the applications we currently envisage, there are many other features that might be desirable, such as packet-level FEC, selective reliability or limited retransmission, and support for multiple data streams in a flow. However all of these features can be supported just as efficiently over the top of a more simple protocol.

CCID 2: TCP-like Congestion Control

TCP's stringent flow-control mechanism is not needed with DCCP. If packet n has been received but not yet read by the application, and packet $n + m$ then arrives, DCCP can choose to drop packet n from its receive buffer and use the buffer space to store the more recent packet. DCCP's TCP-like congestion control still uses the sender's congestion window to limit the number of unacknowledged packets outstanding in the network, but it cannot use a cumulative acknowledgement to control this. Thus some other mechanism is needed to ensure that if packets are lost, the sender halves its sending rate appropriately. One of the limitations of TCP is that there is no congestion control for the acknowledgements sent by the receiver to the sender. Ack congestion control can be useful any time there is congestion on the reverse path, but is particularly important for bandwidth asymmetric networks or packet radio subnetworks . DCCP, unlike TCP, can detect reverse-path congestion using per-packet sequence numbers, and respond to it as appropriate.

Media/Session Control	Media Codecs
SIP │ H.323 │ RTSP	RTP+RTCP
Transport Layer Interface	
CCID 2 │ CCID 3 │ CCID 4 │ …	
DCCP	
IPv4	IPv6

Fig. 1. The architecture of DCCP(8)

In CCID 2, the DCCP sender responds by modifying the ack Ratio, which controls the rate of the acknowledgement stream from the receiver

CCID 3: TFRC Congestion Control

A CCID 3 sender uses a sending rate, and the receiver sends feedback to the sender roughly once per round-trip time reporting the loss event rate calculated by the receiver. The sender uses the reported loss event rate to determine its sending rate. If the sender receives no feedback from the receiver for several round-trip times, then the sender halves its sending rate. a sending application might want to know exactly which packets were received by the receiver for its own reasons. In these cases, a CCID 3 halfconnection can additionally include ack Vectors and acks-of-acks, as in CCID 2.

This DCCP is added with new features with RTT. This protocol is called as Extended DCCP. In extended protocol, the sender has four states Normal State Congestion State, failure State (route change or link failure) , Error State (transmission error). Rate based congestion control is used to avoid the frequent slow starts. The most important task is to design the rate equation for each state, which is the key for throughput. To determine the available end- to-end bandwidth, we adopted the delay based rate estimation mechanism in FAST TCP. The sender maintains two RTT values, one is base RTT (baseRTT), which is the minimum recorded RTT, and the other is exponentially averaged RTT (avgRTT). Each time the sender goes into the failure state, the baseRTT will be reset by the round trip time of a probe packet and its corresponding acknowledgment, after being temporarily saved as old baseRTT. The sending rate after the route establishment is proportional to baseRTT/Old baseRTT.

In the Normal State, the sender adjusts the rate proportional to baseRTT/avgRTT. In the Congestion State, when ECN mark without packet loss happened, the rate adjustment is the same as in Normal State. But when packet loss happened, the sending rate will halve. This idea is based on FAST TCP for High-Speed Long-Distance Networks, which showed proportional fairness under no congestion or mild congested situations when packet loss occurs infrequently. In the Error State, the rate is set to β*rate, calculated using the above scheme, where β ranges from 0.5 to 1, according to the error rate. In the Failure State, probe packets are scheme, where β ranges from 0.5 to 1, according to the error rate. In the Failure State, probe packets are send out to monitor the network situation. The rate of sending probe packets can be set to one packet per RTO like in Fixed RTO, but it should be studied further by experiments. In the implementation, ACKs are sent back to the sender whenever the receiver receives a packet.

ACKs have the ACK Vector option as specified in the DCCP specification. ACK vectors contain packet reception information (whether they are received, not received or ECN marked). Also, the ACK Vector can be used to return information about several packets to make sure the sender receives information though some ACKs may be lost.

4 Conclusion

Congestion control is the major issue of TCP/IP reliable transmission. Specially when we are talking about quality of service in multimedia network as there is heavy traffic due to large amount of data transmission congestion is more. Also many multimedia applications are real time applications. Timely packet delivery is most important, which can be affected by congestion. So the suggested protocol avoids congestion as well as guarantees timely delivery of data for multimedia applications. DCCP, unlike TCP, can detect reverse-path congestion using per-packet sequence numbers, and respond to it as appropriate. The DCCP sender responds by modifying the ack Ratio, which controls the rate of the acknowledgement stream from the receiver. The algorithm used to set the ack Ratio gives an ack sending rate that is very roughly TCP-friendly.

DCCP is simple minimal congestion control protocol upon which other higher-level protocols could be built. DCCP will make it easy to deploy multimedia applications without risking congestion collapse.

5 Future Work

To study and improve throughput when mixed Extended DCCP and TCP flows co-exist. The core congestion control protocol can be further optimized by tuning the rate control formula and retransmission timer to optimize the packet sending rate and adding new features to the implementation in the simulation such as support of ECN, to provide additional information for the sender to identify network condition and to adjust the sending rate accordingly. Finally, we will implement the proposed congestion control protocol in wireless sensor network test bed to verify the simulation results.

References

[1] Jin, C., Wei, D., Low, S.H.: FAST TCP: Motivation, Architecture, Algorithms, Performance. In: Proc. of the 23rd Conf. of the IEEE Communication Society, Hong Kong, China, pp. 8–94 (March 2004)

[2] Xu, K., et al.: TCP Behavior across Multihop Wireless Networks and the Wired Internet. In: Proc. of the 5th Int. Workshop on Wireless Mobile Multimedia, Seattle, USA, pp. 207–218 (September 2002)

[3] Akyildiz, I., Su, W., Sankarasubramaniam, Y., Cayirci, E.: A Survey on Sensor Networks. IEEE Communication Magazine, 102–109 (August 2002)

[4] Wang, F., Zhang, Y.: Improving TCP Performance over Mobile Ad-Hoc Networks withOut-of-Order Detection and Response. In: Proc. of 3rd ACM Int. Symposium on Mobile Ad Hoc Networking & Computing, Lausanne, Switzerland, pp. 217–225 (June 2002)

[5] Holland, G., Vaidya, N.: Analysis of TCP Performance over Mobile Ad Hoc Networks. In: Proc. 5th ACM/IEEE Int. Conf. on Mobile Comp. and Networking, Seattle, USA, pp. 219–230 (1999)

[6] Gracanin, D., Adams, K., Eltoweissy, M.: Data Replication in Collaborative Sensor NetworkSystems. In: Proc. 25th IEEE International Performance, Computing, and Communications Conference (IPCCC 2006), April 10-12, pp. 389–396 (2006)

[7] Kohler, E., Handley, M., Floyd, S.: Datagram Congestion Control Protocol (DCCP). RFC 4340, IETF (March 2006)

[8] Min, L.Y., Jiang, X.: A extended DCCP Congestion Control in WSN. Intelligent System and Applications, 1–4 (2009)

[9] Md, O.R., Muhammad, M.M., Choong, S.H.: A QoS Adaptive Congestion Control in Wireless Sensor Network. In: The 10th International Conference on Advanced Communication Technology (ICACT 2008), Phoenix Park, Korea, pp. 941–946 (February 2008)

[10] Anantharaman, V., Sivakumar, R.: TCP Performance over Mobile Ad Hoc Networks—a Quantitative Study. Wireless Communication and Wireless Networks, 203–222 (2003)

[11] Charfi, W., Masmoudi, M., Derbel, F.: A Layered Model For Wireless Sensor Networks. In: 6th International Multi-Conference on Systems (2009)

Influence of Urban Coastal Region on WiMAX Propagation at 2.3 GHz

Chhaya Dalela[1], M.V.S.N. Prasad[2], P.K. Dalela[3], and Rajeev Saraf[4]

[1] JSS ACADEMY Of Technical Education, C-20/1, Sector-62, Noida-201301, India
chhaya1974@rediffmail.com
[2] National Physical Laboratory, DR K S Krishnan Road, New Delhi-110012, India
mvprasad@mail.nplindia.ernet.in
[3] C-DOT, Mandigaon Road, Opp. New Manglapuri, Chattarpur, Mehraulli,
New Delhi-110030, India
pdalela@gmail.com
[4] Lepton Software Export & Research Pvt. Ltd., New Delhi-110028, India
rajeev.saraf@leptonsoftware.com

Abstract. This paper presents the results of measurements taken at 2.3 GHz using WiMAX transmissions in urban, coastal region environments of western India. Coverage predictions using various models and their comparison with observed data have been carried out. Measured path loss is compared with the theoretical path loss values estimated by COST-231 Hata model, the SUI model, the ECC model, ITU-R(NLOS) model. This investigation is essential to provide last mile Broadband wireless access, before deploying WiMAX. Path loss exponents, mean errors and standard deviations of all the prediction methods have been deduced and suitable models have been identified. The cdf values of prediction errors have also been compared. Different statistical parameters are deduced and the best fit distribution for the cdf curves is found.

Keywords: Path loss, path loss exponent, propagation model, WiMAX.

1 Introduction

In India, incumbent WiMAX operator utilizes the bands of 2.3-3.5 GHz to provide broadband services. Fixed WiMAX services are beneficial to the development of broadband used by consumers and small businesses while mobile WiMAX may be used for mobile services being provisioned by existing fixed line carriers that do not own a 3G spectrum to provide Voice-over-IP (VoIP) or mobile entertainment services [1]. Signal Propagation models are used extensively in network planning, particularly for conducting feasibility studies and performing initial system deployment. Also to increase the robustness of the transmitted information, it is needed to estimate the path loss introduced by a terrain over which the signal will propagate to sufficiently compensate for the power lost during signal propagation. The first major study reporting the comparison of different models with measurements taken at Cambridge, was reported by Abhayawardhana *etal.* [2] at 3.5 GHz. Similar studies were also conducted by Rial *etal.* [3] and Belloul *etal.* [4]. Various countries have conducted radio channel measurements in the 2.3/3.5 GHz band in rural and urban areas [5], [6],

D.C. Wyld et al. (Eds.): NeCoM/WeST/WiMoN 2011, CCIS 197, pp. 252–261, 2011.
© Springer-Verlag Berlin Heidelberg 2011

[7], [8]. A preliminary study involving seven base stations has been reported in [9]. Also comparison of prediction methods with VHF/UHF measurements is performed [10]. Terrestrial communication experiments were performed over various regions of India subcontinent [11]. Path loss measurements in sea port for WiMAX is done for deploying wireless broadband communication in sea ports [12]. Experiments were conducted in an urban zone with one side coastal region of Mumbai in western India. The signal levels have been converted into path loss values using antenna gain, feeder loss etc., and these have been compared with models like COST-231Hata [13], ECC [14], SUI [15] and ITU-R (NLOS) [16]. All these models estimate the mean path loss based on parameters such as antenna heights of the transmitter and receiver, distance between them, etc. Path loss exponents [17] from the observed data have been deduced. The suitable models have been identified after comparing their prediction errors and standard deviations.

In Section 2, data collection and field set up have been provided. In Section 3, we analyzed the measured path loss data and compared with the existing path loss models. The conclusion is presented in Section 4.

2 Data Collection and Field Set Up

2.1 Experimental Set Up

The names of five base stations and the height of transmitting antenna are shown in Table 1. The base stations are Electric Mansion (ETM), Ganga Sagar (CHS-GSC), Geetanzali (GTL), Mistry Chamber (MCB), and Mayfair (MYFY). All sites transmit 43 dBm powers with transmitting antenna gain 8dBi. The transmitter antenna used in the present study was Omni directional antenna, TW2.3/OMNI/8dBi (www.twinantennas.com). The transmitter used for experiment is Tortoise dual band transmitter from Berkeley Varitronics Systems (www.bvsystems.com). The receiver used for present experiment was Coyote dual band receiver. The averaging of 512 samples per second in temporal and spatial zone is done. Omni directional receiver antenna with 2 dBi gain was used for present study. All measurements were taken within a 100m to 3.0 km distance range from the BTS. The calculated average received power was used to estimate the path loss corresponding to each measurement.

Table 1. Experimental Details of Base Stations

S. No.	Site Name	Height of transmitting antenna	Other details	
1.	Electric Mansion (ETM)	35	Height of receiving antenna	1.5m
2.	Gangasagar (CHSGSC)	31	Average Height of building	25m
3.	Geetanzali (GTL)	34	Average street width	15m
4.	Mistry Chambers (MCB)	31	Average separation between buildings	30m
5.	Mayfair (MYFY)	31	Street orientation angle	90 degrees

2.2 Measurement Locations and Routes

All five sites, ETM, CHS-GSC, GTL, MCB and MYFY are situated in urban coastal region of Mumbai, India shown in Fig. 1. The clutter environment of these sites is shown in different colors as indicated in legend part of Fig. 1. CHS-GSC lies in urban region and surrounded by high density vegetation on west side while on east and southern side, it has coastal region which starts at 0.2 Km. GTL and ETM shows presence of urban region and coastal area. MYFY is surrounded by urban environment on north-east side and rest of it is surrounded by water. Eastern side of MCB is coastal zone while urban area is present on western side. MCB and MYFY lies at sea port.

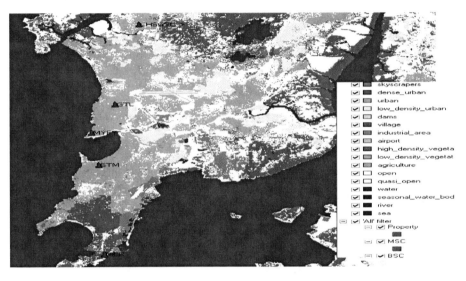

Fig. 1. Clutter Environment for Experimental Sites (ETM, CHS-GSC, GTL, MCB, MYFY)

3   Analysis of Measured Data

3.1 Path Loss Analysis

Figures 2-6 show the comparison of observed path loss values with those predicted by COST-231Hata, ECC, SUI (terrain B), and ITU-R (NLOS) methods. The figures 2-6 also show the least square regression line plotted on the observed data. In these figures close to transmitter observed path losses varied from 100-120 dB and at distances beyond 500 m, path loss was confined in the range of 110-160 dB. In the case of all the base stations ECC and COST231Hata methods gave good agreement and followed the regression line very closely. In fact COST231Hata method gave better agreement than ECC. SUI and ITU-R (NLOS) methods over estimated the loss. In Table II the corresponding error statistics in terms of mean prediction error, μ, and the standard deviation of the prediction errors, σ, are given for each model plotted for different base stations. Least square (LS) Regression Analysis was taken as basis for comparison of the models and path loss at distance d is given by

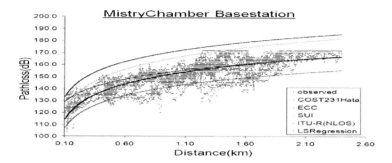

Fig. 2. Comparison of observed path losses with those predicted from different models for MCB

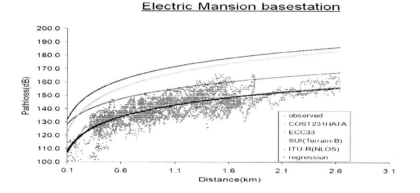

Fig. 3. Comparison of observed path losses with those predicted from different models for ETM

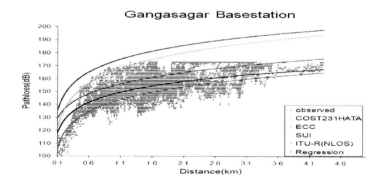

Fig. 4. Comparison of observed path losses with those predicted from different models for CHS-GSC

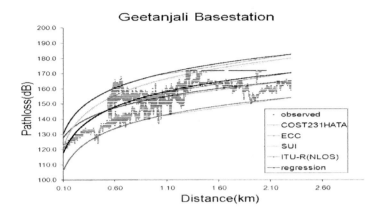

Fig. 5. Comparison of observed path losses with those predicted from different models for GTL

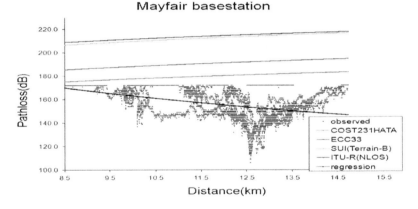

Fig. 6. Comparison of observed path losses with those predicted from different models for MYFY

$$PL(d) = PL(d_O) + 10n \log_{10}(\frac{d}{d_O}) \quad d > d_O \qquad (1)$$

where n denotes the path loss exponent, d is the distance between the transmitter and receiver station, do is the reference distance point at 100m, PL(do) is the path loss at range do . Path loss exponents from the observed data have been deduced based on the above equation (1). An examination of the Table 2 shows that path loss exponents deduced from COST231 Hata, ECC methods agree very well with that of observed values (LS). Exponents from SUI method are around 4 for all base stations and around 3.8 for ITU-R (NLOS). For Mayfair base station, path loss exponent is not evaluated since experiments were conducted from 8.5 km to 15 km. Standard deviations of LS varied from 6.7 to 12.5 which matched well with COST231 Hata method while for dense urban [9], standard deviation of LS varied from 5.9 to 8.6

which is followed by COST231Hata and ECC. Abhayawardana *etal.* [2] observed that SUI model showed large mean path loss prediction errors and COST231 Hata model showed the closest agreement with the measurement results. In present work, compared to the experimental data, while the ECC model overestimates the path loss (Fig. 3, 4), the COST231Hata model showed the best   performance (Fig. 3). For distances up to 600m close to base station, COST231Hata shows better result (Fig. 3,4) while ECC shows better agreement with measured data for distances beyond 1.5 km (Fig. 2). Mardeni [18] based on 2.3GHz measurements in the suburban and open urban urban environments in the Malaysia optimized COST231Hata model. They observed that out of SUI, COST231Hata, Egli, COST231Hata showed closest agreement with observations in terms of path loss exponent prediction and standard deviation error analysis.

Table 2. Error Predictions Compared With LS regression Analysis For Urban Coastal Environment

Sites	LS		COST231HATA			ECC			SUI			ITU-R(NLOS)		
	n	σ	n	μ	σ	n	μ	σ	n	μ	σ	n	μ	σ
ETM	3.4	6.7	3.5	-0.2	6.7	3.2	-12.9	6.8	4.3	-23.3	7.1	3.8	-28.4	6.8
CHS-GSC	3.0	5.9	3.5	4.9	5.9	3.3	-6.7	5.9	4.4	-20.1	6.2	3.8	-26.6	6.0
GTL	3.8	6.7	3.5	14.9	6.8	3.2	1.9	7.9	4.2	-8.1	6.8	3.8	-12.3	6.7
MCB	3.8	7.3	3.5	10.7	7.3	3.3	-2.2	7.6	4.3	-13.2	7.3	3.8	-18.6	7.1
MYFY	-9.7	12.5	3.5	24.4	14.6	3.9	-35.4	14.	4.4	-57.1	14.8	3.8	-58.6	14.6

3.2 Some More Statistical Analysis

In figures 7 and 8 the comparison of standard deviation for   COST231Hata and ECC model for all five base stations is represented by histogram and the cdf (cumulative distribution function, i.e., Prob [signal level < abscissa] of the prediction error of path loss of different models for MCB site is shown in Figure 9. Due to paucity of space, figures for other base stations were not included.   For MCB base station, the prediction error values of COST231 Hata and ECC model (median value of 12.0dB and 8.0dB) are closer to LS regression (median value of 8.0) than SUI and ITU-R NLOS (median value of 16.0 and 20.0dB). Comparative analysis is shown for all five base stations in Table 3. For CHS-GSC base station, the prediction error values of COST231 Hata and ECC model (median value of 8.0dB each) are closer to LS regression (median value of 8.0) than SUI and ITU-R NLOS (median value of 24.0 and 28.0dB). For CHS-GSC, the cdf curve for LS regression (n=3 p=0.32557), COST231Hata (n=7 p=0.47752) and ECC (n=5 p=0.44375) follow negative Binomial distribution while SUI (λ=23.064) and ITU-R (NLOS) (λ=28.645) follow Poisson distribution. However for GTL, MCB, MYFY & ETM all the path loss models, COST231Hata, ECC, SUI, ITU-R (NLOS) along with LS regression lie on negative binomial distribution. In the previous study reported in [9], it has been found that cdf curve for LS regression and COST231Hata follow Poisson distribution while cdf curves of ECC, SUI and ITU-R (NLOS) lie on negative binomial distribution.

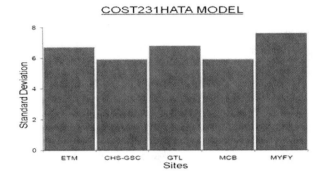

Fig. 7. Standard Deviation Of Prediction Error Of Path Loss Of COST231Hata Model

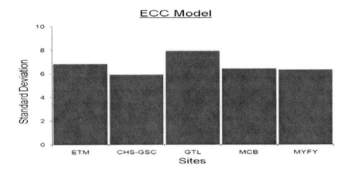

Fig. 8. Standard Deviation Of Prediction Error Of Path Loss Of ECC Model

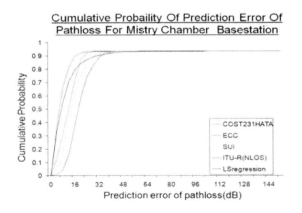

Fig. 9. CDF of Prediction Error Of Path Loss of MCB base station

Table 3. Statistical Values Compared With LS Regression Analysis for Urban Coastal Environment

S.No.	Sites	Models/ Statistics	Mean	Variance	Coeff. of Variation	Std. Error	Skewness	Excess Kurtosis	Median
1	Electric Mansion (ETM)	LS Regression	7.4	23.4	0.5	1.4	1.4	2.9	8.0
		COST231 Hata	18.0	96.0	0.5	3.4	0.0	-1.2	18.0
		ECC	15.1	44.8	0.4	1.9	0.6	1.1	16.0
		SUI (Terrain B)	25.3	50.4	0.2	1.9	0.1	-0.1	24.0
		ITU-R (NLOS)	30.3	46.4	0.2	1.8	0.2	0.3	32.0
2	Gangasagar (CHS-GSC)	LS Regression	8.0	24.5	0.6	1.3	1.4	2.8	8.0
		COST231 Hata	8.5	17.8	0.5	1.6	0.9	1.2	8.0
		ECC	9.6	26.2	0.5	1.6	1.1	1.5	8.0
		SUI (Terrain B)	23.0	39.9	0.2	1.8	0.2	0.7	24.0
		ITU-R (NLOS)	28.6	36.6	0.2	1.6	0.2	0.9	28.0
3	Geetanzali (GTL)	LS Regression	10.1	28.4	0.5	1.8	0.4	-0.8	8.0
		COST231 Hata	16.9	46.4	0.4	2.2	-0.3	-0.9	16.0
		ECC	9.0	18.5	0.4	1.6	0.4	-0.7	8.0
		SUI (Terrain B)	11.5	40.3	0.5	2.2	0.5	-0.8	12.0
		ITU-R (NLOS)	10.1	28.4	0.5	1.8	0.4	-0.8	12.0
4	Mistry Chambers (MCB)	LS Regression	10.8	71.4	0.7	2.2	1.9	4.6	8.0
		COST231 Hata	13.2	37.8	0.4	1.5	0.3	0.6	12.0
		ECC	8.3	22.3	0.5	1.5	1.1	1.3	8.0
		SUI (Terrain B)	16.2	52.8	0.4	2.0	0.6	0.4	16.0
		ITU-R (NLOS)	20.5	53.4	0.3	2.0	0.5	0.1	20.0
5	Mayfair (MYFY)	LS Regression	57.7	220.7	0.2	3.4	0.4	-0.4	56.0
		COST231 Hata	25.2	209.0	0.5	3.4	0.5	-0.3	24.0
		ECC	36.2	209.1	0.4	3.4	0.5	0.3	36.0
		SUI (Terrain B)	59.3	210.8	0.2	3.4	0.5	-0.3	60.0
		ITU-R (NLOS)	19.3	55.8	0.6	2.2	1.4	1.3	12.0

4 Conclusion

An experimental campaign was conducted in the urban, coastal region of Mumbai using WiMAX OFDM transmissions at 2.3 GHz for five base stations. The observed signal levels have been converted into path loss values and plotted as a function of distance. These were compared with various prediction methods like COST231Hata, ECC, SUI (Terrain B), ITU-R (NLOS) along with that of least square regression method. Path loss exponents, mean errors and standard deviations of all the methods have been deduced and compared with observed values. The cdf values of prediction errors have been compared. Different statistical parameters are deduced and the best fit distribution for the cdf curves are found. From the following analysis, it has been observed that the prediction error of SUI, ITU-R NLOS and ECC model is considerably higher than COST231Hata. Negative Binomial distribution is the one that best represent the statistics of prediction error for LS regression analysis and all the models namely COST231Hata, ECC, SUI, ITU-R (NLOS). COST231Hata and ECC method gave good agreement with measured data than other methods.

References

1. Senza Fili Consulting.: Fixed, nomadic, portable and mobile applications for 802.16-2004 and 802.16e WiMAX networks. WiMAX forum (2005)
2. Abhayawardhana, V. S., Wassell, I. J., Crosby, D., Sellars and Brown, M. G.: Comparison of Empirical Propagation Pathloss Models for Fixed   Wireless Access Systems. In: IEEE conference on Vehicular Technology, vol. 1, pp 73-77, Sweden (2005)
3. Rial, V., Kraus, H., Hauck, J., & Buchholz, M.: Measurements and analysis of a. Wimax field trial at 3.5GHz in an urban environment. In: Proceedings of IEEE International Symposium on Broadband (2007)
4. Belloul, B., Aragon-Zaval, A., Saunders, S. R.: Measurements and comparison of WiMAX radio coverage at 2.5GHz and 3.5GHz. EuCAP 2009, 3rd European Conference on Antennas and Propagation (2009)
5. Berlin,. Walden and F. J. Rowsell.: Urban propagation measurements and statistical path loss model at 3.5 GHz. Antennas and Propagation Society International Symposium. IEEE, vol. 1A, pp. 363-366 (2005)
6. B. Geun-Sik and S. Ho-Kyung.: A study of 2.3 GHz bands propagation characteristic measured in Korea. Antennas and Propagation Society International Symposium, IEEE, pp. 995-998 vol.2 (2003)
7. Josip Milanovic, Rimac-Drlje S, Bejuk K. Comparison of propagation models accuracy for WiMAX on 3.5GHz. In: 14th IEEE International conference on electronic circuits and systems, pp. 111-114, Morocco (2007)
8. S Kun, Wang ping, Li Yingze,.: Path Loss Models for Suburban Scenario at 2.3GHz, 2.6GHz and 3.5GHz. IEEE SAPE , pp 438-441 (2008)
9. Chhaya Dalela etal.: A Preliminary Analysis of WiMAX Radio Measurements at 2.3 GHz over Western India. In: 6th International Conference Of Microwaves, Antenna Propagation, and Remote Sensing, Jodhpur, India (2010)
10. M. V. S. N. Prasad and I. Ahmad.: Comparison of some path loss prediction methods with VHF/UHF measurements. IEEE Trans. Broadcasting, vol. 43, no. 4, pp. 459–486 (1997)
11. M. V. S. N. Prasad etal.: Terrestrial communication experiments over various regions of Indian subcontinent and tunig of Hata's model. Annals Telwcommun, vol. 63, pp. 223–235 (2008)
12. Joe,Hazra,Toh and Shankar.: Path loss measurements in sea port for WiMAX. In: *WCNC 2007 proceedings* (2007)
13. Y. Okumuraet ,E. Ohmori,T. Kawano,and K.: Field Strength and Its Variability in UHF and VHF Land Mobile Service. Revi. Elec. Commun .Lab., vol. 16,no. 9,pp 825-873 (1968)
14. Electronic Communication Committee (ECC) within the European Conference of Postal and Telecommunications Administration (CEPT).: The analysis of the coexistence of FWA cells in the 3.4-3.8 GHz band. tech. rep., ECC Report 33, (2003)
15. V. Erceg, K. V. S. Hari, etal.: Channel models for fixed wireless applications. IEEE 802.16 Broadband Wireless Access Working Group, (2001)
16. Recommendation ITU-R P.1411-1.: Propagation data and prediction methods for the planning of short-range outdoor radio communication systems and radio local area networks in the frequency range 300 MHz to 100 GHz. tech. rep., International Telecommunication Union (2001)

17. M. V. S. N. Prasad.: Path loss exponent deduced from VHF &UHF Measurements over India Subcontinent and Model comparison. IEEE Trans. Broadcasting, vol. 52, no. 3, pp. 290-298, (2006)
18. Mardeni.R, T.Siva Priya,: Optimize Cost231 Hata models for Wi-MAX pathloss prediction in Suburban and open urban Environments. Canadian Center Of Science and Education, vol. 4, no. 9, pp 75-89 (2010)

Cognitive Handoff Avoidance and QoS Improvement in WLAN

V. Berlin Hency[1], S. Aravind Prasad[2], Y.RA. Kannan[2], and D. Sridharan[3]

[1] Visiting Faculty, Department of Information Technology, Madras Institute of Technology,
Chennai- 600044
[2] Department of Information Technology, Madras Institute of Technology,
Chennai- 600044
`hencyjoseph@annauniv.edu,`
`{raja.avi,yra.kannan}@gmail.com`
[3] Department of ECE, College of Engineering, Guindy,
Chennai- 600025
`Sridhar@annauniv.edu`

Abstract. With the development of wireless communication technologies, IEEE
802.11 standard (Wi-Fi) has undergone a rapid growth, thanks to low cost and
high-speed connectivity. Hence effective mechanisms need to be developed to
exploit the diversity across a multiple access points and to provide a uniform load
distribution in order to improve the QoS of users and to improve the overall
composite capacity. In this paper, we propose a handoff scheme considering the
current active application in use rather than a single fixed threshold value and
dynamically changing the threshold value depending upon the currently active
applications. In addition to it, we also propose a pro-active Load Balancing
scheme which completely avoids unnecessary overloading of access points by
considering the load at the target access point before associating with it.

Keywords: IEEE 802.11, Handoff, Fixed threshold, QoS, Load Balancing,
Active applications.

1 Introduction

The IEEE 802.11, Wireless Local Area Network (WLAN), have the advantage of
supporting its mobile users with high data rates at much lower costs when compared
with rest of technologies in its class. Main challenge in provisioning of QoS for
WLAN is to provide the support for real-time VoIP with seamless handover since
packet delays and excessive packet losses may be incurred due to dynamic network
conditions. Usually there is always a trade-off between maximizing the overall system
utilization and providing a good QoS to demanding applications. And whenever the
target APs are selected by stations without considering the load capacities, the
composite network capacities will not be able to scale with the increasing number of
APs. This problem is further aggravated by the load distribution in a non-uniform
fashion across APs which is the usual scenario in public hot spots which may lead to
irregular congestions in AP with the strongest signal strength.

D.C. Wyld et al. (Eds.): NeCoM/WeST/WiMoN 2011, CCIS 197, pp. 262–271, 2011.
© Springer-Verlag Berlin Heidelberg 2011

Conventionally the handoff process starts whenever the Mobile Host (MH) moves out of the range of currently associated Access Point (AP) i.e., the RSS received by the MH from the current AP is less than a predefined fixed threshold value. There is also another variation in the mechanisms termed as First Satisfaction First Reservation Handoff (FSFR-HO) Mechanism where the MH selects the AP as soon as it receives the required RSS value from it instead of selecting the AP with maximum RSS value and this scheme essentially removes the scanning for all probable channels and comparing them.

Traditionally all the load balancing algorithms basically deal with utilization of additional system state information which allows them to make use of short-term fluctuations and quality during their decision-making. The load balancing algorithms must have the capability to dynamically change their parameters with respect to current system states. In general the algorithms deal with the mechanisms to transfer stations from heavily to lightly loaded networks. The decisions are generally taken considering the load metrics.

Now all the above mechanisms make use of single fixed threshold value without considering the current active application in use. And the load balancing algorithms previously proposed by various authors are generally reactive in nature and hence implemented only after the AP gets overloaded. In this paper, we propose a handoff scheme considering the current active applications in use rather than a single fixed threshold value and dynamically changing the threshold value depending upon the currently active applications. In addition to it, we also propose a pro-active Load Balancing scheme which completely avoids unnecessary overloading of access points by considering the load at the target access point before associating with it.

The remainder of the paper is organized as follows. Section 2 describes our proposed mechanism. Section 3 illustrates the comparative performance evaluation. Section 4 discusses the related work and Section 5 represents the conclusion.

2   Proposed Mechanism

We propose two influencing factors: 1) Application Specific Threshold (AST) and 2) Load Balancing at each Access point (AP).

2.1   Application Specific Threshold

Usually when the Mobile Host (MH) moves away from the currently associated AP, RSS value from that AP gets reduced below the fixed threshold value and then handoff occurs to another AP by means of active scanning process. Threshold value for handoff process is fixed irrespective of the currently active applications in MH. For e.g. the currently active application in MH requires only less amount of RSS value, say -85 dB and if the threshold value is fixed to -60 dB, then the unnecessary handoff would occur even though the MH is receiving required RSS when it moves away from the currently associated AP. Hence, according to our proposed mechanism each MH should maintain AST i.e. the threshold value with respect to the current active application in use rather than a single fixed threshold value. If the number of applications that are currently in use is more than one then the maximum AST should be selected among AST corresponding to the respective applications. For e.g. if there are three active applications in MH, say AST of Application I is -60 dB, AST of Application II is -90 dB and AST of Application III is -50 dB then AST corresponding to Application III is selected since it is maximum among the three applications. The AST selection is done in the application layer of MH and this selection process should be dynamic in such a way that maximum AST should be selected if there are changes in the number of applications that are currently in use. There should be cross layer communication between Application Layer and MAC layer to deliver the information about AST. The main advantage of AST is when the MH is at the edge of an AP's network coverage area, then RSS from the current AP will be low and if this RSS is greater than required AST then unnecessary handoff can be avoided.

2.2 Load Balancing

Various load metrics can be considered for Load Balancing such as the number of MHs that can be connected to an AP, the bandwidth received by the user from an AP. In our proposed mechanism, we are considering the load metric as number of MHs connected to AP. Load Capacity Threshold (LCT) indicates the maximum number of MHs that can be connected with an AP and Load Capacity of AP (LCAP) indicates the number of MHs that are currently associated with an AP i.e. the number of active connections. Initially, all APs should broadcast its LCAP to its neighboring AP. Hence each AP knows Load Capacity of its neighboring APs. Each AP has to maintain a list which consists of Load Capacity of neighboring APs and the values of LCAP maintained in this list should be sorted in ascending order. Hence, the first LCAP value in the list indicates that AP is under loaded and the last LCAP value in the list indicates that AP is overloaded. If two LCAP values are same then the values are stored as per FCFS procedure. The list maintained by each AP should be dynamic i.e. if there are any changes in the number of MHs that are associated with an AP then the corresponding AP should broadcast its LCAP to its neighboring APs. Hence, each AP maintains an updated list of LCAPs.

Fig. 1. List maintained by each AP

2.3 Overall Process

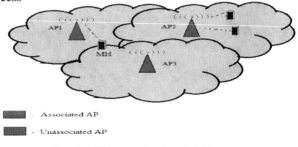

Fig. 2. MH is associated with AP1

Consider MH is currently associated with AP1 and it moves far away from AP1.

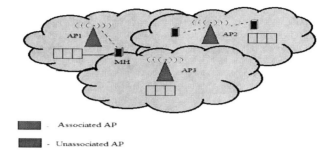

Fig. 3. RSS<AST, MH accesses the list maintained by AP1

Consider the situation that RSS received from AP1 goes below the required AST value. At this time, Handoff will be initiated. Now the MH accesses the list maintained by AP to which it is currently associated as shown in Fig.3.

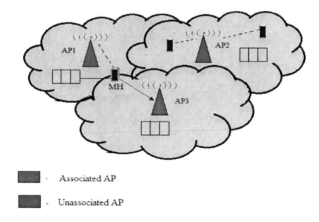

Fig. 4. MH chooses AP with acceptable RSS value > AST value based on FSFR-HO Mechanism

Since the list is maintained in the increasing order of Load Capacity of neighboring APs, MH accesses the list and compares the RSS value received from each AP in the list with its AST. This process is continued as per FSFR-HO mechanism until an AP with an acceptable RSS value is reached. MH selects AP3 by acccessing the list since RSS received from AP3 is greater than AST and also AP3 is not overloaded. MH chooses AP3 by accessing the list that is maintained by AP1. MH checks the RSS value received from AP3 with AST. If RSS value is acceptable then it gets associated with AP3.

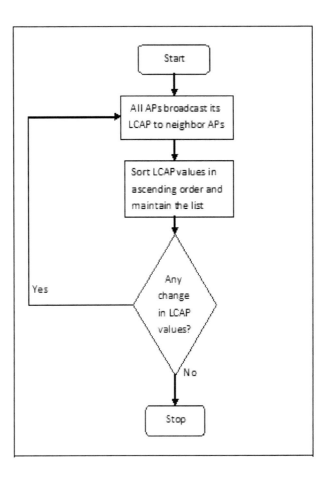

Fig. 5. List Maintenance Procedure at each AP

Fig. 5 shows the List Maintenance Procedure at each AP. This is the initial procedure that should be implemented by each AP and the list should be broadcasted to its neighbor APs. If there are any changes in LCAP value of an AP then that AP should broadcast its LCAP value to its neighboring APs. Therefore the updated list should be maintained by each AP dynamically.

The following Fig. 6 shows the steps in Cognitive Handoff Procedure. Normal Operation in the following figure indicates the normal data transfer operation between MH and AP without any handoff procedure. If RSS from the associated AP falls below AST of MH then the Cognitive Handoff Procedure begins as given in the Fig. 7. After selecting the best target AP according to Cognitive Handoff Procedure, MH will be associated with the selected AP.

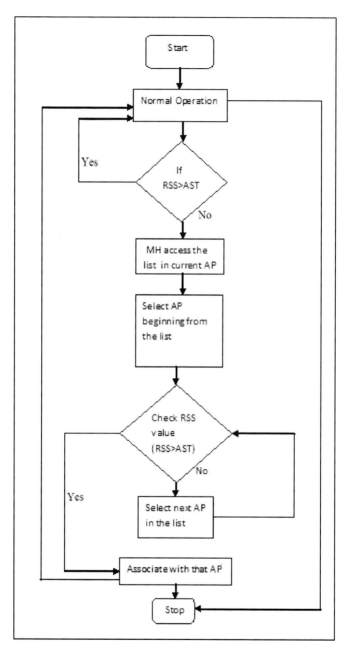

Fig. 6. Cognitive Handoff Procedure

Hence, our proposed mechanism provides three main benefits, viz. (i) avoiding unnecessary handoffs, since the Application Specific Threshold is considered (ii) improving QoS of all MHs connected to each AP since AP with minimum load capacity is considered first (iii) MH will be connected to the best target AP during handoff (AP with minimum load and providing satisfiable RSS).

3 Performance Evaluation

In this section, we show performance evaluation of the proposed Cognitive Handoff Mechanism (CHM) mechanism compared to the Traditional Handoff Mechanism (THM). Fig. 7 and 8 present the average total handoff delay time and the Average Throughput achieved by CHM and THM respectively.

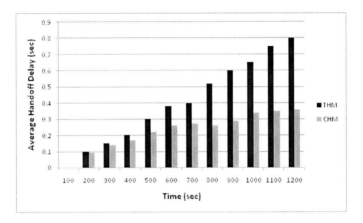

Fig. 7. Average Handoff Delay Vs Time

For our simulations we set the fixed threshold value as -15dB and made use of 3 different applications APP_1, APP_2 and APP_3 with 3 different threshold values of -5 dB, -8 dB, and -13 dB respectively. The Load Capacity Threshold (LCT) for each AP as fixed as 5 and as a whole, 5 APs was used for our simulation purposes. Across our simulations we increased the number of MHs from 3 to upper bound of 20 MHs to stress on the improvement in system performance for large loads.

In THM mechanism, since the handoff occurs depending upon fixed threshold value (-15dB) irrespective of the active application in use, in the extreme situations (i.e. when the MH reaches the edge of the current AP range) handoff would have occurred even though the current active application in MH is able to receive satisfiable RSS. Hence the overall delay time increases due to handoff initiation and scanning for all probable channels. Under similar conditions, the performance of CHM improves greatly since the RSS that the MH receives from the current AP satisfies with AST which, in most situations, is less than the predefined value. Hence with the implementation of CHM mechanism, handoffs could be cognitively avoided which greatly aids in decreasing the overall delay while improving the network throughput and performance.

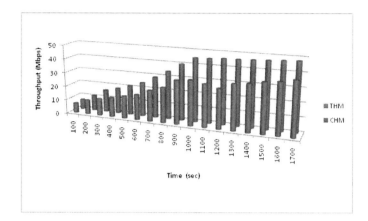

Fig. 8. Throughput Vs Time

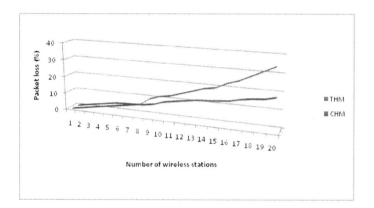

Fig. 9. Packet loss Vs Number of wireless stations

In case of Load balancing too, our proposed pro-active cognitive Load Balancing mechanism (CHM) outperforms the traditionally mechanism (THM) since the load at the target access point is considered before associating with it. The simulation results clearly show that, in case of large loads the performance and overall throughput of THM degrades compared to our proposed scenario. And there is also a significant decrease in the amount of packet losses in the network in our proposed scenario. Additionally in case of traditional mechanisms, there is a possibility of already overloaded AP to be associated with further more MHs (more than its LCT) and which may lead to decrease in QoS of not only the new MH but also for the already associated MHs. Whereas in our proposed mechanism, this possibility is essentially eliminated as the MH has the advantage of selecting the AP in its vicinity with minimum load and receive an acceptable RSS value (RSS>AST).

4 Related Work

Several studies proposed different load balancing schemes with different load balancing metrics. Li-Hsing Yen et al. [6] proposed that balancing AP traffic loads effectively can increase overall system performance. The metrics that had been taken into account for load balancing in several schemes are the number of users associated with an AP, the bandwidth that a new user can get from an AP if that user is connected with that AP. In [1], Yigal Bejerano et al. proposed Cell Breathing Technique for Load Balancing in wireless LAN by controlling the size of WLAN cells. For changing the size of cells, the ability to dynamically change the transmission power of AP beacon messages is required. In this approach, when the AP becomes overloaded then handoff occurs by reducing the cell size. Hence it leads to more handoff occurrence for the mobile nodes.

Ahmed H. Zahran et al. [10] proposed the effect of Application Signal Strength Threshold values depending on the packet delay, bandwidth and number of handoffs. If the Application Signal Strength Threshold value is reduced, the mobile node can be connected with the associated AP for longer duration. In [4], Yang Song et al. proposed that threshold based rate adaptation algorithms play a vital role in IEEE 802.11 services. The System performance can be increased if the threshold is tuned optimally. Eng Hwee Ong et al. [11] proposed the integrated load balancing scheme which includes the QoS based Handover and soft admission control to provide seamless connectivity. But this approach requires the additional Access point controller which gathers the information from each access points and also leads to single point of failure. Yazan M. Allawi et al. [12] proposed First Satisfaction First Reservation Handoff (FSFR-HO) Mechanism i.e. while discovering the next access point during handoff, the access point which has satisfactory Received signal strength value is selected rather than scanning all the access points and choosing the best one. Eng Hwee Ong et al. [2] provided a comparison between three dynamic load distribution algorithms, viz. predictive load balancing (PLB), predictive QoS balancing (PQB) and reactive QoS balancing (RQB) based on opnet simulations QoS metrics considered were packet delay and packet loss rate. It was shown that RQB achieves higher QoS fairness compared to PQB at admission thresholds of 80% to 90%. Our proposal differs from the above mentioned works in the following ways (i) Handoff could be avoided by making use of Application Specific Threshold value, (ii) Improving QoS for each MH by using distributed Load Balancing scheme at each access point based on the load capacity and the application specific threshold value.

5 Conclusion

In this paper, we propose a handoff scheme considering the current active application in use rather than a single fixed threshold value and dynamically changing the threshold value depending upon the currently active applications which greatly helps incase of delay sensitive applications since handoffs can be cognitively avoided in extreme situations thereby avoiding the unnecessary scanning of channels and delays associated with it. In addition to it, we also propose a pro-active Load Balancing scheme which completely avoids unnecessary overloading of access points by considering the load at the target access point before associating with it. Hence, our proposed mechanism provides three main benefits, viz. (i) avoiding unnecessary handoffs (since the Application Specific Threshold is considered) (ii) improving QoS of all MHs connected to each AP (since AP with minimum load capacity is conidered first) (iii) MH will be connected to the best target AP during handoff (AP with minimum load and providing satisfiable RSS).

References

1. Bejerano, Y., Han, S.: Cell Breathing Techniques for Load Balancing in Wireless LANs. IEEE Transactions on Mobile Computing (2009)
2. Ong, E.H., Khan, J.Y., Mahata, K.: On Dynamic Load Distribution Algorithms for Multi-AP WLAN under Diverse Conditions. In: Proceedings of WCNC 2010. IEEE Press, Los Alamitos (2010)
3. Broustis, I., Papagiannaki, K., Krishnamurthy, S.V., Faloutsos, M., Mhatre, V.P.: Measurement-Driven Guidelines for 802.11 WLAN Design. IEEE/ACM Transactions on Networking (2010)
4. Song, Y., Zhu, X., Fang, Y., Zhang, H.: Threshold Optimization for Rate Adaptation Algorithms in IEEE 802.11 WLANs. IEEE Transactions on Wireless Communications (2010)
5. Shin, S., Schulzrinne, H.: Measurement and Analysis of the VoIP Capacity in IEEE 802.11 WLAN. IEEE Transactions on Mobile Computing (2009)
6. Yen, L.H., Yeh, T., Chi, K.H.: Load Balancing in IEEE 802.11 Networks. IEEE Computer Society Press, Los Alamitos (2009)
7. Bshara, M., Orguner, U., Gustafsson, F., Biesen, L.V.: Fingerprinting Localization in Wireless Networks Based on Received-Signal-Strength Measurements. IEEE Transactions on Vehicular Technology (2010)
8. Chitte, S.D., Dasgupta, S., Ding, Z.: Distance Estimation From Received Signal Strength Under Log-Normal Shadowing: Bias and Variance. IEEE Signal Processing Letters (2009)
9. Huang, C.T., Wu, C.H., Lee, Y.N., Chen, J.T.: A Novel Indoor RSS-Based Position Location Algorithm Using Factor Graphs. IEEE Transactions on Wireless Communications (2009)
10. Zahran, A.H., Liang, B., Saleh, A.: Signal Threshold Adaptation for Vertical Handoff in Heterogeneous Wireless Networks. In: ACM/Springer Mobile Networks and Applications (MONET). Springer, Heidelberg (2005)
11. Ong, E.H., Khan, J.Y.: An Integrated Load Balancing Scheme for Future Wireless Networks. IEEE Press, Los Alamitos (2009)
12. Allawi, Y.M., Kim, M.G., Kang, M.: Advanced Handoff Mechanism for Delay Sensitive Applications in IEEE 802.11 Wireless LAN. In: ICACT 2008. IEEE Press, Los Alamitos (2008)

Triangulation Based Clustering for Improving Network Lifetime in Wireless Sensor Networks

Anita Kanavalli[1], G.P. Bharath[1], P. Deepa Shenoy[1],
K.R. Venugopal[1], and L.M. Patnaik[2]

[1] Department of Computer Science and Engineering,
University Visvesvaraya College of Engineering, Bangalore, India
[2] Vice Chancellor, Defence Institute of Advanced Technology (Deemed University)
Pune, India
anita.kanavalli@gmail.com

Abstract. Recent advances in wireless communication have led to rapid development of wireless sensor networks. The power management and power efficiency of the network are the biggest challenges that are to be addressed in this field. One of the most important areas to be concentrated in this field is, the way the sensors communicate with each other such that the energy consumption is reduced. The energy consumption can be reduced by restricting the computation and communication by all the nodes in the network. Clustering of the nodes is one such method used for selection of only specific nodes for communication in the network. In this paper we propose a new clustering protocol which improves the lifetime of the sensor network as compared to the conventional communication protocol used for transmitting directly to the base station. We employ triangulation to cluster the sensor nodes and elect a head node to communicate with base station. The simulation results of our protocol and the conventional protocol shows that our protocol is energy efficient and gives a longer lifetime to the network. Also we give an application of the protocol in the reprogramming of network.

Keywords: Triangulation, Clustering, Reprogramming.

1 Introduction

Wireless sensor network (WSN) has become a very popular area of research and development in recent times. The main cause behind the popularity of WSN is the large number of applications in various fields it can be applied. Sensor networks are used in several places where there is a need to monitor the environment like in military, nature monitoring, traffic monitoring on highways/roads, disaster management to name a few. Due to the popularity of sensor networks, they must be efficient, long lasting and reliable. Sensors are electronic devices that can sense data and have communication capabilities. They are powered by battery whose life is limited. The sensing circuitry does the sensing part like measurement of different parameter from the environment and then converts it into electrical signal. The collected data is then processed locally to some extent and then transmitted to a base station by the communication circuitry.

D.C. Wyld et al. (Eds.): NeCoM/WeST/WiMoN 2011, CCIS 197, pp. 272–284, 2011.
© Springer-Verlag Berlin Heidelberg 2011

One of the main challenges offered by the sensor networks is the power management and efficiency[1]. The sensor network must survive for longer periods without servicing them. One way to ensure this is, by developing better batteries and sensor circuitry which consume less power. Another way is to design power efficient communication protocols so as to reduce the power consumption by the network. By designing efficient routing algorithms, the energy consumption of a sensor network can be reduced[2]. There are many such routing algorithms proposed. These algorithms are highly application based and the algorithms are designed to address only certain set of problems. Due to the large variety of applications that sensor networks can be applied to, designing algorithms and protocols to suite the network for all applications is very difficult and almost impossible. Hence protocols and algorithms are designed keeping certain scenario in mind.

One of the techniques used to reduce the power consumption in a network is by clustering. Clustering is a method of grouping together some sensor nodes by some means and then communicating with each other. This technique improves the power efficiency to a great extent and the lifetime of the network increases considerably. Much work is done on clustering algorithms for various applications. There are various protocols available to implement clustering in sensor networks. In this paper we propose an efficient and simple protocol to implement clustering. We use virtual triangular areas to create clusters and then electing head nodes. The sensor nodes communicate with the head node and the head node communicates with the base station. This reduces the cost of communication in terms of energy consumed. To keep the energy dissipation uniform, the network chooses different head nodes so as to distribute the overload of communication on head nodes equally throughout the network. This protocol is proposed for homogenous system of sensor nodes. The protocol can be implemented for both static and dynamic networks.

One of the uses of this protocol is in the reprogramming of the sensor network. Reprogramming is the method of updating, replacing or modifying the existing code of sensors in the network. We have implemented our protocol in reprogramming the network efficiently addressing all major challenges posed by it. Our protocol, being energy efficient, makes reprogramming use less energy than conventional methods. The first part of this paper deals with the new protocol we propose and a comparison of the protocol is made with the conventional way of routing i.e. each sensor communicating with base station. The next part of the paper discusses the implementation of our protocol in the reprogramming algorithm that we have developed.

2 Related Work

A hierarchical energy efficient communication protocol namely wireless Sensor system for Hierarchical Information gathering through Virtual triangular Areas (SHIVA) is presented in[3]. This approach considers a cluster head set in place of a single cluster head for a cluster. As clustering sensor nodes is an effective topology control approach, a new routing algorithm which can increase the network lifetime is proposed in[4]. Here, the predefined numbers of nodes which have the maximum residual energy are selected as cluster-heads based on special threshold value first and then the members of each cluster are determined based on the distances between the node and the cluster head and also between the cluster head and base station.

A hybrid power saving protocol is presented in[5]. The protocol utilizes the concept of dual-channel and dual-transmission-range clustering. The protocol also utilizes the cluster head dismissal mechanism to avoid the ever-increasing of cluster heads and to adapt to topology changing. An algorithm that elects clusters by using weighted clustering algorithm is presented in[6] which show that this protocol can reduce overall energy consumption and improves network lifetime. A Layered Clustering Hierarchy (LCH) communication protocol for wireless sensor networks is given in[7]. By randomizing the rotation of cluster heads in each layer, the energy load is distributed evenly across sensors in the network. A fuzzy logic approach to cluster-head election is proposed based on three descriptors energy, concentration and centrality is described in [8]. The energy-efficient clustering approach employs optimization technique based on OR (operations research) practices [9]. They adopt a simple hierarchy in which relay nodes forward data messages from cluster head to the sink, thus eliminating the overheads needed to maintain a routing protocol. A centralized adaptive Energy Based Clustering protocol through the application of Self organizing map neural networks (called EBC-S) which can cluster sensor nodes, based on energy level and coordinates of sensor nodes is given in [10]. This algorithm form energy balanced clusters and equally distribute energy consumption. Our protocol uses a simple triangulation method to form the clusters in such a way that the cost of communication is reduced and less energy is consumed.

3 System Model

The model of the sensor network considered in our work is as follows: The field will contain hundreds of sensor networks. The field is considered to be of area $N \times N$ unit area. The field contains of n sensors. The sensors are spread randomly all over the field. The sensor may be static or dynamic and the sensors are moving in the field which is the case in wildlife monitoring. The base station is considered fixed in this work and the location is known. Sensor nodes are electronic devices which are all homogenous, and all sensors are of similar kind and have same capabilities. The sensors have limited memory and processing capabilities. They also are constrained by the limited battery supply available to them. The sensor can put its different parts to sleep and wake them up on receiving appropriate signals.

The base station can be considered to be as a powerful computer with unlimited memory, processing capabilities and unlimited power supply. The base station is stationary. The base station can be in middle of the field or in some corner of the field. We have considered the base station is in one corner of the field. The sensors are deployed in the field and they form a network with the base station in a self-organized manner. It has been assumed that it is possible to know the geographic location of each sensor by itself through a GPS free solution.

4 Proposed Algorithm and Protocol

4.1 Initial Setup

The sensors are deployed in the field initially. After deployment, the base station can broadcast some message making all sensors active. After all sensors are active, the sensors will answer the broadcast message. The geographical positions of all sensors are determined by the base station. In a static sensor network, the position of the sensor does not change. Hence the positions calculated initially can be used throughout the networks lifetime. The relative positions of sensors are known by the base station. In a dynamic sensor network, the sensors are moving around the network frequently. Hence the geographic positions of the sensors must be determined constantly. The positions of all sensors are constantly determined by the base station by some method. Even GPS solution can be used in this case. Else GPS free solutions are available to find the geographic location of the sensors. The frequency of updating the positions of sensors in the base station database depends on the sensor network. If the sensors in the network keep changing positions constantly, like in case of wildlife monitoring, the updating of database must be done very frequently. Else updating can be done in longer interval of time. After the initial setup and finding the locations of all sensor nodes, the base station forms clusters of nodes.

4.2   Clustering of Nodes

The base station forms clusters based on triangular areas it throws. The base station on knowing the geography of the network, starts clustering by throwing triangles in the field. The areas of all the triangles are same but varies in height and breadth. The area of the triangles depends on the area of the field and number of nodes that are deployed. The area of the triangle can change accordingly. The triangle are not thrown randomly around the field, but thrown such that one sensor node is at the centroid of the triangle. All nodes that lie in a triangle together form a cluster. The procedure is continued till all nodes are a part of some cluster. Here is the algorithm of forming clusters in the network:

Step 1.   Get the coordinates or the geographic location of each sensor node. This is done in the initial setup for static network. For dynamic network, the coordinates of nodes are calculated after some specified time period repeatedly.

Step 2.   Calculate the area of the triangle to be thrown. This is done based on the area of deployment of the nodes, number of nodes, etc. The area calculated must be optimum such that it covers at least some sensor nodes in the field. If the area does not cover adequate network area, then the area of the triangle is increased by some factor and the step is repeated again. Triangles are thrown such that one node is at the centroid of each triangle.

Step 3.   All sensors that lie in a triangle are made as one cluster. The base station must keep track of which node is in part of which cluster.

Step 4.   The triangles thrown near all nodes that are not part of any cluster and further groups are created till all nodes are part of a cluster.

If a node belongs to more than one cluster i.e. the node lies in more than one triangle, then the node belongs to that triangle whose centroid is the closest to it. If a node is the sole member of a cluster, then that node is tried to be included in a cluster nearest to it. If there are too few nodes in any cluster, then those nodes are included in cluster nearest to the nodes. If no such cluster exists for any nodes, then those nodes are formed as cluster. Figure 1 shows the formation of clusters through triangular areas.

Figure 1 shows the field with nodes deployed and the formation of clusters using triangular areas. Nodes 1 and 2 are in same triangle. But since their number is small, these nodes are included in clusters nearest to them. Same is the case with nodes 3, 4 and 5. Node 6 is in two triangles. So it belongs to the triangle whose centroid is nearest to it.

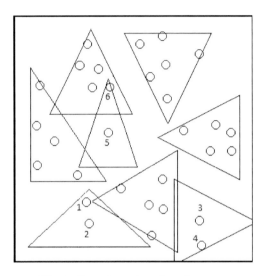

Fig. 1. Clustering using triangular areas

4.3 Selection of Cluster Head

Once the clusters are formed, a cluster head is chosen from the cluster. This node is called the *head node* and all nodes in a cluster communicate with this node and the head node communicates with the base station. Selection of cluster head is based on two factors. It depends on the current energy levels of nodes, distance from the centroid. The algorithm to select a head node is given below:

1. The node with maximum energy in the group is found out. If all the energy of the nodes are the same or nearly same, then the node at the centroid is made the head node.
2. The nodes which are nearest to the centroid are found and the node with the maximum energy among these nodes is made the head node.

Selection of head nodes are made regularly after certain interval of time. The head node has to do maximum amount of work in a cluster and hence takes up a bit more power than usual. Because the protocol is so designed to choose the node with maximum energy remaining and that is nearest to the centroid, changing head node frequently will distribute the consumption of power over the full cluster. This will improve the efficiency of the network in terms of power consumption. The responsibilities of a head node are as follows:

1. Head node must receive all data transmitted from cluster members and process it.
2. The head node must decide what data must be transmitted to the base station.
3. Head node transmits the collected data to the base station. Also during reprogramming, base station send new program to head node which must then distribute the code to cluster.

4.4 Communication between Nodes and Base Station

Once the clusters are formed and the cluster heads selected by the base station, the base station sends signals to all nodes giving details of the cluster and cluster head. The nodes store the details of the nodes to which they must transmit data to. The sensors then collect data and transmit it to the head node after low level of processing. The communication between cluster member and the head node is time division multiple access (TDMA). After one or few rounds of communication, the head node processes the data collected, and sends it to the base station. This can be a single hop communication or multi hop communication. In our work we have considered only single hop communication between any node or node and base station. After head node sends the data and the base station receives it, the base station again elects head node for each cluster. In a dynamic network, the clusters must be reformed and fresh cluster heads must be elected. The base station elects new head nodes and broadcasts the cluster details again. This cycle continues throughout the network lifetime.

Figure 2 shows a cluster and its head node. The figure shows how cluster nodes communicate with head node and head node communicating with the base station. In figure 2, *1* is the head node. All other nodes communicate with the head node in a TDMA fashion. The head node collects all data and transmits the data to the base station.

The clustering of nodes is done throughout the network lifetime. The life time of network can be considered the time where enough nodes are alive to collect enough data from the field, i.e. time when a certain percentage of total nodes deployed are alive. Nodes are considered dead when it has no more energy to do useful work of sensing and transmitting.

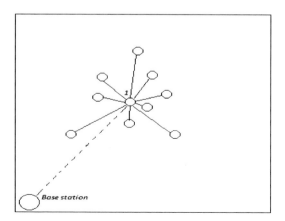

Fig. 2. A cluster with head node showing the communication of data

All nodes communicate with head node of the cluster the nodes belong to. The energy spent on communication is directly proportional to distance squared. Hence lesser distance saves energy drastically. Since most of the nodes communicate with head nodes which are much nearer than base station, the energy spent on communication is decreased to a great extent. The head nodes have to communicate the most in the system. Hence they spend more power compared to rest of the nodes and may die of early. But since the protocol chooses new head nodes frequently, the load of the head nodes is distributed over the network. Thus all nodes are alive for longer period of time as compared to protocols in which nodes communicate directly with the base station. The simulation shows that our protocol is better by at least eight times as compared to conventional method of nodes communicating directly with base station.

5   Simulations and Performance Evaluation

The simulation of the proposed protocol has been carried out in a simulation program written in JAVA. We have considered only the routing algorithm. The program follows TDMA based scheduling for communication. We also compare the protocol with a conventional protocol of nodes communicating with the base stations directly in single hop. The same program and assumptions are used for both protocols. The simulation program uses the algorithms discussed in previous section of the paper and simulates our protocol. The output is the average energy required by the network per data sent to base station and number of data set that a network can send to base station. The program uses conventional protocol i.e. each node communicates with base station in TDMA fashion and the program calculates the energy required by each node based on the equations discussed here. In the simulation, we consider many scenarios wherein the area of the field varies with number of sensor nodes being constant and the number of sensor node varies with the area of the field being same. The results of our protocol and the conventional protocol are compared.

5.1   Energy Considerations

In our simulation we have considered following radio model of first order for the sensor communications[3]. Sensor can turn off their communication module when not required to avoid unnecessary transmissions. The following equation provides the transmission and receiving costs in terms of energy for transmission and receiving a k bit message over a distance of d.

Transmitting:

$$E_{Tx} (k, d) = E_{Tx\text{-elec}} (k) + E_{Tx\text{-amp}} (k, d)$$

$$E_{Tx} (k, d) = E_{elec}*k + \varepsilon_{amp}*k*d2$$

Receiving:

$$E_{Rx} (k) = E_{Rx\text{-elec}} (k)$$

$$E_{Rx} (k) = E_{elec}*k$$

In this radio model we consider,

E_{elec} = 50 nJ/bit (*energy dissipated for transmitting or receiving operation*)

ε_{amp} = 100pJ/bit/m2 (*energy dissipated in the transmitter amplifier*)

5.2 Assumptions Made in Simulations

We have made following assumption in our simulations.

- The sensors are all homogenous.
- The sensors' geographical location can be found by some way.
- There is continuous transmission of data from all nodes and the nodes transmit some data in each round.
- The data to be transmitted is of 32 byte each.
- The sensors have some computing capabilities. The head node sends at most half the amount of data collected.
- Only energy required for transmitting and receiving data are considered.

5.3 Setup

The simulation has following experimental setup for both the protocols: (i) Area of field: varies from 25X25m to 50X50m, (ii) Initial energy of each sensor nodes: *1* joule, (iii) Data size: 32 bytes, and (iv) Number of nodes: Varies from 100 to 1000. The simulation was run for the mentioned setup and following results were found.

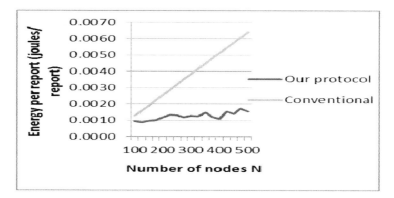

Fig. 3. Comparison of protocols with varying number of nodes for energy required per data

Figure 3 shows the simulation result comparing the energy required per data communicated with the base station by the network by our protocol and the conventional protocol with number of nodes changing and the area of the field being constant. The area of the field is taken 50 X 50 m. The result shows that our protocol takes up less energy than the conventional method. The result improves to great extent as the number of nodes increases. The energy required by our protocol increases very little as the number of nodes increases where as in the conventional method, the increase is linear. Figure 4 shows the simulation result comparing the energy required per data communicated to the base station by the network by our protocol and the conventional protocol, with area of field changing and number of nodes being constant. Number of nodes in the field is taken as 300. The result shows that our protocol takes up less energy than the conventional protocol. Figure 5 shows the simulation result comparing number of data set made to the base station by the network by our protocol and the conventional protocol, with number of nodes changing and area of field being constant. The area of the field is taken as 50 X 50 m. The result shows that our protocol gives more data set than conventional method.

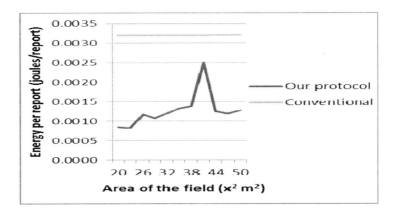

Fig. 4. Comparison of protocols with area of the field varying for energy required per data

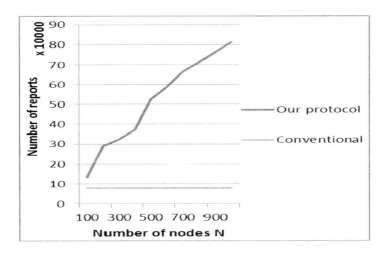

Fig. 5. Comparison of protocol with number of nodes varying for number of data set made in the lifetime of network

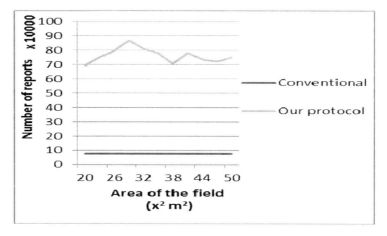

Fig. 6. Comparison of protocol area of the field varying for number of data set made in the lifetime of network

This increases linearly as the number of nodes increases where as in conventional method this is almost constant regardless of number of nodes. This graph also shows that the lifetime of the network increases by applying of our protocol. Figure 6 shows the simulation result comparing number of data set made to the base station by the network by our protocol and the conventional protocol with area of field changing and number of nodes being constant. Number of nodes in the field is taken as 1000. The result shows that our protocol gives more data set than conventional method. Number of data set is 8 to 10 times that of conventional method. One more inference that can be drawn from the graph is that the lifetime of the network has improved more regardless of the size of the field.

6 Application

One of the applications of our protocol is in reprogramming of the network. Reprogramming of network is the method of updating, modifying or deleting existing software in sensor nodes. Code dissemination and code acquisition are two basic schemes to reprogram sensor networks. Code dissemination is usually used by system administrators for updating programs on sensor nodes, fixing bugs, changing network functionality, tuning module parameters, and replacing program modules. Manually reprogramming the sensors are very costly, labor intensive or even impossible since each node has to be collected from the field and physically attach to a computer to burn new codes. In contrast to code dissemination, code acquisition is initiated from individual sensors to fetch and install program modules from the network dynamically and on demand. Dynamic network reprogramming in sensor networks poses several new challenges.

First, network reprogramming requires 100% delivery. But in sensor network applications, occasional loss of data is tolerable and often expected [11]. Second, the problem of concurrent senders needs to be examined. In network reprogramming, code image is propagated from one sensor node to another. Every node that has the new code image like to communicate with all the nodes in the network. Thus, it is likely that several senders are transmitting at the same time. This causes a lot of collisions and congestion of the wireless channel, and possibly the nodes are not reprogrammed. Third, energy efficiency is an important issue of concern. Because sensor nodes have limited energy resources, the amount of energy consumed in network reprogramming will affect the network lifetime. Some of the possible and potential sources of energy consumption component are, message collision, overhearing, control message overhead, and idle listening. Among these, idle listening (using radioactive time unnecessarily) is the major source of energy waste. We have addressed all of the stated problems by using our protocol in reprogramming. The algorithm to reprogram using our protocol is given below.

Step 1.   The base station broadcasts message saying that reprogramming is to be done.
Step 2.   The head nodes respond saying that all are ready to receive the new code. The head nodes' sensing and computing parts are put to sleep.
Step 3.   The base station sends in the new code to all head nodes in a TDMA fashion.
Step 4.   After all head nodes receive new code, the base station sends message saying all nodes to put its sensing and computing parts to sleep.
Step 5.   The head nodes start distributing the code to its cluster nodes in a TDMA fashion.
Step 6.   Once all nodes in a cluster are reprogrammed, head node sends message to base station.
Step 7.   Once the base station receives message from all head nodes, the base station broadcasts another message saying reprogramming is success and telling all nodes to wake up.

The algorithm is so designed that it tackles all problems of reprogramming that was discussed. The algorithm solves the problem of 100% delivery by first putting the sensing and computing parts of the sensor nodes to sleep. This makes the communication part of the sensor made available 100% for the purpose of reprogramming. This also saves lots of energy of the nodes. The problem of concurrent senders is solved by making only head nodes distribute the code. Only the nodes belonging to a cluster can get new program from its head node. Thus message collision and congestion is reduced. The algorithm is energy efficient as mentioned as the sensors are put to sleep. Also the transmission range of nodes is reduced as the head node transmits the codes which are nearer to the recipient nodes.

7   Conclusion

We have introduced a new protocol for communication of sensor nodes in a network through clustering. Our protocol is power efficient and improves the lifetime of the network. The protocol is dynamic and can be used for both static and dynamic networks. The protocol is adaptive in terms of power consumption. By choosing different head nodes frequently, the protocol distributes the power load of the system. By constantly changing the head node, which does more work than usual, we managed to avoid some of the nodes dying early and distributed the share throughout the cluster. The protocol reduces the communication distance for the nodes to transmit data. By transmitting the data to a much nearer head node than the base station, nodes save significant amount of energy. Also the head node processes the collected data from the nodes and sends only most useful information to the base station. So processing of data in the base station is lot easier as the amount of data that is coming in is lesser.

We also used the proposed protocol in reprogramming. Reprogramming with all its challenges was solved quite successfully using our protocol. We designed an algorithm for reprogramming using our protocol at the base station. The reprogramming so done was found to be efficient and faster. Also the energy used for reprogramming was less. For future work, we shall try to remove some of the constraints the protocol has. We will try to bring in heterogeneity in the system i.e. use heterogeneous nodes as opposed to homogenous sensors used in this work. Also using multi hop routing between head node and the base station may reduce more energy. Using sleep time in the protocol may further improve the protocol performance.

References

1. Singh, S., Woo, M., Raghavendra, C.: Power-Aware Routing in Mobile Ad Hoc Networks. In: The Proceedings of the Fourth Annual ACM/IEEE International Conference on Mobile Computing and Networking (MobiCom 1998), pp. 66–75 (October 1998)
2. Rabiner, W., Heinzelman, Chandrakasan, A., Balakrishnan, H.: Energy Efficient Communication Protocol for Wireless Microsensor Networks. In: The Proceedings of the Hawaii International Conference on System Sciences, Maui, Hawaii, January 4-7 (2000)
3. Kumar, H., Sarma, D., Kar, A., Mall, R.: Energy Efficient Communication Protocol for a Mobile Wireless Sensor Network System. IJCSNS Power-Aware Routing in Mobile Ad Hoc Networks International Journal of Computer Science and Network Security 9(2), 384–396 (2009)
4. Golsorkhtabar, M., Hosinzadeh, M., Heydari, M.J., Rasouli, S.: New Power Aware Energy Adaptive Protocol with Hierarchical Clustering for WSN. IJCSNS International Journal of Computer Science and Network Security 2(4), 38–40 (2010)
5. Jiang, J.-R., et al.: A Hybrid Power-Saving Protocol by Dual-Channel and Dual-Transmission-Range Clustering for IEEE 802.11-Based MANETs. International Journal of Pervasive Computing and Communications 3(3) (2005)
6. Zhang, J.-w., Ji, Y.-y., Zhang, J.-j., Yu, C.-l.: A Weighted Clustering Algorithm Based Routing Protocol in Wireless Sensor. In: ISECS International Colloquium on Computing, Communication, Control, and Management, CCCM 2008, vol. (2), pp. 599–602 (2008)
7. Wang, Y., Ramamurthy, B.: Layered Clustering Communication Protocol for Wireless Sensor Networks. In: Proceedings of 16th International Conference on Computer Communications and Networks, pp. 844–849 (August 2007)
8. Gupta, I., Riordan, D., Sampalli, S.: Cluster-head Election using Fuzzy Logic for Wireless Sensor Networks. In: Proceedings of the 3rd Annual Research Conference on Communication Network and Services, pp. 255–260 (May 2005)
9. Aslam, N., Phillips, W., Robertson, W.: A Unified Clustering and Communication Protocol for Wireless Sensor Networks. IAENG International Journal of Computer Science 3(35), 249–258 (2008)

10. Enami, N., Moghadam, R.A.: Energy Based Clustering Self Organizing Map Protocol For extending Wireless Sensor Networks lifetime and coverage. Canadian Journal on Multimedia and Wireless Network 1(4), 42–54 (2010)
11. Kulkarni, S., Wang, L.: Energy-Efficient Multihop Reprogramming for Sensor Networks. ACM Transactions on Sensor Networks 5(2), Article 16 (March 2009)

A Novel Dynamic Cache Invalidation Algorithm for Efficient Data Dissemination in MANET

N. Sabiyath Fatima[1] and P. Sheik Abdul Khader[2]

[1] Department of Computer Science & Engineering, B S A University, Chennai, India
sabiyathfatima@gmail.com
[2] Professor & Head Department of Computer Applications, B S A University, Chennai, India
psakhader@yahoo.com

Abstract. A mobile ad-hoc network (MANET) is a kind of wireless ad-hoc network, and is a self-configuring network of mobile routers (and associated hosts) connected by wireless links – the union of which form an arbitrary topology. Caching the frequently accessed data provides efficient communication in a mobile environment The main objective is to avoid the stale data using invalidation policy based on TTL. This paper discusses Time to Live (TTL) based invalidation. Here we propose an Enhanced Adaptive TTL based invalidation algorithm for maintaining data consistency in MANET. Each 1-hop distance node's to data cache node maintain a hash table for cache invalidation. TTL of the data item is taken as the key factor for invalidation. used as its value. Simulations are carried out in NS-2 to evaluate the performance of the proposed algorithm, also it is compared with fixed TTL and Adaptive TTL approaches.

Keywords: MANET, Cache Consistency, Cache Invalidation, Stale Data, TTL value.

1 Introduction

In the ad-hoc network architecture, there is no pre-existing fixed network infrastructure. MANET can be easily deployed for the applications such as battlefield and disaster recovery. It can also be used as a wireless extension for the users to access the Internet in an area without network infrastructure [1]. The Fig.1 shows a typical adhoc network structure with mobile nodes passing data request to the data source. In this network, out of the seven nodes, two of the nodes acts as cache nodes helping the clients to retrieve data from them, instead of going to the data source which is far away.

Caching reduces average data access latency and access requests are satisfied from the local cache, which makes efficient data accessing [2]. Effective cache invalidation mechanisms are required to ensure the consistency between source node and cached data at the clients. TTL based cache invalidation problem has been well studied in mobile computing environments [3]. The existing strategies use Fixed TTL and Adaptive TTL based techniques for cache invalidation. Maintaining cache invalidation process in cache node produces some additional overhead to cache and also decrease the performance of the network. Cooperative caching service aims to download a copy of a cached data item efficiently and to cooperatively manage the cache space among the mobile nodes [4].

D.C. Wyld et al. (Eds.): NeCoM/WeST/WiMoN 2011, CCIS 197, pp. 285–297, 2011.
© Springer-Verlag Berlin Heidelberg 2011

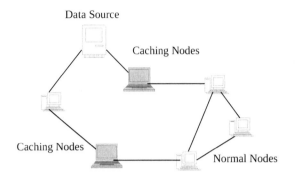

Fig. 1. An Ad Hoc Network Scenario

There are several caching techniques and routing protocols implemented to tackle the problem of node mobility and resource (battery and bandwidth) consumption [5]. But, the policies ignored the important factors such as TTL and distance of the requester from the cache/source satisfying the request.

Caches represent learned portions of the network topology, but a cache entry may become invalid due to changes such as two nodes moving out of wireless transmission range of each other [6]. Even though, periodic routing protocol such as a link-state or distance-vector routing protocol could distribute updated information in a somewhat timely manner, periodic protocols produce higher overhead in a number of studies and periodic protocols still take some amount of time to detect a link failure and to distribute this information. The frequently changing topology make cache consistency a challenging issue [7]. The TTL based cache invalidation scheme is discussed in which a data is considered as invalid if its TTL value expires. In the proposed Ex-ATTL algorithm cache node broadcast the data item's name and data item's TTL to its 1-hop neighbors. Each node invalidates the data according to data items TTL stored in cache invalidation hash table. Here cache nodes computing overhead and the request delay gets reduced, also provides data reliability and avoids stale information.

The rest of this paper is organized as follows. Section 2 reviews the related works for cache invalidation schemes in mobile ad hoc networks. Section 3, presents the system model for data service in MANETs. Section 4, presents the proposed system architecture and Extended Adaptive TTL algorithm. Section 5, discusses the performance evaluation, and simulation results for Ex-ATTL. Finally, Section 6 concludes the paper.

2   Related Works

According to the authors of [8], [9], caching data or path of the data at mobile client side is an essential mechanism for improving system performance in a mobile computing environment. The drawback of these schemes is that if the node is not on the forwarding path of a request to the data center the cache information of a node cannot be shared. The existing studies on cache invalidation strategies for mobile clients are discussed.

As categorized in [10], [11], the two kinds of cache invalidation methods for mobile databases are Temporal-dependent invalidation and Location-dependent invalidation. Location-dependent invalidation depends on the geographical position of the mobile nodes. It supports single hop communication only Generally cellular network uses location dependent invalidation scheme for cache invalidation. Temporal dependent invalidation is carried out by data updates. To carry out temporal-dependent invalidation, the data source keeps track of the update history (for a reasonable length of time) and sends it, in the form of an invalidation report (IR), to the clients, either by periodic / aperiodic broadcasting or upon individual requests from the clients [12]. In the basic IR approach, the server broadcasts a list of IDs for the items that have been changed within a history window. The mobile client, if active, listens to the IRs and updates its cache accordingly.

TTL is the heart of the temporal dependent invalidation scheme. In [13], CachePath and CacheData handle cache consistency using a simple weak consistency model based on the TTL mechanism. In this model, a routing node considers a cached copy up-to-date if its TTL hasn't expired. If the TTL expires, the node removes the map from its routing table (or removes the cached data). As a result, the routing node forwards future requests for this data to the data source. Author's of [14] optimize this model by allowing nodes to refresh a cached data item if a fresh copy of the same data passes by. If the fresh copy contains the same data but a newer TTL, the node updates only the cached data's TTL field. If the data source has updated the data item, the node replaces both the cached data item and its TTL with the fresh copy. This scheme takes more round trip between cache node and data source for invalidation and TTL refreshment. The performance of the overall network decreases due to more round trip between data source and cache node.

In [15], authors use the Adaptive TTL based cache invalidation scheme for Hybrid Cache and Cooperative Cache. In these schemes, if TTL of particular data item expires, some cached data can be invalidated. Usually, the node removes such invalid data from the cache. To save space, when a cached data item expires, it is removed from the cache while its id is kept in "invalid" state as an indication of the node's interest. Certainly, the interest of the node may change, and the expired data should not be kept in the cache forever. For example, caching the data indicates the mobile node's interest in it. While performing data forwarding, if a mobile node finds an invalid copy of that data in its cache, it deletes the old copy and stores new copy for future use. If an expired path or data item has not been refreshed for the duration of its original TTL time, it is removed from the cache.

3   Background System Model and Assumptions

The system model constitutes the mobile node, Data Source Node and the Data Updates. There are n mobile nodes in the system. N= {N1, N2, . . . , Nn} denote the set of mobile nodes. Every node has a cache in its local storage, and may issue queries for data items from the data source. The assumption is that every query requests only one data item. The mobile nodes are free to move in a designated area. One of the mobile nodes act as the data source. The data source is called a server and it contains a database. It is assumed that there are m data items in the database. Data items from

1 to m serve as their identifiers.   D= {D1, D2, . . ., Dm} denotes the set of data items in the database. The data source may repeatedly update the data items in the database. In order to keep track of the version of a cached copy of a data item, each copy of a data item is associated with a TTL and also records the time Tc when the copy is created in the source, where Tc is a data item copy creation time.

4 Proposed TTL Based Cache Algorithm

4.1 Preliminaries

Caching

Generally ad hoc networks are dynamic network. This could often result in shortage of communication bandwidth as well as unacceptable response times. To reduce the number of remote data retrieval operations over long distances, copies of data objects are stored locally. This concept of locally storing copies of remote data objects for faster retrieval is called caching.

Invalidations

When multiple nodes cache the same data item, there is a need to maintain cache consistency. The cached data item needs to be changed when updations occur. These updations cause the data item to become stale in the other cached copies. To rectify this problem it is necessary to propagate the change to all other caches. The policy employed to notify all caches about an update is called invalidation policy.

TTL

TTL is a number indicating the time interval during which the data item is considered to be fresh. Whenever a cached data item is retrieved from the data source, it gets an associated time to live (TTL) with it. When the data item is to be referenced, its TTL value is checked and if the TTL is still valid then the object is retrieved otherwise a new value is requested from the server. The request node caches both the data item and its TTL. Whenever the data item is requested, the client checks the TTL value for that data item. If the TTL has expired, a fresh copy of the object is brought from the source. This is an instance of the weak consistency model. When the data is distributed and replicated, it may have been updated on another client node. The other data items caches shall be informed about the update, only when the TTL for the data item expires. After this TTL has expired on a client, the object is treated as stale and a fresh value is retrieved from the data source.

In the data source, TTL value for the data items are fixed by original nature (application) of the data. For example the whether forecast, stock market, sports news and battle field conditions monitoring update the data item in every short interval of time periods, so these kind of data items are updated very often . Some kind of data items like video films and geographical information of particular places are not updated in short time periods. By the updating nature, the data item's TTL is divided into two categories. They are Short TTL and Long TTL. *Short TTL* has a very little TTL threshold value because of the very fast updating nature of the data item. *Long TTL* has long TTL threshold values for data invalidations.

4.2 System Overview

In Extended Adaptive TTL scheme, each and every node maintains the cache invalidation hash table. This hash contains data item as its key and TTL of the data item as its value. It also store Tc after the node caches the data item. Tc is the time when successful copy of the data item is created in a mobile node. The Fig.2 shows the Block diagram of Cache Invalidation.

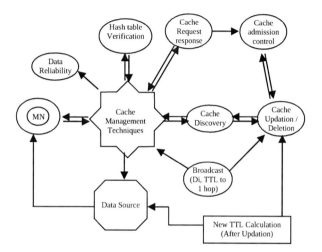

Fig. 2. Block diagram of Cache Invalidation

4.3 Methodology

The proposed scheme is divided into three phases. First phase of the algorithm does the cache invalidation hash table verification for current request. Second phase of the algorithm retrieve the data item from appropriate source. In third phase cache node broadcasts the data item name and its current TTL value to its one hop neighbor.

Phase 1

If a node generates a data request then this request is verified from current nodes invalidation hash table. If cache invalidation hash table contains the requested data item then the algorithm retrieves the TTL and T_c from cache table. The request generation time Treq is also cached from the nodes timer then it subtracts the T_{req} from T_c. If this subtracted value is greater than TTL then this also removes the data item, it's TTL and it's T_c from hash table and forwards the request to the data source. The data source calculates the new TTL and sends with the data item. If the subtracted value is less than TTL it moves to the next phase.

Phase 2

In this phase the algorithm checks the local cache for node request. If local cache contains the requested data item, then the request node simply uses its local cache.

Other wise this phase uses the current implementing cache algorithm and retrieve the data item from nearest cache node or from the data source. Again, the TTL of the particular data item is recalculated.

$$NewTTL = T_{req} - T_c$$

It appends the new TTL with corresponding data item and sends the response to the client node. Data cache node also updates the new TTL in its cache table only for the particular data item.

Phase 3

After successful copy of the data item is created in localized cache or in any intermediate cache node for future requests this phase cache the Tc from the cache node's timer and updates this Tc in its cache invalidation hash table. Cache node also broadcasts the new cached data items id, TTL and its Tc only to one hop neighbors.

The pseudo code of Invalidation Algorithm

```
The values of TTL, Tc and Treq are declared.
Get node's current time when request is generated (Treq)
While (true) /* local Hash Table (HT) contains data item*/
/* Loop 1*/
Get from HT data item's TTL
Get from HT data item's Tc
While ((Treq-Tc)> TTL))
      {delete content from HT
       delete data from local cache}
Send Request To Data Source
/* Loop 2*/
Initialize Hopcount(HC) to 1
newTTL = Treq-Tc
Response from data source
Cache (Di)
Update HT with Di newTTL, Tc
Broad Cast data with newTTL,Tc,HC
/* Loop 2*/
Declare newTTL
While (true) /* local Hash Table (HT) contains data item*/
{retrieve From the Local Cache the data}
Initialize HC = 1
Send Request To Data Source
newTTL = Treq-Tc
Response From Server with node id, Di, newTTL
Cache Di
/* Loop 3*/
Update local HT (Di,newTTL,Tc)
broadCast (Di,newTTL,Tc, HC)
endwhile
```

```
endwhile
/* Loop 2*/
Initialize HC = 1
newTTL = T_req-T_c
Response From Server with (node id, D_i, newTTL)
Cache D_i
/* Loop 3*/
Update local HT (D_i,newTTL,T_c)
broadCast (D_i,newTTL,T_c,HC)
endwhile
```

5 Results and Discussions

5.1 The Simulation Setup

In order to evaluate the efficiency of Ex-ATTL invalidation algorithm, a similar system to [4] and [6] is developed in this work. It consists of a single data source that serves multiple client nodes. The database is updated only by the server, whereas the queries are generated and utilized on the client side. There are 1,000 data items in the database, which is divided into two subsets: the short TTL data subset and the Long TTL data subset. The short data subset includes data items from 1 to 150 (out of 1,000 items) and the long data subset includes the remaining data items of the database. Clients have a large probability (75 percent) to access the data in the short TTL set and a low probability (20 percent) to access the data in the Long TTL set. The system parameters are shown in Table 1.

Table 1. Parameter Settings

Simulator	Network Simulator (NS2)
Simulation Time	8000 Sec
Network Size	2000m x 500m
Transmission Range	250m
Mobility Model	Random waypoint
Speed of mobile host	1~20 m/s randomly
Average Query Rate	0.5 / Second
Database Size n	2000 items
Number of Nodes	100
Bandwidth (Mb / s)	1
TTL (secs)	200 to 800
Pause time (secs)	100
Client cache size (kb)	300 to 900
Mean Query Generate Time Tquery (sec)	1 to 200
TTTL (secs)	300

The server generates updates separated by an exponentially distributed update inter arrival time. The updates are randomly distributed inside the short TTL data subset and the Long TTL data subset, 65.5 percent of the updates are applied to the short TTL data subset. Each client generates a single stream of read-only queries. Each new query generated is based on exponentially distributed time. Once the requested data items arrive on the channel, the client brings them into its cache. Client cache management follows the Extended Adaptive TTL based cache invalidation policy.

5.2 Simulation Results

The performance analysis presented here is designed to find the effects of different workload parameters such as mean update arrival time, mean query generate time, and system parameters such as cache size, replicate times (m), and short TTL data access probability (pq). Then the performance comparison is carried out among Adaptive TTL and Ex-ATTL. The performance is measured by the cache hit ratio, the query delay, and the throughput. Note that minimizing the number of uplink requests is a desirable goal as clients in a mobile environment have limited battery power and transmitting data requires a large amount of power.

5.3 The Query Delay Evaluation

The query delay is measured as a function of the mean query generates time and the mean update arrival time. As shown in Fig. 3, Ex-ATTL algorithm significantly outperforms the Adaptive TTL scheme. As explained before, each client generates queries according to the mean query generate time. If the queried data is in the local cache, the client can serve the query locally; otherwise, the client has to request the data from the server. If the client cannot process the generated query due to waiting for the server reply, it queues the generated queries. Since the broadcast bandwidth is fixed, the server can only transmit a limited amount of data during one transaction interval, and then it can only serve a maximum number (α) of queries during one

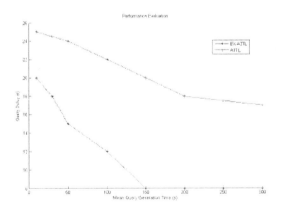

Fig. 3. A comparison of the query delay. The query delay as a function of the mean query generate time ($T_u = 10s$, $c = 100$ items).

transaction interval. If the server receives more than (α) queries during one transaction interval, some queries are delayed to the next transaction interval. If the server receives more than (α) queries during each transaction interval, many queries may not be served, and the query delay may be out of bound. Fig. 3 shows the query delay as a function of the mean query generate time with $T_u = 10s$ and $c = 100$ items. When the query generates time is lower than 70s (e.g., 60s), the query delay of the Adaptive TTL algorithm becomes infinite long.

However, when the query generation time reaches 30s, the query delay of proposed algorithm is still less than 20s. This is due to the fact that the cache hit ratio of Ex-ATTL algorithm is high and a large number of queries can be served locally.

5.4   Comparison of Query Delay with Mean Update Arrival Time

As shown in Fig. 4, as the mean update arrival time increases, the cache hit ratio increases and the query delay decreases.

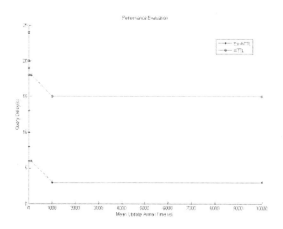

Fig. 4. Query delay comparison with mean update arrival time ($T_u = 100s$, $c = 100$ items)

Since the proposed algorithm has high cache hit ratio than the Adaptive TTL algorithm, the query delay of Ex-ATTL algorithm is shorter than the Adaptive TTL algorithm. For example, with $T_u = 10,000s$, Ex-ATTL algorithm reduces the query delay by a factor of 3 compared to the Adaptive TTL algorithm. Although the cache hit ratio of the Adaptive TTL algorithm is doubled from $T_u = 10s$ to $T_u = 33s$, the query delay of the Adaptive TTL algorithm does not drop too much (from 18.7s to 16.1s). Since the query generated time is exponentially distributed, multiple queries may arrive at a client during one transactional interval. In case of a cache miss, the query delay may be longer than the normal interval 20s; this is due to queue effects. Since requests are generated following an exponential distribution, the server may have a long queue of requests during some period of time. The requests in the back end of the queue will have much higher query latency, and it increases the average query latency.

5.5   Cache Hit Ratio vs. Node Size

The Fig.5. shows cache hit ratio as a function of the number of clients. It is seen that the cache hit ratio of Ex-ATTL algorithm increases as the number of clients increases, but the cache hit ratio of the Adaptive TTL does not change with the number of clients, for e.g., Adaptive TTL (n = 1) and Adaptive (n = 100) have the same cache hit ratio. When the number of clients drops to one, the cache hit ratio of proposed algorithm is similar to the Adaptive TTL algorithm. In the Adaptive TTL algorithm, a client downloads the data and its TTL that it has requested from the server. However, in the proposed algorithm, the client downloads the data with newly calculated TTL. In Ex-ATTL algorithm each and every node maintain the cache invalidation hash table, it increases the cache hit ratio of the data item which does not expire .If data item expires Ex-ATTL algorithm forwards the request to the data source, hence the stale data always gets expired. As the number of clients decreases, clients have less opportunity to download the data requested by others, thus the cache hit ratio decreases. This reveals why Ex-ATTL algorithm has similar cache hit ratio when the number of clients drops to one.

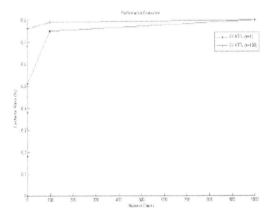

Fig. 5. A comparison of the cache hit ratio (T_{req} = 100s) with number of clients (cache size = 100 items)

5.6   Cache Hit Ratio vs. Different Cache Size

The Fig.6. shows the cache hit ratio under different cache sizes when the number of clients is 100. It is easy to see that the cache hit ratio of Ex-ATTL algorithm is always higher than that of the Adaptive TTL algorithm for one particular cache size (cache size is 50 items, 100 items). The figure shows that the cache hit ratio grows as the cache size increases. However, the growing trend is different between the Adaptive TTL and Ex-ATTL algorithm. For example, in the Adaptive TTL, when the update arrival time is 1s, the cache hit ratio does not have any difference when the cache size changes from 50 data items to 100 data items. However, under the same situation the cache hit ratio increases from about 40 percent to 58 percent in the proposed scheme.

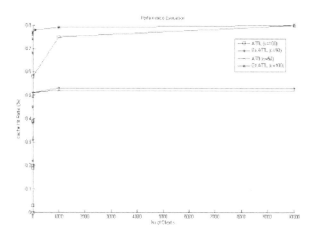

Fig. 6. Cache hit ratio comparison with number of clients

In Ex-ATTL algorithm, clients may need to download interested data for future use, so a large cache size may increase cache hit ratio. When the server updates data frequently, increasing the cache size does not help. This explains why different cache size does not affect the cache hit ratio of the Adaptive TTL when Tu = 1s. As shown in Fig. 6, the cache hit ratio drops as the update arrival time decreases. However, the cache hit ratio of the ATLL algorithm drops much faster than the proposed algorithm.

When the update arrival time is 10,000s, both algorithms have similar cache hit ratio for one particular cache size. With c = 300 items, as the update arrival time reaches 1s, the cache hit ratio of Ex-ATTL algorithm still keeps around 58 percent, whereas the cache hit ratio of the Adaptive TTL drops to near 0. This can be explained as follows: When the update arrival time is very low (e.g., 1s), most of the cache misses are due to short TTL data access; when the update arrival time is very high (e.g., 10,000s), most of the cache misses are due to Long TTL access. Since Ex-ATTL algorithm is very effective to improve cache performance when accessing short TTL data, the cache hit ratio of the proposed scheme can be significantly improved when the update arrival time is low. However, as the mean update arrival time drops further ($T_u < 1$s), the cache hit ratio of the Ex-ATTL drops much faster than before. At this time, the short TTL data changes so fast that the down loaded short data may be updated before the client can use it and, hence, failing to improve the cache hit ratio.

5.7 Analysis Based on the Count of Uplink Requests

The Fig.7, shows uplink cost of both algorithms. Since Ex-ATTL algorithm has a lower cache miss rate than the Adaptive TTL and clients only send uplink requests when there are cache misses, proposed algorithm has lower uplink cost compared to the Adaptive TTL.

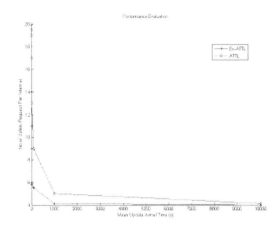

Fig. 7. The number of uplink requests per IR interval (T_q = 100s, c = 100 items)

It is interesting to find that both algorithms have similar uplink cost when the mean update arrival time is very high (e.g., 10,000s), but there is a significant difference when the mean update arrival time is 10s. From Fig.7, it is found that both algorithms have similar cache miss ratio (1 - cache hit ratio) when T_u = 10,000s, but a significant difference when Tu = 10s. As shown in Fig. 7, Ex-ATTL algorithm can cut the uplink cost by a factor of 3 (with T_u = 10s) and, hence, the clients can save a large amount of energy and bandwidth. When the update arrival time is smaller than 1s, the uplink cost of the Adaptive TTL does not increase, but the uplink cost of proposed algorithm increases much faster than before. This can be explained by the fact that the cache hit ratio of the Adaptive TTL already drops to near 0 when T_u = 1s, whereas the cache hit ratio of proposed algorithm drops when T_u < 1s.

6 Conclusions

In this paper, TTL based cache invalidation technique is designed to efficiently support data reliability in ad hoc networks. We have proposed a novel dynamic cache invalidation algorithm for efficient data dissemination in mobile ad hoc network with reduced overheads. This is efficient in the case of dynamic data request. Our experiment have showed through simulation and results, that the proposed algorithm provides reliability, scalability and simple implementation mechanism while comparing with the existing TTL strategies. The algorithm solves the critical issue of data becoming stale. This algorithm supports valid data accessing using clear TTL calculation mechanism. In the proposed scheme, if any node caches the data item, then it broadcast the data items id and its current valid TTL to its one hop neighbor for future request. This advanced mechanism improves the network performance and also reduces the cache nodes overheads. Simulation results showed that Ex-ATTL algorithm can cut the query delay by a factor of 3 and double the throughput compared to the Adaptive TTL. Thus the proposed algorithm performs better than the existing TTL strategies.

References

1. Yin, L., Cao, G.: Supporting cooperative caching in ad hoc networks. IEEE Transactions on Mobile Computing 5(1), 77–89 (2006)
2. Du, Y., Gupta, S.K.S.: A cooperative caching service in MANETs. In: Autonomous Systems and International Conference on Networking and Services, ICAS/ICNS (2005)
3. Abolhasan, M., Wysocki, T., Dutkiewicz, E.: A review of routing protocols for mobile ad hoc networks. Ad Hoc Networks 2, 1–22 (2004)
4. Cao, G., Lin, L., Das, C.: Cooperative cach-based data access in ad hoc networks. IEEE Computer 37(2), 32–39 (2004)
5. Lim, S., Lee, W., Cao, G., Das, C.: Performance Comparison of Cache Invalidation Strategies for Internet based Mobile Ad Hoc Networks. In: IEEE International Conference on Mobile Ad-hoc and Sensor Systems (MASS), pp. 104–113 (2004)
6. Cao, G.: Proactive Power-Aware Cache Management for Mobile Computing Systems. IEEE Trans. Computers 51(6), 608–621 (2002)
7. Kahol, A., Khurana, S., Gupta, S.K.S., Srimani, P.K.: A Strategy to Manage Cache Consistency in a Distributed Mobile Wireless Environment. IEEE Trans. Parallel and Distributed Systems 12(7), 686–700 (2001)
8. Cao, G.: A Scalable Low-Latency Cache Invalidation Strategy for Mobile Environments. In: Proc. Sixth Ann. ACM/IEEE Int'l Conf. Mobile Computing and Networking (MobiCom 2000), pp. 200–209 (2000)
9. Xu, J., Tang, X., Lee, D.L., Hu, Q.L.: Cache Coherency in Location-Dependent Information Services for Mobile Environment. In: Leong, H.V., Li, B., Lee, W.-C., Yin, L. (eds.) MDA 1999. LNCS, vol. 1748, pp. 182–193. Springer, Heidelberg (1999)
10. Vaidya, N., Hameed, S.: Scheduling Data Broadcasts: New metrics and Algorithms. In: ACM/Baltzer Wireless Networks (WINET), pp. 171–182 (1999)
11. Acharya, S., Muthukrishnan, S.: Scheduling On-Demand Broadcasts: New Metrics and Algorithms. In: Proc. ACM MobiCom 1998, pp. 43–54 (1998)
12. Jing, J., Elmagarmid, A.K., Helal, A., Alonso, R.: Bit-Sequences: A New Cache Invalidation Method in Mobile Environments. ACM/Baltzer J. Mobile Networks and Applications (MONET) 2(2), 115–127 (1997)
13. Acharya, S., Alonso, R., Franklin, M., Zdonik, S.: Broadcast Disks: Data Management for Asymmetric Communication Environments. In: Proc. ACM SIGMOD Conference Management of Data, pp. 199–210 (1995)
14. Barbara, D., Imielinski, T.: Sleepers and Workaholics: Caching Strategies for Mobile Environments. In: Proc. ACM SIGMOD, pp. 1–12 (1994)
15. Xu, J., Tang, X., Lee, D.L.: Performance Analysis of Location- Dependent Cache Invalidation Schemes for Mobile Environments. IEEE Transaction on Knowledge and Data Engineering

TinyDB2: Porting a Query Driven Data Extraction System to TinyOS2.x

Bhaskar Biswas and Himanshu Singh

Department of Computer Engineering,
Institute of Technology, Banaras Hindu University
Varanasi, India
{bhaskar.cse,himanshu.singh.cse07}@itbhu.ac.in
http://itbhu.ac.in/cse/index.php/people/faculty/28.html

Abstract. In query driven extraction of data from Wireless Sensor Network (WSNs), application developers can get readings from sensor nodes by using SQL like queries. In normal WSN applications, users need to program the application in WSN specific platform, which not only requires large programming efforts but also makes it difficult to change the application parameters once deployed. SQL like queries present much simplified approach of data collection and changing parameters of application on the air. In this paper, we study one of query driven system – TinyDB. TinyDB was used in TinyOS1.x but due to changes in architecture of TinyOS from TinyOS1.x to TinyOS2.x, TinyDB needed to be ported to newer version of TinyOS. This paper describes the architecture of newer TinyDB system, ported to work with TinyOS2.x, in detail and also presents the major porting changes that were required to make it compatible with TinyOS2.x.

Keywords: Wireless Sensor Networks, Query driven systems, TinyDB, Porting.

1 Introduction

Wireless Sensor Network is becoming a popular research field in distributed systems due to its wide applications. Consider the network requirements of a particular farm scenario. A farmer, having different fields at different locations, may wish to collect data about the field conditions like temperature, water level in the soil and humidity continuously at regular intervals; and would also like to be informed about any event happening on the field like sudden flood or fire. A wired information system would be too costly for this case. The most feasible solution would be to use a wireless sensor network across the fields where nodes (also known as motes) having various sensors attached to it send the data through wireless radio. The requirement for such a network is different. To maximize the network lifetime, energy consumption by batteries should be minimum since it is not feasible to replace the batteries of nodes once deployed in farm. Also, the data delivery time should be very low, especially for fire and flood notifications.

D.C. Wyld et al. (Eds.): NeCoM/WeST/WiMoN 2011, CCIS 197, pp. 298–306, 2011.
© Springer-Verlag Berlin Heidelberg 2011

Now, the farmer may not be educated enough to program the sensor nodes in WSN specific operating systems like TinyOS [1], Contiki [2], MantisOS [3] and to optimize the above mentioned parameters. Two famous techniques which allow the farmers to use WSNs without learning to program the sensor nodes are – macro-programming and query driven data collection. Macro-programming [4] constructs allow the farmer to specify his requirements in the form of a task graph and a network graph. The tasks may be different types of sensing tasks, filtering tasks, routing tasks etc which may be specific to the requirements of a particular field. The network graph consists of sensor nodes on which the tasks have to be executed. The tasks are mapped on sensor nodes and low level programs to execute these tasks are automatically generated. Some of the common macro-programming architectures are KairOS [5], Regiment [6] and COSMOS [7].

The other method – query driven data collection [8], allow the farmer to send SQL like queries and collect data on a GUI interface. The farmer specifies his requirements which are then converted to SQL like queries. The packets containing these queries are routed to the motes which take the data reading from sensors as mentioned in query. The packets containing the sensed data are routed back to the base-station where it is presented on the GUI using visualization techniques. Cougar [9] and TinyDB [10] are such query processing systems. TinyDB was initially designed for TinyOS version 1. Due to evolutionary changes in TinyOS version 2, TinyDB needed to be ported to TinyOS2.x. Section 2 presents previous works in this field. Section 3 of this paper introduces TinyOS2.x and TinyDB. Section 4 presents the detailed system analysis of ported TinyDB. Section 5 highlights major changes that were required in porting and paper concludes with pros and cons of TinyDB.

2   Related Work

There has been a lot of research on query processing in distributed database systems, but only a limited work has been done on query processing for sensor networks. [12] presents need of query processing middleware for sensor networks. It proposes a layered architecture for query processing, focusing on aggregation and join operations. Authors do not address the problem of multi-query optimization. In [13], authors present an algorithm for multi-query optimization, but the work is limited to queries having same frequency of results. The work is targeted mainly towards optimization in energy consumption. Unlike TinyDB, it does not send the new queries immediately, instead they are stored and sent altogether. Cougar Sensor Database project [9] offers similar functionality as TinyDB. Cougar also uses a declarative language to represent the queries and then uses a query optimizer for in-network query processing.

3   Preliminaries

3.1   TinyOS2.x

TinyOS [1] is an operating system, primarily designed to meet the requirements of WSN and written in nesC [11] programming language. One of the main features of

TinyOS is its *Component based architecture*. The functionality of TinyOS is separated and grouped into components [11], which are connected using interfaces. Components contain the command and the event handler implementations. A command is used to perform a particular service whereas events may represent any hardware event such as completion of the service.

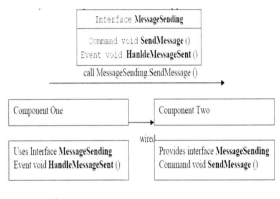

Fig. 1. An example of components and interfaces. It shows an interface, 'MessageSending', used by component 'One' and provided by Component 'Two'.

Along with commands and events, TinyOS also support the concept of tasks, which allow the deferred execution of code [11].

3.2 TinyDB

TinyDB is a query processing system through which information can be extracted from WSNs. TinyDB provides a query interface running on a PC, through which queries having SQL like syntax, referred to as TinySQL, can be sent in the WSN network. The information that needs to be extracted from the network can be defined as the attributes of the query. It is also possible to mention additional parameters in the query, for example the rate for refreshing the data. As shown in figure 2, when a query is sent through the frontend query interface, it propagates through the network nodes which generates results corresponding to the query and send them back towards the root node which forwards the results to the frontend again.

Example of TinyDB query:

> *Select light, temp*
> *Where light>400 AND node-id = 3*
> *For 10, Epoch Duration 1024*

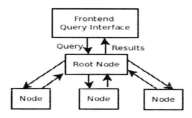

Fig. 2. Overview of TinyDB

3.3 Collection Tree Protocol

CTP [14] is a built in routing protocol in TinyOS 2.x which replaces the routing protocol of TinyDB 1.x. It is a tree-based collection protocol where all nodes try to form a tree to the root node (connected to the base station PC) based upon the link quality information between the node and its neighbors. Such a quality is called routing gradient of link and is measured by Expected Transmissions [14]. CTP needs the application that uses it, to explicitly set the root node of the tree.

4 TinyDB2: System Analysis

TinyDB2 can be classified into two major subsystems: Client Interface (Frontend) that runs on a PC and Sensor Network Software (Backend) that runs on the motes.

4.1 Java-Based Client Interface (Frontend)

It runs on the PC to which the base station node is connected.

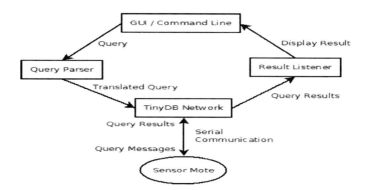

Fig. 3. Component Diagram of the TinyDB Client Interface

After entering the query, the query is assigned a unique query id. A result listener is added to the query to listen for the results of this particular query id. The query is then sent to a query Parser where the query, expressed as a string, is parsed to fill into a 'TinyDBQuery' data structure. The TinyDBQuery data structure consists of the query id, epoch duration and arrays for the selection attributes and the expressions in the query (E.g. WHERE, FOR etc).

The TinyDBQuery object is then passed to the 'TinyDBNetwork' class which is responsible for sending and receiving messages from the sensor network. To send the query over the network, 'TinyDBNetwork' decomposes the query into small query messages each containing one attribute. These messages are then injected into the network one by one over the serial communication interface. After all the query messages have been sent, TinyDBNetwork starts receiving query results. The query id is extracted from these results packets and the message is forwarded to the corresponding result listener and displays the results on GUI.

4.2   Sensor Network Running nesC Code

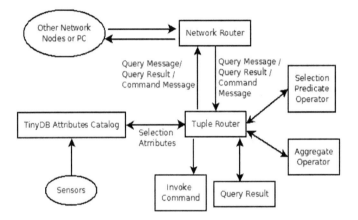

Fig. 4. Component diagram of sensor network software of TinyDB

This part of TinyDB runs on each mote in the network and is described in Figure 4. As shown in figure 4, TinyDB system consists of 2 main components:

1) NetworkRouterM – that forms the routing component of the TinyDB system. It receives and sends the network packets

2) TupleRouterM – that forms the core of the TinyDB system. All the query processing and results formation is done by this component.

The NetworkRouterM on receiving any message checks the type of message and signals the reception of the particular message to the TupleRouterM component. Messages received may be of three types:

1) Command Message – It is received from the frontend or from the parent. E.g. - message to delete a running query or a status command. On receiving a command message, the TupleRouterM invokes the particular command. In case of delete query command, a task 'RemoveQueryTask' is posted and message is rebroadcasted to the other nodes.

2) QueryMessage – It is received at a node from the frontend or from the node one level up in the routing tree. On receipt of query messages, memory is allocated and the fields of which are set as per the information contained in the QueryMessage. After this, the QueryMessage is broadcasted down the routing tree by the Network Router. After all the Query Messages for the query are received, the TupleRouter starts a periodic timer based on required epoch duration of the query. At every timer firing, the TupleRouter invokes the sensors to obtain readings of attributes mentioned in the query and forms a result tuple. The router discards the tuple if it doesn't satisfy any selection predicate present in the query e.g. the WHERE clause. It performs any aggregation operation, if required. The query result component converts this tuple, into QueryResult containing the tuple and metadata information for example – query id, epoch number. The result is then forwarded up the routing tree by the Network Router. TinyDB for TinyOS1.x used NetworkMultiHop whereas TinyDB2 uses CTP, a collection tree protocol provided by TinyOS 2.x, to send the query results up the routing tree. CTP, in turn uses the data link layer of TinyOS to send and receive messages.

3) *QueryResult* – A node receives QueryResult from its children. TupleRouter checks if the QueryResult belongs to an aggregate query and performs aggregation with its local readings, if required. Then the result is forwarded up the routing tree by the NetworkRouter.

5   Porting TinyDB1.x to TinyDB2.x

TinyOS1.x was upgraded to TinyOS2.x. TinyDB system which was designed for TinyOS1.x no longer worked with TinyOS2.x. In TinyOS2.x, several new protocols were adopted. The packets headers and addressing scheme had changed and the protocols defined by IEEE standards were adopted in the implementations. To adapt to these changes, TinyDB1.x needed to be ported according to the changes in TinyOS2.x. This section presents the major changes between TinyOS 1.x and 2.x along with the corresponding porting methodology that was adopted for making TinyDB work with TinyOS2.x.

a) One of the major changes in TinyOS2.x is the use of Collection Tree Protocol as the routing protocol. To plug-in CTP in 'NetworkMultiHopM' and replace the existing routing logic, the upper interfaces provided by CTP and its components were used. The CTP protocol requires its own headers. CTP provides an interface CtpPacket through which packet headers are modified before sending the QueryResults. CTP requires a node to act as root of the tree.

b) In TinyDB1, only the mote with node-id 0 could act as root of topology. In TinyDB2, a new command 'setCTP_Root' is added using which, the user can declare any particular node as the root of the Collection Tree Protocol (CTP).

c) The boot sequence of TinyOS 2.0 follows a different order than in 1.0 version. In 1.0 version there used to be an interface StdControl which had 'init', 'start' and 'stop' commands. The StdControl interface of 1.0 version has been split into StdControl and Init interfaces in 2.0. The StdControl interface now just contains the Start and the Stop commands. After the boot sequence is completed in 2.0 version, Boot.booted event is signaled to the application, which then starts the services accordingly.

d) A component called TinyDBAppC is used to provide the entry point of the mote's execution. This is the component to which the 'MainC' component and 'Boot' interface of TinyOS were wired. On booting the mote, after the TinyOS scheduler finishes initializing all the components having 'Init' interface, the BootC component signals the event Boot.booted. In this event, TupleRouterM is initialized.

e) In TinyOS2.x, Packets have been made abstract data type (ADT) i.e. the fields and the payload of the packet can now, cannot be directly accessed. Instead, TinyOS2.x provides interfaces like AMPacket and Packet to access the packet fields. So, to extract the destination address from the AMPacket, code like "msg -> addr" was replaced with AMPacket.destination( )

f) The removal of query caused runtime errors due to synchronization issues. For example, in case an attempt is made to access a query message of a query that has been just removed, then error is encountered because that query has been de-allocated. Such synchronization issues are resolved in TinyDB2.x with help of synchronization locks like:

IS_RemovingQuery(),
UnSet_RemovingQyeryLock(),
Set_RemovingQueryLock()

g) The TinyOS2 does not define any address for UART (Serial port). In earlier version 'TOS_UART_ADDR' was used to check whether the message is coming from UART. Since there was no such address defined in tinyos2, a flag 'is Message FromUart' is added in QueryMessage. This flag was then used to check whether the message was arriving from UART. Also, 'TOS_LOCAL_ADDRESS' which gives the node id of mote does not exist and is replaced by 'call AMPacket.address( )'.

h) The TOS_msg data structure which was used for representing the packet to be transmitted over the network has changed to message_t [15] data structure.

i) TinyOS 1.x used to assume that the network byte order of the PC and the motes compiler is the same, which actually used to be in case of many platforms. E.g. it is little endian for the mica, micaz motes and the intel PC machines. But to remove this platform dependency, TinyOS 2.x explicitly mentions the endianess of all its data structures to network byte order. e.g. The parameter 'uint8_t data[]' of data structure 'message_t' used for sending messages over the radio changes to 'nx_uint8_t data[]'

Adding nx_ to the variable data type explicitly states its endianess to be big endian. So, because of this endianess mismatch, all the data structures of TinyDB backend were converted to network byte order.

j) In TinyDB1, a query was broadcasted when front-end needed to send it to serial port. Optimization was done in TinyDB2 by unicasting the query to serial port.

k) The 'for' clause of query was masked in TinyDB1. It is now propagated to the nodes and each node keeps a count of the epochs of readings. When the count exceeds the parameter defined by 'for' clause, the query is deleted.

Other porting issues consisted of syntax changes. Some of the syntax changes include header file inclusion, syntax of debug (dbg) statements and conversion of 'result_t' data type into 'error_t'. [16] enlists some of such changes in TinyOS2.x.

6   Testing the Ported TinyDB 2.x

TinyDB2.x has been tested on the *linear topology* of 4 nodes and for *Tree topology* as shown in figure 5.

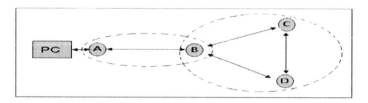

Fig. 5. Sensor network used for testing TinyDB 2.x. Bi-directional arrows show nodes communicating with each other. Dashed eclipses are used to mark the nodes that can communicate with each other.

Testing the tree topology ensured proper functioning of CTP after being plugged in TinyDB. TinyDB2.x was tested to satisfy the case, in the discussed farm scenario. If the farmer wants to collect the temperature of a particular farm area denoted by node-id, periodically, and that too FOR a particular time period only. This was done by mentioning farm area as node-id, periodic interval as epoch duration and time period as number of epochs, resulting into the following query:

select temp, nodeid where nodeid=1 epoch duration 1024 for 10'

7   Conclusion

This paper achieves two different goals. First, it presents an analysis of working of a query processing system in sensor networks and second, it shows the changes that were required in making TinyDB compatible with TinyOS2.x. The ported TinyDB facilitates the new direction of research at the boundary of database systems and sensor networks. It can provide TinyOS2.x users a much simplified approach of data collection. Users do not require knowing nesC language to program TinyOS running motes. The nodes do not need to be reprogrammed for changing the parameter to be sensed, once deployed.

Future work. Due to energy conservative protocols adopted by TinyOS2.x, TinyDB2 is expected give better network lifetime than TinyDB1. We aim to test it by integrating TinyDB with PowerTossim-Z [17], an energy modeling for TinyOS applications. We also aim to provide a method to configure underlying MAC protocols parameters (like sleep period, time slot duration, beacon period etc) through SQL like queries using TinyDB. This will facilitate a user in configuring his application to achieve maximum network lifetime, without requiring knowing about MAC protocols.

References

1. Gay, D., Levis, P., Handziski, V., Hui, J., Wolisz, A.: TinyOS 2.0: A wireless sensor Network operating system,
   `http://www.tinyos.net/tinyos2.x/apps/AntiTheft/tutorial-slides.ppt`
2. Dunkels, A., Gronvall, B., Voigt, T.: Contiki - A Lightweight and Flexible Operating System for Tiny Networked Sensors. In: Proceedings of the 29th Annual IEEE International Conference on Local Computer Networks, LCN, November 16-18. IEEE Computer Society, Washington, DC (2004)
3. Bhatti, S., Carlson, J., Shucker, B., Gruenwald, C., Torgerson, A., Han, R.: MANTIS OS: an embedded multithreaded operating system for wireless micro sensor platforms. Mobile Network Appl. 10, 4 (2005)
4. Pathak, A., Prasanna, V.K.: Energy-efficient task mapping for data-driven sensor network macroprogramming. In: Nikoletseas, S.E., Chlebus, B.S., Johnson, D.B., Krishnamachari, B. (eds.) DCOSS 2008. LNCS, vol. 5067, pp. 516–524. Springer, Heidelberg (2008)
5. Gummadi, R., Gnawali, O., Govindan, R.: Macro-programming wireless sensor networks using kairos. In: Prasanna, V.K., Iyengar, S.S., Spirakis, P.G., Welsh, M. (eds.) DCOSS 2005. LNCS, vol. 3560, pp. 126–140. Springer, Heidelberg (2005)
6. Newton, R., Morrisett, G., Welsh, M.: The regiment macroprogramming system. In: IPSN 2007: Proceedings of the 6th International Conference on Information Processing in Sensor Networks, pp. 489–498. ACM, New York (2007)
7. Awan, A., Jagannathan, S., Grama, A.: Macroprogramming hetero-geneous sensor networks using cosmos. In: EuroSys 2007: Proceedings of the 2nd ACM SIGOPS/EuroSys European Conference on Computer Systems 2007, pp. 159–172. ACM, New York (2007)
8. Madden, S., Hellerstein, J.M.: Distributing queries over low-power wireless sensor networks. In: SIGMOD 2002 (2002)
9. Yao, Y., Gehrke, J.: The cougar approach to in-network query processing in sensor networks. ACM SIGMOD Record 31(3) (September 2002)
10. Madden, S., Al, E.: TinyDB: An acquisitional query processing system for sensor networks. ACM Trans. Database Systems 30 (2005)
11. Gay, D., Levis, P.R., Welsh, M., Brewer, E., Culler, D.: The nesC language: A holistic approach to networked embedded systems. In: Proceedings of the ACM SIGPLAN 2003 Conference on Programming Language Design and Implementation, PLDI 2003, San Diego, California, USA, June 09-11. ACM, New York (2003)
12. Yao, Y., Gehrke, J.: Query Processing for Sensor Networks. In: Proceedings of the 2003 CIDR Conference (2003)
13. Trigoni, N., Yao, Y., Demers, A., Gehrke, J.: Multi-query Optimization for Sensor Networks. Technical Report TR2005-1989, Cornell University (2005)
14. Gnawali, O., Fonseca, R., Jamieson, k., Moss, D., Lewis, P.: Collection Tree Protocol. In: Proceedings of the 7th ACM Conference on Embedded Networked Sensor Systems (November 2009)
15. Lewis, P.: TEP 111 – message_t,
    `http://www.tinyos.net/tinyos-2.x/doc/html/tep111.html`
16. Azim, T., Levis, P.: Porting TinyOS 1.x Code to TinyOS 2.0. Computer Systems Laboratory, Stanford University, Stanford, CA 94305 (October 2006)
17. Perla, E., Catháin, A.Ó., Carbajo, R.S.: PowerTOSSIM z: Realistic Energy Modelling for Wireless Sensor Network Environments. In: Proceedings of the 3nd ACM Workshop on Performance Monitoring and Measurement of Heterogeneous Wireless and Wired Networks. ACM, New York (2008)

Convolutional Coded Selected Mapping Technique for Reducing the PAPR of OFDM Signal

Seema Verma[1], Pawan Sharma[2], Neha Garg[2], and Richa Aggarwal[2]

[1] Electronics and Communication Engineering Department, Banasthali University,
Rajasthan, India
[2] Department of Electronics and Communication Engineering,
Bhagwan Parshuram Institute of Technology, Rohini, New Delhi, India
pawan061971@yahoo.co.in

Abstract. OFDM is a promising broadband technique. However, the implementation disadvantage of OFDM is high peak to average power ratio (PAPR). Selective Mapping (SLM) is an effective method for reducing PAPR in OFDM. The main drawback of this technique is that, it requires side information to be transmitted, which results in some data rate loss. A new modified technique based on SLM using convolution code without side information is presented in this paper. By considering, the example of OFDM with BPSK modulation, simulation results shows that this method performs well in reducing PAPR without the need of any side information.

Keywords: Orthogonal Frequency Division Multiplexing (OFDM), Peak-to-Average-Power-Ratio (PAPR), Selective Mapping (SLM), Complementary Cummulative Distribution Function (CCDF).

1 Introduction

Orthogonal frequency-division multiplexing (OFDM) is a multicarrier modulation technique that can afford high speed transmission and is necessary in the next-generation mobile radio communication system. It has good performance in spectral efficiency and can overcome the effects of frequency selective fading. By transmitting the signal simultaneously across multiple orthogonal sub channels, the system's robustness is improved [1]. OFDM has been adopted for many standards, such as IEEE 802.11a, IEEE 802.11g, IEEE 802.16, HIPERLAN 2, Digital Audio Broadcast, Digital Video Broadcast, and so on. Not only in wireless system, but also in the wired environment, we can see OFDM, such as Discrete Multitone (DMT) in Asymmetric Digital Subscriber Lines (ADSL).

One of the major drawbacks of OFDM system has been its high Peak-to-Average Power Ratio (PAPR). The high PAPR brings the OFDM signal distortion in the non-linear region of high power amplifier (HPA) and the signal distortion induces the degradation of bit error rate (BER). Moreover, to prevent spectral growth of the multicarrier signal in the form of intermodulation among subcarriers and out-of-band radiation, the transmit power amplifier has to be operated in its linear region [2]. If the

D.C. Wyld et al. (Eds.): NeCoM/WeST/WiMoN 2011, CCIS 197, pp. 307–313, 2011.
© Springer-Verlag Berlin Heidelberg 2011

HPA is not operated in linear region with large power back-offs, it is impossible to keep the out-of-band power below the specified limits. This situation leads to very inefficient amplification and expensive transmitters. Therefore, it has been important and necessary to research on the characteristics of the PAPR, including its distribution and reduction, in OFDM systems, in order to utilize the technical features of the OFDM.

There have been two sorts of approaches to deal with PAPR of OFDM, one includes amplitude clipping [3], clipping and filtering [4], coding [5], active constellation extension (ACE) [6]; and the other one, which can be regarded as multiple signal representation technique, contains partial transmit sequence (PTS) [7], selected mapping (SLM) [8], erasure pattern selection (EPS) [9] and interleaving [10]. The latter type is also called probabilistic method, and attracts most of the attention. The character of this kind of methods is not to eliminate PAPR completely, but to reduce the probability of its occurrence. Selected mapping (SLM) is one of the probabilistic methods with good performance in PAPR reduction. In traditional SLM, the data block is rotated by a set of different phase sequences and generates candidates with the same size and information. The candidate with the lowest PAPR is selected for transmission. SLM is proposed by [8], in which the concept of SLM and the probability of $PAPR > PAPR_0$ is given. Quite a number of papers study the SLM performance, complexity [11], and improvements [12]. [13] investigates SLM combining with coding, this has become an important branch in SLM study [14]. The optimality condition of SLM is derived in [15], which gives a very simple conclusion.

In this paper, we investigate the feasibility of the combination of convolution coding and SLM to produce the OFDM with good performance both in spectral efficiency and PAPR. The analysis and simulation results support this try.

The literature is organized as follows: in Section 2, PAPR Problem and SLM Scheme is defined. Section 3 presents proposed scheme. The simulations are shown in Section 4, and the conclusion is given in Section 5.

2 PAPR Problem and SLM Scheme

In the discrete time domain, an OFDM signal x_n of N subcarriers can be expressed as

$$x_n = \frac{1}{N} \sum_{k=0}^{N-1} X_k \, e^{j2\pi kn/N} \quad , \quad 0 \le n \le N - 1 \tag{1}$$

Where X_k, k = 0,1,2,3....., N-1, are input symbols modulated by BPSK, QPSK or QAM and n is the discrete time index.

The PAPR of an OFDM signal is defined as the ratio of the maximum to the average power of the signal, as follows

$$PAPR(x) = 10 \, log_{10} \frac{max\{|x_n|^2\}}{E\{|x|^2\}} , \quad 0 \le n \le N - 1 \tag{2}$$

Where E{.} denotes the expected value operation and $x = [x_1, x_2, x_3, \ldots \ldots x_{N-1}]^T$

As to the discrete-time signals, since symbol-spaced sampling may sometimes miss some of the signal peaks, signal samples are obtained by oversampling by a factor of L to better approximate the true PAPR. Oversampled time-domain samples are usually obtained by LN-point IFFT of the data block with $(L-1)N$ zero-padding. It is shown in [2] that $L = 4$ is sufficient to capture the peaks.

When the OFDM signal with high PAPR passes through a non-linear device, (power amplifier working in the saturation region), the signal will suffer significant non-linear distortion [16]. This non-linear distortion will result in in-band distortion and out-of-band radiation. The in-band distortion causes system performance degradation and the out-of-band radiation causes adjacent channel interference (ACI) that affects systems working in the neighbour bands. To lessen the signal distortion, it requires a linear power amplifier with large dynamic range. However, this linear power amplifier has poor efficiency and is so expensive. Obviously, the distribution of PAPR bears stochastic characteristics in a practical OFDM system. Usually, Complementary Cumulative Distribution Function (CCDF) can be used to evaluate the performance of any PAPR reduction schemes, given by [17]

$$CCDF(N, PAPR_0) = 1 - (1 - e^{-PAPR_0})^N \qquad (3)$$

In the traditional SLM approach, U statistically-independent phase sequences, say, $P^{(u)} = [P_0^{(u)}, P_1^{(u)}, P_2^{(u)}, \ldots\ldots P_{N-1}^{(u)}]^T$ are generated, where $P_k^{(u)} = \exp(j\Phi_k^{(u)})$, $\Phi_k^{(u)} \in [0, 2\pi]$, , $k = 0,1,2,\ldots\ldots, N-1$, $u = 1,2,3,\ldots\ldots, U$. Then the data block $X = [X_0, X_1, X_2, \ldots\ldots X_{N-1}]^T$ is multiplied component-wise with each one of U different phase sequence $P^{(u)}$, resulting in a set of U different data blocks $X^u = [X_0 P_0^{(u)}, X_1 P_1^{(u)}, X_2 P_2^{(u)}, X_3 P_3^{(u)}, \ldots X_{N-1} P_{N-1}^{(u)}]^T$, $u = 1, 2, 3,\ldots, U$. Then, all U alternative data blocks (one of the alternative subcarrier sequences must be the unchanged original one) are transformed into time domain to get transmitted symbols x^u, $u = 1,2,3,\ldots\ldots,U$ by IFFT, where x^u, $u = 1,2,3,\ldots\ldots,U$ are defined as the candidate signals. Finally, the one with the minimum PAPR is selected for transmitting, shown in Fig. 1.

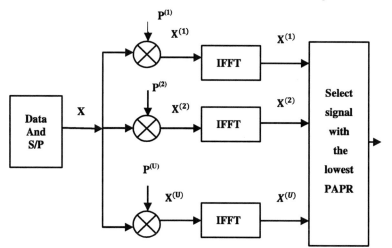

Fig. 1. The block diagram of SLM scheme

At the side of receiver, in order to recover the received signals successfully, the side information is required. This information must be transmitted accompanying with the transmitted signal. When binary symbols are used, $[log_2 U]$ bits are required to represent this side information [2, 18], where operation [.] rounds the elements to the nearest integers toward infinity.

3   Convolutional Coded SLM Using BPSK Modulation

The proposed technique is a modified selective mapping using convolutional codes to generate candidate blocks for transmission with error correcting capability and without explicit side information. In this technique, U statistically independent alternative sequences, which carry same information, are generated, and the sequence with the lowest PAPR is selected for transmission. The probability that the lowest PAPR exceeds a certain threshold $PAPR_0$ is given by

$$Pr\{PAPR > PAPR_0\} = (1 - (1 - e^{-PAPR_0})^N)^U$$

Pr {•} is called complementary cumulative distribution function (ccdf) PAPR. In [19], these sequences are generated by inserting different dummy bits at the beginning of the data. Then all of the sequences are sent into Turbo encoder.

Convolutional codes are generated more simply than Turbo codes. It encodes K bits information into N bits, and this N bits are not only related to current K bits but also related to former (L-1)*N bits, where L is the constraint length. Fig. 1 shows a convolutional encoder with code rate = ½. Viterbi decoding algorithm, which was presented by Viterbi in 1967 [20], is chosen as decoding scheme.

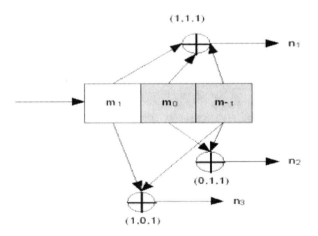

Fig. 2. Convolutional encoder with code rate = 1/2

In this scheme, we use convolutional encoder with code rate = ½, constraint length = 7 to generate different sequences, and at the beginning of each sequence different dummy bits are inserted. Fig.3 shows transmitter side of the system. The first block inserts m dummy bits in the data block and then data block is convolutionally encoded. The encoded data is modulated using BPSK modulation. U different sequences are generated in this scheme where U = 2^m and m is no. of dummy bits inserted. The selector chooses the sequence with the lowest PAPR for transmission among all sequences. Unlike the traditional SLM, to acquire the right data, the receiver only need expunge the dummy bits after decoding without any side information.

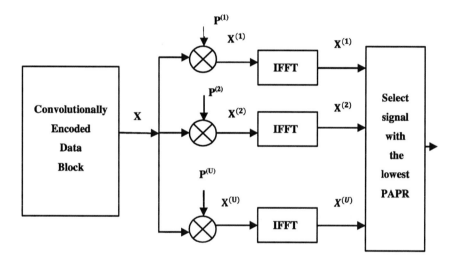

Fig. 3. Convolutional Coded OFDM system Transmitter

4   Simulation Results

In this section, we provide some simulation results of the proposed scheme. The number of subcarriers N is 128 and the constellation - is BPSK. The industry-standard 1/2 rate convolutional code [133 171] is used and the constraint length of this code is 7.

Fig.4 shows the PAPR reduction performance of the proposed scheme. Here, we have used different values of U. U=2^m , m denotes the number of dummy bits inserted and U represents the number of sequences generated of each data block. The figure shows that PAPR has been reduced by 1.4 dB (approx.) with proposed scheme as compared to original OFDM with U=32.

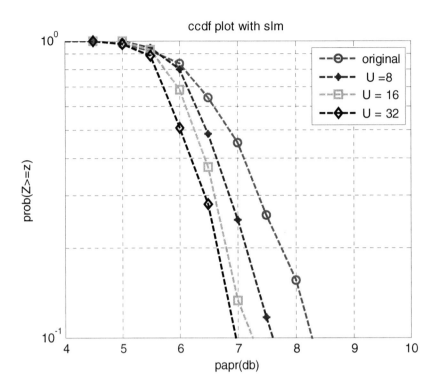

Fig. 4. CCDF of OFDM codes of length 128

5 Conclusion

In this paper, we proposed a PAPR reduction method for coded OFDM system. This scheme is based on the SLM technique. A convolutional code, which is often used in OFDM systems as a channel code, functions as a scrambler and by inserting several dummy bits, it can generate sufficiently different candidate OFDM signals. It is suitable for space-time coded OFDM systems with a convolutional code. Simulation results prove that our scheme can reduce the PAPR of the transmitted OFDM signals effectively.

References

1. Bingham, J.A.C.: Multicarrier modulation for data transmission: An idea whose time has come. IEEE Commun. Mag. 28(5), 5–14 (1990)
2. Jiang, T., Wu, Y.: An Overview: Peak-to-Average Power Ratio Reduction Techniques for OFDM Signals. IEEE Transactions on Broadcasting 54(2), 257–268 (2008)
3. O'Neill, R., Lopes, L.B.: Envelope variations and spectral splatter in clipped multicarrier signals. In: Proc. IEEE PIMRC 1995, Toronto, Canada, pp. 71–75 (1995)

4. Li, X., Cimini Jr., L.J.: Effect of clipping and filtering on the performance of OFDM. IEEE Commun. Lett. 2(5), 131–133 (1998)

5. Jones, E., Wilkinson, T.A., Barton, S.K.: Block coding scheme for reduction of peak to mean envelope power ratio of multicarrier transmission scheme. Elect. Lett. 30(22), 2098–2099 (1994)

6. Krongold, S., Jones, D.L.: PAR reduction in OFDM via active constellation extension. IEEE Trans. Broadcast. 49(3), 258–268 (2003)

7. Muller, S.H., Huber, J.B.: OFDM with reduced peak-to-average power ratio by optimum combination of partial transmit sequences. Elect. Lett. 33(5), 368–369 (1997)

8. Bauml, R.W., Fisher, R.F.H., Huber, J.B.: Reducing the peak- to-average power ratio of multicarrier modulation by selected mapping. Elect. Lett. 32(22), 2056–2057 (1996)

9. Valbonesi, L., Ansari, R.: Frame-based approach for peak-to-average power ratio reduction in OFDM. IEEE Trans. Commun. 54(9), 1604–1613 (2006)

10. Jayalath, D.S., Tellambura, C.: Reducing the peak-to-average power ratio of orthogonal frequency division multiplexing signal through bit or symbol interleaving. Elect. Lett. 36(13), 1161–1163 (2000)

11. Lim, W., et al.: A new SLM OFDM scheme with low complexity for PAPR reduction. IEEE Sig. Proc. Lett. 12(2), 93–96 (2005)

12. Han, S.H., Lee, J.H.: Modified selected mapping technique for PAPR reduction of coded OFDM signal. IEEE Trans. Broadcast. 50(3), 335–341 (2004)

13. Breiling, M., Muller, S.H., Huber, J.B.: SLM peak-power reduction without explicit side information. IEEE Commun. Lett. 5(6), 239–241 (2001)

14. Yue, G., Wang, X.: A hybrid PAPR reduction scheme for coded OFDM. IEEE Trans. Wireless Commun. 5(10), 2712–2722 (2006)

15. Zhou, G.T., Peng, L.: Optimality condition for selected mapping in OFDM. IEEE Trans. Sig. Proc. 54(8), 3159–3165 (2006)

16. Tellambura, C.: Computation of the continuous-time PAR of an OFDM signal with BPSK subcarriers. IEEE Commun. Letter 5(5), 185–187 (2001)

17. Ochiai, H., Imai, H.: On the distribution of the peak-to-average power ratio in OFDM signals. IEEE Trans. Commun. 49, 282–289 (2001)

18. Breiling, H., Muller-Weinfurtner, S.H., Huber, J.B.: SLM Peak-Power Reduction without Explicit Side Information. IEEE Communication Letters 5(5), 239–241 (2001)

19. Abouda, A.A.: PAPR reduction of OFDM signal using Turbo coding and selective mapping. In: Proc. of NORSIG, pp. 239–241 (2004)

20. Viterbi, A.J.: Error bounds for convolutional codes and an asymptotically optimal decoding algorithm. IEEE Trans. on Information Theory, 260–269 (1967)

Energy Efficient Time Synchronization in WSN for Critical Infrastructure Monitoring

Aravinda S. Rao[1], Jayavardhana Gubbi[1], Tuan Ngo[2],
James Nguyen[2], and Marimuthu Palaniswami[1]

[1] ISSNIP, Dept. of Electrical and Electronic Engineering, The University of
Melbourne, Vic - 3010, Australia
{sridhara,jgl,palani}@unimelb.edu.au
[2] Infrastructure Protection Research Group, Dept. of Civil and Environmental
Engineering, The University of Melbourne, Vic - 3010, Australia
dtngo@unimelb.edu.au, james.idt@gmail.com

Abstract. Wireless Sensor Networks (WSN) based Structural Health
Monitoring (SHM) is becoming popular in analyzing the life of critical
infrastructure such as bridges on a continuous basis. For most of the
applications, data aggregation requires high sampling rate. A need for
accurate time synchronization in the order of $0.6-9$ μs every few minutes
is necessary for data collection and analysis. Two-stage energy-efficient
time synchronization is proposed in this paper. Firstly, the network is divided into clusters and a head node is elected using Low-Energy Adaptive
Clustering Hierarchy based algorithm. Later, multiple packets of different
lengths are used to estimate the delay between the elected head and the
entire network hierarchically at different levels. Algorithmic scheme limits error to 3-hop worst case synchronization error. Unlike earlier energy-
efficient time synchronization schemes, the achieved results increase the
lifetime of the network.

Keywords: Time Synchronization, Wireless Sensor Networks, Critical
Infrastructure Monitoring, Structural Health Monitoring, Energy Efficient.

1 Introduction

Time synchronization in WSN has been an important research area over the
past decade. Numerous protocols, benchmarked algorithms and approaches have
been proposed to reduce the synchronization error and also being implemented
to test their viaibility for WSN; Reference Broadcast Synchronization (RBS) [2],
Timing-sync Protocol for Sensor Networks (TPSN) [3], Flooding Time Synchronization Protocol (FTSP) [10], Lightweight Time Synchronization for Sensor
Networks (LTS) [4], Tiny-sync [15] and Mini-sync [15] are widely used.

Time synchronization is an inherent problem in any network. The time between any two networked computers differs due to clock drift and clock offset.
Often the crystal oscillator, provider of appropriate timing signals, is observed
to be drifted from its normal specified frequency. The clock instability is caused

D.C. Wyld et al. (Eds.): NeCoM/WeST/WiMoN 2011, CCIS 197, pp. 314–323, 2011.
© Springer-Verlag Berlin Heidelberg 2011

by many environmental factors, chiefly attributing to temperature variation [13]. The frequency offset is the difference in clock timing between two clocks at any particular instant. As the frequency of the crystal varies, the clock offset varies i.e. offset increases or decreases relative to another clock.

Physical time plays a crucial role in WSN application for Critical Infrastructure Monitoring (CIM) [1,8]. Multiple nodes possessing identical time-stamps of an event are essential. The significance of the physical time with respect to WSNs are detailed in [12] as : (a) interaction between a sensor network and the observer, (b) interaction between nodes, and (c) interface between nodes and the real world. Absence of real-time clock on WSN motes have given rise to software schemes to synchronize their on-board clocks. The Internet uses Network Time Protocol (NTP) [11] having accuracy in the order of nano to pico seconds which can be adapted where there is no power constraint. Numerous solutions exist in literature such as software clocks, unidirectional synchronization, round trip synchronization and reference broadcasting having many advantages and disadvantages; schemes based on high-rate data collection are shown to have decreased failure rate in synchronizing [12]. Power-constrained frequent synchronization is required to tackle drifting, a major contributor to error, with an accuracy of 0.6 to 9 μs for modal analysis [9]. A 5 ms drift in 6 s period was reported by Wang et al. [17] which is on the higher side of acceptability.

In this paper, an energy-efficient time synchronization algorithm is proposed using few existing algorithms, but combines them uniquely to achieve the desired goal. At first, it uses Low-Energy Adaptive Clustering Hierarchy (LEACH) for dividing the network into clusters based on nodes' available energy [5]. Later, a new algorithm is proposed for synchronization. This paper is organized as follows: Section 2 gives brief description of existing protocols, Section 3 contains the proposed approach towards time synchronization followed by Section 4 with results and discussion, and conclusions are given in Section 5.

2   Related Work

There has been substantial amount of work carried out in time synchronization in general [16]. Most of the work has been done in early stage of WSN research and not many of them have been tailored to specific application such as critical infrastructure monitoring. As a result, energy has not been considered as a critical parameter while designing a time synchronization algorithm. As pointed out by Krishnamurthy et al. [9], there is a need to synchronize the clock more frequently than originally intended and this will have a bearing on lifetime on the network. In this context, a few time synchronization methods proposed in literature have been identified to be very useful and are described below.

Reference Broadcast Synchronization (RBS), a pioneering work, is a receiver-to-receiver synchronization in the field. The main drawback of this approach is, as and when the number of receivers grow, the amount of message exchange climbs up [2] which is unsuitable for large networks. Flooding Time Synchronization Protocol (FTSP) floods the network with synchronization packets to the neighbors [10]. However, FTSP cannot compensate the propagation delay.

There have been a few other algorithms proposed similar to FTSP, however, this will not be very energy efficient [16]. Another very popular method on which a lot of methods have been developed is Timing-sync Protocol for Sensor Networks (TPSN) [3]. TPSN has two phases: firstly, during the level discovery phase, the protocol forms a hierarchical network of different levels. Node with level 0 forms the top level followed by level 1, 2 etc. Node in the level i communicates with at least a node in the level above (i-1) it. During the second phase (also called as synchronization phase), the node at level 0 (root node) initiates the synchronization phase using constrained flooding [16,3]. In case of message transmission from a node of higher level, though a node at non-immediate level overhears the message from higher levels, it only synchronizes to the level above it. Lightweight Time Synchronization for Sensor Networks (LTS) uses three messages to synchronize a pair of nodes [4] at the pairwise synchronization stage. It is extended from single-hop synchronization to centralized multi-hop network. The re-synchronization rate in LTS is dependent on the depth of the tree. Also, a bounded-clock drift is assumed and the drifts of all the nodes are considered as equal. Although they discuss distributed multi-hop, energy efficiency is not accomplished as the algorithm focussed only on time synchronization. Shahzad et al. [14] propose EETS algorithm which combines RBS and TPSN for achieving better energy efficiency. Although this improves energy efficiency, in large networks with multi-hops reaching up to 8-10 levels, the synchronization error is higher than required for critical infrastructure monitoring. More recently, Kim et al. [7] have developed an algorithm by reducing the number of packets exchanged thereby conserving power. This again is a combination of RBS, TPSN and LTS methods but reduces the number of packets exchanged. Again, the topology used is identical to TPSN and the best achievable error rate is affected by the number of hops. The second stage of the proposed algorithm uses the above class of algorithms which is a combination of hierarchical levels as TPSN and pairwise synchronization phase of LTS in synchronizing the time after energy efficient clusters are created in the first phase using LEACH based approach. The approach is described in the following section.

3   Approach

Energy efficient time synchronization is carried out in two stages: (a) dividing the network into clusters in an energy-efficient manner using LEACH [5] and (b) synchronizing the time within the cluster using multi-level pairwise synchronization. LEACH elects a cluster head periodically based on the highest energy available live node. The chance of becoming a cluster head is rotated randomly ensuring that energy from a single node is not drained [5]. Upon cluster head election, pairwise transmission range based multilevel, hierarchical sub-clusters are formed in the immediate vicinity of the parent node. Variable-length packets are used to determine the nondeterministic latency between sender and the receiver and is compensated before transmission. The algorithm ensures that the time of a child node is same as that of the its parent. The elected four cluster heads and the cluster formation is pictorially represented in Figure 1. According to LEACH

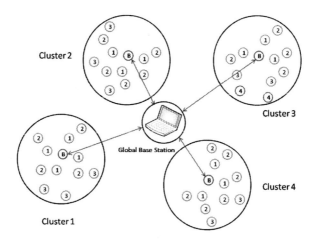

Fig. 1. Schematic of cluster formation using LEACH. Numbers within the node represent levels. B is the chosen cluster-head in any given round.

algorithm [5], the optimal number of nodes to be cluster heads was chosen to be $\hat{N} = 5\%$. In case of the proposed algorithm, as the number of nodes in any cluster is limited to 12 (empirically chosen), $\hat{N} = (\text{Total Number of Nodes})/12 + 1$ is chosen for CIM. The second part of time synchronizing procedure is divided into four phases as explained in the following subsections.

3.1 Initiation

Let there be 'N' nodes neighboring to base station node. Out of 'N' nodes, only 'P' of them are within the communication range of base station and the remaining (N-P) nodes are not. All nodes in the network are switched ON before any communication or network activity is initiated. Node B initiates its routine by synchronizing its time with the base station i.e. with the computer ensuring database connection. It should be noted that the nodes in the topology are placed such that it is in the communication range of at least one node.

3.2 Registration

The process of adding a new node to the topology is called as 'Registration'. Each node has its own ID and is uniquely identifiable. For discussion, let us consider $N = 2$. Nodes in the transmission range of B are therefore 1 and 2 and vice-versa. Therefore, the transmission power for both parent (B) and child nodes (1 and 2) are the same. After initiation process, B broadcasts a READY signal to inform its neighbors that it is ready to accept REQUEST from child nodes. Now, upon hearing B's broadcast signal, both 1 and 2 will send a REQUEST signals. When a READY signal is sent, B will wait for t_w seconds to hear from the nodes. Any message received after t_w is discarded. Suppose, B received both the requests from 1 and 2, then B will serve first node 1 followed by 2 in a Time Division Multiple Access (TDMA) slotted fashion. Nodes 1 and 2 are waiting for the COMMAND signal from B. Nodes 1 and 2 will not proceed further until they receive any signal from B.

3.3 Calculating Nondeterministic Latency

Upon receiving and processing the COMMAND signal from B, node 1 will wait for the t_{start}. At t_{start}, it will send message $M1$ to B. It is repeated for n times at every t_{repeat} intervals. Packets are time stamped at physical layer of node 1 and are stored in B as and when received. Next, B will send a COMMAND signal with $M2 > M1$ i.e. the message length greater than the previous one. At this time, B records node 1's data. Let δt_n be the time difference between consecutive packets arrived at the base station from a particular node. Let L_{M1} be the message length of $M1$ and the time stamp of the packets' arrival be $t_1...t_n$. Time difference between packets can be calculated as in equation 1, where n is the packet arrived at time t_n. B calculates the average time d_{M1} required by a packet of size $M1$ to reach base station due to send time, access time, propagation time and receive time and is given by equation 2. Let L_{M2} be the length of M2. Now, B sends a second COMMAND signal with $M2 > M1$. Equations 1 and 3 are calculated for $M2$. Then essentially, the time required for packet of size $L_{M2} - L_{M1}$ to be constructed, transferred and received from node 1 (or node 2) to B is given by equation 4. Now B sends t_{Byte} in a REGISTRATION_COMPLETE message to node 1. B accepts packets strictly from level 1, and level 1 nodes accept data from level 2 only, identical to TPSN [3]. After this, node 1 sends a READY command to its neighbors. At the same time, B sends a COMMAND signal to node 2 and the process continues. At the end of REGISTRATION_COMPLETE with 2, B sends an ACCEPT command to accept data from 1 and 2. Node 2 continues to act as parent and starts broadcasting READY signal to its neighbors (child nodes).

$$\delta t_n = |t_n - t_{n-1}| \tag{1}$$

$$d_{M1} = \frac{\sum_{i=1}^{n} \delta t_n}{n} \tag{2}$$

$$d_{M2} = \frac{\sum_{i=1}^{n} \delta t_n}{n} \tag{3}$$

$$t_{byte} = \frac{(d_{M2} - d_{M1})}{(L_{M2} - L_{M1})} \tag{4}$$

3.4 Time Synchronization

After every T seconds predetermined by application and the frequency of data collection, B multi-casts current time to all the registered nodes. T is calculated using equation 5, where t_i is the time required for a ith node to be registered,

t_{accept} is the time for accepting data from all the registered nodes. The typical tree structure formed during time synchronization after selecting the cluster head is illustrated in Figure 2.

$$T = \frac{\sum_{i=1}^{N} t_i}{N} + t_{accept} \tag{5}$$

The term $\frac{\sum_{i=1}^{N} t_i}{N}$ is required if a node child node fails and wants to re-register.

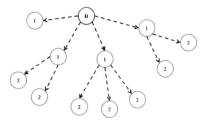

Fig. 2. Hierarchical level creation during proposed second stage of time synchronization

In (5), first part is 'Registration time' and the second part is 'Data acceptance time' in the proposed scheme. Additionally, if there is a new node, then it can register itself in the first part and send data subsequently. In general, T should be selected such that allowances are made for any new node to be added.

3.5   Packets Required to Synchronize a Node

Determining number of packets 'n' in the COMMAND phase is a two-step process. During the first step, B sends COMMAND with n=5. The maximum tolerable synchronization error (E) between two nodes is specified by the user as t_E. During the second step, the node calculates the δE_n and the average of δE_n as in equations 6 and 7 respectively. If δE_{avg} is more than predetermined value δt_E, then B raises its bar and requests more packets during M2 acquisition, otherwise M2 will have 'n' packets as well; B tries to find the delay due to variable-length packet size.

$$\delta E_n = \delta t_n - t_{repeat} \tag{6}$$

$$\delta E_{avg} = \frac{\sum_{i=1}^{n} \delta E_n}{n} \tag{7}$$

4   Results and Discussion

The proposed energy-efficient time synchronization algorithm can be categorized as peer-to-peer, externally synchronized, deterministic, sender-to-sender and clock-corrected approach analogous with table 2 of [16]. It gives an added advantage of selectively using the node head for energy efficiency. Having presented the simulation results in this paper, in future, we plan to validate the proposed algorithm on iMote2 platform and the implementation is underway. At the end of this section, theoretical energy consumption and effect of packet length with respect to iMote2 platform are presented.

LEACH is a very popular clustering-based routing protocol, has been shown to minimize global energy usage by distributing the load among nodes [5]. Theoretically and experimentally, it has been shown that the lifetime of the network is increased 3 times compared to a static topology. In the first stage of the proposed time synchronization, LEACH based clustering is used for dividing the network into clusters. From the results presented in [2,4,3,10], it is very clear that the clock error increases as the number of hops increase. Using cluster-based step at the first stage, ensures that the number of hops required in the second stage of the algorithm will never cross three levels (12 nodes). Hence, the maximum error in time synchronization by the proposed algorithm is the worst case 3-hop error that of TPSN and LTS. According to Krishnamurthy *et al.* [9], anything less than 10 μs error for 30 minutes duration is acceptable for modal analysis using acceleration sensors. By virtue, the proposed algorithm ensures this criterion. Moreover, the clustering algorithm enables data aggregation using energy-efficient routing apart from time synchronization.

4.1   Simulation Analysis

The experiment was conducted using OMNeT++, a component-based discrete event network simulation package. OMNeT++ offer tools to simulate computer networks, queuing networks, processor architectures and for distributed systems. We used NICTA's Castalia 3.1 framework on top of OMNeT++ 4.1 to simulate WSN scenarios [6]. In particular, for this work, we developed three simulation scenarios with three nodes - one base base station node (N0) and two sink nodes (N1, N2). N0 is the head of the nodes and the time-provider for other two nodes. The experiment was simulated for 10 s, with synchronization period of 1 s each for a total period of 10 s. Start up delay for the nodes were initialized to 0.5 ms. Node N0 waited for N1 and N2 for their reply after sending the initiation (READY) signal. The waiting time (t_w) was kept at 400 ms following the broadcast of READY signal to allow sufficient time to respond. Both N1 and N2 nodes replied with REQUEST signal. After t_w seconds, N0 processed REQUEST in ascending order of the node IDs. Node N0 sent a COMMAND signal to N1 with t_{start}=10 ms, t_{repeat}=10 ms, n=5, M1=5, M2=15. N1 sent messages to N0 after adding current time with t_{start} at t_{repeat} intervals (M1=5, M2=15 bytes of data sent 'n' times). Node N0 calculated δt_n for M1 and M2 separately and then the average of δt_n i.e. $dM1$ and $dM2$. t_{Byte} was calculated using equation 4. Node N0 calculated t_{Byte} and δE_{avg}, and sent the t_{Byte} to N1 as variable-length packet delay with REGISTRATION_COMPLETE signal. After processing nodes N1 by N0, N2 was processed by sending COMMAND signal. Further, after processing N2, node N0 sent ACCEPT signal at start of t_{accept}. In our simulation t_{accept}=0 s as only two sink nodes were considered. At

T = 1 s from the start of the READY signal, N0 multi-casts current time to registered nodes. Following this, N0 sent READY signal for the next round of clock synchronization and this process of synchronization was continued at different levels. We simulated for only one level i.e. between N0 and N1-N2. In this simulation for each time synchronization cycle, nodes N0 and N1 sent REQUESTs and participated in registration; however, during implementation, registration will be done once only. Media Access Control (MAC) layer was bypassed in the simulation environment; radio was in Ideal mode with a transmission power level of 0 dBm and configured to zero interference model; wireless channel was set to have bidirectionally identical signal quality links between nodes. One-hop routing was carried out by application layer. The simulation results are presented for three different scenarios of node placements in order to analyze the efficiency of the proposed algorithm.

- **Scenario 1 - Equidistant nodes:** N1 and N2 with distance equal to 14.14 m from N0 and $t_{repeat} = 10$ ms; for Node N1 t_{Byte} was 8.27 ms, $\delta E_{avg} = 67.989$, and $t_{Byte} = 20.65$ ms for N2, $\delta E_{avg} = 33.933$ was obtained by simulation. Using this, nodes N1 and N2 sent 10 messages every 1 s for ten seconds. The message lengths were 5 and 15 bytes. For the two nodes, the results are summarized in table 1 for seven rounds. The nondeterministic delay associated with size of a packet can be calculated as a correction factor ($t_{Byte}*$ Number Of Bytes) and is applied before packet transmission.

Table 1. Synchronization Errors for Node 1 and Node 2

Round	Node ID	Sync Error (ms)	Node ID	Sync Error (ms)
1	1	41.39	2	99.43
2	1	29.82	2	95.55
3	1	41.34	2	91.72
4	1	37.50	2	91.72
5	1	37.52	2	95.56
6	1	41.34	2	95.56
7	1	37.52	2	95.56

- **Scenario 2 - Unequal distance between nodes:** Distance between N0 and N1 was 14.14 m, and between N0 and N2 was 26.92 m; the results obtained from this simulation were same as Scenario 1, with distance having less impact on nondeterministic latency. This can also be justified by the fact the travel times for radio waves remains nearly unvaried for short distances.
- **Scenario 3 - Synchronization error at different levels:** Suppose level i is the base station level, level $i + n$ is the node at level n, then the error at different levels can be calculated relative to base station level as equation 8, where $tByte_{(i+n)-i}$ is the time required from a byte to be transferred between nodes of level n and i; N_i is the number of bytes to be transferred. The error at level $i + n$ is the cumulative error from level $i + n$ to i.

$$Error_{ni} = \sum_{n}^{i} tByte_{(i+n)-i} * N_i \tag{8}$$

4.2 Energy Consumption

Energy consumed by a node in general is essentially due to two main contributors - Processor and the Radio. During active times, the available energy is utilized (by processor and/or RI) up to or less than their stated absolute maximum rating values. During sleep (or idle) times, the nodes conserve their energy by entering into the low-power modes, in particular, sleep modes deactivate RI. Energy consumed by a node for the purpose of the communication, in general, at any particular instant, is given by equation 9; energy consumed by the main processor of the node is given by equation 10 and the total energy consumed by a node (at any instant of time) is given by equation 11

$$E_{RI} = E_{Receiver} + E_{Sender} + E_{Radio\_Process} \tag{9}$$

$$E_P = E_{Process} * [T_{RadioON} + T_{RadioOFF}] + E_{Sleep} * T_{Sleep} \tag{10}$$

$$E_N = E_{Processor} + E_{RI} \tag{11}$$

From equations 9 and 11, for Imote2, $E_{Pmax} = 97$ mA; $E_{Pmin} = 31.387$ mA; $E_{RImax} = 36.626$ mA; $E_{RImin}=27.5$ mA. Energy expended in sending (E_{send}) and receiving ($E_{Receive}$) a packet are 31 mA and 18.1 mA respectively. For the cluster shown in Figure 2, energy consumed will be 32 w per cycle per cluster. For clusters with different spatial orientation, energy consumption entirely depends on number of clusters in the vicinity of each cluster head.

5 Conclusion

Time synchronization is fundamental to data fusion and henceforth to help detect and/or monitor events. The accuracy of synchronized time among nodes, coupling closely (in time), ameliorates the system's ability to determine an event. Synchronization of time among nodes can be achieved by eliminating nondeterministic delays (send time, access time, propagation time, receive time). Adding to nondeterministic delays, frequency drifts due to clock instabilities and offset due to drifts, contribute to increase in synchronization error or mismatch in clock timings among nodes. Though several algorithms and approaches have been proposed by researchers for time synchronization, this proposed approach is also equally useful for energy-efficient, robust, externally synchronized multi-hop networks.

References

1. Elson, J.: Time Synchronization in Wireless Sensor Networks. Ph.D. thesis, UCLA (2003)
2. Elson, J., Girod, L., Estrin, D.: Fine-grained network time synchronization using reference broadcasts. In: Proceedings of the 5ht Symposium on Operating Systems Design and Implementation (OSDI 2002), vol. 36, pp. 11–19. ACM, New York (2002)
3. Ganeriwal, S., Kumar, R., Srivastava, M.B.: Timing-sync protocol for sensor networks. In: Proceedings of the 1st International Conference on Embedded Networked Sensor Systems (SenSys 2003), pp. 138–149. ACM, New York (2003)
4. Greunen, J.V., Rabaey, J.: Lightweight time synchronization for sensor networks. In: Proceedings of the 2nd ACM International Conference on Wireless Sensor Networks and Applications (WSNA 2003), pp. 11–19. ACM, New York (2003)
5. Heinzelman, W.R., Chandrakasan, A., Balakrishnan, H.: Energy-efficient communication protocol for wireless microsensor networks. In: Proceedings of the 33rd Annual Hawaii International Conference on System Sciences, vol. 2, pp. 1–10. IEEE, Los Alamitos (2000)
6. Castalia, http://castalia.npc.nicta.com.au/ (January 2011 (verified on 6th February 2011))
7. Kim, B.K., Hong, S.H., Hur, K., Eom, D.S.: Energy-efficient and rapid time synchronization for wireless sensor networks. IEEE Transactions on Consumer Electronics 56(4), 2258–2266 (2010)
8. Kim, S.: Wireless Sensor Networks for Structural Health Monitoring. Master's thesis, UC-Berkely (2005)
9. Krishnamurthy, V., Fowler, F., Sazonov, E.: The effect of time synchronisation of wireless sensors on the modal analysis of structures. Smart Materials and Structures 17 (August 2008)
10. Maróti, M., Kusy, B., Simon, G., Lédeczi, Á.: The flooding time synchronization protocol. In: Proceedings of the 2nd International Conference on Embedded Networked Sensor Systems (SenSys 2004), pp. 138–149. ACM, New York (2004)
11. Mills, D.L.: Internet time synchronization: The network time protocol. IEEE Transactions on Communications 39, 1482–1493 (1991)
12. Rmer, K., Blum, P., Meier, L.: Time Synchronization and Calibration in Wireless Sensor Networks. In: Handbook of Sensor Networks: Algorithms and Architectures, pp. 199–237. Wiley and Sons, Chichester (2005)
13. Schmid, T., Charbiwala, Z., Friedman, J., Cho, Y.H., Srivastava, M.B.: Exploiting manufacturing variations for compensating environment-induced clock drift in time synchronization. In: Proceedings of the 2008 ACM SIGMETRICS International Conference on Measurement and Modeling of Computer Systems (SIGMETRICS 2008), pp. 97–108. ACM, New York (2008)
14. Shahzad, K., Ali, A., Gohar, N.: Etsp: An energy-efficient time synchronization protocol for wireless sensor networks. In: 22nd International Conference on Advanced Information Networking and Applications - Workshops (Aina Workshops 2008), pp. 971–976 (2008)
15. Sichitiu, M.L., Veerarittiphan, C.: Simple, accurate time synchronization for wireless sensor networks. In: IEEE Wireless Communications and Networks (WCNC 2003), vol. 2, pp. 1266–1273 (2003)
16. Sundararaman, B., Buy, U., Kshemkayani, A.D.: Clock synchronization for wireless sensor networks: A survey. Ad Hoc Networks 3, 281–323 (2005)
17. Wang, Y., Lynch, J.P., Kae, K.H.: A wireless structural health monitoring system with multithreaded sensing devices. Struct. Infrastruct. Eng. 3, 103–120 (2007)

Agent Based Congestion Control Routing for Mobile Ad-hoc Network

Vishnu Kumar Sharma[1] and Sarita Singh Bhadauria[2]

[1] Department of CSE, JUET, Guna, Madhya Pradesh, India
vishnukumarsharmaphd@gmail.com
[2] Department of Elex, MITS Gwalior, Madhya Pradesh, India
saritamits61@yahoo.co.in

Abstract. In Mobile Ad hoc Networks (MANETs) congestion occurs due to the packet loss and it can be effectively reduced by involving congestion control scheme which includes routing algorithm and a flow control at the network layer. In this paper, we propose to design and develop an agent based congestion control technique for MANETs. In our technique, the information about network congestion is collected and distributed by mobile agents (MA). The nodes are classified into four categories based on its traffic class. The MA measures the queue length of the various traffic classes and the channel contention and estimates the total congestion metric to find the minimum congestion level in the network. The congestion metric is applied in the routing protocol to select the minimum congested route. By simulation results, we show that our proposed technique attains high delivery ratio and throughput with reduced delay when compared with the existing technique.

Keywords: Mobile Ad hoc Networks (MANETs), Mobile Agents (MA), Total Congestion Metric (TCM), Enhanced Distributed Channel Access (EDCA), Transmission opportunity limit (TXOP).

1 Introduction

1.1 Congestion Control in MANETs

The mobile ad hoc network is capable of forming a temporary network, without the need of a central administration or standard support devices available in a conventional network, thus forming an infrastructure-less network. In order to guarantee for the future, the mobile ad hoc networks establishes the networks everywhere. To avoid being an ideal candidate during rescue and emergency operations, these networks do not depend on the irrelevant hardware. These networks build, operate and maintain with the help of constituent wireless nodes. Since these nodes have only a limited transmission range, it depends on its neighboring nodes to forward packets [1].

Congestion takes place in MANETs with limited resources. Packet losses and bandwidth degradation are caused due to congestion, and thus, time and energy is wasted during its recovery. Congestion can be prevented using congestion-aware

D.C. Wyld et al. (Eds.): NeCoM/WeST/WiMoN 2011, CCIS 197, pp. 324–333, 2011.
© Springer-Verlag Berlin Heidelberg 2011

protocol through bypassing the affected links [2]. Severe throughput degradation and massive fairness problems are some of the identified congestion related problems. These problems are incurred from MAC, routing and transport layers [3].Congestion control is the major problem in mobile ad hoc networks which is related to controlling traffic entering into a telecommunication network. To avoid congestive collapse or link capabilities of the intermediate nodes and networks and to reduce the rate of sending packets congestion control is used extensively [4]. End system flow control, network congestion control, network based congestion avoidance, and resource allocation includes the basic techniques for congestion control [5].

The congestion non-adaptive routing protocols, leads to the following difficulties:

- Long delay:
- High overhead:
- Many packet losses: [6].

1.2   Problem Identification and Proposed Solution

As explained in the previous section, congestion adaptive routing has been examined in several studies. Estimating or reviewing the level of activity in the intermediate nodes using load or delay measurement, is the common approach in all the studies mentioned. The favorable path is established based upon the collected information, which helps in avoiding the existing and developing congested nodes. The performance of routing protocols is affected by the service type of the traffic carried by the intermediate nodes. But no research has stated this so far.

Before presenting themselves as aspirant to route traffic to the destination, the MANETs do not take the status of the queues into account, for the route discovery process. Because of this, the newly arriving traffic face long delays, packet drops, and fail to be transmit ahead of the already queuing traffic.

Enhanced performance and better congestion control can be achieved only by considering the routing and the flow control together. This was not done in earlier researches [10]. In this paper, we propose to design and develop an agent based congestion control technique.

2   Related Works

Yung Yi et al [7] have developed a fair hop-by-hop congestion control algorithm with the MAC constraint being imposed in the form of a channel access time constraint, using an optimization-based framework. Umut Akyol et al [8] have studied the problem of jointly performing scheduling and congestion control in mobile adhoc networks so that network queues remain bounded and the resulting flow rates satisfy an associated network utility maximization problem. S.Karunakaran et al [9] have presented a Cluster Based Congestion Control (CBCC) protocol that consists of scalable and distributed cluster-based mechanisms for supporting congestion control in mobile ad hoc networks. Xuyang Wang et al [17] proposed a cross layer hop by hop congestion control scheme to improve TCP performance in multihop wireless networks which coordinates the congestion response across the transport, network, and transport layer protocols. Kazuya Nishimura et al [18] proposed a routing protocol that reduces network congestion for MANET using multi-agents. They use two kinds of agents: Routing Agents to collect information about congestion and to update the routing table at each node, and Message Agents to move using this information.

3 Agent Based Congestion Control

3.1 Protocol Overview

In this paper, we propose to design and develop an agent based congestion control technique. In our technique, the information about network congestion is collected and distributed by mobile agents (MA). Each node has a routing table that stores routing information for every destination. MA starts from every node and moves to an adjacent node at every time. The MA updates the routing table of the node it is visiting.

In our technique, the node is classified in one of the four categories depending on whether the traffic belongs to background, best effort, video or voice AC respectively. Then MA estimates the total congestion metric by calculating the queue length and the channel contention and it is applied to the routing protocol to select the minimum congested route.

3.2 EDCA Mechanism of 802.11e

The Hybrid Coordination Function (HCF) which has been sketched by 802.11e labels two new MAC methods. The PCF and DCF modes have been replaced with HCF controlled channel access (HCCA), and enhanced distributed channel access (EDCA) which provides distributed access supplying service differentiation [11].

An extended version of the legacy DCF mechanism is EDCA. Access Categories (AC) or traffic priority classes like voice, video, best effort and background are defined by EDCA [12]. The access categories prioritize themselves from AC3 to AC0. In general, best effort and background traffic are maintained by AC1 and AC0 and real-time applications like voice or video transmission are maintained by AC2 and AC3 [13]. For the purpose of service differentiation, many MAC constraints vary with priority level chosen for each AC.

For the implementation of the EDCA contention algorithm the four transmission queues are applied with each AC being communicated with the others. The minimum idle delay before contention (AIFS), the Contention Windows (CWmin and CWmax), and the Transmission opportunity limit (TXOP) are the various parameters described here.

In the MAC layer, voice traffic is conveyed through AC3 and the video traffic is conveyed through AC2 in accordance with 802.11e EDCA standard. The AC class differentiation in EDCA is very much useful in providing services to the traffic. Superior servicing is done for high-priority traffic and not much importance is given for low-priority traffic. The contention parameters of EDCA are not able to adapt to the network conditions, in spite of the delay sensitivity of real-time traffic taken into account. This leads to limitations in the QOS improvement [14].

ACs pause for diverse values of Arbitration Interframe Space (AIFS) and AIFSi is computed by,

$$AIFSi = SIFS + AIFSNi \times SlotTime$$

where *AIFSi* is a positive integer which is greater than one, *AIFSNi* is the AC-specific AIFS number; SIFS and Slot Time are dependent on physical layer [12]. If the values of the subsequent parameters are small, the channel access delay will become less for the AC which leads the higher priority to approach the medium.

When a particular QoS station (QSTA) has the concession to begin transmissions, then the TXOP is expressed as the time interval in IEEE 802.11e [15].

3.3 Mobile Agent (MA)

A Mobile Agent (MA) starts from every node and moves to an adjacent node at every time. A node visited next is selected at the equivalent probability. The MA brings its own history of movement and updates the routing table of the node it is visiting.

Each MA has its own history which consists of its source node S, the current time Tc, the number of hops *NH* from the starting node, the adjacent node *AN* that the MA has last visited and the number of multiple packets *NP* on AN at *Tc* . When an MA visits a node, it puts the information (S, Tc, NH, AN, NP) in the routing table of that node.

Each node has a routing table that stores k fresh routing information records from itself to every node $S : [S, \{(Tci, NHi, ANi, NPi) \cdots (Tcm, NHm, ANm, NPm)\}]$, where $Tc1 > Tc2 > \cdots > Tm$. We call m the number of entries. For each $i (1 \leq i \leq m)$, Tci is a time of visiting the adjacent node ANi , NHi is the number of hops and NPi is the number of MAs on ANi . When MA with the history (S, Tc, NH, AN, NP) visits a node N , the routing information on that node

$[S, \{(Tci, NHi, ANi, NPi) \cdots (Tcm, NHm, ANm, NPm)\}]$ is updated to

$[S; \{(Tc, NH; AN, NP), (Tci, NHi, ANi, NPi, NPi) \cdots$

$(Tcm - 1, NHm - 1, ANm - 1, NPm - 1)\}]$

3.4 Queue Length Estimation

The traffic rate within the network has to be determined to find the level of congestion. The traffic rate is significantly affected by

- the number of new incoming flows
- the number of existing flows
- the density of the nodes in the network
- Communication abilities of nodes

Our goal is to acquire macroscopic network statistics using a heuristic approach. We compute the traffic rate as follows: Let the value L_o represent the offered load at the queue of node i and it is defined as

$$L_{oi} = \frac{AR_i}{SR_i} \tag{1}$$

where AR_i is the aggregate arrival rate of the packets produced and forwarded at node i while SR_i is the service rate at node i, i.e., $SR_i = 1/T$ where T is the computed exponentially weighted moving average of the packets' waiting time at the head of the service queue. The distribution of the queue length $PR(Q_1)$ (essentially this is the probability that there are Q_l packets in the queue) at the node is computed as

$$PR(Q_1) = (1 - L_{oi})L_{oi}^1 \tag{2}$$

For N distinct queues, the joint distribution is the product

$$PR(Q_{11}, Q_{12} \cdots Q_{1N}) = \prod_{i=1}^{N} (1 - L_{oi})L_{oi}^{li} \tag{3}$$

3.5 Channel Contention Estimation

In this network, we consider IEEE 802.11 MAC with the distributed coordination function (DCF). It has the packet sequence as request-to-send (RTS), clear-to-send (CTS), data and acknowledgement (ACK). The amount of time between the receipt of one packet and the transmission of the next is called a short inter frame space (SIFS). Then the channel occupation due to MAC contention will be

$$C_{OCC} = t_{RTS} + t_{CTS} + 3t_{SIFS} + t_{acc} \tag{4}$$

Where t_{RTS} and t_{CTS} are the time consumed on RTS and CTS, respectively and t_{SIFS} is the $SIFS$ period. t_{acc} is the time taken due to access contention.

The channel occupation is mainly dependent upon the medium access contention, and the number of packet collisions. That is, C_{occ} is strongly related to the congestion around a given node.

C_{occ} can become relatively large if congestion is incurred and not controlled, and it can dramatically decrease the capacity of a congested link.

3.6 Agent Based Congestion Control Routing

The Total Congestion Metric (TCM) can be estimated from the obtained queue length and the channel contention.

$$TCM = PR(Q_1) + C_{occ} \tag{5}$$

The agent based congestion routing can be explained from the following figure:

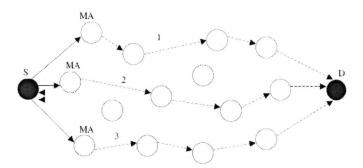

Fig. 1. Agent Based Congestion Routing

Step 1: The source S checks the number of available one hop neighbors and clones the Mobile Agent (MA) to that neighbors.

Step 2: The Mobile Agent selects the shortest path of the route to move towards the destination D as given in the Fig 1 such as P1, P2 and P3.

Step 3: The MA1 moves towards the destination D in a hop-by-hop manner in the path P1 and MA2 in P2 and MA3 in P3 respectively.

Step 4: Then the MA1 calculates the TCM1 of that path P1 and similarly MA2 calculates the TCM2 of P2 and MA3 calculates the TCM3 of P3.

Step 5: Now the destination D sends the total congestion metrics TCM1, TCM2 and TCM3 of the paths P1, P2 and P3 respectively to the source.

Step 6: Now the source selects path using min (TCM1, TCM2, and TCM3) and sends the data through the corresponding path which has the minimum congestion.

4 Simulation Results

4.1 Simulation Model and Parameters

We use NS2 [16] to simulate our proposed technique. In the simulation, the channel capacity of mobile hosts is set to the same value: 11Mbps. In the simulation, mobile nodes move in a 1000 meter x 1000 meter region for 50 seconds simulation time. Initial locations and movements of the nodes are obtained using the random waypoint (RWP) model of NS2. It is assumed that each node moves independently with the same average speed. All nodes have the same transmission range of 250 meters. The node speed is 5 m/s. and pause time is 5 seconds. In the simulation, for class1 traffic video is used and for class2 and Class3, CBR and FTP are used respectively. We compare the performance our Agent Based Congestion Control (ABCC) technique with the Hop by Hop algorithm [7]. The performance is evaluated mainly, according to the metrics: Packet Delivery Fraction, Throughput in terms of number of packets received successfully and Average end-to-end delay:

4.2 Results

A. Effect of Varying Rates

In the initial experiment, we measure the performance of the proposed technique by varying the rate as 250, 500, 750 and 1000Kb.

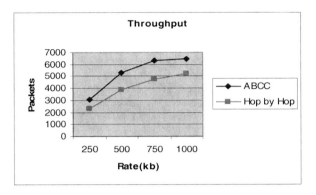

Fig. 2. Rate Vs Throughput

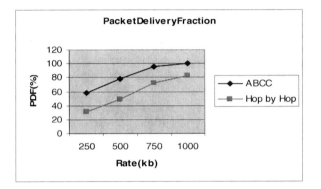

Fig. 3. Rate Vs Packet Delivery Fraction

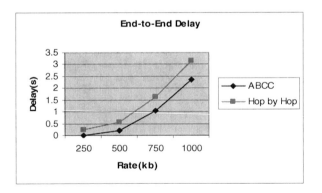

Fig. 4. Rate Vs End-to-End Delay

When the rate is increased, normally, the more number of packets will be sent leading to congestion.

Fig 2 gives the throughput of the proposed technique when the rate is increased. As we can see from the figure, the throughput is more in the case of ABCC when compared to the Hop by Hop algorithm, since it detects the congestion accurately. From Fig 3, we can see that the packet delivery fraction for ABCC is more, when compared to the Hop by Hop algorithm. From Fig 4, we can see that the average end-to-end delay of the proposed ABCC technique is less when compared to the Hop by Hop algorithm, since congestion is quickly detected by the mobile agents.

B. Effect of Varying Flows

In the next experiment, we compare our proposed technique by varying the number of flows as 2, 4, 6, 8 and 10.

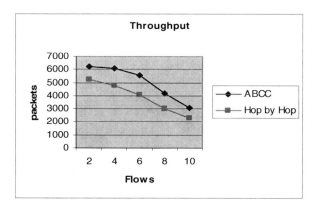

Fig. 5. Flows Vs Throughput

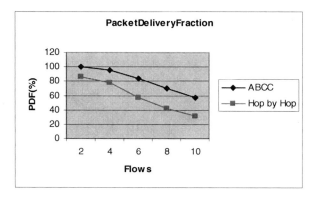

Fig. 6. Flows Vs Packet Delivery Fraction

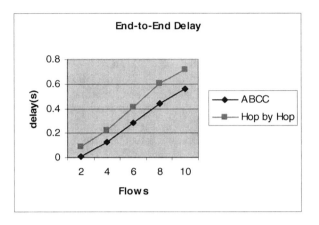

Fig. 7. Flows Vs End-to-End Delay

When the number of flows is increased, it leads to network contention as well as increased queue length, which results in the throughput degradation.

Fig 5 gives the throughput of the proposed technique when the flow is increased. As we can see from the figure, the throughput is more in the case of ABCC when compared to the Hop by Hop algorithm, since it detects the congestion accurately. From Fig 6, we can see that the packet delivery fraction for ABCC is more, when compared to the Hop by Hop algorithm. From Fig 7, we can see that the average end-to-end delay of the proposed ABCC technique is less when compared to the Hop by Hop algorithm, since congestion is quickly detected by the mobile agents.

5   Conclusion

In this paper, we have designed and developed an agent based congestion control technique. In our technique, the information about network congestion is collected and distributed by mobile agents (MA). A mobile agent starts from every node and moves to an adjacent node at every time. The MA updates the routing table of the node it is visiting. In this technique, the node is classified in one of the four categories depending on whether the traffic belongs to background, best effort, video or voice AC respectively. Then MA estimates the queue length of the various traffic classes and the channel contention of each path. Then this total congestion metric is applied to the routing protocol to select the minimum congested route in the network. By simulation results, we have shown that our proposed technique attains high delivery ratio and throughput with reduced delay when compared with the existing technique.

References

1. Baboo, S.S., Narasimhan, B.: A Hop-by-Hop Congestion-Aware Routing Protocol for Heterogeneous Mobile Ad-hoc Networks. International Journal of Computer Science and Information Security (2009)

2. Chen, X., Jones, H.M., Jayalath, A.D.S.: Congestion-Aware Routing Protocol for Mobile Ad Hoc Networks. In: IEEE 66th Conference in Vehicular Technology (2007)
3. Lochert, C., Scheuermann, B., Mauve, M.: A Survey on Congestion Control for Mobile Ad-Hoc Networks. Wireless Communications and Mobile Computing, InterScience (2007)
4. http://en.wikipedia.org/wiki/Congestion_control
5. http://www.linktionary.com/c/congestion.html
6. Tran, D.A., Raghavendra, H.: Congestion Adaptive Routing in Mobile Ad Hoc Networks. IEEE Transactions on Parallel and Distributed Systems (2006)
7. Yi, Y., Shakkottai, S.: Hop-by-Hop Congestion Control Over a Wireless Multi-Hop Network. IEEE/ACM Transactions on Networking (2007)
8. Akyol, U., Andrews, M., Gupta, P., Hobby, J., Saniee, I., Stolyar, A.: Joint Scheduling and Congestion Control in Mobile Ad-Hoc Networks. In: Proceedings of IEEE INFOCOM (2008)
9. Karunakaran, S., Thangaraj, P.: A Cluster Based Congestion Control Protocol for Mobile Adhoc Networks. International Journal of Information Technology and Knowledge Management 2(2), 471–474 (2010)
10. Malika, B., Mustapha, L., Abdelaziz, M., Nordine, T., Mehammed, D., Rachida, A.: Intelligent Routing and Flow Control In MANETs. Journal of Computing and Information Technology, doi:10.2498/cit.1001470
11. Li, J., Li, Z., Mohapatra, P.: APHD: End-to-End Delay Assurance in 802.11e Based MANETs. In: 3rd Annual International Conference Mobile and Ubiquitous Systems – Workshops, pp. 1–8 (2006)
12. Lee, J.F., Liao, W., Chen, M.C.: A Differentiated Service Model for Enhanced Distributed Channel Access (EDCA) of IEEE 802.11e WLANs. In: Proc. IEEE Globecom (2005)
13. Ksentini, A., Naimi, M., Gueroui, A.: Toward an Improvement of H.264 Video Transmission over IEEE 802.11e through a Cross-Layer Architecture. IEEE Communications Magazine (2006)
14. Wu, Y.-J., Chiu, J.-H., Sheu, T.-L.: A Modified EDCA with Dynamic Contention Control for Real-Time Traffic in Multi-hop Ad Hoc Networks. Journal of Information Science and Engineering 24, 1065–1079 (2008)
15. Flaithearta, P.O., Melvin, H.: 802.11e EDCA Parameter Optimization Based on Synchronized Time. MESAQIN (2009)
16. Network Simulator, http://www.isi.edu/nsnam/ns
17. Wang, X., Perkins, D.: Cross-layer Hop-by-hop Congestion Control in Mobile Ad Hoc Networks. In: Proc., IEEE, Wireless Communication and Networking Conference, WCNC, pp. 2456–2461 (2008)
18. Nishimura, K., Takahashi, K.: A Multi-Agent Routing Protocol with Congestion Control for MANET. In: Proceedings 21st European Conference on Modeling and Simulation, ECMS (2007)

VANET Routing Protocols and Mobility Models: A Survey

Dhananjay Sudhakar Gaikwad and Mukesh Zaveri

Computer Engineering Department,
Sardar Vallabhai National Institute of Technology, Surat, Gujarat
India-395007
{g.dhananjay,mazaveri}@coed.svnit.ac.in

Abstract. During the last decade, tremendous progress has been reported in providing network to mobile users. Mobile Ad hoc Network (MANET) is one of the networks that do not require any administrator involvement during the communication. MANET can be deployed in the places, where it is not feasible to install an infrastructure, such as in military area. Vehicular Ad hoc Network (VANET) is an emerging sub-class of MANET. VANET is deployed on the road, where vehicles constitute mobile nodes. Active security and intelligent transportation are important applications of VANET, which need suitable vehicle-to-vehicle communication technology, especially routing technology. Routing protocol needs to design, to address challenges of VANET such as, high mobility of nodes, random topology, and heterogeneous networks. Mobility models reflect the movement pattern of nodes on the road. The mobility models are used during the simulation/implementation of protocols. They should generate movement pattern in such way that, the generated pattern should reflects real world behavior of vehicles on the roads. This paper provides a detailed survey of routing protocols and mobility models in VANET.

Keywords: Mobile Ad hoc Network (MANET), Vehicle Ad hoc Network (VANET), Inter-vehicle communication (IVC), vehicle-to-vehicle (V2V), Global positioning system (GPS).

1 Introduction

Ad hoc network is a collection of wireless mobile nodes without any fixed base station infrastructure and centralized management. Each node acts as both host and router, which moves arbitrarily and communicates with each other via multiple wireless links. It is a multi-hop wireless network, where packets need to pass through several nodes to reach destination [2]. MANET is a class of ad hoc networks. The advantage of ad hoc network is that they can be quickly deployed with no administrator involvement.

Now days, more and more research is dedicated to VANET. VANET allows V2V communication to provide safety and comfort to both drivers and passengers. VANET operates by gathering existing traffic scenarios. Some of the other services provided by VANET such as warning messages to reduce the number of road accidents and

D.C. Wyld et al. (Eds.): NeCoM/WeST/WiMoN 2011, CCIS 197, pp. 334–342, 2011.
© Springer-Verlag Berlin Heidelberg 2011

traffic jam [3]. Apart from these applications, this technology can also used to provide various vehicular services such as transparent connection to Internet and Intranet, telecommunication services, info stations [5].

In order to provide vehicular services, there is a need for good routing protocol, which can deal with all the challenges of VANET. VANET is a dynamic network, so it is challenging issue to be able to get at run time. VANET routing protocols are classified into three categories: proactive routing protocol, reactive routing protocols and position based routing protocols. Proactive routing protocol, which always maintains routes from source to destination by periodically updating routing table example OLSR [24], Where reactive routing protocols initiates route computation only on demand basis, AODV [23]. Position based routing protocol [7] computes routes based on the physical position of the nodes, by using GPS.

Mobility models reflect as possible as real behavior of vehicular traffic on the road. One critical aspect while simulating VANET is the use of mobility models. There are several mobility models such as random pattern, graph constrained commonly used by VANET researchers [9]. But one problem with these types of models is that they do not reflect real behavior of traffic pattern [15]. They ignores some critical aspects of the real world traffic such as queuing of vehicles at road intersection, traffic lights and traffic signs, pedestrian movements, acceleration and deceleration according to neighbor vehicle, overtaking and lane changing behavior of drivers.

This paper provides a detailed survey of routing protocols used in VANET and explained in details advantages and disadvantages of each routing protocol. This paper also provides detailed survey of mobility models and mobility model generation tools with their classification. The certain drawbacks of mobility model and mobility model generation tools have been explained in detail in this paper.

The rest of paper is organized as follows: section 2 describes some currently used routing protocols in VANET. Section 3, describes mobility models and some tools for generation of mobility models with classification; those are used during the simulation of routing protocols and conclusion is drew in section 4.

2 Review of Routing Protocols

Routing protocols in VANET broadly classified into position based routing protocols, proactive routing protocols and reactive routing protocols.

2.1 Position Based Routing Protocols

These types of protocols find the route to destination based on the physical location of the nodes. Several positions based routing protocol have been proposed. Geographic source routing (GSR) protocol [7] uses a city map to find the route from source to destination. The map of city is digitized and stored in a geographic information system (GIS). GSR protocol uses a reactive location service (RLS) to find the position of desired communication partner. The digitized map contains a street and road junction information. Based on that, it finds route that passes through a street and sequence of road functions. The source node floods the network with position request for the specific node identifier. When node corresponds to request identifier receives request, reply back position information to the source node. Then the sending node computes the path through a sequence of road junctions to a destination, by using map of city. GSR performs well in city environments, where generally other position based routing protocols suffer. But GSR does not consider density of nodes during selection of next road junctions.

Greedy perimeter stateless routing (GPSR) [8] is a position based routing protocol. GPSR archives scalability in term of number of nodes in network and mobility rate, by storing little amount of information per node. It stores only node's identifier and physical location of node in a routing table. GPSR works in two modes: i) in greedy forwarding mode, packets are forwarded to a node which is geographically closer to a destination node. ii) if greedy fails, then it switches to perimeter forwarding mode. In this mode, packets are forwarded along the perimeter of the node, where greedy failed. When it finds any node closer to destination, then switches back to greedy mode. This protocol achieves good result at the high mobility rate. But GPSR has a drawback as large number of packet losses due to the formation of routing loops in perimeter forwarding mode.

Greedy Traffic Aware Routing (GySTAR) [21] protocol incorporates vehicle movement prediction method during route selection. It routes packets between the road junctions towards the destination. The difference with GSR is that, junctions are chosen by taking into account the number of vehicles in between the junctions and the range to the next junction. This protocol uses a carry and forward approach, node holds the packets until it finds best hop to forward. It performs well than GSR. This protocol has problem of failure of intermediate nodes due to the holding of packets.

Connectivity Aware Routing (CAR) [6] provides new type beaconing mechanism called, adaptive beaconing. In adaptive beaconing frequency of HELLO beacons depend on the number of neighboring nodes. It uses a preferred group broadcasting (PGB) technique, which is an optimized broadcasting technique. It reduces a control messages overhead by eliminating redundant transmission. This protocol integrates a location service into its route selection process. But due to the integration, it suffers from packet overhead problem.

2.2 Reactive Routing Protocols

These types of protocols initiate route computation only on demand basis, so they give better performance than proactive routing protocols. There are so many reactive routing protocols have been proposed. Ad hoc On Demand Distance Vector (AODV) [24] is reactive routing protocol, which finds the route to destination on demand basis. This protocol invokes route discovery mechanism only when route to a destination is not known. In this protocol each node maintains routing table that contains information about reaching the destination. The size of routing table minimized by storing only next hop information rather than storing entire route to a destination. AODV maintains single route from source to a destination. But this may suffer from a problem of frequent route failures in high mobility of nodes.

Ad hoc On Demand Multi path Distance Vector (AOMDV) [4] overcomes AODV [23] frequent route failure problem by storing multiple routes from source to destination. It is a reactive routing protocol. It creates multiple reverse paths unlike to AODV, which creates only single reverse path. This would give robustness to the protocol, as if one route fails, then packet can be routed through another route. But this AOMDV protocol does not considers real time information during the route discovery process. To overcomes this real time information problem, an improved version of AOMDV proposed [3]. This improved AOMDV is based on the speed metric. The speed metric is a combination of node's speed and direction. This protocol uses speed metrics information, which selects route that based on real time traffic information.

Adaptive routing protocol [2] is a combination of proactive and reactive routing protocol, it is hybrid one. It adapts the transmission range according to the speed and density of nodes. It calculates the density of nodes by taking into account special feature, called link expiration time (LET). If LET is short, means high speed of nodes and low node density and if it is long then low speed of nodes and high density of nodes. This protocol suffers from a message overhead problem due to periodically exchange of speed and location information.

2.3 Proactive Routing Protocols

Proactive protocols always maintain routes from source to destination by periodically updating routing table. Density aware routing [1] protocol uses available road hierarchies' information to route the packets. Road is classified as high density road-street road, minimum density road – secondary roads and low density - freeway. In that two routes are maintained. In case failure of first route, packet is routed through another route. It considers the real time traffic information i.e. it calculates the density of the nodes on that route by sending test packet first. The test packet contains the density of nodes on that route. After that, route is selected. It selects the route based on real time information. But it has a drawback as the consumption of the bandwidth due to test and original packets.

Optimized Link state routing (OLSR) [24] is a proactive routing protocol stores the entire route from source to destination. Due to that size of routing can be increases drastically as the number of node increases in the network. They periodically update routing table by exchanging each other fresh copy of the routes. When ever source node wants to send packet to a particular destination, it searches its own routing table. If route to destination not available, then source node invokes route discovery processes. It finds the best route from source to destination by using Bellman ford algorithm. This algorithm solves routing loop problem. The problem with this, OLSR requires a regular update of its routing tables, which uses up battery power and a small amount of bandwidth even if the network is idle.

3 Review of Mobility Models

Several mobility models and tools are proposed for the generation of traffic pattern. The mobility model is designed to describe the movement pattern of mobile users, and how their location, velocity and acceleration change over time. Here we review some mobility models and mobility model generation tools. Mobility models are usually classified into macroscopic mobility model and Microscopic mobility models [17].

3.1 Macroscopic Mobility Model

This type of mobility models considers the motion constraints such as street, roads, crossroads and traffic lights during the generation of vehicle movement traces. They define the generation of vehicle traffic such as traffic flow, traffic density and initial distribution of vehicles. In following section we review mobility models that generate vehicular traffic in macroscopic way.

Random mobility model: In Random way point model [16], mobile nodes move randomly and freely without any restrictions. In this model, the destination, speed and direction all are chosen randomly and independent of other nodes. The fraction of nodes in network remains static for the entire simulation time. The velocity of node is uniformly chosen at random from the interval [Vmin, Vmax]. The node moves towards destination with a velocity v. When it reaches to destination, it remains static for the predefined pause time and moving again according to same rule. The mobility behavior of nodes very much depends on the pause time and maximum speed of nodes. The following parameters describe a simulation setup of model.

- Size and shape of the deployment region Q,
- initial spatial node distribution $f_{int}(x)$,
- static parameter ps, with 0< p_s<1,
- Probability density function $f_{Tp}(tp)$ of pause time, and
- Minimum and maximum speed: 0 < Vmin ≤ Vmax.

The components of node distribution $f_x(x)$ is composed of three distinct components:

$$f_x(x) = f_s(x) + f_p(x) + f_m(x) \tag{1}$$

Gauss morkev model: The random way-point model can generate speed and direction of nodes independent on previous history. It directly selects from its predefined range, so this can create a sudden stop and sharp turn problem. Gauss morkev model [21] first calculates the speed and direction of movement for each node. Then nodes move with the calculated speed and direction for a period. After that period similar movements begins again. The time that is used in the movement in each interval before the change in speed and direction, is constant. The current speed and direction related to the previous speed and direction by following equation.

$$s_n = \alpha s_{n-1} + (1-\alpha) * s + (1-\alpha^2) * s_{xn-1}\frac{1}{2}. \tag{2}$$

$$d_n = \alpha d_{n-1} + (1-\alpha)*d + (1-\alpha^2) * s_{dn-1}\frac{1}{2}. \tag{3}$$

Where, s_n and d_n are the values of speed and direction for movement in the period time n, s_{n-1} and d_{n-1} are the values of speed and direction for movement in the period time n-1, α is the constant value in the range [0, 1], s and d are constants representing the mean speed and direction, αs_{n-1} and αd_{n-1} are variables from a Gaussian distribution.

This Gauss morkev model calculates current speed and direction of mobile node based on the previous speed and direction values, so due to this gauss morkev model overcomes sudden stop and sharp turn problems of Random way point model [16].

Mobility model generation tool: Several tools are proposed for the generation of mobility models. These tools generate movement traces, to describe the behavior of vehicle on the road. Following tools generate vehicular traffic in a macroscopic way.

Mobility model generator for Vehicular Network (MOVE) facilitates users to rapidly generate realistic mobility models for VANET simulation with a visualization property. This model works with another micro-simulator traffic model, called SUMO [23]. MOV model consists of two main components: Map Editor and Vehicle Movement Editor. Map Editor is used to create the road topology, which is either created by manually, automatically or by importing the maps from databases such as TIGER ((Topologically Integrated Geographic Encoding and Referencing). The Vehicle Movement Editor used for the generation of vehicle movement. The output of MOVE is a mobility trace file which contains the information on vehicle movement that can be used by network simulator. All the parameter configuration of vehicle movement is done in a static way. This model does not consider micro – mobility features. Micro- mobility feature is related to the modeling behavior of single vehicle over the all the vehicles on the road. This feature gives model more realistic that reflects behavior of the real world.

The IMPORTANT tool [27] implements several random mobility models and Manhattan model. The IMPORTANT tool includes the car following model, which includes the basic car to car interaction model based on the distance. It describes the controlling mechanisms such as acceleration and deceleration based on the distance between two cars. It describes the all the physical parameters of cars, such as length and width of car. Based on these parameters, it calculates the acceleration and deceleration of cars. But when related to framework, we can see that the structure of tool is definitely too simple to represent realistic motions, it models only basic motion constrains.

3.2 Microscopic Mobility Model

Street Random Way point (STRAW) is a tool [11] that generates the mobility patterns with extraction of urban topologies from the TIGER database. It supports for the micro – mobility features of models. STRAW implements a complex intersection management using traffic lights and traffic signs. Due to this characteristic, vehicle shows a more realistic behavior when reaching at intersection. It includes a traffic control mechanisms that force drivers to follow deterministic admission control protocol when encountering intersection. Drawback of STRAW model is it does not give details about the traffic flows. Also it does not specify the lane changing behavior.

CanuMobiSim [13] is a tool for the generation of movement traces in a variety of conditions. This tool provides a GUI for the generation of mobility models and it can generate mobility traces for Network simulator [25] and GloMoSim [26]. CanuMobiSim tool keeps micro – mobility in consideration and implements several car to car interaction models that adjust speed of vehicle according to the density of vehicles. It also implements an Intelligent Driver Model (IDM), which adapts the velocity depending on movements between neighboring vehicles. CanuMobiSim tool includes complex traffic generators that can implements basic source-destination paths using Dijkstra shortest path algorithms. But due to its generic structure, it suffers from a problem of reduced level of details in specific scenarios.

VanetMobiSim [15] is a tool that generates a realistic vehicular movement traces. It is an extension to the CanuMobiSim [13]. As CanuMobiSim provides efficient and easily extensible mobility architecture, but due to its genral purpose nature, it suffers from a reduced level of detail in specific scenarios. VanetMobiSim is aimed at extending the vehicular mobility support of CanuMobiSim to a higher degree of realism. In VanetMobiSim the micro – mobility feature takes into account, the road topology, the road structure (Unidirectional or Bidirectional, single lane or multilane), the road characteristics (speed limits, vehicle classes restrictions) and the presence of traffic signs. This tool includes Intelligent Driver Model with Intersection Management (IDM-IM) which gives intersection handling capabilities to the vehicles driven by the IDM (Intelligent Driver Model).

4 Conclusion

In this paper, we have reviewed routing protocols in Vehicular Ad hoc Network, with their classification. Proactive routing protocols such as OLSR, suffers from a problem of tremendous increase in the size of routing table, by increasing number of nodes in the network. Reactive routing protocol such as AODV suffers from frequent route failure problems and additional time required during the route discovery process. AOMDV has real time traffic problems. The position based routing protocols perform well in highway environment but suffer in the city environment due to signal blockage and multi-path effects. GPSR suffers from a packet losses and routing loops in perimeter mode. GySTAR uses carry and forward approach, but leads to intermediate node failure problem. CAR suffers from packet overhead problems. We have reviewed that every protocol has some drawback. It is necessary to design routing protocol that will adderess all these problems.

We reviewed several mobility models and tools. Random way point has sudden stop and sharp turn problem. Random way point and gauss morkev model useful in MANET, but not in VANET. They do not reflect real world mobility pattern. Mobility model generated by tool suffer from a micro –mobility feature problem, road intersection handling problem. It is needed to develop such model that will overcome all the problems and will generate real mobility model.

References

1. Mouzna, J., Uppoor, S., Boussedjra, M., Pai, M.M.M.: Density aware routing using road hierarchy for vehicular networks. In: IEEE/INFORMS International Conference Service Operations, Logistics and Informatics, SOLI 2009, July 22-24, pp. 443–448 (2009)
2. Azarmi, M., Sabaei, M., Pedram, H.: Adaptive routing protocols for vehicular ad hoc networks. In: Telecommunications, IST 2008, August 27-28, pp. 825–830 (2008)
3. Chen, Y., Xiang, Z., Jian, W., Jiang, W.: An improved AOMDV routing protocol for V2V communication. In: 2009 IEEE Intelligent Vehicles Symposium, June 3-5, pp. 1115–1120 (2009)
4. Marina, M.K., Das, S.R.: On-demand multipath distance vector routing in Ad Hoc networks. In: Proc. 9th International Conference on Network Protocols, California, USA, pp. 14–23 (2001)

5. http://en.wikipedia.org/wiki/Vehicular_ad-hoc_network
6. Naumov, V., Gross, T.R.: Connectivity-Aware Routing (CAR) in Vehicular Ad-hoc Networks. In: 26th IEEE International Conference on Computer Communications, INFOCOM 2007, May 6-12, pp. 1919–1927. IEEE, Los Alamitos (2007)
7. Lochert, C., Hartenstein, H., Tian, 1., FiiBler, H., Herrmann, D., Mauve, M.: A Routing Strategy for Vehicular Ad Hoc Networks in City Environments. In: Proc. of the IEEE Intelligent Vehicles Symposium (IV 2003), Ohio, USA, pp. 156–161 (June 2003)
8. Karp, B., Kung, H.T.: GPSR: Greedy Perimeter Stateless Routing for Wireless Networks. In: Proc. of ACM/IEEE MOBICOM'OO, Boston, Massachusetts, USA, pp. 243–254 (2009)
9. http://en.wikipedia.org/wiki/Mobility_model
10. Lan, K.-c., Chou, C.-M.: Realistic mobility models for Vehicular Ad hoc Network (VANET) simulations. In: 8th International Conference on Advantage Telecommunications, ITST 2008, October 24-24, pp. 362–366 (2008)
11. Choffnes, D., Bustamante, F.: An Integrated Mobility and Traffic Model for Vehicular Wireless Networks. In: 2nd ACM Workshop on Vehicular Ad Hoc Networks, VANET 2005 (September 2005)
12. Mangharam, R., Wellerand, D.S., Stancil, D.D., Rajkumar, R., Parikh, J.S.: GrooveSim: a topography-accurate simulator for geographic routing in vehicular networks. In: 2nd ACM Workshop on Vehicular Ad Hoc Networks, VANET 2005 (September 2005)
13. CANU Project Home Page, http://canu.informatik.uni-stuttgart.de
14. Uchiyama, A.: Mobile Ad-hoc Network Simulator based on Realistic Behavior Model. Demo Session in MobiHoc 2005 (2005)
15. Gainaru, A., Dobre, C., Cristea, V.: A Realistic Mobility Model Based on Social Networks for the Simulation of VANETs. In: IEEE 69th Vehicular Technology Conference, VTC Spring 2009, April 26-29, pp. 1–5 (2009)
16. Bettstetter, C., Rasta, G., Santi, P.: The Node Distribution of the Random Waypoint Mobility Model for Wireless Ad Hoc Networks. IEEE Transactions on Mobile Computing 2(3) (July-September 2003)
17. Harri, J., filali, f., Bonnet, C.: Mobility models for vehicular Adhoc Networks: A survey and Taxonomy. Researcher report RR-06-168 (March 2006)
18. Yousefi, S., Mousavi, M.S., Fathy, M.: Vehicular Ad Hoc Networks (VANETs): challenges and perspectives. In: Proc. 6th International Conference on ITS Telecommunications, Chengdu, China, pp. 761–766 (2006)
19. Naumov, V., Baumann, R., Gross, T.: An evaluation of inter-vehicle ad hoc networks based on realistic vehicular traces. In: Proc. 7th ACM International Symposium on Mobile Ad Hoc Networking and Computing (MobiHoc), Florence, Italy, pp. 108–119 (2006)
20. Jardosh, A., Belding-Royer, E., et al.: Towards realistic mobility models for mobile ad hoc networks. In: Proc. of the 9th Annual International Conference on Mobile Computing and Networking, MobiCom 2003 (September 2003) ISBN:1-58113-753-2
21. Jerbi, M., Senouci, S.M., G.-Doudane, Y., Meraihi, R.: GyTAR: Improved Greedy Traffic Aware Routing protocol for Vehicular Ad hoc Networks in City Environments. In: Poster: The Third ACM International Workshop on Vehicular Ad Hoc Networks (VANET 2006), Los Angeles, CA, USA, pp. 88–89 (September 2006)
22. SUMO, http://sourceforge.net/apps/mediawiki/sumo/index.php?title=Main_Page

23. Marina, M.K., Das, S.R.: On-demand multi path distance vector routing in Ad Hoc networks. In: Proc. 9th International Conference on Network Protocols, California, USA, pp. 14–23 (2001)
24. Kumar, S., Sengupta, J.: AODV and OLSR routing protocols for Wireless Ad-hoc and Mesh Networks. In: 2010 International Conference on Computer and Communication Technology (ICCCT), September 17-19, pp. 402–407 (2010)
25. http://www.isi.edu/nsnam/ns/index.html
26. http://pcl.cs.ucla.edu/projects/glomosim/
27. Bai, F., Sadagopan, N., Helmy, A.: The IMPORTANT Framework for Analyzing the Impact of Mobility on Performance of Routing for Ad Hoc Networks. Ad Hoc Networks Journal - Elsevier Science 1(4), 383–403 (2003)

Efficient Key Distribution Schemes for Wireless Sensor Networks Using LDU' Composition of Symmetric Matrices

Sanjay Kumar and Deepti Dohare

Indian Institute of Science, Bangalore
{sanjay08,deeptidohare}@csa.iisc.ernet.in

Abstract. Wireless sensor network (WSNs) is highly vulnerable to attacks because it consists of various resource-constrained sensor nodes which communicates among themselves via wireless links. Establishment of pairwise keys between sensor nodes is used to realize many of the security services for wireless sensor networks. Hence, securely distributing keys among sensor nodes is a fundamental challenge for providing security services in WSNs. Even though the random key pre-distribution approach is suitable for low power and resource constrained sensor nodes, a shared key between a pair of nodes is not guaranteed and thus, they may not be able to communicate with each other. Matrix based scheme for key pre-distribution essentially use LU decomposition of matrix which can provide keys between any pair of nodes but are quite vulnerable to attack. This paper proposes a new robust key pre-distribution schemes based on LDU' composition of matrices. In the first scheme, we use integer as elements of symmetric matrices and in the second scheme we use polynomials over finite fields as elements of the symmetric matrices. The existing approach use decomposition of matrices which is compute intensive but our proposed scheme uses composition of matrices. The analysis shows that the proposed scheme allows almost 100% connectivity regardless of the number of keys and provides 100% resilience against node capture.

1 Introduction

Wireless sensor networks (WSNs) have potential to provide economical solutions to many problems of practical importance. Some of the applications where WSNs can be used are: Emergency Response System, Energy Management, Battlefield Management, Health Monitoring, Logistics and Inventory management etc. For example, power load that should be carried over an electrical line depends on the temperature of the wire and the environmental conditions. If the parameters are monitored by remote sensors and transmitted to a base station, it would be possible to meet load requirements optimally. Wireless sensor network (WSN) consists of various resource-constrained sensor nodes. Each sensor node has low battery power, less memory and very less computational capability. Same battery is used throughout the life time of a sensor node. Typical Mica2Dot sensor node has 4K RAM with 128K flash memory and processor speed of 8 MHz. WSNs are usually deployed in hostile environments. Environmental conditions along with resource-constraints give rise to many type of security threats or attacks.

D.C. Wyld et al. (Eds.): NeCoM/WeST/WiMoN 2011, CCIS 197, pp. 343–357, 2011.

Adversary can physically capture and get the information contained in the sensor node, eavesdrop and inject new messages, modify messages, listen and analyze the messages to obtain the information contained in a message etc. Since solution to physical capture of a node is possible in our approach, we can provide solutions to other security attacks. To defend against false data injection, authenticity of the sender must be checked so that sensor nodes will not listen to unauthorized nodes. Modification of a message is detected by checking integrity of the message. To ensure confidentiality, the information contained in the message should not be displayed to any node other than sender and receiver. The message is sent encrypted with a key that is shared by sender and receiver. Keys play a central role in realizing security services like authenticity, integrity, confidentiality etc. Keys need to be distributed securely among sensor nodes. A new key pre-distribution scheme solving this problem was recently proposed in [7]. It uses key assignment with LU decomposition of the symmetric matrix of the keys. One pitfall of this scheme is, however, that some data needs to be exchanged between the nodes for key authentication. This may compromise the security if the exchanged data are tapped by an adversary. In this paper, thus, we further enhance the security of the approach by employing LDU' composition with polynomial pool, which still allows high security even when the exchanged data are tapped and nodes are captured. A general form of solution for constructing the L, D, and U' matrix is developed in order to minimize the time overhead of LDU' composition in the key pre-distribution steps.

The rest of the paper is organized as follows: Related work and Motivation is given in Section 2. In Section 4 and 5, we describe the proposed schemes. In Section 6, we describe the key distribution scheme for addition of a new node. Section 7 contains the performance analysis of our schemes and comparison with existing schemes. Section 8 ends the paper with conclusions and directions for future work.

2   Related Work

Key distribution schemes available in literature can be broadly divided into the following two categories:

1. Probabilistic key distribution schemes [10]
2. Deterministic key distribution schemes [2,4,7,8]

There are some other schemes which can't be put in these categories directly, like key management schemes using public key cryptography that uses elliptic curve cryptography, and consumes less power and less memory [5]. Other schemes are location based schemes [6]. Eschenauer and Gligor [7] proposed a probabilistic key pre-distribution scheme for pairwise key establishment. For each sensor node, a set of keys are chosen from a big pool of keys and given to each node before deployment. In order to establish a pairwise key [3], two sensor nodes only need to identify the common keys they share. Deterministic key distribution schemes have the advantage that the graph is fully connected because every node in the network can establish a key with any other node. Basically deterministic algorithms are of three types: master key based, matrix based and polynomial based key distribution schemes. Broadcast session key negotiation protocol (BROSK) is based on a single master key which is pre-deployed in each sensor node. This master key is used to establish a key between a pair of sensor nodes. Master key based scheme is very simple to implement but it has no resilience. Lightweight key management system proposes a solution with slightly better resilience where more than one master keys are employed. It also does not give full resilience to node capture. Blom [9] has proposed a key pre-distribution scheme that allows any pair of nodes in a network to be able to find a pairwise secret key. As long as no more than t nodes are compromised, the network is perfectly secure (this is called the t-collision resistance property). Multiple space key pre-distribution scheme [1] improves the resilience of Bloms scheme. The central idea is, for any node, there is no need to establish a key with any other node. Park, Choi, and Youn [3] proposed a new scheme called "A noble key pre-distribution scheme with lu matrix for secure wireless sensor networks" [3]. According to this scheme, the base station creates a large pool of elements and randomly selects some elements from the pool to construct a symmetric matrix A. After constructing this symmetric matrix, the base station applies LU decomposition for calculating L and U matrices by using some formula, i.e., $L = E_1.E_2.E_3....E_n \cdot A$ and $U = E_1^{-1}.E_2^{-1}.E_3^{-1}....E_n^{-1}$, where $E_1, E_2, E_3, \ldots E_n$ are elementary matrices. The main disadvantages of this scheme is that it takes lot of computational overhead, memory overhead and also takes more time in $O(k^2)$. To overcome this problem, Choi and Youn proposed another scheme called "Mkps: A multi-level key pre-distribution scheme for secure wireless sensor networks" [1]. According to this scheme, the base station creates a large pool of elements and randomly selects some number of elements from the pool, and construct a lower triangular matrix. After that the base station constructs an upper triangular matrix based on the lower triangular matrix by applying the formula as follows. For the first row elements, $u_{1j} = (l_{j1}/l_{11}).u_{11}$ and for other rows elements, $u_{ij} = \sum_{a=1}^{j-1} l_{ja} u_{ai} - \sum_{a=1}^{i-1} l_{ia}.u_{aj}/l_{ii}$, where $1 < i < j \leq m$. The main disadvantages of this scheme is that it takes lot of computational overhead and memory overhead, but the total time taken is reduced to $O(k)$. In this paper, we improvised our approach over previous two schemes by reducing the computational overhead, and also increased confidentiality by changing the order of elements of matrix and provide the security for capturing the nodes in the network by the adversary. To address this problem of compromising a network by capturing nodes, we have devised a new approach that is efficient and provide full resilience to network against node capture. Performance analysis shows that it consumes less energy than probabilistic key pre-distribution schemes and completely secure in the sense that compromising any number of nodes will not have any effect on the remaining network. Even a single link will not be compromised between non-compromised nodes.

3   Definitions and Assumption

In this section we present the preliminaries and some assumption of the proposed schemes.

3.1   Preliminaries

We start with a brief description of various concepts and definitions used in this paper.

- **Definition 1:** If a square matrix A has the property $A^T = A$, where transpose of matrix A is denoted by A^T, we say that A is a symmetric matrix. A is a symmetric matrix means $A_{ij} = A_{ji}$, where A_{ij} is the element in the ith row and j^{th} column of matrix A [3].
- **Definition 2:** LU decomposition of an $m \times m$ matrix A decomposes it into two matrices L and U such that $A = LU$, where L is an $m \times m$ lower triangular matrix and U is an $m \times m$ upper triangular matrix, respectively [1].
- **Definition 3:** Now suppose that A is a square matrix with $A = LU$, and the pivots on the diagonal of U are all nonzero. By dividing i^{th} $(1 \leq i \leq m)$ row of U by the nonzero pivot d_i, the matrix U is decomposed into a diagonal matrix D whose diagonals are just the pivots $d_1, d_2, ..., d_n$ and a new upper triangular matrix, denoted by U', whose diagonal elements are all 1. Then $A = LDU'$ [3].
- **Definition 4:** A hash function (H) is any well-defined procedure or mathematical function that converts a large, possibly variable-sized amount of data into a small datum, usually a single integer that may serve as an index to an array. The values returned by a hash function are called hash values, hash codes, hash sums, or simply hashes.
- **Definition 5:** A Circular shift function (CS) is a function that defines an operation of rearranging the entries in a tuple, by moving the final entry to the first position. $CS(tuple, n)$ indicates that n circular shifts are applied to a given tuple. For example, $CS((a, b, c, d), 2) = (c, d, a, b)$.
- **Definition 6:** A Reverse function (R) is a function that rearranges the entries of a tuple in a reverse order. For example, $R((a, b, c, d)) = (d, c, b, a)$.

3.2   Assumption

- Network topology is not known prior to deployment.
- Before deployment each node doesn't know its own location and about its neighbors.
- Initial deployment of the network takes place safely in the sense that adversary cannot capture any node even for a small period of time.
- There is a lower bound T_{min} to compromise a node.
- Time to discover the neighbors for a new node is T_{est} and $T_{est} < T_{min}$.

4   Proposed First Key Distribution Scheme

To remove the drawbacks of the existing schemes, we proposed a new key pre-distribution scheme called **A Key Pre-Distribution Scheme with LDU' Composition of Matrix for WSNs**. The following procedure is executed by base station in order to construct *L, D, U* and *U'* matrices.

- **Step 1:** *Generation of large pool of keys ($2^{18} \sim 2^{21}$ keys):* Base station generates a large pool of keys as shown in Figure 1. Those generated keys are then used to construct a symmetric matrix in further steps.

- **Step 2:** *Forming a lower triangular matrix using the pool of elements:* Construct a lower triangular matrix using the randomly selected elements from the key pool. This can be an $m \times m$ dimension matrix as given below. The first condition for selecting elements from the large pool is that all elements present in a column should be multiple of the diagonal element of the same column, some elements should be zero, some elements should be same as diagonal element and all the selected elements should be large. One more condition for this matrix is that summation of all the diagonal elements should not be divisible by the number of columns of the lower triangular matrix.

$$L = \begin{bmatrix} L_{11} & 0 & 0 & 0 \\ L_{21} & L_{22} & 0 & 0 \\ L_{31} & L_{32} & L_{33} & 0 \\ L_{41} & L_{42} & L_{43} & L_{44} \end{bmatrix}$$

- **Step 3:** *Forming an upper triangular matrix using lower triangular matrix:* Upper triangular matrix is formed by taking the simple transpose of lower triangular matrix, i.e., $U = L^T$, and this matrix is formed in a linear time as given below.

$$U = \begin{bmatrix} U_{11} & U_{12} & U_{13} & U_{14} \\ 0 & U_{22} & U_{23} & U_{24} \\ 0 & 0 & U_{33} & U_{34} \\ 0 & 0 & 0 & U_{44} \end{bmatrix}$$

- **Step 4:** *Forming a diagonal D matrix using U matrix:* Diagonal matrix D is constructed by choosing diagonal elements from matrix U and also generates a U' matrix, where $U = DU'$. Both D and U' are shown below.

$$D = \begin{bmatrix} U_{11} & 0 & 0 & 0 \\ 0 & U_{22} & 0 & 0 \\ 0 & 0 & U_{33} & 0 \\ 0 & 0 & 0 & U_{44} \end{bmatrix} \quad U' = \begin{bmatrix} 1 & U_{12}/U_{11} & U_{13}/U_{11} & U_{14}/U_{11} \\ 0 & 1 & U_{23}/U_{22} & U_{24}/U_{22} \\ 0 & 0 & 1 & U_{34}/U_{33} \\ 0 & 0 & 0 & 1 \end{bmatrix}$$

- **Step 5:** After computing L, U, D, and U' matrices, the base station selects one row, L_{r_i} from lower triangular matrix, L and one column, U'_{c_i} from upper triangular matrix, U' for each node and sends both the tuples along with diagonal matrix D to each node in the network. This is done by using the condition that the row number and column number selected for a particular node should be equal. The following example is given for more clarification:

Example: Suppose we have limited pool of keys $(-20 \sim 20)$. From this pool, we randomly select a subset of elements $(2,3,9,7,3,2,5,1,4,6,\ldots,20)$. Using these elements, we construct a lower triangular matrix, L shown in Figure 1(a). Upper triangular matrix, U is generated by taking simple transpose of L matrix (Figure 1(b)). Then we select the diagonal elements from U matrix and generate diagonal matrix, D shown in Figure 1(c). Finally, we construct U matrix such that $U = DU$ shown in Figure 1(d).

$$L = \begin{bmatrix} 2 & 0 & 0 & 0 \\ 4 & 5 & 0 & 0 \\ 16 & 15 & 6 & 0 \\ 20 & 10 & 12 & 9 \end{bmatrix} \quad U = \begin{bmatrix} 2 & 4 & 16 & 20 \\ 0 & 5 & 15 & 10 \\ 0 & 0 & 6 & 12 \\ 0 & 0 & 0 & 9 \end{bmatrix} \quad D = \begin{bmatrix} 2 & 0 & 0 & 0 \\ 0 & 5 & 0 & 0 \\ 0 & 0 & 6 & 0 \\ 0 & 0 & 0 & 9 \end{bmatrix} \quad U' = \begin{bmatrix} 1 & 2 & 8 & 10 \\ 0 & 1 & 3 & 2 \\ 0 & 0 & 1 & 2 \\ 0 & 0 & 0 & 1 \end{bmatrix}$$

Fig. 1. (a) Lower triangular matrix, L (b)Upper triangular matrix, U (c)Diagonal matrix, D (d)Upper triangular matrix, U'

4.1   Node to Node Pairwise Key Establishment

The existing random key pre-distribution schemes [3,1] allow node to node pairwise key establishment but these schemes have some drawbacks as discussed in section 2. As per [3,1], sending a direct key K_{ij} or k_{ji} between any pair of nodes is not secure because adversary can tamper the key. If the adversary captures the columns send by any node then she can calculate the original matrix by calculating the dimension of the matrix, and the column number in the matrix. The adversary can also put her node in place of actual node in the network and communicate with other nodes. To overcome these problems, we propose a new scheme for node to node mutual authentication by using a hash function, circular shift function and reverse function on L, U, D, and U' matrices which is described in the following steps:

- **Step 1:** Let $Node_A$ and $Node_B$ are in the network. Initially $Node_A$ applies Reverse function (R) on the selected column elements U'_{c_i} and after that it applies right circular shift (CS) function on the reversed data $R(U'_{c_i})$ for $(\sum_{i=1}^{n} D_{i,i} \bmod n)$ times and sends it to the $Node_B$.
- **Step 2:** $Node_B$ applies CS function on the data received from $Node_A$ and then applies reverse function to calculate U'_{c_i}. Then $Node_B$ computes the cross product $U_{c_i} = D \times U'_{c_i}$. After computing this cross product, $Node_B$ generates a key K_{ji} by multiplying L_{r_j} with U_{c_i}, and apply hash function on key K_{ji}, i.e., $H(K_{ji})$.
- **Step 3:** Now $Node_B$ applies the same process as done by $Node_A$ in step 1 on its own column U'_{c_j} and send this value with the generated hash key $H(K_{ji})$ to $Node_A$.
- **Step 4:** After receiving data from $Node_B$, $Node_A$ calculates K_{ij} similarly as $Node_B$ calculated in step 2 and apply the hash function H on K_{ij}.
- **Step 5:** After calculating the key $H(k_{ij})$, $Node_A$ checks whether $H(K_{ij})$ and $H(K_{ji})$ are equal or not. If $H(K_{ij})$ and $H(K_{ji})$ are equal then $Node_A$ sends *Yes* message along with $H(K_{ij})$ to $Node_B$ otherwise sends *errmsg* to $Node_B$. If the response is yes then $Node_B$ verifies $H(K_{ij})$ with $H(K_{ji})$ to establish a secure channel.

The above scheme is explained using an example in Table 1.

Advantages: The main advantages of the first scheme is the use of Circular Shift Function, Diagonal Matrix and Hash Function. When a node exchanges the column with other nodes, the adversary may capture the exchanged column. But the column is sent after applying reverse function and then circular shift function, thus the adversary cannot predict anything about the original matrix. Diagonal matrix is constructed by taking out diagonal elements from the upper triangular matrix U such that $U = D \times U'$. Even

Table 1. Node to Node Pairwise Key establishment

$Sensor\,Node_A$	Messages	$Sensor\,Node_B$
$L_{r_i} = (4, 5, 0, 0), i = 2$ $U'_{c_i} = (2, 1, 0, 0), i = 2$ $D_{n.n} = (2, 5, 6, 9), n = 1..4.$ Hash function CS function		$L_{r_j} = (16, 15, 6, 0), j = 3$ $U'_{c_j} = (8, 3, 1, 0), j = 3$ $D_{n.n} = (2, 5, 6, 9), n = 1..4.$ Hash function CS function
$U'_{r_i} = R\left(U'_{c_i}\right) = (0, 0, 1, 2)$ $U'_{cs_i} = CS\left(U'_{r_i}, 2\right) = (1, 2, 0, 0)$	$\xrightarrow{U'_{cs_i}}$	$U'_{c_i} = R\left(CS\left(U'_{cs_i}, 2\right)\right)$ $U_{c_i} = D \times U'_{c_i}$ $K_{ji} = L_{r_j} \times U_{c_i}$ $K_{ji} = 139$ apply hash on key $H(K_{ji})$
$U'_{c_j} = R\left(CS\left(U'_{cs_j}, 2\right)\right)$ $U_{c_j} = D \times U'_{c_j}$ $K_{ij} = L_{r_i} \times U_{c_j}$ $K_{ij} = 139$	$\xleftarrow{U'_{cs_j} = (3, 8, 0, 1),\, H(K_{ji})}$	$H(K_{ji}), U'_{cs_j} = CS(R(U'_{c_j}), 2)$
Apply Hash function on key $H(K_{ij})$		
Check $H(K_{ij}) = H(K_{ji})$		
If (*yes*)	$[yes, H(K_{ij})] \longrightarrow$	$H(K_{ji}) = H(K_{ij})$
If (*no*)	$[no, errmsg] \longrightarrow$	Connection discarded
	Secure communication established.	

if adversary captures this U'_{c_i} column, she cannot predict anything about upper triangular matrix U. Hash function is a one-way function, so it should be hard to find any message m, such that $h = H(m)$. It is easy to compute the hash value for any given message, but it is infeasible to find a message from a given hash.

In the first approach, if each node will delete its information then a new node cannot be added in the network but provide full resilience to node capture. In second way nodes do not delete all information regarding establishment of key, we can add new node in the network but not provide the resilience to node capture. The main disadvantage of this approach is that this scheme is not proving security for physical capture of nodes. In this approach we provided secure data exchange between nodes.

5   Proposed Second Key Pre-Distribution Scheme

To overcome the drawbacks of our previous scheme we have proposed a new key pre-distribution scheme called **A Key Pre-Distribution Scheme Based on Polynomial Pool Symmetric Matrix with LDU' composition for WSNs**. The following procedure is executed by the base station in order to construct *L, D, U* and U' matrices.

- **Step 1.** *Generation of large pool of polynomials ($-2^{18} \sim 2^{21}$ degree):* Base station generates large pool of polynomials over the finite field F_q, where q is a large prime number. The *t*-degree polynomial is of the form: $P_i(x) = \sum_{i=0}^{t} a_i x^i$ where a_i is the polynomial's i^{th} coefficient. These polynomials are then used to construct

a symmetric matrix A. Let us take an example for generating a large pool of polynomials of degree t $(-20 \sim 20)$. From this limit, we took $(P_1(x), P_2(x), P_3(x),$
$P_{10}(x), \ldots P_{20}(x))$ etc.

- **Step 2.** *Forming a lower triangular matrix using the pool of polynomials:* Randomly select polynomials from the above generated pool to construct a lower triangular matrix as shown below. The first condition for selecting polynomials from
the large pool is that all polynomials present in a column should be multiple of the
diagonal polynomial of that column and the degree of all the selected polynomial
should be large.

$$L = \begin{bmatrix} P_2(x) & 0 & 0 & 0 \\ P_4(x) & P_5(x) & 0 & 0 \\ P_{16}(x) & P_{15}(x) & P_6(x) & 0 \\ P_{20}(x) & P_{10}(x) & P_{12}(x) & P_9(x) \end{bmatrix}$$

- **Step 3.** *Forming an upper triangular matrix using lower triangular matrix:* Upper
triangular matrix is formed by taking the transpose of the above lower triangular
matrix L, i.e., $U = L^T$ as given below. This operation takes linear time thus it
minimizes the computational overhead.

$$U = \begin{bmatrix} P_2(x) & P_4(x) & P_{16}(x) & P_{20}(x) \\ 0 & P_5(x) & P_{15}(x) & P_{10}(x) \\ 0 & 0 & P_6(x) & P_{12}(x) \\ 0 & 0 & 0 & P_9(x) \end{bmatrix}$$

- **Step 4.** *Forming a diagonal matrix D and a new upper triangular matrix U':* We
take the diagonal polynomials from the upper triangular matrix U to construct the
diagonal matrix as shown below:

$$D = \begin{bmatrix} P_2(x) & 0 & 0 & 0 \\ 0 & P_5(x) & 0 & 0 \\ 0 & 0 & P_6(x) & 0 \\ 0 & 0 & 0 & P_9(x) \end{bmatrix} \quad U' = \begin{bmatrix} 1 & P_2(x) & P_8(x) & P_{20}(x) \\ 0 & 1 & P_3(x) & P_2(x) \\ 0 & 0 & 1 & P_2(x) \\ 0 & 0 & 0 & 1 \end{bmatrix}$$

The upper triangular matrix U can be written in the form $U = DU'$, where the new
upper triangular matrix U' is used for key establishment.

- **Step 5.** *Finding the Common Key:* Assume that $Node_A$ and $Node_B$ are in the network. In order to find a common key, the base station randomly selects a row L_{r_i}
from lower triangular matrix L and a column U'_{c_i} from upper triangular matrix U'
and send these two tuples along with diagonal matrix D to $Node_A$. The row number
and column number selected by the base station for $Node_A$ must be equal. Similarly the base station performs the same operation for other nodes in the network.
Then $Node_A$ and $Node_B$ calculate key K_{ij} and key K_{ji} respectively as shown in
Table 2. Since A is a symmetric matrix and $A = LDU'$ as per the definition given
in section 4, so K_{ij} and K_{ji} should be equal.

5.1   Node to Node Pairwise Key Establishment

The proposed scheme provides node to node pairwise key establishment which is explained in the following steps. These steps are also given in table 2. Here we have two nodes, $Node_A$ and $Node_B$, which perform the following operations:

1. $Node_A$ sends column U'_{c_i} to $Node_B$. $Node_A \rightarrow Node_B : U'_{c_i}$
2. $Node_B$ receives U'_{c_i} and calculates U_{c_i} by multiplying diagonal matrix D with U'_{c_i} and computes the key K_{ji}. $U_{c_i} = D \times U'_{c_i}$.
   $K_{ji}(x) = L_{r_j} \times U_{r_i}$
   $Node_B$ randomly generates a large number α' and applies hash function H on α'.
   $\alpha = H(\alpha')$
   $Node_B$ calculates the key K_{ji} by replacing α in place of x in $K_{ji}(x)$.
   $K_{ji} = K_{ji}(\alpha)$
3. After calculating the key K_{ji}, $Node_B$ computes $H(K_{ji})$ and sends it along with α' and U'_{c_j} to $Node_A$. $Node_B \rightarrow Node_A: U'_{c_j}, H(K_{ji}), \alpha'$
   K_{ji} should be the common between $Node_A$ and $Node_B$.
4. Similarly $Node_A$ calculates K_{ij} and apply hash function H on K_{ij} and calculate $H(K_{ij})$.
5. Then $Node_A$ perform some check operation as:
   $Node_A$ check whether $H(K_{ij})$ and $H(K_{ji})$ are equal or not.
   if $(H(k_{ij}) = H(k_{ji}))$ send $[Yes, H(k_{ij})]$ to $Node_B$ else send $[No, errmsg]$ to $Node_B$

After establishment of key among the nodes, each node deletes all of its information which is used during the establishment of keys.

6   Proposed Key Distribution Scheme for Addition of a New Node

After the completion of key establishment over the network, each node deletes its information related to the key establishment. So the addition of new node in the network will create a problem because at that moment every node has already deleted the information related to the key establishment. To solve this problem we proposed a scheme for addition of new nodes.

6.1   Lower Triangular Matrix Based

We proposed a new approach based on lower triangular matrix, for adding new nodes in the network. We take a lower triangular matrix L of polynomials, which are randomly selected from large polynomial pool. These polynomials are different from the polynomials which are used in the previous scheme in the sense that the degree of each polynomial selected from the pool, should be different i.e. for any two polynomial $p_i(x)$ and $p_j(x)$, their corresponding degree t_i and t_j should not be equal. Let L be a lower triangular matrix of polynomials.

$$L = \begin{bmatrix} P_7(x), t_7 & 0 & 0 & 0 \\ P_6(x), t_6 & P_5(x), t_5 & 0 & 0 \\ P_1(x), t_1 & P_2(x), t_2 & P_3(x), t_3 & 0 \\ P_8(x), t_8 & P_{10}(x), t_{10} & P_4(x), t_4 & P_9(x), t_9 \end{bmatrix}$$

Table 2. Node to Node mutual Authentication

$Sensor\,Node_A$	messages	$Sensor\,Node_B$
$L_{r_i} = (P_{16}(x), P_{15}(x), P_6(x), 0), i = 3$ $U'_{c_i} = (P_8(x), P_3(x), 1, 0), i = 3$ $D_{n,n} = (P_2(x), P_5(x), P_6(x), P_9(x)), n = 1..4$ Hash function		$L_{r_j}(P_4(x), P_5(x), 0, 0), j = 2$ $U'_{c_j}(P_2(x), 1, 0, 0), j = 2$ $D_{n,n} = (P_2(x), P_5(x), P_6(x), P_9(x)), n = 1..4$ Hash function
$U'_{c_i} = (P_8(x), P_3(X), 1, 0))$	$\xrightarrow{U'_{c_i}}$	$U_{c_i} = D \times U'_{c_i}$ $K_{ji} = L_{r_j} \times U_{c_i}$ $K_{ji}(x) = P_4(x) \cdot P_{16}(x) + P_{15}(x) \cdot P_5(x)$ Generate a number α' Apply hash function on α', i.e., $\alpha = H(\alpha')$ $K_{ji} = K_{ji}(\alpha)$. Apply Hash on K_{ji}, i.e., $H(K_{ji})$ $H(K_{ji}).U'_{c_j}$
$U_{c_j} = D \times U'_{c_j}$ $K_{ij} = L_{r_i} \times U_{c_j}$ $K_{ij}(x) = P_4(x) \cdot P_{16}(x) + P_{15}(x) \cdot P_5(x)$ $K_{ij} = K_{ij}(H(\alpha'))$	$U'_{c_j}, \alpha'. H(K_{ji})$	
Apply Hash function on key $H(K_{ij})$		
Check $H(K_{ij}) = H(K_{ji})$		
If (yes)	$yes, H(K_{ij})$	$H(K_{ji}) = H(K_{ij})$
If (no)	$no, errmsg$	Connection discarded
Secure communication established. Node delete all information after established keys.		

Before the deployment of the network, we randomly select a polynomial and its corresponding degree from the above lower triangular matrix, L and give it to a particular node in the network. After distributing different polynomials to different nodes, we apply the efficient sorting algorithm to sort the polynomial elements of the lower triangular matrix in order of their degree. Then, we construct a new sorted lower triangular matrix L_{sort} by using the above sorted polynomials. As per matrix L_{sort}, $P_i(x), t_i < P_j(x), t_j$ if $i < j$ for $\forall i, j$.

$$L_{sort} = \begin{bmatrix} P_1(x), t_1 & 0 & 0 & 0 \\ P_2(x), t_2 & P_3(x), t_3 & 0 & 0 \\ P_4(x), t_4 & P_5(x), t_5 & P_6(x), t_6 & 0 \\ P_7(x), t_7 & P_8(x), t_8 & P_9(x), t_9 & P_{10}(x), t_{10} \end{bmatrix}$$

Now each node V_j will evaluate its polynomial on its own id ID_{V_j}. After that each node will erase the polynomial and keep the evaluated value $P_i(ID_V)$ and polynomial's degree t_i.

When a new node U is being added to the network, the sorted lower triangular matrix L_{sort} is given to the new node U. For key establishment with node U, every neighbor node V_j will send a randomly generated value α, ID_{V_j}, t_j and encrypted value of α, i.e., $ENC_{P_i(ID_{V_j})}(\alpha)$ to node U. After receiving key related information from its neighbor, the new node U will search the polynomial of degree t_j using diagonal search on the sorted lower triangular matrix L_{sort}. Now node U will evaluate this polynomial on ID of node V_j and compute α by decrypting the received message with $P_i(ID_{V_j})$. Then the node U compare the computed α with the α received from its neighbor V_j. If it matches then $P_i(ID_{V_j})$ is the common key between U and V_j. For the sake of simplicity, we have used the notation K_{SV_j} for $P_i(ID_{V_j})$. It will first search the polynomial from the

```
 1: Give sorted lower triangular matrix to node U
 2: for each node in the network do
 3:    Randomly select a polynomial Pk(X) from sorted lower triangular matrix, eval-
       uate it on IDVj i.e. Pk(IDVj) and give it to each node
       / * V1, V2........Vm are neighbors of node U */
 4: end for
 5: for j = 1 to m do
 6:    Send α , ENCKSVj (α) , IDVj, tj to new node U.
 7:    for i = 1 to |k| do
 8:       New node U will search the polynomial of degree tj in the sorted lower trian-
          gular matrix Lsort using diagonal search. If found, evaluate the polynomial
          on IDVj. K'U.Vj = Pi(IDVj) that equals to KSVj
 9:       Decrypt ENCKSVj (α) with K'U.Vj which gives α'
10:       if α' = α then
11:          U randomly generates a key KU.Vj, encrypt it with K'U.Vj and send as
             ENCK'U.Vj (KU.Vj)
12:          Node Vj will decrypt it with KSVj and will get the key KU.Vj.
13:          Erase K = Pi(IDVj)
14:          break;
15:       end if
16:       Erase K = Pi(IDVj)
17:    end for
18: end for
19: Erase all the polynomials
```

Fig. 2. Algorithm for Addition of new node U

matrix L_{sort} and put ID_{V_j} in that polynomial. By using this newly established common key $K_{S_{V_j}}$, the node U and neighbor node V_j share a new key K_{U,V_j}. After establishing the new key K_{U,V_j}, both the nodes delete the previously established common key $K_{S_{V_j}}$. Now both U and V_j have same key K_{U,V_j} for further communication. This process is repeated for each node. The new node U also randomly choose a polynomial from lower triangular matrix L_{sort} and evaluates on its own id, i.e., ID_U. After that the node U deletes all information regarding key establishment. The complete algorithm for addition of new node in the network is given in Figure 2.

Advantages: The main advantage of this scheme is that the establishment of key between the new node U and all its neighbors takes very less time and less computational overhead. If the adversary captures some node in the network, she will not get any information regarding the polynomials as the polynomials are different for each node in the network and the new node will also delete all its information after establishment of key with all its neighboring nodes.

7 Performance Analysis and Comparison

In this section, we present the evaluation of the performances of our schemes, and compare the scheme with Eschenauer and Gligor scheme[8]. Our focus are on analysis of the network connectivity, analysis of resilience against nodes capture and Analysis memory usage by each node in the network.

7.1   Analysis of Network Connectivity

In this subsection, we will evaluate the network connectivity and compare it with Eschenauer and Gligor scheme [8]. In our proposed scheme network connectivity is the probability (P) of sharing at least one key between any two sensor nodes. We define an event in which a pair of nodes that does not have a common any one key by an [Event], and $P_r[Event]$ is the probability of such event. The network connectivity P is:

$$P = 1 - P_r[Event]$$
$$P = 1 - (1 - K/S)^{2S-2K+1}/(1 - 2K/S)^{S-2K+1/2}$$

where S= total number of node in network and K is the number of keys in each node.

In the first and second scheme, we have shown that any two sensor nodes can always find a shared key between themselves using LDU' composition. In other word, we can say that the probability of not sharing a common key between any two network sensor nodes is zero. Figure 3(a) compares network connectivity P of our proposed scheme

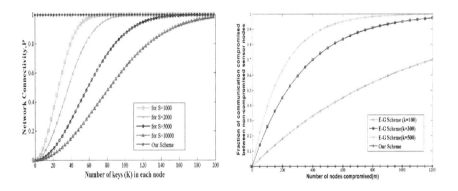

Fig. 3. (a) Analysis of network connectivity and (b) Network resilience comparison between E-G scheme and our scheme

with the Eschenauer and Gligor schemes [8]. In the performance analysis, we assume that the size of key pool for each node is 1000, 2000, 5000 and 10000. The result shows that the proposed scheme has hundred percent connectivity without concern for the number of keys per node. In addition, keys in our scheme occupy less memory space in sensor nodes.

7.2   Analysis of Resilience Against Node Capture

In wireless sensor networks, an adversary can easily calculate the information of compromised nodes, intentionally provide misleading information to the entire network, and break the whole network security. In this subsection we evaluated that the proposed scheme improves WSNs resilience by calculating the fraction of compromised nodes among non-compromised nodes. In addition, we plan to compare our scheme with Eschenauer and Gligor schemes [8] based on performance. In Eschenauer and Gligor schemes [8], the probability of compromising the shared keys between any two non-compromised nodes is following:

$$P_{compromised} = (1 - (1 - k/S)^m)$$

where S is the total number of node in network and K is the number of keys in each node. In the proposed scheme, rows from lower triangular matrix L, column from upper triangular matrix U', diagonal matrix D, hash function H and circular shift function (CS) are deleted after the Establishment of the keys. Polynomials which are pre-distributed to each node are randomly selected from the lower triangular matrix L and its degree will be left in each node for the purpose of addition of new nodes in network. If m nodes are compromised, the probability of compromising the shared keys between any two non-compromised nodes is equal to the probability of compromising the shared polynomials between any two non-compromised nodes But in our scheme, adversary will not get any information from compromised nodes about non-compromised nodes, so we can say that m is equal to zero. Thus in our scheme, the probability of compromising the shared keys between any two non-compromised nodes is:

$$P_{compromised} = (1 - (1 - k/S)^0)$$
$$P_{compromised} = (1 - 1) = 0$$

In case, if adversary captures one node and get the degree of polynomial and key generated by polynomial then there is no effect on other nodes in the network. Thus, our scheme provide 100% resilience against node capture. In the figure 3(b) shows the comparison between Eschenauer and Gligor schemes [8] and the proposed scheme.

7.3   Memory Usage Analysis

In the proposed scheme, any two sensor nodes establish the shared key by using polynomial with LDU' composition based key pre-distribution scheme. The major part of memory is used in storing the polynomial information. We proposed an efficient method to store the row and column information of L, D, and U' matrices. Our scheme will store each element in the non-zero-element part and one value specifying the maximum number of zeros in zero-element part of L and U matrices. This technique is specially suitable for large wireless senor networks. The notations, used in estimating the storage efficiency, are given below:

- M_b:The number of bits to store each polynomial information in L, D, and U' matrix.
- S: The maximum number of sensor nodes deployed in the network.
- Z_{ni}: The total number of nonzero elements in a row of L and in a column of U' and diagonal D stored in sensor node with node ID_i.
- Z_o: The number of bits, needed to store the number of zero elements in zero element part in row of L or in a column of U' could be represented.

- U_{total}: The total memory required using the above method.
- U_{saving}: Memory saved using the above method.
- $U_{without}$: The total memory required without using our method.
- λ_i: The sum of total bits needed to store the polynomial information in each node in the network.

Now the memory usage to store polynomial information in sensor node is:
$\lambda_i = (Z_{ni} \times M_b + 2 \times Z_o + M_b + S \times M_b)$
Memory usage for S number of node in networks:
$U_{total} = \sum_{i=1}^{S} \lambda_i$
$U_{total} = M_b \sum_{i=1}^{S} Z_{ni} + S \times (2 \times Z_o) + S \times M_b + S^2 \times M_b$
$U_{total} = M_b \times 2(1 + 2 + 3 + 4 + ...S) + S \times (2 \times Z_o) + S \times M_b + S^2 \times M_b$
$U_{total} = M_b \times 2.S(S+1)/2 + S \times (2 \times Z_o) + S \times M_b + S^2 \times M_b$
$U_{total} = M_b \times S(S+1) + S \times (2 \times Z_o) + S \times M_b + S^2 \times M_b$
$U_{total} = M_b \times S(S+1) + S \times (2 \times \lceil log_2(S-1) \rceil) + S \times M_b + S^2 \times M_b$
where $Z_o = \lceil log_2(S-1) \rceil$
In our proposed scheme, the memory saving is done by encoding the zeros in the zero-element parts of the L, D, and U' matrices. Hence, the memory saved could be computed as:
Memory usage with out our scheme:
$U_{without} = 2S^2 \times M_b + S \times M_b + S^2 \times M_b$
Now we can calculate saving memory by $U_{saving} = U_{without} - U_{total}$
$U_{saving} = 2S^2 \times M_b + S \times M_b + S^2 \times M_b - (M_b \times S(S+1) + S \times (2 \times \lceil log_2(S-1) \rceil) + S \times M_b + S^2 \times M_b)$
$U_{saving} = 2S^2 \times M_b - M_b(S(S+1)) - 2SZ_o$
$U_{saving} = SM_b(2S - (S+1)) - 2SZ_o$
$U_{saving} = SM_b(S-1) - 2SZ_o$
we know that $Z_o = \lceil log_2(S-1) \rceil$
$U_{saving} = SM_b(S-1) - 2S(\lceil log_2(S-1) \rceil)$

In Eschenauer and Gligor [8] scheme, to maintain the certain network connectivity, which is the probability that two neighboring sensor nodes can establish a direct shared key, the number of keys cannot be too small. However, large number of keys means the adversary can obtain more secrets each time she compromises one more node. The contradiction of memory requirements make it difficult to optimize both security and network connectivity given fixed memory resource. A merit of our scheme is that the memory usage is unrelated with network connectivity, and any two sensor nodes always find a shared key between them by using our scheme.

8 Conclusion

The first key distribution scheme that has been proposed in this paper has very good resilience to data exchanged between the nodes and also took very less time to establishment of key between the nodes. This proposed scheme has very less computational overhead to calculate the key in the network. In our first approach, if every node deletes all its information then a new node cannot be added in the network but still it provides full resilience to the node capture. In other way, if nodes do not delete their information regarding establishment of key, then we can add a new node in the network without providing the resilience to node capture. So in this approach we consider that each node deletes all its information regarding key establishment and proposed new scheme to add new node in the network. In our second approach, we have proposed a new key pre-distribution scheme based on polynomials pool of a symmetric matrix with LDU' composition. This scheme guaranteed that any pair of nodes can find a common key between themselves and also it allows more security enhancement on node-to-node pairwise key establishment. In this paper we showed that both the approaches give many advantages over probabilistic key distribution scheme and deterministic key distribution scheme and our approach requires less memory space for keying material and provide full network connectivity, even after compromising any number of nodes in the network. Our proposed scheme requires very less time to establish a common key between any two nodes while other existing schemes require O(k) [1] and O(k^2) [3]. Our proposed scheme makes a significant improvement in the performance and energy efficiency of the sensor nodes. There is some scope to improve upon our algorithm. Developing a scheme, that provides better path key establishment while retaining good features of our algorithm, would be future work.

References

1. Choi, S.J., Youn, H.Y.: Mkps: A multi-level key pre- distribution scheme for secure wireless sensor networks. In: HCI, vol. (2), pp. 808–817 (2007)
2. Naik, P., Ravichandran, K., Sivalingam, K.M.: Cryptographic key exchange based on locationing information. Pervasive Mob. Comput. 3(1), 15–35 (2007)
3. Park, C.-W., Choi, S.J., Youn, H.Y.: A noble key pre- distribution scheme with lu matrix for secure wireless sensor networks. CIS (2), 494–499 (2005)
4. Zhu, S., Xu, S., Setia, S., Jajodia, S.: Establishing pairwise keys for secure communication in ad hoc networks: A probabilistic approach. In: ICNP, pp. 326–335 (2003)
5. Akyildiz, I.F., Su, W., Sankarasubramaniam, Y., Cayirci, E.: Wireless sensor networks: a survey Arch. Rat. Mech. Anal. 78, 393–422 (1982)
6. Stajano, F.: Security for Ubiquitous Computing. John Wiley and Sons, Chichester (2002)
7. Rivest, R.L., Shamir, A., Adleman, L.: A Method for Obtaining Digital Signatures and Public-Key Cryptosystems. Communications of the ACM 21(2), 120–126 (1978)
8. Eschenauer, L., Gligor, V.D.: A key-management scheme for distributed sensor networks. In: ACM Conference on Computer and Communications Security, pp. 41–47 (2002)
9. Blom, R.: An optimal class of symmetric key generation systems. In: Eurocrypt 1976 (1976)
10. Perrig, A., Szewczyk, R., Wen, V., Culler, D., Tygar, J.D.: Spins: security protocols for sensor networks. In: MobiCom 2001: Proceedings of the 7th Annual International Conference on Mobile Computing and Networking, pp. 189–199. ACM, New York (2001)

Energy Efficient Multi Channel MAC Protocols for Wireless Ad Hoc Networks

B. Nithya, Ashok Kumar Alluri, and C. Mala

Department of Computer Science and Engineering,
National Institute of Technology,
Tiruchirapalli 620 015, Tamil Nadu, India
{nithya,mala}@nitt.edu, ashok.alluri8011@gmail.com

Abstract. Wireless ad-hoc networks are expected to support a variety of services with diverse Quality-of-service (QoS) requirements. For example, a mixture of delay-sensitive applications and delay-tolerant ones must be supported. Given that the two principal wireless network resources, i.e., bandwidth and energy, are scarce, the main challenge in designing wireless networks is to use network resources as efficiently as possible while providing the QoS required by the users. This paper presents an overview of energy efficient Multi channel MAC protocols and summarizes them in a technical way.

Keywords: Wireless Ad-Hoc networks, QoS, Multi channel, Energy efficient.

1 Introduction

A wireless ad hoc network is a collection of wireless nodes that can dynamically self-organize into an arbitrary and temporary topology to form a decentralized network without necessarily using any pre-established infrastructure. It is one of the challenging and more innovative areas of wireless networking with many applications in different fields especially in emergencies, telemedicine, military, entertainment, and out-door business environments where instant fixed infrastructure or centralized administration is too difficult or too expensive to install.

The most popular MAC layer protocol for Ad Hoc networks is IEEE 802.11. It uses the CSMA/CA (carrier sense multiple access with collision avoidance) protocol where RTS/CTS mechanism is used to transmit the packets. RTS (Request to send) and CTS (clear to send) packets will be exchanged in order to reduce the collisions due to hidden and exposed terminal problems. But this mechanism has its own drawbacks i) This mechanism does not allow simultaneous transmissions ii) The fixed power method may lead to more receiving power than required SINR(signal to noise ratio) and hence life time of node will get reduced.

Energy efficiency continues to be a key performance metric as efficient utilization of energy increases the network longevity hence critical in enhancing the network capacity [1].The main objective of this paper is to review the some approaches for energy efficient multi channel MAC protocols that have been proposed in the literature. The rest of the paper structured as follows. Section 2 focuses on issues

D.C. Wyld et al. (Eds.): NeCoM/WeST/WiMoN 2011, CCIS 197, pp. 358–367, 2011.
© Springer-Verlag Berlin Heidelberg 2011

related with single channel and multi channel MAC protocols. Energy efficient techniques are discussed in section 3. The following protocols and their comparisons are presented in Section 4 and 5 respectively.

Dual Reservation CDMA-based MAC Protocol with Power Control (DRCPC) [4] is proposed for power control in multi channel protocol along with improved throughput and to reduce the near-far interference. TDMA based multi-channel MAC protocol (TMMAC) [5] is proposed to save the energy and to improve the communication throughput. Two-phase coding multichannel protocol with power control (TPCPC) [6] is proposed based on CDMA technique to improve the throughput when the network is overloaded. Dynamic Channel Assignment with power control (DCA-PC) [7] assigns channels on demand and supports node mobility, frequency reusability and network scalability. Multi channel based power control (MCBPC) [8] combines power control, multi channel MAC protocol and minimum energy route protocol together.

Finally section 6 concludes the paper.

2 Single Channel vs. Multi Channel MAC Protocols

2.1 Design Issues in Single Channel MAC Protocols

Many MAC protocols which use a single common channel to be shared by mobile hosts are called as Single Channel MAC protocols. Widely accepted single channel protocol is the IEEE 802.11 [3]. The most serious problem is that the network performance will degrade as the network load increases due to the rapidly raised contentions and collisions of the transmitted packets because of hidden-terminal, exposed-terminal problems and near-far terminals. To overcome these problems, usage of multiple channels is a better solution.

2.2 Design Issues in Multichannel MAC Protocols

Using Multi Channel MAC protocols, a mobile host with CDMA technology can utilize multiple codes simultaneously or dynamically switch from one code to another. This leads to increased throughput, decreased probability of collisions and QoS support. There are two tasks to be addressed by Multi Channel MAC protocols: i. Channel Assignment (to decide which channel can be used by which hosts) and ii. Medium access (to resolve the potential contention or collision problem when communicating in a particular channel). The issues are

1. Hardware Cost
2. Channel Assignment
3. Synchronization
4. Losing channel information
5. Disordered Channel Reuse

3 Energy Efficient MAC Protocols

Power of the wireless device is temporally supported by the battery. Energy Saving is hence become important consideration in MAC protocol design. With the increase in the number of mobile devices, and with communication being the major cause of energy consumption, the power savings of a MAC protocol becomes a pertinent issue. There are mainly two categories of power-saving schemes for MAC protocol design namely (i) Power Saving and (ii) Transmission Power Control (TPC). In Power Saving, nodes enter into a sleep state by turning off their radio to avoid overhearing cross-traffic. TPC involves reducing the signal transmission power to a minimum level that enables the destination to clearly receive the message. TPC not only reduces the energy consumed for each data packet transmission, but also improves the network throughput by means of increasing the channel spatial reuse. Advantages of having energy efficient MAC protocols:

1. The precious battery energy of portable devices may sustain for longer time.
2. The co-channel interference with neighboring nodes will be avoided.
3. Near far problem is solved by power control significantly.
4. It increases channel re usability (Figure 1).

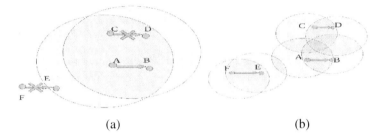

(a)   (b)

Fig. 1. Transmission scenarios a) when there is no power control (only one transmission) b) when there is a power control (three communications simultaneously)

The factors to be considered while designing power efficient MAC protocols

1. All packets that causes the collisions have to be discarded and their re-transmissions which increase the energy consumption.
2. Idle listening period must be minimized.
3. Unnecessary overhearing must be minimized.
4. Minimal number of control packets should be used to make data transmissions in order to reduce control overhead.
5. Explore the tradeoff between bandwidth utilization and energy consumption.
6. The transmission of a message when the destination node is not ready is called over emitting and this need to be reduced.

4   Energy Efficient Multi Channel MAC Protocols

MAC protocols which bring the concepts of power control and multi channel medium access together are described briefly by stating the essential behavior of these protocols. Moreover, the advantages and disadvantages of these protocols are presented.

4.1 DRCPC (Dual Reservation CDMA Based MAC Protocol with Power Control)

DRCPC [4] is a CDMA based MAC protocol with power control and proposed to reduce collisions and near-far interference. The various states of the nodes are Idle, Data, DR (Dual Reservation) and Broadcast state. If the node is in idle state, it listens onto Common Channel (cm). If it is either in Data or Dr state, it listens onto Data channel (cd), else it listens onto Broadcast Channel (cb) to reduce the collisions between broadcast message and RTS/CTS message by using a narrow bandwidth out-of-band Busy Tone (BT) transceiver. Since this protocol is based on CDMA, either static spreading code or dynamic spreading code protocol should be used. In static spreading code protocol, code should be pre allocated and this is unsuitable for the decentralized network. Therefore dynamic spreading code protocol is used. It is easy to implement because nodes just listen on the common channel in idle state.

Simulation Result & Drawback: It has been shown that [4] DRCPC minimizes collision and retransmission as arrival rate increased and achieves better performance that 802.11 DCF. However if number of nodes is increased, common channel will be saturated very soon because of RTS/CTS overhead. Expensive simulation study is needed with different routing protocols to analyze the performance.

Table 1. States and Channel Details (Transmission from A to B)

S. no	State/channel used	Source node	Destination node	Other nodes
1	Idle / cm	Sends RTS (+its ACL) using P_{max}. After receiving CTS, it goes to Data State.	After receiving RTS, it compares A's ACL with its ACL, reply CTS (+ cd + p_{min}) using P_{max} and goes to Data State.	Overhear RTS and/or CTS, updates their code lists and remains in Idle State.
2	Data / cd	Sends data with p_{min}	Receive data and send ACK using p_{min} with reservation flag as 0, if there is no reverse flow. If it is, send piggybacking ACK with reservation flag as 1 and goes to DR state.	
3	DR / cd	After receiving ACK, it waits for the reverse flow of data if the flag is 1.	Transmit data packet as reverse flow until it reaches the reservation threshold.	
4	Broadcast/cb	BT transceiver is turned on to produce a sine wave on cm, goes to cb state.	Idle nodes sensing BT signal will switch to cb.	

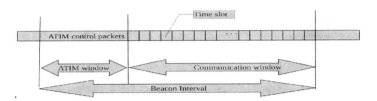

Fig. 2. Overall architecture of TMMAC

4.2 TMMAC (TDMA Based Multi Channel MAC)

TMMAC [5] is a traffic adaptive and energy efficient TDMA scheduling algorithm Its main features are explicit frequency and time negotiation, dynamic ATIM window and broadcast support. Time is divided into fixed length beacon interval which consists of ATIM window and communication window. The communication window is further divided into time slot and the duration of the time slot is long enough to accommodate data packet and ACK transmission and time needed to switch the channel. During the ATIM window all nodes listen to the same default channel to decide which channel to use, which time slot, size of ATIM window and number of data packets to be sent with the help of control packets ATIM, ATIM-ACK, ATIM-RES and ATIM-BRD. Each node maintains CUB (channel Usage Bitmap) and that is transmitted along with ATIM packets. It is used to keep track of the allocations of all the previous negotiations in the current ATIM Window. Time slots allotted by the current negotiation are maintained by CAB (Channel Allocation Bitmap). It is not maintained at the node, and transmitted along with ATIM-ACK, ATIM-REs or ATIM-BRD packets.

Dynamic ATIM Window algorithm:

Finite set of ATIM window sizes is maintained as { $ATIM_1$,........,$ATIM_i$, $ATIM_{i+1}$,...., $ATIM_m$} where $ATIM_1$ is a minimal window size and $ATIM_m$ is the maximal window size and $ATIM_i$ - $ATIM_{i+1}$ = length of the time slot. Assume the transmission from A to B

    if (A knows B's ATIM window size)
       if(min{A's ATIM window size,B's ATIM window size} is enough for negotiation)
           A send the ATIM packet to B
      else
           A waits for the next beacon interval
    else
      if ($ATIM_1$ (minimal window size) is   enough for the negotiation)
           A sends ATIM to B
      else
           A waits for the next beacon interval

After ATIM window, nodes can send, receive packets or go to doze mode to save power. If a node has negotiated to send or receive, it first switches its channel to the negotiated channel and waits for the data packet. After receiving, receiver sends ACK in the same time slot. If the sender doesn't hear an ACK, it retransmits in the next scheduled time slot, which is negotiated with the same receiver. In case of unicast negotiation, source node sends ATIM with its CUBs and number of packets to be sent. After receiving, destination node decides which channel and time slot to be used based on its CUBs and source's CUBs. If there are multiple available channel at one time slot, destination select at most one channel randomly. If destination can't allocate enough time slots as the number of packets specified in the ATIM packet, it allocates as many time slots as possible. After deciding channel and time slots to be used destination will send ATIM ACK with corresponding CAB. Once source the node receives, it will update its CUBs and sends ATIM RES to destination. Nodes overhearing ACK/RES will update their current channel usage information. In case of broadcast negotiation, node randomly selects the time slots in which all the channels are not used by any of its neighbors yet. Then it randomly selects a channel for each chosen time slot and updates its CUBs and generates the corresponding CABs. It broadcasts the ATIM-BRD with CABs. By overhearing other nodes know which time slot and channel to be used and update their CUBs.

Simulation Result and Drawback : It has been shown [5] that per packet energy consumption is reduced compared to MMAC when the network is overloaded. Because TMMAC allows a node to switch to doze mode slot whenever it is not scheduled to transmit or receive a packet. It dynamically adjusts the ATIM window size based on different traffic patterns. TMMAC achieves higher aggregate throughput and lower energy consumption. But each node has to maintain necessary data structure such as CUBs, ATIM window size. As well as tight time synchronization is needed.

4.3 TPCPC (Two Phase Coding with Power Control)

CDMA based TPCPC [6] uses a Common control channel and one data channel with multiple codes. Each node has GPS to know its approximate geographical position and multimode transceiver. It assumes that any one hop neighbors know the codes of each other through broadcast. First phase codes are used to differentiate between different cells that are distributed according to hexagonal cellular structure. Second phase code is used to differentiate between nodes in the same cell. Cell size and number of available codes are determined by using Poisson distribution. Each node communicates with its neighbors using unique codes that can be reused only if two nodes are more than 2-hops away.

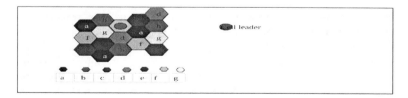

Fig. 3. The Distribution of First Phase Codes

Channel usage: In Common Control Channel (CCC) control packets (CAR, CAS, ACS) are transmitted. Contention only happens in CCC during their contending to obtain the second phase codes. In data channel (DC), no contention and collision will exist since in a specific cell different nodes take their unique codes with them.

Within a cluster, there will be a cell leader to coordinate the operation of all other nodes in that cluster (Figure 3). The central part is the area in which the cell leader mostly stays in. Nodes that come into this central part will get the chance for becoming a cell leader. If the cell leader moves, it sets want-to-retire signal in broadcast signal and the receivers will judge if they are suitable to assume this responsibility. The former cell leader can turn its leader role to the responding receiver. Any node in the central part may consult if current cell leader is willing to hand over this right.

Selecting second phase code: When a node moves from one cell to another cell, it must release the old code before requesting a new code. It tunes its transmitting and receiving corresponding to different first phase codes inherent to that cell and sends Code Request Signal(CRS) to the cell leader on common control channel for maximum of three times. Each time the transmitting power is increased gradually. If the cell leader is not in cross cell area, it allocates a unique code to the requesting node with Code Allocation Reply (CAR). If it is in cross cell area, it sends its updated Available Code Set(ACS) to the requesting node. The node listens to all responses from the adjacent cell leaders and select from the intersection of these ACSs. After that, it sends ACK to all cell leaders so that they can timely update the ACS.

If the requesting node cannot receive CAR, it follows 802.11 back o_ mechanism and the maximum count is set as 3. If it still can't receive CAR, then the node will assume itself as the first node appearing in the current cell and upgrade as the cell leader. Then it selects its unique code randomly and updates the whole code set. CRS and ACK are modulated with different specific orthogonal codes and with implicit first phase code of the cell. CAR is transmitted with only first phase code.

Power Control aspects: The cell leader and other nodes adjust their transmitting power according to its receiving signal strength and current transmitting power from the demanding nodes.

Simulation Result and Drawback: It has been shown that [6] Average throughput and aggregate throughput is increased when the network load is increased compared to 802.11.But frequent movement of cell leader will affect the performance. Each node must maintain code synchronization with other nodes.

4.4 Dynamic Channel Assignment with Power Control (DCA-PC)

A Dynamic Channel Assignment with Power Control (DCA-PC) [7] is an extension of DCA[9]. It combines channel assignment, medium access and power control aspects. Every node is assigned channels dynamically and equipped with two transceivers. One transceiver is used to listen the control traffic (RTS, CTS, RES etc) on control channel (using maximum power) and other switches between the data channels for exchanging data and ack using proper power level. The pair of source and destination nodes uses a RTS/CTS dialog to decide which channel to grab and which power level to use for data transmission. A RES message is used to reserve the data channel. Then data packets and ACKs are transmitted on the reserved data channel using the assigned power level.

Algorithm:

Assume the transmission from A to B.

1. A selects the free channel based on the information stored in the above three data structures.
2. A sends RTS (FCL, length of the data packet to be sent) to B with P_{max} on control channel and waits for B's CTS with a timeout period.
3. B selects the data channel based on A's FCL and its own FCL's and sends CTS on control channel either with data channel to be used, duration and power level of A or with error message indicating no free channel. In later case, A has to go back to step1.
4. Nodes receiving RTS / CTS , update their channel lists and power table.
5. If A receives CTS from B within timeout period, it updates its channel list and broadcasts RES with channel to be used, duration and power level using p_{max} on control channel. If it is not, A will retry until the maximum number of retries is reached.
6. A sends data packet to B on the selected data channel with power level of B.
7. After receiving data packets from A, B sends an ACK on the selected data channel with power level of A.

Simulation Results & Drawbacks: DCA-PC has been shown [7] to achieve higher throughput than DCA. However, it is observed that when the number of channels is increased beyond a point (usually less than 7 channels are beneficial) , the effect of power control is less significant due to overloading of the control channel

4.5 MCBPC (Multi-Channel Based Power Control protocol)

MCBPC [8] combines power control, multi channel MAC protocol and minimum energy route protocol together. It uses one dedicated control channel with maximum power level to exchange all the broadcast packets, RTS, CTS, PREQ and hello packets and separate N data channels to exchange data and acknowledgment the collisions with proper power level. The modified AODV is used as an on-demand minimum energy routing protocol to choose the minimum energy conservation route.

When there are no packets to transmit, nodes listen on public channel. After receiving broadcast packets, node can measure the received power and it can determine the proper transmitting power it needs to reach its neighbors. Transmit power is divided into several levels. Only when a power changing exceeds its current level and lasts for a period of time, the change will be reported to upper layer and will triggers route or topology maintenance. Instead of hop count as a route metric, modified AODV uses a route cost for selecting the best route.

$$Route\ cost_j = \propto \sum_{i,i+1 \in j} P^{i,i+1}_{prop\_t} + (1-\propto)H_j$$

Hello messages sent once per second are used for route maintenance. If the node fails to receives 3 consecutive hello messages from its neighbors, it is taken as an indication that the link to that neighbor is down. When a node detects transmission power level change in 3 consecutive hello messages, it confirms that the distance to this neighbor has been changed and adjusts its route table accordingly.

Simulation results & Drawbacks: It has been shown [8] that the packet delivery ratio is increased compared to AODV in 802.11. Based on end-to-end delay, 802.11 with AODV is better than MCBPC. Because in MCBPC, modified AODV may select longer route as the energy route , so it will increase end-to-end delay. But it can reduce collisions in data transmission by which it avoids delay brought by retransmission.

5   Comparison

In many cases, it is difficult to compare them directly since each method has a different goal with different assumptions and uses different ways to achieve the goal. For example, when the transmission power is controllable, the optimal adjustment of the power level is essential not only for energy conservation but also for the interference control and additional hardware is needed(such as DRCPC,TPCPC and DCA-PC). The sleep/ power-down mode approach focuses on inactivity energy. Although it reduces energy consumption, it needs precious synchronization and prediction of traffic pattern in advance (for example, TMMAC). When the both energy efficient MAC and routing algorithm are combined, most of the cases it will bring more delay, because routing paths involved in this process may reduce total energy consumptions (for example MCBPC). Table 2 gives the comparisons of the discussed protocols with their pros and cons.

Table 2. Comparison of the protocols

Protocol Name	Features	Hardware Requirement	Channels	Information to be stored in a node (or shared by nodes)	Advantages	Disadvantages
DRCPC	CDMA based power control	Nodes to be equipped with separate busy tone transceiver	Common Channel (cm). Data channel (cd),Broadcast Channel (cb)	Available code list(ACL),Occupied Code list(OCL), Forbidden Code list(FCL)	Decreases the collision probability/ broadcast messages and control messages	RTS,CTS overhead, a separate busy tone transceiver is needed
TMMAC	TDMA based DATIM + Broadcast support	Single half duplex transceiver per node	N data channels	CUB(Channel Usage Bitmap) data structure	Per packet energy consumption is reduced. Dynamic adjustment of the ATIM window size	Extra info required, synchronization needed
TPCPC	CDMA based power control + eliminates HT,ET & near far interference	Multicode transceiver, code synchronization and GPS	1 control channel and 1 data channel with multiple code	Available Code Set	Good scalability	Code synchronization needed
DCA-PC	Channel assignment+medium access + power control	2 half duplex transceiver per node	1 control channel and n data channels	- Power information -CUL -FCL	Higher throughput than DCA.	Increase in the number of channels will lead to overload of control channel
MCBPC	power control, and minimum energy route protocol	Single transceiver per node	one dedicated control channel & N data channels	Route metric	Gives the minimum energy efficient routing path	Longer path results in more delay

6 Conclusion

In this paper, we reviewed some of the multi channel protocols MAC layer protocol used in wireless ad hoc network considering energy as the key issue. It is found that there will be always the tradeoffs related with network optimization for energy constrained nodes such as Power tradeoffs for processing vs. transmitting bits, Longevity vs. network function and Energy-conserving modes. For example, changing of transmit power will result in change of network connectivity and affects node's view of network topology. So power conservation within the wireless protocol stack remains a very crucial research area for the viability of wireless services in the future.

References

[1] Liu, F., Xing, K., Cheng, X., Rotenstreich, S.: Energy-Efficient MAC Layer Protocols in Ad Hoc Networks, Department of Computer Science The George Washington University Washington, DC (2005)

[2] Ray, N.K., Turuk, A.K.: Energy Efficient Techniques for Wireless Ad Hoc Network. In: Proceedings of First International Joint Conference on Information and Communication Technology, IJclCT 2010, pp. 105–111 (January 2010)

[3] IEEE Std 802.11-1997: Wireless LAN Medium Access Control (MAC) and Physical Layer (PHY) Specifications. Institute of Electrical and Electronics Enginneres, Inc., New York, USA (1997)

[4] Chen, H., Jia, M., Chen, X., Yuan, Y.: A New Multi-channel MAC Protocol with Power Control for Ad hoc Networks. In: Proceedings of the 20th International Conference on Advanced Information Networking and Applications, AINA 2006 (2006)

[5] Zhang, J., Zhou, G., Huang, C., Son, S.H., Stankovic, J.A.: TMMAC: An Energy Efficient Multi-Channel MAC Protocol for Ad Hoc Networks

[6] Zhang, L., Soong, B.-H., Xiao, W.: A New Multi-Channel MAC Protocol for Ad Hoc Networks Based on Two-phase Coding with Power Control (TPCPC)

[7] Wu, S.L., Tseng, Y.C., Lin, C.Y., Sheu, J.P.: A multi-channel MAC protocol with power control for multi-hop mobile ad hoc networks. The Computer Journal (SCI) 45(1), 101–110 (2002)

[8] Li, D., Xiang, Y., Shi, M.: A Multi-channel Based Power Control Protocol for Mobile Ad-hoc Networks (2004)

[9] Wu, S.-L., Lin, C.-Y., Tseng, Y.-C., Sheu, J.-P.: A new multi-channel MAC protocol with on-demand channel assignment for mobile ad hoc networks, Dallas/Richardson, TX, December 7-9, pp. 232–237. IEEE, Piscataway (2000)

A Decentralized Approach towards Location Tracking of Mobile Users in Opportunistic Networks

Sudipa Batabyal[1], Apratim Mukherjee[2], and Somprakash Bandyopadhyay[3]

[1] Cognizant Technology Solutions, Salt Lake, Kolkata 700091, India
[2] BPP Institute of Management & Technology, VIP Road, Kolkata 700052, India
[3] Indian Institute of Management Calcutta, Joka, Kolkata 700104, India

Abstract. In existing models of opportunistic networks, nodes are not usually topology-aware. In this paper, we have developed a distributed mechanism in order to make each node in the network topology aware, i.e. aware of the approximate location-related GPS information of other nodes. The mechanism proposed in this paper is primarily developed on mobile agent based framework. It is assumed that each node has a dedicated *satellite agent*. Task of this agent is to help exchanging GPS information between its host node and its neighboring nodes only. This nearest neighbor interaction rule will eventually enable each node to have approximate location information about other nodes. As a direct consequence of topology-awareness, data forwarding schemes becomes far more efficient. We have introduced a parameter W (degree of disconnectedness) and show that our system is robust against wide variation of W. The performance evaluation results establish the effectiveness of the proposed scheme.

Keywords: Opportunistic Networks, Multi-Agent System, Location Tracking.

1 Introduction

Opportunistic networks and opportunistic computing have drawn significant attention of researchers in the recent past. In opportunistic networks, the devices (PDA, multi-radio cell-phones and similar devices) spread across an environment form the network. In this type of networks, end-to-end route connecting any two nodes usually does not exist and a source node communicates with its destination node following hop-by-hop, store-wait-forward cycle. In this type of networks, the mobility of devices is an opportunity for communication rather than a challenge. Thus, a mobile node can communicate with other nodes even if an end-to-end route connecting them never exists; any possible node can opportunistically be used as the next hop, if it is likely to bring the message closer to the final destination(s). Designing routing and forwarding schemes is one of the main challenges in this environment [1,2].

In existing models of opportunistic networks, nodes are not usually topology-aware i.e. nodes are not aware about the geographic locations and connectivity patterns of other nodes. However, in many applications, it is important to track the location of mobile users for effective communication. For example, in the context of disaster management (e.g. flood or earthquake), let us assume that fixed infrastructure (mobile

D.C. Wyld et al. (Eds.): NeCoM/WeST/WiMoN 2011, CCIS 197, pp. 368–377, 2011.
© Springer-Verlag Berlin Heidelberg 2011

towers, etc.) is non-functional and rescue workers with their wireless personal mobile communication devices form an opportunistic network. In this context, public health department, after reaching the site with a team of medical expert, must be able to locate other health workers, who are already working in the field. Secondly, in order to distribute relief resources to the designated rescue workers, those workers must be located and the agency carrying the relief resources must be able to send a query to those designated workers in order to assess the requirements. Also, the organizers need to delegate tasks to volunteers working in the field, and therefore those volunteers need to be located. Once the approximate location information of destination node is known to a source node, message communication can be implemented using Geographic Routing [3].

In this paper, we have developed a distributed mechanism in order to make each node in the network aware of the approximate location-related GPS information of other nodes. The degree of accuracy of this information would depend on the inter-node distance and connectivity pattern of the opportunistic network. The mechanism proposed in this paper is primarily based on mobile agent based framework [4]. It is assumed that each node has a dedicated *satellite agent*. Task of this agent is to help exchanging GPS information between its host node and its neighboring nodes. This nearest neighbor interaction rule will eventually enable each node to have approximate location information about other nodes. .

2 Related Work

In opportunistic networks, the notion of data forwarding and routing are merged, because routes are actually built while messages are forwarded [2]. The forwarding scheme has been primarily referred as "store, carry, and forward". Each intermediate node evaluates the suitability of encountered nodes to be a good next hop towards the destination. Another form of routing technique exploits some form of flooding. The heuristic behind this policy is that, when there is no knowledge about a possible path towards the destination or of an appropriate next-hop node, a message should be disseminated as widely as possible. The most representative protocol of this type is Epidemic Routing [5] and some optimizations of the same [e.g.,6]

However, flooding-based approach generates multiple copies of the same message. In Forwarding-based approach, though there is only one single custodian for each message, it may suffer long delays and low delivery ratios. Several schemes have been proposed considering mobility pattern / context information into account. The Haggle Project [7] has developed mechanisms for measuring and modeling pair-wise contacts between users and devices by means of two parameters: contact durations and inter-contact times. The statistical properties of these parameters are used to drive the design of forwarding policies. *Probabilistic Routing* scheme [8] calculates the *delivery predictability* from a node to a particular destination node based on the observed contact history, and it forwards a message to its neighboring node if and only if that neighbor node has a higher delivery predictability value. Leguay *et al.* [9] have taken *mobility pattern* into account, i.e., a message is forwarded to a neighbor node if and only if the neighbor node has a mobility pattern more similar to the destination. However, in many application scenarios (such as ours), mobility patterns are largely unpredictable.

Ghosh et al [10] propose routing based on the predefined infrastructure, such as the places that device holders often visited; they call them "solar-hub". This takes the advantage of user mobility profiles to perform "hub-level"-based routing. However, in this scenario, it is necessary to know about the places visited by the receiver. Exploiting context information related to the social behavior of people is also one of the most promising research directions in the area [11].

However, data forwarding schemes becomes far more efficient, if approximate locations of nodes are known to other nodes. In this paper, we will address this issue using mobile agent-based framework. Use of mobile agents are an effective paradigm for distributed applications, and are particularly attractive in a dynamic network environment involving partially connected computing elements. Intensive research on the "Insect-like Agent Systems" has been done over the last few years. Of particular interest is a technique for indirect inter-agent communication, called stigmergy, in which agents leave information in the cache (which other agent can use) of the nodes they have visited. Stigmergy serves as a robust mechanism for information sharing [4].

As indicated earlier, we propose to use *satellite agents* for distributed location tracking. In a seminal paper in Physical Review Letters, Vicsek et al.[12, 13] propose a simple model of n autonomous agents moving in the plane with the same speed but with different headings. Each agent's heading is updated using a local rule based on the average of its own heading plus the headings of its "neighbors." In their paper, Vicsek et al. demonstrated that the nearest neighbor rule can cause all agents to eventually move in the same direction despite the absence of centralized coordination and despite the fact that each agent's set of nearest neighbors change with time as the system evolves. Other studies also indicate that multi-agent systems that interact through nearest-neighbor rules can synchronize their states regardless of the size of communication delays [14]. We have applied this concept in our system and the performance evaluation results indicate the effectiveness of our approach.

3 System Description

An Opportunistic Network is modeled as a time-dependent disconnected graph $G(t) = (N, L, \tau)$ where N is a finite set of nodes, L is a finite set of unidirectional links and τ is a set of time-values indicating life-span associated with the links. Each link $L_i \in L$ is associated with $\tau_i \in \tau$, indicating life-span of L_i at time t.

Since the graph represents an opportunistic network, graph $G(t)$ should usually be disconnected. $G(t)$ consists of multiple connected pieces called components $C(t)$. When $G(t)$ is fully connected, $C(t) = 1$; when $G(t)$ is fully disconnected, $C(t) =$ number of nodes N.

To characterize an opportunistic network, it is important to define a parameter W that indicates the degree of disconnectedness over a period of time T. W is said to be 0%, if, for each pair of nodes, there always exists a path between them between <0..T>. W is said to be 100%, if, for each pair of nodes, no path exists between them at any point of time between <0..T>. In the first case, the network is always connected and *ceases to be an opportunistic network*. In the other extreme, the graph is fully disconnected and the set of nodes will never form a network.

In order to quantify W, we need to take a set of snap-shots of G(t). $G(t_i)$ is snap-shot of G at $t=t_i$. W_i, the degree of disconnectedness for $G(t_i) = \{C(t_i)-1\}/(N-1)$. When $G(t_i)$ is fully connected, $W_i = 0$; When $G(t_i)$ is fully disconnected, $W_i = 100\%$;

W is the average of W_i over the number of snap-shots taken. So, if number of snap-shots taken is α,

$$W = [\Sigma_{i=1 \text{ to } \alpha} W_i] / \alpha$$

While designing and testing the robustness of any algorithm designed in the context of opportunistic networks, it is important to consider the parameter W. Specially, while testing and validating algorithms designed for opportunistic network in a simulated network environment, disregarding the parameter W may result in a network condition where nodes are always forming a network or forming a network with a few numbers of disconnected components. Any algorithm designed for opportunistic network should work well for a wide range of W.

We define the *physical neighbors* of node n at time t as $N_n(t) \Subset N$, where $N_n(t)$ is the set of nodes within the transmission range of n at time t. It is assumed that each node knows its position, velocity and direction of movement using Global Positioning System (GPS). It is also assumed that each node periodically broadcast a beacon with its id to all its physical neighbors at that instant of time.

The mechanism proposed in this paper is primarily based on a mobile multi-agent based framework. We assume that each node n_i has a dedicated *satellite agent* S_i. Task of S_i is to help exchanging information between its host node n_i and each of the neighboring nodes of n_i. To do this, the satellite agent S_i periodically hops from n_i to one of its neighbors with all location-related information as perceived by n_i. The neighboring node has a different perception regarding location-related information of other nodes. S_i and the neighboring node mutually exchange this information, forms a "consensus view" regarding the location related information of other nodes and S_i then comes back to the host node n_i with this "consensus view". This would then change the perception of n_i about location-related information of other nodes. In the next time-slots, S_i visits other neighboring node of n_i and the process is repeated.

4   Agent-Based Mechanism for Location Tracking

In our mechanism, each *satellite agent* interacts with their respective neighboring nodes only and come back to the respective host node with a localized "consensus view" about location-related information of other nodes. The technique used here for indirect inter-agent communication is *stigmergy*, in which agents leave information in the cache (which other agent can use) of the nodes they have visited.

Structure and Behavior of a Node

In order to facilitate agent-based distributed location tracking, each node is assumed to have the following structure:

- Node Id (n_i)
- Current Location (x_i, y_i)
- Neighborhood List : <for all k : list of n_k>
- Information about all nodes (n_p) $\rightarrow$ (for all p : n_p, x_p, y_p , $timer_p \uparrow$)

Each node is assumed to know its id and current location (through GPS). Each node broadcast a periodic beacon to its neighbors to inform its id. This would help a node to form Neighborhood List. Initially, the Location Table of a node would contain only the location information of itself only. Location Table of node n_i would be augmented by : (i) visits of satellite agents from other neighboring nodes containing the neighborhoods' perception (ii) returning of satellite agent of node n_i from a neighboring node containing the "consensus view" of n_i and that neighboring node.

It is to be noted that the entire scheme is based on multi-agent interaction via Location Table of nodes. Since navigation of satellite agents is asynchronous and there is an obvious time gap between the updation of information by one satellite agent in one node and carrying this information to another node by another satellite agent, there is a notion of timer↑ with each entry, depicting the ageing of information. The information is aging as agents percolates from one node to another and the nodes will therefore have new information about close neighbors and old information about remote nodes.The symbol ↑ indicates that each timer is counting up locally, unless overwritten by more recent information about that entry.

This is illustrated in figure 1. For the sake of simplicity, we are assuming unidirectional communication and we only show percolation of location information of node n1 to node n4. In figure 1, current location of node N_1 is x_1, y_1. Since this information is always recent, no aging factor is associated with it and timer value is 0. Let us assume, this information is taken to node N_2 by N_1's satellite agent S1 at $t_1=0$. The timer associated with x_1, y_1 now starts getting incremented at node N_2, indicating that the location information of N_1 at N_2 is aging. At $t_2=10$, say, N_2's satellite agent S_2 carries this information to N_3. The timer associated with x_1, y_1 at N_3 now starts getting incremented at node N_3 with a starting value of 10. Let us assume further that after 25 time-unit, i.e. at $t_3=25$, N_3's satellite agent S_3 carries this information to N_4. The timer associated with x_1, y_1 at N_4 now starts getting incremented at node N_4 with a starting value of 35. This implies that the perception of node N_4 about the location of N_1 is 35 time-unit old and it is aging, unless overwritten by some more recent location information of N_1.

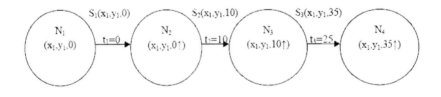

Fig. 1. Percolation of Location Information

Structure and Behavior of a Satellite Agent

As explained earlier, satellite agent is a dedicated agent for any node. Its task is to carry information from its host node to neighboring nodes in a time-sequenced fashion (i.e. one neighbor at a time) and return to its host node with information of that neighboring node. For example, if node N_2's satellite agent has not visited N_1 in the recent past, the satellite agent of Node N_1 visits Node N_2, updates N_2's table to form a consensus view between N_1's and N_2's perception, then comes back to N_1 with this information. After some time, it again collects the latest information from N_1, and moves to another neighboring node, say N_3, provided N_3's satellite agent has not visited N_1 in the recent past. This process occurs for every node since each node has a dedicated satellite agent.

If a satellite agent loses its host node due to mobility of host node, it kills itself. The host node, on the other hand, generates a new satellite agent if the satellite agent doesn't come back after a certain time. The structure of a satellite agent is given below:

- Host Node Id (n_i)
- Current Location of Host Node (x_i, y_i)
- Location of Target Neighbor to be visited now
- Information about all nodes (n_p) $\rightarrow$ (for all p : n_p, x_p, y_p , $timer_p \uparrow$)

5 Performance Evaluation

5.1 Evaluation Criteria

Average Perception Deviation of a node: We have developed a metric Average Perception Deviation of a node i, denoted by P_i (t), to quantify the deviation of actual node position of each node with the node-position of corresponding node perceived by node i at any instant of time t. Let us assume that (x_k, y_k) is the actual co-ordinates of node k at time t. Let (x_k^i, y_k^i) be the coordinate of node k as perceived by node i.
$$P_i(t) = \Sigma_{k=1 \text{ to } n} [(x_k - x_k^i)^2 + (y_k - y_k^i)^2]^{1/2} / n$$

Average Perception Deviation of a network *N* with n number of node, denoted by $P_N(t)$, is defined as
$$P_N(t) = \Sigma_{i=1 \text{ to } n} P_i(t) / n$$

Wait-before-Migrate (WbM): In order to control agent-traffic in the network, a satellite agent, after finishing its first visit to a neighboring node of its host node , is not allowed to migrate immediately to another neighboring node. A satellite agent will be forced to wait in its host node for a pre-specified period of time, termed as *Wait-before-Migrate (WbM)* before migrating to another neighboring node. By controlling WbM, the network congestion due to satellite agent traffic can be controlled. For example, if WbM = 200 msec, and an agent takes approximately 4 msec. to physically migrate from one node to another, the agent traffic (going from and coming back to host node) would occupy 8 ms out of 200 msec. i.e 4%. So, any host node would be free to communicate 98 percent of the time. On the other hand, increasing WbM reduces information percolation efficiency. Thus, the trade off is between congestion and convergence.

Degree of Disconnectedness: In section 3, we have introduced a parameter W that indicates the degree of disconnectedness over a period of time T. In our simulation, by controlling the transmission range, we have controlled W and evaluated the performance.

5.2 Simulation Setup

The proposed schemes are evaluated on a simulated environment under a variety of conditions to estimate average perception deviation against time. In the simulation, the environment is assumed to be a closed area of 1500 x 1500 square meters in which mobile nodes are distributed randomly. We present simulations for networks with 40 mobile hosts, operating at a transmission range from 150 to 250 meters. In order to study the time-related parameters, every simulated action is associated with a simulated clock. The speed of movement of individual node ranges from 2 m/sec (walking) to 10 m/sec (vehicle). Each node starts from a starting location, selects a random direction and moves with a uniform, predetermined velocity along that direction. We define a set of 10 waiting-zones within the area. Once a node reaches a waiting-zones, it waits there for a pre-specified amount of time, selects randomly another direction of movement and moves towards that.

5.3 Results and Discussions

Figure 2 shows the average perception deviation $P_N(t)$ w.r.t time at different Wait-before-Migrate where mobility is randomized between of 2 m/ sec and 10 m/ sec. With 40 nodes in the system, transmission range is adjusted to get an approximate average degree of disconnectedness W= 28%, indicating that the network is having around 10 to 12 disconnected components (fig. 3).

At WbM=120 to 200 msec., average perception deviation is around 75 to 100 meters. So, considering the maximum possible perception deviation to be 2100 meters in a 1500 m x 1500 m area, the perception deviation is around 3.5 % to 5 %. However, when WbM is low (=40 msec)., perception deviation is higher because of congestion due to agent traffic. Perception deviation is also higher, when WbM = 280 msec, although the value is not significantly high even at WbM = 280 Msec ($P_N(t) <$ 125 meters i.e. 6%).

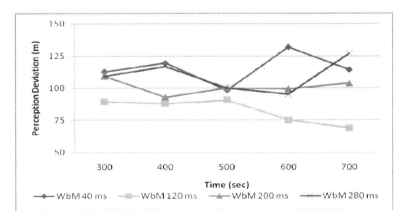

Fig. 2. Average Perception Deviation with time at different WbM

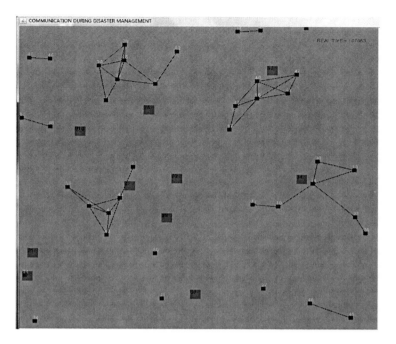

Fig. 3. A snap-shot of the opportunistic network in our simulator: squares are the waiting-zones and dots are the nodes

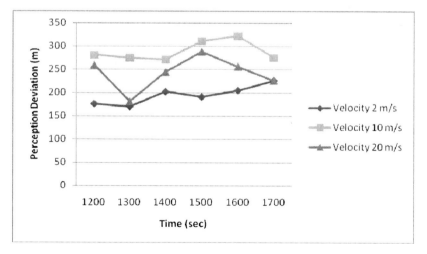

Fig. 4. Effect of Mobility on Perception deviation at W=50%

Next, we have adjusted the transmission range to get a degree of disconnectedness W=50% (approximately). i.e. number of average disconnected components = 20 in a 40-node network. We have studied the average perception deviation against time at different mobility. In the graph (figure 4), we can see that the perception deviation generally increases when velocity is increased from 2 m/s to 10 m/s. It is mainly due to increased rate of change of actual position with increased velocity. So due to this, the perception deviation tends to be high. But as we increase the velocity even higher to as high as 20 m/s, the perception deviation seems to decrease. The reason is that, although the rate of change of actual positions is high (as it was with velocity 10 m/s), at the same time, due to increased mobility, information is percolated faster over longer distances. The up-down trends in the graph indicate the information convergence-divergence pattern. Because of mobility, the information stability would never happen, but at the same time, it would also never diverge away beyond a certain point; information will again start converging. This up-down pattern is more pronounced when mobility is high.

6 Conclusion

In this study, we have designed a mobile agent based mechanism to make the nodes position-aware about other nodes in the network. It has been assumed that each node knows its position and velocity at any instant of time using GPS and this information is getting distributed to other nodes through agents. We have assumed that agents do not get lost in transit nor suffer from any kind of errors in transmission and reception. We have introduced a parameter W (degree of disconnectedness) and show that our system is robust against wide variation of W. Even when the mobility is as high as 20m/ sec (72 km/hr), average perception deviation is 10 to 12 % (figure 4), indicating the success of the proposed mechanism.

References

1. Conti, M., Kumar, M.: Opportunities in Opportunistic Computing. IEEE Computer 43(1), 42–50 (2010)
2. Conti, M., Giordano, S., May, M., Passarella, A.: From opportunistic networks to opportunistic computing. IEEE Communications Magazine 48(9) (September 2010)
3. Bandyopadhyay, S., Paul, K.: Evaluating The performance of mobile agent based message communication among mobile hosts in large ad hoc wireless network. In: Proc. of the Second ACM International Workshop on Modeling and Simulation of Wireless and Mobile Systems (In Conjunction with IEEE/ACM MobiCom 1999), Seattle, Washington, USA, August 15-19 (1999)
4. RoyChoudhury, R., Paul, K., Bandyopadhyay, S.: MARP: A Multi-Agent Routing Protocol for Mobile Wireless Ad Hoc Networks. Autonomous Agents and Multi-Agent Systems (Kluwer) 8(1), 47–68 (2004)
5. Vahdat, Becker, D.: Epidemic routing for partially-connected ad hoc networks. Technical Report CS-2000-06, Duke University (2000)
6. Harras, K.A., Almeroth, K.C., Belding-Royer, E.M.: Delay tolerant mobile networks (dtmns): Controlled flooding in sparse mobile networks. In: IFIP Networking (2005)
7. Chaintreau, A., Hui, P., Crowcroft, J., Diot, C.: Impact of Human Mobility on the Design of Opportunistic Forwarding Algorithms. In: IEEE INFOCOM 2006, Barcelona, Spain, April 23-29 (2006)

8. Lindgren, Doria, A.: Probabilistic routing protocol for intermittently connected networks. Technical report, draft-lindgren-dtnrgprophet-01.txt, IETF Internet draft (July 2005)
9. Leguay, J., Friedman, T., Conan, V.: Dtn routing in a mobility pattern space. In: ACM SIGCOMM Workshop on Delay Tolerant Networks (2005)
10. Ghosh, J., Philip, S.J., Qiao, C.: Sociological Orbit aware Location Approximation and Routing (SOLAR). Manet. Elsevier Ad Hoc Networks Journal 5(2), 189–209 (2007)
11. Hui, P., Crowcroft, J., Yoneki, E.: Bubble rap: Social-based forwarding in delay tolerant networks. Paper Presented in the Proceedings of the 9th ACM International Symposium on Mobile Ad Hoc Networking & Computing (MobiHoc 2008) (May 2008)
12. Vicsek, T., Czirok, A., Ben Jacob, E., Cohen, I., Schochet, O.: Novel type of phase transitions in a system of self-driven particles. Physical Review Letters 75, 1226–1229 (1995)
13. Czirok, Barabasi, A.L., Vicsek, T.: Collective motion of self-propelled particles:kinetic phase transition in one dimension. Physical Review Letters 82, 209–212 (1999)
14. Tanner, H.G., Christodoulakis, D.K.: The stability of synchronization in local-interaction networks is robust with respect to time delays. In: 44th IEEE Conference on Decision and Control (2005)

A Novel VLSI Implementation of K-Best LSD for 3GPP LTE

K. Kalyani, R. Raghuram, V. Raghunandhan, and S. Rajaram

Department of Electronics and Communication Engineering
Thiagarajar College of Engineering, Madurai, India
k_kalyani@tce.edu, raghu77ram@gmail.com,
veeyar287@yahoo.com, rajaram_siva@tce.edu

Abstract. In this paper, Distributed Arithmetic (DA) based K-best List Sphere Detector (LSD) for a 3GPP Long Term Evolution (LTE) receiver is proposed. The K-best LSD block implemented with the use of DA, reduces the size of the parallel hardware multiply-accumulate. These DA based blocks are compared with conventional multiplier based blocks and found that the proposed design has an improvement in terms of area. This design has minimal hardware and computational complexity to meet the requirements of LTE standard. The VHDL coding for K-best LSD using DA for LTE is downloaded onto Xilinx xc3s100e-4vq100 and results were verified.

Keywords: Multiple-Input Multiple-Output (MIMO) - Orthogonal Frequency-Division Multiplexing (OFDM), 3rd Generation Partnership Project (3GPP), Long Term Evolution (LTE), sphere detector(SD), list sphere detector(LSD), Distributed Arithmetic(DA).

1 Introduction

Wireless communications has developed into a key element of modern society. Mobile wireless communication devices have expanded dramatically from their inception as mobile telephones. The LTE is used to provide an extremely high performance radio-access technology that offers full vehicular speed mobility and that can readily coexist with HSPA and earlier networks. Because of scalable bandwidth, operators will be able to easily migrate their networks and users from HSPA to LTE over time.

The 3GPP LTE receiver systems with multiple transmit and receive antennas (MIMO) present a better performance on two different angles, the diversity and the multiplexing [1]. MIMO exploits higher transmission rates, higher spectral efficiencies, greater coverage, improved link robustness, without increasing total transmission power or bandwidth [5]. But, the 3GPP LTE receiver also increases the computational and the hardware complexities greatly. It is a challenge to realize the receiver with the MIMO OFDM system with minimal hardware complexity and power consumption—especially the computational complexity—in VLSI implementation. The Symbol detection is one of the the highest computational complexity modules in the baseband function of 3GPP LTE receiver.

D.C. Wyld et al. (Eds.): NeCoM/WeST/WiMoN 2011, CCIS 197, pp. 378–387, 2011.
© Springer-Verlag Berlin Heidelberg 2011

K-best LSD algorithm[6] in general approximates a breadth-first search by keeping only K best branches (with the smallest partial Euclidean distance) at each level. Sorting circuits are inserted between stages to keep the K best branches. The path with the smallest Euclidean distance is chosen as the best estimate. K data paths at the same time are processed through parallel architecture computing. This approach has the advantages of design simplicity and high-speed operations. However, the required multipliers to implement K-best algorithm incur high area overhead.

Distributed Arithmetic algorithm is an efficient realization of K-Best LSD. It is a bit level rearrangement of a multiply accumulate to hide the multiplications. It is a powerful technique for reducing the size of a parallel hardware multiply-accumulate that is well suited to FPGA designs. This approach has the advantages of design simplicity and high-speed operations. However, the required multipliers to implement K-best algorithm incur high area overhead.

In this work, in order to reduce overhead, and to realize 3GPP LTE receiver with the MIMO-OFDM with minimal hardware and computational complexity, we propose a DA algorithm and its architectures tailored for K-best LSD computations. The proposed K-best LSD for 3GPP LTE receiver will consume less area and has minimal hardware and computational complexity than conventional units.

2   Design Issue of K-Best LSD for MIMO-OFDM

A high-level description of the targeted 2-antenna MIMO OFDM receiver is presented in Figure 1. The input ports are connected to radio-frequency functions of the receiver. The upcoming 3GPP long term evolution (LTE) standard receiver will support data rates up to 100 Mbps [2]. Such a high data rate will be achieved in 20MHz bandwidth by using transmission techniques like orthogonal frequency division multiplexing (OFDM) , multiple-input multiple-output (MIMO) , that is, the use of multiple antennas, and an efficient forward error correction method, the turbo coding [2]. As these techniques are applied, the receiver needs to realize very sophisticated algorithms.

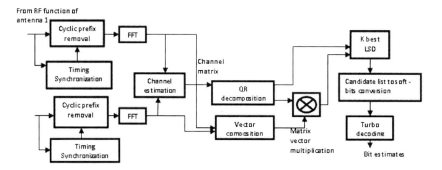

Fig. 1. A Simplified Diagram of Base Band Processing of a Two Antenna MIMO OFDM Receiver

The 3GPP LTE standard based on the MIMO-OFDM system provides very high data throughput rate because the technique of the MIMO can increase the data rate by extending an OFDM based system. However, the 3GPP LTE standard also increases the computational and the hardware complexities greatly, compared with the current WLAN standards. The K-best is one of the highest computational complexity module in the physical layer of the LTE standard. Thus, a DA based K-best LSD was proposed will reduce area, computational and hardware complexity of the receiver of 3GPP LTE standard than conventional K-best LSD.

2.1 MIMO System Modeling and Detection

In principle, an MIMO system with a complex-valued channel matrix, H, noise vector, n, transmitted symbol, s, and received symbol, y, can be described with

$$y = Hs + n \tag{1}$$

The number of receive and transmit antennas equals the numbers of rows and columns of H, respectively. The transmitted symbol s' can be estimated by ML detection by solving

$$s' = \arg\min \| y - Hs \|^2 \tag{2}$$

which gives the optimal result. However, solving (2) is intractable with multiple antennas and large constellations. Instead of solving (2), the symbol estimation can be simplified by using QR decomposition of H. With this practice, the computational complexity is lowered. Instead of ML detection, a substitute

$$s' = \arg\min \| y' - Rs \|^2 \quad \text{where } y' = Q^H y \tag{3}$$

is used. As the R is in upper triangular form, approximation of s' is computationally simpler with the aid of (3). The simplified approximation is based on computing the Euclidean distance in (3) by gradually increasing the dimensions of the symbol vector. Basically, there will be partial solutions which are too far away from the received symbols and when such partial solutions are discarded, the search space is efficiently limited. The K-best LSD[2] applies the aforementioned principles by maintaining a K-length list of the best partial solutions found so far.

2.2 K-Best Algorithm

The signal detected at the receiver after QR decomposition is given by,

$$s' = \arg\min_{s \in M} \sum_{i=1}^{M_T} | y_i - \sum_{j=i}^{M_T} R_{ij} s_j |^2$$

The above equation was implemented with algorithm [4] given below.

Algorithm

1. $P_M = 0$
2. $K = M-1$
3. Calculate PED(Partial euclidean distances)for all admissible symbols at level k

$$P_k = P_{k+1} + \| y_k - \sum_{i=k}^{M-1} R_{k,j} s_j \|^2$$

4. Choose the K best symbol vectors with the smallest PEDs . Save the partial symbol vectors and the corresponding PEDs. If k=0 solution is foundstop the algorithm; else k=k-1 goto 3.

The architecture for the algorithm is given below.

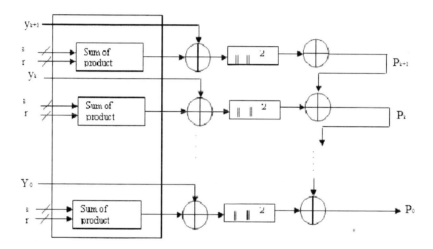

Fig. 2. Architecture for K-Best LSD Algorithm

In this existing architecture, the sum of product term is given by,

$$\sum_{i=k}^{m-1} r(k,i) \times s(i) \qquad (1)$$

Where s(i) is a n-bit scaled input and r(k,i) represents upper triangular matrix formed by QR decomposition of channel matrix H.

When the above equation is implemented in hardware, the architecture looks as given below.

In this case, 'm' number of parallel scaling accumulators with unique serialized data is fed. Each multiplies that data by a possibly unique constant, and the resulting products are summed in an adder tree. If consider that the scaling accumulator multiplier is really just a sum of vectors, then it becomes obvious that the circuit can be rearranged with use of DA algorithm.

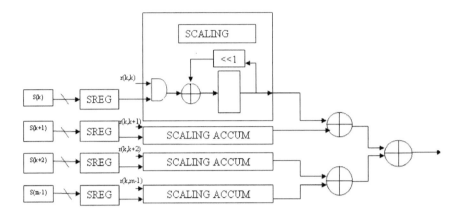

Fig. 3. Existing MAC Architecture in K-Best LSD without Using DA

The Sum Of Product (SOP) of s and r also takes $\dfrac{m(m+1)}{2}$ MAC cycles with use of the conventional arithmetic. These numbers of cycles increase the computational complexity, design area and reduce the speed. This appears to be a fundamental problem when this SOP is implemented with use of general purpose multipliers. To overcome these problems, the proposed architecture is implemented with use of DA algorithm explained below.

2.3 Distributed Arithmetic Algorithm

Distributed Arithmetic (DA) is a bit level rearrangement of a multiply accumulate to hide the multiplications. It is a powerful technique for reducing the size of a parallel hardware multiply-accumulate that is well suited to FPGA designs. It is an important algorithm for DSP applications [3]. It is based on a bit level rearrangement of the MAC "multiply accumulate" operation to replace it with set of addition and shifting operations.

In most of the multiply accumulate applications in signal processing, one of the multiplicands for each product is a constant. Usually each multiplication uses a different constant. If one of the multiplicands are known apriori, then technically the partial product term becomes a multiplication with a constant (ie.,scaling). Using most compact multiplier, the scaling accumulator, a multiple product term parallel multiply-accumulate function in a relatively small space is constructed if a serial input is accepted.

3   Architecture of K-Best LSD Using DA Algorithm

DISTRIBUTED ARITHMETIC (DA) is an important FPGA technology and an efficient technique for calculation of sum of products or vector dot product or inner product or multiply and accumulate (MAC). The "basic" DA technique is bit-serial in nature. DA is basically a bit-level rearrangement of the multiply and accumulate operation. DA hides the explicit multiplications by ROM look-ups an efficient technique to implement on Field Programmable Gate Arrays (FPGAs). This DA algorithm is used for the proposed architecture of K-best LSD which is explained below.

In K-best algorithm, the main equation to compute the Euclidian distance is given by,

$$P_k = P_{k+1} + \left\| y_k - \sum_{i=k}^{m-1} r(k,i) \times s(i) \right\|^2$$

In this equation, the sum of product term is given by,

$$\sum_{i=k}^{m-1} r(k,i) \times s(i) \tag{1}$$

By applying DA algorithm, express $s(i)$ as

$$s(i) = \sum_{0}^{n-1} s(i,n) 2^n \tag{2}$$

where n represents the nth bit of the input vector symbol s(i). substituting S(i) in equation (1) we obtain….

$$= \sum_{i=k}^{m-1} \sum_{n=0}^{n-1} (r(k,i) \times s(i,n)) 2^n$$

Rearranging the above equation on a bit level using DA, we obtain

$$= \sum_{=k}^{n-1} (r(k, i) \times s(i,0)2^0 + r(k, i) \times s(i,1)2^1 + r(k, i) \times s(i,2)2^2 + \ldots \ldots \ldots$$
$$+ r(k, i) \times s(i, n-1)2^{n-1})$$
$$= ((r(k, k) \times s(k,0))2^0 + (r(k, k) \times s(k,1))2^1 + (r(k, k) \times s(k,2))2^2 + \ldots \ldots \ldots \ldots \ldots \ldots$$
$$. + (r(k, k) \times s(k, n-1)) 2^{n-1})$$
$$+ ((r(k, k+1) \times s(k+1,0))2^0 + (r(k, k+1) \times s(k+1,1))2^1 + (r(k, k+1) \times s(k+1,2))2^2$$
$$+ \ldots \ldots \ldots \ldots + (r(k, k+1) \times s(k+1, n-1)) 2^{n-1}) + \ldots \ldots \ldots \ldots \ldots \ldots \ldots$$
$$+ ((r(k, m-1) \times s(m-1,0)) 2^0 + (r(k, m-1) \times s(m-1,1))2^1 + (r(k, m-1) \times s(m-1,2))2^2$$
$$+ \ldots \ldots \ldots \ldots \ldots \ldots \ldots + (r(k, m-1) \times s(m-1, n-1))2^{n-1})$$
$$= (((r(k, k) \times s(k,0)) + (r(k, k+1) \times s(k+1,0)) + \ldots \ldots + (r(k, m-1) \times s(m-1,0))2^0$$
$$+ ((r(k, k) \times s(k,1)) + (r(k, k+1) \times s(k+1,1)) + \ldots \ldots + (r(k, m-1) \times s(m-1,1))) 2^1$$
$$+ ((r(k, k) \times s(k,2)) + (r(k, k+1) \times s(k+1,2)) + \ldots \ldots + (r(k, m-1) \times s(m-1,2))) 2^2$$
$$+ \ldots \ldots \ldots \ldots \ldots \ldots \ldots \ldots \ldots$$
$$+ ((r(k, k) \times s(k, n-1)) + (r(k, k+1) \times s(k+1, n-1)) + \ldots \ldots + (r(k, m-1) \times s(m-1, n-1))) 2^{n-1})$$
$$= \sum_{n=0}^{n-1} (\sum_{=k}^{m-1} r(k, i) \times s(i, n))) 2^n .$$

This is the final equation obtained by applying DA algorithm. When this equation is directly implemented then the hardware looks like as given below.

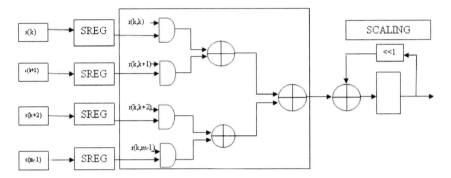

Fig. 4. Proposed MAC Architecture In K-Best LSD Using DA

Here, the adder tree combines the 1 bit partial products before they are accumulated by the scaling accumulator. The order in which the 1xm partial products are summed is rearranged. Now instead of individually accumulating each partial product and then summing the results, the accumulate function is postponed until after all the 1xm partials are summed at a particular bit time. This simple rearrangement of the order of the adds has effectively replaced 'm' multiplies followed by an 'm' input add with a series of 'm' input adds followed by a multiply. This arithmetic manipulation directly eliminates m-1 Adders in an m product term multiply-accumulate function.

Thus number of scaling accumulators used for this proposed architecture gets reduced. If the channel coefficients r(k,i) are known apriori ,then the SOP terms r(k,i) and s(i) becomes a multiplication with a constant and this is an important pre requisite for DA implementation.

3.1 Implementation on FPGA

Further reduction of this hardware architecture is done when this architecture is implemented on FPGA. Though FPGA have Look Up Table (LUT) based logic blocks, sum of product of r and s in the above equation is replaced by LUT. The sum of product part, which computes $\sum_{i=k}^{m-1} r(k,i) \times s(i,n)$ has only 2^n possible values..(ie)....

$$\sum_{i=k}^{m-1} r(k,i) \times s(i,n) = \text{fn}(\text{bkn}, \text{b}(k+1)\text{n}, \ldots, \text{b}(m-1)\text{n}) \ldots \ldots$$

This equation can be precalculated for all possible values of the above bit combinations. We can store these in a look-up table of 2^n words addressed by n-bits. That is a 2^n-word LUT is preprogrammed to accept n-bit input vectors. Then the individual mappings of function fn(bkn,b(k+1)n,.....,b(m-1)n) are weighted by appropriate powers of 2 using scaling accumulators and shift adders. At the maximum of after 'm' lookup cycles the inner product of the SOP expression is computed.This reduces the number of MAC cycles required to compute SOP in the equation of Euclidian distance calculation of K-best LSD algorithm.

In this proposed work, arithmetic manipulation directly eliminates 'm-1' adders in an 'm' product term multiply-accumulate function. For larger numbers of product terms, the savings becomes significant. In DA, a Look Up Table(LUT) for all the combinations of multiplication of 'r' and 's' is created. Hence by selecting one of value from LUT and further process of K-best LSD reduces the computational complexity also. The access time for LUT is less compared to perform conventional MAC operation. Thus speed of the proposed architecture is also higher than existing architecture.

4   Simulation and Implementation

The VHDL coding for K-BEST LSD for LTE is simulated and downloaded onto Xilinx xc3s100e-4vq100. The simulated results and comparison result were given below.

4.1   Simulation Results

4.1.1   Simulation Result for K-BEST LSD Using DA

4.1.2   Simulation Result for CONVENTIONAL K-BEST LSD

4.2 Implementation on FPGA

The VHDL coding for conventional and DA based K-Best LSD was downloaded onto Spartan xc3s100e-4vq100 and the comparison result was given below.

Table 1 shows the comparison of the synthesis reports of conventional and DA based K-best LSD. From the report, DA based K-best LSD have improvement in terms of area. So the proposed DA based K-best LSD consume less area and from the implementation of algorithm, computational complexity also gets reduced.

Table 1. Comparison of Conventional and DA Based K-Best LSD

Logic Utilization	Conventional K-Best LSD	K-Best LSD using DA	Improvement in Efficiency (%)
Number of Slices	73	30	58
Number of 4 input LUTs	126	56	55
Number of MULTI8X18SIOs	4	3	25

5 Conclusion

Thus the proposed architecture reduces the overhead of hardware and computational complexity of 3GPP LTE receiver. Thus it is evident from the comparison result that the number of slices, lookup tables and other components that are required in FPGA implementation of k best LSD is tremendously reduced thereby making the proposed design cost effective and computationally efficient with use of DA algorithm.

By reduction of complexity the highest computational module the 3GPP LTE standard will become efficient. The proposed K-Best LSD using DA blocks can meet the specifications of most OFDM communication systems, including VDSL, 802.16, DAB and DVB. The proposed K-Best LSD was synthesized and implemented on FPGA. In future, this work will be extended to implement other blocks of 3GPP LTE receiver on FPGA.

References

1. Lee, K.F., Williams, D.B.: A space-frequency transmitter diversity technique for OFDM systems. In: Proc. Global Telecommunications Conf., San Francisco, CA, pp. 1473–1477 (November 2000)
2. Salmela, P., Antikainen, J., Anen, T.P., Siv'en, O., Takala, J.: 3G Long TermEvolution Baseband Processing with Application-Specific Processors. International Journal of Digital Multimedia Broadcasting, Article ID 503130, 13 (2009)
3. Timmermann, D., Hahn, H., Hosticka, B.J.: The Role of Distributed Arithmetic in FPGA-based Signal Processing. IEEE Transactions on Computers (August 1992)

4. Antikainen, J., Salmela, P., Silvent, O.: Fine-grained Application-specific Instruction Set Processor Design for the K-best List Sphere Detector Algorithm. In: Proc. Global Telecommunications Conf., San Francisco, CA, pp. 1473–1477 (November 2000)
5. Paulraj, A., Gore, D.A., Nabar, R.U., Bolcskei, H.: An overview of MIMO communications - A key to gigabit wireless. Proc. IEEE 92(2), 198–218 (2004)
6. Wong, K., Tsui, C., Cheng, R.K., Mow, W.: A VLSI architecture of a K-best lattice decoding algorithm for MIMO channels. In: Proc. IEEE Int. Symp. Circuits and Systems, Scottsdale, AZ, May 26-29, vol. 3, pp. 273–276 (2002)

Design of Unified Scrambler for
IEEE 802.11a and 802.16a

Devashish Raval[1], Nilesh Ranpura[2], Ekata Mehul[3],
Rachana Jani[1], and Zuber Saiyed[2]

The Third International Conference on Wireless
& Mobile Networks (WiMoN-2011)
[1] Department of Electronics and communication, Charotar Institute of Technology, Changa,
Anand, Gujarat, India
[2] Department of Electronics Engineering, Sardar Vallabhbhai National Institute of
Technology, Surat, Gujarat, India
[3] ASIC Division, Einfochips Pvt. Ltd., Ahmedabad, Gujarat, India

Abstract. IEEE 802.11a and 802.16a PHY specifications are used in WiFi and
WiMAX technologies and are based on OFDM (Orthogonal Frequency
Division Multiplexing) technology. The PHY layers contains scrambler block
with different hardware parameters for both the technologies. In this paper we
developed a scrambler design compatible to both PHY specifications. This
design saves hardware and proposes a way to unify the OFDM hardware blocks
in similar manner, finally which can be a part of unified physical layer
controlled by SDR (Software Defined Radio) combining both the technologies.

Keywords: IEEE 802.11a, IEEE 802.16a, OFDM, SDR.

1 Introduction

The scrambler is a device that transposes or inverts signals or otherwise encodes a
message at the transmitter to make the message unintelligible at a receiver.
Scrambling is accomplished by the addition of components to the original signal or
the changing of some important component of the original signal in order to make
extraction of the original signal difficult. Examples of the scrambling might include
removing or changing vertical or horizontal sync pulses in television signals;
televisions will not be able to display a picture from such a signal. Some modern
scramblers are actually encryption devices, the name remaining due to the similarities
in use, as opposed to internal operation.

In telecommunications and recording, a scrambler (also referred to as a
randomizer) is a device that manipulates a data stream before transmitting. The
manipulations are reversed by a descrambler at the receiving side. Applications of
scrambling are in satellite and radio relay communications modems. A scrambler can
be placed just before a FEC (Forward Error Correction) coder, or it can be placed
after the FEC, just before the modulation or line code.

A scrambler in this context has nothing to do with encrypting, as the intent is not to
render the message unintelligible, but to give the transmitted data useful engineering

D.C. Wyld et al. (Eds.): NeCoM/WeST/WiMoN 2011, CCIS 197, pp. 388–395, 2011.
© Springer-Verlag Berlin Heidelberg 2011

properties. A scrambler replaces sequences into other sequences without removing undesirable sequences, and as a result it changes the probability of occurrence of vexatious sequences. Clearly it is not foolproof as there are input sequences that yield all-zeros, all-ones, or other undesirable periodic output sequences.

Section 1 gives general introduction about scrambler working. Section 2 describes the hardware architecture of scrambler of IEEE 802.11a and 16a. Section 3 describes the Verilog HDL implementation and simulation results. We conclude in section 4 and references are given at the end of the paper. In this paper 11a notation is used for IEEE 802.11a and 16a is used for 802.16a.

2   Hardware Architecture of Scrambler for 11a and 16a PHY Layers

2.1   Scrambler for IEEE 802.11a

The DATA field, composed of SERVICE, PSDU, tail, and pad parts, shall be scrambled with a length-127 frame-synchronous scrambler. The octets of the PSDU are placed in the transmit serial bit stream, bit 0 first and bit 7 last. The frame synchronous scrambler uses the generator polynomial $S(x)$ as follows, and is illustrated in Figure 1.

$$S(x) = x^7 + x^4 + 1$$

The 127-bit sequence generated repeatedly by the scrambler shall be (leftmost used first), 00001110 11110010 11001001 00000010 00100110 00101110 10110110 00001100 11010100 11100111 10110100 00101010 11111010 01010001 10111000 1111111, when the all ones initial state is used. The same scrambler is used to scramble transmit data and to descramble receive data. When transmitting, the initial state of the scrambler will be set to a pseudo-random nonzero state. The seven LSBs of the SERVICE field will be set to all zeros prior to scrambling to enable estimation of the initial state of the scrambler in the receiver.

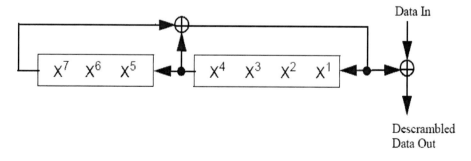

Fig. 1. Scrambler for IEEE 802.11a PHY layer

2.2 Scrambler for IEEE 802.16a

This standard uses 15 bit scrambler [2]. Data randomization is performed on each burst of data on the DL(Down Link) and UL(Up Link). The randomization is performed on each allocation (DL or UL); in other words, for each allocation of a data block (sub-channels on the frequency domain and OFDM symbols on the time domain), the randomizer shall be used independently. If the amount of data to transmit does not fit exactly the amount of data allocated, padding of 0xFF ("1" only) shall be added to the end of the transmission block for the unused integer bytes. The polynomial used for the ex or connections is as follows.

$$S(x) = 1 + x^{14} + x^{15}$$

The shift-register of the randomizer shall be initialized for each new allocation. The PRBS generator shall be as shown in Figure 2. Each data byte to be transmitted shall enter sequentially into the randomizer, MSB first. Preambles are not randomized. The seed value shall be used to calculate the randomization bits, which are combined in an XOR operation with the serialized bit stream of each burst. The randomizer sequence is applied only to information bits.

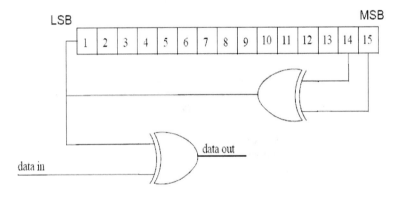

Fig. 2. Scrambler for 802.16a

2.3 Unified Scrambler for 11a and 16a

The unification strategy for the combined hardware is as follows.

Unified hardware for both scramblers = hardware for 802.16a (the greater one) + additional combinational and sequential hardware to extract 802.11a functionalities

Following above strategy we made below design for combined scrambler of 11a and 16a PHY specifications.

The structure exhibits functionalities of scramblers of 11a and 16a. The WiFi/WiMAX line selects which scrambling pattern will randomize the input data. For high level on WiFi/WiMAX line the unified design configures to WiFi structure, as the 4th and 7th bits are ex ored and fed to the upper input of 2:1 mux.

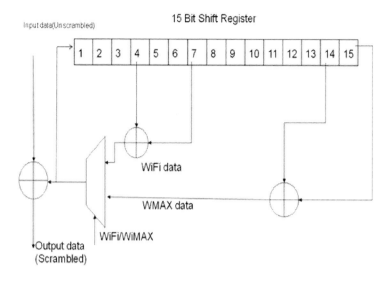

Fig. 3. Unified scrambler for 11a and 16a PHY specifications

Similarly the 14th and 15th inputs are ex or-ed and the output to the second input of 2:1 mux. Thus the low level on WiFI/WiMAX line will configure the unified scrambler to WiMAX configuration.

3   Verilog HDL Implementation and SIMULATION RESULTS

We used Xilinx 12.1i for design and simulation of unified scrambler. Data flow coding style is opted for design and hence the RTL saved much of the hardware than it would be for behavioral style. We also provided the measures of testability by providing test output ports for the shift register and the two output of ex or gates connected to the shift register. These ports along with the module input and output ports are shown in the waveforms in fig 6,7,8.

The RTL schematic is shown in Fig 5. It shows the actual connections of the hardware parts to each other.

We simulated four test cases as shown below for unified scrambler.

1) Long streams of zeros for WiFi configuration
2) Long streams of ones for WiFi configuration
3) Long streams of zeros for WiMAX configuration
4) Long streams of ones for WiMAX configuration

1) Test case 1: Long streams of zeros in input for WiFi configuration

Here the rst_i line is high for 200 ps and then it is pulled low. Wifi_nwimax_i line has been assigned high level and hence the scrambler is configured to wifi configuration.

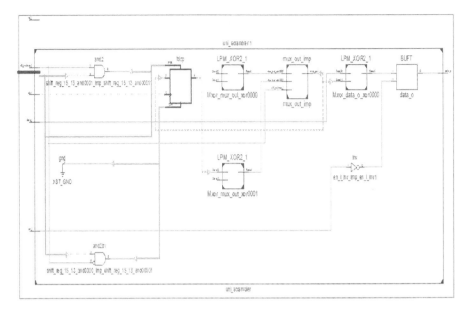

Fig. 4. RTL schematic of unified scrambler

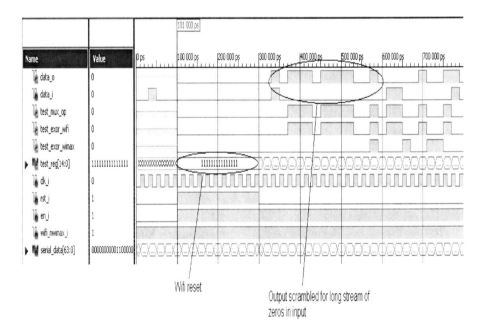

Fig. 5. Waveforms for long streams of zeros in input for WiFi configuration

The input pattern applied for long streams of zeros in input is as follows.
64'b0000_1100_0000_0000_0010_0011_1000_0001_0000_0010_1110_1111_100
0_0001_1010_0101.

From fig 6 it is clear that the output shows the predicted scrambling pattern for consecutive zeros for WiFi configuration.

2) Test case 2:Long streams of ones in input for WiFi configuration

Fig 6 shows the scrambling of long ones in output.
The input pattern given is
64'b0000_1111_1111_1111_1111_0011_1011_1100_1110_1111_0000_0001_0
111_1010_1100_0011.

3) Test case 3: Long streams of zeros in input for WiMAX configuration

Here the rst_i line is high for 200 ps and then it is pulled low. Wifi_nwimax_i line has been assigned low level and hence the scrambler is configured to WiMAX configuration. The output is seen to be scrambled for long streams of zeros. The pattern given to input is
64'b0000_1100_0000_0000_0010_0011_1000_0001_0000_0010_1110_1111_100
0_0001_1010_0101.

4) Test case 4:Long streams of ones in input for WiMAX configuration

The input pattern given is64'b0000_1111_1111_1111_1111_0011_1011_1100_1110_
1111_0000_0001_0111_1010_1100_0011.

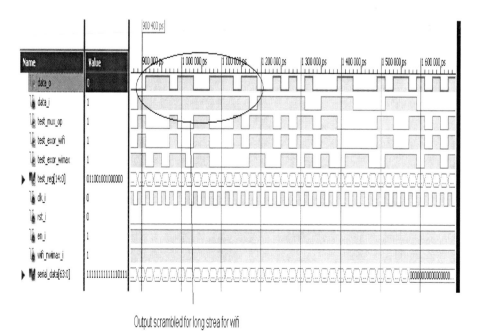

Fig. 6. Scrambling for long streams of ones in input for WiFi configuration

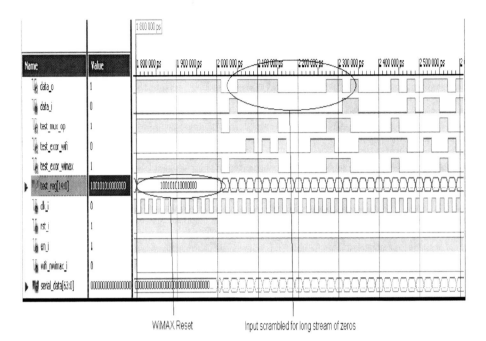

WiMAX Reset   Input scrambled for long stream of zeros

Fig. 7. Waveforms for long zeros for WiMAX configuration

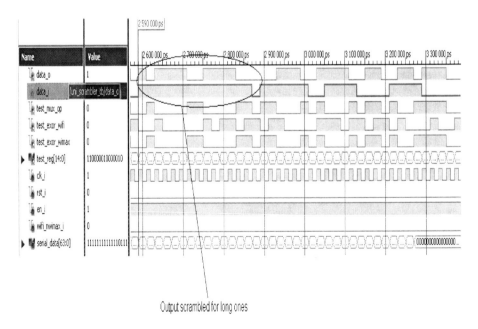

Output scrambled for long ones

Fig. 8. Waveforms for long ones for WiMAX configuration

4 Conclusion

The unified scrambler is verified for all four test cases and waveforms are analyzed and checked against the predicted output of unified scrambler. Here we saved the hardware for 7 bit shift register required for WiFi functionality. We can now assume that in similar way we can also unify interleaver, de-interleaver, IFFT and FFT blocks of IEEE 802.11a and 802.16a PHY layers.

References

1. IEEE Std 802.11a, Part 11: Wireless LAN Medium Access Control(MAC) and Physical Layer (PHY) Specifications, High-Speed Physical Layer in the 5 GHz Band (2007)
2. IEEE Standard for Local and metropolitan area networks Part 16: Air Interface for Broadband Wireless Access Systems (2009)
3. Ryan, P., et al.: A Single Chip PHY COFDM Modem for IEEE 802.11a with Integrated ADCs and DACs. In: IEEE Proc. ISSCC 2001, pp. 338–339 (February 2001)
4. Nogee, A.: WLAN Chipset Market - The Incredible Journey Is Just Beginning. In-Stat rep. no. IN020271WY (2002)
5. Meeuwsen, M., et al.: A full-rate software implementation of an IEEE 802.11a compliant digital baseband transmitter. In: IEEE Workshop on Signal Processing Systems, pp. 124–129 (2004)
6. Tang, Y., Qian, L., Wang, Y.: Optimized Software Implementation of Full-Rate IEEE 802.11a Compliant Digital Baseband Transmitter on Digital Signal Processor. In: GLOBECOMÂ 2005 (2005)
7. Krstic, M., et al.: Baseband processor for IEEE 802.11a Standard with Embedded BIST. Facta

Secure Conversation Using Cryptographic Algorithms in 3G Mobile Communication

Alpesh R. Sankaliya, V. Mishra, and Abhilash Mandloi

Department of Electronics
Sardar Vallabhbhai National Institute of Technology, Surat-395007
Gujarat, India
alpeshrs@yahoo.com, vive@eced.svnit.ac.in, asm@eced.svnit.ac.in

Abstract. Cryptographic algorithms used by Mobile Subscribers to protect the privacy of their cellular voice and data communication. Mobile network is the shared media. When media are shared, privacy and authentication are lost unless some method is established to regain it. Ciphering provides the mean to regain control over privacy and authentication. A5/x are the encryption algorithms used in order to ensure privacy of conversations on mobile phones. The strong version A5/1 is used in most countries. A5/2 is weaker version used in countries on which export restrictions apply. A5/3 encryption algorithm used for 3G and GEA3 encryption algorithm used for GPRS. f8 is confidentiality algorithms developed by 3GPP, bringing out the commonality between A5/3 and GEA3 algorithms. The following paper is based on simulation of A5/1, A5/3 and f8 algorithms.

Keywords: Speech Encryption, Security, Cryptography, Stream Cipher, A5/1, A5/3, f8.

1 Introduction

Secret key cryptographic systems can be categorized into either block or stream ciphers. Block ciphers are memory less algorithms that permute N-bits blocks of plaintext data under the influence of the secret key and generate N-bits blocks of encrypted data[1]. Stream ciphers contain internal states and typically operate serially by generation a stream of pseudo-random key bits, the keystream (stream ciphers are also called *keystream Generators*). The keystream is then bitwise XORed with the data to encrypt/decrypt. Stream ciphers do not suffer from the error propagation, as in the block ones, because each bit is independently encrypted/decrypted from any other. They are generally much faster than block ciphers and they have greater software efficiency [5].

In the Mobile communication, A5 stream cipher is used, which employs a 64-bit secret key [2]. Versions A5/1 and A5/2 were kept secret for a long period of time. Since the GSM *A5* algorithm was developed, the climate for cryptography has changed substantially [1]. Recently, *A5/1* and *A5/2* were reverse-engineered from a GSM handset and published by Briceno et al. [1]. Afterwards A5/2 was cryptanalysis and proved to be completely insecure. The attack required very few pseudo random

D.C. Wyld et al. (Eds.): NeCoM/WeST/WiMoN 2011, CCIS 197, pp. 396–406, 2011.
© Springer-Verlag Berlin Heidelberg 2011

bits and only 216 steps [4]. A new security algorithm, known as A5/3 and f8 provides users of mobile phones with an even higher level of protection against eavesdropping than they have already [18].

A5/3 and f8 have been developed by a joint working party between the GSM Association Security Group and the 3'rd Generation Partnership Project (3GPP)[10]. It will also be applicable for the General Packet Radio Service (GPRS) where it will be known as GEA3, and other modes such as High Speed Circuit Switched Data (HSCSD) and Enhanced Data Rates for GSM Evolution (EDGE) [5][6]. The A5/3 and f8 encryption algorithm specifically supplies signaling protection, so that sensitive information is protected over the radio path, and user data protection, to protect voice calls and other user generated data passing over the radio path [18].

2   Ciphering Algorithm for 2G System

A Mobile conversation is sent as a sequence of frames every 4.6 millisecond. Each frame contains 114 bits representing the digitized X to Y communication and 114 bits representing the digitized Y to X communication. Each conversation can be encrypted by a new session key Kc. For each frame, Kc is mixed with a publicly known frame counter Fn, and the result serves as the initial state of a generator which produces 228 pseudo random bits. These bits are XOR'ed by the two parties with the 114+114 bits of the plaintext to produce the 114+114 bits of the cipher text[5][7].

A5/1 stream cipher is a binary linear feedback shift registers (LFSR) based key stream generator. It combines three LFSRs of lengths 19, 22, and 23 bits, which are denoted by $R1$, $R2$ and $R3$ respectively. All of these registers have primitive feedback polynomials and each register is updated according to its own feedback polynomials. Each LFSR is shifted, using clock cycles that are determined by a majority function. The majority function uses three bits; $C1$, $C2$, and $C3$. Among these bits, if two or more of them are 0 then the majority $m = 0$. Similarly, if two or more of them are 1, then the majority $m = 1$. If $Ck = m$ then Rk is shifted, where k=1, 2, 3. The feedback polynomials for $R1$, $R2$, $R3$ are: $x^{19} + x^5 + x^2 + x + 1$, $x^{22} + x + 1$ and $x^{23} + x^{15} + x^2 + x + 1$, respectively. At each clock cycle, after the initialization phase, the last bits of each LFSR are XORed to produce one output bit. The proposed architecture for the hardware implementation of the A5/1 cipher is shown in Fig. 1.

The process of generating pseudo random bits from the session key Kc and the frame number Fn is carried out in four steps.

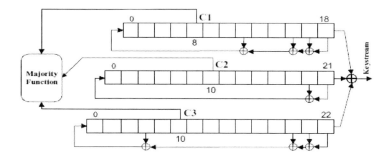

Fig. 1. A5/1 stream cipher architecture

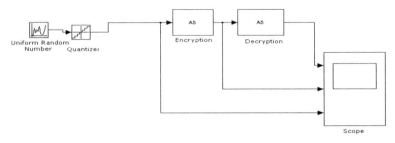

Fig. 2. Simulation of A5/1 Algorithm using Matlab

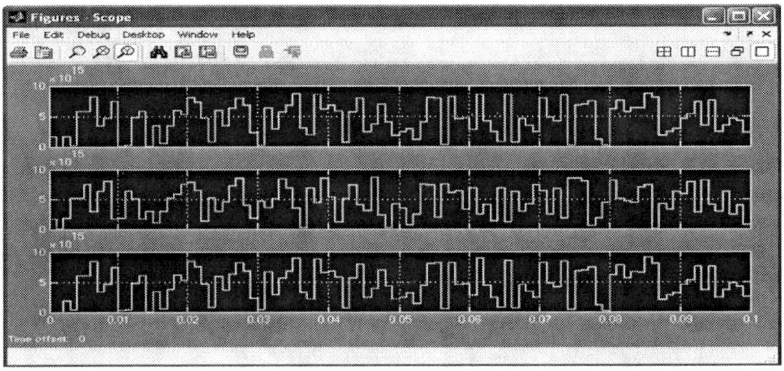

Fig. 3. Simulation result for A5/1 Algorithm

In *step 1*, The Three LFSRs are initialized to zero. Then, clocked for 64 cycles, ignoring the majority function. During each cycle, the each bit from *Kc* is XORed in parallel into the lsb's of the three registers.

In *step 2*, the three registers are clocked for 22 additional cycles (ignoring the majority function). During this period the successive bits of *Fn* (from lsb to msb) are again XOR'ed in parallel into the lsb's of the three registers. The content of the three registers at the end of this step is called the **initial state** of the frame. In *step 3*, the three registers are clocked for 100 additional clock cycles with the majority function but without producing any outputs. Finally in *step 4*, The three registers are clocked for 228 additional clock cycles with the majority function in order to produce the 228 output bits. At each clock cycle, one output bit is produced as the XOR of the msb's of the three registers. Fig 2 gives the simulation of *A5/1* algorithm.

The idea behind the *A5/1* is good. It is very efficient. It passes all known statistical test; it's only known weakness is that its registers are short enough to make exhaustive search feasible. Fig. 3 gives the simulation result by using the *Sample time* = 0.1ms, *KEY* = [1 2 3 4 5 6 7 8].

3   Ciphering Algorithm for 3G System

3G mobile system offering mobile users content rich services, wireless broadband access to internet, and worldwide roaming. However, this includes serious security vulnerabilities. The algorithms are stream ciphers that are used to encrypt/decrypt blocks of data under a confidentiality key **KC**. Each of these algorithms is based on the **KASUMI** algorithm which is a block cipher that produces a 64-bit output from a 64-bit input under the control of a 128-bit key.[10][13] The algorithms defined here use **KASUMI** in a form of output-feedback mode as a keystream generator. The three algorithms are all very similar. **KGCORE** function is shown in Fig.4. Table 1 gives the detail of variables used in figure. Each of these algorithms is based on the KASUMI. KASUMI is a block cipher that produces a 64-bit output from a 64-bit input under the control of a 128-bit key. KASUMI used in these algorithms is the Feistel cipher with eight rounds with associated subkeys (KL, KI and KO)[10] this is generated from CK using rounding manner. It operates on a 64-bit data block and uses a 128-bit key. Its eight rounds are shown in Fig 5. Each KASUMI operator uses FL and FO functions. In each odd round of KASUMI operator uses $R_i=FO(FL(L_{i-1}, KL_i), KO_i, KI_i)$ function and for each even round uses $R_i =FL(FO(L_{i-1}, KO_i, KI_i), KL_i)$.

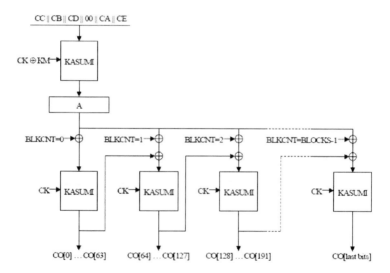

Fig. 4. KGCORE Core Keystream Generator Function with KM=0x5555555555555555555555555555 555555 (in hex)

Table 1. GSM A5/4, GSM A5/3, ECSD A5/3, GEA3 in terms of KGCORE

	GEA3	A5/3	F8
CA	11111111	00001111	00000000
CB	00000	00000	BEARER
CC	INPUT	0…0‖COUNT	COUNT
CD	DIRECTION	0	DIRECTION
CE		0000000000000000	
CK	Cipher Key repeated to fill 128 bits		Kc
CO	Output	Block1‖Block2(114 bit‖114bit)	Ks(Key stream)

The FL and FO algorithms based on number of iteration round with substitutions (S-Boxes) and permutations (PBoxes) shown in Fig 6 and 7.

In FL algorithm $R'=R$ exor ROL (L bit-and $KL_{i1,1}$) , $L'=L$ ex-or ROL(R bit-or $KL_{i2,1}$). In FO algorithm $R_j=FI(L_j-1$ ex-or $KO_{ij},KI_{ij})$ ex-or R_{j-1}, $L_j=R_{j-1}$. In FI algorithm shown in Fig 7 for odd round $R_i=L_{i-1}$, $L_i= S9[L_{i-1}]$ ex-or $ZE(R_{i-1})$, for 2nd round $L_i= R_{i-1}$ ex-or $KI_{i,j,2}$, $R_i= S7[R_{i-1}]$ ex-or $TR(L_{i-1})$ ex-or $KI_{i,j,1}$, for 4th round out = $S7[L_{i-1}]$ ex-or $TR(L_{i-1})$.[10]

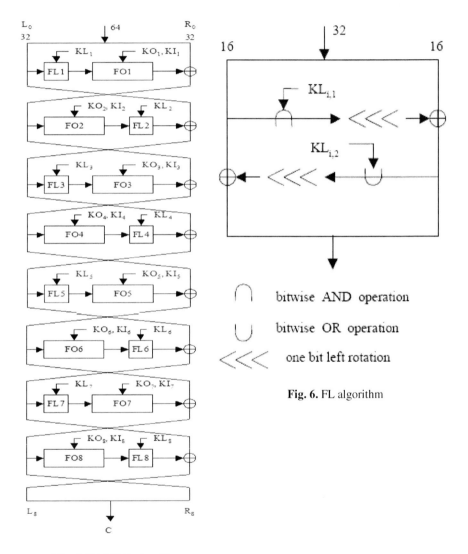

bitwise AND operation

bitwise OR operation

one bit left rotation

Fig. 6. FL algorithm

Fig. 5. KASUMI algorithm

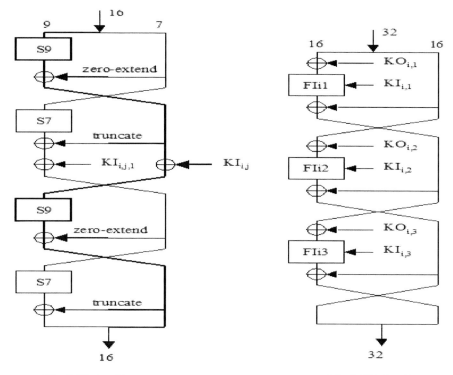

Fig. 7. FI algorithm   **Fig. 8.** FO algorithm

A5/3   Ciphering Algorithm

The GSM **A5/3** algorithm produces two 114-bit keystream strings, one of which is used for uplink encryption/decryption and the other for downlink encryption/decryption. Figure 9 shows simulation of A5/3 algorithm.

Result of Simulation block of *A5/3* algorithm is shown in Fig. 10 by taking sampling time=0.1ms, key=[1 2 3 4 5 6 7 8 9 10 11 12 13 14 15 16], count=32.

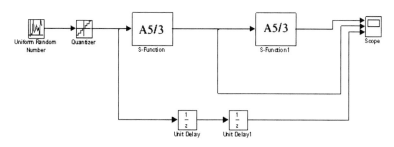

Fig. 9. Simulation of A5/3 Algorithm using Matlab

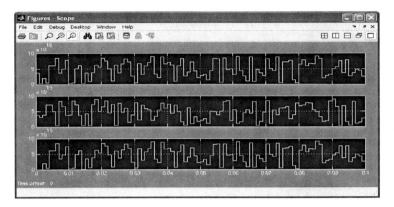

Fig. 10. Simulation result of A5/3 Algorithm

F8 Ciphering Algorithm

Simulation of f8 algorithm is shown in Figure 11 and 12 by taking sampling time = 0.1ms, key=[1 2 3 4 5 6 7 8 9 10 11 12 13 14 15 16], count=140, bearer=32 and direction of transmission upward.

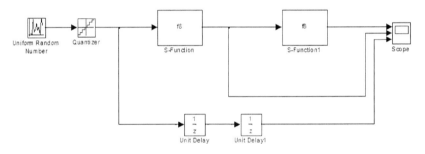

Fig. 11. Simulation of f8 Algorithm

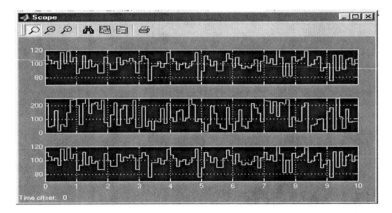

Fig. 12. Simulation result of f8 Algorithm

4   Performance Analysis

The simulation works were carried out on a Pentium Core 2 Duo processor with 3 GB of RAM running on Window7. Codes for A5/1, A5/3 and f8 were written and executed in MATLAB 7.8

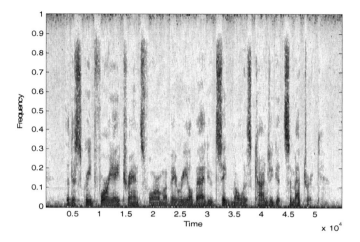

Fig. 13. Spectrogram of plain speech

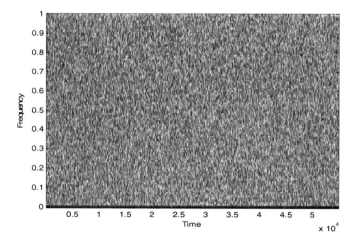

Fig. 14. Speech ciphered by A5/1 algorithm

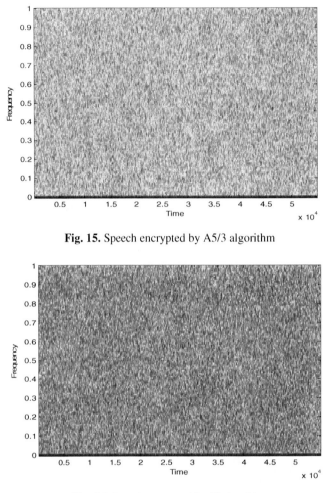

Fig. 15. Speech encrypted by A5/3 algorithm

Fig. 16. Speech encrypted by f8 algorithm

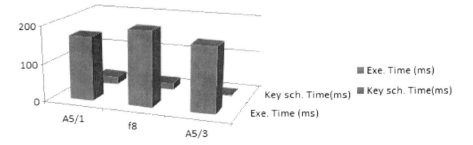

Fig. 17. Total execution time and key scheduling time for all algorithms

Speech is the very complex signal representing different kind of sound voiced, unvoiced and silence. For processing speech one can work with the function x(t) which represents the time information containing time and amplitude. Other information is obtained in frequency domain representation using FFT (Fast Fourier Transform). The speech signal can be visualized well through a spectrogram, which is the three dimensional representation that has time, frequency and energy density as dimension as a dimension. Fig.13 shows the spectrogram of speech_dft.wav sound in Matlab. The dark bands in Fig 13 are called formants and are frequency of resonance. The darkness of these bands is energy, which serves as the third dimension in the spectrogram [9]. Modern speech secrecy systems are mainly based on digital enciphering techniques. In the area of speech ciphers, mainly symmetric key algorithms are used. Fig 14, 15 and 16 shows the spectrograms of the plain speech ciphered by *A5/1, A5/3* and f8 algorithms respectively and easily compared the energy band of ciphered signals. Figure 17 shows the comparison of the total execution time and key scheduling time for 20 consecutive runs of all three algorithms. We can see that total execution time is higher for f8 algorithm compared to A5/1 and A5/3. *A5/3* provides very low key set up time than others.

We can see in *A5/1* ciphering still having the originality of speech and we can hear some voice sound superimposed with some spidery noise. While in *A5/3* and f8, we can only hear non-voice sound. Hence, no one can clearly understand the original plain speech. Normally the length and characteristic of the key specify the depth of encryption. As the key length of A5/1 is only 64 bit while f8 is 128 bit. Hence f8 provides more security than A5/1. A5/3 is the variable length encryption with key length varies from 64-128 bit. so, it is very difficult to guess the key. Hence, *A5/3* is more security than others. We can also see that the spectrogram of *A5/3* is very much different.

The security provided by *A5/3* and *f8* relies almost entirely on the security provided by Kasumi. To allow us to measure how effective the algorithms are at mixing up bits and thus estimate a 'security margin', a voice encryption simulation was carried out and the degree of correlation between the original and encrypted voice was calculated. The correlation coefficient ρ between two speech signal P (original speech) and C (ciphered speech) is computed as:

$$\rho = \frac{\Sigma(P - P_{MEAN})(C - C_{MEAN})}{\sqrt{\Sigma(P - P_{MEAN})^2(C - C_{MEAN})^2}}$$

where P_{MEAN} and C_{MEAN} are respective mean elements of P and C. The correlation coefficient between the original speech waveform of figure 13 and A5/1 encrypted speech waveform of figure 14 is calculated and equals to 0.00409. Similarly, correlation coefficient with A5/3 algorithm is 0.00298 and correlation coefficient of f8 algorithm is =0.00321.

5   Conclusion

From the correlation coefficient values obtained, we can conclude that (i) f8 is about 21.5% more secure than A5/1(ii) A5/3 is about 27.1% more secure than A5/1 and (iii) A5/3 is about 7.1% more secure than f8.

Exponential increase in mobile subscribers has rendered the Mobile communication system vulnerable to attack by unauthorised users. A number of vendors are operating around the world and they employ various operating standards and equipments. It has been estimated that computing power doubles every two years. An algorithm that is secure today may be breakable after 6-8 years. Since any algorithms being designed today must work for many years after design. We conclude that secure communication is essential but operators are operating commercially and switching to newer standards needs a transition from older equipments and interfaces to newer ones. This transition can take higher costs and operator may also lose customers. ITU-T can play a pivotal role to develop a standard for equipments and algorithms.

References

[1] Pandya, R.: Mobile and Personal Communication Systems and Service's. IEEE Press, New York (2001)
[2] Schneier, B.: Applied Cryptography. John Wiley & Sons Inc., New York (1996)
[3] Feher, K.: Wireless Digital Communication - Modulation and Spread Spectrum Applications. Prentice Hall of India Private Ltd., New Delhi (2000)
[4] Garg, V.K.: Wireless and Personal Communication System. Prentice Hall of India Private Ltd., New Delhi (1997)
[5] Stallings, W.: Cryptography and Network Security. Prentice Hall, New Jersey (2006)
[6] Haykin, S.: Communication System. In: 2001 Library of Congress in publication Cataloging Data, Singapore (2001)
[7] Uylessblock: Wireless and personal communications system. PHI, New Delhi (2000)
[8] Veni Madhavan, C.E., Saxena, P.K.: Recent Trends in Applied Cryptology. IETE Technical Review 20(2) (March-April 2003)
[9] Briceno, M., Goldberg, I., Wagner, D.: A Pedagogical Implementation of the A5/1 (1999)
[10] Technical specification of 3GPP TS 55.216 V6.2.0 (2003-2009)
[11] Biham, E., Dunkelmna, O.: Cryptanalysis of the A5/1GSM stream Cipher (2000)
[12] Anderson, R., Roe, M.: A5-The GSM Encryption Algorithm (1994)
[13] Pitz, S., Schmitz, R., Martin, T.: Security mechanism in UMTS. Datenschutz and Datensicherheit (DUD) 25, 1–10 (2001)
[14] Wei, L., Zibin, D., Longmei, N.: Research and Implementation of a High speed Reconfigurable A5 Algorithm. IEEE, Los Alamitos (2008)
[15] Huang, X., Shah, P.G., Sharma, D.: Protecting from Attacking the man-in-middle in wireless sensor Network with elliptic curve cryptography key exchange. In: 2010 Fourth International Conference on Network and System Security (2010)
[16] Ahmed, F., Imran, M.: Cryptographic Analysis of GSM Network. IEEE, Los Alamitos (2009)
[17] Ahmad, M., Izharuddin: Enhanced A5/1 Cipher with improved linear Complexity. IEEE, Los Alamitos (2009)
[18] Pitz, S., Schmitz, R., Martin, T.: Security mechanism in UMTS. Datenschutz and Datensicherheit (DUD) 25, 1–10 (2001)

Performance Evaluation of Transport Layer VPN on IEEE 802.11g WLAN

Praveen Likhar, Ravi Shankar Yadav, and M. Keshava Rao

Centre for Artificial Intelligence and Robotics (CAIR)
Defence Research and Development Organisation (DRDO)
Bangalore-93, India
{praveen.likhar,ravi.yadav,keshava}@cair.drdo.in

Abstract. With the increasing popularity of Wireless Local Area Network (WLAN) in various sectors, security has become a primary concern. This has been necessitated by the fact that free-space radio transmission in wireless networks makes eavesdropping easy and consequently a security breach may result in unauthorized access, information theft, interference and service degradation. Virtual Private Networks (VPNs) have emerged as an important solution to security threats surrounding the use of public networks for private communications. While VPNs for wired line networks have matured in both research and commercial environments, the design and deployment of VPNs for WLAN is still an evolving field. This paper consist a brief description of OpenVPN, a transport layer tunneling VPN solution, used for securing IEEE 802.11g WLAN. In this paper we have presented experimental evaluation of OpenVPN with an analysis of its impact on performance of IEEE 802.11g.

Keywords: WLAN, 802.11g, VPN, performance evaluation, security.

1 Introduction

The IEEE 802.11g WLAN technology is one of the fastest growing segment of the communications market today. It provides always-on network connectivity without, of course, requiring a network cable. Home or remote workers can set up networks without worrying about how to run wires through houses that never were designed to support network infrastructure. WLAN components plug into the existing infrastructure as simply as extending a phone line with a wireless phone. By removing the need to wire a network in the home, the cost of adoption and benefit of mobility within the home and the low cost of components make wireless networking a low-cost and efficient way to install a home network. But many users of WLAN technology are not aware or concerned about the security implications associated with wireless networks. On the other hand, wireless adoption within the corporate and medium-sized businesses has been severely inhibited by security concerns associated with sending sensitive corporate data over the air. Unlike its wired network counterpart, where the data remains in the cables, the wireless network uses open air as a medium. This broadcast nature of WLAN introduces a greater risk from intruders.

D.C. Wyld et al. (Eds.): NeCoM/WeST/WiMoN 2011, CCIS 197, pp. 407–415, 2011.
© Springer-Verlag Berlin Heidelberg 2011

In particular, with the evolution of wireless networking in recent years has raised the serious security issues [1], [2]. These security issues are of great concern for this technology as it is being subjected to numerous attacks [3], [4], [5]. The most common attacks on wireless LANs are unwanted or automatic connection to the wrong network, man-in-the-middle attack with a fake Access Point (AP), theft of information by illegal tapping of the network, intrusion from open air, scrambling of the WLAN and consumption of device batteries.

The Wired Equivalent Privacy (WEP) is a standard security mechanism for IEEE 802.11g WLAN. When it was introduced, it was considered as a secured algorithm. But later it was found that it can be cracked easily [3], [6], [7], [8]. VPN technology has been used successfully to securely transmit data in wired networks especially when using Internet as the medium. This success of VPN in wired networks and the inherent security limitations of wireless networks have prompted developers and administrators to deploy it in case of wireless networks. A VPN works by creating a tunnel, on top of a protocol such as IP. In this paper we evaluated the impact of OpenVPN [9], transport layer VPN solution, on performance of IEEE 802.11g WLAN.

2   Wireless LAN Standards

The IEEE 802.11 is a set of standards for wireless local area network (WLAN) computer communications in the 2.4, 3.6 and 5 GHz frequency bands [10]. The 802.11a, b, and g standards are the most common for home wireless access points and large business wireless systems. The working frequency for 802.11a is 5GHz and for 802.11b & g it is 2.4 GHz. The maximum speed for 802.11a & g is 54Mbps and for 802.11b it is 11Mbps.

3   OpenVPN

The OpenVPN is free and open source user space VPN solution which tunnels the traffic through transport layer using TCP or UDP protocol for encapsulation and transfer of data. It uses virtual network interface (VNI) to receive outgoing traffic from user space program and then perform the cryptographic operations and compression before sending it to other communication end. It also uses VNI to send the incoming traffic to user space program after performing reverse cryptographic operations and decompression. Security in OpenVPN is handled by the OpenSSL [11] cryptographic library which provides strong security over Secure Socket Layer (SSL) using standard algorithms such as Advanced Encryption Standard (AES). The OpenVPN uses a mode called Cipher Block Chaining (CBC), this prevents an attacker from seeing patterns between blocks with identical plaintext messages and manipulating one or more of these blocks.

The VNI appears as actual network interface to all applications and users. Packets of incoming traffic sent via a VNI are delivered to a user-space program attached to the VNI. A user-space program may also pass packets into a VNI. In this case the VNI injects these packets to the operating system network stack to send it to the

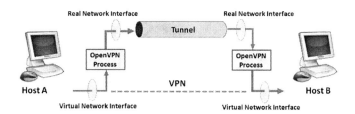

Fig. 1. OpenVPN Tunnel between two end points

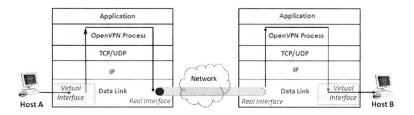

Fig. 2. OpenVPN – Data Flow

location mentioned in destination address field of the packets. The TUN and TAP [12], [13] are open source VNI. The TAP simulates an Ethernet device and it operates with layer 2 packets such as Ethernet frames. The TUN simulates a network layer device and it operates with layer 3 packets such as IP packets.

In Figure 1, the working of OpenVPN is explained and in Figure 2, the data flow in OpenVPN environment is shown.

The OpenVPN performs the following to secure the communications:

- Receives the packets of outgoing plain traffic from user space program by using the VNI. After receiving the packets, it compresses the packets using LZO compression.
- After compression, it encrypts the packets using cryptographic algorithm. For our experimentation we are using AES-128. It also applies sliding window method to provide replay protection. Then it tunnels the packet using UDP or TCP protocol to the other end.
- On receiving the encrypted traffic at other end, the OpenVPN performs the reverse of cryptographic operations to verify integrity, authenticity etc.
- After successful completion of reverse cryptographic operations, it decompresses the packet. The decompressed packet is then passed via VNI to the user space program.

4   Experiment Setup for Performance Measurement

For analyzing the impact of OpenVPN on performance of IEEE 802.11g WLAN we created two experiment scenarios. First was for measuring the throughput under normal conditions and the second was to analyze the variation of traffic throughputs over an IEEE 802.11g WLAN when OpenVPN is implemented in WLAN. The following parameters were used as metrics for performance measurement during our experiments:

- Throughput is the rate at which bulk of data transfers can be transmitted from one host to another over a sufficiently long period of time.
- Latency is the total time required for a packet to travel from one host to another, generally from a transmitter through a network to a receiver.
- Packet delay variation is measured for packets belonging to the same packet stream and shows the difference in the one-way delay that packets experience in the network.

4.1 Standard Followed for Performance Measurement

We followed the IP Performance Metrics (IPPM) RFC 4148 [14], to measure the performance. The following is the list of metrics we have used along with the standard followed to measure these metrics.

1. Maximum throughput achieved as per RFC 2544 [15]
2. One-way Delay as per RFC 2679 [16]
3. IP Packet Delay Variation Metric as per RFC 3393 [17]

4.2 Requirements for Experimentation

The following is a list of the general Software and Hardware requirements for our experiments:

1. Two laptops loaded with Red Hat Enterprise Linux 5
2. Ethernet Cables
3. TL-WA601G 108M TP-Link Wireless Access point
4. SPT-2000A Spirent test center

4.3 Experiment Setup

In our experiment setup two laptops are connected using TP-Link Access point. The distance between the AP and the laptops is set to 4 meters to keep the signal strength high. Port-1 of Spirent test center is connected to laptop-1 and port-2 of Spirent is connected to laptop-2 using Ethernet cables of length 3 meters. These ports act as clients for laptops. These ports are used for traffic generation and analysis purpose. Port-1 of Spirent test center is used to generate the desired traffic for various data rates, frame sizes etc. Port-2 receives the traffic and analyses it. The analysis includes max throughput achieved, latency and packet delay variation with respect to various frame sizes. The 802.11g WLAN standard does not have inbuilt compression feature. OpenVPN supports both modes without compression and with compression, in our study we experimented both modes.

4.3.1 Performance without OpenVPN

The experiment setup for this is shown in Figure 3. We carried out this experiment for measuring the baseline performance of IEEE 802.11g WLAN. This experiment comprises of two steps. The first step measures the throughput with respect to UDP traffic, while the second step measures the throughput with respect to TCP traffic. In the first step, port-1 of Spirent test center sends UDP traffic of different frame sizes to laptop-1, which is connected to laptop-2 through wireless link using an Access Point (AP). Laptop-1 forwards this data to laptop-2 through AP and then laptop-2 send this data to port-2 of the Spirent test center. The second step of the experiment was conducted using the same environment variables described above, but this time TCP traffic was generated using port-1 to send traffic with different frame sizes from laptop1 to laptop2. We varied the size of the frame from 512 bytes to 1518 bytes.

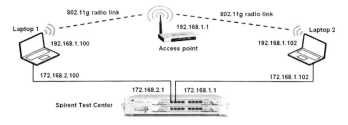

Fig. 3. Experiment setup without OpenVPN

4.3.2 Performance with OpenVPN

Now our next aim is to analyze the impact of applying OpenVPN security solution to 802.11g WLAN. In this scenario first we have to run our OpenVPN solution on both the laptops. OpenVPN configuration files [18] for both laptops are given below in Table 1.

The setup for this experiment is shown in Figure 4. To analyze the impact of applying OpenVPN security to 802.11g WLAN on the throughput of UDP and TCP traffic in IEEE 802.11g WLAN, we performed the experiments in two steps. In first step we measured the impact on UDP traffic over IEEE 802.11g and in second step we measured the impact on TCP traffic over IEEE 802.11g. Experimentation was carried out in the same manner as for baseline performance measurement.

Table 1. OpenVPN configuration files

Configuration file – Laptop-1	Configuration file – Laptop-1
Port 5002	Port 5002
Proto udp	Proto udp
Dev tun0	Dev tun0
Remote 192.168.1.102	Remote 192.168.1.102
Ifconfig 20.20.20.1 20.20.20.2	Ifconfig 20.20.20.1 20.20.20.2
Cipher AES-128-CBC	Cipher AES-128-CBC
Secret static.key	Secret static.key
Comp-lzo	Comp-lzo
Keepalive 5 20	Keepalive 5 20
Persist-tun	Persist-tun

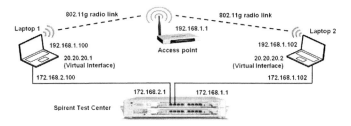

Fig. 4. Experiment setup with OpenVPN

5 Experment Result and Analysis

The results for all test scenarios of our experiment were collected from the test bed illustrated in the experiment setup section. Each experiment was repeated for twenty iterations to find the average performance values.

5.1 Throughput

The UDP and TCP throughput are measured as per RFC 2544 standards for different frame sizes. The results of these experiments are presented in Table 2 & Figure 5. Figure-5 indicates that the throughput increases for both UDP and TCP traffic with increased frame size. Throughput increases because when the data transmitted using large frames the total overhead for transmitting the data due to frame headers will be less as compare to when the data is transmitted using small frames. The throughput is decreased slightly when OpenVPN is applied because of the increased overhead which is due to encapsulation and cryptographic operations used by OpenVPN. When compression is used with OpenVPN throughput increases since compression reduces the packet size in physical interface. Throughput in this case is better than the throughput in normal case i.e. without OpenVPN because IEEE 802.11g does not has inbuilt compression and after compression packet size reduces considerably if data is not randomly distributed which is true most of the time.

Table 2. Throughput results

Frame Size (bytes)	UDP Average Throughput (Mbps)			TCP Average Throughput (Mbps)		
	Without OpenVPN	With OpenVPN		Without OpenVPN	With OpenVPN	
		Without compression	With compression		Without compression	With compression
512	3.847	3.627	5.429	3.135	2.601	4.796
1024	5.429	4.574	11.238	4.796	4.065	10.929
1280	6.062	5.389	13.915	5.429	4.961	12.936
1518	6.906	6.062	16.09	6.062	5.62	16.09

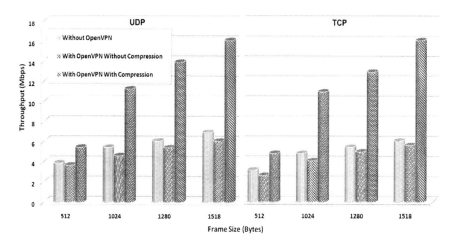

Fig. 5. UDP and TCP Throughput according to frame size

5.2   Average Latency

The average latency is measured as per RFC 2679 standards for UDP and TCP traffic for various frame size. The results of these experiments are presented in Figure 6 and Figure 7. These figures indicate that as we increase the frame size, the latency increases for both UDP and TCP traffic since the round trip time is proportional to the size of frame. The figures clearly indicate that latency is less for normal case as compare to other two cases because additional processing is required for cryptographic operation, compression and encapsulation in OpenVPN mode. It is also analyzed that the latency in case of OpenVPN without compression is more than in case of OpenVPN with compression. Even though compression takes some processing time it reduces the frame size which results in decreased transmission time as compare to the transmission time when frame is not compressed.

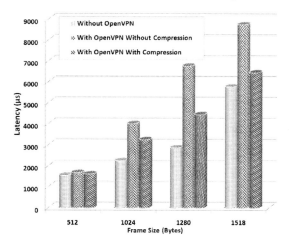

Fig. 6. UDP Average Latency according to frame size

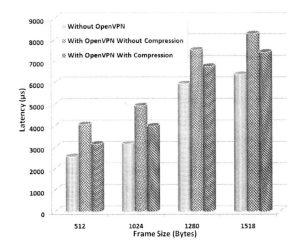

Fig. 7. TCP Average latency according to frame size

5.3 Packet Delay Variation

The IP Packet delay variation is measured as per RFC 3393 standards for UDP traffic for different frame size with different transmission rates. The result of this experiment is presented in Figure 8. This figure indicates that as we increase the load the IP Packet delay variation increases. From the above figures we observe that with the use of compression with OpenVPN, the IP Packet delay variation decreased as compared to normal case because compression reduces the payload size of packet.

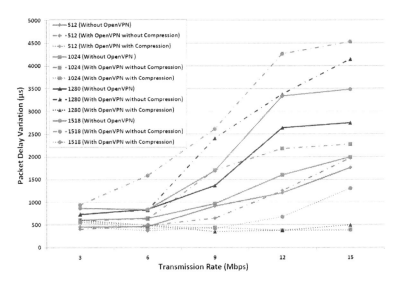

Fig. 8. UDP IP Packet Delay Variation according to frame size

6 Conclusion

In this work OpenVPN, a transport layer tunneling based VPN solution was adopted and implemented for 802.11g WLAN. For a more detailed description of impact of OpenVPN on performance of 802.11g WLAN, performance analysis was done for the UDP and TCP traffic with respect to various data rates and frame sizes using Spirent test center. From the above experimental results we can conclude that there is slight decrease in performance with the implementation of OpenVPN in 802.11g WLAN and there is increase in the performance of 802.11g WLAN with the use of compression in OpenVPN.

Acknowledgments. We would like to thank Director CAIR for supporting us to work in this area. We would also like to thank Dr. G. Athithan for his help and constructive suggestions throughout.

References

1. Karygiannis, T., Owens, L.: Wireless Network Security 802.11, Bluetooth and Handheld Devices, National Institute of technology. In: Special Publication, pp. 800–848 (2002)
2. Zahur, Y., Yang, T.A.: Wireless LAN Security and Laboratory Designs. Journal of Computing Sciences in Colleges 19, 44–60 (2004)
3. Borisov, N., Goldberg, I., Wagner, D.: Intercepting Mobile Communications: The Insecurity of 802.11. In: Proceedings of the Seventh Annual International Conference on Mobile Computing and Networking (2001)
4. Faria, D.B., Cheriton, D.R.: DoS and Authentication in Wireless Public Access Networks. In: Proceedings of ACM Workshop on Wireless Security, pp. 47–56 (2002)
5. Arbaugh, W.A., Shankar, N., Wang, J., Zhang, K.: Your 802.11 network has no clothes. IEEE Wireless Communications Magazine (2002)
6. Fluhrer, S.R., Mantin, I., Shamir, A.: Weaknesses in the Key Scheduling Algorithm of RC4. In: Selected Areas in Cryptography, pp. 1–24 (2001)
7. Stubblefield, A., Ioannidis, J., Rubin, A.D.: Using the Fluhrer, Mantin, and Shamir Attack to Break WEP. In: AT&T Labs Technical Report TD-4ZCPZZ (2001)
8. Hong, J., Lemachheche, R.: WEP protocol Weaknesses and Vulnerabilities. In: ECE 578 Computer Networks and Security (2003)
9. OpenVPN, http://openvpn.net/
10. IEEE Std 802.11™-2007 (Revision of IEEE Std 802.11-199)
11. OpenSSL-The Open Source toolkit for SSL/TLS, http://www.openssl.org
12. TUN-TAP, http://en.wikipedia.org/wiki/TUN/TAP
13. TUN-TAP FAQ, http://vtun.sourceforge.net/tun/faq.html
14. Stephan, E.: IP Performance Metrics (IIPM) Metrics Registry. In: RFC 4148 (2005)
15. Bradner, S., McQuaid, J.: Benchmarking Methodology for Network Interconnect Devices. In: RFC 2544 (2005)
16. Almes, G., Kalidindi, S., Zekauskas, M.: A One-way Delay Metric for IPPM. In: RFC 2679 (1999)
17. Demichelis, C., Chimento, P.: IP Packet Delay Variation. In: RFC 3393 (2002)
18. Feilner, M.: OpenVPN: Building and Integrating Virtual Private Networks, pp. 127–154. Packt Publishing (2006)

Implementation of Hierarchical Model in Ptolemy for Wireless Sensor Networks

Stuti Shah[1] and Ekata Mehul[2]

[1] Computer Science and Engineering Department,
Nirma University, Ahmedabad, India
[2] ASIC Division, eInfochips Pvt. Ltd., Ahmedabad, India
`stutiv23@gmail.com, ekata.mehul@einfochips.com`

Abstract. With the complexity of developing embedded Systems and sensor networks, modeling is essential. Modeling before implementation enables designers to explore ideas and verify the correctness of their design early in the design cycle thus reducing iterations during the final stage. This paper deals with implementation of hierarchical model using open source modeling tool Ptolemy. Different directors available with Ptolemy for implementation of sensor networks and embedded systems such as wireless director, discrete event director, and finite state machine director are used. Hierarchical modeling is used for implementing entire system which is combination of different subsystems already implemented with different directors. Wireless director is used as system level director to provide communication between nodes and in turn finite state machine and discrete event directors are used for realizing different modes of system.

Keywords: Embedded Systems, Sensor Networks, Ptolemy, Hierarchical Model.

1 Introduction

The underlying goal of this paper is to show implementation of systems which is combination of sensor networks and embedded systems. Ptolemy provides different directors which can be used to realize behavior of different modes of systems. Hierarchical modeling of Ptolemy can be used to combine different types of sub systems and realize entire system behavior. One example is explained which gives reader a detail explanation on how Ptolemy can be used to realize system behavior.

Section 1 elaborates on system's introduction which is taken for implementation in section 2 and 3. Section 2 presents Related work. section 3 elaborates use of Ptolemy's different directors for implementing different modes of system on Ptolemy. Section 4 elaborates use of Hierarchical modeling to combine different modes which will give realization of system described in section 1.

D.C. Wyld et al. (Eds.): NeCoM/WeST/WiMoN 2011, CCIS 197, pp. 416–423, 2011.

1.1 Requirement Description of System Which Is Taken for Implementation

Real time systems require modeling before they can be actually implemented due to the complexity they have. This section gives reader a quick overview of which types of systems can be selected for implementation on Ptolemy for behavior modeling and one simple system is taken as example for showing implementation.

Systems which are combination of Embedded systems and sensor networks require support of different domains for modeling. Ptolemy provides large number of domain support as well as it provides tool called visual sense which provides support for sensor network modeling so it is highly suitable for modeling systems which is combination of embedded systems and sensor networks.

For understanding implementation on Ptolemy we are taking one system which is explained below in simple diagram

- System is having two sensor nodes which will be communicating with each other. Wireless communication and wireless channel is required and wireless protocol is requiring for implementation.
- This system provides controlling door functionality for which switch would be operated by node 2. Whenever door needs to be operated that signal is given by node 1 to node 2. Then that would operate switch. This will work on discrete time
- Sensor node 1 will also have functionality of emergency calling to doctor.When that mode would be called by node1 it will send emergency message to doctor. Sensor node 1 will have phone attached to it.
- Emergency mode can be easily realized with the help of finite state machine
- This way this subsystem requires use of different directors of Ptolemy. For communication wireless director can be used, for realizing controlling door operation discrete event director can be used and for realizing emergency calling to doctor finite state machine is used.

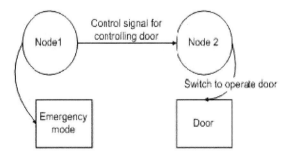

Fig. 1. System Functionality

2   Related Work

The Ptolemy is a modeling tool for simulation, and design of concurrent, real-time, embedded systems. The focus is on assembly of concurrent components. The key underlying principle in the Ptolemy is the use of well-defined models of computation that govern the interaction between components. A major problem area being addressed is the use of heterogeneous mixtures of models of computation. Ptolemy II is being constructed in Java and Ptolemy is open source so it can be enhanced according to system specific requirements.

VisualSense is a modeling and simulation framework for wireless and sensor networks that builds on and leverages Ptolemy II. Modeling of wireless networks requires sophisticated representation and analysis of communication channels, sensors, ad-hoc networking protocols, localization strategies, media access control protocols, energy consumption in sensor nodes, etc. This modeling framework is designed to support a component-based construction of such models. It supports actor-oriented definition of network nodes, wireless communication channels, physical media such as acoustic channels, and wired subsystems. The software architecture consists of a set of base classes for defining channels and sensor nodes, a library of subclasses that provide certain specific channel models and node models, and an extensible visualization framework. Custom nodes can be defined by subclassing the base classes and defining the behavior in Java or by creating composite models using any of several Ptolemy II modeling environments. Custom channels can be defined by subclassing the Wireless Channel base class and by attaching functionality defined in Ptolemy II models.

Viptos, a joint modeling and design environment for wireless networks and sensor node software. Viptos is built on Ptolemy II, a graphical modeling and simulation environment for embedded systems, and TOSSIM, an interrupt-level discrete event simulator for homogeneous TinyOS networks. Viptos includes the full capabilities of VisualSense, a Ptolemy II environment that can model communication channels, networks, and non-TinyOS nodes. Viptos presents a major improvement over VisualSense by allowing developers to refine high-level wireless sensor network simulations down to real-code simulation and deployment, and adds much-needed capabilities to TOSSIM by allowing simulation of heterogeneous networks. Viptos provides a bridge between Ptolemy II and TOSSIM by providing interrupt-level simulation of actual TinyOS programs, with packet-level simulation of the network, while allowing the developer to use other models of computation available in Ptolemy II for modeling the physical environment and other parts of the system.

3   Implementation of Different Modes of System

Ptolemy provides large number of domain polymorphic components which can be used in different domains. Also it provides domain specific components which can only be used for particular domain.System is implemented with VisualSense. Steps followed for implementation of different subsystems are as follows.

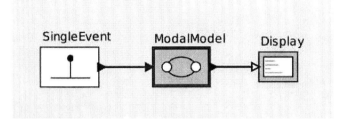

Fig. 2. Modal model component

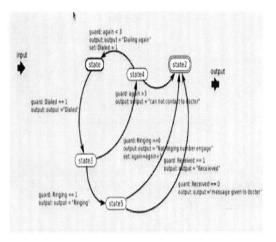

Fig. 3. Finite state machine for emergency mode

1. Emergency mode of system introduced in section I can be realized with finite state machine
2. Ptolemy provides modal model component in it's library which provides implementation of finite state machine inside that component. Modal model component can take variables values from out side and it can also send output to port that can be used as input to other component. Figure 2 shows modal model component of Ptolemy.
3. Modal model contains finite state machine which shows function behavior. Figure 3 shows finite state machine for the system's emergency mode.
4. Finite state machine runs on inputs. Inputs to finite state machine are given at discrete time interval. Inputs to finite state machine are setting of require variables by reading predefined file. File will contain entire string of 0 and 1's. Which are separated using sub string component and that separated values are used to set values of variable. Figure 4 shows final working mode implementation implemented as finite state machine.

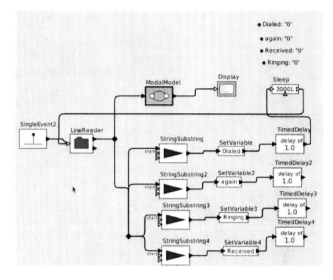

Fig. 4. FSM with inputs from file

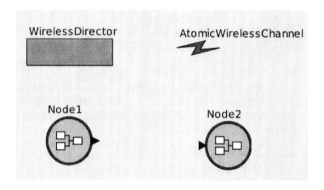

Fig. 5. Communication between two sensor nodes

5. For communication between two nodes wireless director of Ptolemy is required which provides wireless communication between two nodes. It also provides different channels which can be configured by user. Figure 5 shows communications between two nodes

6. One mode of the system is having functionality of operating Door. For that node1 will give signal to node 2. Node 2 is having switch on it which will control Door. This functionality is realized with discrete event director as shown in figure 6.

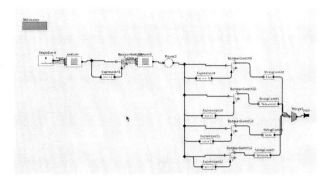

Fig. 6. controlling door implementation with discrete event

4   Integration of Modes Using Hierarchical Modeling

Below mentioned are the steps followed for integration of entire system:

1. As basic goal of this system is to communicate with other sensor node, wireless director is taken as system level director for integration.
2. When we are taking any wireless composite actor from library (node 1 or node 2) , we will find discrete event director inside that because any sensor node run on discrete events.
3. The mode which is used for controlling Door also uses discrete event director so that functionality can be added to this sensor node discrete event director.
4. For invoking finite state machine for emergency mode, discrete event director can be used which invokes emergency mode and sets variables requires for finite state machine transitions.The hierarchy of directors used can be shown in figure 7

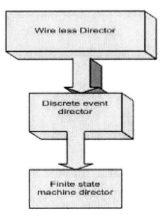

Fig. 7. Hierarchy of Directors

Below figure 8 shows entire system which is combined using hierarchical modeling approach in Ptolemy.

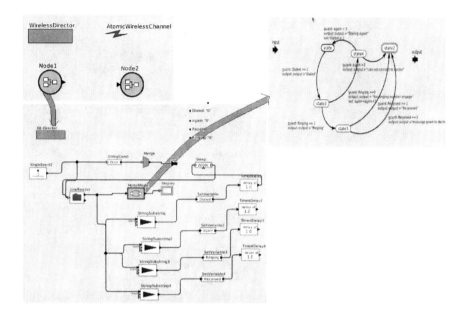

Fig. 8. Integration of modes using hierarchal modeling in Ptolemy

5   Conclusion

Ptolemy is the most suitable open source modeling tool to realize embedded systems. It has VisualSense tool for simulating sensor networks. With the help of hierarchical modeling in VisualSense, systems which are combination of embedded systems and sensor networks can be realized.Ptolemy has large component library which is polymorphic for many domains available in Ptolemy. Ptolemy also gives facility of code generation up to some extent which can be further used for hardware implementation Simulation of embedded sensor networks can be easily done with Ptolemy which in turn reduces time require to design any system.

6   Future Work

Ptolemy is open source modeling tool which can be enhanced according to systems requirement so if any component which is required for embedded systems and sensor networks and not available with Ptolemy, can be implemented on Ptolemy and can be added in to Ptolemy library for further use. Similarly any domain required for embedded systems and sensor networks and not available with Ptolemy, also can be added in to Ptolemy.

References

1. Liu, J., Lee, E.A.: Component-Based Hierarchical Modeling of Systems with Continuous and Discrete Dynamics. In: IEEE International Symposium on Computer-Aided Control System Design Anchorage, Alaska, USA, September 25-27, pp. 95–100 (2000)
2. Girault, A., Lee, B., Lee, E.A.: Hierarchical Finite State Machines with Multiple Concurrency Models. IEEE Transaction on Computer Aided Design of Integrated Circuits and Systems 18(6) (June 1999)
3. Girault, A., Lee, B., Lee, E.A.: A Preliminary Study of Hierarchical Finite State Machines with Multiple Concurrency Models. University of California, Berkeley
4. Eker, J., Lee, E., The Ptolemy group: Heterogeneous Modeling and Design in Ptolemy II, November 29. ECE Seminar Series (2001)
5. Liu, X., Liu, J., Eker, J., Lee, E.A.: Heterogeneous Modeling and Design of Control Systems. University of California, Berkeley
6. Feng, T.H.: Model Transformation with Hierarchical Discrete-Event Control. Technical Report No. UCB/EECS-2009-77, May 20 (2009)
7. Baldwin, P., Kohli, S., Lee, E.A., Liu, X., Zhao, Y.: Modeling of Sensor Nets in Ptolemy II
8. Lee, B., Lee, E.A.: Interaction of Finite State Machines and Concurrency Models. In: Proceeding of Thirty Second Annual Asilomar Conference on Signals, Systems, and Computers, Pacific Grove, California (November 1998)
9. Lygeros, J.: Lecture Notes on Hybrid Systems, February 2-6. University of Patras (2004)
10. Lee, E.A.: Finite State Machines and Modal Models in Ptolemy II, November 1. University of California, Berkeley (2009)
11. Liu, J., Lee, E.A.: A Component-Based Approach to Modeling and Simulating Mixed-Signal and Hybrid Systems. University of California, Berkeley
12. Liu, J., Liu, X., Lee, E.A.: Modeling Distributed Hybrid Systems in Ptolemy II. University of California, Berkeley
13. Lee, B., Lee, E.A.: Hierarchical Concurrent Finite State Machines in Ptolemy. In: Proceeding of International Conference on Application of Concurrency to System Design, Fukushima, Japan, pp. 34–40 (March 1998)

Power and Crosstalk Reduction Using Bus Encoding Technique for *RLC* Modeled VLSI Interconnect

G. Nagendra Babu, Deepika Agarwal, B.K. Kaushik, and S.K. Manhas

Department of Electronics and Computer Engineering,
Indian Institute of Technology-Roorkee, Roorkee-247667, India
na955pec@iitr.ernet.in,deepikaagarwal0987@gmail.com,
bkk23fec@iitr.ernet.in, samanfec@iitr.ernet.in

Abstract. This paper uses bus-invert method to reduce power dissipation, crosstalk and delay for *RLC* modeled VLSI Interconnect. The previously used encoding schemes based on *RC* models worsen crosstalk and delay parameters when the inductive effects become dominant. The proposed method focuses on reducing Type-0 and Type-1 couplings. The results obtained using proposed design of encoder and decoder demonstrates overall reduction in power, crosstalk and delay by reducing switching activity by 40.7%. Furthermore, the chip area and complexity of the circuit is also reduced by more than 25%.

Keywords: Bus-invert method, crosstalk, inductive effect, switching activity, chip area.

1   Introduction

The performance of a high-speed chip is highly dependent on the interconnects, which connect different macro cells within a VLSI/ULSI chip [1]. With ever-growing length of interconnects and clock frequency on a chip, the effects of interconnects cannot be restricted to *RC* models. The importance of on-chip inductance is continuously increasing with faster on-chip rise times, wider wires, and the introduction of new materials for low resistance interconnects. It has become well accepted that interconnect delay dominates gate delay in current deep sub micrometer VLSI circuits. With the continuous scaling of technology and increased die area, this behavior is expected to continue. On-chip inductance has turned out to be significant in designs with giga-hertz clock frequencies [2, 3]. This increased importance of inductive effects in on-chip interconnects, traditional lumped and distributed *RC* models [4] of interconnects are no longer accurate as they result in substantial errors in predicting delay and crosstalk. There has been recent work to include the impact of self-inductance during interconnect delay prediction. However, one aspect of on-chip inductance that has not been well studied is mutual-inductive coupling. Mutual inductance causes signal-integrity issues by injecting noise pulses on a victim line [6, 7]. Most of the existing noise models and avoidance techniques consider only capacitive coupling. However, at current operating frequencies, inductive-crosstalk effects can be substantial and should be included for complete coupling-noise analysis. This diminished the performance of circuit by increasing in wire delay [7, 8].

D.C. Wyld et al. (Eds.): NeCoM/WeST/WiMoN 2011, CCIS 197, pp. 424–434, 2011.
© Springer-Verlag Berlin Heidelberg 2011

In *RC* model, the dominant factor is coupling capacitance, but for *RLC* model, mutual-inductance coupling becomes dominant. Mutual-inductance coupling occurs when both of the interconnect lines which are adjacent have same transition (i.e. either from 0 to 1 ($\uparrow\uparrow$) or from 1 to 0 ($\downarrow\downarrow$)). In that case leftmost aggressor wire induces magnetic field on the victim wire which tends to flow a current which is in opposition to the original current [9, 10]. So crosstalk occurs between the two interconnects which is the present major problem in the submicron technology. However for *RC* modeled, the worst case crosstalk delay occurs when the adjacent wires have an opposite transition. On the contrary, this worst case pattern is the best case for *RLC* model [7]. Most existing works focus on reducing the effects resulting from coupling capacitance on the bus structure by introducing many bus encoding techniques [4, 5]. There is not much work in the literature considering inductive effects on the bus structure.

This paper mainly focuses on reducing power dissipation, crosstalk, delay and chip size of encoder and decoder of *RLC* modeled interconnects. Here the proposed method reduces the two undesirable types of crosstalk i.e. Type-0 and Type-1 couplings which are the worst cases in *RLC* type of interconnects. This design reduces the power dissipation by reducing switching activity using bus invert coding method. Results show that the power dissipation, crosstalk, delay and size of proposed method which are implemented is occupy less area in layout as compared with Fan *et al.*[12] *RC* modeled.

The rest of the paper is described as follows. Section 2 describes crosstalk and dynamic power dissipation expression and their dependence on different parameter. Section 3 describes the working of proposed method. Sections 4 discuss the results of *RLC* model. Finally, Section 5 draws important conclusions.

2   Power Expression and Crosstalk of *RLC* Model

Power dissipation of a circuit can be classified as static power dissipation and dynamic power dissipation. The static power dissipation of a circuit being too small can be neglected. The dynamic power dissipated by the circuit is in the form of [13, 14]:

$$P_{D,bus} = \alpha V_{dd}^2 f\, C_L \qquad (1)$$

where C_L is load capacitance, V_{dd} is supply voltage, f is the clock frequency and α is the average switching activity which lies between 0 and 1. For achieving low power in circuits one or more terms V_{dd}, f, C_L and α must be minimized. Here V_{dd} and f is assumed to be already optimized for low power. Therefore, dynamic power dissipation is proportional to the number of signal transition.

Symbols and terminologies which are used throughout the paper as follows

$B(t)$: The bus value to be sent presently on the bus line i.e. at time t.
$B(t-1)$: The bus value sent previously on bus line i.e. at time $t-1$.
$INV(t)$: Control line for data bus to be sent at time t.
$INV(t-1)$: Control line for data bus sent at time $t-1$.

Coupling between interconnects can be classified into five types i.e. Type-0, Type-1, Type-2, Type-3 and Type-4 as shown in Table 1. Type-0 coupling occurs when $(B(t), INV(t))$ present data bits and previous data bits $(B(t-1), INV(t))$ have transitions in all bit positions i.e. (from 000 to 111 (↑↑↑)) or (from 111 to 000(↓↓↓)). Three conditions causes Type-0 coupling. In this, coupling capacitance is zero but the mutual inductance is very high. Type-1 coupling occurs when there is one or two transitions in the same direction i.e. present data and the previous data have same transitions in one or two bit positions (i.e. transition from 000 to 011 (-↑↑) or from 110 to 111(- -↓)). Eight conditions causes Type-1 coupling. In Type-1, simultaneous transition of two bits causes coupling is lesser as comparison with Type-0. A Type-2 coupling occurs if the center wire is having opposite transition with one of its adjacent wires (from 011 to 100(↑↓↓)) or when the other lines undergo the same state transition with the center wire as quiet (i.e. data change from 100 to 001 (↓-↑)). Ten conditions causes Type-2 coupling. A Type-3 coupling occurs when the center wire undergoes opposite transition with one of the adjacent wire while the other wires are quiet i.e. when the data changes from 010 to 001 (i.e. -↓↑). In this case the mutual inductance is very less. In Type-4 coupling, all three-wires are having transitions in opposite direction with respect to each other i.e. from 010 to 101 (i.e. ↑↓↑). Here mutual inductance coupling is zero but it is the worst case of *RC* model. With the findings of the best case and worst case patterns, we propose a new encoding scheme for on-chip buses to minimize coupling delay with the dominance of inductance effects. The key idea is that inductive coupling effects should be alleviated by transforming the data sequences transmitting through on-chip buses. However, the architectures of the encoder and decoder should be of low complexity so that the power and delay overheads due to the codec circuitry can be compensated by the significant reduction of bus delay.

Table 1. 3-Bit Bus Crosstalk when Considering *RLC* Effects

Type-0	Type-1	Type-2	Type-3	Type-4
- - -	- - ↑	- ↑ -	- ↑↓	↑↓↑
↑↑↑	- ↑↑	↑ - ↑	- ↓↑	↓↑↓
↓↓↓	↑ - -	↑ - ↓	↑↓ -	
	↑↑ -	↑↑↓	↓↑ -	
	- - ↓	↑↓↓		
	- ↓↓	- ↓ -		
	↓ - -	↓ - ↓		
	↓↓ -	↓ - ↑		
		↓↓↑		
		↓↑↑		

↑: switching from 0 to 1, ↓: switching from 1 to 0, - : no transition;

3 Implementation of Proposed Scheme

Inspired by Fan *et al.* [12] *RC* low-power bus invert method for reducing cross talk and power dissipation, a method is proposed which reduces the crosstalk delay and power dissipation of the *RLC* modeled interconnect. Approaching similarly like Fan *et al.* [12] using this proposed method and found that both the power dissipation and crosstalk are reducing greatly.

In this proposed method the data bus is divided into different clusters. Each cluster has 4-bit width with one extra control bit. Extra control bit known as invert pin i.e. $INV(t)$. Bus invert method [16] is based on the invert pin. To limit the number of transmitting transitions, it uses an extra control line i.e. if the number of transitions that are being transmitted are more than half of the bus width, then the original data is inverted and the control line ($INV(t)$) is set to "High", otherwise, the original data is transmitted and the control line ($INV(t)$) is set to "Low". Similarly, in this paper also if the original input data causes crosstalk then the inverted data is transmitted and control line is set to "High" and so the present data is compared with the previous data and depending on the transition of data bits a decision is made.

The proposed method is shown in Fig. 1. It shows the block diagram of encoder. The 5-bit bus encoder architecture is composed of a N0_COUNTER, two N1_COUNTERS, inverter for complementing the original data, a 2-bit comparator, a multiplexer and a latch. N0_COUNTER and N1_COUNTER is called crosstalk module. The purpose of N0_COUNTER is that it detects the Type-0 coupling and on the contrary N1_COUNTER detects the Type-1 coupling. N1_COUNTER counts the Type-1 coupling and as there are 8 such cases (4 of high to low transition and 4 of low to high transition), which can be grouped to two. Finally there are only 4 Type-1 couplings (either ↑ or ↓) and so the output of N1_COUNTER is having 2-bits. 2-bit comparator is used to generate 1-bit output (i.e. *N1*) which compares the count of both the N1_COUNTERS.

3.1 Working of 5-Bit Bus Encoder

Firstly, the original data which is to be transmitted is inverted and so both the original data $(B(t), INV(t))$ and the complemented data $(\overline{B(t)}, \overline{INV(t)})$ are available. Next, the data which is to be transmitted and the data which is previously transmitted are fed back to the N0_COUNTER and N1_COUNTER_1 through latch. N0_COUNTER module judges whether the $(B(t), INV(t))$ data will cause the Type-0 coupling with respect to the previous bus state $(B(t-1), INV(t))$, if any coupling condition occurs then the output of the N0_COUNTER *(N0)* is set to "High".

Similarly, N1_COUNTER_1 counts the number of Type-1 couplings that occurs with the original data and previous data and generates the output as 2-bits *(N1 (1) _1, N1 (0) _1)*. On the other hand the complemented data and the previously transmitted are fed into N1_COUNTER_2. This counter will count the number of Type-1 couplings that occur with the inverted data and generates the output as 2-bits *(N1 (1) _2, N1 (0) _2)*. Now the counts from the two N1_COUNTERS are compared in a 2-bit comparator. The comparator output *(N1)* goes high if and only if the count of N1_COUNTER_1 is greater than the N1_COUNTER_2.

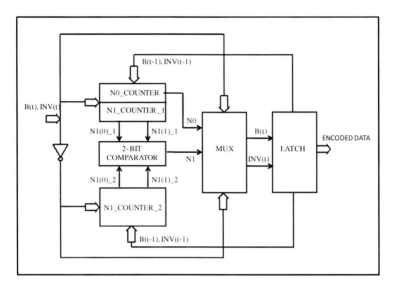

Fig. 1. Block Diagram of 5-Bit Bus Encoder

The next block is the multiplexer which decides the data to be transmitted depending on the inputs *N0 and N1*. If any one of the inputs i.e. *N0 or N1* becomes high, this means that the input data has a crosstalk effect. Hence the inverted data must be sent to reduce that crosstalk effect and the control line *INV(t)* will go high indicating that the inverted data is sent. If both the inputs of the multiplexer are low means that there is no crosstalk effect with the data and so the original data is transmitted as it is without any inversion.

3.1.1 N0_COUNTER

Logic diagram of N0_COUNTER is shown in Fig. 2. It is composed of ten two-input AND gates, eight three-input NAND gates and one two-input OR gate. This circuitry consists of less number of transistors as compared to Fan *et al.* [12] *RC* model. The function of the N0_counter is that firstly, the design will check whether there is any transition or not using the level-1 AND gates. A "High" logic is present at the output if there is any transition otherwise represent "Low" logic. Here the proposed method uses top five AND gates to sense low to high transition (↑) and bottom five AND gate to high to low transition (↓). As Type-0 coupling occurs when three consecutive lines are having same transition (i.e. ↑↑↑ or ↓↓↓) so these lines are fed to one AND gate. As 5 lines are present (including the control line), the method divides them into 3 combinations ($S_A S_B S_C$, $S_B S_C S_D$, $S_C S_D S_E$). The outputs of these three AND gates are given to an OR gate. Hence, if any combination becomes "High" the output L_0 (↑↑↑) should go "High" on the other hand L_1 goes "High" when there are three consecutive high to low transitions (↓↓↓). Finally L_0 and L_1 are fed to OR gate so that if there is any three consecutive transition in the same direction then the N0_COUNTER output (*N0*) goes "High" indicating a Type-0 cross talk and hence the inverted data is transmitted and control line is made "High".

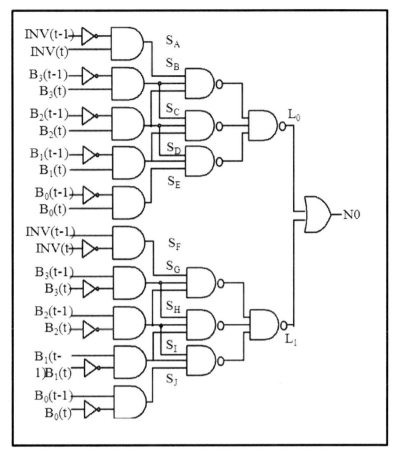

Fig. 2. Logic Diagram of N0_ COUNTER

3.1.2 N1_COUNTER

Logic diagram of N1_COUNTER is shown in the Fig. 3. The proposed method uses the outputs of level-1 AND gates of N0_COUNTER itself to check whether there are any transitions. N1_COUNTER is composed of five 2-input OR gates, five 2-input XOR gates and three 2-input NAND gates. As Type-1 coupling occurs when one or two lines are having transitions in the same direction while the rest (i.e. remaining two or the third one respectively) are having no transition. Hence, the outputs of level-1 AND gates which indicate transitions are fed to five two-input OR gates whose output goes "High" when there is Type-1 coupling. By noticing that Type-1 coupling occurs when the first line is having transition and the third line is in idle state (no-transition) and vice-versa, which clearly assure that these two lines must be given to an XOR gate to verify the condition. These five OR gate outputs divided into 3 groups of two alternate lines *(i.e. K_0 and K_2, K_1 and K_3, K_2 and K_4).* The outputs of these three XOR gates are added binarily using a full adder, the method implements the full adder using two half adders and an OR gate and the output of the full adder represents the number of counts that causes Type-1 coupling *(NI(1), NI(0)).* As the proposed method uses two N1_COUNTERS in which N1_COUNTER_1 counts the number of Type-1 couplings of the original data $(B(t), INV(t))$ whose output is $(NI(1)\_1, NI(0)\_1)$ and the second counter N1_COUNTER_2 counts the number of Type-1 couplings of the inverted data whose output is $(NI(1)\_2, NI(0)\_2)$.

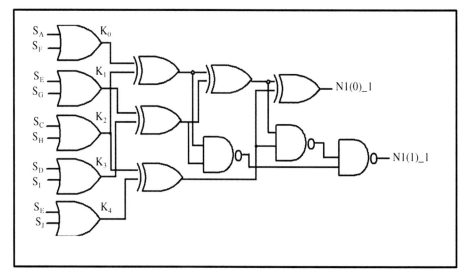

Fig. 3. Logic Diagram of N1_COUNTER

3.1.3 2-Bit Comparator

The internal circuit of 2-bit comparator is shown in Fig. 4. It compares the counts of the two N1_COUNTERS (*i.e.* $(NI(1)\_1, NI(0)\_1)$ and $(NI(1)\_2, NI(0)\_2)$) and generates the output NI as a logic "High" when the count of N1_COUNTER_1 is greater than N1_COUNTER_2 indicating that there are more number of Type-1 couplings with the original data than the inverted data. When NI becomes "High" then the inverted data must be sent and if it is "Low" indicating that the original signal must be transmitted.

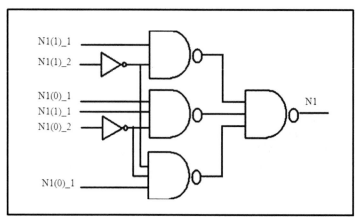

Fig. 4. 2-Bit Comparator

3.1.4 Multiplexer

The truth table of the multiplexer is shown in Table.2. When either *N0* or *N1* is "High" inverted data $(\overline{B(t)}, 1)$ must be transmitted otherwise original data $(B(t), 0)$ must be transmitted. The internal circuit of multiplexer is shown in Fig.5. Truth table of MUX tells that when either *N0* or *N1* is "High" the inverted data is to be transmitted so it is fed as one of the input to the AND gate whose enable pin is output of OR gate (ORing *N0* and *N1*). On the other hand if both *N0* and *N1* goes "Low" original data is to be transmitted so the method uses four more AND gates whose inputs are original data and the output of NOR gate. After that logical addition of both using OR gates gives the final encoded data $(ENC\_B(t))$.

Table 2. Truth Table of multiplexer

N0	*N1*	MUX OUTPUT
0	0	$(B(t), 0)$
1	0	$(\overline{B(t)}, 1)$
0	1	$(\overline{B(t)}, 1)$
1	1	$(\overline{B(t)}, 1)$

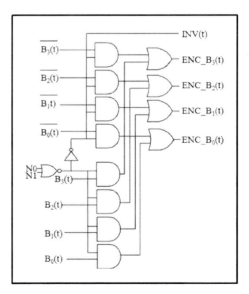

Fig. 5. Internal Diagram of Multiplexer

3.1.5 Latch

Here the proposed design is comparing the present data with the previously transmitted which means there is a necessity for storing the previously transmitted data. For this purpose latches are necessary [15] which are implemented using transmission gates in this paper as shown in Fig. 6. This latch is made of two transmission gates (T_1 and T_2) which work complementarily and two inverters (one inverter is forward and another one is backward inverter). The transmission gate consists of both PMOS and NMOS transistors whose drains and sources are shorted together. When CLK is in "High" condition, transmission gate T_1 goes into ON condition and then the input data is transmitted to output of T_1 (i.e. $B(t)$ output). This data is retained until CLK becomes high for the next time. But when CLK goes "Low" then T_2 goes into ON and T_1 goes to OFF condition and so the data is retained using the inverters which are connected in feedback.

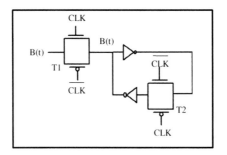

Fig. 6. Latch using Transmission Gates

4 Decoder

The internal circuit of decoder is shown in Fig. 7. The function of decoder is to decode the encoded data. The encoded data is fed as one of the input for the XOR gate and control line ($INV(t)$) is given as second input for the 2-input XOR gate. If the ($INV(t)$) line is "High" then it indicates that the inverted data has been transmitted and ($ENC\_B(t)$) must be inverted to get the original data and if it is "Low" which indicates that the original data has been transmitted.

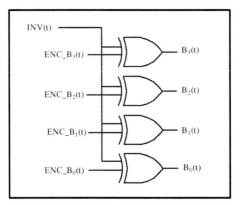

Fig. 7. Decoder

5   Results

The functionality of proposed circuit design has been simulated in 0.18-μm technology with H-SPICE simulator. Power dissipation and crosstalk of the proposed circuit is also evaluated. Total power dissipation includes the power dissipated by encoder, by interconnects and the decoder (i.e. $P_{enc} + P_{dec} + P_{D,coded}$). $P_{D,coded}$ is the dynamic power dissipated (which depends on the switching activities of the data) after the data is encoded. In 0.18-μm technology, when the load capacitance value is less than 0.1pF/bit, then coding method consumes more power than un-coded method. But as the load capacitance is increased i.e. beyond 1.5pF/bit, then coded data consumes lesser power than the uncoded data. The proposed design reduces power dissipation from 33.2% to 42.6% for a load capacitance of 4pF/bit.

The crosstalk effect is reduced by inverting the original data and which in turn also reduces the switching activity. Here, the proposed method reduces both the Type-0 and Type-1 coupling.   As Type-0 coupling is caused in two cases and Type-1 coupling is caused in eight cases. Therefore switching activity reduces by 40.7% which is more as compared to Fan *et al.* [12] *RC* model.

Our proposed method has greatly reduced the chip area by reduction in number of transistor as compared to Fan *et al.* [12] *RC* model as shown in Table 3. By reduction in chip area the complexity of circuit diminished by more than 25%.

Fan *et al.* [12] *RC* model uses four input AND gates whose input capacitance is very high which in turn increases the propagation delay. The proposed model uses 2-input AND gates to decrease the propagation delay which may cause due to encoder. Moreover Fan *et al.* [12] *RC* model uses two 6-bit adders which is comprised of four full adders and four half adders which makes the circuit more complex and also occupies more area and increases the power dissipation. The Proposed method uses only two half adders for counting Type-1 couplings. As all the lines are parallel, the signal is likely to pass through only 3 or 4 gates which shows very less propagation delay due to the encoder insertion. The power consumed by the Encoder & Decoder is very less and so, this method can be used efficiently to reduce crosstalk .

Table 3. Comparison of Proposed Model with the Fan *et al.* [12] *RC* Model

Components	Fan *et al.* [12] *RC* model	Proposed Method
AND gate	4-input	2-input
6-bit adder	2	0
N0_COUNTER	2	1
XOR gate	18	8
Total no. of transistors	664	484

6   Conclusion

This paper demonstrated overall reduction in power dissipation, crosstalk and chip size by using bus-invert method for *RLC* modeled VLSI interconnects. The proposed method is having less number of transistors which decrease the chip area. The results shows the reduction in power dissipation by 33.2% to 42.6%, switching activities by 40.7% and chip size by more than 25% in comparison to previously available research work.

References

1. Trevillyan, L., Kung, D., Puri, R., Reddy, L.N., Kazda, M.A.: An integration environment for technology closure of deep-submicron IC designs. IEEE Des. Test. Comput. 21(1), 14–22 (2004)
2. International Technology Roadmap for Semiconductors (2003)
3. Elgamel, M.A., Bayoumi, M.A.: Interconnect noise analysis and optimization in deep submicron technology. IEEE Circuits Syst. Mag. 3(4), 6–17 (2003)
4. Victor, B., Keutzer, K.: Bus encoding to prevent crosstalk delay. In: Int. Conf. Computer-Aided Design, San Jose, CA, pp. 57–63 (2001)
5. Hirose, K., Yasuura, H.: A bus delay reduction technique considering crosstalk. In: Proc. Design Automation and Test Eur. (DATE), Paris, France, pp. 441–445 (2000)
6. He, L., Lepak, K.M.: Simultaneous Shield Insertion and Net ordering for Capacitive and Inductive Coupling Minimization. In: Int. Symp. Physical Design, pp. 55–60 (2000)
7. Ismail, Y.I.: On-Chip Inductance Cons and Pros. IEEE Trans. VLSI Syst., 685–694 (2002)
8. Chowdhury, M.H., Ismail, Y.I., Kashyap, C.V., Krauter, B.L.: Performance Analysis of Deep Sub micron VLSI Circuits in the Presence of Self and Mutual Inductance. In: IEEE Int. Symp. Circuits Syst., pp. 197–200 (2002)
9. Baek, K.H., Kim, K.W., Kang, S.M.: A Low Energy Encoding Technique for Reduction of Coupling Effects in SOC Interconnects. In: Proc. 43rd IEEE Midwest Symp. Circuits Syst., pp. 80–83 (2000)
10. Deutsch, A., Kopcsay, G.V., Restle, P.J., Smith, H.H., Katopis, G., Becker, W.D., Coteus, P.W., Surovic, C.W., Rubin, B.J., Dunne, R.P., Gallo Jr., T., Jenkins, K.A., Terman, L.M., Dennard, R.H., Sai-Halasz, G.A., Krauter, B.L., Knebel, D.R.: When are transmission-line effects important for on-chip interconnections. IEEE Trans. on Microwave Theory and Techniques 45(10), part-2, 1836–1846 (1997)
11. Tu, S.-W., Chang, Y.-W., Jou, J.-Y.: RLC Coupling-Aware Simulation and On-Chip Bus Encoding for Delay Reduction. IEEE Transaction 25(10) (2006)
12. Fan, C.-P., Fang, C.-H.: Efficient RC low-power bus encoding methods for crosstalk reduction. Integration, the VLSI Journal, Elsevier 44(1), 75–86 (2011)
13. Weste, N., Eshraghian, K.: Principles of CMOS VLSI Design. A Systems Perspective. Addison-Wesley Publishing Company, Reading (1988)
14. Najm, F.: Transition density, a stochastic measure of activity in digital circuits. In: Proc. 28th DAC, Anaheim, CA, pp. 644–649 (1991)
15. Rabaey, J.M., Chandrakasan, A., Nikolic, B.: Digital integrated Circuits, A Design Perspective, 2nd edn. Prentice Hall Publication, Englewood Cliffs (2003)
16. Stan, M.R., Burleson, W.P.: Bus-Invert Coding for Low-Power I/O. IEEE Trans. VLSI Syst. 3, 49–58 (2005)

Novel Bus Encoding Scheme for *RC* Coupled VLSI Interconnects

S.K. Verma[1] and B.K. Kaushik[2]

[1] Department of Computer Science and Engineering,
G. B. Pant Engineering College, Pauri-Garhwal, India
`skverma.gbpec@rediffmail.com`
[2] Department of Electronics and Computer Engineering,
Indian Institute of Technology, Roorkee, India
`bkk23fec@iitr.ernet.in`

Abstract. For System on-chip (SoC) designs in current Deep Submicron (DSM) era, the performance factors such as propagation delay, power dissipation and crosstalk in *RC* modeled interconnects are the major design concerns. The crosstalk effect is a consequence of coupling and switching activities that is encountered when there is a transition in previous state of wire as well as when there are transitions in adjacent wires. Therefore, minimization or elimination of switching and coupling activities is crucial in enhancing the performance of SoC designs. This paper proposes encoding schemes to achieve overall reduction in transitions. The reduction in transition improves the performance in terms of reduced power dissipation, coupling activity and delay in on-chip buses.

Keywords: Coupling, VLSI, SoC, Bus Encoding, Interconnects.

1   Introduction

The feature size of integrated circuits has been consistently reduced in the pursuit of improved speed, power, silicon area and cost characteristics. Semiconductor technologies with feature sizes of several tens of nanometers are currently in development. As per International Technology Roadmap for Semiconductors (ITRS), the future nanometer scale circuits will contain more than a billion transistors and operate at clock speeds well over 10GHz. Distribution of robust and reliable power and ground lines; clock; data and address; and other control signals through interconnects in such a high-speed, high-complexity environment, is a challenging task. The function of wiring systems or interconnects is to distribute clock and other signals and to provide power/ground to and among the various circuits/systems functions on the chip. The performance parameters i.e. time delay and power dissipation of a high-speed chip is highly dependent on interconnects, which connect different macro cells within a VLSI chip.

In current DSM (Deep Submicron) technology, coupling capacitance plays an important role for deciding the behavior of on-chip interconnects. Due to the coupling capacitance, crosstalk, delay and power consumption problems will arise. The above

D.C. Wyld et al. (Eds.): NeCoM/WeST/WiMoN 2011, CCIS 197, pp. 435–444, 2011.

problems are very much dependent on the frequency of signal used, length of interconnects etc. Interconnects can be modeled as the transmission line. Transmission line may be modeled as RC or RLC network. The effect of inductance plays an important role as the length and used frequency signal increases. [1-4, 8-16] This paper considers RC network for the implementation and study of the behavior of interconnects due to coupling capacitance.

The components that affect the behavior of the on-chip bus are internal parasitic capacitances of the transistors, interconnect capacitances and input capacitances of the fan-out gates.

The most common methods to reduce crosstalk, propagation delay and power are:

- Insertion of repeaters
- Insertion of shielding between adjacent wires
- Minimizing spacing between signal and ground lines.
- Isolating clocks and other critical signals from other lines (larger line spacing) or isolation with ground traces.
- In backplane or wire-wrap applications, use twisted pair for sensitive applications such as clocks and asynchronous set or clear functions. While using ribbon or flat cable, make every other line a ground line.
- Introduction of intentional delay among coupled signal transmission.
- Bus Encoding methods
- The use of tight geometry in most systems can reduce crosstalk significantly although it cannot eliminate it entirely. Some preventive design measures can be used to minimize crosstalk.
- Using maximum allowable spacing between signal lines.
- Terminating signal lines into their characteristic impedance.

The Bus encoding method is widely used technique to reduce dynamic switching power and the effects of crosstalk (signal noise, delay) during data transmission on buses [15]. Low power encoding techniques aim to transform the data being transmitted on buses in such a manner so that the self and coupling switching activity on buses are reduced. Crosstalk aware encoding techniques can also modify the switching patterns of a group of wires to reduce crosstalk coupling effect. These techniques are quite effective in reducing power consumption, improving transmission reliability, and increasing system performance. For any encoding scheme, the encoder and decoder functions are the inverse of each other. Bus encoding schemes can be classified according to several criteria, such as the amount of extra information needed for coding (redundant or irredundant coding), and the method of encoding implementation (hardware, software, or a combination of the two), Type of code used (algebraic, permutation, or probability based), the degree of encoding adaptability (static or dynamically adaptable encoding), the targeted capacitance for switching reduction (self, coupling or both). Encoding techniques are often aimed at power reduction, signal transmission delay reduction and reliability improvement, or a combination of these due to the reduction in the transition. Certain optimizations such as crosstalk reduction can have multiple benefits associated with them such as power reduction, signal delay reduction and noise reduction.

This paper presents an encoding method for the reduction of coupling transitions. The crosstalk is classified as the types [1, 2, 15, 16] depending upon the transitions of the signal in the wire. This paper proposes encoding schemes which reduces data lines hence there is reduction in power consumption. The encoding scheme presented in the paper reduced the redundancy. It also considers the worst case crosstalk effects due to transitions in the group of lines.

2 Estimation of Power and Crosstalk in *RC* Bus Model

The total power consumption in the VLSI chip comprises of dynamic power, short circuit power, static power and leakage power. It can be simply described as summation of all these components i.e.

$$P_{Dissipation} = P_{Static} + P_{Dynamic} + P_{Leakage} + P_{Shortckt} \tag{1}$$

The capacitance of interconnect can be classified as coupling capacitance and self-capacitance. The coupling capacitance is the capacitance between the adjacent wires while the self-capacitance refers to the capacitance between the substrate and the wire itself. The dynamic power in VLSI chip decides the behavior of chip and is highly dependent on the load capacitance and coupling capacitance i.e. bus line signal transitions. Dynamic power dissipation on a coded bus thus can be defined as following equation

$$P_{D,Coded} = (\alpha_{cl} \times C_L + \alpha_{cc} \times C_C) \times V_{DD}^2 \times f$$

$$= (\alpha_{cl} + \alpha_{cc} \times \lambda) \times C_L \times V_{DD}^2 \times f) \tag{2}$$

where C_L is the load capacitance, C_c is the coupling capacitance, V_{DD} is the supplying voltage, f is the clock frequency, λ is the capacitance ratio defined as: $\lambda = C_c / C_L$. λ is dependent on the technology which is being used hence its value depends on the physical parameters. α_{cl} is the value of average switching activity for the load capacitance. For un-encoded buses α_{cl} is 1. α_{cc} is the value of average coupling activity for the coupling capacitance. For un-encoded buses α_{cc} is 1. Hence for un-encoded data the power dissipation can be defined by following equation

$$P_{D,un-coded} = (1 + \lambda) \times C_L \times V_{DD}^2 \times f \tag{3}$$

Effective crosstalk capacitance is determined by

$$C_{eff} = C_c \times \frac{\Delta V_2 - \Delta V_1}{V_{DD}} + C_c \times \frac{\Delta V_2 - \Delta V_3}{V_{DD}} \tag{4}$$

where ΔV_2 is voltage variation of the centre wire. ΔV_1 and ΔV_3 are voltage variations in the adjacent wires. V_{DD} is power supply voltage which equals rail-to-rail signal voltage in CMOS circuits. C_{eff} is effective coupling capacitance variation [1, 2].

The coupling between the groups of the three wires is classified into five types depending upon the nature of transitions of signals in the wire that are Type-0, Type-1, Type-2, Type-3 and Type-4. The Type-0 coupling occurs when all of the 3-bit wires are in the same state transition. A transition from 000 to 111 (i.e. ↑↑↑) causes a

Type-0 coupling. For Type-0, coupling capacitance is zero. Type-1 coupling occurs when there is a transition in one or the two wires (including the centre wire) and the third wire remains quite. There are eight possibilities by which Type-1 condition occurs. The coupling capacitance in this case is C_C. A Type-2 coupling occurs when the centre wire is in the opposite state transition with one of its adjacent wires while the other wires undergo the same state transition as the centre wire i.e.100 to 011. Ten different conditions are possible for Type-2 coupling. The coupling capacitance is $2C_C$ in this case. A Type-3 coupling occurs when the central wire undergoes the opposite state transition with one of the two wires while the other wires are quiet i.e. 010 to 001. Coupling capacitance in the case of Type-3 coupling is $3C_C$ and there are four possibilities that cause Type-3 coupling. For a Type-4 coupling, all three wire transitions are in the opposite states with respect to each other. Two conditions cause Type-4 coupling with a coupling capacitance effect of $4C_C$. All the five Types of couplings are shown in Table-1 [2].

It can be concluded from the above description that power and crosstalk highly depend upon the transitions of the signal in the wires. If the number of transitions occurring in the signals by encoding methods is reduced, the dynamic power dissipation as well as crosstalk will also be reduced. Different encoding methods are proposed by different researchers. An efficient encoding proposed by Stan and Burleson [3] includes the concept of counting the number of transitions, with respect to the previous states of group of lines. Data is transmitted in original form or in inverted form depending upon the number of state transition of the lines as compared to previous states.

Table 1. Crosstalk Types for a 3-Bit Bus Considering *RC* Model of Interconnect [2]

Type-0	Type-1	Type-2	Type-3	Type-4
– – –	– – ↑	– ↑ –	– ↑ ↓	↑ ↓ ↑
↓ ↓ ↓	– ↑ ↑	↑ – ↑	– ↓ ↑	↓ ↑ ↓
↑ ↑ ↑	↑ – –	↑ – ↓	↑ ↓ –	
	↑ ↑ –	↑ ↑ ↓	↓ ↑ –	
	– – ↓	↑ ↓ ↓		
	– ↓ ↓	– ↓ –		
	↓ – –	↓ – ↓		
	↓ ↓ –	↓ – ↑		
		↓ ↓ ↑		
		↓ ↑ ↑		

↑ : switch from 0 to 1,   ↓ : switch from 1 to 0,   – : no transition

3   Encoding Method

The proposed encoding method transforms the bus signals for the reduction or elimination of the worst case crosstalk by reducing the 7-bit lines into 4-bit lines. The encoder deals with the coupling transitions among the group of seven bits. It identifies the higher number of 0's and 1's. Output line is set according to higher number of 1's or 0's. The proposed encoder can be depicted as in Fig.1. The components of the encoder circuit include a counter module, controller, a 7-bit comparator module and register,

Firstly, the number of 1's and 0's are counted using a counter module. If the number of 1's is more than the number of 0's, the comparator module sets output line in high state (1). If the number of 0's is more than the number of 1's this module sets output line in low state (0). There are two best cases possible; either all lines are in one state or all lines are in zero state. As said earlier, it is needed to convert all the seven input lines to a single line, either 0 or 1. In order to do this, the position of bits are flipped to either 0 or 1 depending upon the value of 1's or 0's, whichever is higher as discussed above. There are maximum three flips possible.

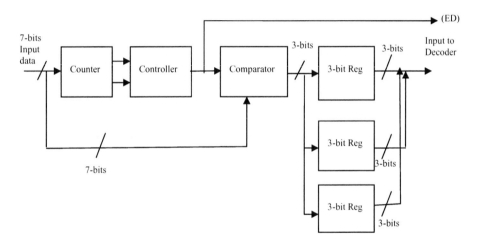

Fig. 1. Block Diagram of Encoding Method

The single output line of controller is compared with initial 7-bit input line and finds the flipped bit positions. The number of flipped bits could be 0 (best case; when all the inputs are either 0 or 1), or 1 or 2 or 3 (worst case). After identification of the flipped bits positions, and stored in the 3-bit registers.

The number of the registers is chosen to be three in order to work for the best as well as the worst cases. The best case is one when all the input lines are 0 or 1. In this case all the registers are empty as there is no change in any of the bits. Thus there is significant reduction in crosstalk as all three registers have same null value. Otherwise the value of the registers can vary from zero to maximum three. Seven bits of input have been given to the encoder. So, three bits have taken to indicate the flips in the seven lines. All the equivalent positions for these 8 combinations are shown in Table.2.

Table 2. Register Values Indicating the Positions of Flipping

Register Value	Flipped I/P Line Position
000	0
001	1
010	2
011	3
100	4
101	5
110	6
111	7

Each of the register value sends in three different clock cycles. At each clock cycle, contents of one register are sent to the decoder. Another register contents are sent in the next clock cycle and so on. Since the maximum flips that can be possible are three so maximum three clock cycles are required for decoding the 7-bit line at decoder side.

3.1 Counter Module

The counter module is for the determination of the number of 0's and 1's in the input sequence of seven bits line. The input to the counter module is 7-bit input. Each of these lines is selected and then compared with '0' and '1'. Two variables are initialized for storing the values of the number of 0's and 1's in the input sequence. The first variable stores the value of the number of 0's and the other one store the number of the 1's in the input sequence. These two lines are then fed into the Controller modules along with two variables and are passed to the Controller; it then decides whether the number of value of 1st or the 2nd variable is higher. The one with higher value is forwarded to the comparator module of the encoder.

3.2 Controller

As seen in Fig.1 the two output lines of the counter represent the number of 1's and the number of 0's. These two inputs are fed in to the controller. The Controller decides for the number of occurrences of 0's and 1's as provided by counter module. This module decides the output as '0' or '1' based on the values input to this. If number of 0's is higher as compared to the number of 1's the output of the controller will be '0'. If number of 1's is higher as compared to the number of 0's the output of the controller will be '1'.

3.3 Comparator

The single output line is fed to the comparator along with the initial 7-bit inputs. This single output line is compared with each of the initial 7-bits. This is to compare whether the value of the bit is the same or different from the single line. This signal is XORed with each of the 7 lines to identify the flipping. These flipped positions are stored for the decoding purpose.

The final output of this module is three 3-bit registers as shown in Fig. 1. Three registers as discussed before are meant for transfer of the three flipped positions if present or whatever the number of flipped bit positions is from 0 to a maximum of 3 positions.

3.4   Registers

This module is used for storing the position of flipped bit. This ascertains the proper interpretation of the input bits where a 000 value in the register stands for the 0th bit position, 001 represents the 1st bit and likewise 111 represents 7th position. These three registers are meant for the simultaneous storage of the flipped bit positions. These lines along with the single input equivalent line from the controller are transmitted to the decoder.

The encoder provides the output in four lines for the decoding purpose i.e. one line from the controller and the other three lines from the register, although three clock cycles are needed for complete decoding of the input sequence.

4   Decoder

The decoder of the proposed encoding method is shown in Fig.2. The decoder of the proposed encoding method consists of the three 3-bit registers, splitter, inversion module and line identifier.

Four lines from the encoder are fed to the decoder. In the first clock cycle the contents of the first register from encoder are stored in the first register of the decoder and so on. The maximum flips that can be possible are three, so maximum three clock cycles are required for complete decoding of the 7-bit data.

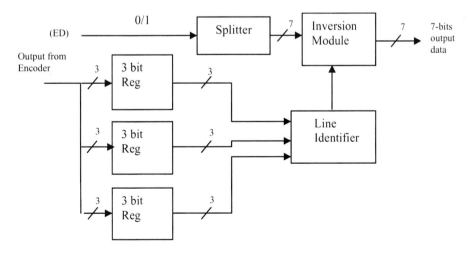

Fig. 2. Decoder of Encoding Method

Although, single 3-bit register can be used in the encoder and decoder side instead of three 3-bit registers, three registers are used for the compensation of delay generated by the clock cycles for the transmission of flipped bit positions to decoder side.

The output line taken from the comparater of encoder side is fed to the spliter module of the decoder. The splitter module splits the 1-bit input line to seven bits of output lines. All the seven output lines have similar value as that of the input i.e. if the input to the spliter is '1' then output of the splitter is of seven lines having value of each line as '1'. Similarily when input of the splitter is '0' all the seven lines will have output value '0'.

The line identifier module takes the input from the three 3-bit registers sequentially. The sequence is managed by the clock cycle. Line identifier gets the content of 3-bit register and identifies the line to be flipped as per Table 2. These identification indications are then fed to the inversion module. The inversion module inverts the indentified line. In next turn this process is repeated. And after three iterations the final decoded data of seven bits is taken as the output of the decoder.

5   Simulation and Results

Encoder and decoder are implemented in VHDL[5]. In the encoder described in the previous sections have a 7-bit input sequence and the task was to reduce the crosstalk and power dissipation using bus encoding schemes. The designed encoder reduces the 7-bit input sequence to a 4-bit output sequence.

The number of wires is reduced by 57.14%. Therefore, redundancy is reduced by 57.14%. However, in other encoding schemes, redundancy increases by 25%. This encoding scheme not only reduced the redundancy but reduced the power consumption too. After the implementation of encoding mechanism it was observed that the crosstalk reduces by 35 to 40%. The encoder is tested on the random 7-bit sequences and it was found that the worst case crosstalk reduced by 40%. There was also a decrease in power dissipation as compared to the initial sequence.

Further, as two out of the three parameters, i.e. power dissipation and crosstalk are decreased, the delay is introduced. This delay can therefore be allowed as the overall implementation is better than the initial input sequence transmission method. Hence, it is evident that this method is acceptable. This encoder considers only the coupling transitions in the input 7-bit sequence.

6   Conclusion

The proposed method of bus encoder significantly eliminates or reduces the worst case crosstalk. Reduction of crosstalk is because of the reduction in the number of lines from 7 bits to 4 bits as an output of the Encoder. This reduces the crosstalk effectively by 35 to 40 percent. The transitions in the state of buses decide the behavior of the switching and coupling activities. It is shown that reduction in the coupling and switching activity reduces the dynamic power dissipation and crosstalk. Thereby the power dissipation is also reduced as compared to the initial input sequence. Hence the performance of the VLSI chip is improved. For all possible 128 combinations of the input sequence the output is seen manually and via the implemented mechanism. It is finally found that the method is implemented successfully and serves its purpose to a great extent.

Acknowledgments

Special thanks to Mr. Kanwaljeet Kathait, Ms. Sushila Mishra and their group members for their valuable efforts and cooperation.

References

[1] Duan, C., Calle, V.H.C., Khatri, S.P.: Efficient On-Chip Crosstalk Avoidance CODEC Design. IEEE Transactions on Very Large Scale Integration (VLSI) Systems 17(4), 551–560 (2009) ISSN: 1063-8210

[2] Khan, Z., Arslan, T., Erdogan, A.T.: A Low Power System on Chip Bus Encoding Scheme with Crosstalk Noise Reduction Capability. IEEE Proc. Computer & Digital Techniques (2005)

[3] Stan, M.R., Burleson, W.P.: Bus-invert coding for low power I/O. IEEE Transactions on Very Large Scale Integration Systems (TVLSI), 49–58 (1995)

[4] Shin, Y., Chae, S., Choi, K.: Partial Bus-Invert Coding for Power Optimization of System Level Bus. In: Proceedings of the 1998 International Symposium on Low Power Electronics and Design, pp. 127–129 (1998)

[5] VHDL Reference Guide, Xilinx, Inc. (1999),
   `http://toolbox.xilinx.com/docsan/`

[6] Perry, D.L.: VHDL, Programming by example, 4th edn. McGraw-Hill, New York

[7] Mano, M., Kime, C.: Logic and Computer Design Fundamentals, 2nd edn. Prentice Hall, Upper Saddle River (2001)

[8] Aghaghiri, Y., Fallah, F., Pedram, M.: Transition reduction in memory buses using sector based encoding techniques. IEEE Transactions on Computer-Aided Design of Integrated Circuits and Systems 23(8), 1174–1184 (2004)

[9] Satyanarayana, N., VinayaBabu, A., Mutyam, M.: Delay-efficient bus encoding techniques. Microprocessors & Microsystems 33(5-6), 365–373 (2009)

[10] Lin, T., Shang, T., Jou, J.: On-Chip Bus Encoding for Power Minimization under Delay Constraint. In: IEEE International Symposium on VLSI Design, Automation, and Test, VLSI-DAT (2007)

[11] Kaushik, B.K., Sarkar, S.: Crosstalk Analysis for a CMOS-Gate-Driven Coupled Interconnects. IEEE Trans. on Computer-Aided Design of Integrated Circuits and Systems 27(6), 1150–1154 (2008)

[12] Kaushik, B.K., Sarkar, S., Agarwal, R.P.: Waveform Analysis and Delay Prediction for a CMOS Gate Driving RLC Interconnect Load. Integration, the VLSI Journal 40(4), 394–405 (2007)

[13] Kaushik, B.K., Sarkar, S., Agarwal, R.P., Joshi, R.C.: Crosstalk Analysis of Simultaneously Switching Interconnects. International Journal of Electronics 96(10), 1095–1114 (2009)

[14] Kaushik, B.K., Sarkar, S., Agarwal, R.P., Joshi, R.C.: Effect of Line Resistance and Driver Width on Crosstalk in Coupled VLSI Interconnects. Microelectronics International 24(3), 42–45 (2007)

[15] Verma, S.K., Kaushik, B.K.: Encoding Schemes for the Reduction of Power Dissipation, Crosstalk and Delay: A Review. International Journal of Recent Trends in Engineering 3(4), 74–79, ISSN 1797-9617

[16] Verma, S.K., Kaushik, B.K.: Reduction of transitions in RC coupled systems in VLSI interconnects. In: International Conference on Emerging Trends in Engineering & Technology ICETET, pp. 735–740. IEEE Computer Society, Los Alamitos (2010)

Performance Driven VLSI Floorplanning with B*Tree Representation Using Differential Evolutionary Algorithm

D. Gracia Nirmala Rani and S. Rajaram

Department of Electronics and Communication Engineering,
Thiagarajar College of Engineering College, Madurai-625015, India

Abstract. In this paper, we present a floorplanning algorithm based on B *Tree representation. Our floorplanner has explicitly designed for fixed-frame floorplanning, which is different from traditional minarea floorplanning. Moreover, we also show that it can be adapted to minimize total area. It addresses the problem of handling alignment constraint which arises in bus structure. It deals with performance constraint such as bounded net delay, while many existing floorplanners just minimize total wire length. More importantly, even with all these constraints the Differential evolutionary algorithm (DE) is very fast in the sense that it can quickly produce optimal solutions.Experimental results based on MCNC benchmark with constraints show that Differential Evolutionary (DE) can quickly produce optimal solutions.

Keywords: VLSI CAD, Floorplanning, B*tree representation, Alignment and Performance constraints, Differential Evolutionary Algorithm (DE).

1 Introduction

Floorplan design is an important step in physical design of very large scale integration circuits. It is the problem of placing a set of circuit modules on a chip to minimize the total area and interconnect cost. In this early stage of physical design, most of the modules are not yet designed and, thus, are flexible in shape (soft modules), while some are reused modules and their shapes are fixed (hard modules). There are two kinds of floorplans: slicing and nonslicing. Many existing floorplanners are based on slicing floorplans [1]. There are several advantages of using slicing floorplans. Firstly, focusing only on slicing floorplans significantly reduces the search space which in turn leads to a faster runtime, especially when the simulated annealing method is used. Secondly, the shape flexibility of the soft modules can be fully exploited to give a tight packing based on an efficient shape curve computational technique.It has been shown mathematically that a tight packing is achievable for slicing floorplans.Slicing structure has advantages, but typical floorplan is non-slicing.

The modeling for the non-slicing structures (and also the slicing structures) have been proposed recently. Among them, sequence pair [2], BSG [3], and TCG [4] specify the topological relative positions between blocks. From these representations,

D.C. Wyld et al. (Eds.): NeCoM/WeST/WiMoN 2011, CCIS 197, pp. 445–456, 2011.
© Springer-Verlag Berlin Heidelberg 2011

we can easily identify the geometric relation between two blocks, such as below, above, left-to and right-to. O-tree [5] and B*-tree [6] give partial topological relations among blocks by using ordered trees. In the trees,a node represent a block and an edge describes the relation between the parent node and the child node.Problems related to floorplanning/placement with the performance and alignment constraints, such as pre-placed and range constraints and rectilinear blocks, were studied earlier. The floorplan design with the pre-defined range constraint was proposed by Young and Wong [7]. Unlike pre-placed blocks,the constrained blocks are required to place within a pre-defined range. Chang *et al.* in [6] applied the B*-tree to handle this constraint by keeping a *location constraint* between nodes associated with the sub-blocks of a rectilinear block.

Similar operations can be found based on the O-tree and Xu *et al.* [8] based on sequence pair.Tang and Wong [7] recently extended the range constraint to the performance constraint, and the rectilinear constraint to the alignment constraint. With the performance constraint, blocks are placed in a movable bounding box to reduce the net delay and minimize the total wire length as well.

1.2 Our Contribution

In this paper, we handle the floorplanning based on B*-tree representation with the alignment and performance constraints using the Differential Evolutionary (DE) optimization algorithm. We first explore the feasibility conditions with the alignment and performance constraints, and then propose algorithms that can guarantee a feasible placement with alignment constraints and generate a good placement with performance constraints during each operation. We use Differential Evolutionary (DE) algorithm to search for optimal floorplan satisfying given constraints, where a novel cost function is used to unify the evaluation of feasible and infeasible tree representations. The algorithm is very fast. Experimental results based on the MCNC benchmark with the constraints show that our method significantly outperforms the previous work.

The remainder of this paper is organized as follows. Section 2 reviews B*- trees. Section 3 gives the definitions of the alignment and performance constraints. The methods for solving these constraints are proposed using Differential Evolutionary algorithm in Section 4.In Section 5 and 6 exhibits the implementation and experiment results. Finally, we give conclusions in Section 7.

2 B*-Tree Representation

To handle non-slicing floor plans, we propose in this paper an ordered binary-tree based representation, called B*-tree representation [9]. Given an admissible placement P, we can represent it by a unique (horizontal) B*-tree. (See Fig 1 for the B*-tree representing the placement shown in Figure 2) A B*-tree is an ordered binary tree whose root corresponds to the module on the bottom-left corner. Similar to the depth first search (DFS) procedure, we construct the B*-tree for an admissible Placement P in a recursive fashion.

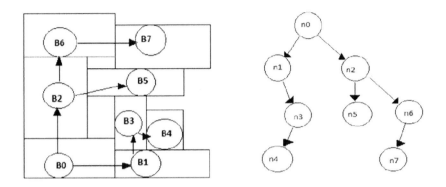

Fig. 1. Admissible Placement   **Fig. 2.** B*tree representation

Starting from the root, we first recursively construct the left sub tree and then the right sub tree. Let R_i denote the set of modules located on the right-hand side and adjacent to bi. The left child of the node n_i corresponds to the lowest module in R_i that is unvisited. The right child of n_i represents the lowest module located above bi with its x-coordinate equal to that of bi and its y-coordinate less than that of the top boundary of the module on the left-hand side and adjacent to b_i, if any. The B*-tree keeps the geometric relationship between two modules as follows. If node n_i is the left child of node n_i module bi must be located on the right-hand side and adjacent to module b_i in the admissible placement; i.e., $x_j = x_i + w_i$. Besides, if node nj is the right child of n_i module b_j must be located above and adjacent to module bi, with the x-coordinate of b_j equal to that of b_i; i.e. $x_j = x_i$, Also, since the root of tree (T) represents the bottom-left module, the x- and y-coordinates of the module associated with the root $(x_{root}, y_{root}) = (0\ 0)$.

We make n_0 the root of T since b_0 is on the bottom-left corner. Constructing the left sub tree of n_0 recursively, we make n_7 the left child of n_0. Since the left child of n_7 does not exist, we then construct the right sub tree of n7 (which is rooted by n_7. The construction is recursively performed in the DFS order. After completing the left sub tree of n_0, the same procedure applies to the right sub tree of n_0. Fig 1 illustrates the resulting B*- tree for the placement shown in Fig 2. The construction takes only linear time.

3   Floorplanning with Alignment and Performance Constraints

In this section, we first define the alignment and performance constraints and then formulate the placement problem with constraints.

3.1   B*-Trees with Alignment Blocks

The alignment blocks have two properties: (1) Alignment blocks must abut one by one; (2) These blocks have to be located in an alignment range. First, we give solutions for abutment placement. For a B*-tree, the left child n_j of the node n_i represents the lowest adjacent block b_j which is right to block b_i

Therefore, blocks can abut one by one if their corresponding nodes form a left-skewed sub-tree in a B*-tree. An example shown in Fig 1, the four sets of abutment blocks b_0 and b_1, b_3 and b_4, b_2 and b_6, and b_7 correspond to four left-skewed sub-trees.

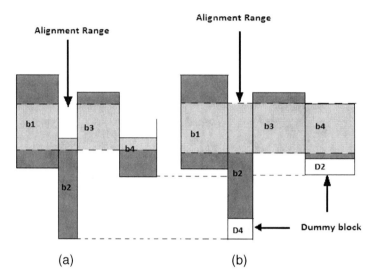

Fig. 3. (a) An infeasible placement with blocks falling out of the alignment range; block b_2 and b_4 are not in the alignment range. (b) Inserting dummy blocks, we obtain a feasible placement without any block violating the alignment constraint.

After packing, blocks are compacted to the bottom and left. The blocks associated with a left-skew sub-tree of a B*-tree may be aligned together if no block falls down during packing. To solve the falling down problem, we introduce *dummy blocks* to fix it. A dummy block comes for an alignment block. The dummy block has the same x-coordinate with the alignment block and right below it. The width of the dummy block is equal to its corresponding alignment block, and its height can be adjusted to make a displaced alignment block shift into the right alignment range. As illustrated in Fig 3(a), the blocks b_2 and b_4 fall out of the alignment range. As shown in Fig 3(b), we adjust the heights of the two dummy blocks to shift the displaced alignment blocks into the correct alignment range. After adjusting the heights of the dummy blocks, we can guarantee that the resulting placement is feasible with the alignment constraints.

3.1.1 Feasibility Condition for Alignment Constraints

The properties mentioned in the preceding section provide the way to develop the feasibility condition of a B*-tree with the alignment constraints. Consequently, we can take advantage of the feasibility condition to transform an infeasible placement to a feasible one of alignment blocks. Given a B*-tree, we refer to the node representing an alignment block as an *alignment node*. For each alignment node, we introduce a *dummy node* in the B*-tree and make the alignment node the right child of its corresponding dummy node. By the definition of the B*-tree, this will make a dummy block right under its corresponding alignment block, and we can thus adjust the height of the dummy block to change the y-coordinate of the alignment block, if needed. We refer to a set of an alignment node and its corresponding dummy node as a *cluster node*, i.e., each cluster node consists of an alignment node and a dummy node. To make a set of alignment blocks abut one by one, by Property 1, we further require that the corresponding cluster nodes form a left-skewed sub-tree. We say that the cluster nodes form an *alignment shape* if they form a left-skewed sub-tree. As an example shown in Fig 4(a), the three cluster nodes c_3, c_4 and c_5 form a left-skewed sub-tree and thus an alignment shape, for which the corresponding placement for the alignment blocks b_3, b_4 and b_5 can abut one by one, as shown in Fig 4(b). In Fig 4(b), the placement is obtained by packing the blocks corresponding to the B*-tree of Fig 4(a) and adjusting the heights of the dummy blocks to satisfy the alignment constraints. We have the following theorem for the feasibility condition of a B*-tree with alignment constraints.

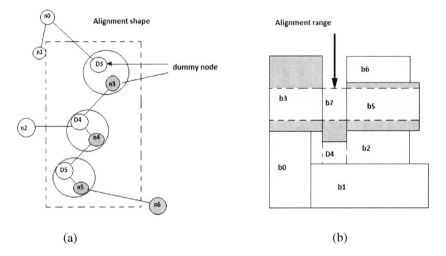

(a)   (b)

Fig. 4. (a) The alignment shape in a B*-tree (b) The corresponding placement of (a)

To deal with the alignment constraints, we need two passes to pack blocks correctly. In the first pass, we compute the coordinate for each non-dummy block (a regular block or an alignment block). Then, we verify whether every alignment block is in the alignment range. If there is any violation of the alignment constraints, we compute in the second pass the minimum movement (height) for the corresponding alignment (dummy) block to shift into the alignment range. Given m alignment blocks and the alignment range r, the equation for computing the minimum movement (height) Δ_i for the alignment block bi, i =1,2,3,.. , m, in H-alignment is as follows:

$$\Delta_t = \begin{cases} (Y_{max}+r)-(y_i+h_i) & \text{if } (y_{max}+r)>(y_i+h_i) \\ 0 & \text{otherwise} \end{cases} \quad (1)$$

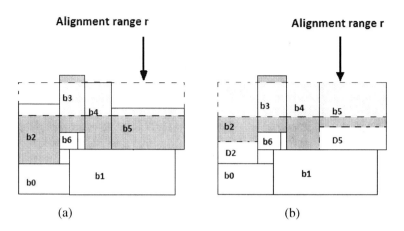

(a)   (b)

Fig. 5. (a) The placement obtained in the 1st pass, where blocks 2 and 5 fall out of the alignment range. (b) The placement obtained in the 2nd pass, where those blocks violating the alignment constraint are adjusted by inserting corresponding dummy blocks with appropriate heights.

After getting the minimum movement for each alignment block, we set the height of the corresponding dummy block to Δ_i to shift the alignment block upward to the alignment range. Using such a two-pass packing scheme, we can guarantee that the final placement is feasible without violating any alignment constraint. As shown in Figure 5(a), the alignment blocks b_2, b_3, b_4 and b_5, abut one by one, but the blocks b_2 and b_5 fall out of the alignment range after the 1st-pass packing. Then, we compute the minimum movement (height) for each alignment (dummy) block i, Δ_i, and shift b_2 and b_5 upward by Δ_2 and δ_5, respectively. Fig 5(b) gives a feasible placement after the adjustment.

3.2 B*Tree with Performance Constraints

Traditional floorplanners try to minimize total wire length but cannot guarantee that critical nets meet the delay constraint. In order to make critical net delay satisfy the delay constraint, we need to place the blocks, called *performance blocks*, connected by critical nets near each other. The delay $D_{s,t}$ of a two-pin net from the source at (x_s, y_s) to a sink at (x_t, y_t) at the floorplanning stage can be approximated by the following equation:

$$D_{s,t} = \delta \left(| x_t - x_s | + | y_t - y_s | \right) \tag{2}$$

where δ is a constant to scale the distance to timing. Note that we can use the above linear function to estimate the delay because the actual delay is close to linear to the source-sink distance with appropriate buffer insertions. (Of course, more sophisticated approximation can also be used for this purpose by trading off the running time.) From the above equation and the given delay bound, D_{max}, the distance from the source s to the sink t, $I_{s,t}$, must satisfy the following inequality to meet the performance constraint:

$$I_{s,t} =\mid x_t - x_s \mid + \mid y_t - y_s \mid = D_{s,t} \leq \frac{D_{max}}{\delta} \tag{3}$$

For a net, we use the popular approximation that the distance of pins is given by half of the perimeter of the minimum bounding box of the blocks connected by the net. To meet the performance constraints, we shall place the constrained blocks in a bounding box whose half of the perimeter is smaller than the distance with the delay bound. In Fig 6(a), the bounding box (dotted lines) of the blocks is smaller than the bounding box (dash lines) with the delay bound, so the placement is feasible for the given performance constraint. The placement of Fig 6(b) is infeasible because the bounding box of the blocks is greater than that with the delay bound. In Fig 6(c), we obtain a feasible placement with the performance constraint from Fig 6(a). Then we cluster the blocks as a rectilinear super block and fix the shape of the rectilinear super block. Therefore, the performance constraint will be satisfied afterwards. We can repartition the rectilinear super block into a set of new blocks for further processing with other blocks.

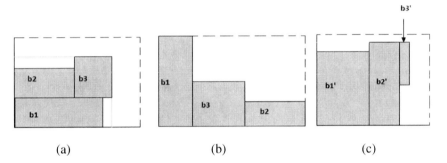

(a)   (b)   (c)

Fig. 6. (a) A placement with performance blocks only.. (b) An infeasible placement with the blocks and the delay bound given in (a). (c) We can cluster the feasible placement in (a) into a new rectilinear block and repartition the rectilinear block into a set of new blocks for further processing with other blocks.

3.2.1   Feasibility Conditions for Performance Constraints

Given a set of blocks and performance constraints, we call the nodes representing performance blocks as *performance nodes* in a B*-tree. To meet the performance constraint, the performance blocks shall be located near each other. We take advantage of the processing for a rectilinear block presented in [9] to guarantee a feasible placement with the performance constraint. Given a placement P of k performance blocks whose areas are A_i, i = 1, 2, ..., k, the width u, the height v, and the dead space $S_{per\ f}$ of the placement P, the sub-placement of the performance blocks must satisfy the following inequality:

$$u + v = I_{bound} \leq I_{max} \tag{4}$$

We do not restrict u or v so that the ratio of the bounding box can be adjusted. If the bounding distance of sub-placement is greater than the distance bound, the sub-placement cannot meet the performance constraints and thus the placement with the sub-placement either. Thus, we shall modify the sub-placement until it is smaller than the distance bound. By doing so, we obtain a set of feasible sub-placements for the performance blocks. Among these sub-placements, we pick the one with the minimum and treat the sub placement as a rectilinear block.

$$S_{perf} = u \times v - \sum_{i=1}^{k} A_i \qquad (5)$$

Then we fix the rectilinear block (and thus fix the delay) for further processing with other blocks. By clustering performance blocks into an appropriate rectilinear block and fixing its shape, we can guarantee that the performance constraint will be satisfied throughout the remaining processing.

4 Differential Evolutionary Algorithm

4.1 Differential Evolution Algorithm

The DE algorithm [10] is a population based algorithm like genetic algorithms using the similar operators; crossover, mutation and selection. The main difference in constructing better solutions is that genetic algorithms rely on crossover while DE relies on mutation operation. The main operation is based on the divergences of randomly sampled pairs of solutions in the population. The algorithm uses mutation operation as a search mechanism and selection operation to direct the search toward the prospective regions in the search space. The DE algorithm also uses a non-uniform crossover that can take child vector parameters from one parent more often than it does from others. By using the components of the existing population members to construct trial vectors, the recombination (crossover) operator efficiently shuffles information about successful combinations, enabling the search for a better solution space. An optimization task consisting of D parameters can be represented by a D-dimensional vector. In DE, a population of NP solution vectors is randomly created at the start. This population is successfully improved by applying mutation, crossover and selection operators.

4.1.1 Mutation
For each target vector $x_{i,G}$, a mutant vector is generated according to,

$$V_{i,G-1} = X_{r1,G} + F(X_{r2,G} - X_{r3,G}) \qquad (6)$$

randomly chosen indexes r1 ,r2, r3 $\varepsilon\{1,2,3...NP\}$. Note that indexes have to be different from each other and from the running index. Therefore, the number of parameter vectors in a population must be at least four is a real and constant factor ε [0, 2] A that controls the amplification of the difference vector $(x_{r2,G}-x_{r3,G})$. Note that the smaller the differences between parameters of parent r_2 and r3, the smaller the difference vector and therefore the perturbation. That means if the population gets close to the optimum, the step length is automatically decreased. This is similar to the automatic step size control found in standard evolution strategies.

4.1.2 Crossover

The target vector is mixed with the mutated vector using the following scheme to yield the trial vector $u_{i,G-1}=(u_{1i,G+1}, u_{2i,G+1}.\ldots\ldots u_{Di,G+1})$ where

$$u_{ij,G-1} = \begin{cases} v_{i,G-1} & \text{If } (r(j){\leq}CR \text{ or } j{=}(i) \\ x_{ji,G} & \text{If } (r(j)){>}CR \text{ and } j{\neq}rn(j) \end{cases} \qquad (7)$$

Evaluation of a uniform random number generator. CR is the crossover constant ε [0, 1] CR=0 means no crossover. rn(i) ε (1,2,...D) is a randomly chosen index which ensures that $u_{i,G-1}$ gets at least one element from $v_{i,G-1}$.Otherwise no new parent vector would be produced and the population would not alter.

4.1.3 Selection

A "greedy" selection scheme is used: If and only if the trial vector yields a better cost function value compared to the parameter vector $x_{i,G}$ is it accepted as a new parent vector for the following G+1.Otherwise,the target vector is retained to serve as a parent vector for generation G+1 once again.

5   The Algorithm

Our floor plan design algorithm is based on the Differential Evolution method [10, 11, 12]. The algorithm can consider not only hard modules, but also pre-placed, soft, and rectilinear ones. We perturb a B*-tree (a feasible solution) to another B*-tree by using the following four operations.

> Op1: Rotate a module.
> Op2: Move a module to another place.
> Op3: Swap two modules.
> Op4: Remove a soft module and insert it into the
>   best internal or external position.

We have discussed Op1 is rotate a module. Op2 deletes and inserts a module. If the deleted node is associated with a rectangular module, we simply delete the node from the B*-tree. Otherwise, there will be several nodes associated with a rectilinear module, and we treat them as a whole and maintain their Location Constraints (LC) relations. Op4 deletes a soft module, tries all possible internal and external positions, inserts it into the best position, and changes its shape and the shapes of the other soft modules. Op2, Op3, and Op4 need to apply the Insert and Delete operations for inserting and deleting a node to and from a B*-tree. We explain the two operations in the following.

5.1 Deletion

There are three cases for the deletion operation.

> Case 1: A leaf node.
> Case 2: A node with one child.
> Case 3: A node with two children.

In Case 1, we simply delete the target leaf node. In Case 2, we remove the target node and then place its only child at the position of the removed node. The tree update can be performed in O (1) time. In Case 3, we replace the target node n_t by either its right child or left child n_c. Then we move a child of n_c to the original position of n_c. The process Proceeds until the corresponding leaf node is handled. It is obvious that such a deletion peration requires O (h) time, where h is the height of the B*-tree. Note that in Cases 2 and 3, the relative positions of the modules might be changed after the operation, and thus we might need to reconstruct a corresponding placement for further processing. Also, if the deleted node corresponds to a sub-module of a rectilinear module b_R, we should also delete other sub-modules of b_R.

5.2   Insertion

When adding a module, we may place it around some module, but not between the sub-modules that belong to a rectilinear module. Only internal and external positions can be used for inserting a new node. For a rectangular module, we can insert it into an internal or an external position directly. For a rectilinear module b_R consisting of the sub-modules b_1, b_2....... b_n ordered from left to right, the sub-modules must be inserted simultaneously, and bi+1 must be the left child of bi to satisfy the LC relation.The DE algorithm starts by randomly choosing an initial B*-tree. Then it perturbs a B*-tree (a feasible solution) to another B*-tree based on the aforementioned Op1–Op4 until a predefined "frozen" state is reached. At last, we transform the resulting B*- tree to the corresponding final admissible placement.

Algorithm: Floorplanning with Alignment and Performance Constraints (blocks and constraints)
Input: A set of blocks and alignment and performance constraints.
Output: A floorplanning without violating the given constraints.
1. Generate the rectilinear blocks for performance blocks
2. Initialize a B*-tree for the input blocks and constraints;
3. Differential Evolution process;
4. **do**
5.   perturb();
6.   first-packing();
7.   adjust _-coordinates of the sub-blocks for rectilinear blocks.
8.   **if** alignment blocks fall out of the required area
9.   **then** adjust heights of dummy blocks to fix alignment violations
10.   final-packing();
11. evaluate the B*-tree cost;
12. **until** converged;
13. **return** the best solution;

Fig. 7. The Design Flow: B*tree with alignment an performance using DE

6 Experiment Results

The experiment employed MCNC benchmarks for the VLSI floorplanning with alignment and performance constraints. The differential evolution (DE) experiments with the following initializations parameter F=0.5, CR=0.9 and used different number of particles and compared with Simulated Annealing [13]. The results obtained for DE is better compared to other techniques. The experimental results are shown in Table 1 for Area estimation and Table 2 for runtime estimation.

Table 1. Area Comparisons

Circuit	Blocks	Constrained blocks		Simulated Annealing(SA) Area (mm_2)	Ours; Differential Evolution(DE) Area (mm_2)
		Align	Perf		
Apte	9	4	0	46.92	45.639
Xerox	10	4	2	20.08	19.19
Hp	11	4	2	9.20	8.95
ami33	33	4	3	1.183	1.15
ami49	49	4	3	36.64	35.56

Table 2. Run Time Comparisons

Circuit	Blocks	Constrained blocks		Simulated Annealing(SA) Run Time(sec)	Ours; Differential Evolution(DE) Run Time(sec)
		Align	Perf		
apte	9	4	0	3.6	1.48
xerox	10	4	2	6.4	4.09
hp	11	4	2	6.1	3.58
ami33	33	4	3	52.6	15.08
ami49	49	4	3	97.9	20.05

7 Conclusions

We have presented an efficient and effective algorithm to deal with the floorplanning with the alignment and performance constraints. The algorithm is based on the B*-tree representation and the Differential Evolution (DE) scheme. We have derived the feasibility conditions with the alignment and performance constraints. We have also proposed an algorithm that can guarantee a feasible placement with alignment constraints and generate a good placement with performance constraints during each operation. To evaluate a B*-tree with the constraints, it takes only amortized linear time (number of groups of constrained blocks is constant), which achieves the best published time complexity for the evaluation operation. The experimental results have shown the effectiveness and efficiency of our algorithm.

References

1. Bazargan, K., Kim, S., Sarrafzadeh, M.: Nostradamus: A floorplanner of uncertain design. In: Proc. Int. Symp. Physical Design, pp. 18–23 (1998)
2. Murata, H., Fujiyoshi, K., Nakatake, S., Kajitani, Y.: Rectangle-packing based module placement. In: Proc. ICCAD, pp. 472–479 (1995)
3. Nakatake, S., Murata, H., Fujiyoshi, K., Kajitani, Y.: VLSI module placement on BSG-structure. and IC layour applications. In: Proc. ICCAD, pp. 484–491 (1996)
4. Lin, J.M., Chang, Y.W.: TCG: A transitive closure graph-based representation for non-slicing floorplans. In: Proc. DAC, pp. 764–769 (2001)
5. Guo, P.N., Cheng, C.K., Yoshimura, T.: An O-tree representation of non-slicing floorplans and its applications. In: Proc. DAC, pp. 268–273 (1999)
6. Chang, Y.C., Chang, Y.W., Wu, G.M., Wu, S.W.: B*-trees: A new representation for non-slicing floorplans. In: Proc. DAC, pp. 458–463 (2000)
7. Tang, X., Wong, D.F.: Floorplanning with alignment and performance constraints. In: DAC, pp. 848–853 (2002)
8. Tang, X., Wong, D.F.: FAST-SP: A fast algorithm for block placement based sequence pair. In: Proc. APS-DAC, pp. 521–526 (2001)
9. Pang, Y., Cheng, C.-K., Lampaert, K., Xie, W.: Rectilinear block packing using O-tree representation. In: Proc. ISPD, pp. 156–161 (2001)
10. Stron, R.: Differential evolutation design of an IIRfilter with requirements for magnitude and group delay. Proc. IEEE, 268–273 (May 1996)
11. Price, K.V.: an Introduction to Differential evolution. In: Corne, D., Dorido, M., Glover, F. (eds.) New Ideas Optimization, ch. 6, McGraw Hill, London
12. Stron, R., Price, K.: Differential evolution-a simple and efficient adaptive scheme for global ptimization over continuopus spaces, Tech. Rep. TR-95-102, International computer science Institute (ICSI), Berkely, Calif., USA (March 1995)
13. Wu, M.-c., Chang, Y.-w.: Placement with alignment and performance constraints Using the B*tree Representations. National council of science

Power Reduction Techniques Applied to FSM Architecture Using Different Technologies

Himani Mittal, Dinesh Chandra, and Sampath Kumar

J.S.S. Academy Of Technical Education, Noida, U.P., India
himanimit@yahoo.co.in, dinesshc@gmail.com,
sampath_sams@yahoo.com

Abstract. As in today's date fuel consumption is important in everything from scooters to oil tankers, power consumption is a key parameter in most electronics applications. The most obvious applications for which power consumption is critical are battery-powered applications, such as home thermostats and security systems, in which the battery must last for years. Low power also leads to smaller power supplies, less expensive batteries, and enables products to be powered by signal lines (such as fire alarm wires) lowering the cost of the end-product. As a result, low power consumption has become a key parameter of microcontroller designs . The purpose of this paper is to summarize, mainly by way of examples,what in our experience are the most trustful approaches to lowpower design. In other words, our contribution should not be intended as an exhaustive survey of the existing literature on low-power esign; rather, we would like to provide insights a designer can rely upon when power consumption is a critical constraint.We will focus on the reduction of power consumption on different technologies for different values of capacitance and also compare power saving in technologies .

Keywords: FSM Decomposition[2] ,Mealy and Moore Machines, Capacitance[5], Power saving.

1 Introduction

Methods of low power realization of FSMs are of great interest since FSMs are important components of digital systems and power is a design constraint.

Power dissipated by FSMs can be controlled by the way the codes are assigned to the states of an FSM.Such attempts are reported in [4] and [6]. In [4], the weighted graph is constructed depending upon the steady state probability distribution, where the states are nodes. A high weight on an edge between a pair of nodes implies that they should be given codes with less Hamming distance, since there is a high probability of transition among them. In [6], a heuristic !- Silicon Automation Systems, India. algorithm is given to embed the state transition graph (STG) in a hypercube such that minimum number of flip-flops will be switched whenever there is a state transition. Recently, attempts using decomposition for low power realization of FSMs were also reported [1,2, 3]. In [2, 3], an STG is partitioned into several pieces, each piece being implemented as a separatemachine with a wait state. In this

D.C. Wyld et al. (Eds.): NeCoM/WeST/WiMoN 2011, CCIS 197, pp. 457–465, 2011.
© Springer-Verlag Berlin Heidelberg 2011

case, only one of the sub-machines is active and other sub-machines are in the reset state. In CMOS circuits, power is dissipated in a gate when the gate output changes from 0 to 1 or from 1 to 0. Minimization of power dissipation can be considered at algorithmic, architectural, logic, and circuit levels. In sequential circuit design, an effective approach to reduce power dissipation is to "turn off" portions of the circuit, and hence reduce the switching activities in the circuit. In this article we propose a technique that is also based on selectively turning off portions of a circuit. Our approach is motivated by the observation that, for an FSM, active transitions occur only within a subset of states in a period of time. Therefore, if we synthesize an FSM in such a way that only the part of the circuit which computes the state transitions and outputs will be turned on while all other parts will be turned off, power consumption will be reduced. In a CMOS circuit, generally, the switching activity of the gate output contributes most to the total power dissipation. For FSM low power design, partitioning technique proves to be effective for reducing switching activity. That is, partition the original FSM into several smaller sub FSMs and only one of them is active at a time.

Designers should use components that deploy the latest developments in low-power technology. The most effective power savings can be achieved by making the right choices early on during the system and architectural level of abstraction. In addition to using power-conscious hardware design techniques, it is important to save power through careful design of the operating system and application programs.Objective of this paper is :

(1) Computing the Power consumption in original FSM
(2) Compute value of Power for different technologies with frequency taken from FSM computation
(3) Take capacitance value for different technologies and from original computaion of FSM find power
(4) Plot graphs for Technologies vs Power .
(5) Plot graphs for Capacitor vs Power

1.1 Dissipation of Power

The sources of energy consumption on a CMOS chip can be classified as static and dynamic power dissipation. The dominant component of energy consumption in CMOS is dynamic power consumption caused by the actual effort of the circuit to switch. A first order approximation of the dynamic power consumption of CMOS circuitry is given by the formula[3]:

$$P = C * V^2 * f \qquad (1)$$

where P is the power, C is the effective switch capacitance, V is the supply voltage, and f is the frequency of operation. The power dissipation arises from the charging and discharging of the circuit node capacitances found on the output of every logic gate. Every low-to-high logic transition in a digital circuit incurs a change of voltage, drawing energy from the power supply.A designer at the technological and architectural level can try to minimize the variables in these equations to minimize the overall energy consumption. However, power minimization is often a complex process of trade-offs between speed, area, and power consumption.

Static energy consumption is caused by short circuit currents, bias, and leakage currents. During the transition on the input of a CMOS gate both p and n channel devices may conduct simultaneously, briefly establishing a short from the supply voltage to ground. While statically-biased gates are usually found in a few specialized circuits such as PLAs, their use has been dramatically reduced. Leakage current is becoming the dominant component of static energy consumption. Until recently, it was seen as a secondary order effect; however, the total amount of static power consumption doubles with every new process node.

Energy consumption in CMOS circuitry is proportional to capacitance; therefore, a technique that can be used to reduce energy consumption is to minimize the capacitance. This can be achieved at the architectural level of design as well as at the logic and physical implementation level.Connections to external components, such as external memory, typically have much greater capacitance than connections to on-chip resources. As a result, accessing external memory can increase energy consumption. Consequently, a way to reduce capacitance is to reduce external accesses and optimize the system by using on-chip resources such as caches and registers. In addition, use of fewer external outputs and infrequent switching will result in dynamic power savings.

Routing capacitance is the main cause of the limitation in clock frequency. Circuits that are able to run faster can do so because of a lower routing capacitance. Consequently, they dissipate less power at a given clock frequency. So, energy reduction can be achieved by optimizing the clock frequency of the design, even if the resulting performance is far in excess of the requirements.

1.2   Methods And Approaches

The key steps in our approach are:

(1) Finding the number of happening states then find the probability Of FSM.

(2) Take different technologies and its related value of voltage.

(3) Find the frequency by using the formula :

$F = P(1-P)$

(4) With calculations based on FSM find power savings in different technologies and compare them .

(5) With different value of capacitor find the power savings.

(6) An effective approach to reduce power dissipation is to "turn off" portions of the circuit, and hence reduces the switching activities in the circuit. We synthesize an FSM in such a way that only the part of the circuit which computes the state transitions and outputs will be turned on while all other parts will be turned off.

(7) In general, since the combinational circuit for each submachine is smaller than that for the original machine, power consumption in the decomposed machine will be smaller than that of the original machine

1.3   Basic Principles

Entropy is a measure of the randomness carried by a set of discrete events observed over time. In the studies of the information theory, a method to quantify the information content C_i of an event E_i in this manner is o take logarithmic of the event probability

$$C_i = \log_2 (1/P_i) \tag{2}$$

Since $0 \leq P_i \leq 1$, the logarithmic term is non negative and we have $C_i > 0$.

The average information contents of the system is the weighted sum of the information content of C_i by its occurrence probability This is also called the entropy[4] of the system.

$$H(X) = \sum_{i=1}^{m-1} p_i \log_2 \frac{1}{p_i} \tag{3}$$

1.4 Estimated Power

Entropy is a measure of the randomness carried by a set of discrete events observed over time. In the studies of the information theory, a method to quantify the information content Ci of an event E_i in this manner is o take logarithmic of the event probability

$C_i = \log_2 (1/P_i)$

Since $0 \leq P_i \leq 1$, the logarithmic term is non negative and we have $C_i > 0$.

The average information contents of the system is the weighted sum of the information content of C_i by its occurrence probability This is also called the entropy of the system.

1.5 Challenges in Physical Design

As technology is directly related to physical size , it is clear that as technology advances power also reduces but there are other constraints that come while designing it at nano level so care should be taken and optimized designing is the demand of the day.Since capacitance, a function of fanout, wirelength, and transistor size , reducing capacitance means reducing it physically . But there are challenges in reducing it. The challenge of low-power physical design is to create, optimize, and verify the physical layout so that it meets the power budget along with traditional timing, SI, performance, and area goals. The design tool must find the best tradeoffs when implementing any number of low-power techniques.

While low-power design starts at the architectural level, the low-power design techniques continue through place and route. Physical design tools must interpret the power intent and implement the layout correctly, from placement of special cells to routing and optimization across power domains in the presence of multiple corners, modes, and power states, plus manufacturing variability. While many tools support the more common low-power techniques, such as clock gating, designers run into difficulty with more advanced techniques, such as the use of multiple voltage domains, which cause the design size and complexity to explode

1.6 Reduction Approach

(1) For a particular technology take its power supply voltage
(2) Take different value of capacitance like 1μF , 0.5 μF , 0.25 μF , 0.1 μF.
(3) By using formula P= CV^2f calculate power dissipation in 180nm , 130nm , 90nm technologies
(4) Compare the results.

1.7   Results

Keeping capacitor constant @ 15(µF) , it is clear from Fig. 1 that as technology grows power consumption reduces from 0.49 µW   to 3.9 µW. Innovation in technology is being riven by the shrinking size which leads to reduction in capacitor values .

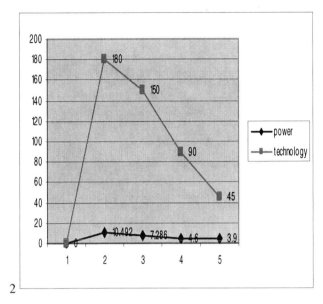

Fig. 1. Technology vs Power @ 15 µF

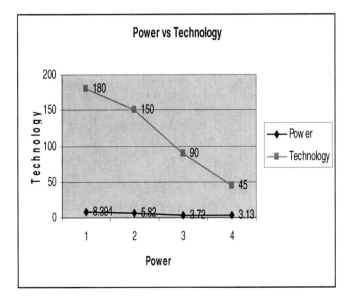

Fig. 2. Technology vs Power @ 12 µF

As observed in Fig. 1 ,in Fig. 2 also keeping capacitor @ 12 µF it is observed that power reduces as technology advances from 8.39 µW to 3.13 µW.

As we move on to advances technology we find that power reduces considerably . As shown in Fig. 3 it is shown that by keeping capacitor constant power reduces from 6.995 µW to 2.612 µW as technology grows .

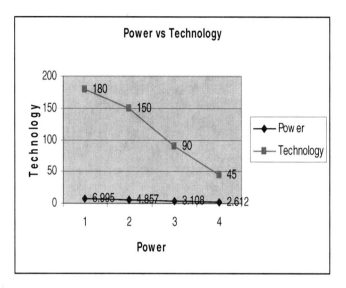

Fig. 3. Technology vs Power @ 10 µF

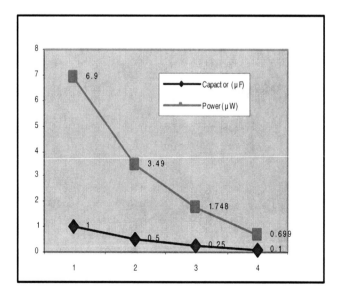

Fig. 4. Cap. vs Power in 180nm tech

As shown in Fig. 4, as capacitor value reduces from 1 μF to 0.1 μF, po wer also get reduces from 0.2612 μW to 0.0261 μW. This is called switched capacitance reduction technique. But designer cannot reduce blindfoldly the value of capacitance as it worsens the performance but it should be according to technology library.

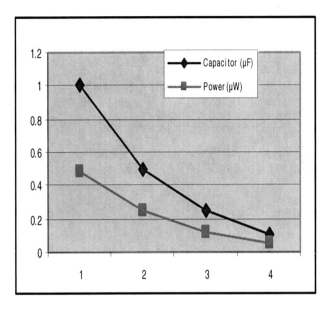

Fig. 5. Cap. vs Power in 130nm tech

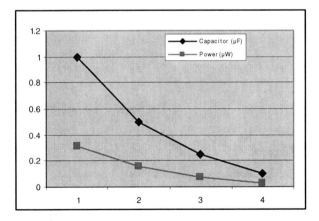

Fig. 6. Cap. vs Power in 90nm tech

Table 1

Power(μW)	Technology(nm)
10.492	180
7.286	150
4.6	90
3.9	45

Table 2

Power	Technology
8.394	180
5.82	150
3.72	90
3.13	45

Table 3

Power	Technology
6.995	180
4.857	150
3.108	90
2.612	45

Table 4

VDD(V)	Frequency(hz)	Capacitor(μF)	Power(μW)
1.8	0.2159	1	6.9
1.8	0.2519	0.5	3.49
1.8	0.2519	0.25	1.748
1.8	0.2519	0.1	0.699

2 Conclusion

Saving with decrease in capacitor and with latest technology leads to more power saving. This is power in original FSM . If we decompose machines in more sub machines then frequency reduces and we can get more reduction in powerThe Decomposed FSM[2] technique leads in a 34.13% average reduction in switching activity of the state variables, and 12% average reduction of the total switching activity of the implemented circuit. Although the solution is heuristic, and does not guarantee the minimum power consumption, these results leads to a reduction in the power consumption in the complete circuit.

References

1. Chow, S.-H., Ho, Y.-C., Hwang, T., Liu, C.L.: Low power realization of finite state machines- a decomposition approach. ACM Trans. Des. Autom. Electron. Syst. 1(3), 315–340 (1996)
2. Benini, L., Bogliolo, A., De Micheli, G.: A survey of Design Techniques for System-Level Dynamic Power Management. IEEE Trans. on VLSI Systems 8(3), 299–316 (2000)
3. Benini, L., De Micheli, G., Macii, E.: Designing Low-Power Circuits: Practical Recipes. IEEE Circuits and Systems Magazine 1(1), 7–25 (2001)
4. Benini, L., De Michelli, G.: State assignment for Low Power. IEEE Trans. on Computer Aided Design 30(3), 258–268 (1995)
5. Benini, L., De Micheli, G.: Transformation and synthesis of FSM for low-power gated-clock implementation. IEEE Trans. Computer (1995b)
6. Wang, S.J., Horng, M.D.: State assignment of finite state machine s for low power applications. Electronics Letters 32 (December 1996)
7. Benini, L., De Micheli, G., Macii, E.: Designing Low-Power Circuits: Practical Recipes

Effect of Temperature and Gate Stack on the Linearity and Analog Performance of Double Gate Tunnel FET

Rakhi Narang[1], Manoj Saxena[2], R.S. Gupta[3], and Mridula Gupta[1,*]

[1] Semiconductor Device Research Laboratory, Department of Electronic Science
University of Delhi, South Campus,
New Delhi 110 021, India
Tel.: +91-11-24115580, Fax:-+91-11-24110606
[2] Department of Electronics, Deen Dayal Upadhyaya College
University of Delhi, New Delhi 110 015, India
[3] Department of Electronics and Communication Engineering,
Maharaja Agrasen Institute of Technology,
Sector-22, Rohini, Delhi 110 086, India
rakhinarang@gmail.com, saxena_manoj77@yahoo.co.in,
rsgu@bol.net.in, mridula@south.du.ac.in

Abstract. The linearity and analog performance of a Silicon Double Gate Tunnel Field Effect Transistor (DG-TFET) is investigated and the impact of elevated temperature on the device performance degradation has been studied. The impact on the device performance due to the rise in temperature has also been investigated for the case of Silicon DG-MOSFET and a comparison with DG-TFET is made. The parameters governing the analog performance and linearity has been studied and the impact of a gate stack (GS) architecture has also been investigated for the same.

Keywords: Analog, DG-TFET, Gate Stack, Linearity.

1 Introduction

With the advancements in the wireless and mobile communication demand of high levels of integration and cost effective technologies are needed. The continuous scaling of CMOS technology has resulted in high speed MOS devices suitable for analog RF applications [1]. The modern day communication requires low distortion and linear systems as a building block for their design. But today the challenges CMOS technology is facing in terms of severe Short channel effects (SCEs), punch through arising from the extremely scaled dimensions has resulted in the need to explore new device architectures and design [2]. There are several experimental and simulation based studies showing TFETs as a potential candidate for the deep sub micron regime. The immunity against the SCEs, low leakage current and CMOS compatible technology makes it an attractive alternative for conventional MOSFETs. The earlier studies on TFETs are focused on achieving high I_{on}/I_{off} [3], sub 60mV/dec subthreshold slope [4], low power supply operation [5], device performance mainly

---

* Corresponding author.

targeted for the digital applications. The analog and linearity performance is still an unexplored area and needs to be investigated too. So the focus of this study is on studying the linearity and analog performance of TFETs to determine their suitability for analog/ RF applications. Tunnel FETs has been demonstrated experimentally as a device with immunity against temperature variations over a wide range [6-9]. The earlier studies have reported weak temperature dependent TFET characteristics and the temperature independent behavior of Subthreshold swing. To address the issue of low ON currents in TFETs several device designs and optimizations are reported, use of a high-k dielectric being one of the possible solutions [10-11]. In the present work, the effect of two parameters namely the impact of temperature variations and the impact of a Gate Stack architecture has been studied on the linearity, distortion and analog performance metrics like VIP_2, VIP_3, IMD_3, device efficiency g_m/I_{ds}, drain output resistance R_{out}, intrinsic device gain g_m/g_d. The effect of temperature has also been studied for DG-MOSFET through the above mentioned parameters in order to make a comparison with DG-TFET in terms of its capability to sustain the temperature variations.

The paper has been divided into two sections. In first part, the impact of temperature has been analyzed and in the second part the effect of Gate Stack architecture is considered and finally the results are concluded.

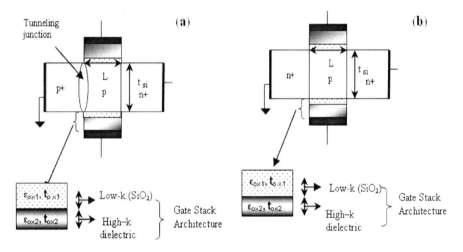

Fig. 1. Schematic of the simulated devices (a) DG-TFET and (b) DG-MOSFET

2 Device Design and Simulation Tools

The schematic for the simulated devices DG-TFET and DG-MOSFET are shown in fig 1. All the simulations have been carried out using the numerical device simulation software ATLAS 3D [12]. Kane's Band to Band tunneling model is employed for DG-TFET. Physical models activated for simulation comprises of concentration and field dependent and surface mobility models, Shockley Read Hall recombination models, and Fermi Dirac statistics. Source and drain junctions are considered to be abrupt. Quantum corrections are neglected. A uniform and asymmetric source and drain doping are chosen for DG-TFET (p+ source $N_A=10^{20}cm^{-3}$, n+ drain

$N_D=5\times10^{18}cm^{-3}$ and a lightly doped p type channel $N_i=10^{15}cm^{-3}$) in order to suppress the ambipolar behavior. Silicon channel thickness (t_{si}) is considered as 10nm with a gate oxide thickness t_{ox} of 3nm SiO_2 and channel length L=70nm. The gate stack architecture consists of a 2nm high-k (t_{ox2}) and 1nm of SiO_2 (t_{ox1}). For DG-MOSFET a symmetric doping profile is chosen with source and drain doping (n+) of $N_D=10^{20}cm^{-3}$ and channel doping similar to DG-TFET. Both the devices (DG-MOSFET and DG-TFET) are optimized for same threshold voltage i.e $V_{th}=0.33V$ @ $V_{ds}=1V$ (evaluated using the constant current method V_{th} @ $V_{ds}=1V$ @ $I_{ds}=10^{-7}A/um$). For Gate Stack architecture, 1nm of SiO_2 ($\varepsilon_{ox1}=3.9$) and a 2nm of high-k gate with dielectric constant $\varepsilon_{ox2}=10$ is considered.

3   Linearity and Analog Performance Metrics

The important device parameters for linearity and analog applications are transconductance (g_m) and drain output conductance (g_d). Transconductance (g_m) determine the various Figure of Merits (FoM) namely VIP$_2$, VIP$_3$, IMD$_3$ used to assess linearity and distortion as well as gain and cut-off frequencies. For analog design the crucial parameters are device efficiency g_m/I_{ds}, intrinsic dc gain g_m/g_d and drain output resistance R_{out} [13-15].

$$VIP_2 = 4*g_{m1}/g_{m2}\big|_{constant\ V_{ds}} . \tag{1}$$

$$VIP_3 = \sqrt{24*g_{m1}/g_{m3}}\big|_{constant\ V_{ds}} . \tag{2}$$

$$IMD_3 = R_L*\left(4.5*(VIP_3)^3*g_{m3}\right)^2 . \tag{3}$$

$$g_{m1}=\partial I_{ds}/\partial V_{gs},\ g_{m2}=\partial^2 I_{ds}/\partial V_{gs}^2,\ g_{m3}=\partial^3 I_{ds}/\partial V_{gs}^3 \tag{4}$$

3.1   Impact of Temperature

The transfer characteristics of DG-MOSFET and DG-TFET and the impact of temperature on drain current is shown in fig. 2. It is observed that the effect of temperature in case of DG-TFET is weak and it results in the increase of drain current both in ON and OFF state, although very small. This increase in value of drain current can be understood by the Kane's band to band tunneling equation given by

$$I_{ds} \propto G_{btbt} = A\frac{|E|^2}{E_g^{1/2}}\exp\left(\frac{-BE_g^{3/2}}{|E|}\right) . \tag{5}$$

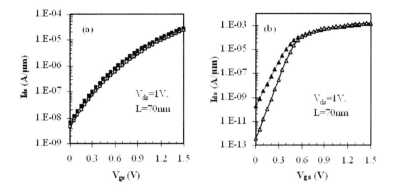

Fig. 2. Transfer characteristics (I_{ds}-V_{gs}) of (a) DG-TFET and (b) DG-MOSFET at two different temperatures. Symbols: (□□□) for DGTFET, (△△△) for DG-MOSFET where Open symbols for 300K, Solid symbols for 400K.

where E is the electric field which is V_{gs} dependent, E_g is the band gap, A and B are the material dependent parameters having default values defined in the simulator.

Since the current depends on the band gap which is a function of temperature [16] as modeled in ATLAS and given by eq. 6, where the default values of alpha and beta are material dependent. With rise in temperature the band gap value reduces which leads to the increase in the band to band tunneling current of the DG-TFET.

The reduction in the threshold voltage (V_{th}) is also minimum in case of DG-TFETs. The threshold voltage reduces *to 0.296 @V_{ds}=1V and T= 400K from its value 0.33V @ V_{ds}=1V and T=300K*. While in case of DG-MOSFET, due to increase in temperature the carriers generated in the channel increases thus leading to significant reduction of threshold voltage (*V_{th} @ V_{ds}=1V and T= 400K is 0.22V and V_{th} @ V_{ds}=1V and T=300K is 0.33V*) but the current degrades due to channel mobility degradation at high temperature arising due to the increased phonon scattering.

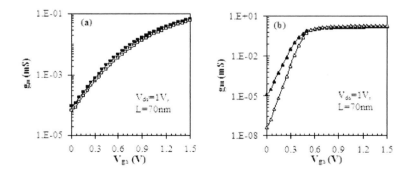

Fig. 3. Variation of Transconductance (g_m) with V_{gs} at two different temperatures 300 and 400K a) DG-TFET b) DG-MOSFET. Symbols: (□□□) for DGTFET, (△△△) for DG-MOSFET where Open symbols for 300K, Solid symbols for 400K.

Fig 3. show the impact of temperature on the transconductance characteristics of DG-TFET and DG-MOSFET. As clearly observed there is a very insignificant change in the magnitude for the case of DG-TFET in contrast with that of DG-MOSFET in which the transconductance has significantly enhanced only in the subthreshold region due to degraded subthreshold characteristics of DG-MOSFET at elevated temperatures.

$$E_g(T) = E_g(0) - \frac{alpha\ T^2}{T + beta} . \qquad (6)$$

For better linearity performance and effective suppression of nonlinear behavior introduced by g_{m3}, the optimum bias point is determined by the zero crossover point of g_{m3} (third order derivative of Transconductance g_{m1}) where its value is minimum and thereby suppressing the distortion created by g_{m3}. The maxima in the VIP_3 curve (corresponding to $g_{m3} = 0$) determines the selection of optimum bias point for device operation for MOSFETs. But for DG-TFET the peak in the VIP_3 curve is obtained at higher gate bias values as shown in fig. 4 (a). The peak has shifted to a lower gate bias with elevated temperature in case of DG-TFET. In case of DG-MOSFET there are two peaks appearing one at a higher gate bias and a local maxima at lower V_{gs} value. However for circuit applications the device operation in the moderate inversion regime is preferred so the maxima appearing at V_{gs}=0.5V can be considered as an optimum bias point for DG-MOSFETs. But as the temperature rises to 400 K the peak of the VIP_3 curve shifts further to lower V_{gs} (0.45V) as shown in fig. 4(b). This indicates the shifting of optimum bias point with temperature variation. Since in case of DG-TFET there is no peak appearing for the VIP_3 curve at the lower gate bias values we need to choose the optimum bias point on the basis of some other parameter, which is in this study is considered to be the intrinsic dc gain as will be discussed in the later part.

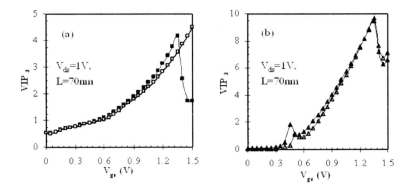

Fig. 4. VIP_3 variation with V_{gs} for a) DG-TFET and b) DG-MOSFET. Symbols: (□□□) for DGTFET, (ΔΔΔ) for DG-MOSFET where Open symbols for 300K, Solid symbols for 400K.

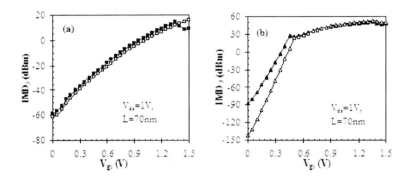

Fig. 5. IMD$_3$ variation with V$_{gs}$ for a) DG-TFET and b) DG-MOSFET. Symbols: (□□□) for DGTFET, (△△△) for DG-MOSFET where Open symbols for 300K, Solid symbols for 400K.

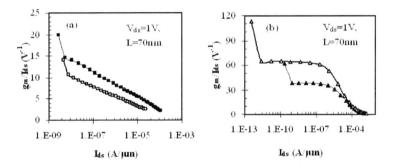

Fig. 6. Device efficiency (g$_m$/I$_{ds}$) Vs I$_{ds}$ for a) DG-TFET and b) DG-MOSFET. Symbols: (□□□) for DGTFET, (△△△) for DG-MOSFET where Open symbols for 300K, Solid symbols for 400K.

Fig. 5 shows the variation of IMD$_3$ with V$_{gs}$ which determines the distortion performance of a device. For minimization of distortion this parameter should be low. As depicted, there is a very insignificant change in IMD$_3$ with rise in temperature in case of DG-TFET while it has degraded in the subthreshold to moderate inversion regime in case of DG-MOSFET. Moreover the value of IMD$_3$ is lower in comparison to DG-MOSFET near the bias point determined by VIP$_3$ in case of DG-MOSFET thus indicating better distortion suppression. Since in case DG-TFET, current increases with rise in temperature, thus a rise in the device efficiency (g$_m$/I$_{ds}$) can also be seen as shown in fig 6(a). In case of DG-MOSFET the device efficiency has degraded severely at elevated temperature as can be observed by fig. 6 (b), this is due to the degradation of I$_{ds}$-V$_{gs}$ characteristics for high temperatures.

One of the important device parameter for analog circuit design is intrinsic dc gain g$_m$/g$_d$. The effect of temperature on g$_m$/g$_d$ is shown in fig. 7. It is observed that the device gain does not degrade much in case of DG-TFET but the range of V$_{gs}$ values over which the gain remains fairly constant and appreciable is reduced for higher temperature. But we can still choose the V$_{gs}$ value where gain is appreciably higher

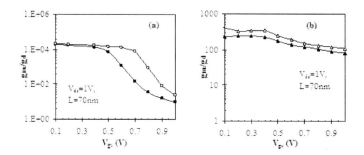

Fig. 7. Intrinsic dc gain (g_m/g_d) Vs V_{gs} a) DG-TFET b) DG-MOSFET. Symbols: (□□□) for DGTFET, (ΔΔΔ) for DG-MOSFET where Open symbols for 300K, Solid symbols for 400K.

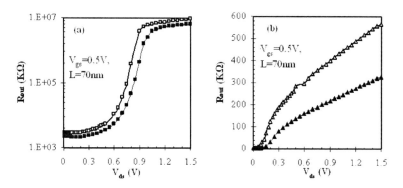

Fig. 8. Output resistance (R_{out}) vs V_{ds} for a) DGTFET b) DGMOSFET. Symbols: (□□□) for DGTFET, (ΔΔΔ) for DG-MOSFET where Open symbols for 300K, Solid symbols for 400K

and hence we can consider the g_m/g_d to be the parameter to determine the bias point at which a fairly high gain value is achieved with a decent linearity and distortion performance. In case of DG-MOSFET the gain reduces at elevated temperature.

The drain output resistance degrades rapidly for a DG-MOSFET at higher temperature while the reduction is nominal in case of DG-TFET as shown in fig 8.

3.2 Impact of Gate Stack Architecture

In this section, the impact of Gate Stack architecture on various linearity and analog performance parameters are studied. Since use of high-k is considered to be an alternative to overcome the impediments of low ON currents in case of TFETs. So in view of that the performance of DG-TFET has been studied with Gate Stack architecture and the possible enhancements brought about are investigated.

As can be seen from fig 9 (a) the transconductance has improved with the usage of a high-k dielectric Gate Stack architecture due to the enhanced gate control and current driving capability. The linearity FoM, VIP_2 has also enhanced for a Gate Stack DG-TFET. Similarly the impact can also be depicted by the shifting of the peak of VIP_3 to lower gate bias and improvement in the magnitude at the lower V_{gs} values (fig. 10(a). The IMD_3 parameter degrades for Gate Stack DG-TFET as shown by fig. 10(b).

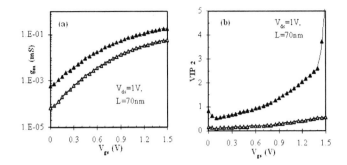

Fig. 9. a) Transconductance (g_m) variation with V_{gs} (b) VIP$_2$ variation with V_{gs} for DG-TFET with SiO$_2$ and Gate Stack architecture. Open symbols ($\triangle\triangle\triangle$) for DG-TFET with ε_{ox2} =3.9 Solid symbols ($\blacktriangle\blacktriangle\blacktriangle$) for GS-DG-TFET with ε_{ox2} =10.

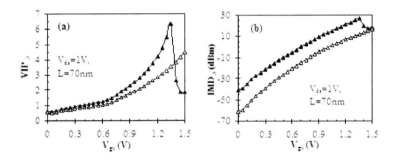

Fig. 10. VIP$_3$ variation with V_{gs} (b) IMD$_3$ variation with V_{gs} for DGTFET with SiO$_2$ and Gate Stack architecture. Open symbols ($\triangle\triangle\triangle$) for DG-TFET with ε_{ox2} =3.9 Solid symbols ($\blacktriangle\blacktriangle\blacktriangle$) for GS-DG-TFET with ε_{ox2} =10.

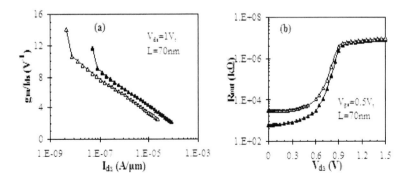

Fig. 11. (a) Device efficiency (g_m/I_{ds}) variation with I_{ds} (b) Output resistance R_{out} variation with V_{ds} for DGTFET with SiO$_2$ and Gate Stack architecture. Open symbols ($\triangle\triangle\triangle$) for DG-TFET with ε_{ox2} =3.9 Solid symbols ($\blacktriangle\blacktriangle\blacktriangle$) for GS-DG-TFET with ε_{ox2} =10.

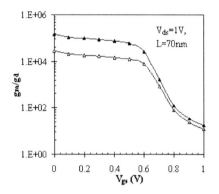

Fig. 12. Intrinsic dc gain (g_m/g_d) comparison for a DG-TFET and Gate Stack-DG-TFET. Open symbols (ΔΔΔ) for DG-TFET with ε_{ox2} =3.9 Solid symbols (▲▲▲) for GS-DG-TFET with ε_{ox2} =10.

The drain output resistance (fig. 11(a)) degrades at lower V_{ds} values for a GS-DGTFET as compared to without gate stack DG-TFET implying an increased effect of drain voltage at the source side due to the improved gate control over the channel.

As fig. 11 (b) shows, that the device efficiency has improved for higher drain current value (inversion regime) for Gate Stack architecture as compared to a low k dielectric (SiO_2) based DG-TFET. This improvement is also reflected in the intrinsic dc gain value (fig. 12) which has significantly improved for GS-DGTFET. This improvement is due to the enhanced current and Transconductance (g_m) due to the improvement of gate control introduced by gate stack.

4 Conclusion

The impact of temperature variation and introduction of Gate Stack architecture on the linearity and analog performance of a DG-TFET has been studied. It has been shown that TFETs are more immune to temperature variations in terms of its stable bias point selection based on achieving high dc gain value, which is an advantage as compared to DG-MOSFET in which the bias point chosen varies with temperature variations. The suppression of distortion is better in case of DG-TFET as compared to DG-MOSFET and they also offer a high drain output resistance (due to a lower DIBL effect) which does not significantly degrade even at high temperature range. Further improvement in terms of linearity and higher gain can also be obtained by using Gate Stack architecture.

Acknowledgment. Author (Rakhi Narang) would like to thank University Grants Commission (UGC), Government of India, for financially supporting this research work.

References

1. Nauta, B., Annema, A.-J.: Analog/RF Circuit Design Techniques for Nanometerscale IC Technologies. In: Proceedings of 31st European Solid-State Circuits Conference, ESSCIRC, pp. 45–53 (2005)
2. Zhang, Q., Seabaugh, A.: Can the Interband Tunnel FET Outperform Si CMOS? In: Proceedings of Device Research Conference, pp. 73–74 (2008)
3. Kim, S.H., Kam, H., Hu, C., Liu, T.J.K.: Germanium-source tunnel field effect transistors with record high ION/IOFF. In: Symposium on VLSI Technology, pp. 178–179 (2009)
4. Choi, W.Y., Park, B.G., Lee, J.D., Liu, T.K.: Tunneling field effect transistors (TFETs) with subthreshold swing (SS) less than 60 mV/dec. IEEE Electron Device Lett. 28, 743–745 (2007)
5. Mookerjea, S., Datta, S.: Comparative study of Si, Ge and InAs based steep subthreshold slope tunnel transistors for 0.25V supply voltage logic applications. In: Proceedings of 63rd Device Research Conference, pp. 47–48 (2008)
6. Born, M., Bhuwalka, K.K., Schindler, M., Abilene, U., Schmidt, M., Sulima, T., Eisele, I.: Tunnel FET: A CMOS Device for high Temperature Applications. In: 25th International Conference on Microelectronics, pp. 124–127 (2006)
7. Guo, P.-F., Yang, L.-T., Yang, Y., Fan, L., Han, G.-Q., Samudra, G.S., Yeo, Y.-C.: Tunneling Field-Effect Transistor: Effect of Strain and Temperature on Tunneling Current. IEEE Electron Device Letters 30, 981–983 (2009)
8. Wan, J., Royer, C.L., Zaslavsky, A., Cristoloveanu, S.: SOI TFETs: Suppression of ambipolar leakage and low-frequency noise behavior. In: Proceedings of the European Solid-State Device Research Conference (ESSDERC), pp. 341–344 (2010)
9. Nirschl, T., Wang, P.-F., Hansch, W., Schmitt-Landsiedel, D.: The tunneling field effect transistors (TFET): the temperature dependence, the simulation model, and its application. In: Proceedings of the 2004 International Symposium on Circuits and Systems, pp. 713–716 (2004)
10. Anghel, C., Chilagani, P., Amara, A., Vladimirescu, A.: Tunnel field effect transistor with increased ON current, low-k spacer and high-k dielectric. Applied Physics Letters 96, 122104 (2010)
11. Boucart, K., Ionescu, A.M.: Double-gate tunnel FET with high- k gate dielectric. IEEE Trans. Electron Devices 54(7), 1725–1733 (2007)
12. ATLAS Device Simulation Software, Silvaco Int., Version 5.14.0.R
13. Woerlee, P.H., Knitel, M.J., van Langevelde, R., Klaassen, D.B.M., Tiemeijer, L.F., Scholten, A.J., Zegers-van Duijnhoven, A.T.A.: RF-CMOS performance trends. IEEE Transactions on Electron Devices 48(8), 1776–1782 (2001)
14. Ma, W., Kaya, S.: Study of RF Linearity in sub-50nm MOSFETs using Simulations. Journal of Computational Electronics 2, 347–352 (2003)
15. Kaya, S., Ma, W., Asenov, A.: Design of DG-MOSFETs for High Linearity Performance. In: IEEE International SOI Conference, pp. 68–69 (2003)
16. Sze, S.M.: Physics of Semiconductor Devices. Wiley, New York (1981)

Channel Material Engineered Nanoscale Cylindrical Surrounding Gate MOSFET with Interface Fixed Charges

Rajni Gautam[1], Manoj Saxena[2], R.S. Gupta[3], and Mridula Gupta[1]

[1] Semiconductor Device Research Laboratory, Department Of Electronic Science,
University Of Delhi, South Campus, Benito Juarez Road, New Delhi, India
[2] Department Of Electronics, Deen Dayal Upadhyaya college,
University Of Delhi, Karampura, New Delhi, India
[3] Department Of Electronics and communication Engineering,
Maharaja Agrasen Institute Of Technology, Sector 22, Rohini, Delhi, India
rajni7986@gmail.com, saxena_manoj77@yahoo.co.in,
mridula@south.du.ac.in, rsgu@bol.net.in

Abstract. The paper presents a simulation study of effect of interface fixed charges on the performance of the Metal Semiconductor Field Effect Transistor (MESFET) for different channel materials (Si, GaAs and Ge). The objective of the present work is to study the effect of hot carrier induced fixed charges at the semiconductor-oxide interface of the nanoscale cylindrical surrounding gate (SRG) MOSFET. Also the circuit reliability issues of the device are discussed in terms of the performance degradation due to interface fixed interface charges and the performance has been compared for the three materials.

Keywords: ATLAS-3D, channel length modulation, hot carrier Effect, interface traps, fixed Charges, SRG MOSFET.

1 Introduction

Silicon technology is all pervasive and underpins the IT revolution that is now reshaping society. The technology keeps improving year on year as chip sizes are being continually reduced and transistor speeds increase. However as we reduce the dimensions SCEs cause several problems such as threshold voltage lowering, increased substrate bias effect while the narrow width transistors cause a decrease of current derivability and reliability degradation due to large fields. To continue the scaling of Si CMOS in the sub-65nm regime, innovative device structures and new materials have to be created in order to continue the historic progress in information processing and transmission. Examples of novel device structures being investigated are double gate or surround gate MOS and examples of novel materials are high mobility channel materials like strained Si, Ge and GaAs, high-k gate dielectrics and metal gate electrodes. As the semiconductor industry approaches the limits of traditional silicon CMOS scaling, introduction of performance boosters like novel materials and innovative device structures has become necessary for the future of

D.C. Wyld et al. (Eds.): NeCoM/WeST/WiMoN 2011, CCIS 197, pp. 476–485, 2011.
© Springer-Verlag Berlin Heidelberg 2011

CMOS. High mobility materials are being considered to replace Si in the channel to achieve higher drive currents and switching speeds. Ge [1]-[2] has particularly become of great interest as a channel material, owing to its high bulk hole and electron mobilities. MOSFETs based on III-V semiconductors promise to combine III-V high frequency performance with scalability and integration known from silicon. GaAs MOSFET technology is used where high RF power is required at low voltage and high efficiency, i.e. wireless and mobile products. The technology also have a unique advantage in regard to integration of RF power, switching, and power control functions. This is of interest where integration lowers cost and enables new functionality. GaAs MOSFET [3]-[4] has many advantages over Silicon MOSFET such as higher electron mobility, shorter transit time, higher resistivity. But as GaAs has no native oxide thereby it limits the voltage that can be applied to the gate. Also, GaAs has lower thermal conductance. Besides the channel material engineering in order to overcome scaling limitations several novel geometrical device structures were proposed. One such structure is the surrounding cylindrical gate MOSFET where gate has greater influence over the channel potential and reduces the short channel effects and improves subthreshold slope [5]. Several papers have been reported on analytical modeling of SRG MOSFET [6]-[8]. Device aging is becoming a big problem for the optimum performance of the recent age devices. There are many factors responsible for device aging problems: (1)hot carrier induced damage, (2) stress induced damage, (3) damage caused by the processing techniques at different levels. The degradation of short-channel MOSFET characteristics due to the injection of hot carriers into the gate oxide stands as one of the most important challenges to further progress of device down-scaling [9]-[11]. The device aging induced by hot-electron injection is summarized in the formation of a narrow defective interface region. The interface trap or oxide-trapped charges which exist at the semiconductor-oxide interface can be transformed into equivalent interface fixed charges Recently hot carrier effect has been studied in SOI MOSFET [12] and pi-gate p-MOSFET [13]. F.Djeffal et al. studied the effects of hot carrier induced interface fixed interface charges for DG and Gate All Around (GAA) MOSFET [14]. Yu et al. [15] proposed an analytical model for Surrounding gate MOSFET with interface fixed charges using ECPE approach. In this paper three different channel materials i.e. Si, Ge and GaAs have been used to compare the performance of the nanoscale cylindrical SRG MOSFET in two cases: damaged and undamaged device. The effect of interface fixed charges on the device characteristics (Potential, Drain current, Transconductance,) has been analyzed by extensive simulation using ATLAS 3-D device simulator [16].

2 Simulation Results

The interface near the drain side is susceptible to strongest electric field and the high field-induced hot carriers will create permanent damage. As the interface traps appears at the semiconductor-oxide interface, it is known that it will accept an electron if the trap level is located beneath the fermi level for an acceptor-type interface trap. In this situation, it acts as a fixed negative charge. Similarly for a donor type interface trap it acts as fixed positive interface charge. Therefore, hot carrier induced interface traps can be transformed into equivalent interface fixed charges.

Nanoscale surrounding cylindrical gate MOSFET with interface interface fixed charges has been simulated using ATLAS-3D device simulator [14] and the models activated in simulation comprise field dependent mobility, concentration dependent mobility model along with the Shockley– Read–Hall (SRH) models for minority carrier recombination. All the simulations have been performed at room temperature. The schematic cross section of the structure with interface fixed charges is shown in Fig.1. Channel has divided into two regions, i.e.L_2 (length of damaged region) and L_1 (damage free part i.e. $L-L_2$).

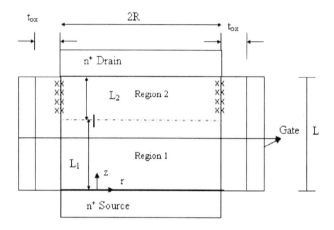

Fig. 1. Schematic cross section of the simulated Nanowire MOSFET structure. Other parameters Channel Length (L)=70 nm, Length of damaged region (L_2)=35nm, Oxide thickness (t_{ox})=1.5 nm, Radius of Silicon pillar (R=t_{si}/2)=15nm, Source/Drain doping (N_d)=1x10^{26}m^{-3}, Substrate Doping (N_a)=1x10^{21}m^{-3}.

There is a band banding due to the work function difference between the metal and the semiconductor in MOS device. Fixed charges at the interface causes additional band bending under the gate which in turn causes change in flat band voltage in the damaged region. Thus surface potential is lowered (raised) in case of negative (positive) interface fixed charges in the damaged region w.r.t the undamaged device as shown in fig.2. It can be shown that minimum surface potential and its position remains nearly unchanged for positive fixed charges but it gets shifted towards drain side for negative fixed charges. Fig.3 shows the surface potential when the fixed charges are located near the source side for all the three materials. In case of fixed charges present near the source side minimum potential and its position is changed (unchanged) for positive (negative) interface fixed charges. Also positive (negative) fixed charges provides screening to the undamaged region from the higher V_{ds} effects in case of fixed charges are present near the drain (source) side just as in case of DMG structure. Thus minimum surface potential and its position changes and induces a shift in the threshold voltage. Although magnitude of surface potential is different because of the different values of semiconductor work function for the three materials but the change in surface potential due to fixed charges is same as it depends only on the oxide properties (relative permittivity and thickness) and the density of fixed charges.

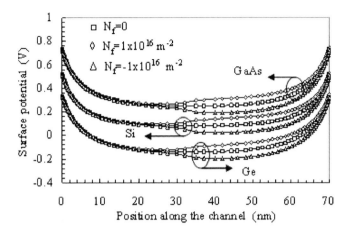

Fig. 2. Surface Potential as a function of distance along the channel when fixed charges are located at the drain side. Other parameters are: t_{ox} =1.5 nm, R=15nm, N_d =1x10^{26} m^{-3}, N_a=1x10^{21} m^{-3}, V_{gs}=0V, V_{ds}=0V, L_1=L_2=L/2.

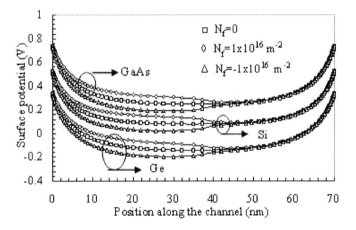

Fig. 3. Surface Potential as a function of distance along the channel when fixed charges are located at source side. Other parameters are: t_{ox} =1.5 nm, R=15nm, N_d =1x10^{26} m^{-3}, N_a=1x10^{21} m^{-3}, V_{gs}=0V, V_{ds}=0V, L_1=L_2=L/2.

All the three devices i.e. Si, Ge and GaAs SRG MOSFETs have been optimized to have same threshold voltage (i.e. V_{th}= 0.3V) by adjusting the metal work function so as to compare their performance in terms of degradation caused due to interface fixed charges. Fig.4 and 5 shows the effect of fixed charges on the transfer characteristics. Performance is compared taking Si as the reference. It clearly shows that the among the three channel materials GaAs shows highest current driving capability then Ge followed by Si. Its because of higher mobility. Also the drain current degradation is there for damaged device. Although drain current is increased (decreased) for positive (negative) interface fixed charges in all regions i.e. subthreshold, linear and saturation but the order of change in off current is greater than the on current. Thus overall effect

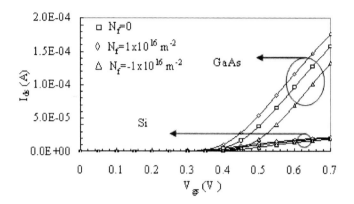

Fig. 4. Drain current as a function of gate to source voltage for Si and GaAs. Other parameters are: t_{ox} =1.5 nm, R =15nm, N_d =1x10^{26} m^{-3}, N_a=1x10^{21} m^{-3}, L_1=L_2=L/2, V_{ds}=0.05V.

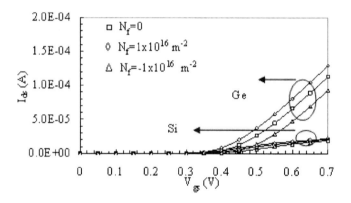

Fig. 5. Drain current as a function of gate to source voltage for Si and Ge. Other parameters are: t_{ox} =1.5 nm, R =15nm, N_d =1x10^{26} m^{-3}, N_a=1x10^{21} m^{-3}, L_1=L_2=L/2, V_{ds}=0.05V.

is enhanced I_{on}/I_{off} ratio in case of negative fixed charges and reduced I_{on}/I_{off} ration in case of positive fixed charges. Fig. 6 shows the I_{on}/I_{off} ration for all cases i.e. all three materials both undamaged and damaged device.

Fig. 7 and 8 illustrate the I_{ds}-V_{ds} characteristics of the device in inversion region i.e. at V_{gs}=0.6V. Taking Si as the reference it can be shown that GaAs shows better output characteristics. Important observation here is the increase in drain current with drain bias and a reduction of output resistance in saturation region. This is due to the CLM effect i.e. shortening the length of the channel region at higher drain bias. This variation in drain current can be better understood by studying the early voltage. Fig. 9, 10 and 11 illustrate the impact of fixed charges on the early voltage for Si, GaAs and Ge respectively. As can be seen from the figures Si has the highest early voltage and Ge has the lowest. Thus Si has better immunity against CLM effect. Also positive (negative) fixed charges lead to enhanced (reduced) early voltage because of the screening effect provided by the damaged region to the undamaged region.

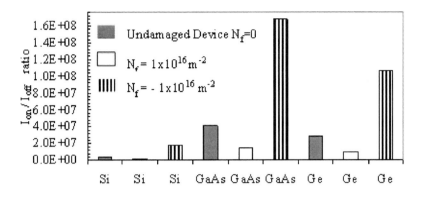

Fig. 6. I_{on}/I_{off} ratio for all materials. Other parameters are: t_{ox} =1.5 nm, R=15nm, N_d =1x10^{26}m^{-3}, N_a=1x10^{21} m^{-3}, L=70nm, N_f=± 1x10^{16} m^{-2}, L_1=L_2=L/2, V_{ds}=0.05V.

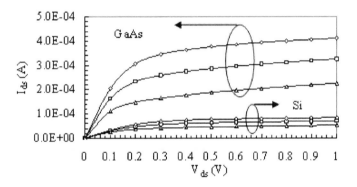

Fig. 7. Drain current as a function of drain to source voltage for Si and GaAs. Other parameters are: t_{ox} =1.5 nm, R =15nm, N_d =1x10^{26} m^{-3}, N_a=1x10^{21} m^{-3}, L_1=L_2=L/2, V_{gs}=0.6V.

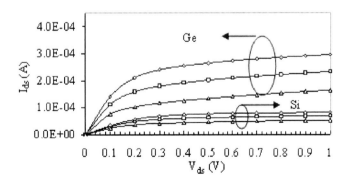

Fig. 8. Drain current as a function of drain to source voltage for Si and Ge. Other parameters are: t_{ox} =1.5 nm, R =15nm, N_d =1x10^{26} m^{-3}, N_a=1x10^{21} m^{-3}, L_1=L_2=L/2, V_{gs}=0.6V.

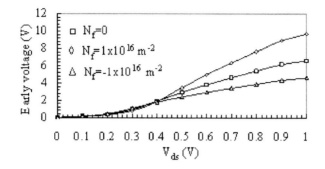

Fig. 9. Early voltage as a function of drain to source voltage for Si. Other parameters are: t_{ox} =1.5 nm, R=15nm, N_d =1x10²⁶ m⁻³, N_a=1x10²¹ m⁻³, L_1=L_2=L/2, V_{gs}=0.6V.

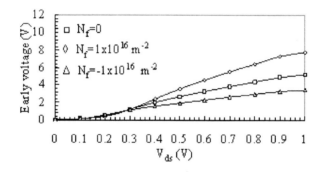

Fig. 10. Early voltage as a function of drain to source voltage for GaAs. Other parameters are: t_{ox} =1.5 nm, R =15nm, N_d =1x10²⁶ m⁻³, N_a=1x10²¹ m⁻³, L_1=L_2=L/2, V_{gs}=0.6V.

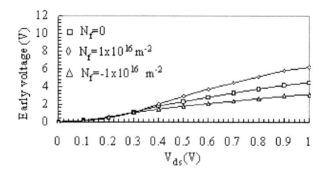

Fig. 11. Early voltage as a function of drain to source voltage for Ge. Other parameters are: t_{ox} =1.5 nm, R =15nm, N_d =1x10²⁶ m⁻³, N_a=1x10²¹ m⁻³, L_1=L_2=L/2, V_{gs}=0.6V.

Gain of any device is given by its transconductance and peak of transconductance curve gives the optimum bias point if device is used to be as an amplifier. Fig.12 and 13 shows the impact of interface fixed charges on the transconductance of the device.

As can be seen positive (negative) fixed charges result in enhanced (reduced) transconductance in subthreshold and weak inversion regions. Also the peak of the transconductance curve shifts towards lower (higher) Vgs values. This has a serious impact on the circuit reliability of the device since it changes the bias point of the device. Also GaAs (Si) has the highest (lowest) transconductance and hence highest (lowest) gain among the three channel materials used.

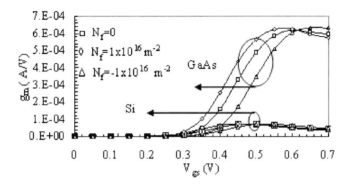

Fig. 12. Transconductance as a function of gate to source voltage for Si and GaAs. Other parameters are: t_{ox} =1.5 nm, R =15nm, N_d =1x10^{26} m^{-3}, N_a=1x10^{21}m^{-3}, L_1=L_2=L/2, V_{ds}=0.05V.

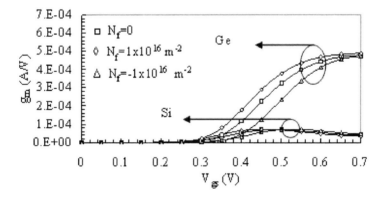

Fig. 13. Transconductance as a function of gate to source voltage for Si and Ge. Other parameters are: t_{ox} =1.5 nm, R =15nm, N_d =1x10^{26} m^{-3}, N_a=1x10^{21}m^{-3}, L_1=L_2=L/2, V_{ds}=0.05V.

3 Conclusion

Impact of hot carrier induced/stress induced/process damage induced interface fixed charges has been studied for three channel materials Si, Ge and GaAs optimized to have same threshold voltage. Presence of fixed charges at semiconductor-oxide interface causes a step in the potential profile which results in the shift of threshold voltage, degradation of drain current and gain of the device. In terms of current driving capability and gain, GaAs is found to be a better material then Ge and Si.

Acknowledgement

Thanks are due to University Grants Commission (UGC), Government of India for necessary financial assistance to carry out this research work.

References

[1] Saraswat, K.C., Chui, C.O., Krishnamohan, T., Nayfeh, A., McIntyre, P.: Ge based high performance nanoscale MOSFETs. Microelectronic Engineering 80, 15–21 (2005)

[2] Wang, D., Wang, Q., Javey, A., Tu, R., Dai, H., Kim, H., McIntyre, P.C., Krishnamohan, T., Saraswat, K.C.: Germanium nanowire field-effect transistors with SiO2 and high-k HfO2 gate dielectrics. Applied Physics Letters 83, 2432–2434 (2003)

[3] Wu, J.-Y., Wang, H.-H., Wang, Y.-H., Houng, M.-P.: GaAs MOSFET's Fabrication with a Selective Liquid Phase Oxidized Gate. IEEE Transactions on Electron Devices 48(4) (April 2001)

[4] Passlack, M., Droopad, R., Rajagopalan, K., Abrokwah, J., Zurcher, P.: High Mobility III-V Mosfet Technology. In: Cs Mantech Conference, Austin, Texas, USA, May 14-17 (2007)

[5] Colinge, J.P.: Multiple-gate SOI MOSFETs. Solid State Electronics 48(6), 897–905 (2004)

[6] He, J., Zhang, X., Zhang, G., Chan, M., Wang, Y.: A carrier-based analytic DCIV model for long channel undoped cylindrical surrounding-gate MOSFETs. Solid State Electronics 50(3), 416–421 (2006)

[7] Yu, B., Yuan, Y., Song, J., Taur, Y.: A Two-Dimensional Analytical Solution for Short-Channel Effects in Nanowire MOSFETs. IEEE Transactions on Electron Devices 56(10), 2357–2362 (2009)

[8] Chiang, T.K.: A new compact subthreshold behavior model for dual-material surrounding gate (DMSG) MOSFETs. Solid State Electronics 53(5), 490–496 (2009)

[9] Ng, K.K., Taylor, G.W.: Effects of hot-carrier trapping in n- and p-channel MOSFET's. IEEE Transactions on Electron Devices ED-30, 871–876 (1983)

[10] Bracchitta, J., Honan, T.L., Anderson, R.L.: Hot-electron-induced degradation in MOSFET's at 77 K. IEEE Transactions on Electron Devices ED-32(9), 1850–1857 (1985)

[11] Hofmann, K.R., Werner, C., Weber, W., Dorda, G.: Hot-electron and hole emission effects in short-channel MOSFET's. IEEE Transactions on Electron Devices ED-32(3), 691–699 (1985)

[12] Jang, S.J., Ka, D.H., Yu, C.G., Cho, W.J., Park, J.T.: Hot-carrier effects as a function of silicon film thickness in nanometer-scale SOI pMOSFETs. Solid State Electronics 52(5), 824–829 (2008)

[13] Lee, C.W., Ferain, I., Afzalian, A., Yan, R., Dehdashti, N., Razavi, P., Colinge, J.P., Park, J.T.: NBTI and hot-carrier effects in accumulation-mode Pi-gate pMOSFETs. In: Proceedings of 20th European Symposium on the Reliability of Electron Devices, Failure Physics and Analysis, Microelectronics Reliability, vol. 49(9-11), pp. 1044–1047 (September-November 2009)

[14] Djeffal, F., Ghoggali, Z., Dibi, Z., Lakhdar, N.: Analytical analysis of nanoscale multiple gate MOSFETs including effects of hot-carrier induced interface charges. Microelectronics Reliability 49(4), 377–381 (2009)

[15] Yu, Y.S., Cho, N., Hwang, S.W., Ahn, D.: Analytical Threshold Voltage Model Including Effective Conducting Path Effect (ECPE) for Surrounding-Gate MOSFETs (SGMOSFETs) With Interface fixed Charges. IEEE Transactions on Electron Devices 57(11), 3176–3180 (2010)
[16] ATLAS User's Manual: 3-D Device Simulator, SILVACO International, Version 5.14.0.R (2010)

FPGA Implementation of Braun's Multiplier Using Spartan-3E, Virtex – 4, Virtex-5 and Virtex-6

R. Anitha and V. Bagyaveereswaran

VIT University, Vellore, India
eranitharavi@gmail.com,
vbagyaveereswaran@vit.ac.in

Abstract. The developing an Application Specific Integrated Circuits (ASICs) will cost very high, the circuits should be proved and then it would be optimized before implementation. Multiplication which is the basic building block for several DSP processors, Image processing and many other. The Braun multipliers can easily be implemented using Field Programmable Gate Array (FPGA) devices. This research presented the comparative study of Spartan-3E, Virtex-4, Virtex-5 and Virtex-6 Low Power FPGA devices. The implementation of Braun multipliers and its bypassing techniques is done using Verilog HDL. We are proposing that adder block which we implemented our design (fast addition) and we compared the results of that so that our proposed method is effective when compare to the conventional design. There is the reduction in the resources like delay LUTs, number of slices used. Results are showed and it is verified using the Spartan-3E, Virtex-4 and Virtex-5 devices. The Virtex-5 FPGA has shown the good performance as compared to Spartan-3E and Virtex-4 FPGA devices.

Keywords: Digital Signal Processing (DSP), Field Programmable Gate Array (FPGA), fast addition, Spartan-3E, truncated multiplier, Verilog HDL, Virtex-4, Virtex-5, Virtex – 6 Low power.

1 Introduction

Multiplication – an important fundamental function in arithmetic operation. Currently implemented in many DSP applications such as FFT, Filtering etc., and usually contribute significantly to time delay and take up a great deal of silicon area in DSP system. Now – a – days time is still an important issue for the determination of the instruction cycle time of the DSP chip. Both the multiplication and the DSP play a vital role in the implementation of VLSI system.

Multiplication – Repeated addition of n – bits will give the solution for the multiplication. ie. Multi-operand addition process. The multi – operand addition process needs two n – bit operands. It can be realized in n- cycles of shifting and adding. This can be performed by using parallel or serial methods. This will be simple to implement in two's complement representation, since they are independent of the signs. It is advantageous to exploit other number systems to improve speed and reduce the chip area and power consumption.

D.C. Wyld et al. (Eds.): NeCoM/WeST/WiMoN 2011, CCIS 197, pp. 486–494, 2011.
© Springer-Verlag Berlin Heidelberg 2011

Generally multiplications can be carried out in all the types of number system. The one which carried out for the Binary number system is the Digital Multiplier.

A **Field-programmable Gate Array** (**FPGA**) is an integrated circuit designed to be configured by the customer or designer after manufacturing. Field Programmable means that the FPGA's function is defined by a user's program rather than by the manufacturer of the device. A typical integrated circuit performs a particular function defined at the time of manufacture. In contrast, the FPGA's function is defined by a program written by someone other than the device manufacturer. Depending on the particular device, the program is either 'burned' in permanently or semi-permanently as part of a board assembly process, or is loaded from an external memory each time the device is powered up. This user programmability gives the user access to complex integrated designs without the high engineering costs associated with application specific integrated circuits (ASIC).

2 Braun Multipliers

It is a simple parallel multiplier generally called as carry save array multiplier. It has been restricted to perform signed bits. The structure consists of array of AND gates and adders arranged in the iterative manner and no need of logic registers. This can be called as non – addictive multipliers. **Architecture:**

An n*n bit Braun multiplier [9] & [10] is constructed with n (n-1) adders and n^2 AND gates as shown in the fig.1, where,

X: 4-bit multiplicand

Y: 4-bit multiplier

P: 8-bit product of X and Y

$P_n = X_iY_j$ is a product bit

The internal structure of the full adder can be realized using FPGA. Each products can be generated in parallel with the AND gates. Each partial product can be added with the sum of partial product which has previously produced by using the row of adders. The carry out will be shifted one bit to the left or right and then it will be added to the sum which is generated by the first adder and the newly generated partial product.

The shifting would carry out with the help of Carry Save Adder (CSA) and the Ripple carry adder should be used for the final stage of the output. Braun multiplier performs well for the unsigned operands that are less than 16 bits in terms of speed, power and area. But it is simple structure when compared to the other multipliers. The main drawback of this multiplier is that the potential susceptibility of Glitching problem due to the Ripple Carry Adder in the last stage. The delay depends on the delay of the Full Adder and also a final adder in the last. The power and area can also be reduced by using two bypassing techniques called **Row bypassing technique (fig. 2) [4 & 3]** and **Column bypassing technique (fig. 3) [4]**.

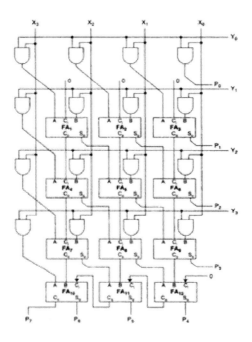

Fig. 1. Braun Muliplier

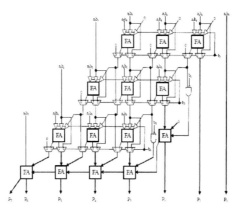

Fig. 2. 4*4 row bypassing

In this paper we have simulated and synthesized the Braun's multiplier and the bypassing multipliers (row bypassing and column bypassing) and then we compare the results of the multipliers. The objective of this study is to present a comparative study of Braun's multiplier and bypassing technique using Spartan-3E, Virtex-4, Virtex-5 and Virtex 6 low power FPGA devices.

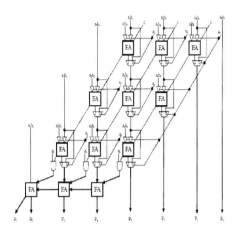

Fig. 3. 4*4 column bypassing

3   Proposed Method

The Braun's Multiplier (fig. 1) which uses the full adder block adding the PP. in the proposed method we have used the fast addition [9] method so that we are reducing the number of slices, LUTs, and the delay is getting reduced. The fig. 4 which shows the proposed method of the Braun's multiplier.

In the proposed method the number of LUTs, slices are reduced and mainly the delay has been very less when compare to the conventional method. The table.1 will give the comparison result of the all the methods which is simulated and synthesized and tested in the FPGA boards.

The Row bypassing and the Column bypassing method also simulated and synthesized by using the proposed method. Table 1 will show the result of those multipliers.

4   Implementation Using Spartan 3e, Virtex 4, Virtex 5 and Virtex 6 Low Power FPGA Devices [11]

4.1   FPGA Design and Implementation Results

The design of standard, row bypassing, column bypassing and the proposed 4×4 multipliers are simulated and synthesis using Verilog HDL and implemented in the Xilinx Spartan – 3E (xc3s500e-4ft256), Virtex – 4 (xc4vlx15-10-sf363), Virtex – 5 (xc5vlx30-1-ff324), and Virtex – 6 ((xc6vlx75tl-1L-ff484) FPGAs using the Xilinx ISE 12.4 design tool and as well as simulated using the Design Architect tool of Mentor Graphics.

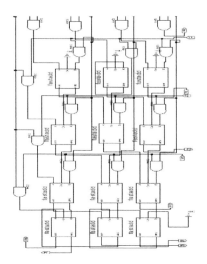

Fig. 4. Proposed 4*4 Braun's Multiplier

Table 1. FPGA resource utilization for standard, row and column bypassing and proposed 4*4 multiplier for Spartan-3E (xc3s500e-4ft256)

Multipliers	% of No. of LUTs	% of No. of Slices	% of bonded IOBs 190	Combinational delay (ns)	Average pin delay (ns)
	9,312	4,656			
Standard Braun's Multiplier	36	22	16	21.224	7.555
Row bypassing	33	21	15	22.340	6.506
Column bypassing	33	20	16	24.757	6.570
Proposed multiplier	31	21	13	20.757	6.444

Table 2. FPGA resource utilization for standard, row and column bypassing and proposed 4*4 multiplier for Virtex – 4(xc4vlx15-10-sf363)

Multipliers	% of No. of LUTs	% of No. of Slices 6144	% of bonded IOBs 240	Combinational path delay (ns)	Average pin delay (ns)
	12288				
Standard Braun's Multiplier	31	19	16	20.726	6.691
Row bypassing	31	17	14	18.786	6.021
Column bypassing	32	17	15	19.112	6.634
Proposed multiplier	28	16	16	19.43	6.1

Table 3. FPGA resource utilization for standard, row and column bypassing and proposed 4*4 multiplier for Virtex – 5(xc5vlx30-1-ff324)

Multipliers	% of No. of LUTs 19200	% of No. of Slices 4800	% of bonded IOBs 220	Combinational path delay (ns)	Average pin delay (ns)
Standard Braun's Multiplier	29	18	14	17.670	6.873
Row bypassing	29	16	15	19.647	6.334
Column bypassing	28	15	13	16.008	6.1
Proposed multiplier	27	15	14	15.967	5.656

Table 4. FPGA resource utilization for standard, row and column bypassing and proposed 4*4 multiplier for Virtex – 6 Low power (xc6vlx75tl-1L-ff484)

Multipliers	% of No. of LUTs 46560	% of No. of Slices 46560	% of bonded IOBs 240	Combinational path delay (ns)	Average pin delay (ns)
Standard Braun's Multiplier	25	16	14	16.87	6.890
Row bypassing	24	15	12	13.543	6.023
Column bypassing	21	13	12	15.76	5.784
Proposed multiplier	19	12	13	9.214	4.032

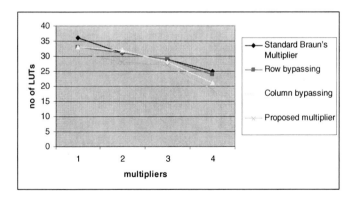

Fig. 5. The LUTs for Spartan-3AN, Virtex-4, Virtex - 5 and Virtex-6 for standard, row and column bypassing and proposed 4*4 Braun's multipliers

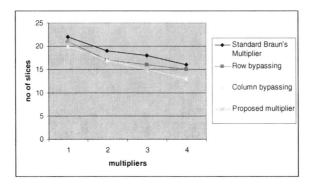

Fig. 6. The Slices for Spartan-3AN, Virtex-4, Virtex - 5 and Virtex-6 for standard, row and column bypassing and proposed 4*4 Braun's multipliers

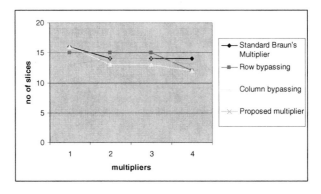

Fig. 7. The bonded IOBs for Spartan-3AN, Virtex-4, Virtex - 5 and Virtex-6 for standard, row and column bypassing and proposed 4*4 Braun's multipliers

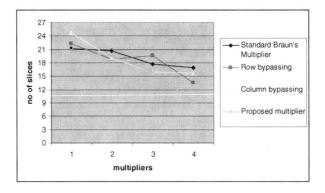

Fig. 8. The combinational path delay for Spartan-3AN, Virtex-4, Virtex - 5 and Virtex-6 for standard, row and column bypassing and proposed 4*4 Braun's multipliers

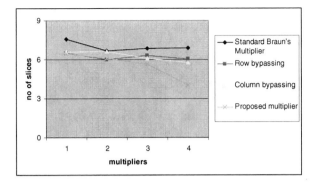

Fig. 9. The average pin delay for Spartan-3AN, Virtex-4, Virtex - 5 and Virtex-6 for standard, row and column bypassing and proposed 4*4 Braun's multipliers

Table 1-4 summarize the FPGA devices resources utilization for standard, row and column bypassing and proposed 4*4 Braun's multipliers.

Figure 5 shows the comparison of number of LUTs for Spartan-3E, Virtex-4, Virtex - 5 and Virtex-6 FPGA devices for standard, row and column bypassing and proposed 4*4 Braun's multipliers, which clearly indicates that the virtex-6 FPGA device utilizes fewer resources than Spartan-3E, Virtex-4, and Virtex - 5 devices.

The number of slices and the bonded IOBs are compared in the fig. 6 and fig. 7, the figure clearly shows that Virtex 6 has the less percentage of among all the FPGAs.

The table 1 -4 is showing the comparison result of the total combinational path delay of the multipliers and the graph has been plotted as shown in the fig. 8. It shows that Virtex -6 showing the less delay so that speed of the multiplier can increase. And the fig. 9 showing that the average timing delay between the pins which is used in the multipliers.

5 Conclusion

In this paper we have presented the hardware implementation of the Multipliers in the FPGA devices using Verilog HDL. The design was implemented on the Xilinx Spartan – 3E (xc3s500e-4ft256), Virtex – 4 (xc4vlx15-10-sf363), Virtex – 5 (xc5vlx30-1-ff324), and Virtex – 6 ((xc6vlx75tl-1L-ff484) FPGAs. The proposed Multiplier shows that reduced utilization when compare to all other multipliers. The average pin delay and combinational path delay has been reduced in the Virtex – 6 Low power FPGA device. So the Virtex – 6 Low power is obtained the best result when compare to the other FPGA devices. And it is feasible for the DSP Processor, Image processing and multimedia technology.

6 Future Work

Braun Multiplier can be modified using the 2- dimensional bypassing technique which will give the best result then the proposed one which is given in the paper. And the adder cell can be replaced with the Kogge Stone adder/non linear carry select adder can be designed using the RTL complier where we can draw the layout and then validation can also be done.

References

1. Rais, M.H.: Hardware Implementation of Truncated Multipliers Using Spartan-3AN, Virtex-4 and Virtex-5 FPGA Devices. Am. J. Engg. & Applied Sci. 3(1), 201–206 (2010)
2. Ashour, M.A., Saleh, H.I.: An FPGA implementation guide for some different types of serial–parallel multiplier structures. Microelectronics Journal 31, 161–168 (2000)
3. Yan, J.T., Chen, Z.W.: Low-power multiplier design with row and column bypassing. In: IEEE International SOC Conference, pp. 227–230 (2009)
4. Yan, J.T., Chen, Z.W.: Low-Cost Low- Power Bypassing-Based Multiplier Design. IEEE, Los Alamitos (2010)
5. Wen, M.C., Wang, S.J., Lin, Y.M.: Low power parallel multiplier with column bypassing. In: IEEE International Symposium on Circuits and Systems, pp. 1638–1641 (2005)
6. Mangal, S.K., Badghare, R.M., Deshmukh, R.B., Patrikar, R.M.: FPGA Implementation of Low Power Parallel Multiplier. In: 20th International Conference on VLSI Design (VLSID 2007). IEEE, Los Alamitos (2007)
7. Hwang, Y.-T., Lin, J.-F., Sheu, M.-H., Sheu, C.-J.: Low Power Multipliers Using Enhenced Row Bypassing Schemes. IEEE, Los Alamitos (2007)
8. Weste, N.H.E., Harris, D., Banerjee, A.: CMOS VLSI Design, A circuits and system perspective. Pearson Education, London (2009)
9. Yeo, K.-S., Roy, K.: Low Voltage, Low Power VLSI Subsystems. TMC (2009)
10. Wanhannar, L.: DSP Integrated Circuits. Academic Press, London
11. http://www.xilinx.com
12. Chen, K.: Types of adders. M. Eng. Project_2005

A Novel Approach towards BDD Generation and CNF Conversion for Half Adder

Deepak Kumar Verma[*] and Pankaj Srivastava

ABV- Indian Institute of Information Technology and Management (ABV-IIITM),
Gwalior 474010, India
deepak20.verma@gmail.com, pankajs@iiitm.ac.in

Abstract. We have proposed a method for generation of Binary Decision Diagram (BDD). This approach follows Depth First Search (DFS) which is based upon the traversal of data structure. This approach is applied on data structure which is actually stored in the form of bits. To analyze results of the program for generating BDD, we have traversed BDD in the form of DFS. Conjunctive Normal Form (CNF) summarizes the logic function of the circuit which tells about how much literals are needed and by these literals understanding of circuit will be obtained. CNF also controls that out of all literals which one(s) will be enough for finding the true output. Our result revealed that it is a better approach for generating BDD from the implementation done for half adder. While for CNF that is obtained through conventional approach, the results are satisfactory.

Keywords: BDD, CNF, DFS.

1 Introduction

Generation of BDD for circuit is being done by various approaches and it also used to reduce the size of the representation of the combinational circuit. It has been proposed that use of BDD can be used to express combinational circuit which seems very effective. In the recent years, the theory for BDD has been improved [1-3] which made a great impact on generation of BDD.

BDDs are extensively used in various softwares, for example CAD software to synthesize circuit (also called logic synthesis) and also in formal verification [4]. These software's are broadly used for various graph of the circuit to test synthesizes [5]. There are several lesser known applications of BDD, including fault tree analysis. Every arbitrary BDD [6-8], even if it is not reduced or ordered can be directly implemented by replacing each node with a 2 to 1 multiplexer; each multiplexer can be directly implemented by a 4-LUT in a field programmable gate array (FPGA). It is not so simple to convert from an arbitrary network of logic gates to a BDD. The size of the BDD is determined by both the function being represented and the chosen ordering of the variables.

---

[*] Corresponding author.

D.C. Wyld et al. (Eds.): NeCoM/WeST/WiMoN 2011, CCIS 197, pp. 495–499, 2011.
© Springer-Verlag Berlin Heidelberg 2011

For BDD to CNF conversion, CNF shows we can also express the combinational circuit in term of propositional logic. This propositional logic can be compressed (or say it can be reduced). Every propositional formula can be converted into an equivalent formula in CNF. This transformation is based on rules about logical equivalences: the double negative law, De Morgan's laws, and the distributive law.

In this paper, BDD is being generated for half adder separately for SUM and CARRY part. Then expression for BDD is being used as an input for converting to CNF. The programming methodology is being used for both BDD generation and CNF clauses conversion [9]. We have used logic for programming which follows DFS showing complexity logarithmically.

2 Preliminary Ideas

2.1 BDD

BDD [6-7] is a directed acyclic graph with a root vertex G= (V, E), where V is the vertex set, and E is the edge set. There are two types of vertexes: terminal vertexes and non-terminal vertexes. A non-terminal vertex is represented by a circle containing the index with the two children indicated by branches labeled 0 (low) and 1 (high). A terminal vertex is represented by a square containing the value. E set is made up of the branches from the father vertexes to the children vertexes. For a Boolean function depending upon the ordering of the variables we would end up with getting a graph whose number of nodes would be linear at the best and exponential at the worst case. Then variable ordering of BDD is also known as Ordered Binary Decision Diagram (OBDD) [10], which is mostly not solvable in given polynomial time. A Reduced Ordered Binary Decision Diagram (ROBDD) is an ordered BDD where each node represents a distinct Boolean expression.

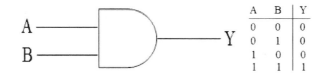

Fig. 1. AND gate and its truth table

Nowadays these BDD are in more reliable form than earlier it was known as Phase Mission System (PMS) [11-12]. PMS is defined as a system subject to multiple, consecutive, non-overlapping phases of operation. During each phase, the PMS has to accomplish a specified task. Thus, the system configuration, failure criterion, and/or failure behavior can change from phase to phase.

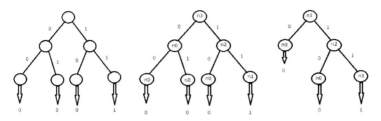

Fig. 2. Various phase of BDD reduction of AND gate

Figure 2 shows an example of BDD reduction for AND gate firstly BDD is generated as per the operation perform by AND gate. Then all nodes in graph has been assigned node number and after that BDD has reduced due to reason that output of the both child of left sub-tree is having same output.

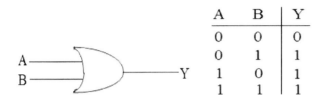

A	B	Y
0	0	0
0	1	1
1	0	1
1	1	1

Fig. 3. OR gate and its truth table

In figure 4 we have shown the example of BDD reduction for OR gate same as for AND gate was done. In this case, reduction is done on right sub-tree.

2.2   CNF

In Boolean logic, a formula is in CNF if it is a conjunction of clauses, where a clause is a disjunction of literals. Literal and its complement cannot appear in the same clause. CNF are generated by converting clauses [9, 13]. As a normal form, it is useful in automated theorem proving. It is similar to the canonical Product Of Sum (POS) form used in circuit theory.

All conjunction of literals and all disjunction of literals are in CNF, as they can be seen as conjunctions of one-literal clauses and conjunctions of a single clause, respectively.

As in the Disjunctive Normal Form (DNF), the only propositional connectives formula in CNF can contain are   'and', 'or', and 'not'. The not operator can only be used as part of a literal, which means that it can only precede the propositional variable.

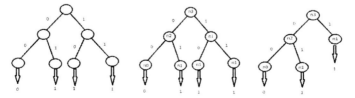

Fig. 4. Various phase of BDD reduction of OR gate

Example of some formulas which are CNF

    I.   ~A ∧ (B ∨ C)
    II.   (A ∨ B) ∧ (~B ∨ C ∨ ~D)∧(D ∨ E)
    III. ~B ∧ ~C
    IV. (A ∨ C) ∧ (B ∨ C)

Since all logical formulae can be converted into an equivalent formula in CNF, proofs are often based on the assumption that all formulae are CNF. However, in some cases, this conversion to CNF can lead to an exponential explosion of the formula. For example, translating the following non-CNF formula into CNF produces a formula with 2^n clauses:

$$(X_1 \wedge Y_1) \vee (X_2 \wedge Y_2) \vee \ldots \ldots \vee (X_n \wedge Y_n)$$

Above formula contain 2^n clauses with each of the clauses contains either X or Y or both. CNF are actually used for expressing true part of function or logic function of the combinational circuit. This is the main reason why the CNF conversions are done.

3 Results and Discussion

We have implemented in C++ to generate BDD and also conversion from logic function to CNF for the half adder. BDD is generated separately for the SUM(S) and CARRY(C) part of the half adder. The output of the program is in the BFS order such that for figure 2 the order at which the output for BDD will be n3, n0, n2, n0, n0, n0, n1. Order is being written from left to right. This order shows how BDD data structure of the circuit is done.

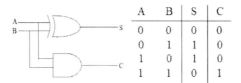

A	B	S	C
0	0	0	0
0	1	1	0
1	0	1	0
1	1	0	1

Fig. 5. Half Adder and its truth table

And for the CARRY part referring to figure 2 which shows carry of half adder and we know carry is equivalent to output of two inputs AND gate.

For CNF conversion

Input given   ((a ∧ ~b) ∨ (~a ∧ b))

Output (((a ∨ a) ∧ (b ∨ a)) ∧ ((a ∨ b) ∧ (b ∨ b)))

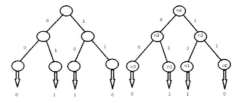

Fig. 6. Various phases for BDD reduction of SUM of half adder

For CNF the input was given dynamically. Respective CNF for the given expression of sum and carry was for CNF. Mainly CNF summarizes the logic function of the circuit which tells about how much literals are needed to describe the circuit. These CNF can be used in automated theorem also.

4 Conclusion

We have implemented half adder for the generation of BDD and converted BDD logic expression to CNF. Both BDD generation and CNF conversion have been implemented in C++. We have adopted an extensive approach to generate BDD and CNF taking half adder to generate smaller CNF and BDD in efficient way. Keeping in mind a large scope in this area, we are planning to do some work in test pattern generation for extending this paper work and also we are looking for some improvement in CNF generation. There is a good scope for researchers to do test pattern generation for single stuck-at-fault and multiple stuck-at-faults for various combinational circuits. Finally, BDD generation and CNF conversion is reaching a performance plateau, we need to look elsewhere for new improvements.

References

1. Hardy, G., Lucet, C., Limnios, N.: K-Terminal Network Reliability Measures with Binary Decision Diagrams. IEEE Trans. on Reliability 56(3) (2007)
2. Lafferty, J., Vardy, A.: Ordered Binary Decision Diagrams and Minimal Trellises. IEEE Trans. on Computers 48(9) (1999)
3. Heinrich-Litan, L., Molitor, P.: Least Upper Bounds for the Size of OBDDs using Symmetries. IEEE Trans. on Computers 49, 360 (2000)
4. Minato, S.: Binary Decision Diagrams and Applications for VLSI CAD, p. 141. Kluwer Academic Publishers, Dordrecht (1996)
5. Ubar, R.: Test Synthesis with Alternative Graphs. IEEE Design & Test of Computers, 48 (Spring 1996)
6. Bryant, R.: Graph-Based algorithms for Boolean function manipulation. IEEE Trans. on Computers 35(8), 677 (1986)
7. Lee, C.Y.: Representation of Switching Circuits by Binary Decision Diagrams. Bell System Techs. J. 38(7), 985 (1959)
8. Akers, S.: Binary Decision Diagrams. IEEE Trans. on Comp. 27, 509 (1978)
9. Jackson, P., Sheridan, D.: Clause Form Conversions for Boolean Circuits. In: H. Hoos, H., Mitchell, D.G. (eds.) SAT 2004. LNCS, vol. 3542, pp. 183–198. Springer, Heidelberg (2005)
10. Bollig, B., Wegener, I.: Improving the variable ordering of OBDDs is NP-Complete. IEEE Trans. Computers 45(9), 993 (1996)
11. Mo, Y.c.: New Insights into the BDD- Based Reliability Analysis of Phased-Mission Systems. IEEE Trans. on Reliability 58(4) (2009)
12. Xing, L., Dugan, J.B.: A separable ternary decision diagram based analysis of generalized phased-mission reliability. IEEE Trans. Reliability 53, 174 (2004)
13. Chambers, B., Manolios, P.: Faster SAT Solving with better CNF Generation. EDAA (2009)

Floating Gate Wilson Current Mirror for Low Power Applications

M. Madhushankara[1] and Prashanth Kumar Shetty[2]

[1] Assistant Professor, Manipal Centre for Information Sciences, Manipal
[2] Associate Professor, Manipal Centre for Information Sciences, Manipal
{madhushankar.m,pk.shetty}@manipal.edu

Abstract. The paper discusses the application of floating gate techniques to Wilson current mirror to reduce power dissipation. With floating gate technique, it is possible to modify the effective threshold voltage of the MOSFET. This will be helpful in reducing the leakage current. This technique is also useful in reducing the power supply voltage required for a MOSFET to operate in a saturation region, which in turn minimizes the dynamic power dissipation. The proposed circuit is simulated using HSPICE for 0.18um CMOS technology and the results are compared with those obtained for simple Wilson current mirror circuit.

Keywords: Floating gate, Wilson current mirror, Low power.

1 Introduction

The CMOS technology has evolved to reduce the overall power dissipation of the device over its predecessor logic families. The main issues related to CMOS logic family were the device speed, cost and the dependability. But the shrinking device size has raised a concern over the power dissipation [1]. The inability to scale down the threshold voltage with the same rate as that of channel length of the device has raised a concern over overall power dissipation. Several circuit techniques have been used to encounter this problem [2].

The threshold voltage is the key in deciding supply voltage of a circuit. The minimum power supply must be equal to or greater than the sum of magnitudes of threshold voltages of NMOS and PMOS [4] which is given by,

$$|V_{DD} - V_{SS}| >= V_{THN} + |V_{THP}| \tag{1}$$

A thorough attention is required to develop a circuit for low power applications. The scaling down of the devices using constant electric field technique, does not consider leakage current which has major role in total power dissipation [3].

This paper aims at the design of current mirror using floating gate technology which has higher performance than the conventional current mirrors and dissipates lesser power.

The paper is organized as below: In section 2, the operation of simple Wilson Current Mirror is explained. In Section 3, floating gate technique is described. In

D.C. Wyld et al. (Eds.): NeCoM/WeST/WiMoN 2011, CCIS 197, pp. 500–507, 2011.
© Springer-Verlag Berlin Heidelberg 2011

section 4, floating gate technique is applied to Wilson current mirror. In section 5, results and comparison of the techniques are given.

2   Wilson Current Mirror

The Wilson current mirror as shown in Fig 1, works on the principle of negative feedback [4]. It has higher output impedence than the basic current mirrors. The gate terminal of transistor M_3 is connected to the point A, which has a stable reference voltage due to the constant current I_{IN}. This voltage initiates the flow of drain current through M_3. If the output voltage V_{OUT} increases, causes I_{OUT} to increase. Due to this, the current through drain - gate connected transistor M_2 increases. By current mirror principle, the drain current of M_1 also increases. To compensate for the increase in current through M_1, the voltage at node A drops and thereby reducing the gate voltage of M_3. Therefore overall reduction in drain current of M_3 decreases which stabilizes the output current, I_{OUT}.

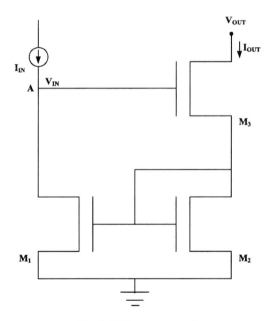

Fig. 1. Wilson current mirror

3   Floating Gate Technique

The floating gate technique [5 - 9] is one of the techniques employed in low power analog circuit design. Its structure is very similar to the traditional MOSFET except that its gate is electrically isolated and multiple inputs can be connected to it. Here the floating gate voltage is influenced by the control inputs through capacitive coupling. The general structure of a floating gate MOSFET is as shown Fig 2.

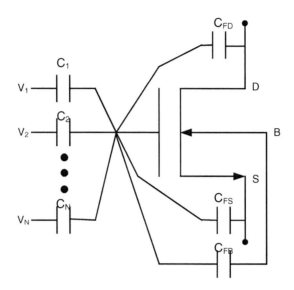

Fig. 2. Floating gate MOSFET

The floating gate voltage [10] is given by equation (2),

$$V_{FG} = \frac{C_{FD}V_{DS} + C_{FS}V_{SS} + C_{FB}V_{SS} + Q_{FG} + \Sigma_1^N C_i V_{GS}}{C_{TOTAL}} \qquad (2)$$

Where,

$$\Sigma_1^N C_i = C_1 + C_2 + C_3 + ...C_N \qquad (3)$$

are the input capacitances

Q_{FG}, the stationary charge on the floating gate, N is the number of inputs. C_{FB}, C_{FS}, C_{FD} are the capacitances between floating gate and bulk, source and drain terminals respectively. The total capacitance,

$$C_{TOTAL} = \Sigma_1^N C_i + C_{FD} + C_{FS} + C_{FB} \qquad (4)$$

The residual charge Q_{FG} can be reduced to zero using the method specified in [11]. Thus the equation of floating gate voltage reduces to,

$$V_{FG} = \frac{C_{FD}V_{DS} + C_{FS}V_{SS} + C_{FB}V_{SS} + \Sigma_1^N C_i V_{GS}}{C_{TOTAL}} \qquad (5)$$

If only 2 inputs are considered for floating gate MOSFET as shown in Fig 3, a bias input (V_{BIAS}) and the signal input (V_{IN}), the charge accumulated will be the sum of the charges due to those input voltages, voltages at the floating gate is considered as in equation (6),

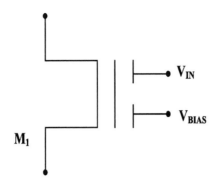

Fig. 3. 2-Input Floating gate MOSFET

$$Q_{FGT} = Q_{BIAS} + Q_{VIN} \tag{6}$$

From equation (6), the voltage at the floating gate (V_{FGT}) will be

$$V_{FGT} = \frac{V_{BIAS} * C_1 + V_{IN} * C_2}{C_1 + C_2} \tag{7}$$

The effective minimum voltage for conduction of current ($V_{TH, E}$) can be adjusted by varying the bias voltage as,

$$V_{TH,E} = \frac{[V_{TH} - C_1/(C_1 + C_2) * V_{BIAS}]}{C_2/(C_1 + C_2)} \tag{8}$$

4   Floating Gate Wilson Current Mirror

The proposed structure of floating gate Wilson current mirror is as shown Fig 4. The transistors M_1, M_2 and M_3 are 2-input MOSFETs and are of equal aspect ratios. The

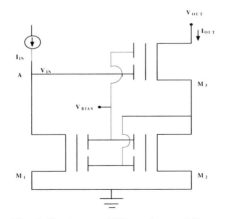

Fig. 4. Floating gate Wilson Current Mirror

voltage, V_{BIAS} is applied to form the conduction channel at one input gate and the other gate is used the normal input gate. The gate source voltages of transistors M_1 and M_2 are made equal by connecting one of their gate inputs together ($V_{GS1} = V_{GS2}$). The source of M_3 is connected to the drain of M_2 so that V_{S3} becomes equal to V_{GS2} and the drain current I_{OUT} is measured.

5   Results

The proposed floating gate Wilson current mirror and Wilson current mirror are simulated using HSPICE for 0.18um CMOS technology. The results are as shown in Fig 5 – 9. Table1 contains the comparison of those two circuits.

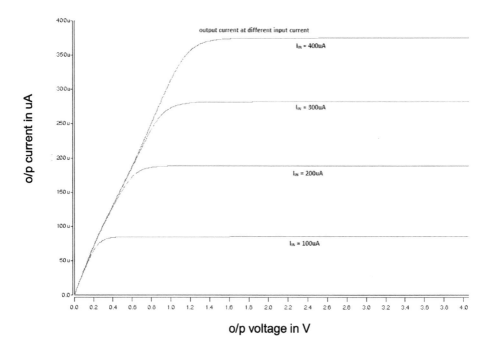

Fig. 5. Output Current v/s Output Voltage at various reference currents, I_{IN}

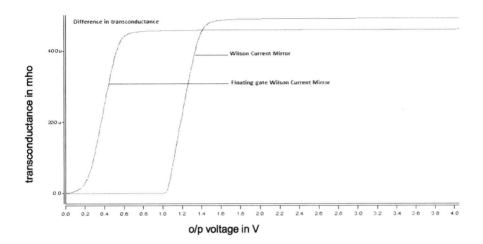

Fig. 6. Comparison: – Transconductance of Floating gate Wilson current mirror and Wilson current mirror v/s O/p Voltage at a reference current of 100uA

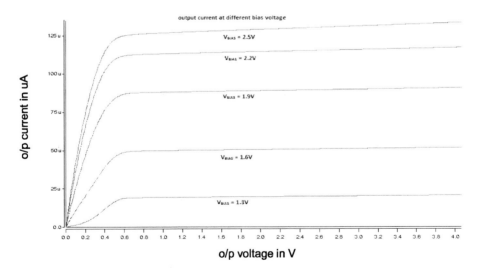

Fig. 7. Output Current v/s Output Voltage at various Gate Bias Voltages, V_{BIAS}

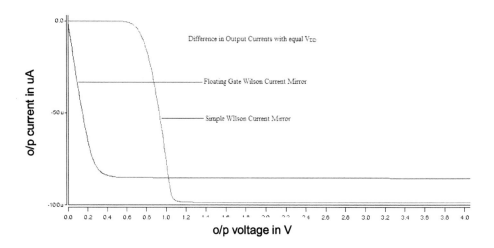

Fig. 8. Comparison: – O/P current of Floating gate Wilson current mirror and Wilson current mirror v/s O/p Voltage at a reference current of 100uA

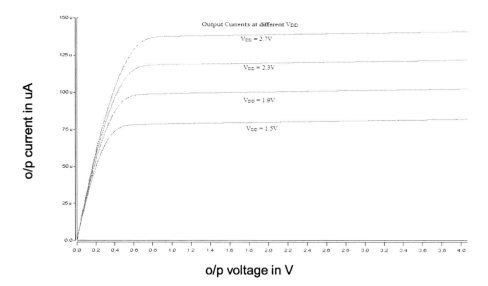

Fig. 9. Output Current v/s Output Voltage at various Supply Voltages, V_{DD}

Table 1.

Parameters	Wilson Current Mirror	Floating gate Wilson current mirror
Supply voltage	3.3V	1.8V
Power dissipation	521.5uW	413.4uW
Transconductance	453.6ul/V	445.6ul/V

6 Conclusion

The Floating gate technique is applied to Wilson current mirror and the simulation result are compared. The threshold voltage of the transistor is increased by applying this technique. This forces the device to move into saturation region early. Thus reducing the power supply required for the operation as well as power dissipation of the circuit. Hence the low power operation is achieved.

References

1. Darwish, T., Bayoumi, M.: Trends in low power design. In: Chen, W.-K. (ed.) The Electrical Engineering Handbook, Chicago (2005)
2. Rajput, S.S., Jamuar, S.S.: Low Voltage analog circuit design techniques. IEEE, Los Alamitos (2002)
3. Islam, S.K., Haider, M.R.: Sensors and Low-Power Signal Processing, USA (2010)
4. Jacob Baker, R., Li, H.W., Boyce, D.E.: CMOS, Circuit Design, Layout and Simulation, 2nd edn. IEEE Press, Los Alamitos (2008)
5. Rodriguez-Villegas, E., Barnes, H.: Solution to trapped charge in FGMOS transistors. IEEE Electronics Letters 39(19) (September 2003)
6. Özalevli, E.: Exploiting floating-gate transistor properties in analog and mixed-signal circuit design. School of Electrical and Computer Engineering Georgia Institute of Technology (December 2006)
7. Silveira, F., Flandre, D., Jespers, P.G.A.: A g_m/I_D Based Methodology for the Design of CMOS Analog Circuits and its application to the synthesis of a Silicon-on-Insulator Micropower OTA. IEEE Journal of Solid-state Circuits 31(9) (September 1996)
8. Shibata, T., Ohmi, T.: A Functional MOS Transistor Featuring Gate-Level Weighted Sum and Threshold Operations. IEEE Transactions on Electron Devices 39(6) (June 1992)
9. Thomsen, A., Brooke, M.A.: A Floating-Gate MOSFET with Tunneling Injector Fabricated Using a Standard Double-Polysilicon CMOS Process. IEEE Electron Device Letters 12(3) (March 1991)
10. Wang, S.T.: On the I-V Characteristics of Floating-Gate MOS Transistors. IEEE Transactions on Electron Devices Ed-26(9) (September 1979)
11. Rajput, S.S., Jamuar, S.S.: Low Voltage analog circuit design techniques. IEEE, Los Alamitos (2002)

Power Aware Physical Design for 3D Chips

Yasmeen Hasan

Dept. of ECE, Integral University, Lucknow, India
yasmeen.hasan9@gmail.com

Abstract. In this work we have proposed a geometric model that is employed to devise a scheme for identifying the hotspots and zones in a chip. These spots or zone need to be guarded thermally to ensure performance and reliability of the chip. The model namely continuous unit sphere model has been presented taking into account that the 3D region of the chip is uniform, thereby reflecting on the possible locations of heat sources and the target observation points. The experimental results for the – continuous domain establish that a region which does not contain any heat sources may become hotter than the regions containing the thermal sources. Thus a hotspot may appear away from the active sources, and placing heat sinks on the active thermal sources alone may not suffice to tackle thermal imbalance. Power management techniques aid in obtaining a uniform power profile throughout the chip, but we propose an algorithm using minimum bipartite matching where we try to move the sources minimally (with minimum perturbation in the chip floor plan) near cooler points (blocks) to obtain a uniform power profile due to diffusion of heat from hotter point to cooler ones.

Keywords: 3D chips, Hotspots, Floorplaning, Continuous domain, Integrated circuits, Power management, Target point, Source point, Heat sink, Coarse mesh (CM), Fine mesh (FM), etc.

1 Introduction

In the recent years the power density of integrated circuits(IC's) has doubled every three years. Because energy consumed by the chip is converted into heat, this continuing exponential rise in power density creates vast difficulties in cooling costs [1][2]. The most critical challenge of 3D IC design is heat dissipation, which has already been realized and studied even for 2D IC designs. There have been several existing works on 3D power and temperature aware physical designs and management. In order to device a scheme for identifying the hotspots and zones in a chip S. Majumder and S.S. Kolay[3] proposed two different geometric models, namely continuous and discrete to take into account whether the 2D plane of the chip floor is gridless or a uniform grid, thereby reflecting on the possible locations of the heat sources and target observation points. These spots or zones need to be guarded thermally to ensure performance and reliability. Some researchers have addressed the problem of identification of hotspots in VLSI chips [4] whereas others have proposed an alternative placement scheme to cool down a hot chip[5].Kang has highlighted the

D.C. Wyld et al. (Eds.): NeCoM/WeST/WiMoN 2011, CCIS 197, pp. 508–515, 2011.

need for new thermal designs in order to cope up with the challenging scenarios ensuing from the high-scale integration[6]. Miranda et al. had successfully used the finite volume method approach to investigate maximum temperature rising on a CPU motherboard [7]. Jing Li and Hiroshi Miyashita (2006) [8] proposed a finite difference thermal model, where it was assumed that every heat source that overlaps the effective area Aeff of a grid point serves as a power source feeding into the grid and the corresponding power value of the grid is calculated based on the ratio of the source area within Aeff to the total area of the source.

In this paper we have proposed a geometric model which is employed to devise a scheme for identifying the hotspots in a three dimensional integrated circuit(IC).

We propose a model here which may facilitate in identifying the hot spots/zones in a VLSI chip. In the continuous domain we have used the concept of a unit sphere model to calculate the local thermal effect at a point due to the heat being dissipated from several point heat sources distributed over the chip plane. We establish that a point on a chip can become very hot due to the conduction effects of other heat sources, although it may not have a heat source in its immediate vicinity. In this model, the heat loss due to radiation has been ignored. If it is to be considered, an appropriate heat loss has to be incorporated functions.

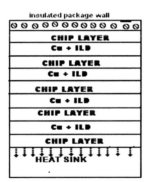

Fig. 1. 3D IC technology

1.1   Time Invariant Heat Sources

The study is made with the assumption that there are constantly active (i.e. always on) heat generating sources placed randomly throughout the chip. For continuous thermal sources; we also assume that the heat from the sources is being propagated through the 3D surface of the chip without being dissipated in the ambience. The objective is to identify the zones in the chip, which have heat content greater than a certain threshold.

2   Continuous Spatial Domain

The position of a heat source may be any point on the chip which is assumed to be a 3D integrated circuit (IC). In the unit sphere model, the contribution of a point heat source S at any target point T is expressed as the amount of heat from S received within the unit sphere centered at the point T. This unit is the same as that of the distance between S and T, and may be related to the minimum dimension of the chip. The cumulative heat received at the point T is evaluated as the linear superposition of the amounts received at T from all heat – generating sources on the chip. As illustrated with Fig. 2, let a heat source at a point S generate an amount Q, henceforth denoted as the strength of the source S. Let the target point T be at a Euclidian distance d from S. Let C_T and C_s intersect at the two points A and B.

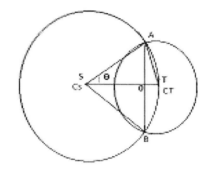

Fig. 2. Unit Sphere Model of Heat Received at a Point T

Then the area cut out on the surface of the sphere C_S is equal to the product of solid angle with its vertex at the center of the sphere C_s and the square of the sphere's radius.

$$A = \tau \times d^2 \tag{1}$$

Where τ *is the solid angle*   formed by the conical surface of the spherical sector and d is the radius of the source sphere [10].

A complete sphere forms a solid angle of 4π.(If the solid angle is not formed by the entire sphere, but only by a conical surface of a spherical sector, the angle in this case is equal to the ratio of the sector's spherical surface to the square of the sphere's radius [11][12].)

By denoting the plane angle at the vertex of the spherical sector as θ, it is possible to express its height h as

$$h = d - d\cos\theta = d(1 - \cos\theta) = 2d\sin^2\frac{\theta}{2} \tag{2}$$

where r is the radius of the source sphere.

Therefore the spherical area of the sector can be represented as

$$A = 2\pi d^2 (1 - \cos\theta) = 4\pi d^2 \sin^2\frac{\theta}{2} \tag{3}$$

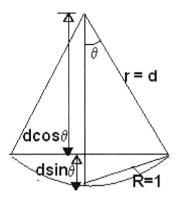

Fig. 3. Section of a cone and a spherical cap inside a sphere

By denoting the solid angle which subtends the spherical surface of the sector as we obtain

$$\tau = 4\pi sin^2 \frac{\theta}{2} = 2\pi(1 - cos\theta) \tag{4}$$

Thus the contribution of heat from S at T is

$$Q \times \frac{2\pi d^2(1-cos\theta)}{4\pi d^2} \tag{5}$$

Where is the surface area of the sphere S.
Consider OC_TB in the figure 10

$$(C_TB)^2 = (OB)^2 + (OC_T)^2$$

$$1 = 2d^2(1-cos\theta) \tag{6}$$

Putting eqn (6) in eqn (5) we get
The contribution of heat from S to T is

$$= Q \times \frac{1}{4d^2} \tag{7}$$

Our concerns are the hottest points on the chip. Intuitively, the source points definitely belong to the above class. But the more pertinent question is whether these are the only points that need to be considered. The question may be re-phrased as follows: does there exist any non-source point on the floor with heat content greater than that of any of the source points?

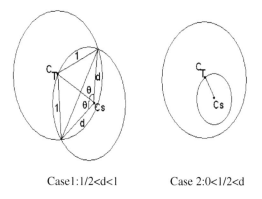

Case1:1/2<d<1   Case 2:0<1/2<d

Fig. 4. Special cases of the unit sphere model

The observations reported, answer in the affirmative. Before we proceed further, we point out two special cases of the unit sphere model fig 4 based on the distance d between S and T:

$$0.5 < d < 1 \qquad \text{and} \qquad (2)\ 0 < d < 0.5$$

In the boundary case when S lies on C_T is equal to, as SAT becomes an equilateral triangle

$$Q = \frac{Q_o}{2}(1 - \cos\theta)$$

$$= \frac{Q_o}{2}(1 - \frac{1}{2}) \qquad = \frac{Q_o}{4} \qquad (8)$$

Hence in case (1) the angle 2θ as defined earlier will be greater than, and consequently more than of the heat emanating from S reaches the unit sphere centered at T. In case (2) T is nearer to S and hence the sphere with radius 'd 'around S will now lie entirely within the Unit sphere at T. Hence the unit sphere C_T receives the entire heat of S in this case.

3   Experimental Results for the Continuous Domain

We performed more experiments in the continuous domain model implemented in C to simulate the effect of active sources placed at random points on the 3D floor. Keeping the dimensions of the 3D structure the same we varied the number of sources from 5 to 50.We have studied five trail runs, keeping the number and range of the power strength of the active sources fixed, just allowing the position of the sources to vary.

We observed that the results did not depend much on the randomness of the position of the active sources. As in the previous experiment we have observed that in the continuous domain the relatively hot points lie near the active source.

During simulation we considered more of those points for evaluation of the cumulative power. We actually considered a fine grid around each source point and evaluated the cumulative power at each of those points along with the source points. Also across the whole floor we considered a relatively coarse grid and evaluated the power at all the grid points of this coarse grid.

In the result we also found the coordinates and cumulative power of the target points. Here we observed that there were some target points whose cumulative power exceeded the cumulative power of the active source nearest to it. The result of our experiments confirm that in 3D IC 's as the number of power sources increases there is an increase in the power density. This means that in 3D IC's there is a need of efficient power management techniques.

4   Conclusion

In this work we have proposed a model in the continuous domain to model the thermal behavior in a 3D VLSI chip. The hotspots were usually concentrated near the active source points, but some points away from the source were found to be much hotter than the sources itself. The randomness of the source did not affect the result much. One important aspect we have observed in all the models is that there are zones in the chip which become much hotter even without containing a heat source. We conclude that it may not be enough to guard only the active regions to make the chip thermally stronger. This also requires the need for more efficient power and thermal management techniques[13][14][15].

Table 1. Results For The Continuous Domain

NO OF SOURCES	THRESHOLD VALUE	TOTAL PROBES POINTS	PROBES POINTS IN FM	PROBE POINTS IN CM	HOTSPOT IN FM	HOTSPOT IN CM	%HOTSPOT IN FM	%HOTSPOT IN CM
5	1.24876	2029160	29160	2000000	9198	2562	0.45%	0.19%
10	1.24338	2058320	58320	2000000	16798	8376	0.81%	0.41%
20	1.26821	2116640	116640	2000000	42238	12048	1.72%	0.68%
40	1.26441	2233280	233280	2000000	93972	19030	4.21%	0.82%
50	1.20101	2291600	291600	2000000	118262	25969	5.16%	1.13%

We also observed that the numbers of hotspots reported in our model were very high compared to those found in the 2D case[3], which shows that the problem of increased power density with the increase in number of sources becomes more grave in the 3D case. We try to propose an algorithm using minimum bipartite matching where we try to move the sources minimally (with minimum perturbation in the chip floorplan) near cooler points (blocks) to obtain a uniform power profile due to diffusion of heat from hotter point to cooler ones, thus reduce the maximum temperature.

4.1   The Minimum Weight Bipartite Matching Problem

The minimum weight bipartite matching problem occupies a central position in combinational optimization, and a variety of applications to transshipment problems.
   The problem is formally defined as follows:
   Obtain a minimum weight perfect matching in an edge-weighted bipartite graph.

1) Let T denote the threshold value. The threshold value is the minimum of the cumulative power of all source points.
2) Let A = [ ] denote a matrix giving the power density at each of the grid points
3) We calculate

$$T - A = S = [\ ] = \text{Excess at each grid point}$$

   Where S denotes a matrix giving the excess at each grid point
   (Some grid points will have positive excess, some negative excess and some zero excess)
4) Identify the sources with their cumulative power. Let the sources be placed at (x_s, y_s).

   Perform minimum weight bipartite matching
   Given: A bipartite graph, $G = (V, E)$ where $V = V_1 \cup V_2$
   V_1 = Set containing the sources;
   V_2 = Set containing all empty grid (target) positions having Excess $\geq$ [max

(excess of source points)]

   For each $e \in E$ and $e = (v_i, v_j)$, where $v_i \in V_1$ and $v_j \in V_2$

   For an edge e $(v_i, v_j) \in E$ from each vertex $v_i \in V_1$ to all vertices $v_j \in V_2$

   Wt (e) = weight is minimum Manhattan distance from the original position of each source $v_i \in V_2$ to the grid corresponding to $v_j \in V_2$

   A min weighted bipartite matching is performed to obtain assignment of each source $v_i \in V_1$ to a target new location $v_j \in V_2$.

   The running time of the minimum weighted bipartite matching algorithm[25] is
$$O(m\sqrt{n}) = O(n^{2.5})$$

   However a detailed study of the algorithm remains an area of future work.

   In this work we have considered a uniform propagation of heat in all the directions. But due to the different thermal conductivities of the different layers, if we take into consideration this non uniform propagation of heat in different layers, we can obtain a more accurate power distribution profile in the model. We have done some work in this regard but a detailed study remains an area for future work.

References

[1] Eichelberger, C.W.: Three-dimensional multichip module system, US. Patent 5 111 278 (1992)
[2] Roos, G., Hoefflinger, B., Schubert, M., Zingg, R.: Manufacturability of 3D-epitaxial-lateral-overgrowth CMOS circuits with three stacked channels. Microelectron (1991)

[3] Mujumdar, S., Kolay, S.S.: Hot spots and zones in a chip: A geometrician's View, pp. 1063–9667 (2005)

[4] Cheng, Y.K., Kang, S.M.: An Efficient Method for Hot-spot Identification in ULSI Circuits. In: Proc. of IEEE Int. Conf. on Computer Aided (ICCAD), pp. 124–127 (1999)

[5] Tsai, C.-H., Kang, S.-M.: Cell-Level Placement for Improving Substrate Thermal Distribution. IEEE Trans. on Computer-Aided Design of Integrated Circuits and Systems 19, 253–266 (2000)

[6] Kang, S.M.: On Chip Thermal Engineering for Peta .scale Integration. In: ISPD, p. 76 (2002)

[7] Miranda, G., Luna, H.P.L., Meteus, G.R., Ferreira, R.P.M.: A Performance Guarantee Heuristic for Electronic Components Placement Problems including Thermal Effects (2004) (in press)

[8] Li, J., Miyashita, H.: Post placement thermal via placement for 3D integrated circuit, pp. 1-4244-0387-1 (2006)

[9] Szek'ely, V., Renzc, M., Torok, S., Ress, S.: Calculating Effective Board Thermal Parameters from Transient Measurement, pp. 1521-3331/01 (2001)

[10] Weisstein, E.W.: Solid Angle, at Math world

[11] Solid Angle, on the Wikipedia, the free encyclopedia Website

[12] Teplov, A.V.: Measurement of Solid Angles, pp. 63–64 (December 1965)

[13] Skadron, K., Stan, M.R., Huang, W., Velusamy, S., Sankaranarayanan, K., Tarjan, D.: Temperature-aware microarhitecture. In: Proceedings of the 30th Annual International Symposium

[14] Hu, J., Shin, Y., Dhanwada, N., Marculescu, R.: Architecting Voltage Islands in Core-based System-on-a-Chip Designs. In: ISLPED (2004)

[15] Singhal, L., Oh, S., Bozorgzadeh, E.: Statistical Power Profile Correlation for Realistic Thermal Estimation, pp. 978-1-4244-1922-7 (2008)

Universal Crypting-Decrypting Algorithm

Geetesh More

VLSI dept., Institute of Technology and Management, Gwalior
more_geetesh@yahoo.co.in

Abstract. This paper presents the universal algorithm for the generation of cyclic code for an n bit binary word. As well as it also provides the algorithm for decrypting the code generated. It is important for the built in self test (BIST) and for memory ROM testing. They are extensively used for encoding and decoding communication channel burst errors.

Keywords: Boolean polynomial multiplier, Boolean polynomial divider, Galois field, test pattern generator, encoder, decoder.

1 Introduction

Till now unique generator polynomial is required for coding and decoding particular set of bits. For generating the code for n-bit binary word generator polynomial of degree (k-n) is obtained, where k is the number of bits in complete code word. In coding theory, a polynomial code is a type of linear code whose set of valid code words consists of those polynomials (usually of some fixed length) that are divisible by a given fixed polynomial (of shorter length, called the generator polynomial). We express the binary vector $D = RmRm\text{-}1Rm\text{-}2\ldots\ldots R0$ as the polynomial $D(x) = Rmx^m + R(m\text{-}1)x^{(m\text{-}1)} + \ldots + R0$.

As a example, suppose $D = 1101$

Then, $D(x) = x^3 + x^2 + 1$. The degree of the polynomial is the superscript of the highest non-zero term. Polynomial addition or subtraction is performed by modulo-2 addition or subtraction, i.e., XORing without carry or borrow. This polynomial resembles the divisor in a polynomial long division, which takes the message as the dividend, and in which the quotient is discarded and the remainder becomes the result, with the important distinction that the polynomial coefficients are calculated according to the carry-less arithmetic of a finite field. The length of the remainder is always less than the length of the generator polynomial, which therefore determines how long the result can be.

1.1 Polynomial Multiplier

Figure1 shows the Boolean polynomial multiplier with internal XOR gate. Here

D.C. Wyld et al. (Eds.): NeCoM/WeST/WiMoN 2011, CCIS 197, pp. 516–525, 2011.

D(x) = binary word polynomial

V(x) = code word polynomial

$h_1.....h_{n-1}$ = 1 when they are connected to D(x).

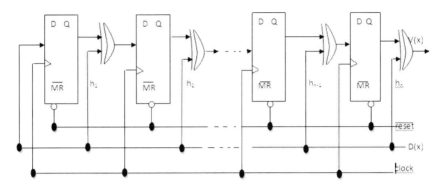

Fig. 1. Boolean polynomial realization

In this number system, we implement the multiplication by x with a time shift using D-flip flop and implement modulo-2 addition operator with an XOR gate. The data to be encoded appears serially on D(x), and the bits of the encoded word appear serially on V(x)[2]. Here serial data transmission is done to ensure the correctness of data. Generator polynomial has a degree of the length of the shift register and has a coefficient that is either 0 or 1, corresponding to the taps of the register that feed the XOR gate. Bits in the multiplier that influences the input are called taps. Following things must be remembered:

- The multiplier will only be maximum length if the number of tap is even, just 2 or 4 taps can suffice even for an extremely long sequence.

- The sets of taps must be relatively prime and share no common divisor to all taps.

- There can be more than one maximum length tap sequence for a given multiplier

From the figure1 we can derive the generator polynomial expression:

$$V(x) = \{x^n....\{x\{xD(x) + h_1D(x)\}+ h_2D(x)\}+..\}+h_{n-1}D(x)\}$$

$$=> G(x) = 1+h_1x^1+.....+h_{n-1}x^n$$

$$=> V(x) = G(x)*D(x) + S(x)$$

S(x) = syndrome polynomial which is zero during encoding.

1.2 Polynomial Divider

Polynomial divider is used as a decoding circuit. It is the companion or mirror circuit to figure1. In the decoding procedure, we treat the code word as a Boolean polynomial, but this time we divide it by generator polynomial and determine the remainder, as well as quotient, of the division. If the remainder is zero, then the code word was valid. A non zero remainder indicates the transmission error.

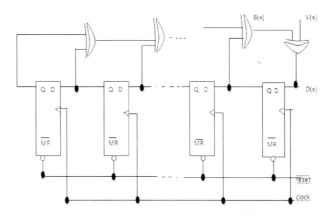

Fig. 2. Boolean polynomial divider realization

Here $D(x) = V(x) + B(x)$

$B(x) = h_1x^1 + \ldots + h_{n-1}x^n$

$D(x) = V(x)/G(x)$

2   Mathematical Evaluation

Instead of generating separate generator polynomial for each binary sequence set, we can generate a universal, simple and less tedious polynomial required for generating code for all bit patterns. But the polynomial must be such that the code polynomial generated by it can be decoded by the decoder also. The multiplier is made of D-type flip-flops and XOR gates in its shift path. The position of XOR gates determine the poly of this circuit, which is poly = 1011.

Polynomial determine bit values that are generated on the serial output of the circuit (poly determine bit values that are generated on the serial output of the circuit V, as serial input bits (D) are being shifted in.

Here

$$V(x) = x\{x\{xD(x)\}+D(x)\}+D(x) \qquad (1)$$

$$V(x) = (1+x+x^3)D(x) \qquad (2)$$

$$\Rightarrow \quad G(x) = 1+x+x^3 \qquad (3)$$

Initially all D flip flop are reset. As 1st starting from MSB of original information bit enters the multiplier, left most flip flop i.e R3 takes the value of D. R2 takes the previous value of R3 and use this as input to R1. R1 takes the XORed value of previous value of R2 with the current value of D(information bit). Output code word V takes the XORed value of previous value of R1 with current value of D. After all 4bits of the data polynomial have entered the multiplier, flip flop will keep on shifting right taking 0 as D till all 3 flip flop regains the 000 state as shown in table3 example.

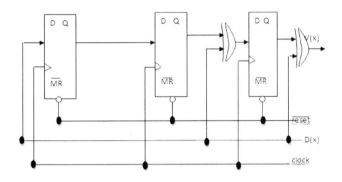

Fig. 3. Digital circuit of Boolean polynomial multiplier for mathematical evaluation

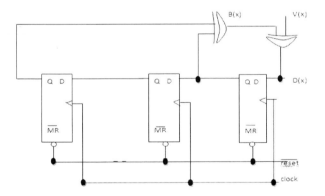

Fig. 4. Digital circuit of Boolean polynomial divider for mathematical evaluation

Using $G(x) = 1 + x + x^3$

$$B(x) = xD(x) + x^3D(x) \tag{4}$$

$$D(x) = V(x) + B(x) \tag{5}$$

$$D(x) = V(x) / G(x) \tag{6}$$

Now instead of generating the polynomial of separate degree every time, we use the above polynomial as universal one.

Suppose we want to code the binary word of n bit. $D(x) = x_{n-1} \ldots\ldots x_0$

Where x represent either 1 or 0, and n represents number of bits. One way is by generating the polynomial of degree $\geq n$. but this will take lot of time and calculation.

Another way we can do is as follows:

$$D(x) = \{D_{n-1}(x), \ldots\ldots\ldots, D_1(x), D_0(x)\} \qquad (7)$$

Where $D_{n-1}(x) = x_{n-1}x_{n-2}x_{n-3}x_{n-4}$

$D_1(x) = x_7x_6x_5x_4$

$D_0(x) = x_3x_2x_1x_0$

Now placing each bit of $D_0(x)$ serially in figure 3, we will get code polynomial for word polynomial $D_0(x)$. Similarly we can obtain the code polynomial for all the other word polynomials.

Finally our final code polynomial will be the concatenation of all the previous code polynomial obtained. [2]

$$V(x) = \{V_{n-1}(x), \ldots\ldots\ldots, V_1(x), V_0(x)\} \qquad (8)$$

At the decoding stage we place our code words from V_0 to V_{n-1} sequentially to obtain the original transmitted information. Here V_{00}, B_{00}, D_{00} corresponds to coefficients of $V_0(x)$, $B_0(x)$, $D_0(x)$ respectively. Figure5 shows the decoding of code polynomial serially at every clock pulse. The same way other polynomials $V_{n-1}(x)$ to $V_1(x)$ can be decoded to obtain original information through verilog coding.[1]

3 Algorithm

After generating the logic for crypting 4bit information, next approach is towards the practical implementation. Flowchart shown in figure6 shows the algorithm involved in crypting n- bit information using simple digital circuit that was used for crypting 4bit data. Figure5 illustrates the algorithm for generating the coding polynomial of the n bit information. To divide the binary word in the set of 4bits each, the word is concatenated with the remaining zero bits to make the n number of bits multiple of 4.

SupposeD=000100100011010001010110011110001001 10101011110
01101111011   (9)

It is a 58 bit binary word information needed to be coded. To make the set of 4bits we concatenate D with 2`b00 as $D_{new} = \{D,2`b00\}$ which is 60 bits now. This is done by dividing the number of bits by 4 and adding the remainder to quotient till the remainder becomes zero.[2]

This 60 bit data will make 15 set of 4bit data as follows:

$D_{14}=0001,D_{13}=0010,D_{12}=0011,D_{11}=0100,D_{10}=0101,D_9=0110,D_8=0111,D_7=1000,$
$D_6=1001, D_5=1010,D_4=1011,D_3=1100,D_2=1101,D_1=1110, D_0=1100$

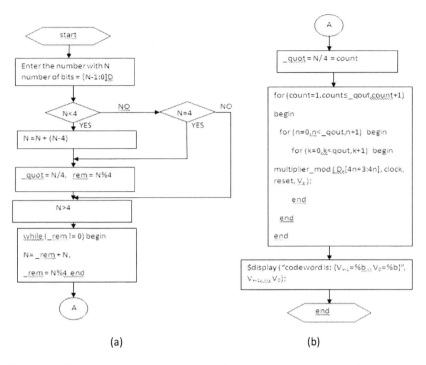

(a)   (b)

Fig. 5. (a), (b): Flowchart showing the algorithm for generating coding polynomial

Data word from D_0 to D_{14} will be passed through the multiplier 15 times and at every iteration step corresponding code word is generated. Finally by concatenating all the code words we get our final code polynomial. Suppose D_{14} bit data is entered in the figure3. This gives $V_{14} = 0001101$.

Table 1. Coding process for $D_{14}(x)$ polynomial

Clock	D	R3=D	R2=previous state R3	R1=(previous state R2)^D	V=(previous state R1)^D
0		0	0	0	
1	$D_{00}=0$	0	0	0	0
2	$D_{01}=0$	0	0	0	0
3	$D_{02}=0$	0	0	0	0
4	$D_{03}=1$	1	0	1	1
5	$D_{04}=0$	0	1	0	1
6	$D_{05}=0$	0	0	1	0
7	$D_{06}=0$	0	0	0	1
	Original information				Code polynomial

Similarly we can obtain the code polynomial for other data words.

In the table1 shown above $D_{00} - D_{06}$ corresponds to coefficient of $D(x)$ polynomial. Finally we obtained:

$$V = \{V_{14}, V_{13}, V_{12}, V_{11}, V_{10}, V_9, V_8, V_7, V_6, V_5, V_4, V_3, V_2, V_1, V_0\}$$

V=000110100110100010111011010001110010101110010001111010001100101111
00101111111011001010001100011010111100   (10)

Now entering the code word sequentially in the Boolean divider from V_{14} to V_0 15 times we get our original information. Suppose we take the code word V_{14}. Putting the code word in our decrypter we obtain the original information as $D_{14} = 0001$.

4   Practical Implementation

4.1   Multiplier

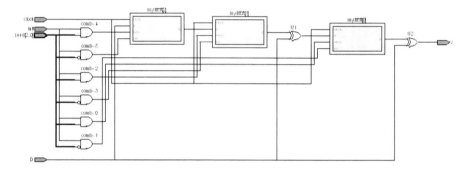

Fig. 6. Structural design of Boolean polynomial multiplier

Fig.6 shows the practical structural design of our Boolean polynomial multiplier. The position of XOR gates determine the poly of this circuit, which is poly = 1011. The seed, which is the initial value of the register, affects set and reset inputs of the individual flip flops of the shift register. The multiplier seed and poly determine bit values that are generated on the serial output of the circuit (V), as serial input bits (D) are being shifted in. This describes the structure of multiplier using XOR gates and positive edge D-type flip-flops with asynchronous set and reset inputs.[3]

4.1.1   Behavioral Coding

Fig.7 shows a generic Verilog code for an multiplier. This behavioral code uses poly and seed parameters. The poly 4-bit parameter specifies where between flip-flops XOR gates are inserted. Here seed is the initial value for the register of multiplier. An always block in the behavioral_ multiplier module of Fig.7 handles initialization, multiplier configuration, and shift-in and shift-out of data. The im_data reg holds the contents of the multiplier register. The D serial input, and is clocked into the left-most bit of the multiplier. Inputs of all remaining multiplier bits are either taken directly from flip-flops to their left (Fig.6) or from the XOR result of the D input and the output of the flip-flop to their left. The XOR result will be taken if the corresponding poly bit is 1. For example if poly[1] is 1, D is selected and XORed with im_data[2] and is used for input of im_data[1].

```
module behav_multiplier
#(parameter[3:0]poly=1011,parameter [2:0]seed=0)
             (input clock, init, D,output reg V);
reg [2:0]im_data;
always @(posedge clock or posedge init)
begin
 if(init)
 im_data = seed;
 else
 im_data ={D, im_data[2:1] ^ (poly[2:1]& {2{D}})};
 V = im_data[0]^D;
 end
endmodule
```

Fig. 7. Verilog code of behavioral multiplier

```
module behav_multiplier
#(parameter[3:0]poly=4`b1011,parameter[2:0]seed=0)
(input clock,init,input [6:0]D, output reg[6:0]V);
reg [2:0]im_data;
integer count,j;
always @(posedge clock or posedge init)
begin
 if(init)
 im_data = seed;    else
 for(count=1;count<7;count=count+1) begin
 for(j=6;j>=0;j=j-1) begin
 im_data = {D[j],im_data[2:1]^(poly[2:1]& {2{D[j]}})};
 V[j] = im_data[0]^D[j];
 end
 end
 end
 endmodule
```

Fig. 8. Verilog code for coding 4bit of original information

4.2 Divider

Decrypting of code word requires the companion circuit of that of multiplier. If the tap sequence in an n bit multiplier is [n, A, B, C, 0)] where 0 indicates the input, then the corresponding mirror sequence will be [n, n-C, n-B, n-A, 0]. For example for the tap sequence[3, 1, 0] i.e1011, we have mirror sequence [3, 2, 0] i.e 1101.

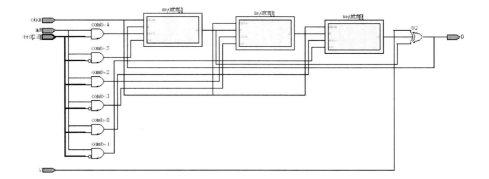

Fig. 9. Design of Boolean polynomial divider

```
module behav_divider #(parameter[3:0]poly=4`b1101,
parameter[2:0]seed=0)

        (input clock, init, V, output reg D);

reg [2:0]im_data;

always @(posedge clock or posedge init)

begin

 if(init)

 im_data = seed;

 else

im_data = {V^(im_data[0]^im_data[2]),im_data[2:1]^ (
poly[2:1]& {2{im_data[0]}}) };

 D = V^(im_data[0]^im_data[2]);

 end

endmodule
```

Fig. 10. Verilog code of behavioral divider

5 Conclusion

By generating the one algorithm for all bit patterns, we not only provide simplicity in calculation but also in design. Here we used single hardware design for different bit pattern. Earlier a separate and complex hardware design was implemented in crypting and decrypting. Mathematical analysis of this division-like process reveals how to pick a divisor that guarantees good error-detection properties. In this analysis, the digits of the bit strings are thought of as the coefficients of a polynomial in some variable x—coefficients that are elements of the finite field GF (2) instead of more familiar numbers. This binary polynomial is treated as a ring. A ring is, loosely speaking, a set of elements somewhat like numbers, that can be operated on by an operation that somewhat resembles addition and another operation that somewhat resembles multiplication. Ring theory is part of Abstract Algebra. Here we have shown how a simple polynomial of just degree 4 can be used to code the information of n bit data. After generating the algorithm we are designing the hardware for cryptic purpose. Ultimately implementing PLI of C with verilog we are generating complete practical structure. This can be further used to simplify LFSR required for generating the pattern for built in self test (BIST) and even memory ROM testing.

Acknowledgement. Success is the manifestation of perseverance and inspiration, motivation. I am deeply grateful to Dr.Vishwani D.Agrawal for guiding me at every step through his books and papers. This work is the reflection of his thought, ideas and concepts and above all his effort that can be seen from his books.

References

1. Peterson, W.W., Brown, D.T.: Cyclic Codes for Error Detection. Proceedings of the IRE 49, 228 (1961), doi:10.1109/JRPROC.1961.287814
2. Bushnell, M.L., Agrawal, V.D.: Essentials of electronic testing, ISBN: 0792379918
3. Navabi, Z.: Verilog Digital system Design, doi:10.1036/0071445641
4. Cook, G.: Catalogue of parametrised CRC algorithms, March 26 (2010), http://regregex.bbcmicro.net/crc-catalogue.htm (retrieved June 5, 2010)
5. Gammel, B.M.: Crypto - Codes, October 31 (2005), http://users.physik.tu-muenchen.de/gammel/matpack/html/LibDoc/Crypto/MpCRC.html (retrieved February 10, 2011)
6. Noda, M., Shinagawa, M., Kondou, K.: CRC generator polynomial select method, CRC coding method and CRC coding circuit. IPC8 Class: AH03M1300FI
7. Brown, S., Vranesic, Z.: Fundamental of Digital Logic, ISBN 0-07-052899-3

Design of 8-Bit Programmable Crossbar Switch for Network-on-Chip Router

Mohammad Ayoub Khan[1] and Abdul Quaiyum Ansari[2]

[1] Centre for Development of Advanced Computing,
Ministry of Communications and Information Techology, Govt. of India
B-30, Sector 62, Noida, UP, India
[2] Department of Electrical Engineering, Jamia Millia Islamia, New Delhi, India
{ayoub,aqansari}@ieee.org

Abstract. The Network-on-Chip (NoC) uses multiple processors, usually targeted for embedded applications. This is widely accepted that NoC represents a promising solution for forthcoming complex embedded systems. The current SoC Solutions are built from heterogeneous hardware and Software components integrated around a complex communication infrastructure. The crossbar is a vital component of in any NoC router. The crossbar allocates requested output channel. Hence, switches must include an efficient arbiter that allocates crossbar's resources(channel). In this paper, we present a novel 8-bit wide 8 x 8 crossbar that is implemented on FPGA. This high performance crossbar is coined with Diagonal Propagation Arbiter (DPA). The presented crossbar requires a two-dimensional arbitration that incorporates a diagonally rotated priority to provide fair arbitration. The arbiter is capable of performing arbitration in 1ns on Vertex 6 FPGA technology for an 8 x 8 crossbar. The proposed architecture of crossbar is implemented in RTL model using verilog language.

Keywords: NoC, DPA, FPGA, RTL.

1 Introduction

The System-on-Chip (SoC) platform has evolved into multiprocessor computing paradigm on a single chip. The multiprocessor computing improves throughput, scalability, and reliability of the system-on-chip [3, 4]. The multiprocessor have already established a theory and set of practices on the parallel computer. The multiprocessor paradigm in parallel computing environment split the computing into two categories as (a) Centralized computing (b) Distributed computing. The Centralized computing is used to construct the super computer, is more appropriate for System-on-Chip environment. The Flynn's classification of architecture for multiprocessor is as (a) SISD (Single Instruction Single Data) (b) SIMD (Single Instruction Multiple Data (c) MISD (Multiple Instruction Single Data) (d) MIMD (Multiple Instruction Multiple Data). Other classification methods are distinguished by having a shared common memory or unshared distributed memories, as shown in figure 1. Among the four different architectures, MIMD architecture is most appropriate to system-on-Chip. The MIMD architecture can be regarded as an

D.C. Wyld et al. (Eds.): NeCoM/WeST/WiMoN 2011, CCIS 197, pp. 526–535, 2011.
© Springer-Verlag Berlin Heidelberg 2011

extension of the uniprocessor single memory and single processor architecture. There are two alternatives for assembling the multiple processors and memory modules. One simple way is to make the processors and memories as pairs and then connect them via an interconnection network. The processor, memory pair, or a PE, works rather independently of each other, and the memory inside one PE is hardly accessible directly by the other. This class of MIMD may be called as distributed-memory MIMD or message passing MIMD architecture. The other way is to group the processors and memories into separate modules, every processor can access any memory through the interconnection network. The set of memories makes up a global address space, which is shared by the processors. This type of MIMD is called shared-memory MIMD.

In system-on-chip, all the processors are different from one another, so it is more complicated than parallel computing. Processors may be of different types, its memories may be different from one another and distributed heterogeneously on the chip, and the interconnection network between the PEs may be heterogeneous.

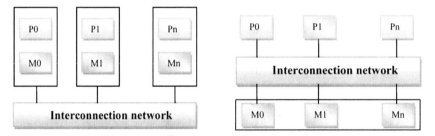

(a) Distributed Memory architecture for Multiprocessor   (b) Shared Memory architecture for Multiprocessor

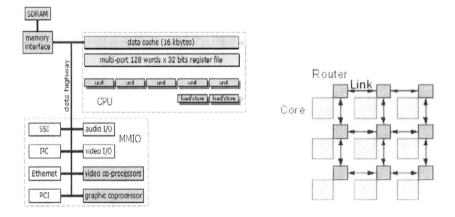

(c) System-on-Chip architecture for multiprocessor   (d) NoC architecture for multiprocessor

Fig. 1. Communication architecture for multiprocessors

Interconnection structure among the memories and processing elements determines the performance of the system. There are three basic interconnection structures (a) Shared bus (b) Crossbar switch network (c) Shared (multiport) memories. Among available interconnection structures, shared-bus system is simple and easy to implement. But, at a time only one processing element can access a particular resource; otherwise, bus contention occurs. To avoid contention, a bus controller with an arbiter switch limits bus access to one processor at a time. The bus is not scalable and the system efficiency is low.

The crossbar switch is the interconnecting architecture for high performance systems. In crossbar m vertical processing elements are connected to n horizontal links, whereas n horizontal memories are connected to m vertical links. At each cross section, a switch connects the junctions with control signals. In this network, every processor can access a free memory or resource independent of other processors. Also, several processors can have access to the memory or resource at the same time. If more than one processor tries to access the same memory or resources, the scheduler in the crossbar should determine which one to connect to. The drawback of the crossbar switch is the number of switches, in this case, $m \times n$. The multiport memory can be used as an interconnection network. All processors have a direct access path to every memory, and the controller inside the memory determines which processor to connect to. The complexity that is present in the crossbar is now shifted inside the memory. The realization of memory with such complex logic and multiport is very expensive, even impractical.

Network-on-Chip has a different outlook from conventional interconnection methods as not only it requires the interconnection technology but two more technologies (networking and packet switching fabric technologies) are required for NoC. This requires more advanced interconnection e.g., high-speed and low-power signaling, and on-chip serializer/deserializer. Switching fabric requires buffer and scheduler technologies. Networking technology includes network topology, routing algorithm, flow control and network performance analysis.

The paper is organized as follows: The section 2 discusses the basics of crossbar and arbitration logic using DPA. The section 3 presents RTL simulation, synthesis and power analysis results. Finally, a conclusion is presented in last section.

2 Design of Crossbar Switch

The crossbar consists of N rows and N vertical columns. Each row is connected to an input port and each column is connected to an output port. The crossbar based systems can be significantly less expensive than bus or ring systems with equivalent performance because the crossbar allows multiple data transfers to take place simultaneously. The crossbar switches are of special interest in packet switch designs. The crossbar switch consists of three major blocks: ports, a crossbar scheduler, and a crossbar fabric. The overall functionality of the switch can be described as follows: the packets first enter the input ports of the switch where they are queued. Each port has a routing computation unit that determines the destination of a packet based on the packet header. The port then sends a request to the scheduler for the destination output port. The scheduler grants a request based on a priority algorithm that ensures fair service to all the input ports. Once a grant is issued, the crossbar fabric is configured to map the granted input ports to their destination output ports.

2.1 2-D Diagonal Propagation Arbiter for 8 x 8 Crossbar

The crossbar schedulers accept one request from each input port and grant some of those requests according to a priority algorithm. The main goal of scheduling algorithm is to be fair to all the inputs. There are many ways of implementing crossbar scheduler. But, here we will present DPA for our design. The DPA arbiter offers less delay and mechanism to rotate the priority as much as possible. The cells are arranged in a diagonal manner to offer independence as shown in Figure 2. For example, cells (1,1),(4,2), (3,3) and (2,4) are independent of each other and so are the cells (2,1), (1,2), (4,3) and (3,4).

The arbitration process in the DPA architecture begins by considering the first diagonal. If there is a request for every cell in the first diagonal of Figure 2, they can all be granted. Then, in the next time slot, the arbitration process moves to the second diagonal. The cells with requests in the second diagonal will only receive grants if no cells on the top or on the left of them have yet received grants.

In this design, the arbitration delay for an n x n switch is nD, D being the delay of a single arbiter cell which is smaller comparably to others. The ripple-carry design gives the priority to the cells that are higher and to the left. It gives the highest priority to cell (1, 1) [1]. Similarly, in the DPA architecture the highest priority is always given to the cells in the first diagonal [1]. But it will rotate the priorities by adding mask active window.

Therefore, these two designs are not the optimal one. Optimally one should be able to rotate the priority so that every cell has the chance of being the highest priority cell. In this new architecture, shown in Figure 2, the first (n-1) diagonals of an n × n DPA scheduler are repeated after the last row [1]. The W signals of the first column and the N signals of the first diagonal are assigned to logic one. At every time slot only n^2 cells are active. The red window is "the active window". The cells on the first diagonal inside the active window have the highest priority. The active window moves one step down in every time slot to rotate the priority.

The algorithm for priority rotations in DPA is:

The algorithm for DPA is

- The first *(n-1)* diagonals of an *n × n* DPA scheduler are repeated after the last row.

- The *W* signals of the first column and the *N* signals of the first diagonal are assigned to logic one.

- N^2 cells (marked by the n*n bold window) are active. We call the bold window "the active window" called MASK

- The active window moves one step down in every time slot to rotate the priority. When the top most diagonal is diagonal n, the active window has traveled all the way through the DPA scheduler and, therefore, goes back to its starting position shown

- To implement priority rotations in this design, vector P is introduced.

The algorithm for priority rotations is:

```
set P = "111111110000000".
if P = "000000011111111" then
        set P = "111111110000000"
else
        rotate P one position to the right.
end if
```

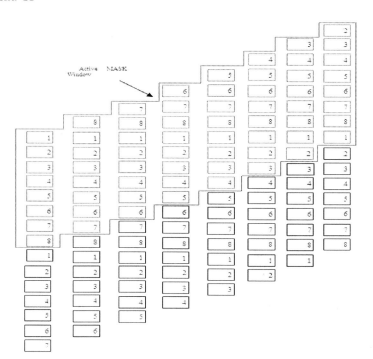

Fig. 2. DPA Scheduler for 8 x 8 Crossbar

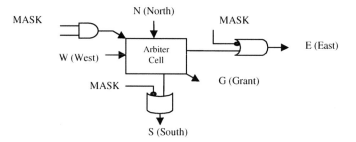

Fig. 3. Modified DPA with Mask

2.2 Design of 8-Bit Fabric

The crossbar fabric module is responsible for physically connecting an input port to its designated output port, based on the grants issued by the scheduler. The inputs of fabric (except for the grant input) are connected to the input port modules of switch. The outputs of fabric are connected to the output ports of the switch. The fabric makes the appropriate connection between each input and its corresponding output port.

The grant comes from the crossbar scheduler and it is the same as the one given to the ports. It determines the output port to which input data is routed. .The cross points are controlled by the grant input of the fabric module (Figure 5). Each bit of the grant input corresponds to one of the cross points of the crossbar.

If a certain grant bit is at logic high, then the corresponding cross point is closed.

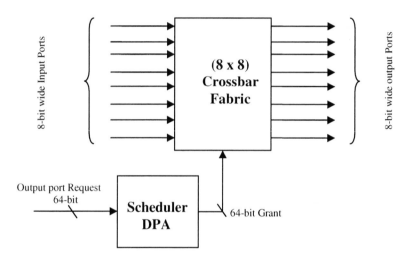

Fig. 4. 8-bit wide 8 x 8 Switch

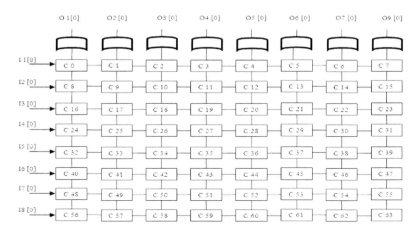

Fig. 5. 8-copies of Crossbar for 8-bit input port

2.3 Control Logic of Cross Points

Each bit of the output is constructed from inputs 1 to 8 AND'ed with the grant lines in the column corresponding to the output, and OR'ed at the end.

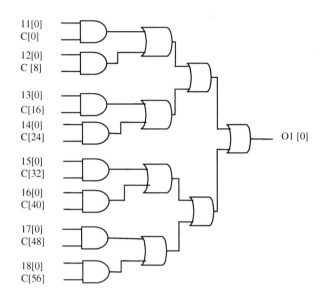

Fig. 6. Internal structure of Cross points

3 Simulation Results and Analysis

We have simulated the crossbar switch for 8-bit wide data. The result is presented in table 1. We have supplied 8-bit data with different priorities. The configuration of the crossbar is shown using control bits

Table 1. Input and control bits

Input data Bits	Control Bits								Output data bit
11111111	C0=0	C1=1	C2=0	C3=0	C4=0	C5=0	C6=0	C7=0	00000000
00000001	C8=0	C9=1	C10=0	C11=0	C12=0	C13=0	C14=0	C15=0	00000000
00000011	C16=0	C17=1	C18=0	C19=0	C20=0	C21=0	C22=0	C23=0	00000000
00000111	C24=1	C25=0	C26=0	C27=0	C28=0	C29=0	C30=0	C31=0	11111111
00001111	C32=0	C33=0	C34=0	C35=1	C36=0	C37=0	C38=0	C39=0	00000111
00011111	C40=0	C41=1	C42=0	C43=0	C44=0	C45=0	C46=1	C47=0	00111111
00111111	C48=0	C49=0	C50=1	C51=0	C52=0	C53=0	C54=0	C55=0	00000011
01111111	C56=0	C57=1	C58=0	C59=0	C60=0	C61=0	C62=0	C63=0	0000001

The correctness of the proposed design is shown through the following waveform generated from mentor graphics ModelSim. In the 8-bit 8x8 crossbar switch, we have 8-bit input and output ports. The waveform shows the multiple transfers of data from input to output port if there is no contention.

The switch has been realized on field programmable gate array. The table 2 summarizes the device utilization of FPAG vertex 6 series.

The schematic generated from Xilinx Synthesis Tool (XST) is shown in figure 8. The schematic has main block known as fabric and a front end circuit known as DPA. The DPA resolves the contention among the input request for the output channel. In DPA the multiple requests for the same output port will be served in the next arbitration cycle.

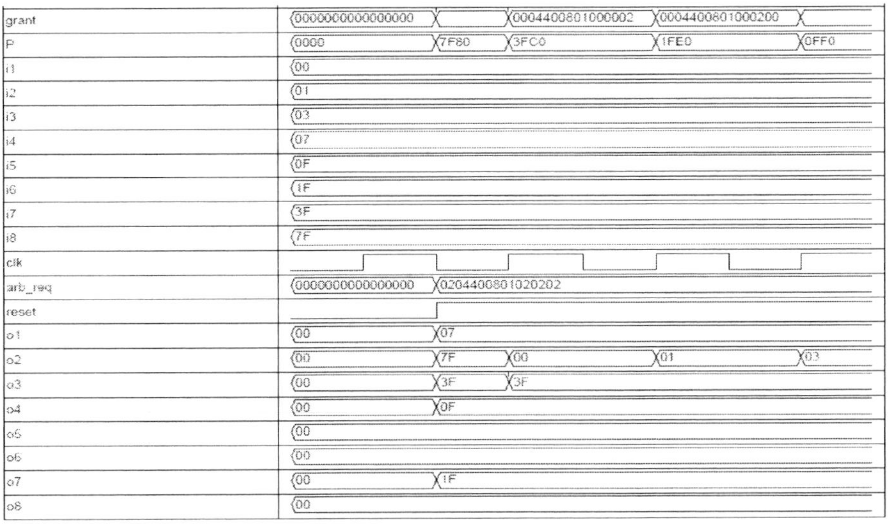

Fig. 7. Simulation waveform of 8 x 8 Switch

Table 2. Device utilization summary

Resources	Used	Avail	Utilization (%)
IOs	8	240	3.3
Global Buffers	4	32	12.5
Function Generators	300	46560	6.4
CLBs Slices	100	11640	0.85
DFF/Latches	20	93120	0.02
Block RAMs	0	156	0
DSP48E1	0	288	0

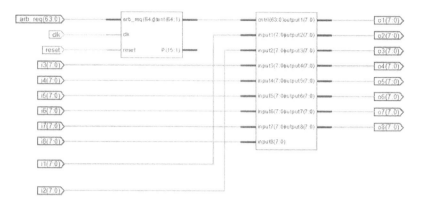

Fig. 8. RTL of 8-bit 8 x 8 Crossbar

The following graph shows the increase of power as the temperature is increased. We have calculated the power at 350nm technology of TSMC.

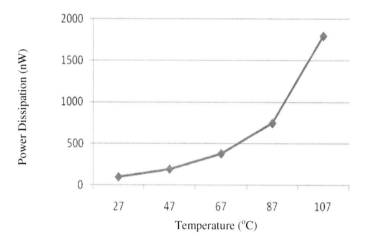

Fig. 9. Temperature Vs Power Dissipation of 8-cross bar at 350nm Technology

4 Conclusions

We have presented a 8-bit crossbar switch for Network-on-Chip (NoC) for parallel data transfer. The presented design has an advantage rotation of priority using Diagonal Propagation Arbiter. This provides fairness in the on-chip network communcation. The high performance crossbar is coined with Diagonal Propagation Arbiter. The presented crossbar requires a two-dimensional arbitration that incorporates a diagonally rotated priority to provide fair arbitration. The arbiter has aceived a propogation delay of 1 ns for Vertex 6 FPGA device.

Acknowledgments. The authors wish to acknowledge the financial support received from University Grants Commission, Ministry of Human Resource Development, Govt. of India, during the course of this project under the Grant F. No. 39-895/2010(SR) to Department of Electrical Engineering, Jamia Millia Islamia, New Delhi, India.

References

1. Hurt, J., May, A., Zhu, X., Lin, B.: Design and implementation of high-speed symmetric crossbar schedulers. In: Proc. ICC 1999, Vancouver, Canada (June 1999)
2. Mullins, R., West, A., Moore, S.: Low-latency virtual-channel routers for on-chip networks. In: Proc. Int. Symp. Comput. Architecture, Cambridge, UK, pp. 188–197 (June 2004)
3. Pasricha, S., Dutt, N.: On-Chip Communication Architectures. Morgan Kaufmann Publications, U.S. (2008)
4. Dally, W.J.: Virtual-channel flow control. IEEE Trans. Parallel Distrib. Syst. 3(2), 194–205 (1992)
5. Kumar, Peh, L., Kundu, P., Jha, N.K.: Express virtual channels: Towards the ideal interconnection fabric. In: Proc. Int. Symp. Comput. Architecture, pp. 150–161 (June 2007)
6. Nicopoulos, et al.: ViChaR: A dynamic virtual channel regulator for network-on-chip routers. In: Proc. Int. Symp. Microarchitecture, pp. 333–346 (December 2006)
7. Enright-Jerger, N., Peh, L.-S., Lipasti, M.: Virtual circuit tree multicasting: A case for on-chip hardware multicast support. In: Proc. Int. Symp. Comput. Architecture, pp. 229–240 (June 2008)
8. McKeown, N., Izzard, M., Mekkittikul, A., Ellersick, W., Horowitz, M.: Tiny Tera: a packet switch core. IEEE Micro, 26–33 (January/February 1997)
9. Dally, W.J., Towles, B.: Principles and Practices of Interconnection Networks. Morgan Kaufmann Publishers, U.S. (2004)
10. Eggers, H., lysaght, P., Dick, H., McGrefor, G.: Fast reconfigurable crossbar switching in FPGA's. In: Hartenstein, R.W., Glesner, M. (eds.) FPL 1996. LNCS, vol. 1142, pp. 297–306. Springer, Heidelberg (1996)
11. Alfke, P., Fewer, C., McMillan, S., Blodget, B., Levi, D., Young, S.: A high I/O reconfigurable crossbar switch. In: Field-Programmable Custom Computing Machines, pp. 3–10 (2003)
12. Fewer, C.: Cross Bar Switch Implemented in FPGA. Xilinx White Paper WP166 (September 2002)
13. Singhal, V., Le, R.: High-Speed Buffered Crossbar Switch Design Using Virtex-EM Devices, Xilinx paper XAPP240 (v1.0), March 14, pp. 1–7 (2000)
14. Fischer, T.: FPGA Crossbar Switch Architecture for Partially Reconfigurable Systems, pp. 1–88. Karlsruhe Institute of Technology (May 7, 2010)
15. A Parameterized Model of a Crossbar Switch In Bluespec System Verilog (TM) June 30, 2005 © Copyright Bluespec, Inc. (2005)

Energy Management for Energy Harvesting Real Time System with Dynamic Voltage Scaling

Ranvijay[1], Rama Shankar Yadav[1], Arvind Kumar[1], and Smriti Agrawal[2]

[1] Department of Computer Science and Engineering,
Motilal Nehru National Institute of Technology, Allahabad, India
[2] Department of Computer Science and Engineering,
Jaypee University of Information Technology, Solan, India
ranvijaymnnit@gmail.com, rsy@mnnit.ac.in,
arvinddagur@gmail.com, smriti.agrawal@juit.ac.in

Abstract. Energy harvesting has recently emerged as a feasible option to increase the operating time of battery based real time embedded systems. In this paper, we propose a scheduling algorithm that offers lesser energy consumption for battery powered dynamic real time system modeled with aperiodic tasks and energy harvesting constraints. As the harvested energy is highly dependent on the environment thus, available power/energy of storage changes over the time. The proposed approach has to decide which speed or voltage level is to be to select leading to reduction in energy overhead as well as timing overhead due to the speed switching. We further, improve the quality of service to accept more number of aperiodic tasks and improve the system performance in terms of remaining energy. Theorem is being derived to show the effectiveness our approach having lesser energy consumption as compared to existing one. The simulation results and examples illustrate that our approach can effectively reduce the overall system energy consumption and improve the system performance in terms of remaining energy as well as reduce the rejection ratio of aperiodic tasks.

Keywords: Real time systems, energy aware scheduling, harvested energy, dynamic voltage scaling, and quality of service (QoS).

1 Introduction

Energy minimization is a key issue for designing of real time embedded systems. This is especially important for battery powered systems. As the advancement of technology chip area reduces. Thus, less energy is storable on board. If deployed bigger battery on a chip as a result leading to their size as well as cost still severely limits the system's lifespan. The emerging technology of energy harvesting has earned much interest recently to provide a means for sustainable embedded systems [1] one of the important domain is wireless sensor network. Wireless sensor networks consisting of numerous minuscule sensors that are unobtrusively embedded in their environment. That sensor nodes scavenging ambient energy may operate perpetually, that has been constrained by their limited power supply. Most of the time in sensor network, recharging or replacing nodes' batteries is not practical due to inaccessibility

D.C. Wyld et al. (Eds.): NeCoM/WeST/WiMoN 2011, CCIS 197, pp. 536–548, 2011.
© Springer-Verlag Berlin Heidelberg 2011

and sheer number of the sensor nodes. In order to solve the energy problem and increase the system operating time, environmental energy harvesting is deemed a promising approach. There are various source of harvesting energy such as solar, thermal, kinetic or vibrational energy, etc. most of the environmental energy sources varied over time [4]. For example, the harvested energy of a solar cell at a sunny noon is much higher than that at dawn. The feasibility of battery based real time system depends upon timing constraint as well as energy constraint. Energy constraint depends upon the stored energy as well as harvested energy from environment. The author [3, 5] is to maximize the utilization of solar energy, in this paper the authors sagest an algorithm, when the scavenged energy is low decrease the duty cycle in time (e.g.at night) and increase the duty cycle when scavenged energy is high (e.g. during the day). Author [2, 7] has been presented which demonstrate both feasibility and usefulness of sensors nodes which are powered by solar or vibrational energy. Kansal et al. [5] explore how to maximize the utilization of solar energy by minimizing the roundtrip losses of the battery. Moser et al. [6] develop lazy-scheduling to avoid deadline violation in energy-harvesting systems.

Existing strategy for energy minimization in support of aperiodic tasks [10, 11, 16] do not solve all this issues completely. For example, uncontrolled occasional deadline misses are possible by using the slacked EDF [13]. W. Yuan et al.[17] proposed energy aware algorithm for dynamic soft real-time multimedia applications. Author [19] provides offline energy aware scheduling approach for mixed task set. The algorithm presented by Shin and Choi in [18] also sets the initial voltage level using Static Voltage Scaling. Then they lower the voltage level further whenever a single task is eligible for execution. Lee et al. [20] developed their DVS algorithms using only two voltage levels and distributing the tasks into two sets, each corresponding to one of the voltage levels: High and Low.

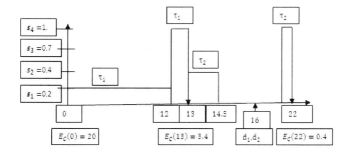

Fig. 1. schedule of existing approach(EA-DVFSA)[]

Liu et al. [21] extend the results in [6] to taking into account dynamic voltage scaling processor to reduce the rate of deadline misses due to the shortage of energy. In this paper author propose energy aware dynamic voltage and frequency selection algorithm (EA-DVFA). According to EA-DVFA [21] when system have not enough energy execute some portion of the computation (execution) time on slower speed and some portion are scheduled at maximum speed level. This leading to more energy consumption due to the speed switching overhead and execute some portion of task at maximum speed level. As a consequence, future tasks have to violet their deadlines due to the shortage of energy.

In this paper, we aim to improve the quality of service (QoS) by accepting more number of aperiodic task as well minimize the energy consumption leading to elongate the operating time of battery. So, we will find the tradeoff between timing conflicts and energy conflicts for that we proposed the modified energy aware dynamic voltage and speed selection algorithm (MEA-DVSA). In this paper we reduce the energy overhead as well as timing overhead by utilizing the speed in such a way that response time of task is less than or equal to the existing approach even though on the cost of lesser energy consumption. The rest of the paper is organized as follows: in section 2, we describe our preliminary, followed by motivational example and system model. Sections 3 discuss our contribution. Section 4 and section 5 elaborates our proposed approach followed by results and analysis in section 6. Finally, paper concludes with section 7.

2 Preliminaries

Here, we provide the system model followed by the motivations for our approach.

2.1 Motivational Example

Consider a real time system with two aperiodic tasks, τ_1 (0, 16, 4), τ_2 (5, 16, 1.5), where the triplet of attributes denotes arrival time(a_i), deadline (d_i) and worst case execution time at maximum speed $e_i(s_{max})$. Assuming at time instance $= 0$, the stored energy $E_C(t) = 20$. The harvested power from time interval 0 to 25 is set to 0.5. System having four normalized speed level say ($s_1 = 0.25$, $s_2 = 0.40$, $s_3 = 0.70$ and $s_4 = 1.0$). the power consumption at corresponding speed level are 1joule, 1.75 joule, 3.8 joule and 7joule per unit time Energy overhead due to the speed/voltage switching are as follows: $\beta_1^2 = 1.8\ \mu\,joule$, $\beta_1^3 = 2.1\ \mu\,joule$, $\beta_1^3 = 2.6\ \mu\,joule$, $\beta_1^4 = 3.1\ \mu\,joule$, $\beta_2^3 = 1.5\ \mu\,joule$, $\beta_2^4 = 1.9\ \mu\,joule$ and $\beta_3^4 = 1.2\ \mu\,joule$.

Energy Aware Dynamic Voltage and Frequency Selection (Existing approach)
Here, at time t=0 the total stored energy is $E_C(t) = 20$. When first task τ_1 arrive at time t=0 it required 4 unit computation time at s_{max} speed level. The energy consumption of task τ_1 at s_{max} speed is 32 joule which is more than the available energy. Existing approach compute execute the some portion at lower speed and some portion run at maximum speed level to provide the time opportunity for future tasks. We can observe from the schedule system starts running task τ_1 at speed level s_1 up to time $t = 12$ and remaining computation time i.e. 1 unit at s_{max} from time $t = 12$ to time $t = 13$ and finish at time $t = 13$. Hence the energy consumption for the task τ_1. $E_{consumption}(\tau_1) =$ task processing energy consumption plus energy overhead due to energy switching. $E_{consumption}(\tau_1) = 12 * 1 + 1 * 7.5 + 3.1 = 23.1$ joule. Thus response time of task τ_1 is 13. The harvested energy $E_{Source}(0,13) = 6.5$ and $E_C(0) = 20$. Hence energy available at time t=13: $E_C(t) = E_C(0) + E_{Source}(0,13) - E_D(0,13) - \beta_1^4 E_C(13) = 20 + 6.5 - 19.5 - 3.1 = 3.4\ joule$.

The time t=13 to time t=16 the harvested energy $E_{Source}(13,16) = 1.5$ so the total available energy from time t= 13 to time t=16 is 4.9 joule leading to miss the deadline of task τ_2 because existing approach starts τ_1 at time t=13 at speed evel s_2 up to time t=14.5, while remaining computation time (0.4) unit executed at maximum speed level s_4. For that it is required $E_{consumption}(\tau_2) = 1.5 * 1.75 + 0.4 * 7.5 + 1.9 = 7.525$ joule of energy where as only 4.9 joule of energy is available up to time t=16. So, deadline of τ_2 is violated due to the shortage of energy.

On the other hand, if we compute a single speed in such away response time of task is same or less without going on maximum speed level. The power consumption increases exponentially at higher speed level as compare to lower speed level as well as energy save due to reducing the speed switching. This provides the better opportunity to insure the timing as well energy constraint of tasks. Thus, we proposed the modified dynamic voltage and speed algorithm that improve the acceptability domain by accepting more aperiodic tasks and minimize the energy consumption.

Before discussing the proposed modified energy aware dynamic voltage and frequency selection algorithm, we describe the system model and assumptions in the next section.

2.2 System Model

This system deals with energy minimization of random arrival pattern aperiodic tasks and is able to operate at different speed level. System modelled with energy source, energy storage, energy drain, DVS processor and real time aperiodic tasks.

Energy Source:
Harvesting source of energy is dependent on environmental factors. Such as solar, wind etc. they are highly varying with time, if (r) is the rate of harvesting power per unit time in any interval [t1, t2]. So total energy harvested in time interval [t1, t2] is as follows:

$$E_{Source}(t1, t2) = (t2 - t1) * r \qquad (1)$$

Energy Storage:
Here, we assume a limited energy storage that may be charged up to its capacity C. If no tasks are executed and the stored energy has reaches its capacity leading to energy overflow.

$$0 \leq EC(t) \leq C \qquad \forall t \qquad (2)$$

For executing the task, power $P_D(t)$ and the respective energy $E_D(t1, t2))$ is drained from the storage to execute tasks. We have the following relation:

$$E_C(t2) \leq E_C(t1) + E_{source}(t1, t2) - E_D(t1, t2) \qquad \forall t2 > t1$$

Therefore,

$$E_D(t1, t2) \leq E_C(t1) + E_{source}(t1, t2) \; \forall t2 > t1 \qquad (3)$$

Energy Drain:
Energy is the function of speed level s_i where, $(s_{low} \leq s_i < s_{max})$. The energy drain in time interval $(t1, t2)$ is given as:

$$E_D(t1, t2) = \int_{t1}^{t2} P_D(s_i)(t)\, dt \qquad (4)$$

Where $P_D(s_i)$ is the power drain at speed level s_i.

The other considerations are as follows:

1. Real time system modeled with aperiodic tasks τ_1, τ_2, τ_3 ... τ_n. Each task τ_i has the attributes, (a_i) is the arrival time, $e_i(s_{max})$ is the worst-case execution time at maximum speed level (s_{max}), and deadline (d_i) are known only after its release.

2. We assume that uni-processorr system.

3. We consider Dynamic priority Scheduling algorithm Earliest deadline first (EDF).

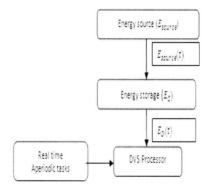

Fig. 2. Energy aware real time scheduling scenario

Table 1. Performance measurement of example 1

Energy Consumption:		
Aperiodic tasks	Energy consumption in existing approach, EA-DVFA [21]	Energy consumption in proposed approach, MEA-DVSA
τ_1	23.1 joule	17.5 joule
τ_2	7.525 joule	7.5 joule
Response time/Status of task		
Aperiodic tasks	EA-DVFA [21]	MEA-DVSA
τ_1	13 (accept)	10 (accept)
τ_2	16.4 (failed)	5 (accept)
Remaining energy after execution of tasks in the system in the schedule length of [0, 22].		
Aperiodic tasks	EA-DVFSA [21]	MEA-DVSA
τ_1	3.4 joule	7.5 joule
τ_2	0.4 joule	4.5 joule

4. DVS processor can operate at $\mathcal{N}$ discrete voltage levels, i.e., $V = \{v_{low}, v_2, v_3 ... v_{max}\}$ where each voltage level is associated with a corresponding speed from

the set $S = \{s_{low}, s_2, s_3 \dots s_{max}\}$. The speed s_{low} is the lowest operating speed level whereas s_{max} is the maximum speed level.

In this figure 2 the energy source harvest the energy from the environment and convert into electrical signal at particular rate of energy. This energy accumulated in the energy storage up to their capacity C; the stored energy at time t is denoted by $E_c(t)$. When the processor executes the real-time task, it has drawn the energy from energy storage. If the energy storage is empty, the processor stops functioning.

3 Contribution

- We proposed energy constrained scheduling algorithm for aperiodic time critical tasks whose energy storage is recharged by environmental source.
- We provide modified dynamic voltage and frequency algorithm to accept more number of tasks while elongate the operating time of battery.
- We present theorem that ensure our existing algorithm for aperiodic task leads to the same or lesser amount of energy consumption as compared to DVFSA.

In this paper we proposed the modified energy aware dynamic voltage and speed selection algorithm (MEA-DVSA). We reduce the energy overhead as well as timing overhead due to the speed switching by utilizing the speed in such a way that response time of task is less than or equal to the existing approach even though on the cost of lesser energy consumption.

4 Energy and Time Overhead

Every time the processor's speed level / supply voltage are switched from one speed/voltage level to other speed/voltage level. The change requires a certain amount of extra energy and time. That extra amount of energy and time is called energy overhead and time overhead respectively [13]. The energy overhead due to the speed /voltage switching form speed level (s_k) to speed level (s_j) is denoted by β_i^j where as α_i^j indicate the timing overhead.

$$\beta_k^j = Cr \cdot |Vdd_k - Vdd_j|^2 + Cs \cdot |Vbs_k - Vbs_j|^2 \qquad (5)$$

$$\alpha_k^j = max(pVdd \cdot |Vdd_k - Vdd_j|, pVbs \cdot |Vbs_k - Vbs_j|) \qquad (6)$$

Where, Cr denotes power rail capacitance, and Cs the total substrate and well capacitance. Since transition times for Vdd and Vbs are different, the two constants $pVdd$ and $pVbs$ are used to calculate both time overheads independently. Vdd indicate the supply voltage whereas, Vbs indicate the body bias voltage. The energy overhead(β_k^j) due to speed switching from speed level (s_k) to speed level (s_j) is as same as for the speed switching from speed level (s_j) to speed level (s_k) i.e.

$$\beta_k^j = \beta_j^k \qquad (7)$$

5 Modified Energy Aware Dynamic Voltage and Speed Selection

In this section we proposed a voltage and speed selection algorithm that reduces the energy as well as timing overhead incurred due to switching between speed levels.

As from example 1 existing approach schedule the some portion of task on lower speed and some portion on maximum speed level to prevent stealing excessive time from future tasks. Due to going on maximum speed level energy consumption increases exponentially (energy consumption is a function of cubic of speed) as well as energy consumption due to the speed switching that leading to miss the deadline due of future task due to the shortage of energy. So we will propose modified dynamic voltage and frequency selection algorithm that compute the speed of task with same or less response time with lesser energy consumption.

Run tasks at maximum speed: when any task τ_k arrived at any time t. its energy requirement at maximum speed level is less than the total available energy $E_C(t)$.

Energy Minimization

Run task at lower speed: when any task τ_k arrived at any time t. its energy requirement at maximum speed level is greater than the total available energy $E_C(t)$. If we start execution at maximum speed that leading to operable Vs non operable time of processor. Tasks start execution at maximum speed until the available energy is zero. When the available energy is zero the system has to stop running the task and delay the task execution until it has a scavenged energy. That's leading to miss the deadline of a task even though it may be feasible at lower speed level.

Assume task τ_k arrives with arrival time a_k , worst case execution time at s_{max} and deadline d_k. The available stored energy is $E_C(a_m)$ and harvested energy from a_k to d_k is $E_{Source}(a_k, a_k + d_k)$. We can calculate the system running time $(Srun_{s_i})$ at any speed level (s_i) as same as the existing author such that all available energy is completed depleted at power P_n until time instance $a_k + d_k$

$$Srun_{s_i} = E_c(a_k) + \frac{E_{Source}(a_k, a_k + d_k)}{P_n} \tag{8}$$

When we slow down the speed of task τ_k, the execution time at any speed level s_i may be less than equal to its deadline and the energy consumption of task must be less than or equal to sum of available energy $E_c(a_k)$ as well as harvested energy $E_{Source}(a_k, a_k + d_k)$. Mathematically

$$e_i/s_i \le d_i - a_i) \tag{9}$$

$$E_{consumption}(a_k(s_i)) \le E_c(a_k) + E_{Source}(a_k, a_k + d_k) \tag{10}$$

So we can find the feasible speed s_i $(s_{low} \le s_i \le s_{max})$ under the constraint of equation 9 and equation 10.

We compute the earliest possible starting running time of task τ_k and as late as possible starting running time under constraint of equation 9 and equation 10 by equation 11 and 12.

$$S_{earlrast}(\tau_k) = max(a_k, a_k + d_k - Srun_i) \tag{11}$$

$$S_{late} = \max(a_k, a_k + d_k - Srun_{max}) \tag{12}$$

Where $Srun_{max}$ is computed by equation 13.

$$Srun_{s_{max}} = E_c(a_k) + \frac{E_{Source}(a_k, a_k + d_k)}{P_{max}} \tag{13}$$

if $S_{earlrast}$ and S_{late} are same it indicates both are equal to a_k. i.e.

$$Srun_i \geq Srun_{max} \geq d_k \tag{14}$$

The equation 13 indicates system running time at maximum power is larger than d_k. Thus, the system has enough energy to run the task at maximum speed level.

If $S_{earlrast}$ less than S_{late} it means the system have not enough energy between the time instances a_k and $a_k + d_k$ to schedule the task τ_k at maximum speed level. In existing approach [21] they execute the task initially at lower speed level (s_i), if task is not finish up to S_{late} the remaining computation time executed at maximum speed level (s_{max}). In our approach we slow down the speed of task and compute the speed level s_i for task τ_k and execute the whole computation time at same computed speed level ($s_{compute}$).

$s_{compute}$ Can be computed as follows:

$$\left(^{e_i}/_{s_i}\right) > (S_{late} - S_{earlrast}) \text{ where } (s_{low} \leq s_i < s_{max}) \tag{15}$$

$$Z_i = \left(e_i - \left(^{S_{late} - S_{earlrast}}/_{s_i}\right)\right) \tag{16}$$

Where Z_i is the remaining computation time.

$$Y_i = Z_i + (S_{late} - S_{earlrast}) \tag{17}$$

Where Y_i is the total required time to complete the task τ_k at speed level s_i as well as speed level s_{max}. Hence, ($s_{compute}$) is computed by equation 11.

$$s_{compute}(\tau_i) = \left(^{e_i}/_{Y_i}\right) \tag{18}$$

Choose the speed level $S_{assigned}$ if it is available otherwise chose the nearest speed level where $\left(^{e_i}/_{s_{compute}}\right) \leq d_i$ and energy drain at speed $S_{assigned}$ in any interval (t1, t2) is less than or equal to $E_D(t1, t2) \leq E_C(t1) + E_{source}(t1, t2)$.

Proposed modified energy aware dynamic voltage and speed selection algorithm (MEA-DVSA) is summarized as below. The effectiveness of proposed modified dynamic voltage and speed selection algorithm (MDVSA) compared to existing dynamic voltage and frequency selection (DVFSA) approach can be seen in example 1. Here, same example 1 is scheduled by the proposed approach. We can observe from the schedule (figure 4) when τ_1 arrives at time $t = 0$ and it required 4 unit of computation time at maximum speed. The power consumption at maximum speed level is 8 joule per unit time. Thus, energy consumption of task τ_1 at maximum speed level is 32 joule while energy available at time instance t=0 is only 20. So it is not process at maximum speed level. Thus, execute the task at lower speed level. We compute the speed ($s_{compute}$) for task τ_1 by equation 18. We get, $s_{compute}(\tau_1) = 0.30$, but this speed level is not available in the system thus, we select the nearest speed level under the constraint of equation 9 and equation 10. So select speed level $s_2 = 0.40$ to run the task τ_1. Thus, task τ_1 finish at time t=10. The energy consumption of task τ_1 $E_{consumption}(\tau_1) = 10 * 1.75 = 17.5$ joule.   the total stored energy at time $t = 10$ is $E_C(10) = 20 + 5 - 17.5 = 7.5$ joule. Thus, task τ_2 run at maximum speed and finish at time $t = 14$ hence, remaining energy in the system at time $t = 16$ is 1.5 joule.

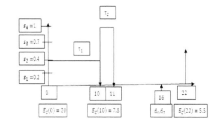

Fig. 3. schedual of existing approach (EAM-DVSA)

Whereas, only task τ_1 is feasible through existing approach [21]. The modified approach not only improves the acceptability domain by accepting more number of tasks it also reduces the response time.The effectiveness of proposed approach has been summarized in table 1.

Theorem: For DVS enable processor, the modified energy aware dynamic voltage frequency scaling (MEA-DVSA) algorithm for aperiodic task leads to the same or lesser amount of energy consumption as compared to EA-DVFA.

Proof: In both the approach we calculate earliest possible start time ($S_{earlrast}$) and as possible as late start time (S_{late}) of task. Case1: when $S_{earlrast} = S_{late}$
Both the approaches execute the task at maximum speed level (s_{max}). Hence, the energy consumption for both approaches is same.
Case2: when ($S_{earlrast} < S_{late}$), scale down the speed.
Start with lowest speed level $s_i \leftarrow s_{low}$ where $s_{low} \leq s_i < s_{max}$ When $\left(e_i/s_i\right) \leq$ $S_{late} - S_{earlrast}) \leq (d_i - a_i)$
Both the approach is able to execute the task at same reduced speed level s_i.
Case3: when ($S_{earlrast} < S_{late}$), scale down the speed Start with lowest speed level $S_i \leftarrow S_{low}$ where, $S_{low} \leq S_i \leq S_{max}$. When $\left(e_i/s_i\right) \geq S_{late} - S_{earlrast}) \leq (d_i - a_i)$ Existing DVFSA start the execution of task at speed level s_i up to s_2 and the remaining computation time are executed at maximum speed.
So there is a speed switching even though there is no higher priority tasks. So the energy consumption of task is the amount of time task running at speed level s_i, remaining computation time executed at maximum speed level (s_{max}) and the energy consumption due to the speed/voltage switching. In proposed MEA-DVSA task executed at $S_{assigned}$ throughout the execution. Energy consumption of task is the amount of time task running at $S_{assigned}$. i.e. only due to the speed level $S_{assigned}$. Energy consumption is a function of cubic of speed level. So energy consumption of task by MEA-DVSA is lesser than existing EA-DVFA. In view of all the three cases we can say MEA-DVSA algorithm for aperiodic task leads to the same or lesser amount of energy consumption as compared to EA-DVFA. Hence, prove. In the view of above theorem we hence have the following corollary.

Algorithm
  1. Maintain a ready task queue Q
  3 $Z_i \leftarrow 0$
  4. $Y_i \leftarrow 0$
  5.$t \leftarrow current\ time$
  3. While (true)
  4.$d_{i\leftarrow} min\{d_j : T_j \in Q\}$
  5. Calculate $S_{earlrast}$ and S_{late} for task τ_i
  6. if $S_{earlrast} = S_{late})$ then
  7. Execute task τ_i at maximum speed of
processor or voltage.
  9 end if
  8. if ($S_{earlrast} < S_{late}$)
  9. Slow down the speed
  10. $s_i \leftarrow s_{low}$
  11. While $(^{e_i}/_{s_i} \le d_i - a_i)$

    {

$$if \left((^{e_i}/_{s_i}) > (S_{late} - S_{earlrast}) \right)$$
$$Z_i = (e_i - (^{S_{late} - S_{earlrast}}/_{s_i}))$$
$$Y_i = Z_i + (S_{late} - S_{earlrast})$$
$$S_{compute} = \left(^{e_i}/_{Y_i} \right)$$

    End if
    }
                  $s_i \leftarrow s_{i+1}$
    Go to level 11
      if
          t=ak
          then add task k to Q
          Goto step 1
            if t=fk
         then remove the task from Q
      End if

  End

Corollary 1: let us consider a system is characterized by energy capacity C, r is the rate of harvesting energy through source Es an interval $[t_1, t_2]$. If our approach can not schedule the given task due to the shortage of energy then existing EA-DVFA is not able to schedule it.

The next section deals with performance measurement of multi budget bandwidth preserving server through simulations.

6 Simulation and Result Discussion

In this section simulation of synthesized tasks are performed to evaluate the performance of the proposed window based lazy scheduling followed by the speed stretching approach to save energy. The processor is capable of voltage and frequency scaling. With five speed level 100 MHz, 200 MHz, 500MHz, 750MHz, and 1000 MHz. We assumed Power consumption at corresponding speed level is 60mW, 180Mw, 750Mw, 1800mW and 3200mW. Aperiodic tasks were generated by the exponential distribution using with inter arrival time ($1/\lambda$) and service time ($1/\mu$) with parameters λ and μ.simulation is run for 10000 .Here, we compare the performance of proposed modified energy aware Dynamic voltage and speed algorithm refer MEA-DVSA with existing energy aware Dynamic voltage and frequency algorithm referred as EA-DVFA [21]. The key parameters for performance measurment are remaning energy and acceptence ratio.

In the following section we measure the effect of variation in aperiodic load on the average energy consumption and acceptense ratio of aperiodic task.

Effect of load on average remaning energy
The effect of load on the remaning energy consumption can be seen from the figure 4. This compare the performance of EA-DVFA and MEA-DVSA. In this we set the storage capacity is to 2000. We observe from the figure 4 when the aperiodic load incress the remaining energy will decreases. When we varies aperiodic load from 10% to 90% we observe from the figure as load increase remaining energy of the system decreases. At lower aperiodic load (10% to 40%) our modified approach have significant saving in energy almost store 15% more energy ac compared to existing EA-DVFA [21] approach. This is due to the at lower aperiodic load our approch run the whole compation of task most of the time at slower speed and same speed level however, existing approach execute some portion at lower speed and remaning comptation time at maximum speed level even there is no any higher priority tasks.

Effect of load on acceptence ratio
The effect of load on the acceptence ratio of aperiodic tasks can be seen from the figure 5. Figure 5 compare the performance of EA-DVFA and MEA-DVSA. In this we set the storage capacity is to 2000. We observe from the figure 6 when the aperiodic load incress the acceptence ratio will decreases. At lower aperiodic load (10% to 40%) our modified approach have accept 10% more aperiodic tasks as compared to existing EA-DVFA [21].

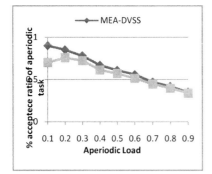

Fig. 4. % Acceptence of aperiodic task

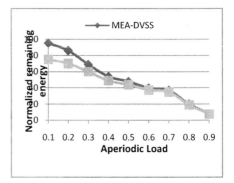

Fig. 5. Average remaining energy

7 Conclusion

In this paper we have presented a general scheduling algorithm that maximize the utility of harvested energy for real time embedded system with voltage scalable processor. The proposed approach judiciously decides operating speed that reducing the energy overhead as well as timing overhead due to the speed switching. The existing EA_DVFA switch the speed level of the task even though there is no any aperiodic task.

The examples and simulation studies shows that the proposed scheduling algorithm (MEA-DVSA) improves the overall average remaining stored energy. The average remaining stored energy of the system is approximately 5 % at aperiodic load varied from 70% to 90% while 20% more energy will be stored at lower aperiodic load varied from 10% to 50%. When the aperiodic load is low say 10% to 50% our praposed approach accept 8 % more task than existing approach. However, at higher aperiodc load both approach performa almost same. Thus, extensive simulation and illustrative example shows that our proposed approach is capable of performing better in terms of average stored remaining energy of the system as well as acceptance ratio of aperiodic tasks.

References

1. Li, D., Chou, P.H.: Application/architecture power co-optimization for embedded systems powered by renewable sources. In: DAC 2005: Proceedings of the 42nd Annual Conference on Design Automation, pp. 618–623. ACM, New York (2005)
2. Ammar, Y., Buhrig, A., Marzencki, M., Charlot, B., Basrour, S., Matou, K., Renaudin, M.: Wireless sensor network node with asynchronous architecture and vibration harvesting micro power generator. In: sOc-EUSAI 2005: Proceedings of the 2005 Joint Conference on Smart Objects and Ambient Intelligence, pp. 287–292. ACM Press, New York (2005)
3. Hsu, J., Zahedi, S., Kansal, A., Srivastava, M.: Raghunathan. Adaptive duty cycling for energy harvesting systems. In: ISLPED 2006: Proceedings of the 2006 International Symposium on Low Power Electronics and Design, pp. 180–185. ACM Press, New York (2006)
4. Roundy, S., Steingart, D., Frechette, L., Wright, P., Rabaey, J.M.: Power sources for wireless sensor networks. In: Karl, H., Wolisz, A., Willig, A. (eds.) EWSN 2004. LNCS, vol. 2920, pp. 1–17. Springer, Heidelberg (2004)
5. Kansal, A., Hsu, J., Zahedi, S., Srivastava, M.B.: Power management in energy harvesting sensor networks. ACM Transactions on Embedded Computing Systems (in revision) (May 2006); also available from: NESL Technical Report Number: TR-UCLA-NESL-200605-01
6. Moser, C., Brunelli, D., Thiele, L., Benini, L.: Real-time scheduling for energy harvesting sensor nodes. Real-Time Systems 37, 233–260 (2007)
7. Jiang, X., Polastre, J., Culler, D.E.: Perpetual environmentally powered sensor networks. In: Proceedings of the Fourth International Symposium on Information Processing in Sensor Networks, UCLA, USA, April 25-27, pp. 463–468 (2005)
8. Mejía-Alvarez, P., Levner, E., Mossé, D.: Adaptive Scheduling Server for Power-Aware Real-Time Tasks. ACM Trans. Embedded Computing Systems 3(2), 284–306 (2004)
9. Aydin, H., Melhem, R.G., Mossé, D., Mejía-Alvarez, P.: Power- Aware Scheduling for Periodic Real-Time Tasks. IEEE Trans. Computers 53(5), 584–600 (2004)

10. Hong, I., Potkonjak, M., Srivastava, M.B.: On-Line Scheduling of Hard Real-Time Tasks on Variable Voltage Voltage Processor. In: Proc. Int'l Conf. Computer-Aided Design, pp. 653–656 (1999)
11. Sharma, V., Thomas, A., Abdelzaher, T., Skadron, K., Lu, Z.: Power-Aware QoS Management in Web Servers. In: Proc. IEEE Real-Time Systems Symp., pp. 63–72 (2003)
12. Pillai, P., Shin, K.G.: Real-Time Dynamic Voltage Scaling for Low-Power Embedded Operating Systems. In: Proc. 18th Symp. Operating Systems Principles, pp. 89–102 (2001)
13. Sinha, A., Chandrakasan, A.P.: Energy Efficient Real-Time Scheduling. In: Proc. Int'l Conf. Computer-Aided Design, pp. 458–470 (2001)
14. Zhu, Y., Mueller, F.: Feedback EDF Scheduling Exploiting Dynamic Voltage Scaling. In: Proc. IEEE Real-Time and Embedded Technology and Applications Symp., pp. 203–212 (2004)
15. Shin, Y., Choi, K.: Power Conscious Fixed Priority Scheduling for Hard Real-Time Systems. In: Proc. Design Automation Conf., pp. 134–139 (1999)
16. Qadi, A., Goddard, S., Farritor, S.: A Dynamic Voltage Scaling Algorithm for Sporadic Tasks. In: Proc. IEEE Real-Time Systems Symp., pp. 52–62 (2003)
17. Doh, Y., Kim, D., Lee, Y.-H., Krishna, C.M.: Constrained Energy Allocation for Mixed Hard and Soft Real-Time Tasks. In: Proc. of Int. Conf. on Real-Time and Embedded Computing Systems and Applications, pp. 533–550 (2003)
18. Shin, Y., Choi, K.: Power Conscious Fixed Priority Scheduling for Hard Real-Time Systems. In: Proceedings of the Design Automation Conference, pp. 134–139 (June 1999)
19. Yuan, W., Nahrstedt, K.: Integration of Dynamic Voltage Scaling and Soft Real-Time Scheduling for Open Mobile systems. In: Proc. of Int. Workshop on Network and Operating Systems Support for Digital Audioand Video, pp. 105–114 (2002)
20. Lee, Y.-H., Krishna, C.M.: Voltage-Clock Scaling for Low Energy onsumption in Real-Time Embedded Systems. In: Proceedings of the Sixth Int'l Conf. on Real Time Computing Systems and Applications, pp. 272–279 (1999)
21. Liu, S., Qiu, Q., Wu, Q.: Energy Aware Dynamic Voltage and Frequency election for Real-Time Systems with Energy Harvesting. In: Design, Automation and Test in Europe, DATE 2008 (2008)

A Natural Language Interface Based on Machine Learning Approach

Himanshu Sharma, Neeraj Kumar, Govind K. Jha, and K.G. Sharma

Assistant Professor, GLA University Mathura
{himanshusharma19,javaneeraj,gvnd.jha,
hollyhoc}@gmail.com

Abstract. This paper deals with natural language interface which accepts a query in natural language and provide answers in the textual form. The paper presents an interface module that converts user's query given in natural language into a corresponding database command. The idea of using natural language instead of SQL has prompted the development of new type of processing method called Natural Language Interface to Database systems (NLIDB). This paper proposes a machine learning approach that replaces previously used approaches based mainly on semantic analysis. The learning interface learns the correct mapping of user's query to corresponding database command based on past data collected.

Keywords: SQL, NLIDB, NLP, Semantic, Database.

1 Introduction

Nowadays there is lot of data that is maintained by organizations, companies and universities, but only the individuals who are familiar with data query methods can directly access that data. It is clear that if people can put their queries in natural language then, the process will continue faster and with higher quality. An important area in this direction is the application of natural language interface for databases (NLIDB). The NLIDB means that a user can use some natural language to create queries and also the answer is presented in the same language. The history of NLIDB goes back as early as 1960's [2]. The era of peak research activity on NLIDB was in the 1980's. In that time, the development of a domain and language independent NLIDB module seemed as a realistic task. The prototype projects showed that the building of a natural language interface is a much more complex task than it was expected.

Over the last years, few approaches have emerged that are based on semantic analysis and grammar and to provide users with a friendly user interface to enable them to ask their queries in some natural language and respond the answers in the same language. Database semantics consists of two concepts; first concept is developed to function as a translation dictionary and second one to contain selection restriction constraints on domain classes. For a target database, the database semantics is semi-automatically obtained from a semantic data model. Based on this

D.C. Wyld et al. (Eds.): NeCoM/WeST/WiMoN 2011, CCIS 197, pp. 549–557, 2011.
© Springer-Verlag Berlin Heidelberg 2011

database semantics, a conceptual NLDBI translation scheme is designed. Translating a natural language question into a database query suffers from translation ambiguity problem. In NLDBI, translation ambiguities occur when a linguistic term is associated with two or more domain classes. That is, a linguistic term has many translation equivalents in physical database structures. This problem must be seriously considered.

We propose to apply the concepts of machine learning to automate the acquisition of linguistic knowledge and present al natural language interface for accessing the databases and let uses ask their queries in their native language.

In our natural language interface architecture we apply the constraint on the linguistic analysis of the user query (input) to the lexical analysis phase. Instead of applying a semantic analysis we associate the input to the correct command class by using a machine learning classifier. Regarding the selection of appropriate machine learning algorithm, we do the comparative study of number of supervised learning algorithms.

2 Related Work

A natural language interface (NLI) is a system that allows a computer user
uses his/her own language when interacting with a computer system. The system accepts an input (speech or text) in a natural language from a user, and transforms it into a formal language statement, in which it can be executed by its processor [16]. With an NLI, a user does not have to remember commands, or lost in a hierarchy of menus.

Since the end of 1960s, there have been a larger number of research works introducing the theories and implementations of Natural Language Interface framework. The first type of framework is based on pattern matching, which is also the first technique applied to NLIDBs, and typical applications of this type of framework include SAVVY [15]. In this, the given input question is matched with the predefined set of pattern of questions and the possible interpretation is made. This can only interpret the questions defined earlier in the pattern. The second type is based on an intermediate representation language. The SQL generator transfers DRS expressions into SQL sentences. One typical example of this type like is MASQUE/SQL [1]. The intermediate language helps us to generate query. Its very difficult to generate SQL queries directly from natural languages however it become quite easier by firstly transforming it in to intermediate language and then from it in to final query language. The third one is based on syntax. The user inputs will be first translated into syntax tree by syntax analysis and parsing, and then it will be translated into SQL. A typical example of this approach is LUNAR [8]. Lunar, a natural language interface to a database containing chemical analyses of Apollo-11 moon rocks by William Woods. It consist of components like parser, syntax analyzer .It also uses an intermediate form before converting it in to query. The intermediate form used here is syntax tree .Since here graphical intermediate form is used it makes it quite easier .The last one is based on semantic grammar. The user inputs will be translated into semantic tree by semantic analysis, then it will be translated into SQL, and a typical example is PLANES [10].In short most of the previous work is based on the grammar and parsing. Consider the figure 1. To process a query, the first step is speech tagging; followed by word tagging. The second step is parsing the tagged sentence by a grammar. The grammar parser analyzes the query sentence according to the tag of each word and generates the grammar tree/s. Finally, the SQL translator processes the grammar tree to obtain the SQL query.

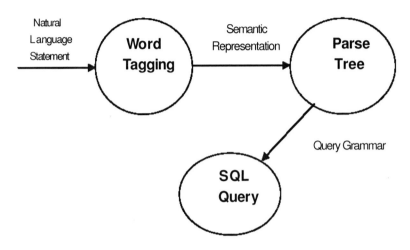

Fig. 1. Query Generation Based on Parsing and Semantic Analysis

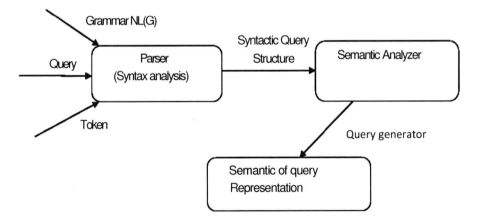

Fig. 2. Different components for developing Natural Language Analyzer (NLA)

3   Proposed Work

In our natural language interface architecture we apply the restrictions on the linguistic analysis of the user query (input) to the lexical analysis phase. Instead of applying a semantic analysis we associate the input to the correct command class by using a machine learning classifier. Our interface architecture is shown in Fig.3. The architecture represents a database interface for the English language which can also be extended to other languages, that is it can be made multilingual interface. That is why, the first step is the detection of user input that is transformed into respective language-specific morphological and lexical analyzer. Morphological and lexical analysis analyse the individual words into their components and non words tokens are separated from the words and thus performs performs the tokenization of the input, i.e. the segmentation into individual words or tokens.

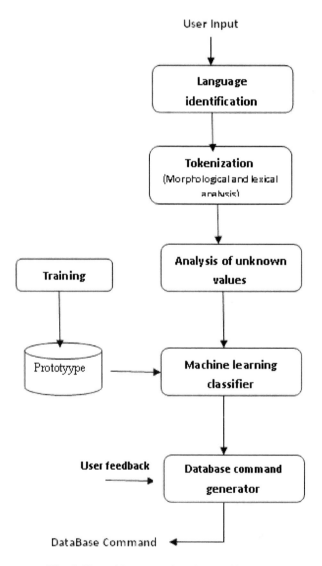

Fig. 3. Natural Language interface architecture

In the next step the input is transformed into a token feature list (TFL), which represents for each token its category, surface form, and semantic token form. For database interfaces, some values which are not known contained in the input may have some importance for the interpretation of a command. Therefore, we consider these values seprately and do their analysis in a analyzer which we call as unknown value analyzer (UVA). This analyzer checks unknown values data types and searches them up in the database to find out whether they represent identifiers of existing entities. In such a case, the entity type is indicated in the resulting UVA; otherwise we use the data type instead.

TFL and UVA are provided as the input to the machine learning (ML) classifier. According to learned classification rules, it assigns a ranked list of command classes to the input sentence. In the last step the classifications are used for generating appropriate database commands.

Thus, an elaborate semantic analysis is replaced by learning task of the user input. Several man-months is required for the design of the corresponding underlying rule base. A realistic real-life application, is represented by learning task. It differs from many other problems studied in machine learning research in a way that it consists of a large number of features and classes. Also, the command classes are very similar and even for human experts very difficult to distinguish. Now, we only make use of the semantic token forms contained in the TFL for the encoding of training data. Then we use English concepts as forms and map them to binary features, i.e. if the token form is a member of the TFL, we map certain feature to 1, and otherwise it equals 0. For the elements of the UVA we apply a more detailed encoding, which maps the type and the number to binary features.

3.1 Algorithm

Rule based learning represents a large category of model-based learning techniques in which the learned language is represented by a theory language that is richer than the language used for the description of the training data [9]. These learning methods construct explicit generalizations of training cases thus resulting in a large reduction of the size of the stored knowledge base and the cost of testing new test cases. Rule based learning aims at deriving a set of rules from the instances of the training set. Rules are learned one at a time. A rule is here defined as a conjunction of literals, which, if satisfied, assigns a class to a new case. For the case of binary features, the literals correspond to feature tests with positive (true) or negative(false) sign. Thus we are checking whether a new case possesses a certain feature (for positive tests) or not (for negative tests). The methods for deriving the rules originate from the field of inductive logic programming [7].

One of the most prominent algorithms for rule-based learning is RIPPER [9], which learns for each class a set of rules by applying a separate-and-conquer strategy. We start with the case of two classes where we talk of positive and negative examples, then later generalize to K > 2 classes. Rules are added to explain positive examples such that if an instance is not covered by any rule, then it is classified as negative. So a rule when it matches is either correct (true positive), or it causes a false positive.The algorithm takes the instances of a certain class as target relation. It

```
type E.literal:
properties:
public:
   litf: feature, sign:
   bool;
ROLL:
   differ(featurelist);
end-type
class E.literal
    public:
            differ(featurelist)
    begin

        differ(Flist) :-
            S == get_sign@self,
            S == true,
            F == get_litf@self,
            ~is_in(F)@Flist;
        differ(Flist) :-
            S == get_sign@self,
            S == false,
            F == get_litf@self,
            is_in(F)@Flist;
    end
end-class
type E.rule:
    properties:
      public:
            rulenr: int,
            ruleclass: int;
        public [literal];
            ROLL:
            differ(featurelist);
end-type
class E.rule
    public:
            differ(featurelist)
                begin

                    differ (Flist) :-
                    is_in(L)@self,
                    differ(Flist)@L;
                end
end-class
```

Fig. 4. ROCK and ROLL code for test of rules

iteratively learns a rule and removes those instances from the target relation that are covered by the rule. This is repeated until no instances are left in the target relation. A rule is grown by repeated specialization, adding literals until the rule does not cover any instances of other classes. In other words, the algorithm tries to find rules that possess some positive bindings, i.e. instances that belong to the target relation, but no negative bindings for instances of other classes. Therefore, the reason for adding a literal is to increase the relative proportion of positive bindings.

We have implemented RIPPER, and besides this, we also developed the algorithm BIN rules with the following weighting function:

$$W_{f,s,c} = b(f)^{+} .(b^{-} - b(f)^{-}) . W_{f,s,c}$$

In this formula, s indicates the sign of the feature test. The number of positive (negative) bindings after adding the literal for the test of feature f is written as $b(f)^{+}$ $b(f)^{-}$ Finally, b- indicates the number of negative bindings before adding the literal so that ($b^{-} - b(f)$) calculates the reduction of negative bindings achieved by adding the literal.

We have implemented the test of rules as deductive ROLL method as shown in fig. 4. The invocation of the method is a query with the parameters fl for the feature list of the new case. The test returns false for those rules that are satisfied by the new case. The result of the query can then be assigned to the set of satisfied rules rs by using the command:

$$rs := [\{R\}|\sim differ (!fl) @R];$$

3.2 Evaluation

For evaluating the feasibility of the implemented machine-learning algorithm, we developed a English natural language interface based on 1500 input sentences that had been collected from users by means of questionnaires. The input sentences were then mapped to 50 command classes (30 for each class). The mapping was performed by elaborate semantic analysis; for the development of the underlying rule base we spent several man-months.

Table 1. Characteristics of rule-based learning

	Rules	Literals	Max Length
RIPPER	300	634	8
BIN Rules	290	788	27

Table 2. Test results for rule based learning

	ENGLISH	
	Success rate	Top 5
RIPPER	90%	96%
BIN rules	93%	96%

As result of the encoding of the training set, we obtained the large number of 400 features, 356 for the TFL and 44 for the UVA. For the evaluation we used as performance measures the success rate, i.e. the proportion of correctly classified test cases, and the top-5 rate. The latter indicates the proportion of cases where the correct classification is among the first three predicted classes. Table 1 shows RIPPER produces a more compact representation of learned knowledge than BIN rules. However, according to Table 2 BIN rules outperforms RIPPER for the ENGLISH language with respect to the success rate.

4   Conclusion and Future Work

By providing an expert system, we are encoding hidden mystery of natural language. Using query language for dealing with databases is always a professional and complex problem. This complexity causes the user's usage of data existing in database limits to use definite reports there are in some pre implemented software's. However, you can create this opportunity that each none professional user transfers his questions and requirements to computer in natural language and derives his desired data by natural language processing. Natural Language Processing can bring powerful enhancements to virtually any computer program interface. This paper proposes a machine learning approach that replaces previously used approaches based mainly on semantic analysis. The learning interface learns the correct mapping of user's input to corresponding database command based on collection of past data.

Future research in this can be development of multilingual natural language interface architecture, which can be used for accessing online product catalogs and other e-commerce applications. By exploiting tools and methods from machine learning and natural language processing we can enhance exciting retrieval tools to take the linguistic context into account

References

[1] Androutsopoulos, I., et al.: Natural language interfaces to databases - an introduction. Journal of Natural Language Engineering 1(1), 29–81 (1995)
[2] Aone, C., Bennett, S.W.: Applying machine learning to anaphora resolution. In: [17], pp. 302–314 (1996)
[3] Barja, M.L., et al.: An effth ctive deductive object oriented database through language integration. In: Proc. of the 20 International Conference on VLDB, Athens, Greece, pp. 63–474. Morgan Kaufmann, California (1994)
[4] Imielinski, T., Mannila, H.: A database perspective on knowledge discovery. Communications of the ACM 39(11), 58–64 (1996)
[5] Mooney, R.J.: Comparative experiments on disambiguating word senses: An illustration of the role of bias in machine learning. In: Proc. of the Conference on Empirical Methods in Natural Language Processing, Philadelphia, Pennsylvania, pp. 82–91 (May 1996)
[6] Moulinier, I., Ganascia, J.-G.: Applying an existing machine learning algorithm to text categorization. In: [14], pp. 343–354 (1996)
[7] Muggleton, S. (ed.): Inductive Logic Programming. Academic Press, London (1992)

[8] Woods, W.A., Kaplan, R.M., Webber, B.N.: The lunar sciences natural language information system: Final Report. BBN Report 2378, Bolt Beranek and Newman Inc., Cambridge, Massachusetts (1972)

[9] Ross Quinlan, J., Michael Cameron-Jones, R.: Induction of logic programs: FOIL and related systems. New Generation Computing 13, 287–312 (1995)

[10] Waltz, D.L.: An english language question answering system for a large relational database. Communications of the ACM, 526–539 (July 1978)

[11] Soderland, S., et al.: Issues in inductive learning of domain-specific text extraction rules. In: [14], pp. 290–301 (1996)

[12] van den Bosch, A., et al.: Morphological analysis as classification: An inductive learning approach. In: Proc. of the 2nd International Conference on New Methods in Language Processing, Ankara, Turkey (September 1996)

[13] Wermter, S., et al. (eds.): Connectionist, Statistical, and Symbolic (1996)

[14] Johnson, T.: Natural language computing: The Commercial Applications. Ovum Ltd., London (1985)

[15] Jusoh, S.: Natural Language Interface for Online Sale Systems. In: International Conference on Intelligent and Advanced Systems (2007)

Analyzing Various Social Networking Approaches for Covert Networks

S. Karthika[1] and S. Bose[2]

[1] Research Scholar
[2] Assistant Professor
Department of Computer Science and Engineering
College of Engineering Guindy, Anna University, Chennai-600096
sk_mailid@yahoo.com
sbs@cs.annauniv.edu

Abstract. The world we live in is a complex socio-technical system and systematically thinking about, representing, modeling and analyzing these systems has been made possible by social network analysis approach. A lot of groups or communities do exist in the society but the terrorist network has been taken for study in this paper because they consist of networks of individuals that span countries, continents, the economic status, and form around specific ideology. In this paper we present a survey to study the terrorist network using the criminal network analysis which is based on dynamic network analysis, destabilizing covert networks, counter terrorism, key player, subgroup detection and criminal network analysis in homeland security. This paper will also discuss various open problems in this area.

Keywords: Criminal Network Analysis (CNA), Social Network Analysis (SNA), and Terrorist network.

1 Introduction

The tragic events of September 11, 2001, attacks on the United States has made both citizens and authorities realize that knowledge about the structure of terrorist networks and how those networks operate will be a key factor in winning the so called "net war", a lower-intensity battle by terrorists, criminals, and extremists with a networked organizational structure [1]. No longer can a structured battle be fought with military power, instead, the war against terrorism will be won with superior knowledge. Due to the changing nature of homeland security problems, a new type of intelligence is needed which is called as Social Network Analysis (SNA). The basis of social network analysis is that individual nodes are connected by complex yet understandable relationships that form networks. These networks are ubiquitous, with an underlying order and simple laws [2]. But a drawback with SNA is that it cannot be considered as a suitable data mining technique because it can discover the patterns from transparent structure and not from hidden structure like terrorist network where the nodes are embedded in a large population. Hence the knowledge discovery process to isolate overt cell from covert cell uses the crime data mining technique and

D.C. Wyld et al. (Eds.): NeCoM/WeST/WiMoN 2011, CCIS 197, pp. 558–566, 2011.
© Springer-Verlag Berlin Heidelberg 2011

the hidden network is analyzed using Criminal Network Analysis (CAN). The terrorist network analysis treats the covert network as an undirected graph and un-weighted graph. The nodes may be individuals, groups (terrorist cells), organizations, or terrorist camps. The ties may fall within a level of analysis (e.g. individual to individual ties) or may cross-levels of analysis (individual-to-group analysis) [3].

The rest of the paper is structured as follows: Section 2 presents a detailed survey of various problems in criminal network analysis. Section 3 outlines the future directions of social network analysis in covert networks. Finally, Section 4 concludes the paper with a summary.

2 Social Engineering Approaches for Covert Networks

In this section we shall discuss various methods of criminal network analysis for terrorist networks.

2.1 Link Analysis

CNA requires the ability to integrate information from multiple crime incidents where the relationships between crimes entities are established using link analysis [5].

Jennifer Schroeder, Jennifer Jie Xu, Hsinchun Chen and Michael Chau [5] establish association path linking using heuristic methods in knowledge engineering which constructs a knowledge base that develops an inference engine. This paper implements a system called as Crime Link Explorer based on a set of structured crime incidents from Tuscan police department. The system has proved that the heuristic weights reflect human judgment more accurately than simple co-occurrence weight because the earlier incorporates domain knowledge of crime investigators.

Robert D. Duval, Kyle Christenseny, Arian Spahiuz [6] in their work have discussed about the problems associated to missing data and the resulting errors like node deletion, node addition, edge deletion and edge addition. The authors prefer to use the bootstrapping methodology which treats the existing network as a sample, and then performs resample from the network. The resample network reduces the size of the network and increases the density. But the problem in this methodology is the removal of a link to more heavily connected nodes, which reduces the total path distances to be counted, and result in decreased centrality. This method is being implemented for Jemaah Islamiyah network collected by Stuart Koschade and 9/11 hijacker network collected by Valdis Krebs [31].

Christopher C. Yang and Tobun D. Ng [7] discuss the challenges in analyzing relationships embedded inside the semantics of bloggers' messages because weblog social network doesn't use page ranking or indexing methods. The authors have developed a crawler called as Dark web, which does link, and content analysis to extract the web log sub-community. It has been experimented for terrorist social network to discover the threat levels based on the activeness of interaction within the community and content development. Jennifer Jie Xu and Hsinchun Chen [8] improve the efficiency of the existing link analysis software that not only provides a visual representation of a criminal network but also uses shortest path algorithm to quickly complete the analysis task. The data set is got from Phoenix police department from which the paths identified are meaningful 80% of the time and provides a complete solution to the problem of identifying the strongest criminal associations between two or more entities.

Boongoen, T., Q. Shen, and C. Price [9] propose an unsupervised hybrid model to detect a false identity problem called as Connected-path that uses link analysis and text based measures in which multiple link properties are proficiently blended to refine the process of similarity estimation. Unlike the existing model, which needs prior linguistic knowledge, the proposed model is language-independent and knowledge-free, and so can be easily adapted to new problem domains. For demonstrating this technique a data set has been constructed with 919 real alias pair from terrorist related web pages and news stories.

2.2 Node Discovery Problem

Criminal network analysis's other main objective is analyzing the covert networks to solve the node discovery problem. Yoshiharu Maeno and Yukio Ohsawa [10] uses the clustering and ranking procedure along with the expert investigator's prior understanding to evaluate the activeness of communication and calculates likeliness of the suspicious inter-cluster relationships due to covert nodes between the clusters respectively. This process if done iteratively invents a hypothesis on the latent structure. This technique helps to reveal the 18 hijackers of 9/11 attacks and also the covert conspirators in the network.

Yoshiharu Maeno [11] presents two methods to solve the node discovery problem. One is a heuristic method in which closeness measure is determined using Jaceard's co-efficient and k-medoids is applied for classification of nodes. Along with these the ranking algorithm is also used to retrieve the suspicious surveillance logs. The next one is statistical inference method that employs the maximal likelihood estimation to infer the topology of the network, and applies an anomaly detection technique to retrieve the suspicious surveillance logs, which are not likely to realize without the covert nodes. The author uses a computationally synthesized network and global mujahedeen organization to generate the test dataset for which the performance evaluation is done.

Nasrullah Memon and Henrik Legind Larsen [4] have developed a prototype called *iMiner* that incorporates several advanced techniques like automatically detecting cells from a network, identifying various roles in a network using newly developed dependence centrality along with the existing ones like degree centrality and eigenvector centrality which also develops a hierarchy of terrorist network, provides facilities for retrieval of information and its presentation in graph form, enable small sub graphs to be retrieved and add to the browsing canvas and may also assist law enforcement about the effect on the network after capturing or killing a terrorist in a network.

Matthew J. Dombroski and Kathleen M. Carley [12] discuss about how the terrorist network structure of 9/11 is estimated, posed for "what if" scenarios to destabilize a network and predict its evolution over time using a tool called as NETEST that combines multiagent technology with hierarchical Bayesian inference models which produces network structure and informant accuracy and biased net models to examine and capture the biases that may exist in a specific network or set of networks.

Christopher E. Hutchins and Marge Benham-Hutchins [13] in this paper show how SNA tools like ORA, Automap stream the information and reduce the time taken for investigation by studying the person-to-person relationship and means for the criminal network in a dynamic environment. The author conducts the study on three networks, which imports the data sets from HIDTASIS, analyzing phone calls based on drug investigation and multimodal network of agents, resources, locations, events and roles.

Matthew Dombroski, Paul Fischbeck and Kathleen M. Carley [14] discuss the possibilities of using the inherent structures observed in social networks to make predictions of networks using limited and missing information. The model is based on empirical network data exhibiting the structural properties of triad closure and adjacency. The model exploits these properties using an inference model to update adjacent dyads given information on a reference dyad. S. Appavu , R. Rajaram, M. Muthupandian, G. Athiappan, K.S. Kashmeera [15] propose a decision tree based classification method to analyze the network by detecting e-mails that contain terrorism information. The proposed classification method is an incremental and user-feedback based extension of a decision tree induction algorithm named Ad Infinitum which uses a supervised learning technique with a set of labeled training example that builds a classifier with which we can predict the category of an unseen incoming e-mail.

2.3 Dynamic Network Analysis

Traditional analysis approaches, such as Social Network Analysis (SNA) and link analysis are limited in their ability to handle multiplex, multimode, large-scale dynamic data that are needed to characterize terror networks. Hence to solve this problem a modern technique called as Dynamic network analysis (DNA) is introduced which not only facilitates the collection, analysis and understanding of the network but also predicts the dynamic relationship and the impact of such dynamics on individual and group behavior.

Kathleen M. Carley [16] discuss about the integrated CASOS dynamic network analysis toolkit which is an interoperable set of scalable software tools for coding, analyzing and forecasting behavior given relational or "network" data. These tools form a tool chain that enables analysts to move from raw texts to meta-networks to the identification of patterns in networks. This toolset contains the following tools: AutoMap is a semi-automated Network Texts Analysis (NTA) that extracts networks from texts using the distance based approach called windowing, ORA for analyzing the extracted networks having meta-matrix data and generates report that identifies key players and can also compare two different networks, and DyNet that is built over a Construct simulation engine for what-if reasoning about the networks. These tools were tested by collecting thousands of open source documents about terrorism and it's being processed by Automap that constructs the database from which particular entities are studies and the resultant data are processed using ORA.

Ian A. McCulloh and Kathleen M. Carley [17] discuss about social network change detection using statistical process control chart that detects when significant changes occur in the network and from the chart the various centrality factors are calculated for several consecutive time periods. The suspected time period when a change has occurred is studied using CUSUM statistics and in depth time period is considered for understanding the degree of change.

Kathleen M. Carley [18] in this paper proposes an approach to estimate vulnerabilities and the impact of eliminating those vulnerabilities in covert networks. Key features of this work include: using detailed network data to supplement high level views of organizations to create a composite image using network metrics and using multiagent simulation to predict change in the composite network view over time. Running the model in a Monte-Carlo fashion to determine the robustness of the results and examining the result by adding and dropping nodes and edges in the underlying networks handle uncertainty.

2.4   Key-Player Identification and Sub-group Detection

To perform any terrorist activity their need to be collaboration between the terrorist and these ties are framed around some nodes, which act as key nodes or leaders who control and command the activity of the group. There are lots of works done to study about how the network is affected if the key nodes are removed. These networks are divided into subgroups and understanding these structures helps to disrupt terrorist network and develop effective control strategies to combat terrorism. Hence key player identification and sub-group detection are some major problem in criminal network analysis.

Stephen P. Borgatti [19] discuss about two problems in key player identification called as KPP1 which finds a set of k nodes if removed, would maximally disrupt communication among the remaining nodes which is solved using graph's cohesion measure and secondly KPP2 finds a kp-set of order k that is maximally connected to all other nodes which quantify the extent to which a node's ties reach into the network. Shou-de Lin and Hans Chalupsky [20] focus on finding abnormal instances in multirelational networks (MNR), which uses unsupervised framework to model semantic profile and detects the suspicious node with the abnormal semantic profile. The authors propose a novel explanation mechanism that facilitates verification of the discovered results by generating human-understandable natural language explanations describing the unique aspects of these nodes.

Nasrullah Memon, Nicholas Harkiolakis and David L. Hicks [21] have introduced the investigative data mining technique to study terrorist networks using descriptive and predictive modeling based on centralities and applied it to the detection of high value individuals by studying the efficiency after removing some nodes, determining how many nodes are dependent on one node and if hidden hierarchy exists find the command structure. The authors have also demonstrated this newly introduced technique with a case study of 7/7 bombing plot.

Nasrullah Memon, Abdul Rasool Qureshi, Uffe Kock Wiil, David L. Hicks [22] discusses about the software iMiner which uses the algorithms for subgroup detection using IDM and demonstrated them with an example of a fictitious terrorist network. The software iMiner can detect all terrorists who are directly or indirectly connected to a specified terrorist, they can detect paths that connect two specified terrorists, they can detect connections between groups of terrorists and they can uncover connections between the root (a node) and a destination (another node in terrorist cell). Yuval Elovici, Bracha Shapira, Mark Last, Omer Zaafrany and Menahem Friedman, Moti Schneider and Abraham Kandel [23] discuss about online tracking system called as Advanced Terrorist Detection System (ATDS) which determines the interest of a set of users based on their web access and it performs the real time monitoring of the web traffic generated by the same set of users and alerts the system if any accessed information is not relevant to the groups interest.

2.5 CNA for Homeland Security

India is at the geographical center of a belt of terrorist, insurgent and separatist violence. Internally, India is faced with terrorist violence in Jammu and Kashmir, in the North East and the South. Militant organizations have links to external agencies, and these links can be surprisingly long [24]. It is necessary for the citizens and the authorities to understand the situation and learn how to face the problem using social network analysis techniques.

Aparna Basu [24] derives a linkage map of terrorist organizations in India, which uses the methods of centrality and the co-occurrence of names of the terrorist organizations to determine the key players and the intensity of the links between them. The groupings affected by SNA based on textual links correctly displayed ideological and regional groupings of the terrorist organizations. Sudhir Saxena, K. Santhanam, Aparna Basu [25] has developed in-house Terrorism Tracker (or T2) which performs systematic search for information on terrorist events from open sources. This paper addresses organization-to-organization links of terrorist organizations operating in the Indian State of Jammu & Kashmir. The SNA software package, Visone, developed in Germany, has been used with the T2 generation of "co-occurrence" pairs where organizations are cited together in an event during the period 2000 – 2003. This output was converted into an adjacency matrix to form the input to Visone for analysis and generation of linkage graphs.

2.6 Counterterrorism

Uffe Kock Wiil, Nasrullah Memon and Jolanta Gniadek [26] present the Crime Fighter toolbox for counterterrorism which performs various processes like data acquition, knowledge management and information processing using a number of tools that are categorized as semi automatic tools which are web harvesting tool, data mining tool, data conversion tool, SNA tools, visualization tools and manual tools which are knowledge base tools and structure analysis tools. Clifford Weinstein, William Campbell, Brian Delaney, Gerald O'Leary [27] has developed the Counter-Terror Social Network Analysis and Intent Recognition (CT-SNAIR) which focuses on development of automated techniques and tools for detection and tracking of dynamically-changing terrorist networks as well as recognition of capability and potential intent. The authors have also simulated the terrorist attack based on real information about past attacks and generating realistic background clutter traffic to enable experiments to estimate performance in the presence of a mix of data. They have developed a new Terror Attack Description Language (TADL) which is used as a basis for modeling and simulation of terrorist attacks.

In order to destabilize and end the terrorist organizations we need to understand the how these networks evolved, the reason behind their origin and what makes them to grow even after removing the leading covert nodes. These are some serious is problems in criminal network analysis which have been studied.

Rebecca Goolsby [29] briefly examines how Al Qaeda evolved from an insurgency assistance group to a terrorist network of sophistication and global reach. It argues that Al Qaeda filled the needs of Islamist insurgencies and then developed into a complex system of networks by co-opting other groups, hijacking their agendas and transforming their ideologies. Al Qaeda thus has global aspects, which in a long run can withstand any disturbances, and local aspects, which are more vulnerable to discovery by local authorities and disruption. They tend to lack the training, professionalism, education and capacity to ensure strict security measures and discipline within their own ranks. Hsinchun Chen, Wingyan Chung, Jialun Qin, Edna Reid, Marc Sageman, Gabriel Weimann [30] discuss how terrorists share their ideology and communicate with members on the "Dark Web"—the reverse side of the Web used by terrorists. To improve understanding of terrorist activities from the web, the information is collected using searching, browsing and spidering. Then it's filtered based on domain and linguistic knowledge. These are then analyzed as domestic and international terrorism based on the group profile, dynamics and relationships. It's been applied for collecting and analyzing information of 39 Jihad web sites.

2.7 Visualization

Terrorist social network analysis is in general a manual process of collecting a large amount of information about the entities and their relationships, which are being maintained in a database. In order to reduce these overheads in data processing and collection, modern systems present the network in the form of graphs. The networks are represented as 2D and 3D graphs from which knowledge could be gained but the network was not analyzed. This poses as a challenge in visualization of terrorist networks.

Christopher C. Yang, Nan Liu, and Marc Sageman [28] discuss about visualization techniques like fisheye views and fractal views of a network using a 2D graph which facilitates the exploration of complex networks by allowing a user to select one or more focus points and dynamically adjusting the graph layout and abstraction level to enhance the view of regions of interest. Combining the two techniques can effectively help an investigator to recognize patterns previously unreadable in the normal display due to the network complexity.

3 Limitations and Future Directions

The major limitation of this area is all the research work has been done under the assumption that the data collected is complete information but in real world the data are incomplete. It's very difficult to collect the complete data about any terrorist activity. A lot of research has been done till now in which some of the following problems have not yet been addressed. In node discovery problem radial transmission is being always used. The hub-and-spoke model could also be implemented for influence transmission. Further study is also needed to solve the discovery of fake node and spoofing node. In DNA the behavioral impacts of social or political context and regional based specialties of the nodes are not represented in the graph. In CNA, the network could be formed not only between the persons but also between locations and properties for which temporal patterns are needed to help us predict the trend and operations of a criminal enterprise. The expansions of such enterprises are to be studied based on cross-regional analysis.

4 Conclusion

In this paper we have presented various social network analysis methods like link analysis, DNA, CNA for homeland security, visualization, exploring network structure of various terrorist networks, counter terrorism, key player identification and sub-group detection for terrorist network.

References

[1] Xu, J.J., Chen, H.: CrimeNet Explorer: A framework for criminal network knowledge discovery. ACM Transactions on Information Systems 23(2), 201–226 (2005)

[2] Ressler, S.: Social network analysis as an approach to combat terrorism: past, present, and future research. Homeland Security Affairs II(2) (July 2006)

[3] Chen, H., Chung, W., Xu, J.J., Qin, G.W.Y., Chau, M.: Crime Data Mining: A general framework and some examples. IEEE Computer Society 37(4), 50–56 (2004)

[4] Memon, N., Larsen, H.L.: Practical approaches for analysis, visualization and destabilizing terrorist networks. Presented at First International Conference on Availability, Reliability and Security (2006)

[5] Schroeder, J., Chen, H., Xu, J., Chau, M.: Automated criminal link analysis based on domain knowledge. Journal of the American Society for Information Science and Technology 58(6), 842–855 (2007)

[6] Duval, R.D., Christenseny, K., Spahiuz, A.: Bootstrapping a terrorist network. Presented in the Conference of Southern Illinois University Carbondale (2010)

[7] Yang, C.C., Ng, T.D.: Terrorism and crime related weblog social network: link, content analysis and information visualization. Presented in IEEE International Conference on Intelligence and Security Informatics, New Brunswick, NJ (2007)

[8] Xu, J.J., Chen, H.: Using shortest path algorithms to identify criminal associations. Decision Support Systems 38, 473–487 (2004)

[9] Boongoen, T., Shen, Q., Price, C.: Disclosing false identity through hybrid link analysis. AI and Law (in press)

[10] Maeno, Y., Ohsawa, Y.: Analyzing covert social network foundation behind terrorism disaster. Int. J. Services Sciences 2(2) (2007)

[11] Maeno, Y.: Node discovery problem for a social network. Connections 29, 62–76 (2009)

[12] Dombroski, M., Carley, K.M.: NETEST: Estimating a terrorist network's structure. Computational & Mathematical Organization Theory 8, 235–241 (2002)

[13] Hutchins, C.E., Benham-Hutchins, M.: Hiding in plain sight: criminal network analysis. Computational & Mathematical Organization Theory 16(1), 89–111 (2009)

[14] Dombroski, M., Fischbeck, P., Carley, K.: Estimating the shape of covert networks. Presented in the Proceedings of 8th International Command and Control Research and Technology Symposium, Washington, DC (June 2003)

[15] Appavu, S., Rajaram, R., Muthupandian, M., Athiappan, G., Kashmeera, K.S.: Data mining based on intelligent analysis of threatening e-mail. Knowledge-Based Systems 22, 392–393 (2009)

[16] Carley, K.M.: A dynamic network approach to the assessment of terrorist groups and the impact of alternative courses of action. In: Visualizing Network Information. Meeting Proceedings RTO-MP-IST-063. Neuilly-sur-Seine, France: RTO, pp. KN1-1 – KN1-10 (2006)

[17] McCulloh, I.A., Carley, K.M.: Social network change detection. Carnegie Mellon University, School of Computer Science, Technical Report, CMU-CS-08-116

[18] Carley, K.M.: Estimating vulnerabilities in large covert networks. Presented in the Proceedings of 9th International Command and Control Research and Technology Symposium held at Loews Corornado Resort, CA. Evidence Based Research, Vienna, VA (2004)

[19] Borgatti, S.: The key player problem. Presented in the Proceedings of the National Academy of Sciences Workshop on Terrorism. National Academy of Sciences, Washington DC (2002)

[20] Lin, S.-d., Chalupsky, H.: Discovering and explaining abnormal nodes in semantic graphs. IEEE Transactions on Knowledge and Data Engineering 20(8), 1039–1052 (2008)

[21] Memon, N., Harkiolakis, N., Hicks, D.L.: Detecting High-Value Individuals in Covert Networks: 7/7 London Bombing Case Study. In: The Proceedings of the IEEE/ACS International Conference on Computer Systems and Applications, pp. 206–215 (2008)

[22] Memon, N., Qureshi, A.R., Wiil, U.K., Hicks, D.L.: Novel algorithms for subgroup detection in terrorist networks. Presented in the International Conference on Availability, Reliability and Security, Fukuoka Institute of Technology, Fukuoka, Japan (2009)

[23] Elovici, Y., Shapira, B., Last, M., Zaafrany, O., Friedman, M., Schneider, M., Kandel, A.: Detection of access to terror-related web sites using an Advanced Terror Detection System (ATDS). Journal of the American Society for Information Science and Technology 61(2), 405–418 (2010)

[24] Basu, A.: Social network analysis of terrorist organizations in India. Paper Presented at the North American Association for Computational Social and Organizational Science (NAACSOS) Conference, Notre Dame, Indiana, pp. 26–28 (2005)

[25] Saxena, S., Santhanam, K., Basu, A.: Application of Social Network Analysis (SNA) to terrorist networks in Jammu & Kashmir. Strategic Analysis 28(1) (2004)

[26] Wiil, U.K., Memon, N., Gniadek, J.: Knowledge management processes, tools and techniques for counterterrorism. Presented in the International Conference on Knowledge Management and Information Sharing, pp. 29–36 (2009)

[27] Weinstein, C., Campbell, W., Delaney, B., O'Leary, J.: Modeling and detection techniques for counter-terror social network analysis and intent recognition. Presented in the Proceedings of the IEEE Aerospace Conference (2009)

[28] Yang, C.C., Liu, N., Sageman, M.: Analyzing the terrorist social networks with visualization tools. In: Mehrotra, S., Zeng, D.D., Chen, H., Thuraisingham, B., Wang, F.-Y. (eds.) ISI 2006. LNCS, vol. 3975, pp. 331–342. Springer, Heidelberg (2006)

[29] Goolsby, R.: Combating terrorist networks: An evolutionary approach. Presented in the Proceedings of the 8th International Command and Control Research and Technology Symposium held at National Defense War College Washington DC, Evidence Based Research Vienna VA (2003)

[30] Chen, H., Chung, W., Qin, J., Reid, E., Sageman, M., Weimann, G.: Uncovering the dark web: A case study of Jihad on the web. Journal of the American Society for Information Science and Technology 59(8), 1347–1359 (2008)

[31] Krebs, V.E.: Mapping networks of terrorist cells. Connections 24(3), 43–52 (2002)

Semantic Data Integration and Querying Using SWRL

Vadivu Ganesan[1], S. Waheeta Hopper[2], and G. BharatRam[3]

[1] Assistant Professor, Department of Information Technology, SRM University
[2] Professor & Head, Department of BioInformatics, SRM University
[3] PG Student, Department of Information Technology, SRM University

Abstract. The semantic Web technology enables users to represent, share and discover heterogeneous data through formal ontologies. Semantic Web technologies also allow to link information thus moving from document centric idea of current Web to more fine grained semantic structures. The biological community requires more sophisticated methods to store, integrate and query their knowledge. This paper is focusing on Ontology construction of Natural Food Resources, Chemicals and Diseases. Semantics should be formally specified to provide a shared understanding of the implied relationships. Semantic Web Rule Language (SWRL) based on Description Logic (DL) is very useful for this formal specification of the ontologies. This enables the retrieval of user-specific semantic querying for topics of interest. This paper describes the works carried out on ontology-driven knowledge base and semantic querying of implicitly related sources from different domain.

Keywords: Semantic Web, **RDF** (Resource Description Framework), **OWL** (Web Ontology Language), **DL** (Description Logic), **SWRL** (Semantic Web Rule Language).

1 Introduction

Semantic Web is increasingly used in the area of health informatics and bioinformatics to get the integrated knowledge. In general many of the chronic diseases are due to the chemical reactions of medicines or food habits in the physiological processes. The balanced intake of natural foods with rich in nutritional factor has impact on curing such kind of chronic diseases such as cancer, diabetes, asthma, and hypertension etc.,. However, for the normal person, the study of relationship among chemical reactions, nutritional factors of the food sources, prevention and disease curing methods are very difficult. And also for the experts finding the alternate methodology, or structure, or similar type of entities are not that much simpler process.

The rise of the Internet has influenced the biologists, chemists, nutritionist and others to store and share their data. However, these distributed data are independent and often used in closed environment. Though the Web is rich of content, the users find difficulty on retrieving data from the large set, which consumes more human effort. If these data were to be linked, it would be possible for finding more inferences. The current Web is hampered with handling advanced applications such as processing, understanding and semantic interoperability of information contained in several Web documents. Semantic Web is the new generation Web that tries to represent information such that it can be

D.C. Wyld et al. (Eds.): NeCoM/WeST/WiMoN 2011, CCIS 197, pp. 567–574, 2011.
© Springer-Verlag Berlin Heidelberg 2011

used by machines, not just for display purposes, but for automation, integration, and reuse across applications (Berners-Lee 2000). Semantic Web is considered to be able to solve all such problems presented by the current web. The semantic web will be able to solve the problems with Ontologies. Ontologies are considered to be the basic building blocks of the Semantic Web.

Ontology is considered as a formal description of the concepts and relationships. The independent nature of Ontologies allows agents to be able to provide intelligent services by combining data from different Ontologies. This is why Ontologies are so popular that they are considered to be the building blocks of semantic web. Ontologies are implemented using OWL (Web Ontology Language) and RDF(Resource Description Framework).

Furthermore, semantic Web is about explicitly declaring the knowledge embedded in many Web based applications, integrating information in an intelligent way, providing semantic based access to the Internet, and extracting information from texts.

1.1 Literature Study

In [15], for foreseeable future, most data will continue to be stored in relational databases. To work with these data in ontology-based applications, tools and techniques that bridge the two models are required. Mapping all relational data to ontology instances is often not practical so dynamic data access approaches are typically employed, though these approaches can still suffer from scalability problems. The use of rules with these systems presents an opportunity to employ optimization techniques that can significantly reduce the amount of data transferred from databases. They express these data requirements by using extensions to OWL's rule language SWRL.

In [13], The SWRLTab is a development environment for working with SWRL rules in Protégé-OWL. It supports the editing and execution of SWRL rules. It also provides mechanisms to allow interoperation with a variety of rule engines and the incorporation of user-defined libraries of methods that can be used in rules. Several built-in libraries are provided, include collections of mathematical, string, and temporal operators, in addition to operators than can be used to effectively turn SWRL into a query language. This language provides a simple but powerful means of extracting information from OWL ontologies.

Our study focuses on developing semantic relationships to the domains of Chemical Compounds, Diseases and Natural Food sources for the better querying and linking of information. The paper is structured as follows: section 2 describes about the choice of ontology language; section 3 describes Knowledge Construction; section 4 outlined about Description Logic and Rule Specification followed by querying the datasets in section 5.

2 Semantic Web Layer

Ontology is defined as explicit and formal specification of conceptualization. Ontology comprises a set of knowledge terms, including the vocabulary, the semantic interconnections, simple rules of inference and logic for some particular topic.

Ontologies applied to the Web are creating the semantic Web. The Semantic Web architecture lists the underlying machine understandable languages for knowledge representation: XML (Extensible Markup Language), RDF (Resource Description Framework), and OWL (Web Ontology Language).

XML with XML namespace and XML schema definitions makes sure that there is a common syntax used in the semantic Web. When it comes to semantic interoperability, however, XML has disadvantages. Using XML, it is not possible to specify more relationships among the data. On top of XML is the RDF, for representing information about resources in a graph form. RDF, follows binary predicates with the format <Subject, Predicate, Object> used to create the relationship in the form of triples. For example, "Adhatoda used to cure Fever", <Adhatoda, usedToCure, Fever> is the triple form. RDF Schema (RDFS) defines the vocabulary of RDF model. It provides a mechanism to describe domain-specific properties and classes of resources to which those properties can be applied, using a set of basic modeling primitives (class, subclass-of, property, subproperty-of, domain, range, type). However, both RDF and RDFS are rather simple and still do not provide exact semantics of a domain. OWL is the next layer used in Semantic Web Architecture, is having more features compared to RDF. OWL is a set of XML elements and attributes, with well-defined meaning, that are used to define terms and their relationships (e.g. Class, equivalentProperty, intersectionOF, unionOF, etc.). Reasoning tasks like verification of ontology consistency, computing inferences and realizations can be easily executed with the OWL representation.

Fig. 1. Class, Subclass, Individual and their Properties

3   Construction of Knowledge Base

In practice, ontologies are often developed using integrated, graphical, ontology authoring tools, such as Protégé, OILed and OntoEdit. Protégé facilitates extensible infrastructure and allows an easy construction of knowledge rich domain ontologies. Protégé tool is used to develop domain ontology and querying since it has adopted the recent recommendation of the W3C, i.e. OWL standard. Protégé is also a knowledge based editor and it is open source Java tool that allows the easy construction of Ontologies.

```
<!-- http://www.owl-ontologies.com/Ontology1271250586.owl#LemonPepper -->
<owl:NamedIndividual rdf:about="&Ontology1271250586;LemonPepper">
  <rdf:type rdf:resource="&Ontology1271250586;Plants"/>
  <hasSodium rdf:datatype="&xsd;string">Low</hasSodium>
</owl:NamedIndividual>

<!-- http://www.owl-ontologies.com/Ontology1271250586.owl#Milk -->

<owl:NamedIndividual rdf:about="&Ontology1271250586;Milk">
  <rdf:type rdf:resource="&Ontology1271250586;DairyProducts"/>
</owl:NamedIndividual>

<!-- http://www.owl-ontologies.com/Ontology1271250586.owl#Mushroom -->

<owl:NamedIndividual rdf:about="&Ontology1271250586;Mushroom">
  <rdf:type rdf:resource="&Ontology1271250586;Herb"/>
  <hasVitamin rdf:datatype="&xsd;string">Vitamin D</hasVitamin>
  <containsChemicalCompound rdf:resource="&Ontology1271250586;VitaminD"/>
</owl:NamedIndividual>
  <!-- http://www.owl-ontologies.com/Ontology1271250586.owl#OcimumSantum -->
<owl:NamedIndividual rdf:about="&Ontology1271250586;OcimumSantum">
  <rdf:type rdf:resource="&Ontology1271250586;Plants"/>
  <isRelatedWith rdf:resource="&Ontology1271250586;fever"/>
  <usedToCure rdf:resource="&Ontology1271250586;fever"/>
</owl:NamedIndividual>
```

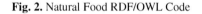

Fig. 2. Natural Food RDF/OWL Code

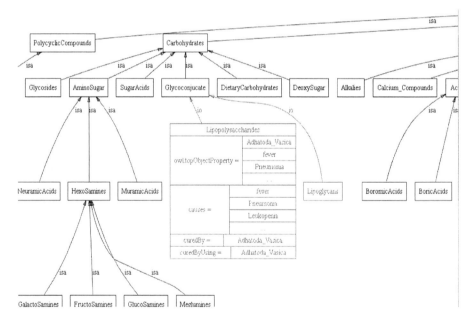

Fig. 3. Part of Chemical Ontology

The effort is taken to provide an explicit specification of the conceptual model. Ontologies are a means to formalize explicit knowledge related to a specific domain. The ontology development focuses on developing design hierarchy towards the explicit specification of relationships. Initially, the identified components of Natural Food, Disease and Chemical compound are represented in the form of class hierarchy using protégé tool. Fig. 1. shows the class, subclass, Individual and their properties creation using Protégé software. Fig. 2. Shows the Natural Food RDF/OWL code. The partial graphical representation of Chemical ontology is shown in Fig 3.

The hyperlinks are added to navigate among html pages. The hyperlink updating is possible only for smaller set of datasets. However, it results cumbersome for larger datasets. The semantic Web performance can be improved through linking of related entities from different datasets and establishing relationships automatically.

The ontology representation in Protégé is mapped on different dimensions. Semantic link is used to connect different datasets. The semantic linking provides more meaningful navigational paths to the users. There are two different types links are used in semantic web. Explicit links are given by the developers to find the relationship among the entities. Implicit relationships among the data cannot be automatically identified by the machines; developers have to find the internal relationships to assist the machine. There is no methodology for specifying implicit relationships. This type of sharing and finding implicit information is more important and also critical.

4 Description Logic

Description Logic (DL) is the formal knowledge representation language and the subset of First Order Logic. A Description Logic used to represent concepts, roles and individuals, and their relationships and is also used to write unambiguous statements. Attributive Language with Complement (ALC) is the simple form of DL has two parts: TBox and ABox. TBox (terminological box) is used to specify the class definition and the ABox (assertional box) is used to specify the relationships. Classes can be defined with many operations applied on it.

(i)   Diseases Ξ ∃causedBy some Microbes

(ii) Diseases Ξ ∃causedBy some Chemicals

(iii) Diseases Ξ ¥preventedBy only (Chemicals or NaturalFood)

(iv) NaturalFood Ξ ∃prevents some Diseases

(i) shows that Diseases can be caused by some of the Microbes. (ii) specifies that Diseases caused by some of the Chemicals. (iii) instances of Diseases can be prevented by only by the instances of Chemicals or NaturalFood. (iv) NaturalFood instances are used to prevent some of the instances of Diseases.

4.1 SWRL

The Semantic Web Rule Language (SWRL) is an expressive OWL-based rule language. SWRL allows users to write their own rules for their domain knowledge to find more relationships between the classes, properties and individuals[9]. This can be expressed in terms of OWL concepts to provide more powerful deductive reasoning capabilities than OWL alone. Using Protégé software the SWRL rules can be included by adding the plug-in SWRL tab. SWRLRules tab can be activated by selecting Project -> configure -> SWRL tab [10].

5 Query the Dataset

The semantic querying is made simple once the rules are specified using SWRL tab. The semantic querying helps the user to identify the related entities with ease.

$$Diseases(?x) \wedge hasTemperature(?x, "High") \rightarrow sqwrl:select(?x)$$

The above rule is used to identify all the Diseases with High Temperature.

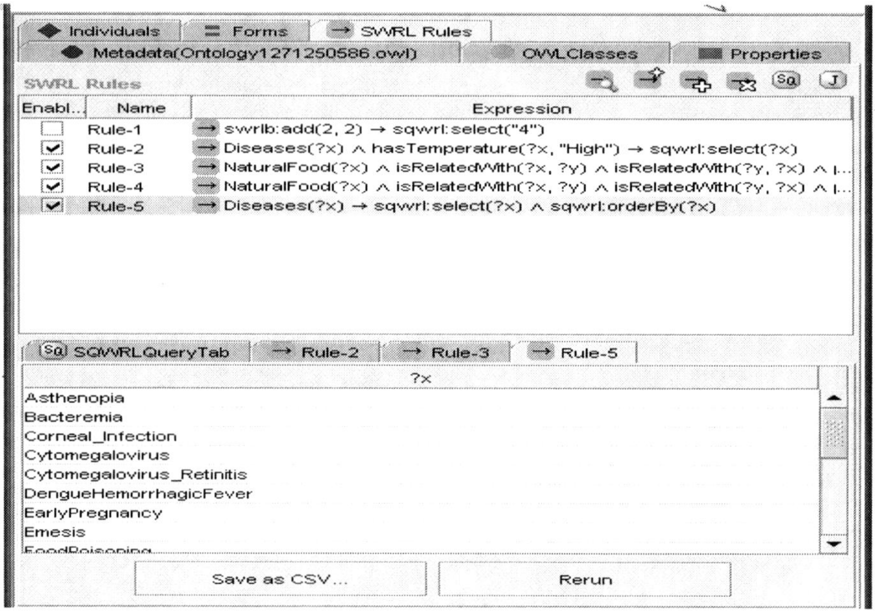

Fig. 4. List of all the Diseases

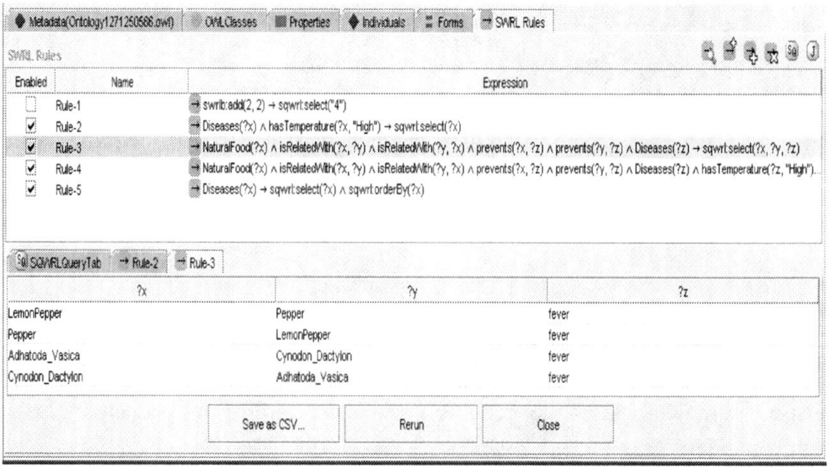

Fig. 5. Related instances

NaturalFood(?x) ^ isRelatedWith(?x, ?y) ^ isRelatedWith(?y, ?x) ^
prevents(?x, ?z) ^ prevents(?y, ?z) ^ Diseases(?z) → sqwrl:select(?x,?y,?z)

This rule is used to find all the Natural Foods those are used to prevent a particular disease. Based on this rule one can identify the implied relationship among the Natural Food sources which are not directly related but is related through a disease.

Diseases(?x) → sqwrl:select(?x) ^ sqwrl:orderBy(?x)

Fig. 4., Fig. 5. Shows the result of finding all the diseases and related instances based on the above mentioned rules.

6 Conclusion

In this paper, the usefulness of semantic representation and querying the data based on rule specification is given. Along with OWL, SWRL is used to specify the rules to find relationships. Thus this method is used to find explicit and implicit relationships among classes and individuals. This approach can be extended with more entities and for complex relationships such as entities without having direct links.

References

1. Berners-Lee, T., Hendler, J., Lasilla, O.: The Semantic Web. Scientific American (2001)
2. Aleman-Meza, B., Halaschek-Wiener, C., Arpinar, I.B., Ramakrishnan, C., Sheth, A.P.: Ranking complex relationships on the semantic web (2005)
3. Bizer, C., Lehmann, J., Kobilarov, G., Auer, S., Becker, C., Cyganiak, R., Hellmann, S.: DBpedia: a crystallization point for the web of data. Web Semantics: Science, Services and Agents on the World Wide Web
4. Lehmann, J., Schuppel, J., Auer, S.: Discovering unknown connections - the DBpedia relationship Finder (2007)
5. Horridge, M., Jupp, S., Moulton, G., Rector, A., Stevens, R., Wroe, C.: A Practical Guide To Building OWL Ontologies Using Protégé 4 and CO-ODE Tools (2007)
6. Cregan, A.M.: Linked Open Data: a new resource for eResearch (2009)
7. Heim, P., Lohmann, S., Stegemann, T.: Interactive Relationship Discovery via the Semantic Web (2010)
8. Heath, T., Hausenblas, M., Bizer, C., Cyganiak, R., Hartig, O.: How to Publish Linked Data on the Web (2009)
9. http://www.w3.org/Submission/SWRL/
10. http://protege.cim3.net/cgi-bin/wiki.pl?SWRLTab
11. Chen, H., Wang, Y., Wang, H., Mao, Y., Tang, J., Zhou, C., Yin, A., Wu, Z.: Towards a Semantic Web of Relational Databases: a Practical Semantic Toolkit and an In-Use Case from Traditional Chinese Medicine. In: Fifth International Semantic Web Conference (2006)
12. Farooq, A., Arshad, M.J., Shah, A.: A Layered approach for Similarity Measurement between Ontologies. Journal of American Science (2010)

13. O'Connor, M.J., Shankar, R.D., Tu, S.W., Nyulas, C., Parrish, D.B., Musen, M.A., Das, A.K.: Using Semantic Web Technologies for Knowledge-Driven Querying of Biomedical Data. In: Bellazzi, R., Abu-Hanna, A., Hunter, J. (eds.) AIME 2007. LNCS (LNAI), vol. 4594, pp. 267–276. Springer, Heidelberg (2007)
14. Horridge, M., Knublauch, H., Rector, A., Stevens, R., Wroe, C.: A Practical Guide To Building OWL Ontologies Using The Protégé-OWL plugin and CO-ODE Tools, Edition 1.0 (2004)
15. Mendes, P.N., Kapanipathi, P., Cameron, D., Sheth, A.P.: Dynamic Associative Relationships on the Linked Open Data Web. In: Web Science Conf. (2010)
16. O'Connor, M., Shankar, R., Tu, S., Nyulas, C., Das, A., Musen, M.: Efficiently Querying Relational Databases Using OWL and SWRL
17. Lohmann, S., Heim, P., Stegemann, T., Ziegler, J.: The RelFinder User Interface: Interactive Exploration of Relationships between Objects of Interest. ACM, New York (2010), 978-1-60558-515-4/10/02

Annotation Based Collective Opinion Analysis

Archana Shukla and B.D. Chaudhary

Department of Computer Science and Enginerring,
Motilal Nehru National Institute of Technology,
Allahabad (UP) -211004, India
`{archana,bdc}@mnnit.ac.in`

Abstract. We present a tool which analyzes annotations on a document to infer collective sentiments of annotators. Annotations may include comments, notes, observation, explanation or question, help etc. Comments are used for evaluative purpose where as others are used either for summarization or for expansion. Further, these comments may be on another annotation, not on the original document and referred as meta-annotations. Collective sentiments of annotators are classified as positive, negative or neutral based on sentiments of words found in annotations. All annotations may not get equal weightage. If an annotation has higher number of meta-annotations on it, it is assigned higher weight. If a comment is on another annotation and negates the sentiments of previous annotator, then the weightage of that annotation is either reduced or annotation is excluded from inference. Our tool computes collective sentiments of annotators in two steps. In first step, it computes sentiment scores of all annotations. In second steps, it computes weighted average of sentiment scores of annotation to obtain the collective sentiments. We demonstrate the use of tool on research papers.

Keywords: sentiment analysis; opinion mining; classification; Annotation; sentiment words; sentiment scores.

1 Introduction

Several degree programs of universities academic institute have research component of varying duration from six months to four-five years. As a first activity in the research, students are advised to survey literature related to their domain of interest to define their proposed activity. They collect research papers and other publication either from web sites of professional societies like IEEE, ACM, and LNCS or from printed copy of journals available in their library. While going through these research publications, they write their notes, observations, remarks, questions etc either on the same document or on the separate sheet of paper. These comments/observation may be about entire paper or part of them. These observation/comments are very valuable knowledge resource not only for the current reader but also for future generation of students who are likely to work in the same area. However, at present these knowledge resources are not available to future generation as they are not available in electronic form and are not sharable.

D.C. Wyld et al. (Eds.): NeCoM/WeST/WiMoN 2011, CCIS 197, pp. 575–584, 2011.
© Springer-Verlag Berlin Heidelberg 2011

Our work is motivated by desire to provide a tool which provides a facility to record their comments, notes, observation, and explanation etc. either on document or on another comments and evaluate the collective sentiments of the researchers over the document. These collective sentiments of annotators may be used as an indicator of quality or usefulness of the documents.

We have developed a tool, KMAD [16], which provides facility to annotate either PDF documents or another annotation. It also creates knowledgebase consisting of annotations and metadata found in the document.

In this paper, we describe augmentations made in KMAD for the analysis of annotations found in the document to infer collective sentiments of annotators. The relationships between annotations are complex. Meta annotation, which is annotation over another annotation, may be comment on annotation which is of type comment, note, explanation, help etc. We only consider those annotation or Meta annotations which are of type comment.

Collective sentiments of annotators are visualized either in terms of positive sense, or negative sense or neutral sense based on adjectives, adverbs, verbs etc using *WordNet*. These collective sentiments of annotators may be used as a characteristic features to judge the quality or usefulness of the document.

Our tool uses *SentiWordNet* to assigns sentiment scores to each word found in annotations. Sentiments of words are assigned three sentiment scores: positivity, Negativity and objectivity with a word and lies in between the range of [0-1].

This paper is organized in seven sections. Section 2 presents the related work. Section 3 briefly describes the services provided by KMAD without augmentation. In Section 4, we describe sentiment analyzer. In section 5, we describe the augmented KMAD tool. In section 6, we present the design and implementation details of our application and last section 7 present the conclusion.

2 Related Work

Several research efforts have been made to analyze documents, comments, annotations on document and web sites to evaluate collective sentiments of readers or evaluators. [1] [2] considered contents of the documents for analysis of sentiments. They extracted the sentiment words consisting of adjectives and nouns using GI (*General Inquirer*) and *WordNet*. They assigned sentiment value to each extracted word based on number of times it appears in the whole document. They assigned sentiment polarity using sentiment lexicon database which include 2500 adjectives and 500 nouns where for each word, sentiment definition was defined in terms of (word, pos, sentiment category). Jiang Kim & Hovy and Weibe & Riloff [3, 4] analyzed the text file related to a given topic. They they used their own dictionary which included 5880 positive adjectives, 6233 negative adjectives, 2840 positive verbs and 3239 negative verbs instead of considering generalized ontology for extracting sentiment words. For unseen word, they assigned sentiment strength by computing probability of word based on count occurrences of word synonyms in the dictionary. YANG et al [5] did analysis of online document of Chinese review based on topic. Topic of a review was identified using n-gram approach. Sentiment words were extracted using four dictionaries such as Positive Word Dictionary, Negative Word Dictionary, A student Positive and Negative Word Dictionary and HowNet. Polarity values were assigned by computing average score based on term frequency of word. Positive and Negative value of words were assigned manually by annotators. [6, 7, 8, 9, 10] extracted the sentiment words consisting of adjectives or adverbs or adjective-adverb both. They proved that subjectivity of a sentence could be judged according to the adjectives/adverb in it. Polarity value for each word was assigned by calculating the probability based on term frequency of word.

Several authors also did classification of document based on annotation. Emmanuel Nauer et al [11] did classification of the HTML document based on the annotation. The content of the document is annotated and similarity will be matched based on the domain Ontology. Michael G. Noll et al [12] did classification of the web document by analyzing the large set of real world data. They interested to find out what kinds of documents are annotated more by the end-users. Anotrea Mazzei [13] did classification of extracted handwritten annotations on machine printed documents based on type of annotations such as underline annotation, highlighted annotation, annotations in margins and blank space, and annotation in between the lines or over the text. Steimle et al [15] developed a system *CoScribe* which provided facility to annotate and classify power point lectures slides based on four types of annotation such as important, to do, question and correction. Sandra Bringay et al [16] did classification of the electronic health record based on both informal and formal annotations for managing knowledge. They had designed a schema for formal annotation which includes author name, date time, place, document, target, annotation type. Annotation type consisted of comment, link between two documents, a message for a precise recipient, an annotation created in order to write a synthesis, a response to a annotation. Informal annotation was used by practitioners when they would like to give some brief history about the patients or disease.

All the above works have contributed significantly in the field of sentiment analysis and classification of document in different domains. We have focused on research academy domain to analyze annotations on research papers to obtain the collective sentiments. Our sentiment words include adjectives, verbs, adverbs, nouns found in comments. We expect that it will give better result because we give bigger set of sentiment words.

Our annotation schema has similarity and difference with the one used in [16]. Our comments reflect evaluative judgment of annotation whereas that of [16] summarizes the content. Our meta-annotation is very similar to [16].

3   KMAD Tool

We have developed a tool named KMAD [14] to annotate a PDF document. We have designed an annotation schema using DTD (Document Type Definition) to capture the information of annotation. These annotations contain *Author*, *Type*, *Annotation_on*, *Comment*, *Date_Time* as elements. *Annotation_id* , *PDF_Paper_id* , *Comment_id* as an attribute. The element *Type* may take either "*note*" or "*comment*" or "*help*" or "*insert*" or "*paragraph*" or "*unknown*" as values. *Note* type indicates that

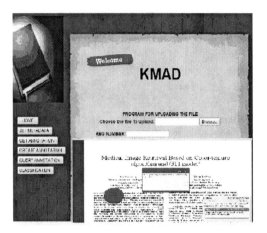

Fig. 1. Annotation Creation Process

annotation summarizes the content whereas *comment* type indicates weather it is an evaluation or criticism of the content. Our tool also captures the relationship between PDF documents and associated annotations and also between annotations and about annotations.

It provides user friendly interface to upload a PDF document and to create annotation on document. Author can either visualize annotation along with document or only annotations. A snap shot for our tool is shown in Fig 1.

Our application creates a relational database for annotations, PDF documents and relationship between them. It also keeps the record of each annotator. This database can be queried to find all annotations with a PDF document or to model the annotators. It also support search on PDF document based on any of the metadata or annotator_id.

4   Sentiment Analyzer

Our tool analyzes annotations to obtain the collective sentiments of annotators. It is a two step process. In first steps, it computes the average scores for all annotations. A detail of this process is given in Algorithm 1. In second steps, it computes the weighted average of score of annotation to infer the collective sentiments of author. A detail of this process is given in Algorithm 2. We have used SentiWordNet to assign polarity scores. Three scores are associated with each sentiment word in terms of positivity, negativity and objectivity.

Algorithm 2 is used to find weighted average of sentiment score to infer the collective sentiments of annotator over the document. This algorithm takes input as sentiment score of each annotation and we also eliminate scores of annotation on which another annotation has contradicting sentiments.

Algorithm 1. Find the average score of each annotation found in PDF document

---

Input: List of sentiment words extracted from comments of annotation
Output: Sentiment score

1. **for** each sentiment word from List **do**

2. Get polarity as well as sentiment scores using *SentiWordNet*.

3. **if** word is preceded with negation word "Not" **then,**

4. Interchange positive and negative sentiment scores of the word which comes after the Not.

5. Record above sentiment scores of each word in Table

4. end if

5. **end for**

6. Get maximum polarity value of each word from the table to compute average score.

7. **if** maximum polarity value is negativity **then** ,

8. Make the score negative.

9. Compute sentiment score such as S.S (sentiment Score) = add (maximum polarity value of each word)/ Total number of words found in comment.

10. Output S.S (Sentiment score).

Algorithm 2. Find weighted average of sentiment score on PDF document

---

Input: sentiment score, number of meta-annotation on annotation
Output: weighted average score of each comment of annotation

1. **for** each sentiment score **do**

2. **if** sentiment score is of annotation on annotation **then,**

3. **if** sentiment score negates the previous sentiment score **then,**

4. Exclude that sentiment score from the computation.

5. **else**

6. Compute weighted average of sentiment score = sentiment score * number of meta-annotation/total number of annotation on a document.

7. **end if ;end if**

8. **end for**

9. **if** weighted average of sentiment score is positive **then,**

10. Result "sentiment of collective annotator over the document is positive".

11. **else**

12. Result "sentiment of collective annotator over the document is negative".

13. **end if**

We demonstrate our algorithm using example annotations on a document. These annotations are given as shown in Fig 2.

> Ann1: This article is quite well but not so good.
> Ann2: I am satisfy with this comment.
> Ann3: It is not a good one.
> Ann4: This is the best article.
> Ann5: It is good article but not best one.
> Ann6: It is bad one.
> Ann7: Not best one but quite well.

Fig. 2. Annotations

List of sentiment words found in annotations of document as shown in Table 1.

Table 1. Words with associated sentiment scores and their maximum polarity

	Word	Positive value	Negative value	Objective value	Max(polarity value)
Ann1	Quite	0	0.625	0.375	-0.625
	Well	0.75	0	0.25	+0.75
	Not	0	0.625	0.375	-0.625
	Good	0.875	0.125	0	-0.875
Ann2	Satisfy	0.5	0	0.5	+0.5
Ann3	Not	0	0.625	0.375	-0.625
	Good	0.875	0.125	0	-0.875
Ann4	Best	0.75	0	0.25	+0.75
Ann5	Good	0.875	0.125	0	+0.875
	Not	0	0.625	0.375	-0.625
	Best	0.75	0	0.25	-0.75
Ann6	Bad	0	0.625	0.375	-0.625
Ann7	Not	0	0.625	0.375	-0.625
	Best	0.75	0	0.25	-0.75
	Quite	0	0.625	0.375	-0.625
	Well	0.75	0	0.25	+0.75

Sentiment score of annotation 1= ((-0.625)+(0.75)+(-0.625)+(-0.875) /4) = -0.34375

Similarly, Average score of annotation 2 = +0.75
Total weighted average of sentiment score of document = +0.29375

So, if the above value is positive then, sentiment of document is positive, otherwise negative. Here, sentiment of collective annotator over document is positive.

5   Augmented KMAD Tool

We describe augmentations made in KMAD tool for the analysis of the annotations. Fig 3 shows the Home Page of our tool.

It provides five clickable buttons to perform different tasks. These tasks include *new*, *view* annotations either page wise or collectively, *Metadata, Query, Sentiments.*

Our application extracts the sentiment words such as adjectives, adverbs or verbs from annotations found in the document to evaluate the collective sentiments of annotators. It also assigns sentiment scores to each sentiment words found in comments of annotations using *SentiWordNet.*

Our application computes total weighted average of sentiment score of annotations found in PDF document to infer the collective sentiments of annotators as shown in Fig 4. It also allows authors to view list of annotation available on PDF document created by them either page wise or collectively. Our application also extracts the metadata such as Title, Author, keywords, summary, date-time using function of PDF BOX API.

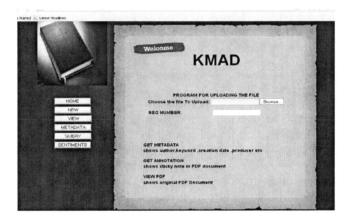

Fig. 3. Home Page

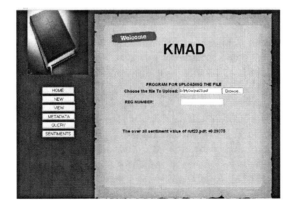

Fig. 4. Collective sentiments over document

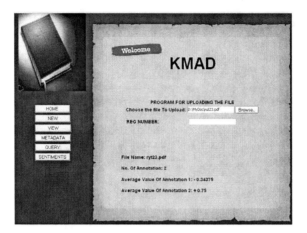

Fig. 5. Sentiment scores of annotations

Our application allows authors to query about sentiment score or collective sentiments of annotator which is available on PDF document either on the basis of annotator-id or on the basis of file name as shown in Fig 5.

6 Design and Implementation

We have used three layer architecture for our augmented KMAD tool. The top most layer is the presentation layer, which manages all the interaction to end user. The middle layer is the application logic layer which includes all the functionalities such as *annotation extractor module, sentiment word extractor module, SentiWordNet* and *WordNet* which are used to manage knowledge resources. The bottom layer is the database layer and contains the database for document, document Metadata, Annotation, annotation relation and sentiment words.

Our tool extracts the annotation using PDF BOX API such as *getDocumentCatalog()* for extracting the page information on which annotation has been done. Total number of pages in the PDF document and their count is listed using *getAllPages()* and *size()* function respectively. Extracts annotation field list available on a PDF document using *getAnnotation()* function. This function maintains the list of all annotation. If annotation field is of type "text", then , for each annotation field in the annotation list extracts information of annotation field such as comment using *getContents()* function. It also removes stop words and performs stemming using one of the module and consider adjectives, nouns, adverbs and verbs based on POS tagging using *WordNet*. It assigns polarity values in terms of positive, negative and objective using *SentiWordNet*.

Sentiment scores lie in between the range of [0.0-1.0]. At the time of assignment of scores, our tool also takes care of negation words such as "Not", "Never". If these words are found before any other word *(Adj)*, then it interchanges +ve and −ve polarity values of that word which comes after "Not".

We have created a relational database as per ER diagram as shown in Fig 11. It shows the entity relationship between Document, Document metadata, Annotation, Annotation relation, Words and their associated sentiments. Our database contains five tables PDF_document, PDF_Annotation, Annotation_Annotation, Sentiments_Words, Sentiments_Annotation.

All the information extracted related to annotations and the relationship between annotations is available in a separate xml file. Our tool also stores all these information in relational database.

7 Conclusion

We have developed an augmented KMAD tool implemented using java server programming language to infer the collective sentiment of annotators and query knowledge base containing metadata, annotations and sentiments. We believe that it is helpful to research community. The relationship between the annotations is complex. We have only considered those annotations or meta annotation which is of type comment. In future we plan to consider more complex type relations.

References

1. Yi, J., Nasukawa, T., Bunescu, R., Niblack, W.: Sentiment Analyzer: Sentiment Analyzer: Extracting Sentiments about a Given Topic using Natural Language Processing Techniques. In: Proceeding of the 3rd IEEE International conference on Data Mining, Melbourne, pp. 427–434 (2003)
2. Yu, H., Hatzivassiloglou, V.: Towards Answering Opinion Questions. In: Proceeding of EMLP 2003, Sapporo, pp. 29–136 (2003)
3. Kim, S., Hovy, E.: Determining the Sentiments of Opinions. In: Proceeding of COLING 2004: The 20th International Conference on Computational Linguistics, Geneva, pp. 1367–1373 (2004)
4. Wiebe, J., Riloff, E.: Creating Subjective and Objective Sentence Classifiers from Unannotated text. In: Gelbukh, A. (ed.) CICLing 2005. LNCS, vol. 3406, pp. 486–497. Springer, Heidelberg (2005)
5. Yang, J., Hou, M., Wang, N.: Recognizing Sentiment Polarity in Chinese Reviews Based on Topic Sentiment Sentences. In: International Conference Natural Language Processing and Knowledge Engineering (NLP-KE), Beijing (2010)
6. Wiebe, J.: Learning Subjectives adjectives from Corpora. In: Proceeding of the 17th National Conference on Artificial Intelligence, Menlo park, pp. 735–740 (2000)
7. Weibe, J., Wilson, T., Bruee, R., Bell, M., Martin, M.: Learning Subjective Language. Computational Linguistics 30, 277–308 (2004)
8. Owsley, S., Sood, S., Hammond, K.J.: Domain Specific Affective Classification of Documents. American Association for Artificial Intelligence (2006)
9. Duan, X., He, T., Song, L.: Research on Sentiment Classification of Blog Based on PMI-IR. In: International Conference on Natural Language Processing and Knowledge Engineerng, NLP-KE (2010)
10. Benamara, F., Cesarano, C., Reforgiato, D.: Sentiment Analysis: Adjectives and Adverbs are better than Adjectives Alone. In: ICWSM 2007, Boulder, Co, USA (2007)

11. Nauer, E., Napoli, A.: A proposal for annotation, semantic similarity and classification of textual documents
12. Noll, M.G., Meinel, C.: Exploring Social Annotations for Web Document Classification. In: Avanzi, R.M., Keliher, L., Sica, F. (eds.) SAC 2008. LNCS, vol. 5381. Springer, Heidelberg (2009)
13. Mazzei, A.: Extraction and Classification of Handwritten Annotations for Pedagogical Use. In: EDIC (2009)
14. Shukla, A.: A metadata and annotation extractor from PDF document for semantic web. In: Proceedings of the 1st Amrita ACM-W Celebration on Women in Computing in India, A2CWiC (2010)
15. Steimle, J., Brdiczka, O., Mühlhäuser, M.: CoScribe: Using Paper for Collaborative Annotations in Lectures. In: Proceedings of the 2008 Eighth IEEE International Conference on Advanced Learning Technologies, ICALT 2008 (2008)
16. Bringay, S., Barry, C., Charlet, J.: Annotations: A functionality to support Cooperation, Coordination and Awareness in the Electronic Medical Record. In: Proceeding of the 2006 Conference on Cooperative Systems Design: Seamless Integration of Artifacts and Conversations Enhanced Concepts of Infrastructure for Communication (2006)

A Novel Social Network Model for Research Collaboration

Sreedhar Bhukya

Department of Computer and Information Sciences
University of Hyderabad, Hyderabad- 500046, India
sr2naik@gmail.com

Abstract. Recent studies on social networks are based on a characteristic which includes assortative mixing, high clustering, short average path lengths, broad degree distributions and the existence of community structure. Here, an application has been developed in the domain of 'research collaboration' which satisfies all the above characteristics, based on some existing social network models. In addition, this application facilitates interaction between various communities (research groups). This application gives very high clustering coefficient by retaining the asymptotically scale-free degree distribution. Here the community structure is raised from a mixture of random attachment and implicit preferential attachment. In addition to earlier works which only considered Neighbor of Initial Contact (NIC) as implicit preferential contact, we have considered Neighbor of Neighbor of Initial Contact (NNIC) also. This application supports the occurrence of a contact between two Initial contacts if the new vertex chooses more than one initial contacts. This ultimately will develop a complex research social network rather than the one that was taken as basic reference.

Keywords: Social networks. Random initial contact. Neighbor of neighbor initial contact. Tertiary contact. Research collaboration.

1 Introduction

Recent days research collaborations becoming domain independent. For example stock market analyst is taking the help of computer simulator for future predictions. Thus there is a necessity of research collaboration between people in different research domains (different communities, in the language of social networking.) Here we develop a domain for collaborations in research communities which gives a possibility of interacting with a research person in a different community, yet retaining the community structure. Social networks are made of nodes that are tied by one or more specific types of relationships. The vertex represents individuals or organizations. Social networks have been intensively studied by Social scientists [3-4], for several decades in order to understand local phenomena such as local formation and their dynamics, as well as network wide process, like transmission of information, spreading disease, spreading rumor, sharing ideas etc. Various types of social networks, such as those related to professional collaboration [6-8], Internet

D.C. Wyld et al. (Eds.): NeCoM/WeST/WiMoN 2011, CCIS 197, pp. 585–592, 2011.
© Springer-Verlag Berlin Heidelberg 2011

dating [9], and opinion formation among people have been studied. Social networks involve Financial, Cultural, Educational, Families, Relations and so on. Social networks create relationship between vertices; Social networks include Sociology, basic Mathematics and graph theory. The basic mathematics structure for a social network is a graph. The main social network properties includes hierarchical community structure [10], small world property [11], power law distribution of nodes degree [19] and the most basic is Barabasi Albert model of scale free networks [12]. The more online social network gains popularity, the more scientific community is attracted by the research opportunities that these new fields give. Most popular online social networks is Facebook, where user can add friends, send them messages, and update their personal profiles to notify friends about themselves. Essential characteristics for social networks are believed to include assortative mixing [13,14], high clustering, short average path lengths, broad degree distributions[15,16], and the existence of community structure. Growing community can be roughly speaking set of vertices with dense internal connection, such that the inter community connection are relatively sparse.

Here we have considered an existing model [2] of social networks and developed it in way which is suitable for collaborations in academic communities.
The model is as follows:

The algorithm consists of two growth processes: (1) random attachment (2) implicit preferential attachment resulting from following edges from the randomly chosen initial contacts.

The existing model lacks in the following two aspects:

1.   There is no connection between initial to initial contacts, if more than one initial contact is chosen.
2.   There is no connection between initial contact and its neighbor of neighbor vertices.

These two aspects we have considered in earlier model [1] from the earlier model we applied application for research collaboration. The advantage of our application can understand from the fallowing example and our earlier model can be applicable to the real-world applications. Let us consider a research person contacting a research person in a research group for his own purpose or research purpose and suppose that he/she didn't get adequate support from that research person or from his neighbors, but he may get required support from some friend of friend for his/her initial contact. Then the only way a new person could get help is that his primary contact has to be updated or create a contact with his friend of friend for supporting his new contact and introduce his new contact to his friend of friend. The same thing will happen in our day to day life also. If a research person contacts us for some research purpose and we are unable to help him, we will try to help him by some contacts of our friends. The extreme case of this nature is that we may try to contact our friend of friend for this purpose. We have implemented the same thing in our application. In the old model [2], information about friends only used to be updated, where as in our application information about friend of friend also has been updated. Of course this application creates a complex research social network but, sharing of information or data will be very fast. This fulfills the actual purpose of research social networking in an efficient way with a faster growth rate by keeping the community structure as it is.

2 Network Growth Algorithm

The algorithm includes three processes: (1) Random attachment (2) Implicit preferential contact with the neighbors of initial contact (3) In addition to the above we are proposing a contact between the initial contact to its Neighbor of Neighbor contact (tertiary). The algorithm of the model is as follows [1,2] in this paper we consider vertices is as a research person.

1) Start with a seed network of N vertices
2) Pick on average $m_r \geq 1$ random vertex as initial contacts
3) Pick on average $m_s \geq 0$ neighbors of each initial contact as secondary contact
4) Pick on average $m_t \geq 1$ neighbors of each secondary contact as tertiary contact
5) Connect the new vertex to the initial, secondary and tertiary contacts
6) Repeat the steps 2-5 until the network has grown to desired size.

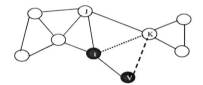

Fig. 1. Growing process of community network: The new vertex 'V' initially connects to random initial contact (*say i*). Now *i*, updates its neighbor of neighbor contact list and hence connects to k. 'V' connects to m_s number of neighbors (*say k*) and m_t number of neighbor of neighbors of i (*say k*).

Below in Fig.2.Visualization of a research network graph with N=45. Number of each secondary contact from each initial contact $n_{2nd} \sim U[0,3)$ (uniformly distributed between 0 and 3), and initial contact is connecting its neighbor of neighbor vertices

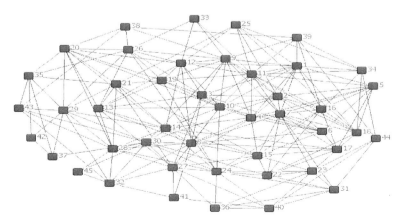

Fig. 2. Showing research social network graph with 45 researchers

U[1-2]. In this model we tried 45 sample research persons and prepared a strong growing research network.

3 Vertex Degree Distribution

We derive approximate value for the vertex degree distribution for growing network model mixing random initial contact, neighbor of neighbor initial contact and neighbor of initial contacts. Power law degree distribution with $p(k) \sim k^\gamma$ with exponent $2 < \gamma < \infty$ have derived [17, 19]. In this model also the lower bound to the degree exponent γ is found to be 3, which is same as in the earlier model.

The rate equation which describes how the degree of a vertex changes on average during one time step of the network growth is constructed. The degree of vertex v_i grows in 3 processes:

1) When a new vertex directly links to v_i at any time t, there will be on average $\sim t$ vertices. Here we are selecting m_r out of them with a probability m_r/t.
2) When a vertex links to v_i as secondary contact, the selection will give rise to preferential attachment. These will be $m_r. m_s$ in number.
3) When a vertex links to v_i as tertiary contact, this will also be a random preferential attachment. These will be $2m_r m_s m_t$ in number.

These three processes lead to following rate equation for the degree of vertex v_i [1,2]

$$\frac{\partial E_i}{\partial t} = \frac{k_i}{t} = \frac{1}{t}\left(m_r + \frac{m_r m_s + 2m_r m_s m_t}{2(m_r + m_r m_s + 2m_r m_s m_t)} k_i\right) \qquad (1)$$

Based on the average initial degree of a vertex is

$$k_{init} = m_r + m_r m_s + 2m_r m_s m_t$$

Separating and integrating from t_i to t, and from k_{init} to k_i, we will get the following time evaluation for the vertex degrees

$$k_i(t) = B\left(\frac{1}{t_i}\right)^{1/A} - C \qquad (2)$$

Where

$$A = 2\left(\frac{m_r + m_r m_s + 2m_r m_s m_t}{m_r m_s + 2m_r m_s m_t}\right), B = A\left(m_r + \frac{1}{2}m_r m_s + m_r m_s m_t\right), C = A m_r$$

From time evolution of vertex $k_i(t)$, we can calculate the degrees of distribution $p(k)$ by forming cumulative distribution $F(k)$ and differentiating with respect to k. Since the mean field approximation[1,2] the degree $k_i(t)$ of a vertex v_i increases monotonously from the time t_i the vertex initially added to the network, the fraction of vertices whose degree is less than $k_i(t)$ at t is equivalent to the fraction of vertices that introduced after time t_i. Since t is evenly distributed, this fraction is $(t-t_i)/2$. These facts lead to the cumulative distribution [1]

$$F\left(k_i\right) = P\left(\tilde{k} \le k_i\right) = P\left(\tilde{t} \ge t_i\right) = \frac{1}{t}\left(t-t_i\right)$$ (3)

Solving for $t_i = t_i\left(k_i, t\right) = B^A\left(k_i + C\right)^{-A} t$ from (2) and inserting it into (3), differentiating $F(k_i)$ with respect to k_i, and replacing the notation k_i by k in the equation, we get the probability density distribution for the degree k as

$$P\left(k\right) = A B^A\left(k+C\right)^{-2}\Big/m_s + 2m_s m_t^{-3}$$ (4)

Here A, B and C are as above. In the limit of large k, the distribution becomes a power law $p(k) \sim k^{-\gamma}$ with $\gamma = 3+2/m_s$, $m_s > 0$, leading to $3 < \gamma < \infty$. Hence the lower bound to the degree exponent is 3. Although the lower bound for degree exponent is same as earlier model. The probability density distribution is larger compared to earlier model, where the denominator of the first term of degree exponent is larger compared to the earlier model.

4   Clustering

The clustering coefficient on vertex degree can also be found by the rate equation method [18]. Let us examine how the number of triangles E_i changes with time. The triangle around v_i are mainly generated by three processes

1.   Vertex v_i is chosen as one of the initial contact with probability m_r/t and new vertex links to some of its neighbors as secondary contact, giving raise to a triangle.
2.   The vertex v_i is chosen as secondary contact and the new vertex links to it as its primary or tertiary contact giving raise to a triangles.
3.   The vertex v_i is chosen as tertiary contact and the new vertex links to it as its primary or secondary contact, giving raise to a triangles.

These three process are described by the rate equation [1]

$$\frac{\partial E_i}{\partial t} = \frac{E_i}{t} = \frac{k_i}{t} - \frac{1}{t}\left(m_r - m_r m_s - 3m_r m_s m_t - \frac{5m_r m_s m_t}{2(m_r + m_r m_s + 2m_r m_s m_t)t} k_i\right)$$ (5)

where second right-hand side obtained by applying Eq. (1) integrating both sides with respect to t, and using initial condition $E_i(k_{init}, t_i) = m_r m_s(1+3m_t)$, we get the time evaluation of triangle around a vertex v_i as

$$E_i(t) = (a+bk_i)\ln\left(\frac{t}{t_i}\right) + \left(\frac{a+bk_i}{b}\right)\ln\left(\frac{a+bk_i}{a+bk_{init}}\right) + E_{init} \qquad (6)$$

Now making use of the previously found dependent of k_i on t_i for finding $c_i(k)$. solving for $\ln(t/t_i)$ in terms of k_i from (2), inserting into it into (6) to get $E_i(k_i)$, and dividing $E_i(k_i)$ by the maximum possible number of triangles, $k_i(k_i-1)/2$, we arrive the clustering the coefficient

$$c_i(k_i) = \frac{2E_i(k_i)}{k_i(k_i-1)} \qquad (7)$$

For this equation detail explanation on refer ref [1]

For large values of degree k, the clustering coefficient thus depend on k as $c(k)\sim\ln k/k$.

This has very large clustering coefficient compared to the earlier work where it was $c(k)\sim 1/k$.

5 Results

Here a comparison has been made between the earlier model and current application by calculating the edge to vertex ratio and triangle to vertex ratio for 45 researchers. The results are given in Table: 1 .here one can see an enormous increase in secondary contacts. In addition tertiary contacts also have been added in earlier model and the earlier model applied in the application of research group, which leads to a faster and complex growth of research network.

Table 1.

Data on our proposed model	Initial Contact (IC)	Secondary Contacts (SC)	Neighbor of Neighbor IC (NNIC)
Vertices	2.55	5.77	4.12
Triangles	0.4	5.30	5.34

5.1 Simulation Results

The below results have been represented graphically by calculating the degree (number of contacts) of a node. This also is shows an enormous growth in degree of nodes.

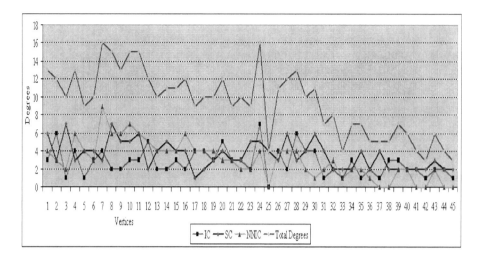

Fig. 3. Comparison results of growing research community network: initial contacts are growing very slow rate compared to secondary contact i.e. ■ indicates initial contact, ◆ indicates secondary contacts, and ▲ indicates neighbor of neighbor of initial contact connects to the vertex v_i, Finally ● indicates degree of each vertices, when initial, secondary and tertiary contact connect to a vertex v_i. Our research community network is growing very fast and complex when compared to existing model, vertices simulation results based on Table: 1.

6   Conclusion

In this paper, an application which reproduces very efficient research networks' compared to real social networks has been developed. And also here, the lower bound to the degree exponent is the same. The probability distribution for the degree k is in agreement with the earlier result for m_t =0. The clustering coefficient got an enormous raise in growth rate of $\ln(k_i)/ k_i$ compared to the earlier result $1/k_i$ for large values of the degree k. This is very useful in the case of research groups, which helps in faster information flow for research and an enormous growth in good research. Thus here an efficient but complex application of research social network has been developed which gives an enormous growth in probability distribution and clustering coefficient and edge to vertex ratio by retaining the community structure. This application can be used to develop a new kind of social networking among various research groups.

Tool

We have used C language, UciNet, NetDraw and Excel for creating graph and simulation.

Notations

Notation	Description
m_r	Initial Contact
m_s	Secondary Contact
k_i	Degree of vertex i
E_i	Number of triangles at vertex i
$P(k)$	Probability density distribution of degree k

References

1. Bhukya, S.: A novel model for social networks. In: BCFIC IEEE, pp. 21–24 (February 16-18, 2011)
2. Toivonen, R., Onnela, J.-P., Saramäki, J., Hyvönen, J., Kaski, K.: A model for social networks. Physica A 371, 851–860 (2006)
3. Milgram, S.: Psychology Today, vol. 2, pp. 60–67 (1967)
4. Granovetter, M.: The Strength of Weak Ties. Am. J. Soc. 78, 1360–1380 (1973)
5. Wasserman, S., Faust, K.: Social Network Analysis. Cambridge University Press, Cambridge (1994)
6. Watts, D.J., Strogatz, S.H.: Collective dynamics of 'small -world' networks. Nature 393, 440 (1998)
7. Newman, M.: The structure of scientific collaboration networks. PNAS 98, 404–409 (2001)
8. Newman, M.: Coauthorship networks and patterns of scientific collaboration. PNAS 101, 5200–5205 (2004)
9. Holme, P., Edling, C.R., Liljeros, F.: Structure and Time-Evolution of an Internet Dating Community. Soc. Networks 26, 155–174 (2004)
10. Girvan, M., Newman, M.E.J.: Community structure in social and biological networks. Proc. Natl. Acad. Sci. USA 99, 7821–7826 (2002)
11. Newman, M.E.J.: The structure and function of complex networks. SIAM Review 45, 167–256 (2003)
12. Barabási, A.-L., Albert, R.: Emergence of scaling in random networks. Science 286, 509–512 (1999)
13. Newman, M.E.J.: Assortative Mixing in Networks. Phys. Rev. Lett. 89, 208701 (2002)
14. Newman, M.E.J., Park, J.: Why social networks are different from other types of networks. Phys. Rev. E 68, 036122 (2003)
15. Amaral, L.A.N., Scala, A., Barth, M., Stanley, H.E.: Classes of small-world networks. PNAS 97, 11149–11152 (2000)
16. Boguna, M., Pastor-Satorras, R., Díaz-Guilera, A., Arenas, A.: Models of social networks based on social distance attachment. Phys. Rev. E 70, 056122 (2004)
17. Evans, T., Saramäki, J.: Scale-free networks from self-organization. Phys. Rev. E 72, 026138 (2005)
18. Szabo, G., Alava, M., Kertesz, J.: Structural transitions in scale-free networks. Phys. Rev. E 67, 056102 (2003)
19. Krapivsky, P.L., Redner, S.: Organization of growing random networks. Phys. Rev. E 63, 066123 (2001)

An Effective Approach for Student Evaluation in E-Learning Based on Semantic Web

Amit Chauhan[1] and Nidhi Shah[2]

[1] Institute of Engineering & Science, IPS, Indore, India
amitcs3786@gmail.com
[2] U & P. U. Patel Department of Computer Engineering, CSPIT, CHARUSAT, Changa,
Gujarat, India
nbshah999@yahoo.com

Abstract. The Semantic Web is not a separate Web but an extension of the current one, in which information is given well-defined meaning, better enabling computers and people to work in cooperation. E-learning is network-enabled transfer of skills and knowledge. E-learning refers to using electronic application and processes to learn. E-learning applications and processes include web-based learning, computer-based learning, virtual classrooms and digital collaboration. E-learning offer obvious advantages for learners by making access to educational resources very fast, just-in- time and relevance, at any time or place. The Semantic Web technology has enabled by a set of suitable agents, which seems to be powerful enough to satisfy the e-learning requirements like fast, just- in-time and relevant learning. A new class of approach inspired by multi agent system and semantic web has been developed that can solve various problem of feedback between student and tutor. It includes personal agents of students and course tutors. Agents of students and tutors don't communicate directly. They send ontological information to informational agent that analyses them and returns the results to students and tutor. In this paper we derive a new approach, by building reference ontology and student domain ontology of physical layer and apply ontology comparison algorithm on them for evaluation of student. Comparison algorithm compares reference ontology and student ontology. By comparing reference ontology and student domain ontology student mistake can be analyzed. Analysis of student mistakes allows proposing them personalized recommendations.

Keywords: Multiagent, Ontology, Semantic Web.

1 Introduction

Student evaluation in E-learning based on semantic web. Student evaluation is necessary for improvement of student skill and check the level of student. Teachers face many difficulties when working with Information and Communication Technology in education. Many of those problems are caused by the lack of conformity between the used technology and the educational requirements. E-learning is not just concerned with providing easy access to learning resources, anytime, anywhere, via a repository of learning resources, but is also concerned with

D.C. Wyld et al. (Eds.): NeCoM/WeST/WiMoN 2011, CCIS 197, pp. 593–602, 2011.
© Springer-Verlag Berlin Heidelberg 2011

supporting such features as the personal definition of learning goals, and the synchronous and asynchronous communication, and collaboration between learners and tutors. So, the aim of e- Learning is to replace old-fashioned learning process with efficient and on-demand process of learning, relevant to the user desires. The current *WWW* is a powerful tool for research and education, but its utility is hindered by the failure of the user to navigate easily the reputable sources for the information he requires. The semantic web is a vision to solve this problem. The new generation of the Web, the so-called Semantic Web, appears as a promising technology for implementing e- Learning. The Semantic Web constitutes an environment in which human and machine agents will communicate on a semantic basis. It is about making the web more understandable by machine. It is also about building an appropriate infrastructure for intelligent agents to run around the web performing complex actions for their users. Furthermore, semantic web is about explicitly declaring the knowledge embedded in many web based applications, integrating information in an intelligent way, providing semantic-web based access to the internet, and extract information from text. Semantic web is about how to implement reliable, large-scale interoperation of web services, to make such services computer interpretable ,*i.e*, to create a web of machine understandable and interoperable services that intelligent agent can discover, execute, and compose automatically[4].

The term ontology has been widely used in recent years in the field of Artificial Intelligence, computer and information science especially in domains such as, cooperative information systems, intelligent information integration, information retrieval and extraction, knowledge representation, and database management systems. Ontology's in the context of the semantic web are specifications of the conceptualization and corresponding vocabulary used to describe a domain. Any semantic on the web is based on an explicitly specified ontology, so 2 different semantic web applications can communicate by exchanging their ontology's.

The reminder of this paper is organized as follows. Section 2 describes about the ontology construction. About Student evaluation in e-learning system using ontology comparison algorithm is discussed in section 3.

2   Ontology Analysis

Ontological analysis is accomplished by examining the vocabulary that is used to discuss the characteristic objects and processes that compose the domain, developing rigorous definitions of the basic terms in that vocabulary, and characterizing the logical connections among those terms. The product of this analysis, ontology, is a domain vocabulary complete with a set of precise definitions, or axioms, that constrain the meanings of the terms sufficiently to enable consistent interpretation of the data that use that vocabulary [7].

An ontology includes a catalogue of terms used in a domain, the rules governing how those terms can be combined to make valid statements about situations in that domain, and the sanctioned inferences that can be made when such statements are used in that domain. In the context of ontology, a relation is a definite descriptor referring to an association in the real world; a term is a definite descriptor that refers to an object or situation-like thing in the real world. Formal model of ontology O is ordered triple of finite sets O = < T, R, F > , where T - the domain terms of which is described by ontology O; R - finite set of the relations between terms of domain; F – the domain interpretation functions on the terms and the relations of ontology O. In process of ontology building students use relations from the fixed set that contains the most widely used relations: R={"is a subclass of", "is a part of", "is a synonym", "has attributes", "has elements"}. It simplifies the ontology building and analyses processes.

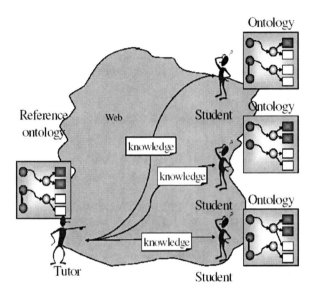

Fig. 1. Ontology building process as a result of learning

Main steps of ontology construction

In ontology building students must perform three tasks:

• Build the set of the domain terms;
• capture the constraints that govern how those terms can be used to make descriptive statements about the domain;
• Build a model that, when provided with a specific descriptive statement, can generate the "appropriate" additional descriptive statements.

The students (as well as the tutor) have to execute four main steps to design the ontology of domain.

2.1 Ontology Construction Algorithm

1) Define the main classes and terms of domain and describe their meaning:
• Define the set of class names T;
• Define the set of relation names R;
• For every class name define the set of attribute names A_t;

• For every attribute name name $a \in A_t$, $t \in T$ define it type – INT, STRING, NUMBER ets. or other class of ontology;

2) Construct the taxonomy of domain terms:

• Define all pairs of classes

$< t_1, t_2 >, t_1 \in T, t_2 \in T, r (t_1, t_2) \rightarrow t_1$ "IS_A_Subclass_Of"t_2, $r \in R$;

3) Define synonymy and other relations between these terms:

• Define all pairs of classes

$< t_1, t_2 >, t_1 \in T, t_2 \in T, r (t_1, t_2) \rightarrow t_1$ "IS_Synonyme_Of"t_2, $r \in R$;

• Define all pairs of classes

$< t_1, t_2 >, t_1 \in T, t_2 \in T, r (t_1, t_2) \rightarrow t_1$ "Related_With"t_2, $r \in R$;

4) Describe the instances of constructed classes:

• Define names of instances a;

• Define meanings of all attributes of instance class

$\forall a \in t, t \in T$

2.2 Classification of Mistake Types in Student Ontologies

Students will receive a mark depending on their mistakes. We consider that the students can make different types of mistakes. We distinguish amongst students' mistakes in the following manner. Here, both semantic and terminological mistakes are considered.

• Wrong direction in hierarchical relations. This is the case of stating that "A is a part of B" when the correct relation is "B is a part of A" as shown in fig 2.

• Wrong instance classification. This is the case when instance a belong to class A in the reference taxonomy and the student states that instance a that belongs to class B as shown in fig 3.

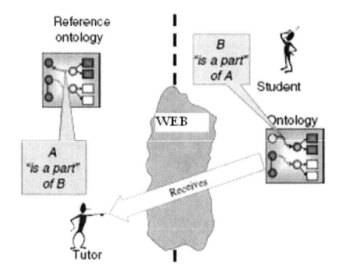

Fig. 2. Hierarchical Direction Class Error

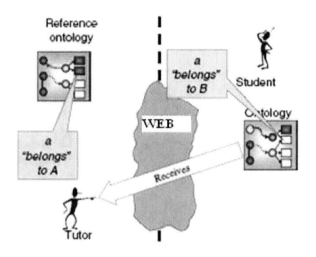

Fig. 3. Instance classification error

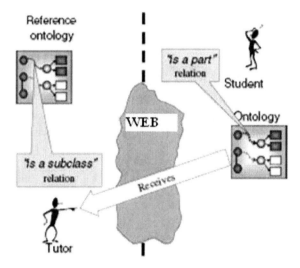

Fig. 4. Class name error

• Wrong Relation. The student uses an improper relation but this one belongs to a group of hierarchical relations (for example, ''A is a part of B'' instead of ''A is a subclass of B'' as shown in fig 4.

• Use of hierarchical relation instead of synonymic relation. This is the case of ''A is a part of B'' instead of ''A is a synonym of B'' as shown in fig 5.

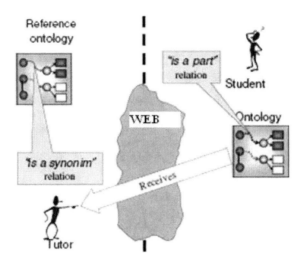

Fig. 5. Hierarchical class errors

3   System Design of E-Learning Based on Multiagent System

Ontological representation of student domain skills can be automatically processed by intelligent software agents. It is appropriate to use software agents for e-learning because they work efficiently in dynamic heterogeneous distributed environment. One of the main properties of an intelligent agent is sociability. Agents are able to communicate between themselves. In that way they can engage in complex dialogues, in which they can negotiate, coordinate their actions and collaborate in the solution of a problem. A set of agents that communicate among themselves to solve problems by using cooperation, coordination and negotiation techniques compose a multi-agent system (MAS).

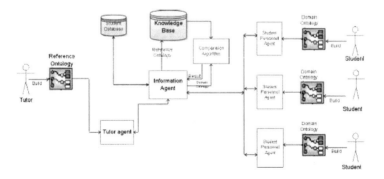

Fig. 6. System design of E-learning using Multiagent system

Description of modules contain in system design:

Tutor

Tutor has to describe the main terms and concepts from which a course is to be constructed. Tutors have precise information about the learning difficulties of their students and tutors can make actions for students to overcome their learning flaws. Main task of tutor is to build reference ontology using ontology construction algorithm.

Student

Student has to build the domain ontology of learning material using ontology construction algorithm.

Database (DB)

It contains general information about students:
Student name
Student e-mail address
Student registration detail
Student learning style

Knowledge Base (KB)

In knowledge base the courses ontological information is stored. Reference ontology build by the tutor is send to the knowledge base via tutor personnel agent.

Student personnel agent

Each student is monitored by a student agent. Student agent contains the information related to the topics visited during the student's e-Learning activities.Student personal agents allow the framework to find situations where a student makes mistakes of the same type in ontology's of different courses.

Tutor agent

Tutor agents will provide the personalization of distributed learning processes. These agents will use the learning history for feedback between students and tutors. A tutor agent is associated with a set of students that are interested in the same topic. A tutor agent is associated with an e-Learning site in order to manage the Learning objects contained in the site. Tutor agent contains the global profiles of all the students associated with it.

Informational agent

Informational agent supports the communication process and facilitates the user interaction with both the DB (database) and the KB (knowledge base). Students and tutors personal agents do not communicate among them directly, but they send the ontological information to the Informational Agent. This informational agent then analyses the received information and returns the results to both, the students and the tutors.

Comparison Algorithm

This algorithm compares the student domain ontology and reference ontology and returns the result to the informational agent.

Reference ontology
It is the ontology of course material of e-learning system.

Domain ontology
Domain ontology plays central role as a resource structuring the learning content. Domain ontology is work as object of examining. It is ontology of learning material of student.

This system works as follows. The reference ontology is sent to knowledge base by the tutor personal agent. Then, when a student forms the domain ontology in OWL format, her/his personal agent connects not with the course tutor personal agent but with the informational agent and sends this ontology for comparing it to the last version of the reference one. After the comparison, the informational agent sends these results to the student and tutor personal agent. If a student or tutor usually prefers certain learning or information presentation method then the personal agent accomplishes all these requirements in new courses without needing to receive direct instructions from the user. After that, the student would receive information in the appropriate way taking into account previous examination results.

Thus, if a student, for example, makes the same mistakes in an ontology (s)he receives a notification about it suggesting to her/him to follow some links that lead to suitable course materials. The use of student personal agents allows the framework to find situations where a student makes mistakes of the same type in ontologies of different courses. (S)he then receives a notification about it and is informed about links with suitable logical course materials. Another important advantage of using multi-agent technology comes from having tutor personal agents. If the majority of students make the same mistakes the course tutor receives a notification this fact, so that (s)he can change suitable course materials.

4   Comparisons of Ontologies

This algorithm is based on some specific conditions.
Student has to use ontological terms for classes and subclasses only from the fixed set corresponding to terms of reference ontology, other terms are considered as mistakes;
Student has to use relations between classes only from the fixed set corresponding to relations of reference ontology, other relations are considered as mistakes too;
If student nevertheless use some term that doesn't exist in reference ontology this term has to correspond to some term of reference ontology (student can use the incorrect name by mistake).

The ontology comparison algorithm
Ontology comparison algorithm compare the student ontology O_s with reference ontology O_e made by tutor

   1. Define the sets of ontology terms T_s and T_e .
   2. Classify terms from T_s on three disjoint categories.
   T_n, T_u and T_w. $T_s = T_n \cup T_u \cup T_w$

- Correctly defined terms
$$T_n \subseteq T_e$$
- Not accurately defined terms
$$T_u \not\subseteq T_e \text{ but}$$
$$\forall t_i \in T_n \; \exists t_j \in T_e, \dots, t \in T_e, t_j \in T_e, m = 1, k$$
  - Incorrectly defined terms
$$T_u \not\subseteq T_e \text{ and } \forall t_i \notin T_n \neg \exists t_j \in T_e$$
  3. Define the sets of ontology relations Rs and Re .
  4. Classify relations from R_s on three disjoint categories: R_n, R_u and R_w.

$$R_s = R_n \cup R_u \cup R_w \quad \text{where}$$
- Correctly defined terms
$$R_n \subseteq R_e$$
  - Not accurately defined terms
$$R_u \not\subseteq R_e \text{ but}$$
$$\forall r_i \in R_n \; \exists r_{jl} \in R_e, \dots, r_{jm} \in R_e, r_{jk} \in R_e, m = 1, k$$
  - Incorrectly defined terms
$$R_u \not\subseteq R_e \text{ and } \forall r_i \notin R_n \neg \exists r_j \in R_e$$

5   Analysis of the Use of Ontology Classes and Relations

We do not consider the use of elements from T_w and relations from R_w. It is very important to take into account the type of relations – hierarchical or improper: A mistake coming from using "is a part" relation instead of "is a subclass" is much less significant than using "is a synonym" relation instead of "is a subclass" one. This step requires the definition of an evaluation function which provides a mark to the students by analyzing the similarity between the sets obtained by the teacher and by the student. In this work, the student receives a mark, written K, which is calculated as follows: K = (Kterm * mterm + Kref * mref + Ktype * mtype) / (mterm + mref + mtype), where Kterm is the % of concepts correctly identified in the student ontology; Krel is the % of relations correctly identified in the student ontol- ogy; Ktype is the % of types of relations correctly identified in the student ontology; mterm is the weight given by system/teacher to the identification of concepts; mrel is the weight given by system/teacher to the identification of relations; mtype is the weight given by system/teacher to the identification of types of relations.

   Ontology comparison algorithm compares the reference ontology and student domain ontology. It compares mainly the classes, relations and type of relations. In first step of algorithm it defines classes of reference ontology as T_s and classes of student ontology as T_e. In third step of algorithm divide the classes of student ontology into three disjoint set as correctly identified classes, not accurately defined classes and incorrectly defined classes. Same concept is used in step three and step four but it is for relations. in step five it calculate the percentage of student ontology correctness by considering only correctly defined classes and not accurately defined classes.

6   Conclusion

The main intension of system is to provide student evaluation in e-learning based semantic web using multiagent system. The Proposed approach is used to generate feedback for student for efficient assessment of student. Feedback generation is also possible through human tutor but it takes time. The Proposed approach provides automatic generation of feedback between student and tutor. It will improve the efficiency of e-learning system.

Few improvements for this approach are possible. An issue that is not addressed here is individual marking and individual ranking of student. Also we improve this approach by ontology integration and provide knowledge sharing between students.

References

1. Saleem, A.: Semantic Web Vision: survey of ontology mapping systems and evaluation progress. In: Clerk Maxwell, J. (ed.) A Treatise on Electricity and Magnetism, Blekinge Institute of Technology, Sweden, 3rd edn., vol. 2, pp. 68–73. Clarendon, Oxford (1892)
2. Malik, H.W.: Visual semantic web: ontology based E- learning Management system. Blekinge Institute of Technology, Sweden
3. Hosam, F., El-Sofany, P.D.: E-Learning Model Based On Semantic Web Technology. Department of Engineering and Computer Science at Qatar University
4. Alsultanny, Y.A.: e-Learning System Overview based on Semantic Web. Graduate College of Computing Studies, Amman, Jordan
5. Fensel, D., Van Harmelen, F.: OIL: An Ontology Infrastructure for Semantic Web. Vrije University, Amsterdam
6. MacDonald, C.J., Stodel, E., Thompson, T.L.: Addressing the eLearning Contradiction:A Collaborative Approach for Developing a Conceptual Framework Learning Object. University of Ottawa, Ottawa
7. Gladun, A., Rogushina, J.: An Application of Intelligent techniques and semantic web technologies in e-learning environment. In: International Research and Training Centre of Information Technologies and Systems. National Academy of Sciences and Ministry of Education, Ukraine
8. Gladun, A., Rogushina, J.: An Ontology based approach to student skills in multiagent e-learning system. Senior Researcher, Institute of Software Systems, National Academy of Sciences, Ukraine
9. Advantage of E-learning,
   http://www.1stopbiztro.com/_mgxroot/page_10751.html

Capturing Popular Opinionated Words with Patterns for Efficient Opinion Detection

K.M. Anil Kumar and Suresha

Department of Studies in Computer Science,
University of Mysore,
Manasagangothri,
Mysore, India
{anilkmsjce,sureshabm}@yahoo.co.in

Abstract. In this paper we present an approach that will identify opinion of web users popularly expressed using short words or sms words. These words are pretty popular with diverse web users and are popular means for expressing their opinion on the web. The study of opinion from web arises to know the diversity of web users. The opinion expressed by web users may be on diverse topics such as politics, sports, products, movies etc. These opinions will be very useful to others such as, leaders of political parties, selection committees of various sports, business analysts and other stake holders of products, directors and producers of movies as well as to the other concerned web users. We use semantic based approach to find users opinion from short words or sms words apart of regular opinionated phrases. Our approach efficiently detects opinion from opinionated texts using extraction patterns and is found to be better than the other approaches on different data sets.

Keywords: Artificial Intelligence, Sentiment Analysis, Opinion Mining.

1   Introduction

The rapid development of web and its related technologies have fueled the popularity of the web with all sections of society. The web has been used by many such as governments, business houses, industries, educational institutions etc., to reach the masses. The individual user's are provided with an opportunity to obtain and share knowledge.

Today many web users document their opinion on different platforms like discussions forums, opinionated sites, e-commerce sites, blogs, personal web pages etc., the opinion expressed may be in a single line or multiple lines in an opinionated text. For last few years, web has seen new forms of written communications, which are quite popular with vast section of the web users. One such form of written communication popular with web users is using short words.

Short words also known as SMS language [8] [9] [10] are quite popular with web users. There are many arguments [8] [9] and counter arguments [10] about its use in communication and its impact on linguistic development of future generations. We believe these short words continue to exist and would conceal facts and opinions important to others.

D.C. Wyld et al. (Eds.): NeCoM/WeST/WiMoN 2011, CCIS 197, pp. 603–611, 2011.
© Springer-Verlag Berlin Heidelberg 2011

For example, word like excellent is written in short words as xllent, xlent etc., the use of short words are found to be very popular as it conveys message at less time. The limitation is that there are no standards for short words, making it very difficult for processing. A few web users use one or more short words in their communication and opinionated text are no exceptions. Following are the examples of opinionated text with regular and short opinionated words collected from opinionated site review centre and retained in same form.

Example 1. Well it is one of the most exciting phones to ever come out. I do think it might be behind the times compared to older phones from Nokia like the N95 etc but it is still a nice phone.

Example 2. A **gr8** TV for the dollar. Samsung has designed and produce a **5n** TV. The picture quality is **xllent** with analog and high definition signal. Sound quality is **gud** to **xllent.** It has a wide angle of picture side vision. It is a very compact design for a TV of this size. Instructions are very **xllent** with simple setup.

Example 1 conveys opinion of a web user with regular opinionated words. Similarly, example 2 conveys opinion of a web user using regular and short opinionated words. The words in bold represent regular opinionated words, those that are bold and underlined represent short opinionated words. The afore used short words like gr8, 5n, gud, xllent are commonly used to represent regular words great, fine, good and excellent.

In this paper we focus on detecting opinions expressed by web users using short and regular opinion words only on products. The remainder of this paper is organized as follows: In Section 2 we give a brief description of related work. Then, in Section 3, we discuss our methodology. In Section 4, the experimental results are discussed. Conclusion is discussed in Section 5.

2   Related Work

Opinion mining is a recent sub discipline of information retrieval which is not about the topic of a document, but with the opinion it expresses [1]. We have referred many literatures on opinion mining, due to space constraint only a few are below mentioned.

Hatzivassiloglou and McKeown [15] have attempted to predict semantic orientation of adjectives by analyzing pairs of adjectives (i.e., adjective pair is adjectives conjoined by and, or, but, either-or, neither-nor) extracted from a large unlabelled document set.

Turney [13] has obtained remarkable results on the sentiment classification of terms by considering the algebraic sum of the orientations of terms as representative of the orientation of the document.

Wang and Araki [16] proposed a variation of the Semantic Orientation-PMI algorithm for Japanese for mining opinion in weblogs. They applied Turney method to Japanese webpage and found results slanting heavily towards positive opinion. They proposed balancing factor and neutral expression detection method and reported a well balanced result.

Kamps et al [11] have focused on the use of lexical relations defined in WordNet. They defined a graph on the adjectives contained in the intersection between the Turney's seed set and WordNet, adding a link between two adjectives whenever WordNet indicate the presence of a synonymy relation between them. The authors defined a distance measure d (t1, t2) between terms t1 and t2, which amounts to the length of the shortest path that connects t1 and t2. The orientation of a term is then determined by its relative distance from the seed terms good and bad.

Opinion observer [6] is the sentiment analysis system for analyzing and comparing opinions on the web. The product features are extracted from noun or noun phrases by the association miner. They use adjectives as opinion words and assign prior polarity of these by WordNet exploring method. The polarity of an opinion expression which is a sentence containing one or more feature terms and one or more opinion words is assigned a dominant orientation. The extracted features are stored in a database in the form of feature, number of positive expression and number of negative expression.

Anil and Suresha [5] proposed an approach for detecting opinion from short words using short word lexicon. It involves in searching an opinionated text with entries of short word lexicon and translating short words with regular words in an opinionated text for opinion detection.

Our work differs from the afore mentioned studies by finding opinion of a user from both regular and short opinionated words in an opinionated text. Our work uses adjectives as well as part-of-speech like verb, adverb etc., to capture opinionated words for efficient opinion detection. Also the use of extraction patterns eliminates searching and translation phases for opinion detection from short opinionated words.

3   Methodology

We collected nearly 2000 opinionated texts from sources such as web search engines like Google, Altavista, Exalead etc., opinionated sites like Amazon, CNet, review centre, bigadda, rediff etc., and from researchers [2][6] for experimentation.

Our data sets comprised of predominantly of normal opinionated words with a few short words used for expressing opinions. We passed these data sets to group of 10 engineering students of diverse disciplines to rephrase regular opinion words with their popular short opinion words, while retaining a copy of original data sets for further processing. We refer to original opinionated texts as Data Set 1 and rephrased opinionated texts as Data set 2. All opinionated texts, both original and rephrased, are subjected to a part of speech tagger. The tagger used is Monty Tagger [7]. The tagged opinionated texts are then subjected to extraction patterns to obtain opinionated phrases that are likely to contain user's opinion. Table 1 shows a few extraction patterns used to find opinionated phrases, where JJ represent adjective, CD represent cardinal and NN/NNS, VB/VBD/VBN/VBG, RB/RBR/RBS represent different forms of noun, verb and ad-verb.

An initial study undertaken by [4] showed that the extracted phrases also contain neutral phrases which can influence opinion of an opinionated text. In order to remove these neutral phrases we use Sentiment Product Lexicon (SPL) for capturing only subjective or opinionated phrases.

Table 1. Extraction patterns

Slno.	First Word	Second Word	Third Word
1	JJ	NN or NNS	anything
2	RB,RBR or RBS	JJ	not NN nor NNS
3	JJ	JJ	not NN nor NNS
4	NN or NNS	JJ	not NN or NNS
5	RB,RBR or RBS	VB,VBD,VBN or VBG	anything
6	NN, NNS or NNP	NN or NNS or NNP	anything
7	RB, RBR or RBZ	VB or VBD or VBG or VBN	anything
8	RB, RBR or RBZ	CD	anything
9	CD	NN, NNS or NNP	anything

Sentiment Product Lexicon is collection of General lexicon and Domain lexicon. General lexicon maintains a list of positive and negative words by collecting opinion words that are positive or negative from sources. Domain lexicon maintains a list of positive or negative words from the domain context. We found words like cool, revolutionary etc., appeared in negative list of General lexicon. These words were used to express positive opinion by web users. Hence we created a domain lexicon to have opinion words from the domain perspective. The details of construction of General lexicon and Domain lexicon are made available in [3].

To capture opinion from popular short words in opinionated texts, we collected 220 short words that were analyzed by a group of 10 engineering students of diverse disciplines for identifying short words which conveys positive or negative opinion. Short words were added to the Domain lexicon, when there is 60% students agreement on the polarity of short words.

We obtained 170 short opinionated words with 92 positive and 78 negative short words. The opinionated phrases from opinionated texts are subjected to Domain lexicon to identify the opinion of short words. Consider the text " this is a gr8 phone". Here gr8 is used to represent great. After part of speech tagging the text, we obtain this/DT is/VBZ a/DT gr8/CD phone/NN. Where DT,VBZ,CD and NN corresponds to determiner, verb, cardinal and noun. Application of extraction patterns from Table 1 obtains gr8/CD phone/NN as opinionated phrases. We use SPL and a list of Intensifiers and diminishers to obtain a score that aids in finding opinion of web users.

When an text with short opinionated words such as This is a gud phone. is passed to a tagger, we obtain the following tagged text This/DT is/VBZ a/DT gud/NN phone/NN ./.". Application of extraction pattern from Table 1 will obtain gud/JJ phone/NN as opinionated phrase from the text. Similarly, an opinionated text such as This is a bad phone. with regular opinionated words is input to the tagger, we get the following tagged text This/DT is/VBZ a/DT bad/JJ phone/NN ./.. Application of extraction patterns from Table 1 will obtain bad/JJ phone/NN as opinionated phrase from the text. SPL is used to detect neutral phrases. We consider the extracted phrases or words namely word1 and word2 from an opinionated text as neutral if none of the extracted words are found in SPL.

From the above example word1 is bad and word2 is phone. We find whether word2 is in positive or negative list of Domain lexicon. If word2 is present in any one of the list in Domain lexicon, polarity of the word will be similar to polarity of list in which it is found. If it is not in positive or negative list of Domain lexicon, then positive and negative list of General lexicon is consulted to find the polarity of a word.

If word2 is neither present in Domain lexicon nor in General lexicon, we assume word2 to have neutral polarity, in such a case we use word1 instead of word2, and find polarity of word1 similar to polarity of word2 afore discussed. If polarity is found, then polarity is for the phrase consisting of both word1 and word2. If polarity is not found, we assume both word1 and word2 to be neutral. If a word, either word1 or word2 is present in both Domain lexicon and General lexicon, polarity of word will be similar to polarity of Domain lexicon. If word1 is a negator such as not, the polarity of word2 will be opposite to an earlier obtained polarity of word2.

For example the phrase "not good", here word1 is not and word2 is good. The polarity of word2 is positive, since word2 is prefixed by word1 i.e. not. The polarity of phrase is negative. We retain only those phrases that have a polarity and discard phrases that are neutral. We assign a score of +2 for positive phrases and -2 for negative phrases. we have used the values as discussed in [12].

The phrases obtained are subjected to a list of intensifiers and diminishers obtained from [14]. The objective is to assign a score to opinionated phrase based on occurrence of phrases that scales positive or negative opinion of the users. For example the opinionated text "this phone is good" is different from "this phone is too good". Here the phrase too is intensifying positive opinion of the user. Similarly, in the text "This phone is barely good" the phrase barely is dimishing the positive opinion of the user.

When the extraction patterns discussed in Table 1 are applied to the text "this phone is too good", the opinionated phrase too good is obtained. The SPL also outputs the phrase too good as positive opinion phrase with score +2. We pass the positive phrase to a list of intensifiers and diminishers.

Our intuition here is that, intensifiers or diminshers precede opinionated phrase. if the phrase is positive and preceded by an intensifier we add 1 to score of positive phrase(1+2). if the phrase is positive and preceded by an diminisher we subtract 1 to score of positive phrase(1-2). Similarly, if the phrase is negative and proceeded by an intensifier we add -1 to score of negative phrase (-1-2). if the phrase is negative and preceded by an diminisher we add 1 to score of negative phrase(1-2). Therefore the score for the phrase too good is 3(1+2) and score for phrase barely good is 1(-1+2). We are unable to provide more examples because of the page limit guidelines of the conference.

We compute the average semantic orientation of the opinionated text by considering all scores of opinionated phrases as shown in Equation 1. We classify opinionated text as positive, if the average semantic orientation of opinionated text is greater than a threshold and negative when the average semantic orientation is less than a threshold. The threshold used here is 0.

$$SO(OpinionatedText) = \frac{1}{n}\sum_{i=1}^{n}(OpinionatedPhrase_i) \qquad (1)$$

Table 2. Results on Data Set 1

Slno.	Approach	Number of opinionated text	Accuracy(%)
1	[16]	400	75
2	[2]	140	69.3
3	Our approach	400	79.5
4	[5]	400	79.5
5	Our approach	140	73.56
6	[5]	140	73.56
7	Our approach	250	89.86
8	[5]	250	89.86
9	Our approach	100	83.14
10	[5]	100	83.14
11	Our approach	34	87.87
12	[5]	34	87.87
13	Our approach	95	89.47
14	[5]	95	89.47
15	Our approach	45	95.55
16	[5]	45	95.55
17	Our approach	97	78.94
18	[5]	97	78.94
19	Our approach	33	96.67
20	[5]	33	96.67

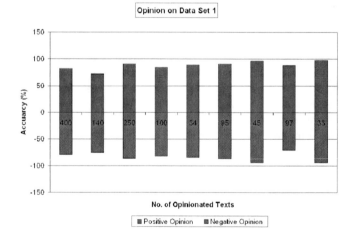

Fig. 1. Summary of Users Opinion on Data Set 1

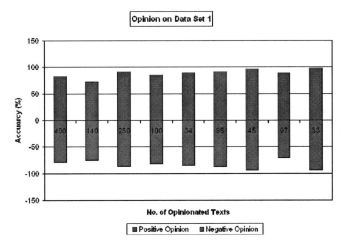

Fig. 2. Summary of Users Opinion on Data Set 2

4   Experiments and Results

We use afore mentioned approach to find opinion from opinionated texts. Table 2 provides result of our approach along with a few published results. Application of extraction patterns defined in [5] yields results similar to our approach on Data Set 1.

When Opinionated texts from Data Set 2 are subjected to opinion detection, the extraction patterns defined in Table 1 provides better opinionated phrases, including regular and short words, than the patterns defined in [5]. For example, consider opinionated text "I am extremely happy with this product. It is grt player with xlent feature." We obtain extremely happy as opinionated phrase with pattern defined in [5] without recognizing popular short words. We get extremely happy, grt player and xlent feature as opinionated phrases using extraction patterns defined in Table 1.

Table 3 provides result of opinion detection from opinionated texts on Data Set 2. We achieve an increased accuracy of 5.83% than the other approach discussed in [5]. Another advantage of our approach is that, it eliminates searching for short words and later translation of short words to regular words. For example, In an opinionated text such as "It is grt player with xlent feature" short words like grt and xlent are translated to normal words with the help of short word lexicon in a few approaches. Our approach eliminates searching and translation phases, thereby significantly reducing the processing time to detect opinion.

We compute the accuracy of our approach by considering true positives and true negatives divided by total number of opinionated texts. True positives represent number of opinionated texts classified correctly as positive. Similarly, true negatives represent number of opinionated texts classified correctly as negatives. Figure 1 and 2 shows positive accuracy and negative accuracy of users opinion on Data Set 1 and Data Set 2.

Table 3. Result on Data Set 2

Slno.	Approaches	Number of opinionated text	Accuracy(%)
1	[5]	400	67.8
2	[5]	140	73.56
3	[5]	250	75.9
4	[5]	100	89.7
5	[5]	34	87.7
6	[5]	95	89.47
7	[5]	45	95.55
8	[5]	97	78.94
9	[5]	33	96.67
10	Our approach	400	**85.6**
11	Our approach	140	**74.45**
12	Our approach	250	**88**
13	Our approach	100	**95.58**
14	Our approach	34	**96.9**
15	Our approach	95	**92.01**
16	Our approach	45	**97.62**
17	Our approach	97	**79.80**
18	Our approach	33	**97.87**

5   Conclusion

We have discussed an approach that detects opinion of a web user from an opinionated text. Today opinions are expressed by the web users using regular words or short words. We find opinion of a web user from both regular and short word and later classifies opinion as positive or negative. Our approach achieves an increased accuracy of 5.83% on opinionated texts comprising of regular and short words. It efficiently detects opinion from opinionated texts using extraction patterns and is found to be better than the other approaches on different data sets.

References

1. Esuli, A., Sebastiani, F.: Determining term subjectivity and term orientation for opinion mining. In: Proceedings of 11th Conference of the European Chapter of the Association for Computational Linguistics, Trento, Italy (2006)
2. Kennedy, A., Inkpen, D.: Sentiment Classification of Movie and Product Reviews Using Contextual Valence Shifters. In: Proceedings of FINEXIN 2005, Workshop on the Analysis of Informal and Formal Information Exchange during Negotiations, Canada (2005)
3. Anil Kumar, K.M., Suresha: Identifying Subjective Phrases From Opinionated Texts Using Sentiment Product Lexicon. International Journal of Advanced Engineering & Applications 2, 63–271 (2010)

4. Anil Kumar, K.M., Suresha: Detection of Neutral Phrases and Polarity Shifting of Few Phrases for Effective Classification of Opinionated Texts. International Journal of Computational Intelligence Research 6, 43–58 (2010)
5. Anil Kumar, K.M., Suresha: Detection of Web Users' Opinion from Normal and Short Opin-ionated Words. In: Proc.: International Conference on Data Engineering and Management, Bishop Heber College (Autonomous), July 29-31 (2010)
6. Liu, B., Hu, M., Cheng, J.: Opinion Observer: Analyzing and Comparing Opinions on the Web, Chiba, Japan (2005)
7. Hugo: MontyLingua: An end-to-end natural language processor with common sense (2003)
8. `http://www.dailymail.co.uk/news/article-483511/-h8-txt-msgs-How-texting-wrecking-language.html`
9. `http://news.bbc.co.uk/2/hi/uknews/education/2197173.stm`
10. `http://entertainment.timesonline.co.uk/tol/artsandentertainment/books/non-fiction/article4356458.ece`
11. Kamps, J., Marx, M., Mokken, R.J., De Rijke, M.: Using wordnet to measure semantic orientation of adjectives. In: Proceedings of 4th International Conference on Language Resources and Evaluation, Lisbon, Portugal, pp. 1115–1118 (2004)
12. Polanyi, L., Zaenen, A.: Contextual Valence Shifters. In: Computing Attitude and Affect in Text: Theory and Applications, pp. 1–10 (2006)
13. Turney, P.D.: Thumbs up or thumbs down? Semantic orientation applied to unsupervised classification of reviews. In: Proceedings of 40th Annual Meeting of the Association for Computational Linguistics, Philadelphia, US, pp. 417–424 (2002)
14. Stone, P.J.: Thematic text analysis: New agendas for analyzing text content. In: Roberts, C. (ed.) Text Analysis for the Social Sciences. Lawrence Erlbaum, Mahwah (1997)
15. Hatzivassiloglou, V., McKeown, K.R.: Predicting the semantic orientation of adjectives. In: Proceedings of 35th Annual Meeting of the Association for Computational Linguistics, Madrid, Spain, pp. 174–181 (1997)
16. Wang, G., Araki, K.: Modifying SO-PMI for Japanese Weblog Opinion Mining by Using a Balancing Factor and Detecting Neutral Expressions. In: Proceedings of NAACL HLT 2007, New York, US, pp. 189–192 (2007)

A Review on the Variants of Information Retrieval

Pothula Sujatha and P. Dhavachelvan

Department of Computer Science, Pondicherry University, Puducherry-605014, India
{spothula,dhavachelvan}@gmail.com

Abstract. In this paper we investigate some of the most important variants of information retrieval. They are Cross-lingual Information Retrieval (CLIR) and Multilingual Information Retrieval (MLIR). CLIR deals with submitting queries in one language and retrieving documents in some other language other than query language. MLIR deals with submitting questions in one or more languages and retrieving documents in one or more diverse languages. With increasing globalized economy, the knack to find information in other languages is becoming a necessity. In short the paper tries to encapsulate the overall review of the research works in Indian and Foreign languages.

Keywords: Cross-Lingual Information Retrieval, Dictionary Based Translation, Machine Translation, Ontology.

1 Introduction

Information Retrieval [IR] is the act of storing, searching, and retrieving information that match a user's request [3]. IR became popular with the start of the Internet, and it is increasingly relevant and researched. Now, almost all internet users use some type of modern IR system every day, whether it is a search engine (Google or Yahoo) or some specially developed system for digital libraries [46]. The variants of the IR are BLIR, CLIR and MLIR. In this paper we concentrate on CLIR and MLIR only. CLIR deals with submitting queries in one language and retrieving documents in some other language other than query language. MLIR deals with submitting questions in one or more languages and retrieving documents in one or more diverse languages. With gradually more globalized economy, the knack to find information in other languages is becoming a necessity.

The rest of the paper is organized as the following. Section 2 introduces the most important IR methods, various works of CLIR are presented in Section 3, and in Section 4 MLIR system and review its previous research works are discussed, at last, we conclude in Section 5.

2 IR Methods

In classical IR search engines, both the query and the retrieved documents are in the same language. The classical IR regards the documents in foreign language as the unwanted "noise" [1]. These needs are introduced in new area of IR which takes into account all the documents received regardless of the languages being used. This is

D.C. Wyld et al. (Eds.): NeCoM/WeST/WiMoN 2011, CCIS 197, pp. 612–621, 2011.
© Springer-Verlag Berlin Heidelberg 2011

where the bilingual, cross-lingual and multi-lingual IR plays a part. But to perform these variants of IR, a variety of translation methods are required. These are described in the following sub-sections.

Translation can be done to the query, the document or both when any retrieval system involved with many languages. Query translation involves translating the query to the target language. Document translation translates the document into the source language (i.e. the language used for the query). There are various methods to translate query, document or both. There are three primary tools for translations are dictionaries, machine translation systems and parallel corpora. Query translation, typically, uses either dictionary based or corpus based translation. Document translation, for the most part, only uses machine translation.

2.1 Dictionary Based

A bilingual dictionary is a catalog of words in the query language and their translations in the document language. However, these dictionaries have translation probabilities assigned that allow for disambiguation and weighting it is an easiest method. Most of the researchers choose this tool. There are plenty of bilingual dictionaries are available in the literature both in Indian and Foreign languages [46]. The drawback of this method is specialized terms and phrases are often not replaced properly.

2.2 Machine Translation

In this method, a machine translation system is used to translate either the document or query. The main weaknesses of this method are translation text or words may be incorrect and computational expensive. This method is not adequate in situations where there is a large collection of documents or when searching for documents on the web.

2.3 Parallel Corpora

The final method of translation is corpus-based method that depends on parallel corpora in the two languages. When compared to dictionary based translation, corpus based translation typically gives much superior performance [5]. The drawback of this translation method is the creation of parallel corpora is convoluted and quite expensive and sometimes it can be extremely hard to find parallel corpora for certain languages or that are large enough to be of use [46].

The main problems with dictionary based and corpus based translation are coverage and quality. Poor quality dictionaries and corpora can greatly diminish the performance of a system [5]. Coverage relates to words that are not present in the dictionary or corpus. These words will have no translation, while in some languages that are related this is no problem in other language pairs such as Chinese and English this is a big problem [6]. Because of this there has been considerable research done on automatically or semi-automatically acquiring parallel corpora or bilingual lexicons [46].

The above described methods are used for CLIR and MLIR systems. These two systems may use translation of all documents into a common language, automatic translation of the queries, or combination of both query and document translations.

3 CLIR

One variant of IR that has made a great deal of interest and has had many exciting advances made in it, is CLIR. The purpose of CLIR is to permit users to make queries in one source language and retrieve target documents in one or more other languages. The resulting target documents can then be translated into the source query language to permit the user to get to know about the information retrieved. For example, a user makes a query in English about "school" and receives documents back in Hindi about "विद्यालय" which is Hindi school.

As stated above most systems in CLIR use some type of translation methods. Apart from translation methods, there exist few non-translation methods, such as cognate matching [2], latent semantic indexing [10], and relevance models [4]. The translation methods are frequently used because of the problem in CLIR in language translation. The most important and major areas of research in CLIR are: What should be translated, how it should be translated, and how to eliminate bad translations, and also an active topic is how to acquire large enough amounts of translation.

3.1 CLIR Survey on Indian and Foreign Languages

In [11], the task is to retrieve relevant documents from an English corpus in response to a query expressed in different Indian languages which includes Hindi, Tamil, Telugu, Bengali and Marathi. A word alignment table have been used that was learnt by a Statistical Machine Translation (SMT) system trained on aligned parallel sentences, to map a query in source language into an equivalent query in the language of the target document collection. The relevant documents are then retrieved using a language modeling based retrieval algorithm. This work has been tested on CLEF 2007 data collection.

The most commonly used vocabulary in Indian language documents found on the web contains a number of words that have Sanskrit, Persian or English origin. In [12] approximate string matching techniques are used to exploit relatively large number of cognates among Indian languages, which are higher when compared to an Indian language and a non-Indian language.

An approach to identify cognates was presented and made use of them for improving dictionary based CLIR where the query and documents both belong to two different Indian languages. Experiments using a Hindi document collection and a set of Telugu queries were conducted and reported the improvement due to cognate recognition and translation.

The main objective of this work [13] is to analyze and evaluate the retrieval effectiveness of various indexing and search strategies based on test collections written in four different languages: English, French, German, and Italian. Data base merging strategies have been used. Experiments are done in CLEF 2000 corpora.

This paper [14] describes an approach that employs user-assisted query translation to help searchers better understand the system's operation.

[15] This paper explores the key issues in dictionary-based CLIR, develops unified frameworks for term selection and term translation. This framework helps to explain the relationships among existing techniques, and demonstrates the effect of those techniques using four contrasting languages for systematic experiments with uniform query translation architecture. The other popular works on CLIR are given in table 1.

Table 1. An overview of CLIR and MLIR research works in foreign languages

Authors	Languages	Method/Technique	Evaluation Initiatives
Fujii, A., Ishikawa, T., 2001[19]	J to E and E to J	Query translation and Document translation	NTCIR -2 Collection
Jialun Qin, Yilu Zhou, Michael Chau, and Hsinchun Chen, 2003 [22]	E to Ch	Dictionary based query translation	TREC Collection
David A. Hull, Gregory Grefenstette, 1996 [29]	E to F	Dictionary based query translation	Documents Collection
Chen-Yu Su, Tien-Chien Lin and Shih-Hung Wu, 2007 [30]	Ch to J and K	Dictionary based query translation	NTCIR -6
Paraic Sheridan, Jean Paul Ballerini, 1996 [31]	G to I	Thesaurus-based query expansion	Documents Collection
Wen-Cheng Lin, Hsin-Hsi Chen, 2003 [20]	J to E and Ch	Query translation	NTCIR-3
David A. Hull , Gregory Grefenstette, 1996 [32]	E to F	Dictionary based query translation	Documents Collection
Peter A. Chew and Ahmed Abdelali, 2008 [33]	E, R, S, F and A	Latent Semantic Analysis	Bible and Quran data
Su Liu, 2001 [34]	E to Ch	Dictionary based query translation	TREC Collection
Mizera-Pietraszko J, 2009 [35]	E to F and F to E	Meta data search	Documents Collection
Turdi Tohti, Winira Musajan, Askar Hamdulla, 2008 [36]	Uyghur, Kazak, Kyrgyz	Query phase reconstruction, character coding	Website data

Table 1. (*continued*)

Marshall Ramsey, Thian-Huat Ong, Hsinchun Chen, 1998 [37]	Ch and J	Dictionary-lookup, phonetic, radical, and mnemonic	Training data
Dong-Mo Zhang, Huan-Ye Sheng, Fang Li and Tian-Fang Yao, 2002 [38]	E, G and Ch	Case based reasoning and machine learning	Documents
Kazuyuki Yoshinaga, Takao Terano, Ning Zhong, 1999 [39]	J and E	Web Information Collector, Document classifier, Ontology generator and Search engine	Web documents
Hsin-Chang Yang, Chung-Hong Lee, 2008 [45]	E and Ch	Parallel corpora	Bilingual corpus documents
Hassina Aliane, 2006 [40]	A, F and E	Ontology based Approach (corpora)	Trilingual corpus documents
Chung-hsin Lin and Hsinchun Chen, 1996 [41]	Ch and E	Indexing and Classification approach	Multilingual Databases
Jeffrey A. Rydberg-Cox, Lara Vetter, Stefan M. Rüger, Daniel Heesch [42]	Greek, Latin and Old Norse	Query translation	Search engine results
Shuang-Qing Yuan, Fang Li, and Huan-Ye Sheng, 2002 [43]	Ch and E	Novel approach for finding terminology translations from hyperlinks	Website Links (parallel or unparallel corpus)
Akiko Aizawa, 2002. [44]	E and J	Evolutionary framework	NTCIR-J1

Table 1 describes the works in foreign languages which are involved in the CLIR/MLIR systems, the translation technique/method and finally the evaluation initiatives/web document collections used in the research work for experiments are enumerated.

Similarly, Table 2 describes the works in Indian languages which are involved in the CLIR/MLIR systems, the translation technique/method and finally the evaluation initiatives/web document collections are used in the reviewed research work experiments are enumerated.

4   MLIR

MLIR facilitates the usage of queries in one language to access documents in different languages. In recent years, large amount of multilingual information is created and disseminated. Due to this reason it attracts the attention of the researchers lately. In order to retrieve this multilingual information efficiently the adaptation of traditional IR systems has been considered. That is query translation and document translations have been used. The problem of MLIR is an extension of the general problem of monolingual IR [16].

MLIR can be thought of as a combination of machine translation and traditional monolingual IR. Most research has focused on locating and exploiting translation resources with which the user's search requests or target documents (or both) are translated into the same language.

A multilingual data collection is a set of documents that are written in different languages. There are two types of multilingual data collection. The first one contains several monolingual document collections. The second one consists of multilingual-documents. The second type of multilingual data collection is written in more than two languages. Some multilingual-documents have a major language, i.e. most part of the document is written in the same language.

4.1   MLIR Survey on Indian and Foreign Languages

In this area, there is almost a nil figure available in Indian languages. It is also hardly available in foreign languages. The few available ones are presented as follows: Most systems in MLIR use some type of translation. While there exist non-translation methods, such as: Translation-free technique is based on an ontological representation of documents and queries. A multilingual ontology for documents/queries representation has been used [18].

Integrate query and document translation with monolingual retrieval to improve retrieval accuracy have been presented in [19], and perform clustering to improve browsing efficiency. Finally, an entropy-driven technique has been used in evaluating clustering methods.

Japanese/English cross-language (J-E and E-J) and multi-lingual (J-JE and E-JE) IR tasks are participated in NTCIR-2. In this paper, performance evaluation is done with respect to the NTCIR-2 collection. The paper [20] deals with Chinese, English and Japanese MLIR run and the merging problem in distributed MLIR is studied. In [21] MLIR based on knowledge representation model is given. This model permits to describe the semantics of document in a multilingual context. This model also, called semantic graph, is an extension of the Sowa's model of conceptual graphs where different vocabularies' are available. In [22] a multilingual English-Chinese Web portal in the business domain is developed and evaluated. This paper used a dictionary-based approach that has been adopted to combine phrasal translation, co-occurrence analysis, and pre- and post-translation query expansion.

Recently, a number of tracks and workshops have evolved to support research in this area. They are TREC (Text Retrieval Conference), CLEF (Cross Language Evaluation Forum) and the NTCIR (NII Test Collection for IR Systems). The NTCIR project is a yearly competition in Japan that covers many topics including CLIR.

Table 2. An Overview of CLIR and MLIR Research Works In Indian Languages

Authors	Languages	Method/Technique	Evaluation Initiatives
Jagadeesh, J. and Kumaran, K , 2007 [11]	(H, Ta, Te, Be, Ma and E) to E	structural query translation, Language Modeling based retrieval algorithm	CLEF 2007
Ranbeer Makin, Nikita Pandey, Prasad Pingali, and Vasudeva Varma,2007 [12]	Te to E	Dictionary based query translation, String matching	Documents Collection
A. Kumaran, Jayant and R. Haritsa, 2005 [23]	E to (Ta and F)	Semantic text matching	Standard SQL:1999 Constructs
Prasad Pingali and Vasudeva Varma, 2006 [24]	(H and Te) to E	Dictionary based query translation, Lucene search engine, vector based ranking model	CLEF 2006
Tune, K. K, Pingali, P., Varma, V., 2007 [25]	Oromo to E	Dictionary based query translation, Approximate string matching	CLEF 2006
Sethuramalingam S and Vasudeva Varma, 2008 [26]	E to H and H to E	Dictionary based query translation, Mapping based approach for transliteration, Lucene's BM25 algorithm for ranking	FIRE-2008
Manoj kumar Chinnakotla and Om P.Damani, 2009 [27]	E to (H, Te, Ta)	Machine Transliteration	NEWS 2009
Anurag Seetha, Sujoy Dos and M. Kumar, 2007 [28]	E to H	Dictionary based query translation	Documents Collection

5 Conclusion

CLIR and MLIR provide new paradigms in searching documents through numerous varieties of languages across the world and it can be the baseline for searching not only between two languages but also in multiple languages. These two represents some of the most active areas of research in IR. This paper describes these two important variants of IR, its challenges, current methods, drawbacks of these methods and the current evaluation tracks. Finally, this paper reviews not all but some of the latest research works in the area of CLIR and MLIR for both foreign and Indian languages. These two presented areas have made great progress and are important for the future.

References

1. Abusalah, M., Tait, J., Oakes, M.: Literature Review of Cross Language Information Retrieval. World Academy of Science, Engineering and Technology 4, 175–177 (2005)
2. Buckley, C., Mitra, M., Walz, J.A., Cardie, C.: Using clustering and super concepts within SMART. TREC 6, Information Processing and Management 36, 109–131 (2000)
3. Korfhage, R.R.: Information Storage and Retrieval. John Wiley and Sons, Chichester (1997)
4. Lavrenko, V., Choquette, M., Croft, W.B.: Cross-lingual relevance models. In: SIGIR 2002: Proceedings of the 25th Annual International ACM SIGIR Conference on Research and Development in Information Retrieval, pp. 175–182 (2002)
5. McNamee, P., Mayfield, J.: Comparing cross-language query expansion techniques by degrading translation resources. In: SIGIR 2002: Proceedings of the 25th Annual International ACM SIGIR Conference on Research and Development in Information Retrieval, pp. 159–166 (2002)
6. Zhang, Y., Vines, P.: Using the web for automated translation extraction in cross-language information retrieval. In: SIGIR 2004: Proceedings of the 27th Annual International ACM SIGIR Conference on Research and Development in Information Retrieval, pp. 162–169 (2004)
7. Belkin, N.J., Dumais, S.T., Scholtz, J., Wilkinson, R.: Evaluating interactive information retrieval systems: opportunities and challenges. In: CHI Extended Abstracts, pp. 1594–1595 (2004)
8. Peters, C., Braschler, M.: Cross Language System Evaluation: The CLEF Campaigns. Journal of the American Soc. for Inf. Sci. and Tech. 52(12), 1067–1072 (2001)
9. Voorhees, E.M., Harman, D.: Overview of TREC 2001. In: NIST Special Publication 500-250: Proceedings of TREC 2001, NIST (2001)
10. Dumais, S.T., Letsche, T.A., Littman, M.L., Landauer, T.K.: Automatic cross-language retrieval using latent semantic indexing. In: AAAI Spring Symposuim on Cross-Language Text and Speech Retrieval (1997)
11. Jagarlamudi, J., Kumaran, A.: Cross-Lingual Information Retrieval System for Indian Languages. In: Peters, C., Jijkoun, V., Mandl, T., Müller, H., Oard, D.W., Peñas, A., Petras, V., Santos, D. (eds.) CLEF 2007. LNCS, vol. 5152, pp. 80–87. Springer, Heidelberg (2008)
12. Makin, R., Pandey, N., Pingali, P., Varma, V.: Approximate String Matching Techniques for Effective CLIR Among Indian Languages. In: Masulli, F., Mitra, S., Pasi, G. (eds.) WILF 2007. LNCS (LNAI), vol. 4578, pp. 430–437. Springer, Heidelberg (2007)
13. Savoy, J.: Cross-language information retrieval: experiments based on CLEF 2000 corpora. Information Processing and Management 39, 75–115 (2001)
14. Oard, D.W., et al.: User-assisted query translation for interactive cross-language information retrieval. Information Processing and Management 44, 181–211 (2008)
15. Levow, G.-A., et al.: Dictionary-based techniques for cross-language information retrieval. Information Processing and Management 41, 523–547 (2005)
16. Abdelali, A., Cowie, J.R., Farwell, D., Ogden, W.C.: UCLIR: a Multilingual Information Retrieval Tool. Inteligencia Artificial, Revista Iberoamericana de Inteligencia Artificial 22, 103–110 (2003)
17. Clough, P., Gonzalo, J., Karlgren, J., Barker, E., Artiles, J., Peinado, V.: Large-Scale Interactive Evaluation of Multilingual Information Access Systems - the iCLEF Flickr Challenge. In: Macdonald, C., Ounis, I., Plachouras, V., Ruthven, I., White, R.W. (eds.) ECIR 2008. LNCS, vol. 4956, pp. 33–38. Springer, Heidelberg (2008)
18. Aliane, H.: An Ontology Based Approach to Multilingual Information Retrieval. In: Artificial Intelligence Division, Research Center on Scientific and Technical Information (2006)

19. Fujii, A., Ishikawa, T.: Evaluating Multi-lingual Information Retrieval and Clustering at ULIS. In: Proceedings of the Second NTCIR Workshop Meeting on Evaluation of Chinese & Japanese Text Retrieval and Text Summarization, Tokyo, Japan, pp. 5-144–5-148 (March 2001)

20. Lin, W.-C., Chen, H.-H.: Description of NTU Approach to NTCIR3 Multilingual Information Retrieval. In: Proceedings of the Third NTCIR Workshop on Research in Information Retrieval Automatic Text Summarization and Question Answering. National Institute of Informatics, Tokyo (2003)

21. Roussey, C., et al.: SyDoM: A Multilingual Information Retrieval System for Digital Libraries. In: Electronics Publishing 2001 – 2001 in the Digital Publishing Odyssey. IOS Press, Amsterdam (2001)

22. Qin, J., Zhou, Y., Chau, M., Chen, H.: Supporting Multilingual Information Retrieval in Web Applications: An English-Chinese Web Portal Experiment. In: Sembok, T.M.T., Zaman, H.B., Chen, H., Urs, S.R., Myaeng, S.-H. (eds.) ICADL 2003. LNCS, vol. 2911, pp. 149–152. Springer, Heidelberg (2003)

23. Kumaran, A., Haritsa, J.R.: SemEQUAL: Multilingual Semantic Matching in Relational Systems. In: Zhou, L.-z., Ooi, B.-C., Meng, X. (eds.) DASFAA 2005. LNCS, vol. 3453, pp. 214–225. Springer, Heidelberg (2005)

24. Pingali, P., Varma, V.: Hindi and Telugu to English Cross Language Information Retrieval at CLEF 2006. In: Peters, C., Clough, P., Gey, F.C., Karlgren, J., Magnini, B., Oard, D.W., de Rijke, M., Stempfhuber, M. (eds.) CLEF 2006. LNCS, vol. 4730, pp. 35–42. Springer, Heidelberg (2007)

25. Pingali, P., Varma, V., Tune, K.K.: Evaluation of Oromo-English Cross-Language. Information Retrieval. In: IJCAI 2007 Workshop on CLIA, Hyderabad, India (2007)

26. Sethuramalingam, S., Varma, V.: IIIT Hyderabad's CLIR experiments for FIRE-2008. In: The working notes of First Workshop of Forum for Information Retrieval Evaluation (FIRE), Kolkata (2008)

27. Chinnakotla, M.K., Damani, O.P.: Experiences with English-Hindi, English-Tamil and English-Kannada Transliteration Tasks at NEWS 2009. In: Proceedings of the 2009 Named Entities Workshop: Shared Task on Transliteration, pp. 44–47 (2009)

28. Seetha, A., Dos, S., Kumar, M.: Evaluation of the English-Hindi Cross Language Information Retrieval System Based on Dictionary Based Query Translation Method. In: Proceedings of the 10th International Conference on Information Technology (2007)

29. Hull, D.A., Grefenstette, G.: Querying Across Languages: A Dictionary-Based Approach to Multilingual Information Retrieval. In: SIGIR 1996, pp. 49–57 (1996)

30. Su, C.-Y., Lin, T.-C., Wu, S.-H.: Using Wikipedia to Translate OOV Terms on MLIR. In: Proceedings of NTCIR-6 Workshop Meeting, Tokyo, Japan, May 15-18 (2007)

31. Sheridan, P., Ballerini, J.P.: Experiments in Multilingual Information Retrieval Using the SPIDER System. In: SIGIR 1996, pp. 58–65 (1996)

32. Hull, D.A., Grefenstette, G.: Experiments in Multilingual Information Retrieval. In: Proceedings of the 19th Annual International ACM SIGIR Conference on Research and Development in Information Retrieval (1996)

33. Chew, P.A., Abdelali, A.: The Effects of Language Relatedness on Multilingual Information Re-trieval: A Case Study With Indo-European and Semitic Languages. In: The Second International Workshop on Cross Lingual Information Access (2008)

34. Liu, S.: ECIRS: an English-Chinese Cross-language Information-retrieval System. In: IEEE International Conference on Systems, Man, and Cybernetics, vol. 2, pp. 954–959 (2002)

35. Mizera-Pietraszko, J.: Interactive Document Retrieval from Multilingual Digital Repositories. In: IEEE Xplore Digital Library. IEEE Computer Society Press, Los Alamitos (2009); ICADIWT 2009, pp. 423–428 (2009)

36. Tohti, T., Musajan, W., Hamdulla, A.: Character Code Conversion and Misspelled Word Processing in Uyghur, Kazak, Kyrgyz Multilingual Information Retrieval System. In: ALPIT 2008, pp. 139–144 (2008)
37. Ramsey, M., Ong, T.-H., Chen, H.: Multilingual Input System for the Web - An Open Multimedia Approach of Keyboard and Handwriting Recognition for Chinese and Japanese. ADL, 188–194 (1998)
38. Zhang, D.-M., Sheng, H.-Y., Li, F., Yao, T.-F.: The model and design of a case-based reasoning multilingual natural language interface for database. In: Proceedings of the First International Conference on Machine Learning and Cybermetics, vol. 3, pp. 1474–1478 (2002)
39. Yoshinaga, K., Terano, T., Zhong, N.: Multi-lingual Intelligent Information Retriever with Automated Ontology Generator. In: Third International Conference on Knowledge Based Intelligent Information Engineering Systems, pp. 62–65 (1999)
40. Yang, H.-C., Lee, C.-H.: Multilingual Information Retrieval Using GHSOM. In: ISDA, vol. (1), pp. 225–228 (2008)
41. Lin, C.-h., Chen, H.: An Automatic Indexing and Neural Network Approach to Concept Retrieval and Classification of Multilingual (Chinese-English) Documents. IEEE Transactions on Systems, Man, and Cybernetics-Part B: Cybernetics 26(1), 75–88 (1996)
42. Rydberg-Cox, J.A., Vetter, L., Rüger, S.M., Heesch, D.: Cross-lingual searching and visualization for greek and latin and old norse texts. JCDL 383 (2004)
43. Yuan, S.-Q., Li, F., Sheng, H.Y.: Finding terminology translations from hyperlinks on the internet. In: Proceedings of the First International Conference on Machine Learning and Cybermetics, vol. 1, pp. 533–535 (2002)
44. Aizawa, A.: A co-evolutionary framework for clustering in information retrieval systems. In: Proceedings of the World Congress on Computational Intelligence, pp. 1787–1792 (2002)
45. Yang, H.-C., Lee, C.-H.: Multilingual Information Retrieval Using GHSOM. In: ISDA, vol. (1), pp. 225–228 (2008)
46. Ren, F., Bracewell, D.B.: Advanced Information Retrieval. Electronic Notes in Theoretical Computer Science 225, 303–317 (2009)

Web Service Suitability Assessment for Cloud Computing

M.S. Nanda Kishore[1], S.K.V. Jayakumar[1], G. Satya Reddy[2],
P. Dhavachelvan[1], D. Chandramohan[1], and N.P. Soumya Reddy[3]

[1] Department of Computer Science and Engineering,
Pondicherry University, Pondicherry, India
[2] IBM Software Group, Bangalore, India
[3] BVB Deemed University, Hubli, India
{nandakishore.ms,skvjey,g.satyareddy,dhavachelvan,
pdchandramohan,npsoumyareddy}@gmail.com

Abstract. Cloud offers its services with the help of web services. This paper addresses the problem of suitability assessment of a particular web service (WS) for cloud, that is whether a particular web service can be deployable over cloud or not. If not what are the requirements it needs to meet so that it can be effectively deployable over cloud. We address this problem with the help of a mathematical model Turing machine with multiple tracks. Here turing machine with three tracks are considered each for SaaS, PaaS, and IaaS. The properties of web services and cloud services are considered as evaluation criteria for suitability assessment. Based on the acceptance of the input the deployment decision of web service over cloud is decided. If input is accepted, web service can be effectively deployed over cloud, otherwise it has to meet certain requirements to be effectively deployed over cloud, and those requirements are also identified.

Keywords: Turing Machine with multiple moves, Suitability Assessment, Scalability, Reusability, Availability, Response Time.

1 Introduction

Cloud computing the new emerged technology of distributed computing systems changed the phase of entire business over internet and set a new trend. The dream of Software as a Service becomes true; cloud offers Software as a Service (SaaS), Platform as a Service (PaaS), and Infrastructure as a Service (IaaS). For more details on cloud computing refer [3] [4] [13] [14] [15]. Cloud offers these services with the help of web services. Cloud and web services are related in two ways. *1. Cloud offers its Core Services as Web Services. 2. Business Services are provided over Cloud as Web Service* [1] [6]. Both *core* and *business services* are charged based on utility. Hence, both can be coined as Utility Services. *Core services* refers to low level services that are owned by cloud and the users do not have access to them where as *Business services* refers to business applications that are deployed over cloud. *Business services* depend on *core services* for their execution. For example, suppose a user requires consuming a business service (SaaS) which also requires JDK software (PaaS) and processor and memory (IaaS) for execution. If the consumer of business application is not having those

D.C. Wyld et al. (Eds.): NeCoM/WeST/WiMoN 2011, CCIS 197, pp. 622–632, 2011.
© Springer-Verlag Berlin Heidelberg 2011

resources and they are also need to be provided by the cloud by charging some amount, then some open challenges needed to be addressed [7].

1. Interoperability between clouds if each service is provided by different cloud providers (Federated Cloud Computing) and

2. Web Service suitability assessment for cloud that is whether a web service can be deployable over cloud.

The same cloud can provide business and core services then the interoperability issue no more exist. If a service is composed and provided by different clouds, that is SaaS from one cloud, PaaS from one cloud and IaaS from other cloud, then interoperability is a major challenge and till now no protocol is designed to address interoperability issue. Every cloud will have its own API or adapters that need to be installed or consumed if anyone wants to use that cloud. Still there is a problem with decision making in the composition of services from different clouds, that is which composition is better, still work is going on to address the first challenge.

This paper address the second challenge web service suitability assessment for Cloud computing. Whether the service is deployed and provided over a single cloud or a single cloud which acquires *core services* from other clouds, the service is needed to be assessed before deploying over cloud so that the performance of the cloud will not be affected and consumers get satisfied with the cloud service providers. Consider the following scenario, suppose a cloud consumer is consuming PaaS from a cloud A, and suppose he also requires IaaS which is not provided by that cloud A, and then the cloud A will take the responsibility of providing the IaaS to the consumer by lending from another cloud B, which is transparent to the consumer. It is no doubt that the cloud A offers maximum runtime scalability of platform services but it is depending on the other cloud B for providing infrastructure services. If this is the case, how a consumer is guaranteed that cloud A is providing maximum run time scalability of platform services which also requires runtime scalability of infrastructure services which is owned by the cloud B. This case is needed to be considered not only for scalability but also for various other properties.

This problem is addressed here by developing a framework for suitability assessment of web service before deploying over the cloud. This framework can also be used as a *test bed* for the applications that are running on the cloud that is it can be used for restricting the user from accessing the resources based on the utilization of the cloud. At the peak time if a request comes for cloud service then with the help of *test bed* the entry decision of providing the service to the user can be predicted. Thus, the framework can be used as a test for deployment of a new service as well as for prediction of the provisioning of the provided services on cloud.

Approach to Solution:

The framework is developed in three stages; here we concentrates only on third stage.

1. Evaluate the Web Services Properties.
2. Evaluate the Cloud Properties.
3. Evaluate the Web Service Suitability Assessment for Cloud Computing.

The rest of the paper discuss about the literature review considering WSs and cloud separately, and how we are combine both for assessing WSs over Cloud. Followed by the description of problem and how solution is acquired. Then follows the description of problem and how solution is acquired. Web Service properties in Cloud is measured in Measuring properties section. Mathematical Model for suitability assessment is discussed followed by simulation and conclusion.

2   Literature Review

More research is available on Web services and Cloud Computing as separate lanes, a very less combined research work is available as of now. Here a combined research is done for evaluating Web services in Cloud. In order to evaluate web service/cloud service properties a clear distinction need to be made between the Quality of Web Service/Cloud Service (QoWS/QoCS) and the Quality of Real Service (QoR). The Quality of the Web Service/Cloud Service refers to implementation properties whereas the Quality of the Service refers to properties of the Service itself. The QoR cannot be tractable because it varies according to user interest and type of selected service whereas QoWS/QoCS is tractable. Here we use QoWS/QoCS for evaluating web services suitability assessment for cloud computing.

2.1   Evaluate the Web Service Properties

The properties of web services shown in fig 1 are not measurable and composition of WSs may include core cloud services also (platform or infrastructure) when they are

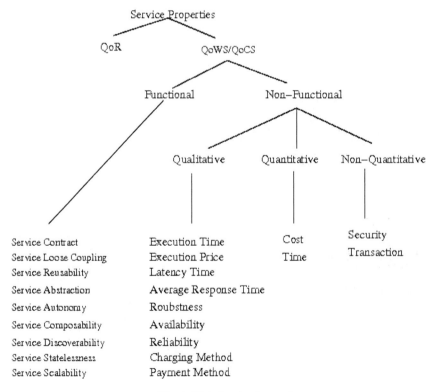

Fig. 1. Web Service Properties

provided over cloud. More details on composition or discoverability of WSs are discussed in [2] [11]. Evaluation of WS properties like Reliability, Scalability, Execution Price, Availability etc is discussed in [12] and the properties of web services are evaluated by using the existing formulae and the result is normalized by using Z – Score Normalization [16] and is given as an input to the third stage for evaluating web service suitability assessment for cloud. For more details on web services go through [5].

2.2   Evaluate the Cloud Properties

Cloud properties that are measurable include Scalability (Elasticity), Virtualization [10], Reliability, Transactions, Response Time etc., and non measurable properties include Up Time, Security etc. Since, the cloud computing research is still in initial stage and it's a distributed environment, up to now no metrics are available to measure the properties of cloud [9]. More research work is going in evaluating the cloud properties; this paper uses some properties of cloud like Scalability and Availability for evaluating web services over cloud. Although, Virtualization is the major property, but measuring virtualization is not possible, because it varies with load on the system and user requests, hence other means of source is taken for consideration to make management decision. The main reason to evaluate cloud properties is web services properties depends on the cloud services (SAAS, PAAS and IAAS) when provided over cloud [3] [8].

2.3   Evaluate the Web Service Suitability Assessment for Cloud Computing

Based on the understanding of web services and cloud up to now the new web service or an extended web service is evaluated for making deployment decision. Evaluation

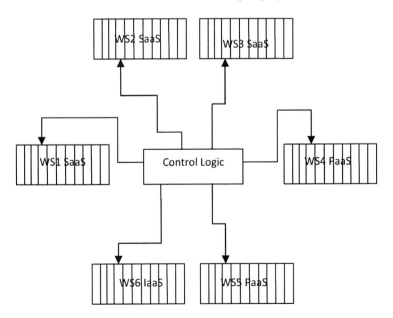

Fig. 2. Cloud Services represented by using Turing Machine

can be done in 3 ways, Measurement, Simulation and Mathematical Methods. This project concentrates on Mathematical Methods later we shift to Simulation and actual Measurement. Turing Machine with Multiple Tracks is used to evaluate the suitability assessment. The Fig 2 represents turing machine to check whether a web service can be deployable over cloud on not. Turing machine with multiple tracks is considered where it represents SaaS, PaaS, IaaS. Each track input evaluates cloud service properties. If the input is accepted and turing machine is in final state then the service can be deployable on cloud. We explain this with the help of an example. Consider a web service which consumes all kinds of services SaaS, PaaS, IaaS.

this scenario can be easily mapped to the turing machine with multiple tracks and each track contains the cloud service properties. Suppose, if the head of SaaS moves one step right corresponding heads on PaaS and IaaS may or may not move. When the Turing Machine halts and all tracks are in final state and if the string is accepted then the web service can be deployable on cloud.

3 Problem Descriptions

To deploy existing services or new services over cloud we need to evaluate whether we can deploy it or not, so there is a need to develop framework which assess the service suitability for cloud computing. This framework should act as an evaluating criterion for deploying a WS over cloud and also for extending the existing WS. Here we have developed a framework which uses turing machine with multiple tracks.

3.1 Key Concepts

Web services provided over cloud may be composed of business services as well as cloud core services. Services that are required to be provided along with the basic services (actual services requested by the consumer) are called supplementary services. These supplementary services are also called reusable or agnostic services. Web service composition over cloud varies as the composition involves cloud services (SAAS, PAAS, and IAAS) also.

3.2 Construction of Turing Machine

The turing machine is designed in such a way that if the first symbol encountered is 1, then it will treat it as a value for SaaS, if the first symbol is 2, then PaaS and if the first symbol is 3 then IaaS. If it encounters 0 symbols, then the turing machine won't accept the input symbols and the web service cannot be deployable over cloud. The language accepted by turing machine with multiple tracks is also accepted by turing machine with single track, but the design is difficult, that requires more restriction. Turing machine with multiple tracks is designed with turing machine with single track by dividing single track into multiple tracks. This paper makes use of turing machine with single track logically partitioned into multiple tracks to assess the web service suitability in cloud computing. The input to each track is the evaluated and normalized properties of web services over cloud. The properties of web services are evaluated and normalized to 0 or 1 for SaaS, similarly 0 or 2 for PaaS and 0 and 3 for IaaS and then the input is provided to turing machine. Control head moves right or left according to logic. If the control head of SaaS moves right the control head of PaaS and IaaS also moves right. The input string is accepted when the turing machine reaches the final state and the service can be deployable otherwise not. Fig3 Explains about the turing machine for web service composed of one SaaS, one PaaS and one IaaS. This can be extended deeper with more WSs at each layer as shown in fig 2. We consider only Scalability and later it is extended to Reusability, Availability, and Response Time for evaluating deployment criteria. Each track of turing machine represents four properties Scalability, Reusability, Availability, Response Time normalized to 0 or 1, 2, 3. This approach can be extended to any number of properties which is also shown in Fig2.

3.3 An Illustrating Example

Consider a new WS that need to be deployed over cloud. NWS depends on other WSs for its successful execution, WS1 represents the actual business service that need to be provided over Cloud, and if the new WS requires search engine for its execution is provided by WS2 with the help of Policy-Oriented Model (SaaS) and policies for the WS is provided by another existing WS3 (SaaS), JDK by WS4 and Oracle by WS5 (PaaS) for executing the NWS, WS6 provides the hardware resources (VM's) for executing the NWS by using Resource-Oriented Model. NWS and is composed of other services not only at SaaS layer but also at PaaS as well as IaaS layer.

$$NWS = WS1 + WS2 + WS3 + WS4 + WS5 + WS6$$

WS1 and WS2 depend on other WS4,WS5,WS6 for its successful deployment and execution. These properties are measured and normalized between 0 and 1 and is given as an input for turing machine, the turing machine takes the responsibility of suitability assessment. We illustrate this with the help of an example with a composite WS with 3 WSs one from SaaS, one from PaaS, one from IaaS, and the properties listed above. This requires turing machine with three tracks, WS=WS1+WS2+WS3 WS1, WS2, WS3 each is given to single track and all these individual tracks are controlled by Master Control Logic based on output of tracks.

Since the turing machine reaches the final state therefore the service can be deployable over cloud. If the first input symbol is 0, then the WS is not meeting scalability requirement and hence the WS cannot be deployable over cloud.

States	1	2	3	X	Y	Z	B
q_0	q_1, X, R	q_2, Y, R	q_3, Z, R		q_4, Y, R		
q_1	q_1, 1, R	q_2, Y, R			q_1, Y, R		
q_2		q_2, 2, R	q_3, Z, L			q_2, Z, R	
q_3	q_3, 1, L	q_3, 2, L	q_3, Z, R	q_0, X, R	q_3, Y, L / q_1, Y, R	q_3, Z, L	q_3, Y, L / q_6, B, R
q_4					q_4, Y, R	q_5, Z, R	
q_5						q_5, Z, R	q_6, B, R
q_6							

Fig. 3. Turing machine Table for Admission Control of Cloud Services

4 Measuring Web Service Properties in Cloud

Here we describe about how to measure WS properties in cloud, because the WS properties vary in cloud which depends on the cloud provider. Providing metrics for measuring properties of WS is beyond scope of this paper, but these metrics are calculated for giving input to turing machine. The concept of every WS depends on supplementary or supporting is used to measure some of these properties.

4.1 Measuring Scalability

Measuring Scalability of a particular web service depends on the number of available instances of the supporting services and how many supporting service instances required for that particular service. Scalability is measured as follows. Consider WS_x is a particular web service that needs to be deployed over cloud and composition of the WS_x is defined as

$$WS_x = WS1 + WS2 + WS3 + WS4 + WS5 + WS6 + WS7 + WS8 + WS9 + WS10.$$

Here, WS1 and WS2 are the actual Web services that are required by the user or that needs to be deployed, WS5 and WS8 provides the necessary platform and infrastructure required for the execution of WS1 and WS2. Hence, WS1, WS2, WS5, WS8 form the actual user required service. For this service to execute it requires supporting services and also the necessary platform and infrastructure for those services. Therefore, a total of 10 services need to be provided. The services can be grouped as follows WS1+WS2+WS5+WS8, WS3+WS6+WS9 and WS4+WS7+WS10. Suppose at a particular instance the demand for a particular web service instance WS_x is 500, then the web service instances availability is calculated as follows:

Table 1. Scaling Factor and NSF for the Cloud

Total number of Web services	Available Web services	Scaling Factor	Normalized Scaled Factor
1200	1200	0.58	0.82
1200	1200	0.58	0.82
100000	20000	0.19	0.32
20000	16000	0.77	1.46
1000	200	-0.30	-0.76
2000	1000	0.25	0.14
1400	400	-0.07	-1.08
22000	5000	0.20	0.29
20000	19000	0.92	2.70
900	300	-0.22	-1.50

Now, these values will provide information about the scaling factor. WS3 = 0.19 means 19% of the available services of total services are used, still it can scale up to 81%. WS5 = -0.3 means it is lagging 30% of scaling. But as the available and total services of the composed service may vary in number, these statistics are not correct for taking decision. Hence, all the values should be normalized to a common value and is calculated by applying Z – Score normalization to the existing values [16].

$$Sf(Standard\,Deviation) = \frac{1}{n(|x1 - mf| + |x2 - mf| + \cdots + |xn - mf|)}$$

$$mf = \frac{1}{n}(x1 + x2 + \cdots + xn)$$

Here, m_f = 0.304, S_f = 0.35
Now, Z – Score Normalization is calculated as follows,

$$Zf = \frac{xf - mf}{Sf}$$

Now, if any service is having negative value, then it is made equal to zero by adding equal number of another equivalent service/s. This new service again requires supporting services, this cycle will continue, first scaling is done for best fit, if not able to provide best fit then for better fit.

Normalized Scaled Factor is used by Turing Machine to take admission control decision:

A service having positive normalized scale value implies that they are enough in number to satisfy the user requests and is scalable. Problem comes with the services having negative normalized scale values. If all values are more than zero then the composed service is scalable, If not the turing machine will search for better fit, that is it will search for services that can make negative normalized scale factor to zero or more than zero. As a result one more turing machine tracks is created to match the Normalized Scaled Factor of these services, this process will continue and if the turing machine is not able to find the services then the service is not scalable and therefore service is not deployable. Fig 4 explains the working of turing machine, here WS5 Normalized Scaling Factor is -0.76, now a new Control Logic is created and that Control Logic will take the responsibility of replacing WS5 with alternate WS or composed service having $\sum NSF \geq 0.76$. If service is found then that service is added for better fit, if that composed service is also having NSF < 0 again new Control Logic is created this process is continued until no service is available. This is for scalability; this can be extended to other properties such as Response Time, Availability, Reliability, and Virtualization etc., Therefore, WS5 having NSF = -0.76 is replaced by another combination of services having $\sum NSF = 1.97$. When the NSF of all the services is greater than zero, then the master control logic shift the pointer one position right in all the tracks, and now control logic will be pointing to the Response Time in all the tracks including new tracks created for new services. Same process is repeated for Response Time but only for the services that are passed scalability test and no new services is created, means no new tracks are created. When the services pass all the tests then the composed cloud service can be deployable or can be provisioned over cloud, otherwise not possible.

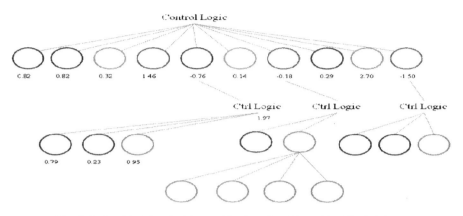

Fig. 4. Turing Machine decision making based on Normalized Scaled Factor

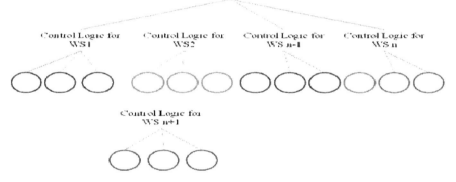

Fig. 5. Working of Master Control Logic

Fig 5 shows how control logic creates control logic and sends the result back to take Admission Control or Provisioning decision. All these control logic are guided by master control logic. Master control logic takes the responsibility of controlling the multiple tracks of turing machine. It assigns each turing machine track to each service as shown in fig5. The control logic for a particular service has to take the responsibility of evaluating the service and the result is sent back to master control logic. Here, we considered two cloud properties for evaluation Scalability, Response Time. Formula for calculating scalability is already discussed; In the next section we discuss about Measuring Response Time. If the master control logic gets positive response from all the subordinate ctrl logic then that service is passed the test and can be deployable or provisioned.

4.2 Measuring Response Time

Response Time in a cloud is unavoidable property, since the service need to be provided from cloud to user it will take certain amount of time to get the service. Delay in *Response Time* may not be tolerated by the user. Hence, admission decision is needed to be based on *Response Time* also. Response time in cloud is calculated as follows.

Response Time = Propagation Time + Virtual Appliance Allocation Time + Latency Time + Execution Time of the WS.

Propagation Time: Whenever a cloud user or an organisation request for a service, first the service need to be transferred to that particular cloud server. Every cloud may have the data centres distributed across the globe but may not have that many number of cloud servers. Hence, the request first need to be transferred to the cloud server, and then based on the IP address of the request cloud server assigns resources from the nearest data centre to that host. The time taken for this communication can be termed as *Propagation Time.* As the request requires communication across the globe, this results in maximum amount of delay, other delay parameters may be proxy settings, delay at gateways, routers etc but they are minimum compared to communication.

Virtual Machine Allocation Time: After forwarding the request to the nearest data centre, data centre takes the responsibility of allocation of Virtual Machines/ Appliances to the request. This will take certain amount of time, suppose if the data centre is not having the requested resource it need to get it from another data centre via cloud server. If that service is not at all available then it may get from another cloud. This time taken by the data centre to allocate resources to the user is called VM Allocation Time.

Latency Time: It refers to the network usage time. It refers number of bytes transferred/bandwidth and delay time if no direct connection between data centre and the user.

Execution Time: Execution Time of WS depends on the WS that is going to be deployed. Each composed WS can be treated as a single virtual appliance, whenever user requests for a service in cloud, the cloud takes the responsibility of providing all the supporting services and all these services are composed to a single WS and a constructor of this service is executed as a single virtual appliance. The supplementary services may be hardware resources, operating systems, and database tables etc; this property of cloud is called Virtualization which is transparency to the user.

5   Conclusion

Here we have proposed how the web services suitability can be assessed for deploying over cloud computing and is verified by using turing machine with multiple tracks to take admission control decisions in terms of scalability and response time. This approach can be applied to other properties as well to assess the entire cloud environment. We are trying to evaluate our proposed system in practical using eucalyptus, Linux.

References

1. Breiter, G., Behrendt, M.: Life cycle and characteristics of services in the world of cloud computing. IBM Journal of Research and Development, Internet and Enterprise Scale Data Centers 53(4), Paper 3 (2009)
2. Hwang, S.-Y., Lim, E.-P., Lim, C.-H.: Dynamic Web Service Selection for Reliable Web Service Composition. IEEE Transactions on Services Computing 1(2), 104–116 (2008)

3. Chou, T.: Introduction to Cloud Computing Business & Technology, 2nd edn. Active Press (printed in United States of America)

4. Reese, G.: Cloud Applications Architectures, Building Applications and Infrastructure in the Cloud. O'Reilly, Sebastopol (2009)

5. Erl, T.: SOA: Principles of Service Design. SOA Systems Inc., Prentice Hall (2008)

6. Naghshineh, M., Ratnaparkhi, R., Dillenberger, D., Doran, J.R., Dorai, C., Anderson, L., Pacifici, G., Snowdon, J.L., Azagury, A., VanderWiele, M., Wolfsthal, Y.: IBM Research Division cloud computing initiative. IBM Journal of Research and Development, Internet and Enterprise-Scale Data Centers 53(4), Paper 1 (2009)

7. Bhuya, R., Ranjan, R., Calheiros, R.N.: Modeling and Siulation of Scalable Cloud Computing Environments and the CloudSim Toolkit: Challenges and Opportunities. In: Proceedings of the 7th High Performance Computing and Simulation Conference, Leipzig, Germany, June 21-24 (2009)

8. Nurmi, D., Wolski, R., Grzegorczyk, C., Obertellli, G., Soman, S., Youseff, L., Zagorodnov, D.: The Eucalyptus Open-source Cloud computing System, http://www.eucalyptus.com/whitepapers

9. Avetisyan, A.I., Campbell, R., Gupta, I., Heath, M.T., Ko, S.Y., Ganger, G.R., Kozuch, M.A., O'Hallaron, D., Kunze, M., Kwan, T.T., Lai, K., Lyons, M., Milojicic, D.S., Lee, H.Y., Soh, Y.C., Ming, N.K., Namgoong, J.-Y.H.: Open Cirrus: A Global Cloud Computing Testbed, pp. 35–43. IEEE Computer Society, Los Alamitos (2010)

10. Braham, P., Dragovic, B., Fraser, K., Hand, S., Harris, T., Ho, A., Neugebauer, R., Pratt, I., Warfield, A.: Xen and the Art of Virtualization. In: SSOP 2003, October 19-22. ACM, New York (2003)

11. Balbiani, P., Cheikh, F., Feuillade, G.: Algorithms and Complexity of Automata Synthesis by Asynchronous Orchestration with Applications to Web Services Composition. Electronic Notes in Theoretical Computer Science 229, 3–18 (2009), http://www.sciencedirect.com

12. Li, M., Huai, J., Guo, H.: An Adaptive Web Services Selection Method Based on the QoS Prediction Mechanism. In: IEEE/WIC/ACM International Joint Conference on Web Intelligence and Intelligence and Intelligent Agent Technology (2009)

13. Amazon Web Services, Amazon Web Services, LLC, http://aws.amazon.com

14. Salesforce.com and Force.com, Inc., http://www.salesforce.com

15. GoogleAppEngine,GoogleCode,Google,Inc., http://code.google.com/appengine

16. Han, J., Kamber, M.: Data Mining Concepts and Techniques, 2nd edn., p. 388. Elsevier Publication, Amsterdam

Computability and Traceability Analysis for Dynamic Web Service Integration

M. Thirumaran[1], P. Dhavachelvan[2], G. Aranganayagi[1], and S. Abarna[1]

[1] Department of Computer Science and Engineering, Pondicherry Engineering College
[2] Department of Computer Science, Pondicherry University

Abstract. The Service Integration has become a critical issue as organizations find a greater need to consistently interact with their partners and share their business logics to carry out the necessities. To accurately and efficiently extract and integrate the required service logic from the rapidly expanding Business Services, developers need to empathize the whole service and must decide on proper approach to merge them which are complex and time-consuming tasks. So the present focus is to have a mechanized system which analyzes the business logics and conveys proper mode to integrate them. One such a model proposed in this paper examines the business logics individually and suggests proper structure to integrate them. One of the innovative concepts of proposed model is Property Evaluation System which scrutinizes the service logics and generates Business Logic Property Schema (BLPS) for the required services. BLPS holds necessary information to recognize the correct structure for integrating the service logics. At the time of integration, System consumes this BLPS schema and suggests the feasible ways to integrate the service logics. Also if the service logics are attempted to integrate in invalid structure, system will throw exception with necessary information. This helps developers to ascertain the efficient structure to integrate the services with least effort.

Keywords: Business Services, Service Integration, Business Logic Property Evaluation System, Enterprise Service Bus, Computability and Traceability Evaluation.

1 Introduction

With the trend in economic globalization and enormous development in information technology, the demand for information and logic sharing has become more serious which urges the companies to collaborate closely with their business partners to gain access to needed information and business logic. Over the past decade, the companies have been using various technologies and products in an attempt to support collaboration. These solutions vary from basic point-to-point connection approach such as EDI, expensive ERP systems such as Rossetanet, ebXML, etc. The current technologies semi-automatically integrate the services and it needs manual intervention in number of areas. It requires developers to analyze the service to identify possible way for integration. It is a complex task which needs developers to understand both service and identify better way for integration. Also the present

D.C. Wyld et al. (Eds.): NeCoM/WeST/WiMoN 2011, CCIS 197, pp. 633–644, 2011.
© Springer-Verlag Berlin Heidelberg 2011

technologies does not consider how to composite of services and how to describe the service contracts. We proposed Business Logic model to face these brutal challenge and complexities.

The proposed model enables the automation of service integration by coordinating sequences of tasks and supports sophisticated exception management. The proposed Business Logic Model uses property evaluator method to evaluate the service to ascertain correct structure for integration. It analyses at which level service fulfills particular property in functionality level and also as per contract, accordingly develops flow diagram as it reflects property evaluation outcome. Then BLP (Business Logic Property) schema is generated from this diagram holding necessary information for integration. While integration, System utilizes this BLP schema to identify proper structure for integration and to spot various actions can be carried out with the service. With this flocked information from BLP schema, it integrates the service automatically. If services are integrated as violating contract or with invalid structure, the system will throw exception with necessary information. End-to-end security is provided by annotating service descriptions with security objectives used to generate convenient Quality of Protection Agreements between partners. Conversely, agreements are processed by a dedicated matching module with respect to security requirements stated by the SLA. In addition to this, we need a mechanism to monitor the resource while sharing to adapt the modifications made by the developers. Source control Management tracks the modification and facilitates impact analysis between the existing and modified services that ensures computability criteria. The source control management system allows us to see the historical background behind the changes made to the business logic of the web services. This helps the developers to see where the changes have been progressively made and include or remove the change as per the need. Thus this would be a powerful and easiest model for developers to integrate the services. Here we demonstrated service integration with BLP schema generation for banking application using Netbeans IDE.

2 Related Works

In this section, we discuss various research work and different solutions exist in the market for service integration. Zuoren Jiang proposed a model called 'Multi-layer Structure for Dynamic Service Integration (MSFDSI)' in SOA which adds authorized institution and a service integration & analysis adapter to achieve the service authorization, service analysis and dynamic service integration. Service integration & analysis adapter analyses and search the service that can meet the service requestor's requests according to service contracts stated by authorized institution [1]. W.J.Yan proposed B2B integration approach for SME which provides a feasible and cost-effective B2Bi solution for SMEs by leveraging the characteristics of Web Services. It utilizes pull and push mechanisms for effective information exchange and sharing between trading partners. This approach has been incorporated in a B2Bi Gateway which enables SMEs to participate in business-to-business collaboration by making use of Web Services [2]. Liyi Zhang proposed a model called WSMX (Web Service Modeling execution), a software system that enables the creation and execution of Semantic Web Services based on the Web Service Modeling Ontology (WSMO) for enterprise application integration. It improves Service discovery, simplifies change management and supports semi-automatic service composition and enhanced interoperability between services [3]. Thomas Haselwanter presented a model based on the WSMX was build to tackle heterogeneities in RosettaNet messages by using the axiomatised knowledge and rules. It supports communication between partners, data and process mediation using WSMX integration middleware[4]. Jianwei Yin proposed an ESB framework for large scale Service Integration, JTangSynergy adopts several mechanisms for providing effective and efficient dependability. It enables automated recovery from component failures and robust execution of composite services by checking service compatibility [5].

Gulnoza Ziyaeva proposed framework to enable the content-based intelligent routing path construction and message routing in ESB which defines the routing tables and mechanisms of message routings and facilitate the service selection based on message content [6]. Soo Ho Chang proposed a framework for dynamic composition on Enterprise Service Bus which consists of four elements; Invocation Listener, Service Router, Service Discoverer, and Interface Adapter. This framework enables the runtime discovery and composition of published services without altering the client side applications [7]. Liu Ying presents a unified service composition framework to support business level service composition. An intelligent service composer based on this unified service composition framework is developed to enable business level service composition by business people under the help of some advanced technologies, including intelligent service components searching, automatic service compliance checking, and template-based service adaptation [8]. In addition, Companies use different solutions exist in the market for Business to business application framework, including EDI, RosettaNet, ebXML etc. EDI: A seminal event in B2B evolution was the development of electronic data interchange (EDI), whereby trading partners established standard formats for the exchange of electronic documents to facilitate electronic transactions. Trading partnerships between two firms using EDI are well defined and is used for automated replenishment and efficient supply chains[9]. RosettaNet: The RosettaNet consortium develops XML-based business standards for supply chain management in the information technology and electronic component industries. It defines the business processes and provides the technical specifications for data interchange. RosettaNet standards comprise Dictionary, RNIF (RosettaNet Implementation Framework) and PIP (Partner Interface Process)[10][11]. ebXML: The electronic business XML (ebXML) provides a complete framework for setting up B2B collaborations. It is a set of documents, with several prototype completed, enabling businesses of any size to do business electronically with anyone else. The ebXML specifications cover almost the entire B2B collaboration process: collaboration Protocol Profile (CPP), Collaboration Protocol Agreement (CPA), Business Process Specification Schemas (BPSS), Messaging, Registry/repository and a core Component [12]. Above works paves way to semi-automatically integrate the services across enterprise. But still there is no mechanism to monitor the services while sharing and to routinely guide the developers to integrate according to SLA. Here we demonstrated service integration with BLP schema generation for banking application using Netbeans IDE.

3 Business Logic Model

Figure 1 depicts detailed architecture and illustrates how enterprises integrate their services dynamically. Let Enterprise A sends request to share Enterprise B's service, Message broker receives and validates the request, identifies required services from service registry by applying set of rules and delivers the necessary information regarding the identified services to communication handler. Communication handler calls integration bus to deliver the created service proxy to the requestor. Integration bus, a key component of SOA, supports asynchronous messaging, document exchange and above all provides powerful platform for connecting different applications together enabling seamless integration between components. Before delivering the service proxy to the requestor, it assesses the security issue by firing the trigger to the Functional analyzer.

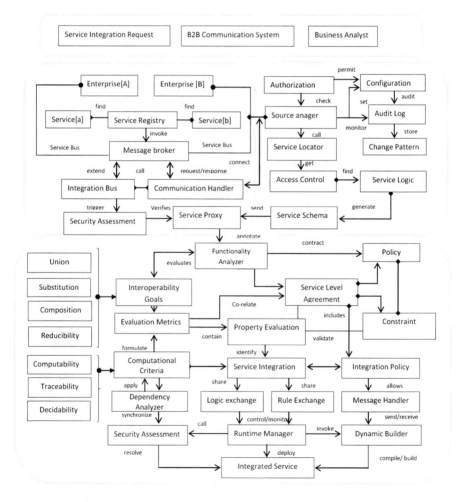

Fig. 1. Detailed Architecture of Dynamic Web Service Integration

Functionality analyzer analyzes Service Level Agreement (SLA) and policy defined between the two enterprises, identifies the list of constraints for integrating the service. Through this it scrutinizes the security gap between approved security policies and created service proxy and transmits the result to integration bus. Subsequently, integration bus handovers the proxy to the requestor. When requestor attempts to integrate the service, Property evaluation, heart of this model, validates integrating service with various constraints listed out by Functional analyzer to achieve the interoperability goals such as union, substitution, composition, finiteness, enhancement and configuration, etc..,. We will see the process of property evaluation detailly in next section. Evaluation metrics holds set of formulas to measure the activities and performance of service integration in order to achieve the interoperability goals efficiently. Business logic and rules are shared in such a way integration policy and interoperability goals are satisfied. Service integration allows sharing the service according to the specified evaluation metrics and integration policy through the created service proxy.

Message handler sends needed information about the service logic to the requestor. Work flow decider evaluates the performance of service integration through formulated metrics and sends the result to Exception handler. Runtime manager monitors the service logic while integrating with theirs, if at any case service integration violates the integration policy or deviates the interoperability goals, it calls exception handler. Exception handler handles and resolves the exception in such a way metric evaluated is also improved. Runtime manger invokes dynamic builder to build the newly integrated service dynamically and deploys the service in server. It monitors the service whenever changes have been done and redeploys dynamically. Source Manager monitors all these activities and adds necessary information to configuration and audit log.

4 Property Evaluation for Service Integration

4.1 Computability

Computability is an essential criterion in web service which determines whether the modified service is computable with in time limit.

Example The requirement is to create a service, e-payment to calculate total price for the list of purchased items and to transact the calculated amount. In the existing shopping application, we have billing service which computes total cost for the purchased items and transaction service in banking application transacts the amount. By integrating these two services, required new service e-payment can be developed. Here integration should be done in such a way that the processing time of the integrated service bounded within a time limit.

logic1
```
BL₁: public string billing(){
BF₁:     String username=username.get();
         String password=password.get();
DRf1:    String sql="select * from shopping where
         username="+username+" and  password="+password;
```

```
          ResultSet rs=st.executeQuery(sql);
CR_r1:     if(rs.next()){
BF_r1:     double amount=calculateamount();
          String accno=accountno.get();
BF_r2      String accno1=123456;
BF_f1:     String result="Amount to be paid="+amount;
P_1:       return result;
          }}
```

logic 2

```
BL_2:  public string transact(){
BF_21      String accno=accno.get();
          String accno1=accno1.get();
          String amount=amount.get();
BF_22      String transid1=transid.set();
DR_f1  Statement st=con.createStatement();
          ResultSet rs=st.executeQuery("select Balance from
          bank where Accountno='"+ accno+"'");
DR_r1  double balance=rs.getDouble("Balance");
CR_r1  if( (balance-amount)>1000 ){
DR_rr1  st.executeUpdate("update bank set balance= balance-
"+amount+" where Accountno='"+accno+"'";);
 DR_rr2  st.executeUpdate(update bank set balance=
balance+"+amount+" where Accountno='"+accno1+"'");
BF_f1      String transid=" Amount"+amount+"transferred
from"+accno+" to "+accno1;
BF_r2      String result= "Ur transaction id is "+transid1+"
Ur transaction completed successfully";
P_2        return result;
}
```

Solution : Integrated logic

```
BL_1 public string ebilling(){
BF_11      String username=username.get();
          String password=password.get();
DR_f11: String sql="select * from shopping where
username="+username+" and
          password="+password;
          ResultSet rs=st.executeQuery(sql);
CR_1fr1 if(rs.next()){
BF_1frr1  double amount=calculateamount();
          String accno=accountno.get();
          String accno1=123456;
BF_1frr1 transact(accno,amt,accno1);}
BL_2   public String transact(String accno, double amt,
String accno1){
BF_11    String transid1=transid.get();
DR_1f1 ResultSet rs=st.executeQuery("select Balance from bank
where Accountno='"+
          accno+"'");
DR_1fr1  double balance=rs.getDouble("Balance");
```

```
CR_lfrr1 if( (balance-amount)>1000 ){
DR_lfrrr1String sql="update bank set balance= balance-
"+amount+" where
       Accountno='"+accno+"'";
       st.executeUpdate(sql);
DR_lfrrrr1 sql="update bank set balance= balance+"+amount+"
where Accountno='"+accno1+"'";
        st.executeUpdate(sql);
P_lfrrrr1String transid=" Amount"+amount+"transferred
from"+accno+" to "+accno1;
P_lfrr2String result= "Ur transaction id is "+transid1+" Ur
transaction completed successfully";
}
```

Logic Flow Diagram

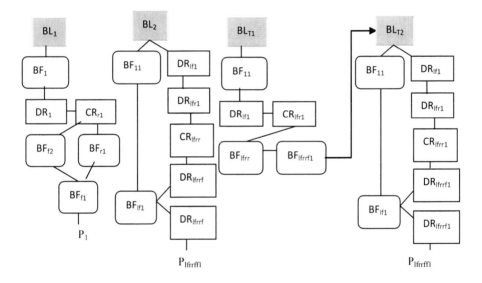

$BL_1 \to \{ BF_1 \}$ $BL_2 \to \{[BF_{lf1}, BF_{11}]\}$ $BL_{T1} \to \{ BF_{11}\}$

$BF_1 \to \{DR_{f1}\}$ $BF_{lf1} \to \{ DR_{lfr1}\} BF_{11} \to \{BF_{lf1}\}$ $BF_{11} \to \{DR_{lf1}\}$

$DR_{f1} \to \{ CR_{r1}\}$ $DR_{lfr1} \to \{CR_{lfrr1}\}$ $DR_{lf1} \to \{ CR_{lfr1}\}$

$CR_{r1} \to \{ BF_{r1}\}$ $CR_{lfrr1} \to \{[DR_{lfrrf1}],[BF_{lf1}]\}$ $CR_{lfr1} \to \{ BF_{lfrr1}\}$

$BF_{r1} \to \{ BF_{f1}\}$ $DR_{lfrrf1} \to \{DR_{lfrrf1}\}$ $BF_{lfrr1} \to \{BF_{lfrrf1}\}$

$BF_{f1} \to \{P_1\}$ $DR_{lfrrf1} \to \{ P_{lfrrf1}\}$ $BF_{lfrr1} \to \{ BL_{T2}\}$

BF_{lfrr1} $BL_{T2} \to \{[BF_{lf1}, BF_{11}]\}, BF_{11} =$

$BF_{lf1} \to \{ DR_{lfr1}\} BF_{11} \to \{BF_{lf1}\}$

$DR_{lfr1} \to \{CR_{lfrr1}\}$

$CR_{lfrr1} \to \{[DR_{lfrrf1}],[BF_{lf1}]\}$

$DR_{lfrrf1} \to \{DR_{lfrrf1}\}$

$DR_{lfrrf1} \to \{ P_{lfrrf1}\}$

billing→{get}	transaction→{get,set}	billing→{get}
get→ {r:select}	get→{ r:select}	get→ {r:select}
r:select →{r:cmp}	r:select→{r:cmp}	r:select →{r:cmp}
r:cmp →{compute}	r:cmp→{r:update1,r:update2}	r:cmp →{compute}
compute→{store}	{r:update1, r:update2}→{store}	compute→{store}
store→{return}	store→{return}	store →{transaction}

transaction→{set,get}
get=compute
get→{ r:select}
 r:select→{r:cmp}
 r:cmp→{[r:update1, r:update2]}
 {r:update1, r:update2}→{store}
 store→{return}

BLPS of Logic 1

```
1 ⊟<service name="billing">
2 ⊟   <property>
3         <computability CF= BF1, BFf1,BFr1,BFr2 ,DR1,CRr1/>
4 ⊟   </property>
5 ⊟   <function name=get type="input" index=BF1>
6         <param1 name=username datatype='string' value=null/>
7         <param2 name=password datatype='string' value=null/>
8     </function>
9 ⊟   <rule index=DR1 name="select' type=' data manipulation' dbname=' shopping" >
10 ⊟       <conditions setStatus=true>
11           <condition1 Lvar= db.username expr= &eq rvar=$username />
12           <condition2  lvar= db.password expr=&eq rvar=$password />
13         </conditions>
14         <retrieve param1=accno/>
15     </rule>
16 ⊟   <rule index=CRr1  name="if' type=" conditional' condition:status=true>
17         <function index=BFr1 name=compute " action='call' target-function=compute() return-type="double" store-result=amount />
18 ⊟       <function index=BFr2 name=set type=set >
19           <param name=accno1 value='123456'/>
20         </function>
21         <function index=BFf1 name=assign type=output> <param name=result returntype=double value=amount/>
22     </rule>
23   </service>
```

BLPS of Logic 2

```
1 ⊟<service name="transact" >
2 ⊟   <property>
3         <computability CF="BF21,DRf1,CRr1,DRrr1, DRrr2"/>
4     </property>
5 ⊟   <function name=get type="input" index=BF21>
6         <param1 name=accno datatype='string' value=null/>
7         <param2 name=accno1 datatype='string' value=null/>
8         <param2 name=amount datatype='double' value=null/>
9     </function>
10 ⊟  <rule index=DRf1 name="select' type="data manipulation' dbname="bank" >
11         <condition1 Lvar= db.accountno expr= &eq rvar=$accountno />
12         <retrieve param1=balance/>
13 ⊟       <rule index=CRr1 name="if' type="conditional'>
14           <condition lvar=$balance-$amount expr=&gt rvar=1000/>
15           <rule index=DRrr1 name='update' type="data manipulation" dbname="bank" >
16           <condition Lvar= db.accountno expr= &eq rvar=$accno />
17           <assign Lvar=balance expr=&eq rvar=($balance-$amount) />
18       </rule>
19 ⊟     <rule index=DRrr2 name="update' type="data manipulation" dbname="bank" >|
20           <condition Lvar= db.accountno expr= &eq rvar=$accno1 />
21           <assign Lvar=balance expr=&eq rvar=($balance+$amount) />
22       </rule>
23         <function index=BFf1 name=assign type=output> <param name=transid returntype=double value=transstat/>
24     </rule>
25   </service>
```

Integrated Service

```
1   <service name="e-billing">
2     <property>
3       <composable CT=BF1, BFf1,BFr1,BFr2,BF21,DR1,CRr1, DRf1,CRr1,DRrr1, DRrr2/>
4     </property>
5     <service name="billing">
6       <function name="get" type="input" index="BF1">
7         <param1 name="username datatype="string" value=null/>
8         <param2 name="password datatype="string" value=null/>
9       </function>
10      <rule index=DR1 name="select" type="Data Manipulation" dbname="shopping">
11        <conditions setStatus=true>
12          <condition1 Lvar= db.username expr= &eq rvar=$username />
13          <condition2 lvar= db.password expr=&eq rvar=$password >
14        </conditions>
15        <retrieve param1=accno>
16      </rule>
17      <rule index=DR1 name="if" type="conditional" condition.status=true>
18        <function index=BFr1 name="compute" action= call target function=compute() return type="double" store result=amount />
19        <function index=BFr2 name="set type="set">
20          <param name=accno1 value="123456"/>
21        </function>
22        <function index=BFf1 name="call type=invoke target-service=transact>
23          <arg name=accno datatype=string>
24          <arg name=accno1 returntype=string>
25          <arg name=amount returntype=double>
26        </function>
27      </rule>
28    </service>
29    <service name=transact>
30      <function name=receive >
31        <arg name=accno datatype=string>
32        <arg name=accno1 returntype=string>
33        <arg name=amount datatype=double>
34      </function>
35      <function name=get type="input" index=BF1>
36        <param1 name=accno datatype=string value=$accno>
37        <param2 name=accno1 datatype=string value=$accno1/>
38        <param3 name=amount datatype= double value=$amount/>
39      </function>
40      <rule index=DR1 name=select type=data manipulation dbname=bank >
41        <condition1 Lvar= db.accountno expr=&eq rvar=$accountno />
42        <retrieve param1=balance />
43      </rule>
44      <rule index=CRr1 name="if" type="conditional" >
45        <condition lvar=$balance $amount expr=&gt rvar=1000>
46          <rule index=DR1 name="update" type=data manipulation dbname=bank >
47            <condition Lvar= db.accountno expr= &eq rvar=$accno />
48            <assign Lvar=balance expr=&eq rvar=($balance-$amount) />
49          </rule>
50        </condition>
51      </rule>
52      <rule index=DR1 name= update type=data manipulation dbname=bank >
53        <condition Lvar= db.accountno expr=&eq rvar=$accno />
54        <assign Lvar=balance expr=&eq rvar=($balance+$amount) />
55      </rule>
56      <function index=BFf1 name=assign type=output>
57        <param name=transid returntype=double value=transtat/>
58      </function>
59    </service>
```

4.2 Traceability

Traceability in general is 'ability to chronologically interrelate the uniquely identifiable entities in a way that matters'. It verifies the flow, assesses the risk, checks completeness and helps to improve the quality by tracing each and every step of the service.

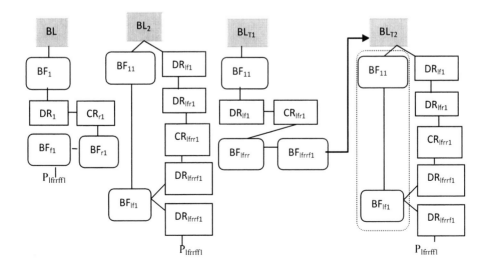

Input 1

```
1  <service name="billing">
2    <properties>
3      <computability CF= BF1, BFf1,BFr1,BFr2 ,DR1,CRr1/>
4    </property>
5    <function name=get type="input"  index=BF1>
6      <param1 name=username datatype='string' value=null/>
7      <param2 name=password datatype='string' value=null/>
8    </function>
9    <rule index=DR1 name="select  type="data manipulation" dbname="shopping" >
10     <conditions setStatus=true>
11       <condition1 Lvar= db.username expr= &eq rvar=$username />
12       <condition2 lvar= db.password expr=&eq rvar=$password />
13     </conditions>
14     <retrieve param1=accno/>
15   </rule>
16   <rule index=CRr1  name="if" type=" conditional" condition:status=true>
17     <function index=BFr1 name=compute  action=`call` target-function=compute() return-type="double"  store-result=amount />
18     <function index=BFr2 name=set type=set>
19       <param name=accno1 value="123456"/>
20     </function>
21     <function index=BFf1 name=assign type=output> <param name=result returntype=double value=amount/>
22   </rule>
23 </service>
```

Input 2

```
1  <service name="transact" >
2    <property>
3      <computability CF="BF21,DRf1,CRr1,DRrr1, DRrr2"/>
4    </property>
5    <function name=get type="input"  index=BF21>
6      <param1 name=accno datatype='string' value=null/>
7      <param2 name=accno1 datatype='string' value=null/>
8      <param2 name=amount datatype='double' value=null/>
9    </function>
10   <rule index=DRf1 name='select' type="data manipulation" dbname="bank" >
11     <condition1 Lvar= db.accountno expr= &eq rvar=$accountno />
12     <retrieve param1=balance/>
13     <rule index=CRr1  name="if" type="conditional">
14       <condition lvar=$balance-$amount expr=&gt rvar=1000/>
15       <rule index=DRrr1 name="update" type="data manipulation" dbname="bank" >
16         <condition Lvar= db.accountno expr= &eq rvar=$accno />
17         <assign Lvar=balance expr=&eq rvar=($balance-$amount) />
18     </rule>
19     <rule index=DRrr2 name="update" type="data manipulation" dbname="bank" >
20       <condition Lvar= db.accountno expr= &eq rvar=$accno1 />
21       <assign Lvar=balance expr=&eq rvar=($balance-$amount) />
22     </rule>
23     <function index=BFf1 name=assign type=output> <param name=transid returntype=double value=transstat/>
24   </rule>
25 </service>
```

Service Integration Solution (BLP Schema)

```
1  <service name" e billing >
2    <property>
3      <traceability TF=" BF1, BFf1  NTF="BFf1,BF11,BFr2, DR1,CRr1, DRf1,CRr1,DRr1, DRrr2"/>
4    <property>
5    <service name=" billing">
6      <function name=get type="input"  index=BF1>
7        <param1 name=username datatype= string value=null/>
8        <param2 name=password datatype=string value=null/>
9      </function>
10     <rule index=DR1 name="select" type="Data Manipulation" dbname="shopping" >
11       <conditions setStatus=true>
12         <condition1 Lvar= db.username expr= &eq rvar=$username />
13         <condition2 lvar= db.password expr=&eq rvar=$password />
14         <retrieve param1=accno>
15     </rule>
16     <rule index=CRr1  name="if" type="conditional" condition:status=true>
17       <function index=BFr1 name=compute  action=`call` target-function=compute() return-type="double"  store-result=amount />
18       <function index=BFr2 name=set type=set>
19         <param name=accno1 value="123456"/>
20       </function>
21       <function index=BFf1 name=call type=invoke target service=transact>
22         <arg name=accno returntype=string/>
23         <arg name=accno1 returntype=string/>
24         <arg name=amount returntype=double/>
25       </function>
26     </rule>
27   </service>
28   <service name=transact>
29     <function name=receive >
30       <arg name=accno datatype=string>
31       <arg name=accno1 datatype=string>
32       <arg name=amount datatype=double>
33     </function>
34     <function name=get type= 'input'  index=BF1>
35       <param1 name=accno datatype= string value=$accno/>
36       <param2 name=accno1 datatype='string' value=$accno1/>
37       <param2 name=amount datatype= double value=$amount/>
38     </function>
39     <rule index=DR1 name="select" type= 'data manipulation' dbname= 'bank' >
40       <conditions setStatus=true>
41         <condition1 Lvar= db.accountno expr= &eq rvar=$accountno />
42         <retrieve param1=balance/>
43     </rule>
44     <rule index=CRr1  name="if" type="conditional">
45       <condition lvar=$balance-$amount expr=&gt rvar=1000>
46       <rule index=DR1 name="update" type="data manipulation" dbname= 'bank' >
47         <condition Lvar= db.accountno expr= &eq rvar=$accno />
48         <assign Lvar=balance expr=&eq rvar=($balance-$amount) />
49       </rule>
50       <rule index=DR1 name="update" type="data manipulation" dbname= 'bank' >
51         <condition Lvar= db.accountno expr= &eq rvar=$accno1 />
52         <assign Lvar=balance expr=&eq rvar=($balance-$amount) />
53       </rule>
54       <function index=BFf1 name=assign type=output>
55         <param name=transid returntype=double value=transstat/>
56       </function>
57     </rule>
58   </service>
```

Example: In the previous case, integrated service might fail due to transaction failure or erroneous calculation of price. So it is necessary to trace the service and verify the transaction status at the end of every transaction. Transaction id gives necessary information of that transaction such as credit, debit, time, etc. So it is enough to trace the transaction id to verify the whole service.

5   Implementation Methodology

E-payment service is developed by integrating existing billing service and transaction service in banking application as discussed above. Computability and traceability properties are verified as discussed in last section. BPEL diagram of newly developed service is depicted in Fig 2.

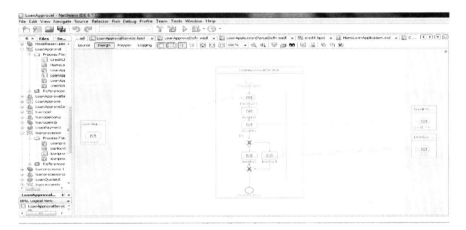

Fig. 2. Service Integration using BLP schema

6   Conclusion

The proposed model provides a powerful platform to share service logic dynamically and securely in such way interoperability between the services is managed. This paper evaluates the services to be integrated with properties such as computability and traceability and integrates in efficient way. Also, this model progressively monitors the changes made in the source code and points out whether the changes made affect the computability and traceability criterias of the web services. Examples given in this paper explains how properties are evaluated for various situations. This would be a standard platform for service providers to share their resources dynamically and securely.

References

1. Jiang, Z., Chen, Y., Yang, M.: A research on multi-layer structure for dynamic service integration. In: IEEE International Conference (2010)
2. Yan, W.J., Tan, P.S., Lee, E.W.: A Web Services-enabled B2B Integration Approach for SMEs. In: IEEE International Conference on Industrial Informatics, July 13-16 (2008)

3. Zhang, L., Zhou, S.: A Semantic Service Oriented Architecture for Enterprise Application Integration. In: Second International Symposium on Electronic Commerce and Security (2009)
4. Haselwanter, T., Kotinurmi, P., Moran, M., Vitvar, T., Zaremba, M.: WSMX: A Semantic Service Oriented Middleware for B2B Integration,
   http://www.vitvar.com/tomas/publications/icsoc2006-WSMX.pdf
5. Yin, J., Chen, H., Deng, S., Wu, Z.: A Dependable ESB framework for Service Integration. In: IEEE Internet Computing (2009)
6. Ziyaeva, G., Choi, E., Min, D.: Content-Based Intelligent Routing and Message Processing in Enterprise Service Bus. In: International Conference on Convergence and Hybrid Information Technology (2008)
7. Chang, S.H., Bae, J.S., Jeon, W.Y., La, H.J., Kim, S.D.: A Practical Framework for Dynamic Composition on Enterprise Service Bus. In: IEEE International conference on Service Computing (2007)
8. Ying, L., Li, W.: An Intelligent Service Composer for Business-level Service Composition. In: Nineth International Conference on Enterprise Computing, E-Commerce and E-Services (2007)
9. http://en.wikipedia.org/wiki/Electronic_Data_Interchange
10. Rossatanet, http://www.rosettanet.org
11. Wang, J., Song, Y.-T.: Architectures Supporting RosettaNet. In: Proceedings of the Fourth International Conference on Software Engineering Research (2006)
12. ebxml, http://www.ebxml.org

Business Logic Evaluation Model for Web Service Reliability Analysis

M. Thirumaran[1], P. Dhavachelvan[2], S. Abarna[1], and P. Lakshmi[1]

[1] Department of computer science and engineering, Pondicherry Engineering College
[2] Department of computer science, Pondicherry University

Abstract. The business logic of a system plays a major role in this ever changing age defined by global competition, rampant change, faster flow of information and communication, increasing business complexity. Business parties have to react to several different competitors by promoting the business process management to the standard level by incorporating the higher-end technology solution such as service oriented business communication and business rule management automation. They realize that it is important to react to the changes faster since the reaction time needs are decreasing every moment. Business Logic Evaluation Model (BLEM) are the proposed solution targeting business logic automation and facilitating business experts to write sophisticated business rules and complex calculations without costly custom programming. BLEM is powerful enough to handle service manageability issues by analyzing and evaluating the computability and traceability and other criteria of modified business logic at run time. The web service and QOS grows expensively based on the reliability of the service. Hence the service provider of today things that reliability is the major factor and any problem in the reliability of the service should overcome then and there in order to achieve the expected level of reliability. In our paper we propose business logic evaluation model for web service reliability analysis using Finite State Machine (FSM). If any change occurs in the business logic the FSM will automatically measure the reliability.

Keywords: Business Process Management, Business Automation, Business Logic Model, Service Oriented Architecture.

1 Introduction

The Business Logic Management system (BLMS) brings about best results if we select a BLMS that is able to reconcile the business methodology of that system. The BLMS has the following features which makes it a better system. BLMS is fully scalable, it can be integrated, and it separates the business logic from the clients who deplete that information. This result in intense levels of code reuse and portability as well as it enables applications to be upgraded without affecting testing and functioning of business logic. It allows the non- technical people to create and alter very detailed levels of business logic without calling for the assistance of the IT Department, by providing a point-and-click or GUI interface that endows the user to

D.C. Wyld et al. (Eds.): NeCoM/WeST/WiMoN 2011, CCIS 197, pp. 645–654, 2011.

manage the logic using easily apprehensible symbols. The system supports a test environment that permits the business analyst or non technical user to test logic changes before deploying the modifications in a live environment. This is the only means to ascertain that changes do not negatively impact business logic integrity or compromise the production system. In support of this test environment, the BLMS has a realistic debugging process that is graphical and easy to understand. The debugger provides a method for adjusting parameters and data, in real time, so that the business analyst can create realistic test cases and validate each one as they are executed.

The BLMS is modular. Each module can be easily integrated with existing modules so that the applications can acquire added functionality as the need arises. Those modules provide built-in support for the core requirements of any advanced business system which includes the ability to automate decision making using a rule-based process, a monitoring engine that lets us configure any number of check points, support for integral workflow and BPM (Business Process Management) capabilities and the ability to communicate with other systems.

BLMS transparently communicates with the information consumers want without forcing those consumers to know anything about the underlying technology of the BLMS including the language it was written in, the version of the compiler used, or the type and structure of any associated databases. In essence, the BLMS is capable of putting up a "black box" interface where the consumer simply sends a query and receives the data back in a format that it can interpret. It is capable of supporting web services and other current technologies like HTML, XML, SOAP, etc. The IT Department does not have to hold out an excessive learning when implementing the BLMS. They have to build a complete documentation and actual code examples to make the transition to a logic-based system easier and to accelerate the implementation and deployment process. It includes accession to a full SDK (Software Developers Kit) that enables developers to easily create and integrate their own custom components into the BLMS without negatively impacting the system's usability, security or stability. Thus, the goal of implementing BLMS is to allow the organization to ultimately reduce the cost by automating tasks that used to require large human intervention. Let us have a detailed look at the essential component of a BLMS namely the Business Rule Management System and the Business Logic Evaluation Model for the automation of services.

2 Literary Survey

Web services used primarily as a means for businesses to communicate with each other and with clients, Web services allow organizations to communicate data without intimate knowledge of each other's IT systems behind the firewall. Unlike traditional client/server models, such as a Web server/Web page system, Web services do not provide the user with a GUI. Web services instead share business logic, data and processes through a programmatic interface across a network. The applications interface, not the users. Developers can then add the Web service to a GUI (such as a Web page or an executable program) to offer specific functionality to users. Web services allow different applications from different sources to communicate with each other without time-consuming custom coding, and because all communication is in XML, Web services are not tied to any one operating system or programming language. For example, Java can talk with Perl, Windows applications can talk with UNIX applications. This is made possible by using technologies such as Jini, UPnP, SLP, etc.

Slim Trabelsi and Yves Roudier proposed a scalable solution to enabling secure and decentralized discovery protocols. It also deals how to extend the WS-Discovery Web Service protocol with these mechanisms [1]. Colin Atkinson and Philipp Bostan proposed the brokerage aspect of the web service vision but it is difficult to involve in setting up and maintaining useful repositories of web services. So they describe a pragmatic approach to web service brokerage based on automated indexing and discuss the required technological foundations [2]. Janette Hicks and Weiyi Meng proposed a current discovery research through use of the Google Web service, UDDI category searching and private registry. They found WSDL documents for a given domain name, parse the desired service document to obtain invocation formats, and automatically invoke the Web service to support enhancements of HTML-dependent search tools by providing access to data inaccessible through surface HTML interfaces [3]. ZHANG Changyou and ZHU Dongfeng invented a web service discovery mechanism on unstructured P2P network. The web services are clustered into communities through functional properties and several query packets will be proliferated and spread through the community. Each service in this community will be evaluated through non-functional properties. The service clustering and experience exchanging enhanced the efficiency in discovery [4]. Henry Song and Doreen Cheng examine better approaches of using general-purpose search engines to discover Web Services. They used Yahoo and Google search engine and the queries were fired to each search engine daily and the top 100 search results returned from every search are collected and analyzed. The results show that for both search engines, embedding a WSDL specification in a Web page that provides semantic description of the service [5].

A QoS-oriented Optimization Model for Web Service Group proposed by Xiaopeng Deng and Chunxiao Xing defines functionality satisfaction degree, performance satisfaction degree, cost satisfaction degree and trust satisfaction degree as the QoS parameters of a Web service. The Web service optimization model is described formally. simulation cases prove that the proposed model is effective and can be used for Web service selection from its group [6]. Zibin Zheng, Hao Ma, Michael R. Lyu, and Irwin King came up with a Collaborative Filtering Based Web Service Recommender System which includes a user-contribution mechanism for Web service QoS information collection and an effective and novel hybrid collaborative filtering algorithm for Web service QoS value prediction. The comprehensive experimental analysis shows that WSRec achieves better prediction accuracy than other approaches [7]. Hao Yang, Junliang Chen, Xiangwu Meng and Ying Zhang put forth a Dynamic Agent based Web Service Invocation Infrastructure which presents a Web service invocation infrastructure based on software agents [8]. Youngkon Lee set forth Web Services Registry implementation for Processing Quality of Service. He proposed the design principle for integrating quality management on Web service registry developed in UDDI specification and Web service quality management system (WSQMS). For representing Web service quality information, the WSQDL(Web Service Quality Description Language), which published by WSQM technical committee in OASIS is adopted. In more detail, this paper also presents the scheme to compose the classification scheme for quality data and to modify the necessary data structure of the registry [9].

3   Business Logic Evaluation Model

Figure 1 depicts Business Logic Evaluation Model with a Business Logic Analyzer dissects the business logic into the rule source and function source that constitutes the logic. The rule source bears a collection of rules. The rule sets from rule source are analyzed by the rule bound analyzer. The function source contains all the functions of the business logic. The function sets from function source are analyzed by the function bound analyzer. The finite state machine simulator evaluates certain properties like computability and traceability whereas the PBF (Primitive Business Function) valuates properties such as configurability and customizability. The change monitor takes charge of Manageability and decidability. The property evaluator appraises the Business Logic with the interoperable goals such as Computability, Traceability, Decidability and Manageability and other goals such as Configurability, Customizability, Serviceability and Extensibility. After being done with the property evaluation the BL schema is generated from the schema generator.

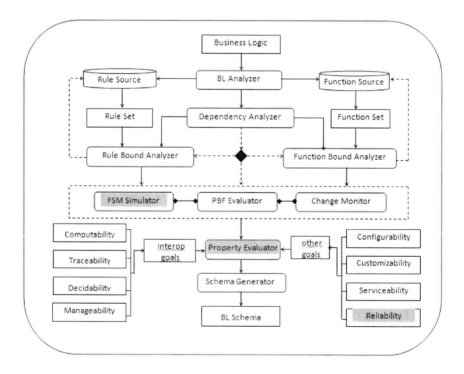

Fig. 1. Business Logic Evaluation Model

3.1 Computability

Computability refers to feasibility of the modification anticipated. Whenever the request is issued, it is being edited by the analyst as a rule in order to bring in action the change request using the rule editor. If the request can be edited as rule using the editor, it means it is computable. And hence computability of a request is determined to be true or false based on whether it can be formed as rule by the editor or not. Therefore rule editor should consider all intricacies of the business product in its construct to effectively able to represent all computable rules. Thus the functional QoS parameter, computability is identified. It is enhanced by the construction of a functionally complete rule editor.

There are also other kinds of computability's defined, partial and complete computability. Say a rule includes a set of actions. If all the requirements of the action are satisfied it is said to be completely computable. If few of the requirements of the action are satisfied it is said to be partially computable. Say an action is composed of a data retrieval statement. If the specified database, table, fields are available, it is said to be computable. So in the editor we have also the space to specify actions constituted by a rule and we can calculate computability to provide more insight into computability of the rule.

3.2 Traceability

Rule traceability refers to tracing of similar rules which were solved before and issue of using its execution plan in solving current issue. Some errors may occur during runtime. The complaint is given by the user in general English and tries to edit it as rule using editor. In case of the same error occurring at two different locations, he may give the complaint in different way. If we manage to store the thread control block of that session then it is easy to identify similar change requests whose origin is due to the same internal operating state of the service. If the request happens to match and the issue was solved, we flag the present request as repeating request and indicate that the issue was not solved completely. If it happens to match partially, say parameters alone, we can make use of execution plan of the change request solved before.

3.3 Decidability

A rule or logic is said to be decidable if they are completely computable. (Each business logic system has both syntactic component which determines the notion of provability and the semantic component which determines the notion of logical validity). A rule or logic which is partially computable is sometimes said to be semi decidable. If we ascertain the rule is completely computable or partially computable we can determine the rule is decidable or semi decidable. This property is particularly useful in program verification, in the verification of reactive, real time or hybrid systems, as well as in databases and ontology. It is therefore important to identify such decidable fragments and design efficient decision procedures for them.

3.4 Manageability

Manageability is defined as a set of capabilities for discovering the existence, availability, performance, and usage, as well as the control and configuration of business logic within the Web services architecture. This implies that business logic can be managed using Web services technologies.

3.5 Configurability

The Configuration provides the functional capability to manage the collection of properties whose values may influence the behavior of a resource. Such deterministic behavior includes cost in terms of code size of business logic, slower algorithms, and so on. Hence these issues have to be managed to have a better configurability.

3.6 Customizability

Customizable solutions may be appropriate for customers whose needs and expectations change from time to time. Here the business analyst is given with customizing options so that he can change the logic according to the user's need.

3.7 Serviceability

Serviceability refers to the ability to identify exceptions or faults, debug or isolate faults to root cause analysis, and provide software maintenance in pursuit of solving a problem and restoring the problem in the logic. Incorporating serviceability facilitating features typically results in more efficient maintenance and reduces operational costs and maintains business continuity.

3.8 Reliability Analysis

Numerous web services are evolving today. Selecting the quality web service is a tedious process and one of the predominant QoS factor is reliability. Reliability is the ability of a system to keep operating over time. Software reliability is "the probability that the software will be functioning without failures under a given environmental condition during a specified period of time". A reliability evaluation framework model is designed. The Reliability depends on user profile. A module in a web service is defined to perform a particular function .Non executed part of codes have no influence on output. Little used modules might be less important for reliability of the system. Reliability of a module is the probability that the module performs the function correctly. A module passes result to next module.It is logical independent for design, programming and testing.

Availability

Determine whether your users need reliability [non-performance has the greatest impact] or availability [downtime has the greatest impact] or both

$$A(t) = \frac{1}{1+t_m \lambda_F} \quad \text{or} \quad \lambda_F = \frac{1-A(t)}{t_m A(t)}$$

A = availability; tm = average downtime per failure

Reliability

If you need to . . . convert from FIO to reliability

$$R = e^{-\lambda t}$$

– where R is reliability, λ = failure intensity, and t = number of natural or time units
    If you need to . . . convert from reliability to FIO

$$\lambda = \frac{-\ln(R)}{t}$$

In this model the conditional states are represented as nodes and each transition is given by a reliability factor R and probability factor P. Reliability factor is a probability that gets to the state C (state that returns correct output), when starting

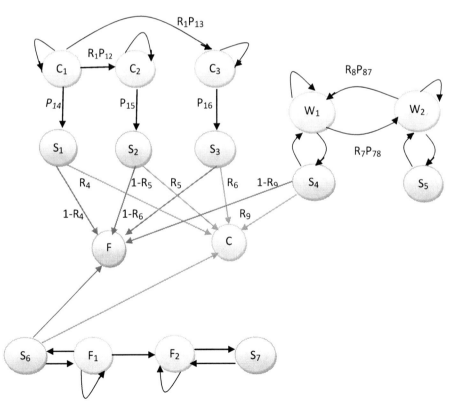

Fig. 2. Reliability Evaluation model

from any node say n. Probability factor values are decided based on the probability that the node performs function correctly and it varies between 0 and 1. In any service if majority of statements are directing to failure states i.e. F that service will be less reliable. Program runs correct only if the correct sequence of functions are executed and every function executed gives the correct result i.e C. Any service is said to be more reliable when modules of that service terminates in correct output C. Let us take an example of a program and evaluate its reliability using this model.

```c
#include<stdio.h>
void main()
{
        int b,p,q,r,x;
        printf("enter the no: of rows : ");
        scanf("%d",&r);
        printf("\n pascals triangle :\n\n");
        b=1;
        q=0;
                while(q<r)
                    {
                    for(p=30-3*q;p>0;p--)
                            printf(" ");
                    for(x=0;x<=q;x++)
                        {
                        if(x==0||q==0)
                                b=1;
                        else
                                b=(b*(q-x+1)/x);
                                printf("%6d",b);
                        }
                    printf("\n");
                    q++;
                    }
                getch();
}
```

W1-while loop
F2- first for loop
S3- statements following F2
F4-second for loop
I5-if statement
E6-else statement
S7-statement following I5
S8-statement following E6
C, F-exit states
C-program returns correct output
F-program has a fault

The reliability evaluation model for this program is given in the above figure. The nodes represent the loops such as while, for followed by if – else statement. The sequence of the program is depicted in the above graph. Their transition represents probability that they will enter the next node. To the node F are the reliability factors $(1-R_i)$ that the loop may have fault and to the node C are the reliability factors of correctness of the output. This program is reliable since the reliability factors of correctness sum to be higher than that of the fault. Thus these factors prove the program to be highly reliable.

4 Conclusion

In this paper we addressed actual need of reliability for an efficient web service. Reliability testing produces failures, particularly when the tests are accelerated with extra loads, and this may be troublesome to have in the records for future lawsuits. Thus it is often to everyone's advantage to perform reliability test under code names to protect against the broad rules of legal discovery. The reliability tests will determine a product's longevity and failure-free performance. This requires data recording and data integrity. Since web service and QOS grows expensively based on the reliability of the service. We have proposed business logic evaluation model for web service reliability analysis using Finite State Machine (FSM). If any changes occur in the business logic of the service the FSM will automatically measure the reliability for the corresponding service.

References

1. Trabelsi, S., Pazzaglia, J.-C., Roudier, Y.: Secure Web service discovery: overcoming challenges of ubiquitous computing. In: The European Conference on Web Services, ECOWS 2006 (2006)
2. Atkinson, C., Bostan, P.: A Practical Approach to Web Service Discovery and Retrieval. In: IEEE International Conference on Web Services, ICWS 2007 (2007)
3. Hicks, J., Govindaraju, M., Meng, W.: Search Algorithms for Discovery of Web Services. In: IEEE International Conference on Web Services, ICWS 2007 (2007)
4. Zhang, C., Zhu, D.: A Web Service Discovery Mechanism Based on Immune Communication. In: International Conference on Convergence Information Technology (2007)
5. Song, H., Cheng, D.: Web Service Discovery Using General Purpose Search Engines. In: IEEE International Conference on Web Services, ICWS 2007 (2007)
6. Deng, X., Xing, C.: A QoS-oriented Optimization Model for Web Service. In: Eigth IEEE/ACIS International Conference on Computer and Information Science (2009)
7. Zheng, Z., Ma, H., Lyu, M.R., King, I.: A Collaborative Filtering Based Web Service Recommender System. In: 2009 IEEE International Conference on Web Services (2009)

8. Treiber, M., Truong, H.-L., Dustdar, S.: Service Evolution Management Framework. In: 34th Euromicro Conference Software Engineering and Advanced Applications
9. Lee, Y.: Web Services Registry implementation for Processing Quality of Service. In: International Conference on Advanced Language Processing and Web Information Technology

Selection Based Comparative Summarization of Search Results Using Concept Based segmentation

Chitra Pasupathi[1], Baskaran Ramachandran[2], and Sarukesi Karunakaran[3]

[1] Dept. of Information Technology, RMK Engineering College, Tamilnadu, India
pce.it@rmkec.ac.in
[2] Dept. of Comp. Sci. & Engg., Anna University, Chennai, Tamilnadu, India
baaski@cs.annauniv.edu
[3] Hindustan University Chennai, Tamilnadu, India
profsaru@gmail.com

Abstract. Search result summarization aims at providing the users with the summary of the contents of single or multiple web pages based on the search query. This paper proposes a novel idea of generating a comparative summary from a set of URLs from the search result. User selects a set of web page links from the search result produced by search engine. Comparative summary of these selected web sites is generated. This method makes use of HTML/XML DOM tree structure of these web pages. HTML documents are segmented into different concept blocks. Sentence score of each concept block is computed according to the query keywords. As per the required compression ratio, the important sentences from the concept blocks of different web pages are extracted to compose the comparative summary on the fly. The comparative summary of the contents of a set of web pages would help the users in quick decision making.

Keywords: Summarization, concept segmentation, query based summary.

1 Introduction

The WWW grows rapidly and caters to a diversified levels and categories of users. Web search engines play a major role in information retrieval and provide thousands of results for a query. Users still have to spend lot of time to read the contents of different results from the set to locate the required information. It is not feasible for the user to open each link in the result set to find out its relevance. The performance improvement of the search engines has become the most important research area to satisfy the needs and expectations of diversified target users.

A small summary generated from the content of web page would be helpful for the users to get an instant feel about the content without going through the entire content. People can have a concise overview in short time. This can greatly enhance the retrieval efficiency. Automatic summary aims to extract some important sentences from original documents to represent the content of the article.

Automatic summary produced by current search engines contains first few sentences of the web page or the set of sentences containing the query key words.

D.C. Wyld et al. (Eds.): NeCoM/WeST/WiMoN 2011, CCIS 197, pp. 655–664, 2011.
© Springer-Verlag Berlin Heidelberg 2011

Using this information, users have to decide which of the listed documents in the search result will be most likely to satisfy their information need.

This paper proposes a summarization technique, which extracts query relevant important sentences from a set of selected web pages to generate a comparative summary which would be beneficial for the users to make informed decisions.

The remainder of this paper is organized as follows: Section 2 provides the motivating examples for this work, Section 3 discusses about the related research works that have been done in this field and Section 4 describes concept based segmentation process guided by the webpage's DOM tree structure. In section 5, we present the framework for the selection based comparative summarization system using concept based segmentation. Section 6 gives experimentation results and performance measures and in section 7, the paper is concluded with a light on further improvement to this system.

2 Motivating Example

Real time decision makers collect all related material and information before they come to the conclusion. For example, to know about the placement activities done in various Engineering College, the user collects placement details of various Engineering Colleges using search engines like Google, prepares a comparative statement manually to find out the best option for admission.

The proposed system generates the comparative summary from the set of URLs selected by user from the search result based on the specified feature set. The comparative summary contains the text relevant to placement and training, infrastructure details, result details and fee structures from the selected URLs. This would definitely be helpful to get instant comparative statement.

Another example could be the comparison between the services offered by various Banks. Set of Banks can be selected from the list of Bank web sites and comparative summary based on feature keywords like home loan, term deposit, etc would be helpful for users to make quick decisions.

3 Related Works

Summarization in general can be categorized into two types as extraction based and abstraction based methods. Extractive summary is created by extracting important sentences from the original content, based on some statistical measures like **TFxIDF, SimWithFirst**[6],etc. Abstractive summary is created by rewriting sentences on understanding the entire content of the original article by applying NLP techniques. The later technique is more computationally intensive for large data-sets.

Concept based automatic summarization directly extracts the sentences, which are related to the main concept of the original document while the query sensitive summarization extracts sentences according to user queries, so as to fit the interests of users. In multi-document summarization the sentences are selected across different documents by considering the concept and diversity of contents in all documents.

Query based summarization system to create a new composed page containing all the query key words was proposed in[2]. Composed page was created by extracting and stitching together the relevant pieces from a particular URL in search result and all its linked documents but not other relevant documents of user's interest.

Segmented topic blocks from HTML DOM tree were utilized to generate summary in [9] by applying a statistical method similar to TFxIDF to measure the importance of sentences and MMR to reduce redundancy. This system focused on the summary of single document.

SimWithFirst (Similarity With First Sentence) and MEAD (Combination of Centroid, Position, and Length Features) called CPSL features were used for both single and multi document text summarization in[6]. Both these techniques show better performance for short document summarization but not suitable for large ones.

Document Graph structure for sentences was used in[3] for text summarization. Similarity scores between the query and each sentence in the graph are computed. Document graph construction is an overhead for the summarization process.

Balanced hierarchical structure[4] was utilized to organize the news documents based on event topics to generate event based summarization. This method focused on news and event summarization.

This research work focuses on the novel idea of generating the aggregation of document summaries. This document summarization makes use of concept based segmentation of DOM tree structure of web pages. This comparative summary is composed of the query sensitive important sentences extracted from concept blocks of different web pages which would be helpful for decision making.

4   Concept Based Segmentation

In general, web page summarization derives from text summarization techniques, while it is a great challenge to summarize Web pages automatically and effectively. Because Web pages differ from traditional text documents in both structure and content. Web pages often have diverse contents such as bullets, images and links.

Web documents may contain diversified subjects and information. Normally, the contents of same subjects will be grouped within the same tag. This system utilizes the Document Object Model (DOM) to analyze the content of the web page. The leaf nodes of DOM tree contain the actual content and the parent nodes generally contain higher level topics or section headings.

4.1   Concept Based Segmentation Process

Figure 1 depicts the concept based segmentation using DOM tree structure. The rectangular nodes represent the HTML tags and the circular nodes represent the information content within the tag. These circular nodes from left to right constitute a coherent semantic string of the content[9].

The DOM trees of the user selected URLs are processed to generate the summary. Leaf nodes are considered as micro blocks which are the basic building blocks of the summary. Adjacent micro blocks of the same parent tag are merged to form the topic blocks.

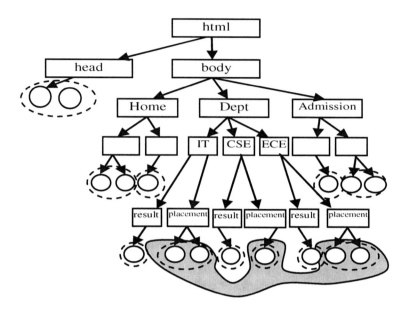

Fig. 1. Concept based segmentation

Each sentence in the topic block is labeled automatically based on the PropBank notations [10]. These sentences are labeled by a semantic role labeler that determines the words which contribute to the sentence semantics associated with their semantic roles in the sentence. ASSERT software which is a publicly distributed semantic labeling tool, is used for this purpose. Each word that has a semantic role in the sentence, is called a concept[1][9]. Concepts can be either words or phrases and are totally dependent on the semantic structure of the sentence. List of concept words for these topic blocks are identified.

Concept based similarity between the topic blocks are measured using the concept lists to identify the similar topics. Topic blocks having similarity above the threshold value α, are combined to form the concept block. Topic blocks having content about the same concept (for example placement and training in a college web site) will be similar to each other. Topic blocks containing information about placement (concept word) are merged to form one concept block (placement block having placement details of all departments in the college).

The concept block formation could be done offline for all web documents in the repository. These concept blocks contain related information content scattered throughout the document. The set of sentences in each of these concept blocks are actually present is different parts of the document.

Since DOM nodes are processed, the time taken for processing is less when compared to other vector based and document graph[8] based models. The processing time required to build the document graph is avoided in this approach.

4.2 Concept Based Segmentation Algorithm

The conceptual term frequency is an important factor in calculating the concept-based similarity measure between topic blocks. The more frequent the concept appears in the verb argument structures[1] of a sentence, the more conceptually similar the topic blocks are. Concept based segmentation algorithm is described below:

Input : Web document d_i

Output : Set of concept blocks $\{Cb_1,..Cb_n\}$ of di,

   Concept list of d_i, $L=\{C_1,..C_m\}$

   Concept list of topic block tb_i, $C_{tbi} =\{c_{k1},..c_{km}\}$, k=1..n

Step1: Mark all leaf nodes as individual micro blocks in the DOM tree.

Step2: Extend the border of the micro block to include all leaf nodes of the same tag to form a topic block so as to have a set of topic blocks $TB=\{tb_1, tb_2, ...tb_n\}$, $TB \subset di$.

Step3: Build concept list for all topic blocks $TB =\{tb_1, tb_2, ...tb_n\}$.

Topic block tb_i is a set of sentences, $tbi=\{s_{i1}, s_{i2}, ..s_{in1}\}$, $s_i \subset tb_i$

Sentence s_i is a string of concepts, $s_i=\{c_{i1},c_{i2} . . . c_{im}\}$, $c_i \subset s_i$, if c_i is a substring of s_i

Concept c_i is a string of words, $c_i = \{w_{i1},w_{i2}, . . .w_{ik}\}$,

   where k: number of words in concept c_i.

   m: number of concepts generated from the verb argument structures in sentences

   n1: total number of sentences in tb_i

   3.1: C_{tbi}, L are empty lists.

   3.2: Build concept list of each sentence in tb_i

      3.2.1: s_i is a new sentence in tbi

      3.2.2: Build concepts list C_i from s_i, $C_i =\{c1,c2,..cm\}$

      3.2.3: Update concept list C_{tbi} of tbi and L of d_i

         3.2.3.1: for each concept $c_i \subset C_i$ do

         3.2.3.2: for each $cj \subset L$, do

         3.2.3.3: if ($c_i == c_j$) then

         3.2.3.4:   update ctf_i of ci // increment conceptual term frequency

         3.2.3.5: else add new concept to C_{tbi}, L // added to both L and C_{tbi}

         3.2.3.6: end if

         3.2.3.7: end for

         3.2.3.8: end for

   3.3: Output the concepts list C_{tbi}

   3.4: Output the concepts list L of document di.

Step4: The concept based similarity between topic blocks are measured by (1) .

$$Sim(tb_1,tb_2) =1- \left| \sum_{t \subset C_{tb1} \cap C_{tb2}} ctf_i \times ctfweight_i - \sum_{t \subset C_{tb1} \cap C_{tb2}} ctf_i \times ctfweight_i \right| \quad (1)$$

Where,

   ctf_{i1}, ctf_{i2} : Frequency of concept c_i in tb_1, tb_2

   t : set of common conceptual terms between tb_1, tb_2

   $ctfweight_{i1}, ctfweight_{i2}$: Weight of concept c_i with respect to topic blocks tb_1, tb_2 normalized by the frequency vectors of tb_1, tb_2 calculated as in (2)

$$ctfweight_i = \frac{ctf_i}{\sqrt{\sum_{k=1}^m (ctf_k)^2}} \quad (2)$$

Step5: Merge the topic blocks having concept based similarity measure above the predefined threshold α.

Concept block Cb_k={set of topic blocks tb_i}|

$\forall tbi, tbj \in Cb_k, sim(tbi, tbj) > \alpha, tb_i \subset TB, tb_j \subset TB, k=1..n$

Step6: Output Concept blocks $Cb_1, Cb_2,..Cb_n$

The concept blocks of each URLs selected by the user are identified. Concept blocks of all URLs in the repository can be identified during preprocessing stage itself. This will reduce the computation complexity at run time.

The next section describes about generating the comparative summary on the fly at run time using these concept blocks of the web document.

5 Comparative Summary Generation

The architecture of the comparative summarization system is given in Figure.2. User enters the generic query string (eg. Engineering College) through the search engine query interface. Search engine identifies the relevant pages and present the search result in rank order. Then the specific feature keywords based on which comparative summary is to be generated and the set of URLs are obtained from the user.

The selected HTML files of the URLs are cleaned by removing unwanted HTML tags (like META tag, ALIGN tag, etc.) which do not contribute much for further processing. Concept blocks of these URLs which were already formed during preprocessing are utilized to generate the summary.

The relevance of the concept blocks Cbi to the feature keywords f is measured by means of similarity between the feature keyword string[7] and the concept list of each of the concept blocks $Cb_{i..}$

$$sim_f(f, Cb_i) = \frac{\sum_{t \in f \cap Cbi} Ctf_{ti}}{\sqrt{\sum_{t \in Cbi} Ctf_{ti}^2}} \qquad (3)$$

Where,

$Sim_f(f, Cb_i)$: Similarity between feature keyword string f and Concept block Cb_i

t   : set of common terms between f and Concept list of Cb_i

Ctf_{it} : frequency of term t in Cb_i

The range of $Sim_f(f, Cbi)$ value lies between 0 and 1, and the similarity increases as this value increases. The concept block with maximum similarity is considered as the superset of the summary to be generated.

The significance of each sentence in this concept block with respect to the query string is measured. The sentences are considered in the descending order of their score. According to the ratio of summarization required or the number of sentences required, the sentences are extracted from these concept blocks to compose the HTML page for comparative summary.

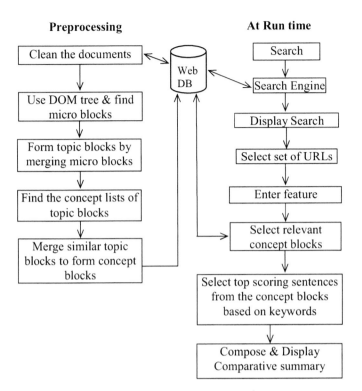

Fig. 2. Framework of comparative summarization system

5.1 Sentence Weight Calculation

Content of these concept blocks are ranked with respect to the query string and the feature keywords, using (4). Sentence weight calculation considers the number of occurrences of feature keywords and their distance and frequency, location of the sentence, tag in which the text appears in the document, uppercase words,etc.

$$W(S_i) = \frac{W(k_i)}{Len(S_i)} + e^{-\gamma(D-1)} + \alpha W_{tag} + \beta W_l \qquad (4)$$

Where,
$W(k_i)$:Weight of certain feature word ki in sentence si
$Len(si)$:number of words contained in the sentence.

W_{tag} :weight determined by the tag to which the sentence belongs
       BOLD, UNDERLINE, ITALICS, CAPTION, PARAGRAPH TITLE : 3
       COLOR CHANGE :2
W_l :weight determined by the location of the Sentence with respect to the parent
       node, set to 1 to the left most node and 0.5 to the right most node of a parent
D   :average distance between feature words α , β and γ :adjusting parameters.

The sentences having frequent occurrences of the feature keywords and enclosed in special tags are given preference. Location based weight is assigned according to the location of the sentence within its immediate parent node. The top scoring sentences are extracted and arranged based on the hierarchical structure of the individual documents. The title or first sentence of the immediate parent of the extracted sentence, is chosen as subtitles for a set of leaf node contents. (for example, IT, CSE, ECE in our example). Hence the resulting summary will contain the SECTION-wise summary sentences of a set of URLs chosen by the user for immediate comparison. This is applicable to various decision making situations which require analysis of various parameters from various sources.

6   Experimentation Results

The experimentation of this work was carried out with the real time dataset containing randomly collected 200 web documents from internet related to the educational institutions, algorithms, banking and household items.

Normally, the summarization systems are evaluated using intrinsic approach or extrinsic approach [5]. Intrinsic approach directly analyzes the quality of the automatic summary through comparing it with the abstract extracted by hand or generated from other different automatic system. Extrinsic approach is a task-oriented approach, which measures the abstract quality according to its contribution.

Intrinsic approach was utilized to conduct the experiment of this system. Users including one engineering student, three naïve users and one expert level user were involved in the experimentation process.

The evaluation feedback collected from the experimentation is listed in table 1.

Table 1. Evaluation feedback measure

User#	Query 1	Feature Keywords	Feed back in 5 point scale
#1	Engineering College, Chennai	Placement, Recruiters	4
#2	Optimization Algorithms	Efficiency, Time Complexity	3.5
#3	Theme Park, Chennai	Entry Fee, Games	4.2
#4	Banks	Home loan rate, services	3.5
#5	Washing Machine	Brands, cost, offers, warranty	3.3

The query result user interface of the system is given in Fig. 3 through which the user selects the URLs and enter feature words for comparative summary generation.

| engineering colleges in chennai | Search |

☑ **SRM Engineering College**
SRM joins the league of IITs & NITs Ranked among the Top 15 in India
www.srmuniv.ac.in

☑ **Sri Krishna Engineering College**
28 Jun 2010 ... Founded in 1999 it is affiliated to Anna University and is approved by All India Council for
Technical Education
www.snkrishna**college**.com/ - Cached - Similar
> No. 27, Near Padappai Viatambaram, Panappakam, Chennai
> 044 42044337

☐ Meenakshi **College** Of **Engineering**
Email: babaiks@yahoo.com.uk, Email: babaiks@yahoo.com.uk, Website: http://www.msec.edu.in/
www.msec.edu.in/
> 363, Arcot Road, Kodambakkam, Chennai
> 044 24801636

☑ Panimalar **Engineering College** 🔍
Email: panitech@md3.vsnl.net.in, Email: panitech@md3.vsnl.net.in, Website:
http://www.panimalar.ac.in/ Email: panitech@md3.vsnl.net.in
www.panimalar.ac.in/
> Bangalore Trunk Road, Varasanathpettai, Taluk -Poonamalle, Varadharaj Apuram
> Chennai

| **FEATURE WORDS FOR SUMMARIZATION** | Placement | → |

Fig. 3. Query result and URL selection interface

SRM ENGINEERING COLLEGE	Sri Krishna Engineering College	Panimalar Engineering College
Placement & Training Cell The Placement and Training Cell, headed by a Senior Professor, helps students plan their career. Placement Cell and Career Guidance Towards the end of the 6th Semester or during the beginning of the 7th, students are exposed to opportunities and get selected in campus interviews with attractive packages. Recruiters Many Corporates have a close relationships with SRM University and many more have come to the campus in search of talent. 3i Infotech 7 Strata Inc ABN Amro ACC Limited Accenture Agilent AIG Systems AIG Systems Solutions	our Training & Placement Drive for our final Students Free Seminar / Workshop @ our premises with prior notification In-Plant Training Certification for pre/final students Global Certification Programme @ college premises Recruiters 1 Tata Consultancy Services 2 Infosys Technologies Ltd 3 Mphasis, an EDS Company 4 Tech Mahindra 5 Siemens Information Systems Ltd	Placement Cell The Panimalar Engineering College fosters an active placement cell that provides excellent future and assured job opportunities to students. The Placement Cell identifies the Industrial requirements and trains the students in areas such as the following: •List of Premier Recruiters: •1. Infosys 2. HP Ltd., 3. Xansa Ltd., 4. Satyam Computer Services Ltd., 5. Computer Science Corporation

Fig. 4. Comparative summary

Summary extracted from these selected URLs are presented to the user as a comparative summary given in Fig 4. This system produces the comparison information required for real time decision making dynamically. The average user satisfaction index is 3.7.

Since DOM tree structure of the web documents are utilized to process the content and generate the summary the time complexity involved is very less when compared to systems making use of vector space model and document graph model.

7 Conclusion and Future Work

This system focused on generating comparative summary from a set of URLs selected by the user. Concept based segmentation is used to identify the relevant block of content in the document and top scoring sentences are extracted, composed and displayed to the user. This summary would definitely be helpful for the users to get the immediate summary and for decision making.

The impact of usage of key words association, document graph model of documents on this system and advanced text clustering techniques for summary generation can be done as a future expansion to this system.

References

[1] Shehata, S., Karray, F., Kamel, M.S.: An Efficient Concept-Based Mining Model for Enhancing Text Clustering. IEEE Transactions on Knowledge and Data Engineering 22(10), 1360–1371 (2010)
[2] Varadarajan, R., Hristidis, V., Li, A.T.: Beyond Single-Page Web Search Results. IEEE Transactions on Knowledge and Data Engineering 20(3), 411–424 (2008)
[3] Mohamed, A.A., Rajasekaran, S.: Improving Query-Based Summarization Using Document Graphs. In: Proceedings of IEEE International Symposium on Signal Processing and Information Technology, pp. 408–410 (2006)
[4] Wa, F.L., Wong, T.-L., Mak, A.N.H.: Organization Of Documents For Multiple Document Summarization. In: Proceedings of the Seventh International Conference on Web-Based Learning, pp. 98–104. IEEE, Los Alamitos (2008)
[5] Mani, I.: Summarization Evaluation: An Overview. In: Proceedings of the NTCIR Workshop Meeting on Evaluation of Chinese and Japanese Text Retrieval and Text Summarization (2001)
[6] Mohsin Ali, M., Ghosh, M.K., Al-Mamun, A.: Multi-Document Text Summarization: Simwithfirst Based Features And Sentence Co-Selection Based Evaluation. In: Proceedings of IEEE International Conference on Future Computer and Communication, pp. 93–96 (2009)
[7] Zhang, Y., Yin, C., Yuan, F.: An Application of Improved PageRank in Focused Crawler. In: Fourth International Conference on Fuzzy Systems and Knowledge Discovery (FSKD 2007). IEEE, Los Alamitos (2007), 0-7695-2874-0/07
[8] Sornil, O., Gree-Ut, K.: An Automatic Text Summarization Approach Using Content-Based and Graph-Based Characteristics. IEEE, Los Alamitos (2006)
[9] Chen, Z., Shen, J.: Research On Query-Based Automatic Summarization Of Webpage. In: ISECS International Colloquium on Computing, Communication, Control, and Management, pp. 173–176 (2009)
[10] Kingsbury, P., Palmer, M.: Propbank: The Next Level of Treebank. In: Proc. Workshop Treebanks and Lexical Theories (2003)

A Novel Way of Invoking Web Services and RESTful Web Services Using Aspect Oriented Programming

Vishnuvardhan Mannava[1] and T. Ramesh[2]

[1] Department of Computer Science and Engineering, KL University,
Vaddeswaram 522502, A.P., India
vishnu@klce.ac.in
[2] Department of Computer Science and Engineering, National Institute of Technology,
Warangal, 506004, A.P., India
rmesht@nitw.ac.in

Abstract. The need for adaptability in software is growing, driven in part by the emergence of autonomic computing. In many cases, it is desirable to enhance existing programs with adaptive behavior, enabling them to execute effectively in dynamic environments. Existing web service invocation and adaptation mechanisms are limited only to the scope of web service choreography in terms of web service selection. Such a scope hardly leaves ground for a participating service in a choreographed flow to re-adjust itself in terms of changed non functional expectations. In this paper we used Aspect oriented programming (AOP) to invoke Web Services (WS) and Representational State Transfer (REST) web services and to enable dynamic adaptation in existing programs. We propose an approach to implement dynamic adaptability especially in Aspect weaving at the time invoking web services and REST web service. We have used AspectJ; Java based language to create aspects in Eclipse supported framework.

Keywords: Dynamic Adaptation, Web Services, RESTful Web Services, Aspect Oriented Programming (AOP), and AspectJ.

1 Introduction

A software application is adaptable if it can change its behavior dynamically (at run time) in response to transient changes in its execution environment or to permanent changes in its requirements. Recent interest in designing adaptable software is driven in part by the demand for autonomic computing. Autonomic computing [1] refers to self-managed, and potentially self-healing, systems that require only high-level human guidance. Autonomic computing is critical to managing the myriad of sensors and other small devices at the wireless edge, but also in managing large-scale computing centers and protecting critical infrastructure (e.g., financial networks, transportation systems, power grids) from hardware component failures, network outages, and security attacks. Developing and maintaining adaptable software are nontrivial tasks. An adaptable application comprises functional code that implements the business logic of the application and supports its imperative behavior, and adaptive code that implements the adaptation logic of the application and supports its

D.C. Wyld et al. (Eds.): NeCoM/WeST/WiMoN 2011, CCIS 197, pp. 665–674, 2011.
© Springer-Verlag Berlin Heidelberg 2011

adaptive behavior. The difficulty in developing and maintaining adaptable applications is largely due to an inherent property of the adaptive code, that is, the adaptive code tends to crosscut the functional code. Example crosscutting concerns include QoS, mobility, fault tolerance, recovery, security, self auditing, and energy consumption. Even more challenging than developing new adaptable applications is enhancing existing applications, such that they execute effectively in new, dynamic environments not envisioned during their design and development. For example, many non-adaptive applications are being ported to mobile computing environments, where they require dynamic adaptation. Many different styles can be used to integrate enterprise applications. The choice between relying on a shared database, using batched file transfer, calling remote procedures, or exchanging asynchronous messages over a message bus is a major architectural decision, which influences the requirements for the underlying middleware platform and the properties of the integrated system. The "Big"1 Web services technology stack [2] (SOAP, WSDL, WS-Addressing, WS-Reliable Messaging, Security, etc.) delivers interoperability for both the Remote Procedure Call (RPC) and messaging integration styles. More recently, an alternative solution has been brought forward to implement remote procedure calls across the Web: so-called RESTful Web services [11] are gaining increased attention not only because of their usage in the Application Programming Interface (API) of many Web 2.0 services, but also because of the presumed simplicity of publishing and consuming a RESTfulWeb service. Key architectural decisions in distributed system design, such as the choice of integration style and technology, should be based on technical arguments and a fair comparison of concrete capabilities delivered by each alternative. Our experience with this system have been proved that use of AspectJ[15] language helps to modularize the crosscutting concerns and improved the productivity, reusability, dynamic adaptability, maintainability and code independence in our aim of invoking Web Services and REstful web services using AOP.

Our paper is organized as follows. We review related work in section 2. Section 3 describes REstful web services Technologies. Section 4 describes the AOP paradigm and the need for a distributed framework to address the problem. In Section 5, we propose the solution framework with a case study. Try to show the Efficiency of AOP by CPU Profiling in section 6. Section 7, Try to show the affect of 'Aspects' on application through Eclipse's Aspect Visualizer. We conclude the paper in section 8 with possible future directions.

2 Related Work

There are a number of publications reporting the possible applications of aspect oriented programming and web services with AOP. Cibrán and Verheecke propose a method for modularizing Web services management with AOP [5]. Charfi have approached this problem from a different direction [6]. They have proposed an extension to the BPEL language, which they called aspect-oriented BPEL (AO4BPEL). Their language brings in modular and dynamic adaptability to BPEL, since mid-flight adaptations can be implemented via advices in AO4BPEL. SOAP vs. REST [9] has been an ongoing discussion for some time on the blogosphere and has also recently gained attention in the academic community. None of the existing work employs a structured and detailed comparison method based on architectural decisions. For example, the ECOWS 2005 keynote [8] focused on the reconciliation of WS-* with REST, whereas [9] gives a comparison of the two approaches from the point of view of their application to workflow systems. A good discussion on whether the Web (and in particular RESTfulWeb services) can fulfill the requirements of enterprise computing can be found in a recent W3C workshop [10]. A comparison of RESTfulWeb services and so-called "Big Web Services" is also found in Chapter 10 of [11].

In it, a critical look to the WS-* stack is given in terms of how it does not fit with the "resource-oriented" paradigm of the Web. The chapter also attempts to show how simpler RESTful techniques can be used to replace the corresponding WS-* technologies. The distinction between "resource-oriented" and "service-oriented" architectures was first introduced by [17]. Unfortunately, the book does not provide a clear definition of the terms services and resources, and its technology comparison is not based on measurable, objective criteria such as software quality attributes, design and development effort, technical risk, and QoS characteristics. Even if HTTP is a synchronous protocol, the comparison presented in [18] argues that RESTful calls are asynchronous from an application layer perspective. Thus, REST can be seen as favorable solution for simple integration scenarios. Additional architectural concerns such as the URL design and payload format are not discussed. In [20] we applied architectural decision modeling concepts to another complex design issue in SOA, that of designing transactional workflows. A framework for the comparison of pre-Web services middleware infrastructures (i.e., CORBA vs. J2EE vs. COM+) has been introduced in [19].

In this paper, we present experimental study of aspect oriented programming to invoke web services and Restful Web Services.

3   Web Services Technologies

3.1   RESTful Web Services

In this section we outline the main characteristics of REST focusing on the current interpretation used to define "RESTful" Web services. For more information we refer the reader to [11].
The REST architectural style is based on four principles:

- Resource identification through URI. A RESTful Web service exposes a set of resources which identify the targets of the interaction with its clients. Resources are identified by URIs [14], which provides a global addressing space for resource and service discovery.
- Uniform interface. Resources are manipulated using a fixed set of four create, read, update, delete operations: PUT, GET, POST, and DELETE. PUT creates a new resource, which can be then deleted using DELETE. GET retrieves the current state of a resource in some representation. POST transfers a new state onto a resource.
- Self-descriptive messages. Resources are decoupled from their representation so that their content can be accessed in a variety of formats (e.g., HTML, XML, plain text, PDF, JPEG, etc.). Metadata about the resource is available

and used, for example, to control caching, detect transmission errors, negotiate the appropriate representation format, and perform authentication or access control.

- Stateful interactions through hyperlinks. Every interaction with a resource is stateless, i.e., request messages are self-contained. Stateful interactions are based on the concept of explicit state transfer. Several techniques exist to exchange state, e.g., URI rewriting, cookies, and hidden form fields. State can be embedded in response messages to point to valid future states of the interaction.

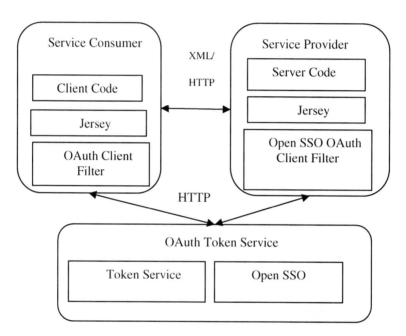

Fig. 1. Traditional REstful Web Service Invocation

4   Aspect Oriented Programming

Aspect-oriented programming (AOP) [4] has been proposed as a technique for improving separation of concerns in software AOP builds on previous technologies, including procedural programming and object-oriented programming that have already made significant improvements in software modularity.

The central idea of AOP is that while the hierarchical modularity mechanisms of object-oriented languages are extremely useful, they are inherently unable to modularize all concerns of interest in complex systems. Instead, we believe that in the implementation of any complex system, there will be concerns that inherently crosscut the natural modularity of the rest of the implementation. AOP does for crosscutting concerns what OOP has done for object encapsulation and inheritance. It provides language mechanisms that explicitly capture crosscutting structure as shown in Fig. 2.

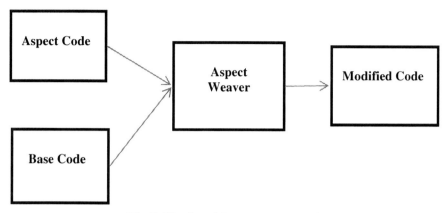

Fig. 2. Weaving of Aspect on source code

This makes it possible to program crosscutting concerns in a modular way, and achieve the usual benefits of improved modularity: simpler code that is easier to develop and maintain, and that has greater potential for reuse. We call a well modularized crosscutting concern an aspect.

5 Case Study

5.1 Invoking Web Services Using Aspect Oriented Programming

```
//aspect code to cross cut specified class and invoke web
services
public aspect Additionws        {
  //cross cut Celsius to Fahrenheit method
    pointcut  ctof(Addws  ad,double  a):call(public  double
    Addws.ctof(..))
    && target(ad)
    && args(a);
  //cross cut Fahrenheit to celsius method
    pointcut  ftoc(Addws  ad,double  a):call(public  double
    Addws.ftoc(..))
    && target(ad)
    && args(a);
  //invoking Celsius to Fahrenheit web service
    before (Addws ad, double a):ctof(ad,a){
    try{String
    endpoint="http://localhost:8088/webservices/services/
    TemperatureConversion";
    Service   service = new Service();
    Call      call    = (Call)service.createCall();
```

```
call.setTargetEndpointAddress(new
java.net.URL(endpoint));
call.setOperationName(new
QName("http://localhost:8088/webservices/services/","
cToF"));
String ret =(String)call.invoke(new Object[] { a } );
double result=Double.parseDouble(ret);
System.out.println("Sent"+a+"got result="+ result);}
catch (Exception e) { System.out.println(e);}}
//invoking Fahrenheit to Celsius web service
before (Addws ad, double a):ftoc(ad,a){
try{String
endpoint="http://localhost:8088/webservices/services/
TemperatureConversion";
Service  service = new Service();
Call     call    = (Call) service.createCall();
call.setTargetEndpointAddress(new
java.net.URL(endpoint));
call.setOperationName(new QName
("http://localhost:8088/webservices/services/",
"fToC"));
String    ret=(String)call.invoke(new    Object[]{a});
double res=Double.parseDouble(ret);
System.out.println("Sent "+a+" got result="+ res);}
 catch (Exception e) {System.out.println(e)
 }}}
```

In the above code, two web services (Celsius to Fahrenheit and Fahrenheit to Celsius) are calling by Additionws which is Aspect Oriented Program. Here aspect will cross cut two methods of Addws. User can select desired Operation from Addws class; he has to give input parameters to specified method, all the methods in Addws class will cross cut by Additionws. So, parameters directly passed to Additionws and then execute related advice i.e., before advice in all pointcuts. Web services are invoking in every before advice, execute successfully if desired web service available. Finally send input parameters to web services, get result value and then print resultant value to client.

Everyone can cross cut their methods in AOP and then pass their parameters to web services and get response via AOP. Hence, we are saying that AOP supports reusability and web services supports distributed environments.

In Fig. 3, as we explained above Aspect code will weave into Base code and then Aspect weaver produces Modified code. From that available modified code we can call web services.

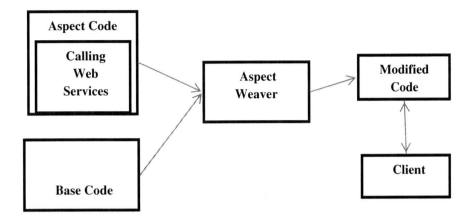

Fig. 3. Invoking Aspect Oriented Web Services

Everyone can use that Aspect code and then it will call web services from aspect code at run time. If particular web service not available, we can change address of web service at runtime also. Here we can say that AOP support dynamic adaptation [15] at run time.

5.2 Invocation of RESTful Web Services Using Aspect Oriented Programming

```
public aspect RestAspetct  {
pointcut read():call(public void Test.read(..));
before():read(){
System.out.println("welcome to restfull world");
ClientConfig config = new DefaultClientConfig();
Client client = Client.create(config);
WebResource service = client.resource(getBaseURI());
// Fluent interfaces
System.out.println(service.path("rest").path("hello").a
ccept(MediaType.TEXT_PLAIN).get(ClientResponse.class).t
oString());// Get plain text
System.out.println(service.path("rest").path("hello").a
ccept(MediaType.TEXT_PLAIN).get(String.class));
// Get XML
System.out.println(service.path("rest").path("hello").a
ccept(MediaType.TEXT_XML).get(String.class));
// The HTML
System.out.println(service.path("rest").path("hello").a
ccept(MediaType.TEXT_HTML).get(String.class));}
private static URI getBaseURI() {
return
UriBuilder.fromUri("http://localhost:8088/MyREstworld")
.build();}}
```

In the above code, we are invoking Restful Web service which is located at local server (http://localhost:8088/MyREstworld/rest/hello). We can call this Restful web service using traditional java code, but if we follow traditional way we cannot provide dynamic adaptability, reusability to our application. So, here we are using Aspect Oriented Programming to provide/support dynamic adaptability and reusability.

RestAspect is an AOP code; it will cross cut read method of Test class. The client write base code and run that code, here aspect weaver will link aspect code and base code together and then generate a class file which is referred as modified code as shown in Fig.4. Here hello Restful web service will support 3different formats to display data on the browser those are plain text, XML and HTML. Client can send request in any format; this service will give response to the user. Like Web Services, no need specify wsdl and soap formats to send request and to get response.

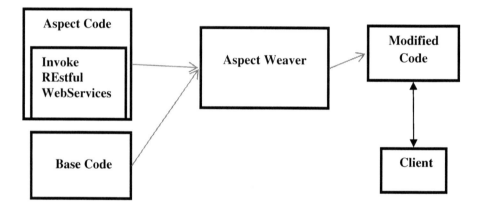

Fig. 4. Invocation of Restful Web Services using AOP

Everyone can use this aspect code by cross cutting their methods in pointcuts and dynamically change Rest full web service end point in before advice as mentioned in above code. Hence we strongly say that AOP always supports reusability and dynamic adaptability [16]. We practically proved above all things using Eclipse platform.

6   Efficiency of AOP by CPU Profiling

The comparison of the differences between AOP and OOP shows results that indicates influence of application quality, especially performance. To demonstrate this Web Service invocation is applied and the CPU profiling data is collected from IDE. It took 4.81 ms to execute the program without AOP and 3.96 ms to execute when AOP is applied.

Here, we have observed practically that execution time analysis comparison of Web Services and RESTful web services invocation without AOP and With AOP by run the above code seven times shows in Fig 5. Both resulted the same memory usage.

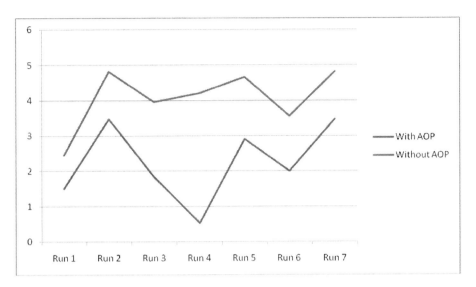

Fig. 5. Execution time analysis of Web Service invocation without and with AOP

7 Conclusion

Aspect Oriented Programming supports reuse of existing programs in new, dynamic environments even though the specific characteristics of such new environments were not necessarily anticipated during the original design of the programs. In particular, many existing programs, not designed to be adaptable, are being ported to dynamic wireless environments, or hardened in other ways to support autonomic computing. We describe an approach how aspect oriented software development (AOSD) is useful to resolve the tangled concerns, reusability and dynamic adaptation specifically for Aspect Weaving in Web Services and Restful Web Services Invocation. The solution extends the existing web services infrastructure to a distributed aspect infrastructure. We demonstrate the use of AspectJ in distributed environment, which is java based tool to encapsulate the crosscutting concerns like distribution, tracing, profiling and exception handling. In future, we will implement autonomic web services using aspect oriented programming and we will also address how Agent based java program communicates with aspect oriented java program with web services.

References

1. Kephart, J.O., Chess, D.M.: The vision of autonomic computing. IEEE Computer 36(1), 41–50 (2003)
2. Alonso, G., Casati, F., Kuno, H., Machiraju, V.: WebServices: Concepts, Architectures, Applications. Springer, Heidelberg (2004)
3. Fielding, R.T.: Architectural Styles and the Design of Network-based Software Architectures, Doctoral dissertation, University of California, Irvine (2000)

4. Kiczales, G., Lamping, J., Mendhekar, A.: Aspect-oriented programming. In: Aksit, M., Auletta, V. (eds.) ECOOP 1997. LNCS, vol. 1241, pp. 220–242. Springer, Heidelberg (1997)
5. Cibrán, M.A., Verheecke, B.: Modularizing Web Services Management with AOP. In: Cardelli, L. (ed.) ECOOP 2003. LNCS, vol. 2743. Springer, Heidelberg (2003)
6. Charfi, A., Schmeling, B., Heizenreder, A., Mezini, M.: Reliable, Secure and Transacted Web Service Compositions with AO4BPEL. In: Proceedings of the 2nd International Conference on Service Oriented Computing, ICSOC 2004, New-York, USA (2004)
7. Kongdenfha, W., Saint-Paul, R., Benatallah, B., Casati, F.: An Aspect-Oriented Framework for Service Adaptation. In: Dan, A., Lamersdorf, W. (eds.) ICSOC 2006. LNCS, vol. 4294, pp. 15–26. Springer, Heidelberg (2006)
8. Haas, H.: Reconciling Web services and REST services (Keynote Address). In: Proc. of the 3rd IEEE Europe Conference on Web Services (ECOWS 2005), Växjö, Sweden (November 2005)
9. zur Muehlen, M., Nickerson, J.V., Swenson, K.D.: Developing Web services choreography standards - the case of REST vs. SOAP. Decision Support Systems 40(1), 9–29 (2005)
10. Laskey, K., Hègaret, P.L., Newcomer, E. (eds.): Workshop on Web of Services for Enterprise Computing. W3C (February 2007)
11. Richardson, L., Ruby, S.: RESTful Web Services. O'Reilly, Sebastopol (2007)
12. Fielding, R.T., Taylor, R.N.: Principled Design of the Modern Web Architecture. ACM Transactions on Internet Technology (TOIT) (New York: Association for Computing Machinery) (2005)
13. Pautasso, C., Zimmermann, O., Leymann, F.: RESTful Web Services vs. Big Web Services: Making the Right Architectural Decision. In: 17th International World Wide Web Conference (WWW 2008), Beijing, China (2008)
14. Berners-Lee, T., Fielding, R., Masinter, L.: Uniform Resource Identifier (URI): generic syntax. IETF RFC 3986 (January 2005)
15. Laddad, R.: AspectJ in Action. Manning Publications Co., Greenwich (2003)
16. Avgustinov, P., Christensen, A.S., Hendren, L., Kuzins, S., Lhoták, J., Lhoták, O., de Moor, O.: An Extensible AspectJ Compiler. In: Proceedings of the 4th International Conference on Aspect-Oriented Software Development, pp. 87–98. ACM Digital Library (2005)
17. Snell, J.: Resource-oriented vs. activity-oriented Web services. IBM Developer Works (October 2004)
18. Landre, E., Wesenberg, H.: Rest versus soap: as architectural style for web services. In: 5th International OOPSLA Workshop on SOA & Web Services Best Practices (2007)
19. Zarras, A.: A comparison for middleware infrastructures. Journal of Object Technology 3(5), 103–123 (2004)
20. Zimmermann, O., Grundler, J., Tai, S., Leymann, F.: Architectural decisions and patterns for transactional worlflows in SOA. In: Krämer, B.J., Lin, K.-J., Narasimhan, P. (eds.) ICSOC 2007. LNCS, vol. 4749, pp. 81–93. Springer, Heidelberg (2007)

A Novel Way of Invoking Agent Services Using Aspect Oriented Programming via Web Service Integration Gateway

Vishnuvardhan Mannava[1] and T. Ramesh[2]

[1] Department of Computer Science and Engineering, KL University,
Vaddeswaram 522502, A.P., India
vishnu@klce.ac.in
[2] Department of Computer Science and Engineering, National Institute of Technology,
Warangal, 506004, A.P., India
rmesht@nitw.ac.in

Abstract. Web services have gained popularity today for enabling universal interoperability among applications. In many scenarios, allowing software agents to access and control Web Services is important and hence the integration between these two platforms. In this paper, we focus on technical aspects of an integration framework of Web Services and Jade agent platform using Aspect Oriented Programming. Agent creates a service and publishes their services in UDDI as Web service. We are communicating with agents using Aspect Oriented Programming to access their services via Web Service Integration Gateway (WSIG). We propose an approach that Aspect weaving during invocation of Agent services using AOP. We have used AspectJ; Java based language to create aspects in Eclipse supported framework, and JADE: is a frame work to create and publish Agent services as web services using WSIG.

Keywords: Aspect Oriented Programming, Agent Oriented Programming, Software Agent, Web services, FIPA, and AspectJ.

1 Introduction

A software application is adaptable, reusable and distributed if it can change its behavior dynamically (at run time) in response to transient changes in its execution environment or to permanent changes in its requirements and everyone can use application functionalities among the world. Developing and maintaining adaptable, reusable and distributed software are nontrivial task. An adaptable application comprises functional code that implements the business logic of the application and supports its imperative behavior, and adaptive code that implements the adaptation logic of the application and supports its adaptive behavior. The difficulty in developing and maintaining adaptable applications is largely due to an inherent property of the adaptive code, that is, the adaptive code tends to crosscut the functional code. Example crosscutting concerns include QoS, mobility, fault tolerance, recovery, security, self auditing, and energy consumption. Even more challenging than developing new adaptable applications is enhancing existing

D.C. Wyld et al. (Eds.): NeCoM/WeST/WiMoN 2011, CCIS 197, pp. 675–684, 2011.
© Springer-Verlag Berlin Heidelberg 2011

applications, such that they execute effectively in new, dynamic environments not envisioned during their design and development. For example, many non-adaptive applications are being ported to mobile computing environments, where they require dynamic adaptation.

This paper reports on the results of preliminary work conducted by members of the IEEE FIPA Agents and Web Services Integration (AWSI) Working Group. This group was formed shortly after the creation of IEEE FIPA with the remit to specify the minimum infrastructure required to facilitate interaction between FIPA compliant agents with W3C compliant Web services. The purpose of this paper is to both inform the community of progress and invocation of particular service using outside technologies. Here we are using Aspect Oriented Programming (AOP) to invoke Agent Service. Our experience with this system have been proved that use of AspectJ[14] language helps to modularize the crosscutting concerns and improved the productivity, reusability, dynamic adaptability, maintainability and code independence in our invoking Agent services using AOP via WSIG.

Our paper is organized as follows. We review related work in section 2. Section 3 we describe Agent Service Technology. Section 4 describes the AOP paradigm and the need for a distributed framework to address the problem. In Section 5, we propose the solution framework with a case study. Try to show the Efficiency of AOP by CPU Profiling in section 6. Section 7, Try to show the affect of 'Aspects' on application through Eclipse's Aspect Visualizer. We conclude the paper in section 8 with possible future directions.

2 Related Work

The agent paradigm assumes interaction between agents and services, of which web services are specific instances. This paper addresses how this interaction can be structured. Integration of web services with agent applications can be considered at two levels: semantic level and management level. Independently, both Greenwood et al. [5] and Shafiq et al. [11] introduce a web service gateway as a (FIPA compliant) solution to web service integration, connecting agents and web services transparently. The operation is fully automatic, allowing web services to invoke agent services and vice versa by translating message encodings and service descriptions between the two technologies. The gateways provides service directory transformation (directory facilitator–UDDI), service description transformation (agent description–WSDL), and communication protocol transformation (ACL–SOAP). An enhanced version of the web service gateway of Greenwood et al. [5] allows agents and web clients to invoke atomic services and composition patterns.

WS2JDADE [6] provides a similar framework for agent–web service integration, but also includes facilities to deploy and control web services as agent services at runtime for deployment flexibility and active service discovery. So to presents a web service based message transport service (WSMTS) [7]. The message transport service enables agents to interact through the web with web services and other agents. WSMTS is a FIPA compliant communication framework where messages are grounded using web services standards (e.g., SOAP, WS-Addressing, etc.). The WSMTS not only allows for web service accessibility as with the other proposals, but provides the possibility to perform complex interaction patterns using SOAP between agents and other agents or Web Services. Dan et al. [16] present a framework for differentiated levels of service through automated management and SLAs. Machiraju et al. [20] introduce architecture for federated service management, which targets management of web services that interact across administrative domains (and involves multiple stakeholders). The potential of web service gateways for consumer side web service management has, however, not yet fully explored. Sahai et al. [18] have also identified this problem: customer side measurement has been neglected relying solely on measurements on the server side. In their article, they propose an automated and distributed SLA monitoring engine to obtain measurements from multiple sites to guarantee SLAs. Ma et al. [19] designed a Web Service Offerings Infrastructure (WSOI) by extending Apache Axis.

3 Agent Service Technology

From 1997 until present FIPA has produced a set of specifications [7] describing various aspects related to the lifecycle support of software agents.

3.1 FIPA Agent Technology

FIPA specifies the FIPA-ACL (Agent Communication Language) language which is used to express messages and allows the specific message content to be expressed using different content languages such as FIPA-SL or FIPA-KIF. FIPA-ACL is grounded in speech act theory resulting in typed messages which represent the action, or performative, the message performs.

FIPA-ACL defines 22 of these performatives, otherwise known as communicative acts, with some of the most commonly used being inform, request, agree, not understood, and refuse. These capture the essence of most forms of basic communication. It is stated in the FIPA standards that to be fully compliant an agent must be able to receive any FIPA-ACL communicative act message and at the very least respond with a not-understood message if the received message cannot be processed. Additionally, based on these communicative acts FIPA defines a set of interaction protocols, each consisting of a sequence of communicative acts to coordinate multi-message actions, such the contract net for establishing agreements and several types of auctions. A critical choice to be made by this integration work is which of these per formatives should be supported within the context of agent to Web service interactions. As Web services conforming to the WSA stack are essentially invokable remote procedures that may return a response, the minimum subset of performatives would consist of Request and Inform used within the context of the FIPA Request interaction protocol.

3.2 JADE WSIG

The JADE Web Services Integration Gateway [4], WSIG, is an open source add-on for the FIPA 2000 compliant JADE platform. The WSIG supports registration and discovery of WSA Web services by JADE agents, registration and discovery of JADE Agents and agent services by Web service clients, automatic and bi-directional cross-translation of UDDI directory entries into DF directory entries and vice versa, invocation of Web services by JADE agents, and invocation of JADE Agent services by Web services. Fig. 1 shows the WSIG, adds a specialized Gateway Agent to a JADE Main Container which acts as the interface point between the agent system and third party Web service technology including a UDDI repository and Axis Web server.

The DF of the hosting JADE agent platform and a third party UDDI directory expose the standard actions of register, deregister, modify and search. All register, deregister and modify actions performed on either repository are automatically echoed onto the counterpart repository, i.e., if an agent service is de-registered from the platform DF, the Gateway Agent will ensure that the corresponding tModel is removed from the UDDI repository. This ensures that the two repositories remain consistent. The WSIG Gateway Agent is responsible for

- Receiving and translating agent service registrations from the DF into corresponding WSDL descriptions and registering these with the UDDI repository as tModels. This also applies to de-registrations and modifications;
- Receiving and translating Web service operation registrations from the UDDI repository into corresponding ACL descriptions and registering these with the DF. This also applies to de-registrations and modifications;
- Receiving and processing Web service invocation requests received from JADE agents. This includes retrieving the appropriate tModel from the UDDI repository, translating the invocation message into SOAP and sending it to the specified Web service. Any response from the Web service will be translated back into ACL and sent to the originating JADE agent;
- Receiving and processing agent service invocation requests received from Web service clients. Processing includes retrieving the appropriate tModel from the UDDI repository, translating the invocation message into ACL and sending it to the specified agent. Any response from the agent will be translated back into SOAP and sent to the originating Web service.

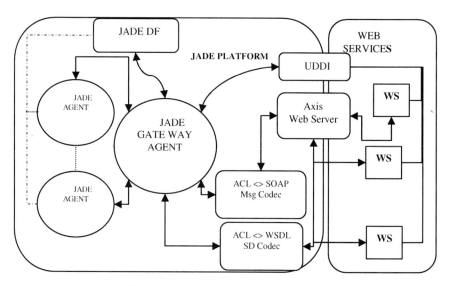

Fig. 1. Web Service Integration Gateway

To invoke a Web service, a JADE agent first seeks its service description in the JADE DF, and then sends an invocation request to the Gateway Agent. To invoke a JADE agent service a Web service first seeks its service description in the UDDI (or otherwise, be provided the description), and then sends an invocation request to the Gateway Agent via the Axis Web server. The JADE WSIG requires no alteration to existing FIPA of WSA-related specifications.

4 Aspect Oriented Programming

Aspect-oriented programming (AOP) [1] has been proposed as a technique for improving separation of concerns in software AOP builds on previous technologies, including procedural programming and object-oriented programming that have already made significant improvements in software modularity.

The central idea of AOP is that while the hierarchical modularity mechanisms of object-oriented languages are extremely useful, they are inherently unable to modularize all concerns of interest in complex systems. Instead, we believe that in the implementation of any complex system, there will be concerns that inherently crosscut the natural modularity of the rest of the implementation. AOP does for crosscutting concerns what OOP has done for object encapsulation and inheritance. It provides language mechanisms that explicitly capture crosscutting structure as shown in Fig. 2.

This makes it possible to program crosscutting concerns in a modular way, and achieve the usual benefits of improved modularity: simpler code that is easier to develop and maintain, and that has greater potential for reuse. We call a well modularized crosscutting concern an aspect.

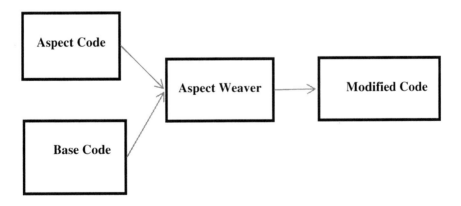

Fig. 2. Weaving of Aspect on source code

5 Case Study

```
Invocation of Agent Service Using AOP
public aspect AgentWs  {
//cross cut multiplication method of Addws class
```

```
pointcut mul(Addws ad,float a,float b):call(public float
Addws.mul(..))
  && target(ad)
  && args(a,b);
//Invoking Multiplication service of Agent
before (Addws ad, float a,float b):mul(ad,a,b){
try{System.out.println("entering      to     call     Agent
services");
String
endpoint="http://localhost:8088/wsig/ws/MathFunctions?wsd
l";
Service service = new Service();
Call call = (Call) service.createCall();
call.setTargetEndpointAddress( new java.net.URL(endpoint)
);call.setOperationName("multiplication");
  System.out.println("entered into webservices");
call.setOperationName(new
QName("http://localhost:8088/wsig/ws/MathFunctions/","mul
tiplication"));
  String ret =(String)call.invoke( new Object[] { a,b} );
  float res=Float.parseFloat(ret);
  System.out.println("Sent    "+a+","+b+"   got    result="+
res);}
  catch (Exception e) {
  System.out.println("Exception cured:\n"+e);
  }}}
```

In the above code, we are invoking Agent Web service which is located at local server (http://localhost:8088/wsig/ws/MathFunctions?wsdl). We can call this web service using traditional java code, but if we follow traditional way we cannot provide dynamic adaptability, reusability to our application. So, here we are using Aspect Oriented Programming to provide/support dynamic adaptability and reusability.

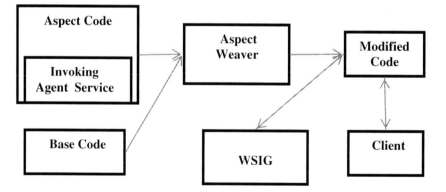

Fig. 3. Invocation of Agent Service using AOP via WSIG

AgentWs is an AOP code; it will cross cut mul method of Addws class. The client write base code and run that code, here aspect weaver will link aspect code and base code together and then generate a class file which is referred as modified code as shown in Fig.3.

Here WSIG will provide communication between AOP and AgentOP. Client can send request for Agent service in traditional way. Aspect code will call for Agent service via WSIG. WSIG will search for requested services is available or not in UDDI. If desired service found then send the request to Directory Facilitator (DF). DF will search for agent who provides specified service. If agent found then send client request details. Agent will process the request and send response to DF vice versa. Everyone can use this aspect code by cross cutting their methods in pointcuts and dynamically change Agent service end point in before advice as mentioned in above code. Hence we strongly say that AOP always supports reusability and dynamic adaptability [13]. We proved practically above all things in Eclipse platform.

6   Efficiency of AOP by CPU Profiling

In some cases, flexibility and reusability of the design comes with the price of decreased efficiency. At the same time, performance is often a key quality attribute of distributed applications. It is therefore beneficial to investigate whether AOP may influence performance of applications. The comparison of the differences between AOP and OOP shows results that indicates influence of application quality, especially performance. To demonstrate this Agent Service calling is applied and the CPU profiling data is collected. It took 4.81 ms to execute the program without AOP and 3.16 ms to execute when AOP is applied.

6.1   Profiling Statistics before Applying AOP

The main method execution took 4.81 ms with 1 invocation. The below figure 4 shows that the complete details of the invocations and time spent by the processor in each time.

6.2   Profiling Statistics after Applying AOP

The main method execution took 3.16 ms with 1 invocation of each method defined. The below figure 4 shows that the complete details of the invocations and the time spent by the processor in each method. By comparing these two call tree graphs we can say that the code having the AOP cross cutting is more efficient in terms of computation power usage. These both resulted has the same for memory usage.

Here, we have observed practically that execution time analysis comparison of JADE Agent Service invocation without AOP and With AOP by run the above code seven times shows in Fig 4. Both result the same memory usage.

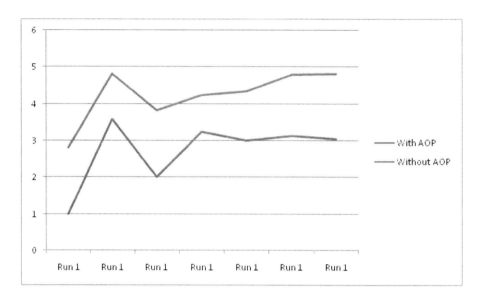

Fig. 4. Execution time analysis for Web Service Calling without AOP and with AOP

7   Eclipse's Aspect Visualiser

Aspect Visualiser is an extensible plugin that can be used to visualize anything that can be represented by bars and stripes. It began as the Aspect Visualiser, which was a part of the popular AspectJ Development Tools (AJDT) plug-in. It was originally created to visualize how aspects were affecting classes in a project. As in Fig. 5 we have shown the member view of distribution, tracing, and profiling aspects with class AgentWs in Addws class. Here bars represent classes and aspects in AOP code and black colored stripes represent advised join points in the execution flow of AOP code, which were matched with defined pointcuts in various aspects.

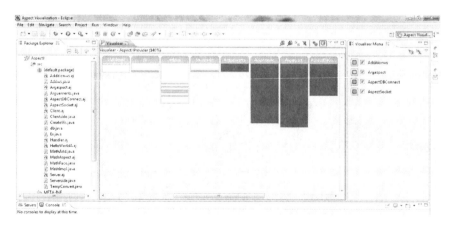

Fig. 5. Aspect Visualizer member view

8 Conclusion

Aspect Oriented Programming supports reuse of existing programs in new, dynamic environments even though the specific characteristics of such new environments were not necessarily anticipated during the original design of the programs. In this paper we are using Aspect Oriented Programming to invoke Agent services via WSIG. Any Program can reuse this aspect code to invoke Agent service. Practically we proved the reusable concept in the above case study. The interoperability of the web service gateway with web service management frameworks as described by Dan et al. [16] and Machiraju et al. [20] will be further studied. Also the inclusion of the other two transormation (directory facilitator–UDDI and agent description–WSDL) is future work. Finally, a more in-depth study into the web services offerings language (WSOL) and the WSAgreements will be performed.

References

1. Kiczales, G., Lamping, J., Mendhekar, A.: Aspect-oriented programming. In: Aksit, M., Auletta, V. (eds.) ECOOP 1997. LNCS, vol. 1241, pp. 220–242. Springer, Heidelberg (1997)
2. Booth, D., Haas, H., McCabe, F., Newcomer, E., Champion, M., Ferris, C., Orchard, D.: Web Service Architecture: W3C Working Group Note (February 2004)
3. Christensen, E., Curbera, F., Meredith, G., Weerawarana, S.: Web Services Description Language (WSDL) 1.1 (March 2001)
4. Greenwood, D., Calisti, M.: Engineering Web Service-Agent Integration. In: Proceedings of the IEEE International Conference on Systems, Man and Cybernetics, The Hague, Netherlands, pp. 1918–1925 (2004)
5. Greenwood, D., Nagy, J., Calisti, M.: Semantic enhancement of a web service integration gateway. In: Proceedings of the Workshop on Service-Oriented Computing and Agent-Based Engineering (SOCABE 2005), Utrecht, The Netherlands (July 2005)
6. Nguyen, X.T., Kowalczyk, R.: WS2JADE: Integrating web service with JADE agents. In: Huang, J., Kowalczyk, R., Maamar, Z., Martin, D., Müller, I., Stoutenburg, S., Sycara, K. (eds.) SOCASE 2007. LNCS, vol. 4504, pp. 147–159. Springer, Heidelberg (2007)
7. Soto, E.L.: Agent communication using web services, a new FIPA message transport service for JADE. In: Petta, P., Müller, J.P., Klusch, M., Georgeff, M. (eds.) MATES 2007. LNCS (LNAI), vol. 4687, pp. 73–84. Springer, Heidelberg (2007)
8. Dickinson, I., Wooldridge, M.: Agents are not (just) web services: Considering BDI agents and web services. In: Proceedings of the Workshop on Service-Oriented Computing and Agent-Based Engineering (SOCABE 2005), Utrecht, the Netherlands (July 2005)
9. Mitra, N.: Simple Object Access Protocol (SOAP) 1.2 Part 0: Primer (June 2003)
10. Clement, L., Hatley, A., von Riegen, C., Rogers, T.: UDDI Specification Version 3.0.2 (October 2004)
11. Shafiq, M., Ding, Y., Fensel, D.: Bridging multi agent systems and web services: Towards interoperability between software agents and semantic web services. In: Proceedings of the 10th IEEE International Conference on Enterprise Distributed Object Computing (EDOC 2006), Hong Kong, China, pp. 85–96 (October 2006)

12. Ortiz, G., Hernandez, J.: Clemente, and P.J.: Decoupling Non-Functional Properties in Web-Services: As Aspect-Oriented Approach. In: Proceedings of the 2nd International Conference on Service Oriented Computing, ICSOC 2004, New-York, USA (2004)
13. Avgustinov, P., Christensen, A.S., Hendren, L., Kuzins, S., Lhoták, J., Lhoták, O., de Moor, O.: An Extensible AspectJ Compiler. In: Proceedings of the 4th International Conference on Aspect-Oriented Software Development, pp. 87–98. ACM Digital Library (2005)
14. Laddad, R.: AspectJ in Action. Manning Publications Co., Greenwich (2003)
15. Sadjadi, S.M., McKinley, P.K., Cheng, B.H.C.: Transparent Shaping of Existing Software to Support Pervasive and Autonomic Computing. ACM, New York (2005)
16. Dan, A., Davis, D., Keamey, R., Keller, A., King, R.: Web services on demand: WSLA-driven automated management. IBM Systems Journal 43(1), 136–158 (2004)
17. Jin, L.-J., Machiraju, V., Sahai, A.: Analysis on service level agreement of web services. Technical Report HPL-2002-180, HP Laboratories, Palo Alto, CA (June 2002)
18. Sahai, A., Machiraju, V., Sayal, M., van Moorsel, A., Casati, F.: Automated SLA monitoring for web services. In: Proceedings of the 13th IFIP/IEEE International Workshop on Distributed Systems, Montreal, Canada, pp. 28–41 (October 2002)
19. Ma, W., Tosic, V., Esfandiari, B., Pagurek, B.: Extending Apache Axis for monitoring of web services offerings. In: Proceedings of the IEEE EEE 2005 International Workshop on Business Services Networks, Hong Kong, China (March 2005)
20. Machiraju, V., Sahai, A., van Moorsel, A.: Web services management network: An overlay network for federated service management. In: IFIP/IEEE Eighth International Symposium on Integrated Network Management, pp. 351–364 (March 2003)

The Goal of Existing Security Mechanisms in 3G

Najiya Sultana and S.S. Sarangdevat

Rajasthan Vidhyapeeth University, Udaipur, India
saara.sultan@gmail.com, drsssarangdevat@yahoo.com

Abstract. Security has become one major concern in wireless networking, with the risk of hampering or delaying the migration of value-critical services towards wireless platforms (e.g., ecommerce, e-banking). Securing wireless networks poses unique research challenge. In this paper, we survey the state-of-the-art approach to providing security for wireless networking paradigm, namely 3G Cellular WWAN. We identify the security threats as well as examine the current solutions. We further discuss open issues and identify future directions.

Keywords: 3G, security, DoS, WLAN, TCP/IP, UMTS.

1 Introduction

The 3G networks are the next-generation wireless telecommunication networks that target wide area wireless data services for global subscribers. Several 3G networks became operational since 2003. In recent years, wireless networking has been experiencing an explosive growth. Wireless networks offer attractive flexibility and coverage to both network operators and users. Ubiquitous network coverage, for both local and wide areas, can be provided without the excessive costs of deploying and maintaining the wires. Mobility support is another salient feature of wireless networks, which grants the users not only "anytime, anywhere" network access but also the freedom of roaming while networking. Recent advances in wireless communication technology have offered ever increasing data rates. In this article we focus on popular wireless networking paradigm, namely 3G Cellular networks. To protect the data delivery functionality of Network, we focus on the following two security goals:

• *Information Security*, i.e., to provide confidentiality, integrity, authentication, and non-repudiation for two entities that communicate with each other.

• *Network Security*, i.e., to protect the networking system as a whole and sustain its capability to provide connectivity between communicating entities.

Although most of the security threats against the TCP/IP stack in a wired network are equally applicable to an IP-based wireless network, the latter possesses a number of unique vulnerabilities which make it more challenging to secure:

• *Open Wireless Access Medium*: The security threats of message eavesdropping and injection are universe in any network; however they are particularly severe in wireless

D.C. Wyld et al. (Eds.): NeCoM/WeST/WiMoN 2011, CCIS 197, pp. 685–693, 2011.
© Springer-Verlag Berlin Heidelberg 2011

networks due to the open wireless medium. With off-the shelf hardware's and little efforts, an attacker can intercept and inject traffic through a wireless channel. There is no physical barrier to separate the attacker from the network, as is the case in wired networks.

• *Limited Bandwidth*: Wireless networks are particularly vulnerable to Denial-of-Service (DoS) attacks due to their limited bandwidth and in-band signaling. Although the wireless channel capacity is continually increasing, the spatial contention problem poses a fundamental limit on network capacity. One can deploy redundant fibers, but everyone must share the same wireless spectrum.

• *System Complexity*: Generally wireless networks are far more complex than their wired counterparts due to the special needs for mobility support and efficient channel utilization. Each piece of complexity added into the system can incur potential security vulnerability, especially in a system with a large user population and a complex infrastructure, such as 3G networks. Due to the open wireless medium, wireless networks require explicit mechanisms to control the membership; the absence of a stringent admission control mechanism may open the door for potential security threats. Recent years have witnessed a lot of efforts on wireless security in both academia and industry, with the outcome of a rich body of proposed solutions. In this article we assess security threats and summarize representative proposal in the context of 3G networks.

2   Security of 3G Networks

In this section we examine the security threats and countermeasures in 3G networks. We first describe the general things of 2G and 3G networks, and then discuss the security threats. Finally we summarize the existing security mechanisms in UMTS, and outline the ongoing work.

1. From 2G to 3G

Public wide-area wireless networks are now migrating from the second-generation systems (2G), developed for low-bandwidth circuit-switched (CS) services, towards third-generation (3G) systems, designed to support higher data rates and packet-switched (PS) services. Several 3G systems are being developed evolving from different 2G roots and with different radio technologies. Despite lack of mutual compatibility, all 3G systems share the same fundamental structure and functionalities, therefore most of the security concepts presented here are common to all 3G platforms [01], [02]. Also we will focus here on the Universal Mobile Telecommunication System (UMTS) for sake of simplicity.

During the migration path from GSM to UMTS, an intermediate phase is General Packet Radio Service (GPRS). With GPRS, the existing GSM Radio Access Network (RAN) is augmented with packet-switching capabilities for data services, and a new packet-switched core network (PS-CN) is added in parallel to the legacy circuit-switched core network (CS-CN) to carry data traffic. Along with the evolved GSM/GPRS RAN, PS-CN will eventually connect to the new UMTS Radio Access Network (UTRAN) based on WCDMA.

The information servers play an important role in the control procedures of 2.5G/3G systems. Among them, the Home Location Register (HLR) maintains all subscriber information's, including location tracking at the SGSN level, while the Authentication Center (AuC) is responsible for the subscriber authentication. The signaling procedure involve communication between the SGSN/GGSN and HLR/AuC. Additionally, a numbers of other IP-based servers (e.g., DNS, DHCP, RADIUS, proxies, etc.) find place within PS-CN for control and management procedures [03].

In 2G/3G networks, each active Mobile Station (MS) embeds two components that are physically and logically distinct: a software/hardware *terminal* (i.e., a cellphone, smartphone, PDA, palmtop, laptop), and a *Subscriber Identity Module* (SIM), which is a tamper-resistant smart-card storing a unique identifier (the IMSI) and associated secret keys. The UMTS SIM (USIM) is endowed with internal processing, and the cryptographic algorithms involved in authentication are executed directly in it since it is the USIM, not the terminal, to be authenticated. The USIM is issued by the network operator. Its secret keys are known to the home AuC, and a trust relationship is in place between the USIM and the AuC. This makes the administrative separation between the terminals and the network less sharp than in other networks such as WLANs.

2 Security Threats

a) Threats to Information Security: USIM is typically associated to a single subscriber, eavesdropping the signaling messages may reveal the subscriber's identity and physical location, which harms the user privacy beyond the content of the data communication.

b) Threats to Network Security: The IP-based 3G networks and terminals are vulnerable to all traditional attacks against the TCP/IP stack. There are specific attacks associated to the intimate nature of a cellular wireless network (e.g., signaling attacks) -

i) Attacks from external wired networks, typically from the Internet (Gi interface)
ii) Attacks from other interconnected CNs (Gp interface)
iii) Attacks from the user plane of the RAN
iv) Attacks from the signaling plane of the RAN

A successful attack on an internal element of CN might have a dramatic impact on a large portion of the network. For example, the attacker can simply inject massive unsolicited traffic towards the terminals. This threat is more severe in 3G networks than in wired networks because:

• The per-cell radio capacity is scarce and shared. Massive traffic to one terminals impacts the services of other users in the same cell, representing a sort of "soft DoS" attack.

• Massive traffic might induce an additional overload on the control plane. For example, with mobile-terminated services, an incoming packet towards an attached terminal triggers a paging procedure over a vast area, which is iterated a few times if the terminal does not respond.

• The 3G users are typically billed per-volume, thus unsolicited traffic causes billing problems resulting in a lower level of perceived service reliability. Such "over-billing attacks" apply to any network implementing volume based billing.

Attacks from the user plane of the RAN might be critical since the terminals communicate with internal CN elements with IP-based protocol stack, like GGSN, proxies, WAP server, etc. From it, the intruder can attempt to gain access to even more critical elements (e.g., AAA system, OAM system). These kinds of attacks, which ultimately exploit loopholes or other software flaws, have been demonstrated in laboratory at least for 2.5G [08] [05].

Another security threat is the Distributed-DoS (DDoS) attacks that send massive amount of malicious IP traffic from the terminal side (e.g., SYN storm, malformed packets), aiming at overloading the network elements or terminals. Generally the network stability might be hampered by macroscopic volumes of malicious traffic, regardless on whether the network elements are directly targeted or not. For example, large worm infections targeted at the terminals might generate large volumes of unwanted traffic, e.g. TCP-SYN probes and backscatter ICMP traffic [06], that collectively builds up a traffic aggregate that deviates   from the "typical" traffic characteristics along several dimensions - e.g. packet size, address distribution, timing, etc. As a result, the network is exposed to a completely different and unexpected traffic pattern at the macroscopic level, and there is no *a priori* guarantee that all network elements will operate correctly in these new conditions. The proof-of-concept of such potential was given in 2001 during the propagation of the Code Red worm, which *indirectly* caused troubles to several routers in the Internet [07], [08] despite the worm was not targeting network elements but just hosts. In principle, similar incidents might occur in 3G network as well.

Another type of potential attacks are those launched via signaling from the RAN. A specific feature of 2.5G/3G is the strong signaling interaction between a large population of terminals and a reduced number of network elements (e.g., BSC, SGSN), which is required primarily for mobility and resource management. The attackers might use malformed or iterated signaling procedure to launch DoS attempts targeting some network elements in the CN or in the RAN itself. In fact, several procedures require a considerable amount of resources - mainly processing power and memory state. In the worst case they might seek to evocate flaws in the network equipments, software bugs or misconfiguration, and drive them to crash.

In general, once that one portion of the network or piece of equipment has been impacted, it is possible to trigger a sequence of cascading failures which ultimately enlarge the scope of the damage in domino effect. Despite no concrete examples have been demonstrated in practice, the potential of latent cascading failures cannot be excluded *a priori* in large-scale systems with a highly complex web of internal interactions - which is exactly the case for a 3G network.

c) Practicality of Network Threats: So far we have presented a number of potential security threats for 3G networks. To launch attacks towards the CN, the attacker should have a deep insight into the specific equipments and an accurate knowledge of the network internals that are unlikely leaked outside the operator and vendor staff. For attacks from the RAN, it is unrealistic to expect that a single misbehaving terminal can impose a critical load, unless hitting a real loophole or triggering a cascade of failures. This is because of the intrinsic resource asymmetry between CN elements and terminals. The maximum signaling load that a terminal can generate is limited by one or more of the following factors:

- Capacity of the signaling or data radio channel
- Processing capacity of the handset
- Processing capacity of the USIM

To overcome the resource limitation of individual terminals, the attacker might have to set up a large pool of misbehaving terminals and attempt large-scale DDoS attacks. To overcome the radio bandwidth bottleneck, particularly of the signaling channels, the set of misbehaving terminals should be distributed over a large geographical area to access multiple cells. They can communicate via some other network (e.g., Internet), since the new generation of terminals tend to have multiple communication interfaces (e.g., a laptop with a GPRS/UMTS card plus legacy wired interfaces). For example, distant terminals could exploit this communication to share a single identity by connecting to a single USIM, then emulate large false mobility procedures. DDoS attacks might also be launched from a number of legitimate terminals that have been corrupted by malicious codes (virus, worms, trojans, backdoors, etc.).

An additional difficulty is associated with DoS attacks via signaling: they generally require hacking the low-layer logics of the terminal where the control plane modules are implemented, which is difficult since it is often implemented in firmware. Regarding DDoS attacks via signaling from infected terminals, to date there is no concrete evidence that a virus might take control of the low-layer logic and affect its signaling behavior. At most, it might indirectly trigger a high rate of legitimate procedures (e.g., attach/detach cycles, PDP-context activation). Other obstacles arise if the attacker seeks to put in place his own set of malicious terminals.

In summary, several features of 3G networks contribute to make the attacks difficult and costly to instruct. However, the security of 3G networks should not rely on such factors, which might eventually change in the future. For instance, in the short term the widespread popularity of 3G data cards for laptops will inevitably import inside the 3G networks all the kinds of malicious code that are currently present in the Internet, along with the associated risks outlined above. In the mid-term, future software platforms might make it easier to compromise the signaling behavior of the terminal, while a higher level of terminal homogeneity will extend the potential of large virus infections to handsets. In a longer term, the advancements in software defined radio [09] will perhaps make it possible to build (malicious) terminals by coupling some general purpose transceiver and some (malicious) protocol stack publicly downloadable from the Internet. Ultimately, the cost of an attack - whether it lies in the cost of setting up a suitable attacking hardware or in the cost of acquiring knowledge about internal network features - is not an obstacle any more in front of an economic motivation for the attack itself, which is likely to grow together with the economic value of the network.

3 UMTS Security Mechanisms

The security specifications in 3GPP follow the assessment of the threats and risks defined in [11]. As specified in [12], 3GPP security mechanisms are built on those adopted in GSM for back compatibility, with improvements to address the limitations and known weaknesses of GSM. For instance, ciphering algorithms in 2G were not robust enough and could be cracked [13], with key lengths perhaps too short and lazy key reuse. Some improvements were already achieved in GPRS by the adoption of the GEA algorithms [14], and in fact no cracks are available in the public literature for them. However, they are kept secret and did not pass the severe testing of the open cryptanalysis community; therefore there is no evidence of their real strength. With 3G a major improvement is introduced with this regard, with the adoption of public and provably robust ciphering algorithms, with longer cipher keys (up to 128 bits) which are frequently refreshed.

The set of cryptographic functions $f0 - f5^*$ used in the AKA are implemented exclusively in the USIM and in the AuC. By the standards they are operator specific, but 3GPP has developed a reference algorithm, called MILENAGE [15], which is in practice the recommended choice. It is built around the Rijndael block cipher, which was successively adopted in the AES standard.

The cryptographic functions $f8 - f9$ are implemented in the terminal equipment and in the RNC, and therefore must be standard in order to ensure interoperability between multiple, vendors. The 3GPP security architecture allows for up to 16 different algorithms for encryption and other 16 for integrity, but so far only one standard algorithm has been defined for encryption (UEA-1), and one for integrity (UIA-1), which is based on the KASUMI block cipher algorithm [16]. Both the Rijndael and Kasumi cryptographic algorithms recommended in 3GPP are considered solid enough at present [10].

While in 2G all critical information (cipher keys, authentication data, signaling messages) were transported without protection on the assumption that external access to the CN is intrinsically restricted, security mechanisms in UMTS are extended to the wired CN (from Rel4).

Finally, to protect the subscriber's identity and location privacy, a temporary identifier (Temporary Mobile Subscriber Identity, TMSI) is assigned by the SGSN to the MS. The TMSI is therefore used for subsequent identification in place of the primary subscriber identifier (i.e., the IMSI), which makes tracking a specific subscriber much more difficult.

4 Ongoing Work

Attacks from the Internet are similar to the external IP attacks that wired corporate networks have to face, and are typically counteracted by middle-boxes such as Intrusion Detection / Prevention Systems (IDS/IPS) and firewalls active on the TCP/IP stack. Certainly some customization is needed to adapt them to the specific characteristics of a 3G network: very large set of hosts (i.e., up to millions of terminals), highly dynamic addressing scheme (a new IP address is assigned for every connection and can be reused within few minutes) etc.

The issue of attacks from the RAN is still a unexplored area for public research. There are a number of studies on DoS/DDoS attacks and countermeasures in the wired networks, and many of these concepts can be applied to 3G networks as well. However, research on 3G-specific DoS/DDoS attacks is still in a pioneering phase. Despite some preliminary works have appeared [18], [19], limited to attacks on the data plane, they do not display real experiments nor analysis of real data. It is likely that experimental investigations are being carried on within industry laboratories [20], however to the best of our knowledge no results have been made public so far.

In assessing the security of 3G networks, one should keep in mind that they do not work in isolation. As a matter of fact the security mechanisms of GSM/GPRS are generally weaker than those specified for UMTS. Since the PS-CN is shared, attacks from one RAN might impact the other as well. Moreover, it is likely that in the near future certain level of integration will emerge between WLAN and 3G infrastructures, as these technologies are complementary under many aspects [21]. 3GPP has already taken the initiative to develop an interworking 3GWLAN architecture [22]. The 3G-WLAN integration involves a number of security issues which greatly depend on the exact form of such integration [23].

5 Summary

To date the security architecture based on cryptographic techniques defined by 3GPP is believed to adequately preserve information security in 3G. Nevertheless, several aspects regarding network security and robustness against malicious traffic have not yet received adequate attention by the research community. For instance, it has not yet been quantified the real exposure of the 3G network to certain types of incidents, including explicit attacks from the terminal side, both on the data plane and on the signaling, and other large-scale events like DDoS or worm infection. In the near future, the introduction of new services and new types of terminals will likely introduce new potential risks for the security of the network infrastructure, and the design of appropriate countermeasures require a ready understanding of the threats and a concrete assessment of the risks. The prominent key factor shaping the success of these efforts will be the availability of experimental data and measurements from real operational networks.

3 Conclusion

In assessing the security of 3G networks, the security mechanisms of GSM/GPRS are generally weaker than those specified for UMTS. Since the PS-CN is shared, attacks from one RAN might impact the other as well.

The cryptographic techniques are an essential ingredient in providing information security, and can serve as the first line of defense against network attacks (e.g., through authentication). However, cryptography alone does not suffice to secure a networking system. Given a specific security requirement, there is neither a systematic process to develop a suitable design nor an automatic way to gauge its vulnerability at this time. One major challenge in network security design is to address various dimensions of performance tradeoff including crypto strength, execution speed, computational overhead, communication cost, energy consumption, operational and configuration complexity, etc. A feasible solution must balance among these partially conflicting goals, yet a systematic way to evaluate these tradeoffs is still missing. Unfortunately, many state-of-the-art solutions still do not possess the properties that networking protocols deem necessary. Finally, the current security solutions are typically based on specific threat models, and operate explicitly or implicitly with a number of assumptions made on the networks. For example 3G network security designs assume a reliable core network. When unexpected failures or unanticipated threats occur, these security solutions are likely to collapse.

Proposed Future Research

Future software platforms might make it easier to compromise the signaling behavior of the terminal, while a higher level of terminal homogeneity will extend the potential of large virus infections to handsets. In a longer term, the advancements in software defined radio [17] will perhaps make it possible to build (malicious) terminals by coupling some general-purpose transceiver and some (malicious) protocol stack publicly downloadable from the Internet. Looking ahead into the future, two directions that need more research and development efforts to build a truly secure wireless networking system:

(a) *Critical evaluation:* In fact, we lack systematic evaluation methods and efforts in the Vulnerability analysis of the current solutions/standards. While the crypto strength of individual ciphering algorithms is relatively well understood, we have no formal analytical tools to assess a system security proposal. In particular, the analysis on the inter-dependency among various system components and security operations poses a major research challenge. (b) *Resilient security:* A truly resilient security solution needs to possess both robustness and resiliency. Most current solutions make idealistic assumptions on the network and individual components. It must be robust against wireless channel errors, transient/permanent network connectivity and topology changes, and user mobility. It must also be resilient against unanticipated attacks, operational errors such as misconfigurations, and compromised devices.

Security is an evolving process, as we have seen in the context of 2G/3G networks. New system vulnerabilities continue to be identified, and new security threats continue to arise. Accordingly new solutions must be developed and integrated into existing systems. The history of security has taught us that a perfectly secure system does not exist. We need continued development of newer and stronger ciphers, but more fundamentally we also need a better understanding of how to architect a secure system that can embrace the security evolution in a flexible, non-intrusive, and efficient manner.

References

1. Chen, J.-C., Zhang, T.: IP-Based Next-Generation Wireless Networks. Wiley, Chichester (2004)
2. Rose, G., Koien, G.: Access Security in CDMA 2000, including a Comparison with UMTS Access Security. IEEE Wireless Communications 11(1) (February 2004)
3. Bannister, J., Mather, P., Coope, S.: Convergence Technologies for 3G Networks: IP, UMTS, EGPRS and ATM. Wiley, Chichester (2004)
4. Whitehouse, O., Murphy, G.: Attacks and Counter Measures in 2.5G and 3G Cellular IP Networks. Research Report by stake Inc. (March 2004),
   http://www.atstake.com/research/reports
5. Whitehouse, O.: GPRS Wireless Security: Not Ready For Prime Time. Research Report by stake Inc. (June 2002), http://www.atstake.com/research/reports

6. Pang, R., Yegneswaran, V., Barford, P., Paxson, V., Peterson, L.: Characteristics of Internet Background Radiation. In: Proc. of the International Measurements Conference (IMC 2004), Taormina, Sicily, Italy (October 2004)
7. Zou, C.C., Gong, W., Towsley, D.: Code Red Worm Propagation Modeling and Analysis. In: Proc. of the 9th ACM Conference on Computer and Communications Security (CCS 2002), Washington, DC, USA (November 2002)
8. Cisco. Dealing with mallocfail and High CPU Utilization Resulting From the "Code Red" Worm (2001),
   http://www.cisco.com/warp/public/63/tscodredworm.pdf
9. GNU Software Radio, http://www.gnu.org/software/gnuradio
10. Koien, G.: An Introduction ro Access Security in UMTS. IEEE Wireless Communications 11(1) (February 2004)
11. 3GPP. TS 21.133. 3G Security. Security threats and requirements
12. 3GPP. TS 33.120. 3G Security. Security principles and objectives
13. Barkan, E., Biham, E., Keller, N.: Instant Ciphertext-Only Cryptanalysis of GSM Encrypted Communications. In: Boneh, D. (ed.) CRYPTO 2003. LNCS, vol. 2729, pp. 600–616. Springer, Heidelberg (2003)
14. 3GPP. TS 01.61. GPRS Ciphering Algorithm Requirements
15. 3GPP. TS 33.205. Specification of the MILEAGE Algorithm Set: an Example Algorithm Set for the 3GPP Authentication ad KEy Generation Functions f1 – f5*. Document 1: General (see also TS 33.206)
16. 3GPP. TS 35.202. 3G Security. Specification of the 3GPP Confidentiality and Integrity Algorithms; Document 2: KASUMI specification
17. GNU Software Radio, http://www.gnu.org/software/gnuradio
18. Huang, Q., Kobayashi, H., Liu, B.: Modeling of Distributed Denial of Service Attacks in Wireless Networks. In: IEEE Pacific Rim Conference on Communications Computers and Signal Processing, PACRIM (2003)
19. Park, J., Liu, F., Kuo, C.: Design of Detection System Against the Denial of Service Attack in 3G1x System. In: IEEE Globecom (2003)
20. METAWIN project, http://www.ftw.at/projects
21. Ahmavaara, K., Haverinen, H., Pichna, R.: Interworking Architecture Between 3GPP and WLAN Systems. IEEE Communications Magazine 14(11) (November 2003)
22. 3GPP. TS 23.234. 3G Security. 3GPP Systems to WLAN Intrworking: System Description
23. Koien, G., Haslestad, T.: Security Aspects of 3G-WLAN Interworking. IEEE Communications Magazine 14(11) (November 2003)

Extracting Concepts for Software Components

Ahmad Kayed[1], Nael Hirzalla[2], Hadeel Ahmad[3], and Enas Faisal[3]

[1] Computer Science, Computing Faculty, Fahad Bin Sultan University, KSA
[2] Computer Engneering, Computing Faculty, Fahad Bin Sultan University, KSA
[3] Computer Science, Amman, Jordan
{Kayed,nhirzallah}@fbsc.edu.sa,
hadeel_ahmed@hotmail.com, enas_faisal@yahoo.com

Abstract. Ontologies enhance searching information on the Web since they provide relationships and semantics among them. Ontology is required to describe the semantics of concepts and properties used in a web document. It is needed to describe products, services, processes and practices for any software components. Software components are essential part of software development process. Using component is essential in nowadays software development. This paper demonstrates several experiments to extract concepts to build ontologies that improve the description process for software components embedded in a web document. In this paper we built ontology (mainly concepts) for some software components then used them to solve some semantic problems. We collected many documents that describe components in .Net and Java from several and different resources. Concepts were extracted and used to decide which domain of any given description (semantic) is close or belong to.

Keywords: Ontology, Semantic Web, Component Description, Software Engineering.

1 Introduction

Ontologies are originated in philosophy, but they are increasingly being used in many scientific and engineering domains. The word ontology can be described as "an explicit specification of a conceptualization" [1]. Conceptualization refers to an abstract model of some phenomenon in the world that identifies that phenomenon's relevant concepts [2]. Ontologies have recently been introduced into higher-level information fusion where they provide a mechanism for describing and reasoning about sensor data, objects, relations and general domain theories [3], [4], [5], and [6]. Ontology is required to describe the semantics of concepts and properties used in web documents. It is needed to describe products, services, processes and practices in any e-application. In the last years there has been a growing recognition of the need to create explicit specifications of conceptualizing of the knowledge in several domains [7].

Software components are essential part of software development process. Wang and Qian [8] define software component as a piece of self-contained, self-deployable computer code with well-defined functionality, and it can be assembled with other components through its interface. According to them, a component is a program or a

D.C. Wyld et al. (Eds.): NeCoM/WeST/WiMoN 2011, CCIS 197, pp. 694–699, 2011.
© Springer-Verlag Berlin Heidelberg 2011

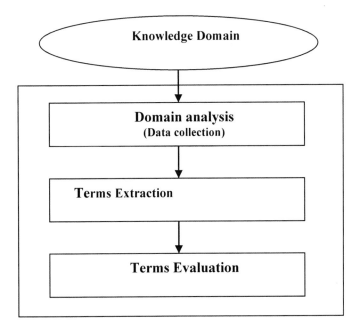

Fig. 1. Building Components Domain Ontology

collection of programs that can be compiled and made executable. Component technologies complying with the above definition include JavaBeans and enterprise Java Beans (EJB) from Sun Microsystems, COM (Component Object Model), DCOM (Distributed Component Object Model), and .NET components from Microsoft Corporation, and CORBA (Common Object Request Broker Architecture) components from the Object Management Group [8] [9]. Microsoft.NET and J2EE are development environments which provide solutions (ready components) to be used in many applications.

This paper extracts concepts to build ontologies in the domain of two well-known software components i.e. .Net and Java. KAON[1] (KArlsruhe ONtology) [10] is used to extract these concepts. KAON is a framework for the development of ontology-based applications. It is an open-source ontology management infrastructure targeted for business applications [11]. We collected many documents that describe components in .Net and Java from several and different resources. All these documents have been converted to text format. KAON has been used to extract concepts that describe these components. These concepts were used to decide the domain for any given description (semantic) that this semantic is close or belong to. This paper proves that ontologies promote common understanding to describe software components. This paper is organized as follows: section 2 describes our ontology building process, section 3 demonstrates our experiments, and section 4 concludes the paper.

---

[1] http://kaon.semanticweb.org/

2 Ontology Building Process

Kayed et al. [12] summarized the methodologies for building ontologies around three major stages of the ontology life cycle i.e. Building-Manipulating-Maintaining. In the building stage, four steps are needed: specification, conceptualization, formalization, and implementation. In the manipulation stage, an ontology query language should be provided for browsing and searching; efficient lattice operation; and domain specific operations. In the maintenance part, developers should be able to syntactically and lexically analyze the ontology, adding, removing, modifying definitions, and also translate from one language to another. The three stages are overlapped. For more details, see [12].

Building ontology to describe software components is not a simple task. We decided to build two domains ontologies: Java and .Net. To evaluate our work, we introduced a new relevancy measure. We used this measure into two ways: first to evaluate the ontology itself and then to evaluate the description of a concept. We called this measure **Relv(D, O)** which will be read as the relevancy of a description **D** according to an ontology **O**. **Relv(D, O)** counts how many concepts in a description **D** belongs to an ontology **O**. It calculates the number of words in a description (**D**) that match concepts in the provided ontology (**O**). A detailed formal definition of this measure will be published in another forum.

KAON's tool has been used in our experiments. It has the ability to change the frequency of concepts in the provided corpus which will give different number of concepts in the yield ontology. Increasing the frequency will reduce the number of concepts in the ontology. For that we applied our relevancy measure on several testing cases with five different frequencies (frequencies=10, 15, 20, 25, and 30).

3 Building Components Domain Ontology

Our methodology to build components domain ontology is summarized in three main steps: Domain analysis, data collection, and terms extraction (see figure 1).

Domain analysis was performed to analyse, identify, and determine source of knowledge to be used in extracting the concepts. Ontology requires minimal ontological commitment sufficient to support the intended knowledge sharing activities. It should describe the essential part of knowledge not the whole knowledge [10]. The task has been simplified by using existing resources that describe .NET and Java components. Data that describes the domain components has been collected from the web. All data has been integrated and converted to text-files to be used as corpuses for KAON's tool. One of the main obstacles was the lack of UDDI (Universal Description, Discovery and Integration) registered descriptions for both .Net and Java. The size of corpuses was too small to conduct the experiment. Therefore, the outcome concepts were not enough to proceed our experiment. It should be pointed out that KAON's tools depend on the most common terms and most frequent terms in a specific domain. We decided to expand our resources and go beyond the UDDI descriptions. The new corpuses were collected from several resources such as online reports, news, and academic research.

Data collection: Collecting the raw data is the essential step in building ontology in any domain. Our methodology was to collect as much as possible of the raw data that is related to both domains i.e. Java and .Net. Then use them as basis to our ontology. The Web was our main source of information about the descriptions of .NET, Java and their components. Microsoft, sun micro system, UDDI, and other sites were among our resources. The collection process has spanned for three months. The size of domain sources was 128 pages for .NET domain and 154 for Java. The resources for both domains were containing many codes which are not helpful in building ontologies. Documents were enhanced by removing irrelevant information and source codes. The comments and the descriptions of some codes were kept. The size of documents of both domains is made close to each other. Table 1 provides some samples of the raw data. This process spanned for another three months.

Table 1. Samples of the .Net and Java raw data

.NET Samples	Java Samples
NET is a A Microsoft operating system platform that incorporates applications, a suite of tools and services and a change in the infrastructure of the company's Web strategy. .NET Framework execute in a software environment that manages the program's runtime requirements. This runtime environment, which is also a part of the .NET Framework, is known as the Common Language Runtime (CLR). The CLR provides the appearance of an application virtual machine, so that programmers need not consider the capabilities of the specific CPU that will execute the program. The CLR also provides other important services such as security mechanisms, memory management, and exception handling. C# Validator2.aspx [Run Sample]	[View Source] LateBreaking Samples: Displaying Validation Errors	J# The System.Web.UI.WebControls namespace includes a Style base class that encapsulates common style attributes (additional style classes, such as TableStyle and TableItemStyle, inherit from this common base class). Many Web server controls expose properties of this type for specifying the style of individual rendering elements of the control. For example, the WebCalendar exposes many such style properties: DayStyle, WeekendDayStyle, TodayDayStyle, SelectedDayStyle, OtherMonthDayStyle, and NextPrevStyle. You can set individual properties of these styles using the subproperty syntax PropertyName-SubPropertyName, as the following sample demonstrates.

Terms extracting: After enhancing both domain resources, we developed our ontologies' concepts using KAON. All documents have been converted into text format to be used as corpuses in KAON. The size of files in text format for both domains was very close to each other. The file size for .Net was 0.6 MB and 0.5 MB for Java. Table 2 presents samples of .Net and Java extracted concepts (i.e. the output of these files from KAON).

We used our measure **Relv(D, O)** to check the quality of these concepts. The measure computes the percentage of how many concepts that covers a description **D** in ontology **O**. If an ontology is claimed to be "good" then the coverage of concepts of that description in that ontology should be better than any other ontology i.e. **Relv(D, O)** is higher. Several descriptions have been selected from both Java and .Net domains. Samples of these descriptions are presented in table 3. We run six cases for each ontology. Table 4 shows that for a frequency 10, the coverage for the .Net description in the .Net Ontology is 10.7 i.e. **Relv(.NET, .NET) = 10.7%**. Also it shows that the coverage for the Java description in the .Net ontology is 5.19%. i.e. **Relv(.Java, .NET)** = 5.19%. It has been noticed that the coverage of .Net descriptions are better that their corresponding to the Java descriptions (table 4). Results indicate that the Java ontology could be enhanced.

Table 2. Samples of .Net and Java Concepts

.NET Concepts	JAVA Concepts
Access, action, addition, application, state, argum , asax, asmx, asp, asp net, common, language, common language runtime, compile, component, web service, window, work, worker, worker process, world, wsdl, xml, xml web service	Call, case, change, child, class, client, client side, interface, JVM, Microsystems, sender, Server, session, set, side, site, Soap, virtual , World Wide Web.

Table 3. Samples of .Net and Java Descriptions

Description 1.: .NET	Description 1.:JAVA:
A programming language developed by Sun Microsystems. It implements a strong security model, which prevents compiled Java programs from illicitly accessing resources on the system where they execute or on the network. Popular World-Wide Web browsers, as well as some World-Wide Web servers and other systems implement Java interpreters. These are used to display interactive user interfaces, and to script behaviour on these systems. It can also be used to build a small application module or applet for use as part of a Web page. Applets make it possible for a Web page user to interact with the page	A programming language developed by Sun Microsystems. It implements a strong security model, which prevents compiled Java programs from illicitly accessing resources on the system where they execute or on the network. Popular World-Wide Web browsers, as well as some World-Wide Web servers and other systems implement Java interpreters. These are used to display interactive user interfaces, and to script behaviour on these systems. It can also be used to build a small application module or applet for use as part of a Web page. Applets make it possible for a Web page user to interact with the page

Table 4. Applying relevancy measures on .Net and Java descriptions using both ontologies with different frequencies

Frequency	Relv(.NET, .NET)	Relv(Java, .NET)	Relv(Java, Java)	Relv(.NET, Java)
10	29/270 = 10.7%	14/270 =5.19%	17/240 = 7.1%	18/240 = 7.5%
15	23/194 =11.9 %	13/194 =6.7%	14/158 =8.9 %	12/158 =7.6 %
20	20/147 =13.6%	10/147 = 6.8 %	14/125 =11.2%	12/125 = 9.6%
25	18/120 =15%	8/120 =6.67%	11/93 = 11.8%	8/93 =8.6%
30	12/89 = 13.5%	7/89 =7.9%	10/77 = 13%	8/77 = 10.4%

4   Conclusion and Future Work

Building "good" ontology needs "good" resources. A relevancy measure is provided to define how we can measure the "goodness" of ontology or its resources. The measure uses the coverage technique to define the relevancy. The more concepts are covered by a knowledge resource, ontology, or a description of the targeted domain, the better of this source, ontology, or description is. The main contributions of this work are: Building domain ontologies (mainly concepts) for software components (Java and .Net) and defining a new relevancy measure to check the quality of resource knowledge and/or ontology.

We chose the domain of Java and .Net since these are well-known frameworks in the domain of components based software but it can be generalized and used in any other domain such as IBM, Oracle, etc.

In this work we measure the quality of a description. In future work we will define standards i.e. list of well-formed descriptions in certain domains then used these descriptions as a benchmark to check the quality of existing domain ontology.

Acknowledgment

The authors wish to thank FBSU for their support.

References

1. Gruber, T.: Towards Principles for the Design of Ontologies Used for Knowledge Sharing. In: Poli, R., Guarino, N. (eds.) International Workshop on Formal Ontology, Padova, Italy (1993)
2. Fensel, D., van Harmelen, F., Horrocks, I., McGuinness, D., Patel-Schneider, F.: OIL: An Ontology Infrastructure for the Semantic Web. IEEE Intelligent Systems (2001)
3. Boury-Brisset, A.: Ontology-based approach for information fusion. In: Proceedings of the Sixth International Conference on Information Fusion, pp. 522–529 (2003)
4. Horney, T., Jungert, E., Folkesson, M.: An ontology controlled data fusion process for a query language. In: Proceedings of the Sixth International Conference on Information Fusion, pp. 530–537 (2003)
5. Sycara, K., Paolucci, M., Lewis, M.: Information discovery and fusion: Semantics on the battlefield. In: Proceedings of the Sixth International Conference on Information Fusion, pp. 538–544 (2003)
6. Matheus, J., Kokar, M., Baclawski, K.: A core ontology for situation awareness. In: Proceedings of the Sixth International Conference on Information Fusion, pp. 545–552 (2003)
7. Bench-Capon, T., Visser, P.: The Need for Explicit Specifications of Domain Conceptualisations. In: Ontologies in Legal Information Systems, pp. 132–141. ACM, New York (1997), doi:10.1145/261618.261646
8. Wang, A., Qian, K.: Component-oriented programming. John Wiley & Sons, Inc., Chichester (2005) ISBN 0-471-64446-3
9. Qawaqenh, Z., Qawasmeh, E., Kayed, A.: New Method for Ranking Arabic Web Sites Using Ontology Concepts. In: The IEEE Second International Conference on Digital Information Management, ICDIM 2007 (2007)
10. Falbo, R., Guizzardi, G., Natali, A., Bertollo, G., Ruy, F., Mian, P.: Towards Semantic Software Engineering Environments (2002)
11. Oberle, D., Staab, S., Studer, R., Volz, R.: Supporting application development in the semantic web. ACM Transactions on Internet Technology (TOIT) 5, 328–358 (2005)
12. Kayed, A., Hirzallah, N., Luai, A., Najjar, M.: Building Ontological Relationships: A new approach. Journal of the American Society for Information Science and Technology (2008) ISSN: 1532-2882

A Review on Web Pages Clustering Techniques

Dipak Patel and Mukesh Zaveri

Computer Engineering Department
Sardar Vallabhbhai National Institute of Technology, Surat, Gujarat
India-395007
{pc.deepak,mazaveri}@coed.svnit.ac.in

Abstract. World Wide Web (WWW) has become largest source of information. This abundance of information with dynamic and heterogeneous nature of the web makes information retrieval a difficult process for the average user. A technique is required that can help the users to organize, summarize and browse the available information from web with the goal of satisfying their information need effectively. Clustering process organizes the collection of objects into related groups. Web page clustering is the key concept for getting desired information quickly from the massive storage of web pages on WWW. Many researchers have proposed various web document clustering techniques. In this paper, we present detail survey on existing web document clustering techniques along with document representation techniques. We have also described some evaluation measures to evaluate the cluster qualities.

Keywords: Web page Clustering, Vector Space model, Feature Extractions, Cluster quality.

1 Introduction

The size of World Wide Web (WWW) has grown largely and still rapidly increasing. From abundance of information on WWW, getting desired information quickly is important for the users. Generally, a user looking for information submits a query to the search engine and the search engine returns the linear list of URLs with short document summaries in the order of documents relevancy to the query. This query list approach has several problems [1][2], of which the most important one is that if query is too general, the search results would contain many different topics, which leads to the situation that users have to go through a large number of irrelevant documents in order to identify the ones they are looking for. Problem increases when users are novice about the topic they are searching (i.e. having no domain knowledge of topic they are looking for) and the search engine retrieves documents on different topics. With many irrelevant documents from search engine user may not get desired information even after spending lots of time in browsing. Therefore, this has led to the requirement of new techniques to help the users to effectively navigate and organize the available web documents. One of the techniques that can play an important role to achieve this objective is web document clustering. In web document clustering web documents on the same topics are gathered in one group so that each clusters contain documents that are very similar to each other and dissimilar to documents in other

D.C. Wyld et al. (Eds.): NeCoM/WeST/WiMoN 2011, CCIS 197, pp. 700–710, 2011.
© Springer-Verlag Berlin Heidelberg 2011

clusters. If search results are clustered into different groups according to documents contents and each cluster is assigned an informative label then the user can select only appropriate cluster of his use.

To understand the importance of web documents clustering, consider the example where User may search with "Apple" key word if he wants information on Apple Company, then search results contains only few documents on Apple Company, the rest of the documents may be related to other topics like apple resort, apple fruit and many other topics that matches the key word "Apple". If all retrieved web pages are clustered on similar topic then users could find the cluster related to Apple Company and thus save valuable browsing time. Web documents clustering clusters the related documents on specific topic into same groups having semantically same meaning and separates unrelated documents. Web documents clustering can also be used to design adaptive website by clustering web page browsed by users [3][4].

2 Formulation of Clustering Problem

Clustering documents basically involve grouping similar documents in one group so that documents in one group have high similarity compare with documents in other groups. Mathematically we can model clustering problem as follows.

Consider that X is the document set to be clustered, $X = \{x_1, x_2, ..., x_N\}$. Each document x_i is a vector of various dimensions, where each dimensions typically correspond to extracted features from the documents. A clustering of documents collection X in "m" sets can be defined as $Q = \{q_1, q_2, ..., q_m\}$, so that the following conditions are satisfied:

$$q_i \neq \emptyset, i=1, ..., m,$$
$$q_1 \cup q_2 \cup ....\cup q_m = X,$$
$$q_i \cap q_j \neq \emptyset \text{ for } i \neq j \text{ and } i, j = 1 \text{ to m.}$$

Here last condition states that no overlapping of the cluster but algorithms like suffix tree [5] and fuzzy based [6] clustering algorithm allows overlapping of the clusters. Overlapping of clusters means that documents do not belongs to one cluster only they may belongs to more than one cluster because documents may shared multiple topics.

3 Categorization of Web Page Clustering Algorithms

The general process of web page clustering is shown in fig 1. In first step of web page clustering data can be collected either in form of original web pages or search results. In next step, preprocessing is done on collected data to transform it into appropriate form so that it can be efficiently used in clustering process. In feature extraction step features are extracted in form of web links or page contents or combination of web contents and links information. In link information numbers of in links and out links of the web documents are extracted as features and for page content, words or terms are extracted as features. In last step, clustering algorithms are applied on extracted features and cluster result is obtained. Based on feature extraction we categorize web page Clustering algorithms in three parts. 1) text-based approach 2) link-based and 3) hybrid approach.

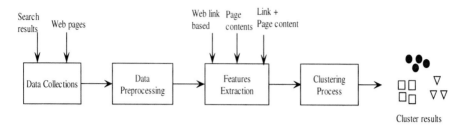

Fig. 1. General Process of Web Page Clustering

3.1 Text Based Approach

In this approach web pages are treated as a text documents that is all HTML and XML tags, special characters and images are removed from the web pages so web pages would be converted into normal documents. Here web documents are clustered according to their contents. As clustering algorithms cannot works on text directly so documents must be presented in correct format.

Most widely used text document representation is based on vector space model (VSM) [7]. In VSM each document is represented by vector of extracted features from the document. Consider the vector for i^{th} document $d_i = (f_{1i}, f_{2i}, f_{3i}, \ldots, f_{mi})$. Here 'm' features are extracted and f_{ji} is the weights of jth feature of document i. The weight is based on contribution of the feature in the semantics of the document. Further the feature can be represented as word, phrase or n-gram types [8][9]. In word representation documents are represented as "set of words" or "bag of the words". This representation of the documents has higher dimensionality. Phrase (set of words) can also be used as a feature in document vector to reduce the dimensionality of document representation. Character N-gram is a language independent text representation technique. It transforms documents into high dimensional feature vectors where each feature corresponds to a contiguous substring. N-Grams are 'n' adjacent characters (substring) from the alphabet A [10]. Hence, the number of distinct N-Grams in a text is less than or equal to $|A|^n$. where $|A|$ represents length of alphabet A. We further categorized Clustering algorithms in text based approach in three parts; Partition based algorithms, Hierarchical and algorithms based on optimization techniques and tree based technique.

3.1.1 Partition Based Clustering Algorithms

The most common partitioned clustering algorithm is k-means [11]. K-means algorithm groups the documents into predefined numbers of the clusters. The algorithm starts by randomly selecting k features as an initial centroid and then it assigns each document to the cluster with the closest centroid. Then centroids of each cluster are updated by calculating the mean of features in the clusters. This process of assignment of documents to nearest cluster centroid and updating of cluster centroids is repeated until cluster centroids remain same or no change in the cluster centroid. The main drawback of the k-means algorithm is that the cluster result is sensitive to the selection of the initial clusters centroids and may converge to the local optima [12]. Even the number of iterations the algorithm runs are also differing based on initial clusters centroids. Complexity of K-means depends on the number of data elements [13], numbers of clusters and numbers of iterations, so change in number of iterations increase the complexity of K-means. To overcome this drawbacks many variation of K-means has been proposed [14][15][16].

A variation to k-means clustering algorithm is presented by K. A. Abdul Nazeer et al. [14] with two methods one for finding the better initial centroids and other method for an efficient way for assigning data points to appropriate clusters with reduced time complexity. This algorithm produces good clusters in less amount of computational time. But to find initial cluster centroids distance is calculated to each data points in the set so its complexity was very high. Then Madhu Yedla et al. [13] described k-means to find the better initial centroids with reduced time complexity. Almost every aspect of k-means like distance measure, initialization of centroid and overall process have been modified by the researchers [15][16].

3.1.2 Hierarchical Clustering Algorithms

In this family, algorithms build the hierarchy bottom-up or top down by iteratively computing the similarity between all pairs of clusters and then merging the most similar pair [11]. Bottom up approach is called agglomerative hierarchical clustering and top down called divisive approach. Fung et al. [17] proposed Frequent Item set based Hierarchical Clustering to handle issues like high dimensionality and giving meaningful cluster labels. The algorithm generates the hierarchy of clusters by applying frequent item set concept this method require to specify number of cluster required. Malik et al. [18] have presented the closed interesting itemset based hierarchical clustering to further reduce the dimensionality and increasing the accuracy. The Hierarchical clustering approaches produce high quality clusters but have very high computational (O (n^2)) requirements.

3.1.3 Tree Based Algorithm

Suffix tree clustering algorithm is the first tree based algorithm that generates the tree from the documents contents. Suffix tree clustering (STC) algorithm for search results clustering is proposed by Zamir et al. [9]. It is incremental clustering approach to suit the nature of the web search results. Hua-Jun et al. [19] introduced an improved suffix tree with N-gram to deal with the problem of long path and memory requirement of the original suffix tree. However, the suffix tree with N-gram can discover only partial common phrases when the length of N-gram is shorter than the length of true phrases. Junze Wang et al. [20] proposed concept of X- gram suffix tree to have variable length in suffix tree. X-gram suffix tree able to recognize whole common phrases those were not recognized by N-gram suffix tree. X-gram suffix tree able to generate better cluster description but it require additional complement operation to identify all common phrases.

3.1.4 Optimization Based Algorithms

In this category we have described genetic algorithm and Particle swarm optimization algorithm. Zahra hossain et al. [21] proposed genetic based clustering with variable size coding and different fitness function to achieve greater accuracy in clustering. Wei Jian-Xiang et al. [22] proposed genetic algorithm for document clustering to refine K-means for searching global optimal value for clustering. But it is for low dimensionality and language specific (Chinese). Dynamic GA for Web Pages clustering is introduced by Zhu Zhengyu et al [23]. It does not require to give number of cluster required in advance it automatically calculate it. The way with which each chromosome is encoded has been modified in the algorithm. The chromosome encoded with cluster instead of document vector.

Particle swarm optimization (PSO) has gained significant attention as an attractive heuristic search method due to its easy implementation, stable convergence characteristics and good computational efficiency. The PSO algorithm searches for the best solution in parallel using a group of particles [24]. Each particle is represented as an n-dimensional vector in the n-dimensional search space and corresponds to a possible solution to the problem under consideration. Each particle is flying with a velocity which is influenced by the social and cognitive components. An alternative KPSO-Clustering algorithm is introduced by Ye and Chen [25] to cluster N data points into k clusters. KPSO is a PSO based k-means algorithm in which each particle represents a possible clustering solution consisting of k cluster centers. The proposed algorithm is more robust and better than the traditional k-means clustering algorithm. However, the PSO and k-means could converge to local optimum. Premalatha, and Natarajan [26] proposed PSO algorithm for document clustering. This algorithm is a hybrid of PSO and GA, which can be used to solve combinatorial optimization problems. In this algorithm PSO has been modified to add reproduction using crossover when stagnation in the movement of particle is identified and carry out local search to improve the goodness of fit. Reproduction has the capability to achieve faster convergence and better solution.

3.2   Link Based Clustering Algorithms

The web pages have hyperlink and metadata attached to them that can be very useful for clustering. The link-based document clustering approaches characterize the documents by information extracted by the link structure of the collection. Basic idea is that when two web pages are connected via a link, it means they may have semantic relationship between them, which can be the basis for the partitioning of the collection into clusters. But the link based clustering algorithms suffers from the facts that pages without sufficient in-links or out-links could not be clustered and results in poor cluster quality.

HITS algorithm based on link information to retrieve authority and hub documents for user query is presented by Kleinberg [27]. Pages with many incoming links are called authorities and are considered very important. The hubs are pages that point to many important pages. A. M. Rahmani et al. [28] proposed fuzzy based clustering by considering just anchor tags of the web pages. The algorithm is based on logic that the anchor tags make a links to other pages that have similar contents as original page or some other important concepts. By using only anchor tags for documents representation they reduced the vector size without decreasing precision. They assign weights to terms, based on occurrences of terms in title, name, id or other part of the anchor tag.

3.3 Hybrid Approach

The web links can be seen as a recommendation of the creator of one page to another page, they do not intend to indicate the content similarity and link based algorithms may suffer from poor or too dense link structures. On the other hand, text-based algorithms have problems of high dimensionality and identification of different languages. To combine the advantages of both text based and hyperlink based approach hybrid document clustering approaches have been proposed.

He et al. [29] proposed hybrid approach for web documents clustering. The algorithm constructs the similarity matrix from hyperlink between documents, co-citation patterns and text contents and apply normalized cut method for partitioning of the web graph (nodes are web pages and edges are hyperlinks) to form the cluster. Ron Bekkerman et al. [30] argued that web pages belong to same cluster if they are similar in content or close to each other in the Web graph. The technique proposed in [30] perform search result clustering using heuristic search in web graph and topology driven heuristic for filtering URLs that connect to unrelated pages. They gave content driven heuristics to combine pages that share the contents. Michael Chau et. al [31] give new metrics of HFIDF ((hyperlink frequency multiplied by inverse document frequency) combined with traditional TFIDF (term frequency multiplied by inverse document frequency) approach to consider link structure of web pages. Cindy et. al [32] state the method for hierarchical web page clustering with combination of in-page link, cross page link and the contents of the web pages. Cross page link structure deals with the co-citation and bibliography-coupling. For in-page link authors build the DOM tree to extract the structure of the web pages. Then method in the paper introduces the new similarity that combines the in-page link, cross page link and the contents of the pages for clustering. Also author have mentioned the new density-based clustering algorithm to group densely linked web pages into semantic clusters and identifying their hierarchical relationships.

4 Comparison of Clustering Techniques

Selecting particular clustering algorithms for any application is always a big issue. Because each method has its own advantages and disadvantages. In this section we compare three types of clustering algorithms that is content based, link based and hybrid clustering algorithms. In content based clustering algorithms, only web page contents are considered and clusters are generated based on matching of each word from different documents. Below table 1 shows the comparison between various clustering algorithms that is used in content based clustering approach. Content based clustering suffers from high dimensionality. Content based clustering may not get sufficient content for clustering if web pages contain only navigation links and images. Whereas Link based clustering exploit the hyperlink structure of the documents. It can consider images, videos and other objects from web pages for clustering that is not possible with content based clustering. Link based clustering is also independent of languages of the web pages as it exploit the document structure rather than its contents. Link based clustering techniques suffer from poor or dense link structure. No cluster can be found if web pages have hyperlink in lower number. Hybrid document clustering considers the page contents as well as link structures taking advantages of both the techniques.

Table 1. Comparison of some clustering algorithms

Algo. \ Parameters	K- means	AHC	STC	PSO	GA
Time Complexity	O(knt) n=No. of Objects k=No. of clusters t=no. of iterations	$O(n^2)$ n=No. of Objects	O(n) n is the size of the text	O(n) n=No. of Objects	O(n) n=No. of Objects
Number of cluster required to specify	YES	NO	NO	YES	YES
Overlap cluster produced?	No	NO	Yes	NO	NO
How clusters Produced	Mostly Based on Euclidean or Cosine similarity	Comparing similarity between each pair of the documents	If common documents between base clusters are greater than similarity threshold then merge base clusters in one cluster	Each particle represents documents and changes their velocity to find optimal centroid for the clusters.	Initial population is created and through crossover and mutation optimum clusters are found
Advantages	1. Efficient and Simple to implement 2. Suitable for large datasets	1.High quality results 2. No requirement of initial clusters	1. Incremental algorithm 2.Fast and allow overlapping of the clusters	1. Find solution faster than GA. 2. It is parallel algorithm 3. can find global and local optimal cluster centroid	1.Perform global search to find optimal centroid for clusters 2.It is inherently parallel algorithm
Disadvantages	1.Sensitive to initial cluster centroids 2.Number of clusters must be known in advance	1. Not suitable to large data sets due to high complexity	1. It's snippets based clustering so snippets may not have good description of documents	1. Setting of Initial parameters (no. of particles, K clusters etc.)required	1.High computation cost 2.Sensitive to selection of various learning parameter

5   Cluster Evaluation Methods

In this section we have described the quality measures for clusters. Most commonly used clusters evaluation measures are as below.

5.1   Precision and Recall

The recall–precision framework is a useful method for evaluating Information retrieval system performance. It is used to measure the quality of search results. The proportion of retrieved relevant documents to all retrieved documents is called precision. If all documents are retrieved then the precision value is 1 and no relevant documents are retrieved then the precision is 0. Same way recall represents the proportion of relevant documents retrieved to all relevant documents. If recall value is 1 it means all relevant documents are retrieved and 0 means no relevant documents are retrieved. Same concept is applied to cluster evaluation if each cluster is treated as if it were the result of a query and each class as if it were the desired set of documents for a query. Then the recall and precision of cluster j for given class is

$$\text{Recall}(i, j) = n_{ij}/n_i \qquad (1)$$

$$\text{Percision}(i, j) = n_{ij}/n_j \qquad (2)$$

Where n_{ij} is the numbers of members of class i in cluster j, n_j is the numbers of members of cluster j and n_i is the number of members of class i.

5.2 F Measure

The F measure which is harmonic mean of precision and recall of cluster j and class i is given by the following:

$$F(i, j) = (2 * \text{Recall}(i, j) * \text{Precision}(i, j)) / ((\text{Precision}(i, j) + \text{Recall}(i, j)) \qquad (3)$$

F measure considers the trade of between recall and precision. It discourages the clustering algorithms that sacrifice one measure for another too drastically. Higher value of F measure indicates good clustering quality. F-measure for the entire clustering is,

$$F = \sum_{i=1}^{m} \frac{n_i}{n} \max_{j=1,\dots,k} F(i, j) \qquad (4)$$

Where n_i is the number of document belonging to class i and "n" is the total number of documents in the collection.

5.3 Entropy

Entropy shows the probabilistic approach for calculation of the cluster quality. It allows us to evaluate the probability distribution of class labels in each cluster. The probability of class i in cluster j can be estimated by the proportion of occurrences of class label i in cluster j.

Formally, we can measure the entropy value for each cluster Cj as follow.

$$\text{Entropy}(C_j) = - \sum_{j=1}^{k} Pr_i(C_j) \log_2 Pr_i(C_j) \qquad (5)$$

Here $Pr_i(c_j)$ is the probability that member of cluster C_j belongs to class "i". Total entropy for all clusters is as follow.

$$\text{ntropy}_{\text{total}}(C) = \sum_{i=1}^{k} \frac{|Di|}{|D|} * \text{entropy}(C_i) \qquad (6)$$

Here D_i is the size of cluster "i" and D is the total number of data objects. Entropy gives the measure of uncertainty so lower value of entropy expected for good clustering algorithms.

5.4 Means Square Error (MSE)

Partition based clustering algorithm try to minimize with in cluster variance. MSE computes the within class variance so for good partition based clustering algorithms should minimize the MSE. The equation for calculating MSE is as below.

$$\text{MSE} = \frac{1}{N} \sum_{j=1}^{K} \sum_{x \in Cj} \| x - m_k \|^2 \tag{7}$$

Here K is the number of clusters and m_k is the mean of cluster C_k.

5.5 Davies-Bouldin Validity Index (DBI)

DBI is defined as [11], given a partition of the N points into K clusters, one first defines the following measure of within-to-between cluster spread for two clusters, C_i and C_j for $1 \leq I,j \leq K$.

$$R_{j,j} = e_i + e_j / D_{ij}$$

where e_i and e_j are the average dispersion of clusters C_i and C_j, and D_{ij} is the Euclidean distance between C_i and C_j. If m_i and m_j are the centers of C_i and C_j respectively, then

$$e_i = \frac{1}{N_i} \sum_{x \in Ci} \| x - m_k \|^2 ,$$

$D_{ij} = \|m_i - m_k\|^2$, where m_i is the center of cluster C_j consisting of N_i points. The term R_k for each C_k is given as
$R_k = \max_{i \neq j} R_{i,j}$,
Now the DBI is defined as:

$$\text{DB}(k) = \frac{1}{K} \sum_{k=1}^{K} R_k \tag{8}$$

Here K is the number of clusters. The DBI takes into account cluster dispersion and the distance between cluster means. Well separated compact clusters are preferred. The DBI favors small numbers of clusters. Optimizing the DBI frequently eliminates clusters by forcing them to be empty.

6 Conclusion and Future Scope

We have surveyed existing web page clustering algorithms with its advantages and limitations. We have shown the comparison of some clustering algorithm with various parameters. We have also described some clustering quality measures. Clustering is very complex process and depends on feature selection and other parameters value depending on clustering algorithms. Up till now much research has been conducted on the field of web document clustering and there are still some open issues like achievement of better quality clusters with readable labels. Handling the high dimensionality and speed of the clustering process are also considerable issues. In addition, another important issue is incrementality, because the web pages change very frequently and new pages are always added to the web. So addition of one page should not repeat whole clustering process it should immediately cluster it. Also, clustering algorithms should generate overlapping clusters because web pages often shared multiple topics.

References

1. Leuski, A.: Evaluating Document Clustering for Interactive. In: 10th International Conference on Information and Knowledge Management, New York, pp. 33–40 (2001)
2. Grouper, E.O., Zamir, O.: Web Document Clustering: A Feasibility Demonstration. In: 19th International ACM SIGIR Conference on Research and Development of Information Retrieval, pp. 46–54 (1998)
3. Govardhan, A., Suresh, K., Vasumathi, D.: Effective Web Personalization Using Clustering. In: International Conference Intelligent Agent & Multi-Agent Systems, pp. 1–7 (2009)
4. Yang, Q., Zhang, H., Xu, X., Hu, Y.-H., Ma, S., Su, Z.: Correlation-Based Web Document Clustering for Adaptive Web Interface Design. Knowledge and Information Systems, 151–167 (2002)
5. Nan-Feng, X., Qion, C., Han, W.: Web Snippets Clustering Based on an Improved Suffix Tree Algorithm. In: Sixth International Conference on Fuzzy Systems and Knowledge Discovery, vol. 1, pp. 542–547 (2009)
6. Fresno, V., Martinez, R., Garcia-Plaza, A.P.: Web Page Clustering Using a Fuzzy Logic Based Representation and Self-Organizing Maps. In: IEEE/WIC/ACM International Conference on Web Intelligence and Intelligent Agent Technology, vol. 1, pp. 851–854 (2008)
7. Buckley, C., Salton, G.: Term Weighting Approaches in Automatic Text Retrieval. Inf. Process. Manage 24(5), 513–523 (1988)
8. Keselj, V., Milios, E., Miao, Y.: Document clustering using character N-grams: a comparative evaluation with term-based and word-based clustering. In: 14th ACM International Conference on Information and Knowledge Management, New York, USA, pp. 357–358 (2005)
9. Grouper, E.O., Zamir, O.: A Dynamic Clustering Interface to Web Search Results. In: Eighth International World Wide Web Conference, pp. 283–296 (1999)
10. Cavnar, W.B.: Using an n-gram-based document representation with a vector processing retrieval model. In: Third Text Retrieval Conference (TREC-3), pp. 269–278 (1994)
11. Jain, A.K., Dubes, R.C.: Algorithms for Clustering Data. Prentice Hall, New Jersey (1998)
12. Ismail, S.Z., Selim, M.A.: K-means type algorithms: A generalized convergence theorem and characterization of local optimality. IEEE Transaction on Pattern Analysis and Machine Intelligence 6(1), 81–87 (1984)
13. Pathakota, S.R., Srinivasa, T.M., Yedla, M.: Enhancing K-means Clustering Algorithm with Improved Initial Center. International Journal of Computer Science and Information Technologies 1(2), 121–125 (2010)
14. Abdul Nazeer, K.A., Sebastian, M.P.: Improving the accuracy and efficiency of the k-means clustering algorithm. In: Data Mining and Knowledge Engineering (ICDMKE), London, UK, pp. 308–312 (2009)

15. Barakbah, A.R., Arai, K.: Hierarchical K-means- an algorithm for centroids initialization for K-means. Technical Reports, Faculty of Science and Engineering 36(1), 25–31 (2007)

16. Duraiswamy, K., Mumtaz, K.: A Novel Density based improved k-means. (IJCSE) International Journal on Computer Science and Engineering 2(2), 213–218 (2010)

17. Wang, K., Ester, M., Fung, B.C.M.: Hierarchical document clustering using frequent itemsets. In: SIAM International Conference on Data Mining, San Francisco, CA, United States, pp. 59–70 (2003)

18. Kender, H.H., Malik, J.R.: High Quality, Efficient Hierarchical Document Clustering Using Closed Interesting Itemsets. In: Sixth International Conference on Data Mining, Washington, DC, USA, pp. 991–996 (2006)

19. He, Q., Chen, Z., Ma, W., Ma, J., Zeng, H.: Learning to Cluster Web Search Results. In: 27th Annual International ACM SIGIR Conference on Research and Development in Information Retrieval, pp. 210–217. Sheffield, South Yorkshire (2004)

20. Mo, Y., Huang, B., Wen, J., He, L., Wang, J.: Web Search Results Clustering Based on a Novel Suffix Tree Structure. In: Rong, C., Jaatun, M.G., Sandnes, F.E., Yang, L.T., Ma, J. (eds.) ATC 2008. LNCS, vol. 5060, pp. 540–554. Springer, Heidelberg (2008)

21. Masoud, A., Setayeshi, S., Hossaini, Z.: A web page classification and clustering by means of Genetic Algorithm- a variable size page representation approach. In: Computational Intelligence for Modelling, pp. 436–440 (2008)

22. Wei, J.-X., Huai, L., Yue-hong, S., Xin-Ning, S.: Application of Genetic Algorithm in Document Clustering. In: Information Technology and Computer Science, pp. 145–148 (2009)

23. Zhengyu, Z., Ping, H., Chunlei, Y., Li, L.: A dynamic genetic algorithm for clustering web pages. In: 2nd International Conference on Software Engineering and Data Mining, pp. 506–511 (2010)

24. Zhenkui, P., Xia, H., Jinfeng, H.: The Clustering Algorithm Based on Particle Swarm Optimization Algorithm. In: International Conference on Intelligent Computation Technology and Automation, Washington, DC, USA, pp. 148–151 (2008)

25. Chen, F., Ye, C.-Y.: Alternative KPSO-Clustering Algorithm. Tamkang Journal of Science and Engineering 8(2), 165–174 (2005)

26. Natarajan, A.M., Premalatha, K.: Procreant PSO for fastening the convergence to optimal solution in the application of document clustering. Current Science 96(1), 137–143 (2009)

27. Kleinberg, J.M.: Authoritative sources in a hyperlinked environment. J. ACM 46(5), 604–632 (1999)

28. Hossaini, Z., Setayeshi, S., Rahmani, A.M.: Link Processing for Fuzzy Web Pages Clustering and Classification. European Journal of Scientific Research 27(4), 620–627 (2009)

29. Zha, H., Ding, C.H.Q., Simon, H.D., He, X.: Web document clustering using hyperlink structures. Computational Statistics & Data Analysis 41(1), 19–45 (2002)

30. Zilberstein, S., Allan, J., Bekkerman, R.: Web Page Clustering using Heuristic Search in the Web Graph. In: 20th International Joint Conference on Artificial Intelligence, Hyderabad, India, pp. 2280–2285 (2007)

31. Chau, P.Y.K., Hu, P., Chau, M.: Incorporating Hyperlink Analysis in Web Page Clustering. In: Sixth Workshop on E-Business, Montreal, Quebec, Canada, pp. 102–109 (2007)

32. Lin, C., Yu, Y., Han, J., Liu, B.: Hierarchical Web-Page Clustering via In-Page and Cross-Page Link Structures. In: Zaki, M.J., Yu, J.X., Ravindran, B., Pudi, V. (eds.) PAKDD 2010. LNCS, vol. 6119, pp. 222–229. Springer, Heidelberg (2010)

Application of Latent Semantic Indexing for Hindi-English CLIR Irrespective of Context Similarity

A.P. SivaKumar[1], P. Premchand[2], and A. Govardhan[3]

[1] Assistant Professor, Department of Computer Science and,
JNTUACE, Anantapur
[2] Professor, Department of Computer Science Engineering, Osmania University, Hyderabad
[3] Principal & Professor, Department of Computer Science Engineering,
JNTUHCE, Nachupalli
sivakumar.ap@gmail.com, p.premchand@uceou.edu,
govardhan_cse@yahoo.co.in

Abstract. Retrieving information from different languages may lead to many problems like polysemy and synonymy, which can be resolved by Latent Semantic Indexing (LSI) techniques. This paper uses the Singular Value Decomposition (SVD) of LSI technique to achieve effective indexing for English and Hindi languages. Parallel corpus consisting of both Hindi and English documents is created and is used for training and testing the system. Removing stop words from the documents is performed followed by stemming and normalization in order to reduce the feature space and to get language relations. Then, cosine similarity method is applied on query document and target document. Based on our experimental results it is proved that LSI based CLIR gets over the non-LSI based retrieval which have retrieval successes of 67% and 9% respectively.

Keywords: Latent semantic indexing, Cross language information retrieval, Indexing, Singular value decomposition.

1 Introduction

Information Retrieval (IR) deals with representing, storing, organizing, and accessing information. This representation and organization of information is useful for user accessing. The main goal of Information Retrieval (IR) is to retrieve the information which is relevant to the users need. This Information Retrieval will be helpful in structuring of the language.

The demand for multilingual information is becoming profound as the users of the internet throughout the world are increasing. This demand creates a problem of retrieving documents in one language by specifying query in other language. This increasing necessity for retrieval of multilingual documents comes up with the new branch called Cross Lingual Information Retrieval (CLIR).

Cross Lingual Information retrieval makes use of user queries in one language (source language) and utilizes them in retrieval of documents in other language (target language). For example, if the user enters a query in Hindi language then relevant

D.C. Wyld et al. (Eds.): NeCoM/WeST/WiMoN 2011, CCIS 197, pp. 711–720, 2011.
© Springer-Verlag Berlin Heidelberg 2011

documents in English will be retrieved. These retrieved documents are semantically equal. Many information retrieval methods depend on the exact match between words in user queries and words in documents. The documents which contain the words in user query are returned to the user. So those methods will fail in retrieving the documents which do not match with the words in the user queries in a proper way. There are many standard methods like, Dictionary based method, Inverted indexing method, Probabilistic based methods are failed due to the consideration of words in user queries. The most familiar dictionary method for CLIR is also not giving efficient information retrieval, due to the limited number of indexing terms or words present in the dictionary method.

The contents of the paper are as follows. Section 2 outlines the previous work done by different institutions on Indexing. Section 3 gives the information regarding proposed system. Section 4 is about the experiment and results. Finally Section 5 includes future work and concludes the paper.

2   Previous Work

Much work has already been done on CLIR systems and presently research is going on in many countries like India, Japan, China, and Portugal. Most of the proposed systems are based on indexing techniques like dictionary based indexing, inverted file system, probabilistic latent semantic indexing, ontology indexing, and language modeling which retrieve the documents based on the index terms. But, by using index terms we won't be able to get the documents which are relevant to the user query.

Using latent semantic indexing, cross language information retrieval can be performed automatically as described in [1].They tested the language independent depiction of the documents, irrespective of the user query, which means it may be short or long query. They used French and English parallel corpus for training and testing the system. They collected the corpus from Hansard collection. 982 documents were collected for training the system and 1500 documents for testing it. Totally they had used nearly 2482 documents. In English documents there are 2482 paragraphs and in French documents also there are 2482 paragraphs. The success rate in finding out the mate documents is 98%.

The reference [2] has used porter stemmer for stemming of the documents in English. Here they removed suffixes from the words. Stemming is done on the Cranfield200 collection. While stemming they calculated precision and recall. They tested porter stemmer algorithm on 10,000 vocabularies. The reduced words out of 10,000 are 1373 and the 3650 were not reduced. So by using porter stemmer the vocabulary size is nearly reduced by 1/3 rd of the original one.

The reference [3] illustrates the method of Turkish-English cross language information retrieval using LSI. In this they experimented on LSI using Singular Value Decomposition. The parallel corpus is collected from Skylife Magazine's website, which contains both Turkish as well as English articles. Those articles are converted by the interpreters. This corpus contains 1056 Turkish documents and 1056 English documents. Here each paragraph is taken as an individual document. They had matched paragraphs to their cross language mates. So finally there are 3602 document pairs and each single term is represented by document matrix. Out of 3602 documents 1801 documents are used for training the system and 1801 for testing the system. Longest Match Stemming algorithm is used for the stemming of the Turkish Documents and for English they used Porter stemmer. They had taken My SQL 5.1.11 Data base server for storing the documents. By using Latent Semantic Indexing the retrieval rate is 3 times more than the direct Matching. The success rate is 69%.

The reference [4] describes Portuguese-English Experiments using LSI. They used Los Angeles Times for English Documents only. Systran (translator) used for translating the 20 % of the English collection to Portuguese. The total documents in the collection are 22000. The success rate of the retrieval is nearly 99%.

The reference [5] describes Indexing by Latent Semantic Analysis. The method Singular Value Decomposition tested in this analysis, it gives the details about how to solve the problem of multiple terms referring to the same object. In this the relevant documents are characterized and identified properly. For example 12 term by 9 document matrix is decomposed by using SVD is given clearly.

The reference [6] describes the method of Latent Semantic Indexing Overview. It described some advantage of Liplike less dimensionality, polysemy, synonym and Term dependence .In the analysis of LSI they used 90,000 terms instead of 70,000 documents. So the term by document contains only 0.001% - 0.002% non zero, entries. To compute a [200], it had taken nearly 18 hours CPU time. In this LSI gave 16% improvement than original keyword method.

The reference [7] describes the method for retrieving of English-Greek documents using Latent Semantic Indexing for Cross Language Information Retrieval. The English and Turkish documents are clustered along the X-axis and Y-axis into a two dimensional vector. Parsing mechanism is used. Here the terms should be appearing at least more than once in the database. This paper mainly focuses on the query matching within the data base. Folding-in is another technique for the LSI generated database already exists. In this Folding- in technique each new document is represented as weighted sum of component document vector, this is appended to the existing documents.

The reference [8] describes the method of Latent semantic Indexing a fast Track Tutorial. The reference [9] describes the method of Singular Value Decomposition Singular Value Decomposition (SVD) is a mathematical technique used for reduce the dimension of a matrix. This tutorial describes how the documents are decomposed from a single matrix. This gives the relation between the correlated documents and uncorrelated documents. In this tutorial they illustrated the two dimensional data points.

The reference [10] describes the method of indexing documents by a combination of keywords neglecting the relationship between semantic words. The reference [11] describes new Chinese term measurement and MLU extractor process that none well on small corpora, and approach to the selection of MLU's in a more accurate manner. The reference [12] describes probabilistic latent semantic indexing (PLSI) models using word segmentation. Their result show that correct word segmentation improve precision of information retrievals and index based on keywords extraction obtains highest accuracy rate to PLSI model.

3 Proposed System

This latent semantic indexing is the best approach for mapping of each document and query vector in to a reduced dimensional space. This is based on concept matching rather than matching of index terms. The proposed system follows many steps in retrieval of documents.

Indexing is a data structure built on the text to speed up searching. This indexing is very simple for a single language, but when coming to multilingual it is quiet difficult. So for this we are proposing Latent Semantic Indexing (LSI), by Using Singular Value Decomposition (SVD). Here input is a set of documents d1, d2, d3... and user query is q=q1, q2..., we are giving the entire document as a query.

We applied a ranking method for the documents retrieval, it gives the order of the documents (top) relevant to the user query.

In this we scale the term frequency by using following formula

$$W(t,d) = 1+\log (tf (t,d)) \qquad\qquad \text{if } tf(t,d) > 0 \qquad (1)$$

$$=0 \qquad\qquad \text{otherwise}$$

$$Idf (t) = \log (N/df(t)).$$

Where Idf = inverted document frequency.

N = number of documents in the collection.

Here first we collect the information which is semantically equal and perform stemming on that corpus. After stemming of the documents both are placed in the same space vector. Each paragraph is considered as a single term-by -document matrix. Latent Semantic Indexing uses a mathematical method called Singular Value Decomposition. This SVD is used for reducing dimensions of the term-by-document matrix. The formula for SVD as follows:

SVD splits a matrix (A) in to 3 matrices.

$$A=UXV^T \qquad\qquad (2)$$

Here,

U is a matrix containing the columns as the eigenvectors of AA^T. It is a concept by term matrix.

X is a matrix, the diagonal elements are singular values of A. It is a concept by concept matrix.

V is a matrix containing the columns as the Eigen vectors of the A^T a matrix. It is a concept by document matrix.

From these observations a suitable rank value (k value) is to be taken to reduce the semantic space. The selection of K value is depending on the parallel corpus that we are using in this experiment.

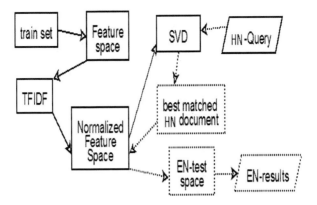

Fig. 1. System overview

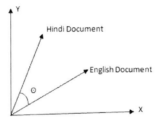

Fig. 2. Cosine Similarity

In this, we have created a system that can search the cross language mate of a given document. First we train the system with bilingual documents. In this stage, we have stemmed the English documents using porter stemmer and we also stem the Hindi documents manually. After stemming the documents using corresponding stemmers we remove the stop words to increase the retrieval performance.

By counting the frequency of each word in documents we created a term-by-document matrix (Feature-space). We Normalized the Feature-space using Term Frequency – Inverse Document Frequency (TF-IDF), because longer documents may affect the retrieval results. Then the normalized term-by-document matrix has been decomposed to U, S, and V matrices using singular values decomposition (SVD). For this we have used JAMA package which contains all the classes and interfaces which are used for decomposing the Feature-space.

After training the system using bilingual documents, the documents in the Hindi database have been queried to find the cross language mates. To find the similarity between the documents we use cosine similarity. For the given query document we retrieve the document which gives the value of cosine similarity almost equal to one.

Cosine similarity can be calculated by the following formula,

$$cosine\ similarity(q, d) = sim(q^T U_k \Sigma_k^{-1}, d^T U_k \Sigma_k^{-1}) \tag{3}$$

Where,

q is the query document
d is the target document
k is the rank value

4 Experiment

In this we have taken parallel corpus. We retrieved documents from India Gov[1]. This contains both Hindi and English documents which are semantically equal. Documents in both languages have been divided into paragraphs. Each paragraph is divided into a single document. So these documents are mapped to the respective translation language paragraphs. The mapping data is stored in MYSQL data base server.

The corpus consists of 180 Hindi and 180 English parallel documents. So for this purpose we used every paragraph as a single document.

Table 1. Example Document

English Document	Hindi Document
India & the World	भारत और विश्व
India's foreign policy seeks to safeguard the country's enlightened self-interest. The primary objective of India's foreign policy is to promote and maintain a peaceful and stable external environment in which the domestic tasks of inclusive economic development and poverty alleviation can progress rapidly and without obstacles. Given the high priority attached by the Government of India to socio-economic development, India has a vital stake in a supportive external environment both in our region and globally.	भारत की विदेश नीति में देश के विवेकपूर्ण स्व-हित की रक्षा करने पर बल दिया जाता है। भारत की विदेश नीति का प्राथमिक उद्देश्य शांतिपूर्ण स्थिर बाहरी परिवेश को बढ़ावा देना और उसे बनाए रखना है. जिसमें समग्र आर्थिक और गरीबी उन्मूलन के घरेलू लक्ष्यों को तेजी से और बाधाओं से मुक्त माहौल में आगे बढ़ाया जा सकें। सरकार द्वारा सामाजिक-आर्थिक विकास को उच्च प्राथमिकता दिए जाने को देखते हुए. क्षेत्रीय और वैश्विक दोनों ही स्तरों पर सहयोगपूर्ण बाहरी वातावरण कायम करने में भारत की महत्वपूर्ण भूमिका है।

Porter stemmer has been used for stemming of English documents. For Hindi documents we performed manual stemming. So after stemming the stop word list is as follows.

---

[1] India Gov http://www.india.gov.in/

Table 2. Top 20 Stop Word List

English		Hindi	
Word	Count	Word	Count
The	969	में	550
Of	577	और	445
And	483	की	378
In	389	को	241
To	337	का	215
A	202	लिए	166
For	161	से	165
With	111	ने	124
Is	108	एक	110
On	105	किया	108
As	102	पर	105
By	100	है	95
Was	73	करने	75
From	63	साथ	72
Has	63	इस	69
Also	57	भी	67
At	56	द्वारा	66
An	43	यह	51

As mentioned earlier each paragraph is taken as an individual document. We have mapped the paragraphs to their cross linguistic mates in the MY SQL data base server. So totally we have 360 document pairs created. In that each of them is represented as a single document in term -by-document relation.

The paragraphs which are present in the same document are semantically equal. So we used 180 documents for training the system and 180 documents for testing the system. The document set is shown in the below table.

Table 3. Corpus Overview

	Number of Documents	
Set	English	Hindi
Corpus	360	360
Training set	180	80
Hindi Test Set	00	180
English Test Set	180	00

After training the system, the documents in the Hindi testing set have been queried to the system to find their cross language mates. Cosine similarity is used to find the similarity among the documents. We also tested the system with different ranks (k values). Based on k value the results are shown in the table below.

Table 4. Cross Language Mate Retrieval Results

k	Return Rank										
	Hindi document as query										
	1	*2*	*3*	*4*	*5*	*6*	*7*	*8*	*9*	*10*	*total*
dm	01	01	01	02	02	-	06	-	01	02	16
40	40	04	01	02	-	-	-	03	-	01	51
80	80	04	02	01		04		01	01		93
120	118	03	01				01				123
160	158	03							01		162

dm: denotes direct match.

The performance of the system is evaluated if we find the mate of query document in the retrieval result. After submission of query, retrieval results are ranked according to their similarity to the query document. We have given 180 test documents one by one as a query and expected to find its mate in the query results. We considered the query results as successful, if the mate of query document appears in the first 10 of ranked retrieval results. The above table shows the number of successful queries according to rank order of the mate document. For example, if we consider k=40 experiment, we obtained the mate of query document at the first rank for 40 documents. The first row in the table shows the results of CLIR, if we make direct match between documents, where no LSI and TFIDF is used. The above table also shows that, using TFIDF and LSI increases the query performance by approximately 3 times when direct matching is considered. The table shows that as k value increases the results are better but compile time is increased.

5   Conclusion and Future Work

Various experiments by other researchers carried out using Latent Semantic Indexing method for other test data and other languages have produced good results. Our study on other Indian languages like Telugu, Tamil and Marathi has proved that using LSI methods increase the retrieval performance. Availability of standard test collect, remain major concern for testing LSI method. And also another important question number and size of documents to be used during training.

In this experiment we have mainly focused on improving a Hindi-English cross language information retrieval using latent semantic indexing. For that we collected parallel corpus from India.gov.in web site [12] and performed singular value decomposition to get a CLIR system. Our tests depicted that the latent semantic indexing improves the results three times to that of direct matching method. We also observed that if the value of k increases then there is no consistent performance improvement.

The CLIR system we have developed will work well for document queries but it was less informative for user generated queries. So, much work needs to be done in order to make this system work for user generated queries.

References

Dumais, S.T., Littman, M.L., Landauer, T.K.: Automatic cross language retrieval using latent semantic indexing

Porter, M.: The Porter Stemmer,
   http://www.tartarus.org/~martin/PorterStemmer/

Sen, B., Gunel, 3.B.: Turkish – English Cross Language Information Retrieval using LSI

Orengo, V.M., Huyck, C.: Portuguese-English Experiments using Latent Semantic Indexing

Deerwester, S.: Indexing by Latent Semantic Analysis; Rosario, B.: Latent Semantic Indexing: An overview

Young, P.G.: Cross Language Information Retrieval Using Latent Semantic Indexing

Garcia, E.: Latent Semantic Indexing (LSI) A Fast Track Tutorial Kirk Baker: Singular Value Decomposition Tutorial

Garcia, E.: Singular Value Decomposition (SVD) A Fast Track Tutorial. In: Ientilucci, E.J. (ed.) Using the Singular Value Decomposition,

Tazzite, N., Yousfi, A.: Design and Implementation of an Information Retrieval System by Integrating Semantic Knowledge in the Indexing Phase

Lu, C., Xu, Y.: Web-Based Query Translation for English-Chinese CLIR

Fang, X., Xiaoguang, L., Quan, H.: Comparison Probabilistic Latent Semantic Indexing Mode In Chinese Information Retrieval

The corpus India Gov., http://www.india.gov.in

Abdullah, M.T., Ahmad, F., Mahmod, R., Tengku, T.M.: Application of Latent Semantic Indexing on Malay-English Cross Language Information Retrieval

Maruf Hasan, M., Matsumoto, Y.: Japanese-Chinese Cross-Language Information Retrieval: An Interlingua Approach

Hofmann, T.: Probabilistic Latent Semantic Indexing

Paltoglou, G., Salampasis, M., Lazarinis, F.: Indexing and Retrieval of a Greek Corpus

Ponte, J.M., Croft, W.B.: A Language Modeling Approach to Information Retrieval

Lin, C.-h., Chen, H.: An Automatic Indexing and Neural Network Approach to Concept Retrieval and Classification Multilingual (Chinese-English) Documents

Xu, J., Weischedel, R., Nguyen, C.: Evaluating a Probabilistic Model for Cross-Lingual Information Retrieval

Schiel, U., Lanna, M.S., de Sousa, F.: Semi-Automatic Indexing of Documents with a Multilingual Thesaurus

Lee, H.-J., Kim, H.-I., Chang, J.-W.: An Efficient High-Dimensional Indexing Scheme using a Clustering Technique for Content-based Retrieval

Lopez, A.: Statistical machine translation. ACM Computing Surveys 40(3), Article 8, 1–49 (2008)

Robertson, S.E., Walker, S.: Some simple effective approximations to the 2-Poisson model for probabilistic weighted retrieval. In: Proceedings of the 17th Annual International ACM SIGIR Conference on Research and Development in Information Retrieval, Dublin, Ireland, pp. 232–241 (1994) ISBN:0-387-19889-X

Jian-Yun, N., Simard, M., Isabelle, P., Durand, R.: Cross-language information retrieval based on parallel texts and automatic mining of parallel texts from the web. In: Proceedings of the 22nd Annual International ACM SIGIR Conference on Research and Development in Information Retrieval, Berkeley, California, United States, pp. 1–58113 (1999) ISBN:1-58113-096-1

Xu, J., Weischedel, R., Nguyen, C.: Evaluating a Probabilistic Model for Cross-Lingual Information Retrieval. In: Proceedings of the 24th Annual International ACM SIGIR Conference on Research and Development in Information Retrieval, New Orleans, Louisiana, United States, pp. 105–110 (2001) ISBN:1-58113-331-6

Chew, P.A., Bader, B.W., Kolda, T.G., Abdelali, A.: Cross-language information retrieval using parafac2. In: Proceedings of the 13th ACM SIGKDD International Conference on Knowledge Discovery and Data Mining, San Jose, California, USA, pp. 143–152 (2007) ISBN:978-1-59593-609-7

Yang, C.C., Wei, C., Li, K.W.: Cross-lingual thesaurus for multilingual knowledge management. Decision Support Systems 45(3), 596–605 (2008) ISSN:0167-9236

Gao, J., Nie, J., Zhou, M.: Statistical query translation model for crosslanguage information retrieval. ACM Transactions on Asian Language Information Processing (TALIP) 5(4), 323–359 (2006) ISSN:1530-0226

COCA: Combining Speedup Techniques Based on Containers and Arc-Flags

Kalpana Ramanujam[1] and Thambidurai Perumal[2]

[1] Department of Computer Science & Engineering,
Pondicherry Engineering College,
Pondicherry, India
[2] Perunthalaivar Kamarajar Institute of Engineering & Technology,
Karaikal, Pondicherry India
rkalpana@pec.edu

Abstract. The Dijkstra's algorithm [1] is applied on many real world network problems like mobile routing, road maps, railway networks, etc,. There are many techniques available to speedup the algorithm while guaranteeing the optimality of the solution. The main focus of this work is to implement the combined speedup technique which is based on containers and arc flags(COCA). The technique is experimented with two different types of LEDA generated graphs namely random graphs, planar graphs and road networks. The performance metric speedup was measured with respect to runtime of the technique and vertex visited during shortest path computation. The COCA technique proves to give best results in planar graphs. Road networks can be effectively processed with shortest path containers

Keywords: Dijkstra's Algorithm, Graph Theory, Containers, Arc flags, Speed-up.

1 Introduction

Finding shortest paths in large, sparse graphs is typically used in wide applications which include route planning systems for cars, bikes and hikers, or timetable information systems for scheduled vehicles like trains and buses, spatial databases and web searching, etc. In these applications, different places are considered as nodes and their distances are considered as edge weight, which constitute a graph structure. The shortest path queries for those applications were originally solved by Dijkstra, Bellman-ford, Johnson etc. The classical algorithm for computing shortest paths in a directed graph with non-negative edge weights is that of Dijkstra's algorithm. Dijkstra's algorithm implemented with Fibonacci heaps is still the fastest known algorithm for the general case of arbitrary nonnegative edge lengths.

A directed simple graph G is a pair (V, E), where V is the set of nodes / vertices and $E \subseteq V \times V$ is a set of edges, where an edge is an ordered pair of nodes of the form (u, v) such that $u, v \in V$. Usually the number of nodes $|V|$ is denoted by n and the number of edges $|E|$ is denoted by m.

D.C. Wyld et al. (Eds.): NeCoM/WeST/WiMoN 2011, CCIS 197, pp. 721–730, 2011.
© Springer-Verlag Berlin Heidelberg 2011

A path in graph G is a sequence of nodes $(u_1, ..., u_k)$ so that $(u_i, u_{i+1}) \in E$ for all $1 \le i < k$. A path in which $u_1 = u_k$ is called a cycle or cyclic path. Given the edge weights $l : E \to R$, the length of the path $P = (u_1, ..., u_k)$ is the sum of the lengths of its edges $l(P) := \sum_{1 \le i < k} l(u_i, u_{i+1})$. For any two nodes $s, t \in V$, a shortest s-t path is a path of minimal length with $u_1 = s$ and $u_k = t$. The distance $d(s, t)$ between s and t is the length of the shortest path s-t. A layout of a graph $G = (V, E)$ is a function $L : V \to R^2$ that assigns each node a position in R^2. A graph is called sparse if $m = O(n)$.

Let G = (V, E) be a directed graph whose edges are weighted by a function $w : E \to R$. The weights are interpreted as the edges' or lengths in the sense that the length of a path is the sum of the weights of its edges. The single-source single-target (SSST) shortest-path problem consists in finding a path of minimum length from a given source $s \in V$ to a given target $t \in V$. The problem is only well defined for all pairs, if G does not contain negative cycles. In the presence of negative weights, but not negative cycles, it is possible, using Johnson's algorithm, to convert in $O(nm + n^2 \log n)$ time the original edge weights $w : E \to R$ to non-negative edge weights $w' : E \to R_0^+$ that result in the same shortest paths. Hence, it can be safely assumed that the edge weights are non-negative. It can also be assumed that for all pairs $(s, t) \in V \times V$, the shortest path from s to t is unique.

In this paper the two basic speedup techniques namely shortest path containers and arc flags were combined, implemented and tested in random graphs, planar graphs and South India Road network.

2 Related Work

2.1 Basic Speedup Techniques

Computing shortest paths between nodes in a given directed graph is classically solved by Dijkstra's algorithm[1],[2]. But besides Dijkstra's algorithm there are many recent algorithms that solve variants and special cases of the shortest-path problem with better running time. This section also focuses on variants of Dijkstra's algorithm (also denoted as speedup techniques in the following) that further exploit the fact that a target is given. Typically, such improvements of Dijkstra's algorithm cannot be proved to be asymptotically faster than the original algorithm, and, in this sense are heuristics. However, it can be empirically shown that they indeed improve the running time drastically for many realistic data sets. An overview of the speedup techniques is as follows

- *Goal-directed search:* The given edge weights are modified to favour edges leading toward the target node [3],[4],[5]. With graphs from timetable information, a speed-up in running time of a factor of roughly 1.5 is reported [3]
- *Bidirectional search:* Start a second search backward, from the target to the source[4],[5],[6]. Both searches stop when their search horizons meet. Using bidirectional search space can be reduced by a factor of 2.
- *Multilevel approach:* This approach takes advantage of hierarchical coarsening[4],[5],[7],[8],[9] of the given graph, where additional edges have to be computed. These edges can be regarded as distributed to multiple levels. Depending on the given query, only a small fraction of these edges have to be considered to find a shortest path. Using this technique, speed-up factors of more than 3.5 were observed for road map and public transport graphs [8]. Timetable information queries could be improved by a factor of 11 [9].
- *Shortest-path containers:* These containers [10] provide a necessary condition for each edge, whether or not it has to be respected during the search. More precisely, the set of all nodes that can be reached on a shortest path using this edge is stored. Speedup factors in the range between 10 and 20 can be achieved.
- *Arc flags:* The partitioning strategy[11] adapted in arc flag approach helps in segregating the graph into regions. Based on the arc flag vector the shortest path regions are mapped to find the shortest path.

2.2 Combining Speedup Techniques

Combining each pair of techniques is outlined in [4] and it is noted that extending these to combinations, including three or all four techniques, are not difficult.

Goal-Directed Search and Bidirectional Search: Combining goal-directed and bidirectional search[4] is not as obvious as it may seem. Simple application of a goal-directed search forward and backward yields a wrong termination condition. In certain situations the search in each direction almost reaches the sources of the other direction. This often results in a slower algorithm. To overcome these deficiencies, it is preferable to use the very same edge weights $l'(v, w) = l(v, w) - \lambda(v) + \lambda(w)$ for both the forward and the backward search. With these weights, the forward search is directed to the target t and the backward search has no preferred direction, but favours edges that are directed towards t. This proceeding always computes shortest paths, as an s-t path is shortest independent of whether l or l' is used for the edge weights.

Goal-Directed Search and Multilevel Approach: The multilevel approach determines, for each query, a subgraph of the multilevel graph on which Dijikstra's algorithm is finally run. The computation of this subgraph does not affect edge lengths and thus a goal-directed search can be simply performed on it[4].

Goal-Directed Search and Shortest-Path Containers[4]: Similar to the multilevel approach, the shortest-path containers approach determines for a given query a subgraph of the original graph. Again, edge lengths are irrelevant for the computation of the subgraph and goal-directed search can be applied readily.

Bidirectional Search and Multilevel Approach[4]: A bidirectional search can be applied to the subgraph defined by the multilevel approach. The subgraph can be computed on the fly during Dijikstra's algorithm: for each node considered, the set of necessary outgoing edges is determined. To perform a bidirectional search on the multilevel subgraph, a symmetric, backward version of the subgraph computation has to be implemented: for each node considered in the backward search, the incoming edges that are part of the subgraph have to be determined. Shortest paths are guaranteed, since bidirectional search is run on a subgraph that preserves optimality, and, by the additional edges, only contains supplementary information consistent with the original graph.

Bidirectional Search and Shortest-Path Containers[4]: In order to take advantage of shortest-path containers in both directions of a bidirectional search a second set of containers is needed. For each edge e ∈ E, the set $S_b(e)$ is computed containing those nodes from which a shortest path ending with e exists. For each edge e ∈ E the bounding box of $S_b(e)$ is stored in an associative array C_b with index set E. The forward search checks whether the target is contained in C(e), the backward search, checks whether the source is in $C_b(e)$. It can be verified that by construction only such edges are pruned that do not form part of any partial shortest path and thus of any shortest *s-t* path.

Multilevel Approach and Shortest-Path containers[4]: The multilevel approach enriches a given graph with additional edges. Each new edge (u_1, u_k) represents a shortest path $(u_1, u_2, ..., u_k)$ in G. Such a new edge (u_1, u_k) is annotated with $C(u_1, u_2)$, the associated bounding box of the first edge on this path. This consistent labelling of new edges, which represent shortcuts in the original graph, ensures still shortest paths.

Hierarchical and Goal-directed speed-up techniques[4]: The combination of hierarchical and goal directed speedup techniques [12],[13] found to give best results for unit disk graphs, grid networks, and time-expanded timetables. It is suggested that the goal directed technique can be applied to higher levels of hierarchy.

3 Combining Speedup Techniques Based on Arc Flag and Containers

The graph G is partitioned into regions[11]. The sub graph within region itself is considered as graph G'. Theorem 2 in [10] holds good for the subgraph. i.e. The Graph G is divided into m sub graphs each residing in one region p. A set of nodes C'⊆ V' is called a container, if for all shortest paths from u' to t' that start with the edge (u',v'), the target t' is in C'.

Theorem 1. Let G' = (V', E'), w': E' → R' be a weighted sub graph in region p_i and for each e' let C'(e) be a consistent container in the subgraph of the region. Then Dijkstra's Algorithm with Pruning[10] finds a shortest path from s' to t' in the sub graph G' in region p_i. Subsequently finds a shortest path from s to t in the graph G considering k<=p regions and k sub graphs in k regions.

Proof. Consider the shortest path P from s to t that is found by Dijkstra's algorithm. If the graph G is divided into p regions, the shortest path P passes through these regions k<=p.

If for all edges e' ∈ P'⊆ P the target t' is in C'(e) in a region p_i ,the path P' subpath in subgraph G' is found by Dijkstra's Algorithm with Pruning[10], because the pruning does not change the order in which the edges are processed. A shortest subpath in sub graph of a graph G is shortest path of path P is again a shortest path, so for all (u', v') ∈ P' the sub path of path P in sub graph G' of graph G, the subpath of P'⊆P from u' to t' is a shortest u'-t'-sub path in path P' of sub graph G', which links all the sub paths in sub graphs from u to t . Then, by the definition of consistent container, t' ∈ C'(u', v') of sub graph G' and Dijkstra's algorithm with arc-flags finds a shortest path from s to t, using a set of consistent containers C_n, if one exists.

The arc-flag speedup technique uses a partitioning strategy to precompute information on whether an arc may be part of a shortest path in a graph[11]. Any possible partitioning can be used for the technique and the accelerated Dijkstra algorithm will always return a correct shortest path. However, different partitions do lead to different accelerations of the algorithm of Dijkstra. Here 2D grid partitioning strategy is adapted.

4 Experimental Analysis

The different speedup techniques for Dijkstra's algorithm were implemented in C++ with the help of LEDA library version 6.2 (Library of Efficient Data Types and Algorithms) [14]. The graph and priority queue data structures as well as other utilities such precise time measurement function provided by LEDA were used in the implementation. The code was compiled using Microsoft ® 32-bit C/C++ Compiler (version 15.00.30729.01) and the experiments were performed on an Intel Core2Duo machine (2.20 GHz) with 1 GB RAM running Windows 7 32-bit operating system.All the speedup techniques were coded as separate functions, for instance, the bidirectional search and traditional Dijkstra's algorithm were kept as separate modules. The random and planar graph generators provided by LEDA were used for generating graphs on which the modules were tested. The number of vertices visited during the shortest path computation and runtime were measured and used as metrics for comparing the different speedup techniques. The time required for preprocessing and shortest path computation was accurately measured by using the functionality offered by LEDA.

The random graph can be considered for network applications or as a model of real-world networks such as the Internet, social networks or biological networks. The planar graphs can be considered in applications like telecommunications - e.g spanning trees, Vehicle routing – e.g. planning routes on roads without underpasses.

The random and planar graphs were tested for maximum of 20000 nodes and the results were analysed. Road Map of TamilNadu was considered for testing the combined speedup technique(COCA). The first data set consists of 17 nodes and 36 edges (Dindivanam to Thiruvarur). The second data set consists of 26 nodes and 62 edges (Dindivanam to Karaikudi). And the third data set consists of 35 nodes and 82 edges (Dindivanam to Tuticorin).

4.1 COCA in Random Graphs

The arc flag method with different partitioning strategy was tested in road networks[11]. Here the arc flags are combined with containers and the running time is high compared to that of traditional Dijkstra in the case of random graphs. The combination doesn't give a big change in the case of number of nodes visited also. The preprocessing time is also very high both for arc flags and containers, as edges identified for the graph is random.

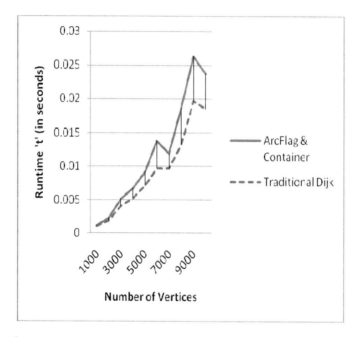

Fig. 1. Runtime during shortest path computation by traditional Dijkstra and search procedure with COCA in Random Graphs

There is a very small difference in the number of nodes visited during the shortest path computation from s to u. But this difference is also appreciable as the number of nodes increases this difference will also increase with respect to the visited vertices.

4.2 COCA in Planar Graphs

Compared to random graphs the planar graphs give a good result in the case of running time and number of nodes visited. The preprocessing time of arc flag is very less compared to that of containers as the number of edges is very less in the case of planar graphs. There is a negligible difference in running time with that of Dijkstra. It gives a good difference in the case of number of nodes visited.

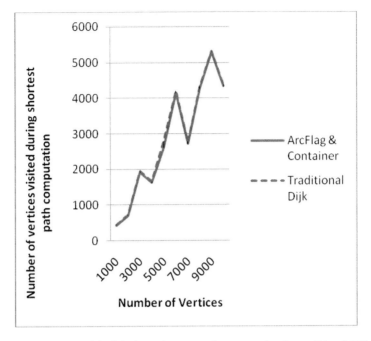

Fig. 2. Number of nodes visited during shortest path computation by traditional Dijkstra and search procedure with COCA in Random Graphs

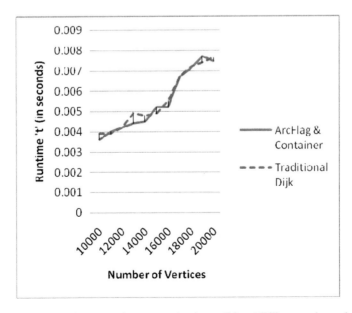

Fig. 3. Runtime during shortest path computation by traditional Dijkstra and search procedure with COCA in Planar Graphs

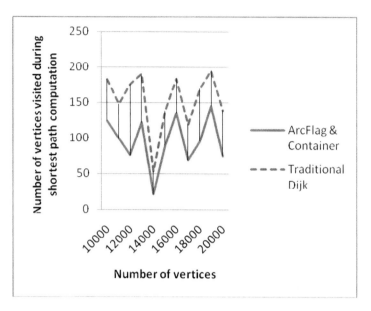

Fig. 4. Number of nodes visited during shortest path computation by traditional Dijkstra and search procedure with COCA in Planar Graphs

4.3 Speedup with Respect to Runtime and Vertex Visited during Shortest Path Computation

The speedup obtained in the individual basic and combined speedup techniques are charted in Fig.5 and Fig.6 respectively.

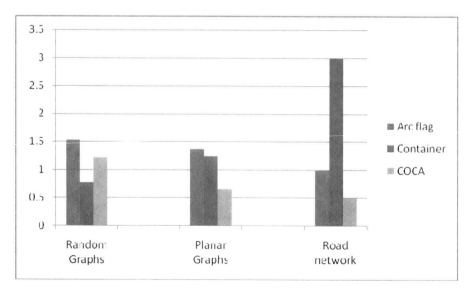

Fig. 5. Speedup with respect to runtime during shortest path computation

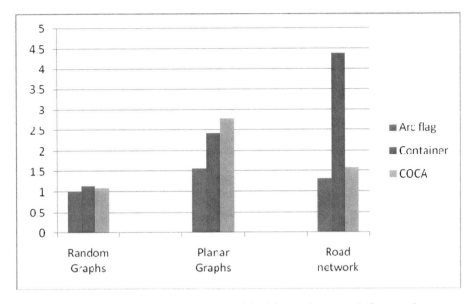

Fig. 6. Speedup with respect to Vertices visited during shortest path Computation

It is observed that the combined speedup technique based on containers and arc flags perform well in planar graphs compared to random graphs in terms of runtime of the technique.

It is understood from the graph that the average performance of combined speedup technique based on containers and arc flags are better in both random and planar graphs in terms number of vertices visited.

The combined speedup technique (COCA) achieves a speedup of 1.018 in the vertices visited during shortest path computation with random graph. This COCA technique achieves 1.016 in its running time and 1.61 in its vertices visited during shortest path computation with planar graphs.

The performance of COCA is appreciable in both random and planar graphs with respect to vertex visited during shortest path computation. This may help in network problems wherever hop count is primary Qos parameter.

5 Conclusion

The combined speedup techniques used for Dijkstra's based on containers and arc flags were analysed with random graphs, planar graphs and road network(South India road network). The key metrics for evaluation of the techniques like speedup based on running time and the number of vertices visited during shortest path computation were considered. The COCA speedup technique works well for a planar type of graph. Shortest path containers perform well in Road networks.

The performance is expected to be improved on real world graphs with more number of nodes compared to the graphs generated by LEDA. The technique can be extended for new combinations. This technique can also be applied to various other graph types.

Acknowledgment. The authors wish to thank Mr. R. Arvind Kumar for his efforts in conducting the experiments.

References

[1] Dijkstra, E.W.: A note on two problems in connection with graphs. Numerische Mathematik 1, 269–271 (1959)

[2] Schulz, F., Wagner, D., Weihe, K.: "Dijkstra's algorithm on-line: An empirical case study from public railroad transport". ACM Journal of Experimental Algorithmics 5, 12 (2000)

[3] Goldberg, A.V., Harrelson, C.: Computing the Shortest Path: A* Search Meets Graph Theory. In: Proc. 16th Annual ACM-SIAM Symposium on Discrete Algorithms (2005)

[4] Holzer, M., Schulz, F., Wagner, D., Willhalm, T.: Combining Speed-up Techniques for Shortest-Path Computations. ACM Journal of Experimental Algorithmics 10, Article No. 2.5 (2005)

[5] Wagner, D., Willhalm, T.: Speed-Up Techniques for Shortest-Path Computations. In: Thomas, W., Weil, P. (eds.) STACS 2007. LNCS, vol. 4393, pp. 23–36. Springer, Heidelberg (2007)

[6] Phol, I.: Bi-directional Search. Machine Intelligence 6, 124–140 (1971)

[7] Holzer, M., Schulz, F., Wagner, D.: Engineering Multilevel Overlay Graphs for Shortest-Path Queries. ACM Journal of Experimental Algorithmics 13, Article No. 2.5 (September 2008)

[8] Holzer, M.: Hierarchical speedup techniques for shortest path algorithms., M, Tech. report, Dept of Informatics, University of Konstanz, Germany (2003)

[9] Schulz, F., Wagner, D., Zaroliagis, C.: Using multi-level graphs for timetable information in railway systems. In: Mount, D.M., Stein, C. (eds.) ALENEX 2002. LNCS, vol. 2409, pp. 43–59. Springer, Heidelberg (2002)

[10] Wagner, D., Willhalm, T., Zaroliagis, C.: Geometric Containers for Efficient Shortest-Path Computation. ACM Journal of Experimental Algorithmics 10(1.3) (2005)

[11] Mohring, R.H., Schilling, H., Schutz, B., Wagner, D., Willhalm, T.: Partitioning graphs to speed up Dijkstra's algorithm. ACM Journal of Experimental Algorithmics 11, Article No. 2.8, 1–29 (2006)

[12] Bauer, R., Delling, D., Sanders, P., Schieferdecker, D., Schultes, D., Wagner, D.: Combining hierarchical and goal-directed speed-up techniques for dijkstra's algorithm. ACM Journal of Experimental Algorithmics 15, Article No. 3 (2010)

[13] Bauer, R., Delling, D., Sanders, P., Schieferdecker, D., Schultes, D., Wagner, D.: Combining hierarchical and goal-directed speed-up techniques for dijkstra's algorithm. In: McGeoch, C.C. (ed.) WEA 2008. LNCS, vol. 5038, pp. 303–318. Springer, Heidelberg (2008)

[14] LEDA, http://www.algorithmic-solutions.com

Author Index